SUBJECT AND STRATEGY

A Rhetoric Reader

Sixth Edition

SUBJECT
AND
STRATEGY

A Rhetoric Reader

Sixth Edition

Editors
PAUL ESCHHOLZ
ALFRED ROSA

University of Vermont

St. Martin's Press   New York

Editor: KAREN ALLANSON
Managing editor: PATRICIA MANSFIELD-PHELAN
Project editor: AMY HOROWITZ
Production supervisor: ALAN FISCHER
Art director: SHEREE GOODMAN
Cover design: JEANNETTE JACOBS DESIGN
Cover art: FRANCES WELLS

For information, write:
St. Martin's Press, Inc.
175 Fifth Avenue
New York, NY 10010

ISBN: 0-312-06541-8

Acknowledgments

Gordon Allport, "The Language of Prejudice" from *The Nature of Prejudice* by
Gordon Allport © 1979 by Addison-Wesley Publishing Company, Inc. Reprinted
with permission of the publisher.

Isaac Asimov, "The Case against Man" from *Science Past–Science Future*. Copyright
© 1970 by Isaac Asimov. Reprinted with permission of Janet Asimov.

Russell Baker, "The Plot against People" Copyright © 1968 by The New York
Times Company. Reprinted by permission.

Bruce A. Baldwin, "Stand Up for Yourself" from *Beyond The Cornucopia Kids: How
to Raise Healthy Achieving Children*, Direction Dynamics, Wilmington, NC, 1988. First
appeared in *Pace* magazine, February, 1987.

M. Stephen Arnold, "Teaching Types," copyright © 1988 by Stephen Arnold.
Reprinted by permission of the author.

Jacqueline Berke, "The Qualities of Good Writing," from *Twenty Questions for the
Writer: A Rhetoric With Readings*, 2d ed., by Jacqueline Berke copyright 1976, 1972
by Harcourt Brace Jovanovich, Inc. Reprinted by permission of the publisher.

Judy Brady, "Why I Want a Wife" Copyright © 1970 by Judy Brady. Reprinted
by permission of the author. First published in *Ms.* magazine.

Suzanne Britt, "Neat People versus Sloppy People," from *Show and Tell* by Suzanne Britt. Copyright © 1982 by Suzanne Britt. Reprinted by permission of the
author.

Acknowledgments and copyrights are continued at the back of the book on pages
645–647, which constitute an extension of the copyright page.

Preface

Subject and Strategy: A Rhetoric Reader is an anthology of essays for college writing courses. In the opening section, "Four Writers on Writing," professional writers offer practical advice on the qualities of good writing and on specific elements of the writing process—getting started, revising, and editing. Each of the next ten sections focuses on a particular rhetorical strategy: narration, description, illustration, process analysis, comparison and contrast, analogy, division and classification, definition, cause and effect analysis, and argumentation. In the final section, "Language, Race, and Gender: A Casebook," we present nine essays on a common theme. The writers of these essays explore various aspects of how language shapes our perceptions of race and gender. Taken together, these essays provide students with an overview of the subject as well as the specific ideas and examples necessary to write a controlled research paper. This section ends with a list of suggested paper topics. Students can either use one of these topics for their own papers or use the list to generate topics of their own choosing. Finally, to assist students with the documentation of their researched papers, we include advice with examples on note taking, integrating sources into a paper, and using the MLA and APA in-text citation systems.

Of the sixty-one readings by professional writers in this sixth edition, twenty-five have been retained from the fifth edition, and thirty-six are new. These selections represent a range of topics and purposes that students in our classes have found consistently exciting and that we believe others will, as well. In addition, we continue to include student essays, at least one for each of the ten rhetorical chapters and two in our general introduction. Each of these essays is on a topic of the student's own choosing and is, we believe, comparable in length and quality to what most instructors expect from students in writing courses today. Of particular interest is an interview following each student essay in which the writer discusses such matters as how the topic was chosen, how ideas were generated, how suitable writing strategies were determined, how many drafts were required, what kinds of revisions were made, and how peer responses were integrated into the writing process. The student essay and interview come at the beginning of each rhetorical grouping in order to help students establish realistic goals and standards for their writing, as well as to suggest ways of identifying and solving the sorts of problems a particular assignment may present.

Our general introduction stresses the role of reading (particularly, analytical reading and critical thinking) in the student writer's development. First, using a brief selection from Laurence Perrine's *Sound and Sense*, we provide an example of how to analyze a text closely and thoughtfully, how to discover the craft involved in its composition and the strategies the writer has employed. Further, we suggest procedures for using the readings in *Subject and Strategy* concurrently and interactively throughout the process of completing a writing assignment. Finally, we provide two student essays. For the first we describe the process the student went through from his initial notes for the assignment to his completed final draft. The second is the final draft of an argumentative essay on homelessness.

We offer specific and focused advice in our introductions to each of the ten rhetorical chapters. Each chapter introduction includes a definition of the rhetorical strategy under discussion and explains in detail why writers use the strategy, how one should read an essay using the strategy, and, finally, how one goes about writing such an essay. Along with the general introduction, these chapter introductions provide samples of professional writing as the basis for discussing how to read analytically.

In the sixth edition of *Subject and Strategy* we retained the organization of the "Argumentation" section we initiated in the fifth edition. Believing that it is important for students to hear a variety of arguments on a specific topic, we have presented three groups of essays on contemporary issues. We believe that your students will find these essays on "Censorship," "Diversity in America," and "The Environment: Conflicting Values" as informative and provocative as our students have.

We have again included an alternate table of contents that groups all the essays in the text according to thirteen broad subject categories. We believe that this listing will provide further opportunities for classroom discussion and student writing, based both on the content of individual essays and on the various rhetorical approaches to common themes.

In selecting the readings for this edition, we have continued to prize readability, whether in such classic selections as Bruce Catton's "Grant and Lee," Rachel Carson's "Our Assault on Nature," Frederick Douglass's "The Last Flogging," and Mark Twain's "Two Ways of Seeing a River," or in such contemporary writings as Jean Shepherd's "Lost at C," Margaret Laurence's "The Shack," Anna Quindlen's "Going to the Gym," Barbara Ehrenreich's "Teach Diversity—with a Smile," and Perri Klass's "Ambition." We have also been conscious of the length of essays, generally preferring those in the three- to five-page range, although several longer ones have demanded to be included. Above all, we have chosen essays that are well written.

Most of the essays in *Subject and Strategy* are followed by four kinds of study questions: "Questions on Subject," "Questions on Strategy," "Questions on Diction and Vocabulary," and "Writing Assignments." In addition, "Writing Suggestions" for each rhetorical mode are provided at the end of each chapter.

Questions on Subject are designed to focus the reader's attention on the content of the essay as well as on the author's purpose. These questions help students check their comprehension of the essays and are useful also as a basis for classroom discussion.

Questions on Strategy focus on the various rhetorical strategies the authors have employed in composing their essays. In answering these questions, students are encouraged to put themselves in the author's place and come to an awareness of how they may employ the same strategies effectively in their own writing.

Questions on Diction and Vocabulary emphasize the importance of each author's choice of appropriate words and phrases. We have tried always to remind students of the importance of the verbal context in which such choices are made. Each set of diction and vocabulary questions ends with an exercise in vocabulary building in which the reader is asked to use a desk dictionary to determine the meanings of words as they are used in the essay.

The Writing Assignments following individual essays are of two types: the first assignment generally focuses on the particular mode under discussion; the second focuses more on the content of the essay, sometimes providing practice in the mode as well. Instructors wishing to have students work on different assignments, or on topics of their own choosing, may find these writing assignments helpful in generating good classroom discussions. Such discussions can often help students discover issues that they wish to pursue on their own. The Writing Suggestions that appear at the end of each rhetorical section offer students an additional range of topics suitable to each particular mode. Instructors may use these writing suggestions as complements to—or substitutes for—the more focused writing suggestions that accompany individual essays.

A "Glossary of Rhetorical Terms," located at the end of the book, provides students with concise definitions of terms useful for discussing the readings and their own writing. Wherever we have felt that information in the glossary might assist students in answering a study question, we have placed a cross-reference to the appropriate glossary entry next to the question.

The arrangement of chapters in *Subject and Strategy*, of course, suggests one possible sequence for using the book: an overview of the writing process followed by the movement from narration and description through exposition to argumentative writing. Because each section is self-contained, however, an instructor may follow any sequence, omitting or giving greater emphasis to a particular chapter according to the special needs of his or her students.

We have been deeply gratified by the acceptance of the five previous editions of *Subject and Strategy*. Our fellow teachers of composition in hundreds of community colleges, liberal arts colleges, and universities have used the book. In preparing this sixth edition, we have benefited inestimably from the comments and suggestions of Kim Bridgford, Fairfield University; Joanne Fattori, University of Massachusetts, Boston Harbor; Kitty Frazier, West Virginia State College; William Gilbert, California State University at Long Beach; Patricia Hutchins, Delta College; Jim Kolsky, Western Nevada State College; Vicki Scheurer, Palm Beach Community College; and Cindy Thomas, College of Du Page. We would also like to thank Karen Allanson of St. Martin's Press for her insightful editorial guidance; Patricia Mansfield-Phelan and Amy Horowitz for their help in seeing the project through from manuscript to bound book; and Patricia Paquin for her assistance in developing the questions and the preparation of the Instructor's Manual that accompanies *Subject and Strategy*.

Our special thanks go to Samuel Feitelberg and the faculty and staff of the Race and Culture program at the University of Vermont for their help in selecting articles on issues of cultural diversity and then testing these articles in their classes.

We are especially proud of those students whose essays appear in *Subject and Strategy* for their willingness to contribute their time and effort on behalf of the book and the students who will use it. Finally, we are grateful to all our writing students at the University of Vermont for their enthusiasm for writing and their invaluable responses to materials included in this book.

Paul Eschholz
Alfred Rosa

Contents

Alternate Table of Contents Arranged by Subject

A Sense of Self

People and Personalities

Places

Education

The World of Work

A Sense of Humor

Contemporary Social Issues

Women and Men

Minorities and the Poor

Health and Medicine

The Natural World

Technology

Language, Reading, and Writing

SUBJECT
AND
STRATEGY

A Rhetoric Reader

Sixth Edition

Introduction

Subject and Strategy is a reader for writers. The selections in this book will entertain you, inform you, even contribute to your self-awareness and understanding of the world around you. But, above all, they have been chosen to help you become a better writer—and especially to help you grasp and master ten versatile and widely used writing strategies. After an opening section in which professional writers offer advice about writing, the next ten sections are devoted to these strategies: narration, description, illustration, process analysis, comparison and contrast, analogy, division and classification, definition, cause and effect analysis, and argumentation. In each section an introduction first defines the strategy, explains its purpose, illustrates it with brief examples, tells how you can analyze the strategy as you read, and finally offers suggestions for using the strategy in your own writing. This leads into a collection of essays that demonstrate how the strategy can be used with various subjects. The first essay in sections 2 through 12 is written by a student in a college writing course and is followed by an interview in which the student writer talks about his or her process of writing the essay and some of the problems that arose during that process. The essays that come next in each section are drawn from various magazines and books, and each is accompanied by questions that direct your attention to aspects of its content and form or that offer writing assignments. At the end

1

of each section are suggested topics for writing to help you continue your practice of the strategy.

Section 12, "Language, Race, and Gender: A Casebook," is a collection of essays linked by the common theme of language and identity. As we state in our introduction to the casebook, these essays explore some of the ways people use language to define themselves and to interact with those around them. Implicitly and explicitly, the essays reinforce the need to both eliminate language bias and find a common ground for greater understanding and more open communication among all people. We have selected the essays in this casebook for you to use in conjunction with your own observations and experiences on the centrality of language in your life to write a controlled research paper. In writing your own paper you will want to quote, paraphrase, and summarize important ideas and information contained in these essays. To help you integrate these borrowed materials into your essay and correctly document your use of them, we have included some brief guidelines on writing a researched paper. These guidelines are presented following the brief introduction to the casebook. At the end of the section, we have included suggested writing topics to start you thinking about your own approach to the theme.

Subject and Strategy, as its title suggests, places equal emphasis on the content and form of an essay—that is, on what an essay has to say and on the strategy used to say it. All readers pay attention to content, to the substance of what an author is saying. Far fewer, however, notice the strategies that authors use to organize their writing, to make it understandable and effective. Yet using these strategies is an essential element of the writer's craft, an element that must be mastered if one is to write well. Because these strategies are such an essential element of the writer's craft, you will need first to become more aware of them and then to master your use of them in order to write well.

There is nothing mysterious or difficult about the strategies themselves. You're probably familiar with some of them already. When you want to tell a story, for example, you naturally use the strategy called *narration.* When you want to make a choice, you naturally *compare and contrast* the things you must choose between. When you want to explain how to make a pizza, you fall automatically into the strategy called *process analysis*. These and the other strategies are ways we think about the world and our experiences in it. What makes them seem mysterious, especially in writing, is that most people use them more or less unconsciously, with little awareness that they're doing so. Sophisticated thinking and writing do not come from simply using these structures—everyone does that—but from using them consciously and purposefully.

A writing strategy, however, is not like a blueprint or a plaster mold that determines in advance exactly how the final product will be shaped. Rather, these forms of thought are flexible and versatile, with only a few simple rules or directions to define their shape, like the rules for basketball, chess, and other strategic games. Such directions leave plenty of room for all the imagination and variety you can put into your writing and for all the many things you may want to write about.

As the readings that make up this text will demonstrate, content and form are unified. Indeed, the two actually help determine one another. A writer who wants to tell what happened, for example, will naturally choose narration; at the same time, the requirements of the narrative form will influence the content of the written story. On the other hand, if the writer wants to tell *why* something happened, no amount of storytelling will do the job: it will be necessary to use the strategy of analyzing *cause and effect*, and this strategy will determine the ultimate content. As you write, you will often tentatively plan your strategy before you start, consciously deciding which one or which combination you think best fits what you have to say and what you want to accomplish. Sooner or later, you will have to look back at what you have written, making sure your choice of strategy was a good one and that it expresses your content accurately and effectively. The sort of reading this text encourages will help you become more skilled at making such decisions about your own writing.

Reading as a Writer

You read for many reasons and in different ways. But reading is most rewarding when you do it actively, in a thoughtful spirit and with an alert and inquiring mind. One of the greatest benefits of active reading is that it can help you become a better writer. To read as a writer, you must know how to analyze what you read. You must be able to discover what is going on in an essay, to figure out the writer's reasons for shaping the essay in a particular way, to decide whether the result works well or poorly—and why. Such digging into an essay may seem odd, and for good reason: like writing itself, analytical reading is a skill that takes time to acquire. But the skill is necessary if you are to understand the craft of a piece of writing.

Another important reason to master the skills of analytical reading is that, for everything you write, you will be your own first reader and critic. How well you are able to analyze your own drafts will powerfully affect how well you revise them; and revising well is crucial to writing well. So reading others' writings analytically is useful and important practice.

Getting the Most Out of Your Reading

Practice in analytical reading requires, first, a commitment of time and effort. Second, you should try to take a positive interest in the act of reading, even if the subject matter is not immediately appealing. Remember, you are reading not for content alone, but also to understand a writer's methods.

Here are some further tips to follow:

READ AND REREAD Always read the selection at least twice, no matter how long it is. The first reading is a chance to get acquainted with the essay and form your first impressions of it. The essay will offer you information, ideas, and arguments—some that you may not have expected; as you read you will find yourself continually modifying your sense of its purpose and its strategy.

Your second reading should be quite different from the first. You will know what the essay is about, where it is going, and how it gets there; now you can relate the parts more accurately to the whole. You can test your first impressions against the words on the page, developing and deepening your sense of how the essay is written, and how well. You can pay special attention to the author's purpose and means of achieving that purpose, looking for features of organization and style that you can learn from and adapt to your own work.

ASK YOURSELF QUESTIONS   As you probe the essay, focus your attention by asking yourself some basic questions about its content and its form. Here are some you may find useful:

1. What does the author want to say? What is his or her main point or thesis?
2. Why does the author want to say it? What is his or her purpose?
3. What strategy or strategies does the author use?
4. Why and how does the author's writing strategy suit both subject and purpose?
5. What, if anything, is noteworthy about the way the author uses the strategy?
6. How effective is the essay? Why?

Each selection in *Subject and Strategy* is followed by questions for analysis similar to the ones suggested here, but usually more specific. These questions will work best when you try to answer them as fully as you can, remembering and considering many details from the selection to support your answers.

ANNOTATE THE TEXT   As you read, keep a pencil in hand and use it. Mark the selection's main point when you find it stated directly. Look for the strategy or strategies the author uses to develop that point, and jot the information down. If you disagree with a fact or a conclusion, object in the margin: *"No!"* If you feel skeptical, indicate that response: *"Why?"* If you are impressed by an argument or a turn of phrase, compliment the author: *"Good!"* Write in whatever marginal notes come naturally to you. These quick, brief responses will help you later when you begin asking and answering for yourself more specific analytical questions.

When annotating a text, don't be timid. Mark up your book as much as you like. Jot down as many responses in your notebook as you think will be helpful. But don't let annotating become burdensome. It should be an aid, not a chore; and a word or phrase is usually as good as a sentence. You may, in fact, want to delay much of your annotating until a second reading, so that your first can be fast and free.

An Example: Reading Laurence Perrine's "Paradox"

The following brief selection is from Laurence Perrine's engaging text *Sound and Sense: An Introduction to Poetry*. First published in 1956, this textbook has introduced generations of high school and college students to the excitement and art of poetry.

As you read this through the first time, try not to stop—take it all in as if in one breath. The second time, however, pause to annotate the text as often as you like, keeping in mind the six basic questions we mentioned earlier:

1. What does Perrine want to say?
2. Why does Perrine want to say it?
3. What strategy or strategies does Perrine use?
4. Why and how does Perrine's strategy suit his subject and purpose?
5. What is noteworthy about Perrine's use of the strategy?
6. How effective is the essay? Why?

Paradox

Aesop tells the tale of a traveler who sought refuge with a Satyr on a bitter winter night. On entering the Satyr's lodging, he blew on his fingers, and was asked by the Satyr what he did it for. "To warm them up," he explained. Later, on being served with a piping hot bowl of porridge, he blew also on it, and again was asked what he did it for. "To cool it off," he explained. The Satyr thereupon thrust him out of doors, for he would have nothing to do with a man who could blow hot and cold with the same breath.

A *paradox* is an apparent contradiction that is nevertheless somehow true. It may be either a situation or a statement. Aesop's tale of the traveler illustrates a paradoxical situation. As a figure of speech, paradox is a statement. When Alexander Pope wrote that a literary critic of his time would "damn with faint praise," he was using a verbal paradox, for how can a man damn by praising?

When we understand all the conditions and circumstances involved in a paradox, we find that what at first seemed impossible is actually entirely plausible and not strange at all. The paradox of the cold hands and hot porridge is not strange to a man who knows that a stream of air directed upon an object of different temperature will tend to bring that object closer to its own temperature. And Pope's paradox is not strange when we realize the *damn* is being used figuratively, and that Pope means only that a too reserved praise may damage an author with the public almost as much as adverse criticism. In a paradoxical statement the contradiction usually stems from one of the words being used figuratively or in more than one sense.

The value of paradox is its shock value. Its seeming impossibility startles the reader into attention and, thus, by the fact of its apparent absurdity, it underscores the truth of what is being said.

Once you have read and reread Perrine's essay, write your own answers to the six basic questions listed earlier. Then compare your answers with the set of answers that follows.

1. What does Perrine want to say?

Perrine wants to tell his readers what paradox is: "An apparent contradiction that is nevertheless somehow true." He also wants to show why paradox can be useful for writers. His main point seems to be that "The value of paradox is its shock value. Its seeming impossibility startles the reader into attention and, thus, by the fact of its apparent absurdity, it underscores the truth of what is being said."

2. Why does Perrine want to say it?

Perrine's purpose is to explain the meaning of the word *paradox* so that his readers can better understand the concept and how it works. He would also like his readers to appreciate how valuable and interesting examples of paradox can be to storytellers, poets, and writers in general. So Perrine's purpose is *to inform* and *to persuade.*

3. What strategy or strategies does Perrine use?

Overall, Perrine uses the strategy of *definition*. He gives what seems like a dictionary definition in the second paragraph ("A *paradox* is an apparent contradiction that is nevertheless somehow true"); but he elaborates on this formal definition in several ways, mainly through *illustration* or examples. The first paragraph is a *narration* that serves as an example of a paradoxical situation, while the quotation from Alexander Pope at the end of paragraph 2 provides an example of a paradoxical statement.

4. Why and how does Perrine's strategy suit his subject and purpose?

It is natural for Perrine to select definition as a strategy, because his purpose is to explain the meaning of a term unfamiliar to his readers. And for a complicated abstraction like *paradox*, the two specific examples he points out are crucial to illustrate his meaning.

5. What is noteworthy about Perrine's use of the strategy?

The concrete examples he includes serve to show rather than merely tell what paradox is and how it works. By beginning his essay with a clever story that provides a good example of his subject, Perrine is able to catch his readers' attention immediately and to prepare them for the formal definition of paradox in paragraph 2.

6. How effective is the essay? Why?

Perrine's essay is effective because it serves its purpose very well. He helps his readers understand what paradox is and appreciate what it does. His definition is to the point and easy to follow, while his examples from Aesop and Pope show how interesting the idea of paradox can be and clearly demonstrate why writers use paradox.

Using Reading in the Writing Process

What does all this have to do with your own writing? Analytical reading is not simply an end in itself; it is also a means to help you become a better writer. At the simplest level, reading stimulates your thinking; it provides you with information and ideas to enliven your writing and often with subjects to write about. In a more subtle way, analytical reading can increase your awareness of how others' writing affects you, and thus can make you more sensitive to how your own writing will affect your readers. If you've ever been impressed by an author who uses convincing supporting evidence to document each one of his or her claims, you might be more likely to back up your own claims carefully. If you've been impressed by an apt turn of phrase or absorbed by a new idea, you might be less inclined to feed your readers clichés and platitudes. Gradually, you will discover yourself becoming more sensitive to how readers will be likely to respond.

More to the point, however, analytical reading of the kind you'll be encouraged to do in this text will help you master important strategies of thinking and writing that you can use very specifically throughout the writing process. During the early stages of your writing, you will need to focus on the large issues of choosing a subject, gathering information, planning a strategy suited to your purpose, and organizing your ideas. As you move from a first draft through further revisions, your concerns will begin to narrow. In conference with your instructor, you may discover a faulty beginning or ending, or realize that your tone is inappropriate, or see that the various parts of your essay are not quite connected, or notice awkward repetitions in your choice of words and phrases. Analytical reading can lead you to solutions for such problems at every stage of the writing process: prewriting, writing a draft, and revising.

Reading while Prewriting

Of course, reading can give you ideas and information. But reading also helps expand your knowledge of the writing strategies available to you and, consequently, can help direct all your prewriting activities. Let us explain how this works.

CHOOSING A TOPIC In a composition course, you may be given the freedom to choose your own subject matter. In selecting your topic, you should consider whether you know something about it and also whether it interests you.

Begin by determining a broad subject that you like to think about and might enjoy writing about—a subject like "music" or "relationships" or "college" or "sports." Something you read—one of the essays in this book, for example—may help bring particular subjects to mind. Or consider the possibilities of your career ambitions: business, journalism, law, sports, medicine, computer programming, whatever. Or list some subjects you like discussing with friends: food, perhaps, or motorcycles or soap operas or the next election. Focus on a likely subject; then let your mind explore its possibilities.

Suppose, for example, you're interested in journalism and have even done some writing for your school newspaper. Here's what you might come up with when you think about possible topics for your writing:

JOURNALISM
print news
television news
press freedom
press control
Time
Newsweek
USA Today
ABC Nightly News
CBS Evening News
NBC Nightly News
CNN
editorial writing
advertising
censorship

Once you have such a list, you can choose from among the possible topics one that interests you most, that you have several ideas about.

GATHERING INFORMATION AND IDEAS   Even the most experienced writers need to generate information and ideas to use in their writing. Once you have begun to read analytically and thus to increase your command of the general writing strategies, you can use those strategies to get your mind working, to make associations, to find meaningful things to say about your topic. Remember that writing strategies are more than composing techniques; they are basic ways of thinking.

Suppose that you decide to write about the different ways your classmates dress. First, you decide to identify the most common stylistic groups—to use the strategy of *division and classification:*

casual
preppie
the cowboy look
mixed
miscellaneous

Next, you might want to use the strategy of *illustration.* In order to do this you would choose one or more students to represent each style of dress, to provide a typical *example* of that style:

casual: me
preppie: Joanie Cabot
the cowboy look: Fred Williams
mixed: Jim Lee
miscellaneous: Emilia Sanchez—the young executive look; Bill Glass—
the punk look; Judy Davidovich—the socialite/fashion model look

Then it would be natural to *describe* a typical outfit for each of your exemplary classmates. You would try to capture specific details of how each looks and, if necessary, to point out clearly why each is representative of a particular style:

Joanie: loose, thick wool sweaters; tweedy skirts; loafers; muted greens
and browns. Right out of the *Lands' End Catalog.*
Bill: black leather jacket and black denim jeans. Lots of metal.
Judy: a different ensemble every day, down to the shoes and accessories;
every one of them looks like it cost hundreds of dollars. Even wears
perfume.

Other strategies you might choose include *narration*—thinking of brief stories or anecdotes that would add interest; *cause and effect*—analyzing how your classmates' dress affects the impression they make on others; even *comparison and contrast*—pointing out points of similarity and difference between the various styles.

Of course, you probably won't use all the material you gather this way; and you won't necessarily organize your writing using the same strategies that helped you find your ideas. At this stage, what you're concerned with is mining your memory for material. The writing strategies you learn through your reading can help immensely.

DETERMINING YOUR STRATEGY   Once you decide what you want to write about and come up with some ideas for what you might like to say, your next task is to jot down the main ideas for your essay in an order that seems both natural and logical to you. In other words, make a scratch outline. This outline will often suggest to you one of the basic writing strategies you have learned from your reading. Or a strategy that was particularly helpful to you in generating ideas may well work for you now as an overall organizing principle.

If you're still confused about what strategy to use for your essay, however, try this: (1) sum up the point you want to make in a single phrase or sentence; (2) restate the point as a question, in effect the question your essay will answer; (3) look closely at both the summary and the question for key words or concepts that go with a particular strategy.

Here are some examples:

SUMMARY: Roger Clemens is the best pitcher in baseball.
QUESTION: How does Clemens compare with other pitchers?
STRATEGY: Comparison and contrast. The writer must compare Clemens and other pitchers to support the claim that Clemens is "the best."

SUMMARY: How to make chili.
QUESTION: How do you make chili?
STRATEGY: Process analysis. The word *how*, especially in the phrase *how to*, implies a procedure that can be explained in steps or stages.

SUMMARY: Systems malfunction and human error made the disaster happen at the Chernobyl nuclear power facility.
QUESTION: Why did the Chernobyl disaster happen?

STRATEGY: Cause and effect. The word *why* demands reasons in the answer, and the strongest kinds of reasons are causes.

SUMMARY: Petroleum and natural gas prices should be federally controlled.

QUESTION: What should be done about petroleum and natural gas prices?

STRATEGY: Argument or persuasion. The word *should* signals an argument, calling for evidence and reasoning in support of the conclusion.

These are just a few examples of how to decide on a writing strategy that is suitable for your topic and what you want to say about that topic. In every case, your reading can guide you in recognizing the best plan to follow.

ORGANIZING THE PAPER Before you start a draft, it's a good idea to organize your material according to the strategy you will use—to create a working plan. Different strategies, of course, will suggest different kinds of working plans. An *argumentative* essay, for example, might be mapped out in this way:

Point to be proved: _____

Supporting arguments:

1. _____

2. _____

3. _____

Opposing arguments: _____

Rebuttal: _____

Final argument: _____

A working plan for an essay in *comparison and contrast*, however, would naturally look quite different—perhaps like this:

OBJECT A

Point 1: _____
Point 2: _____
Point 3: _____
Point 4: _____

OBJECT B

Point 1: _____
Point 2: _____
Point 3: _____
Point 4: _____

A working plan for a *process analysis,* on the other hand, might look like this:

Step 1: _____

Step 2: _____

Step 3: _____

Step 4: _____

A working plan is similar to a scratch outline; but it is determined much more specifically by the requirements of the particular writing strategy you intend to use. You have a great deal of flexibility in determining the format of your working plan—the models provided here are only suggestions. Your reading will help you understand the kinds of modifications that are acceptable and useful for a given strategy.

Reading while Writing Your First Draft

First drafts are exploratory and sometimes unpredictable. While writing your first draft, you may find yourself getting away from your original plan; for example, what started as a definition may develop as you write into a process analysis or an effort at persuasion. If you notice something like this happening, don't force yourself to revert to your original plan. Allow your inspiration to take you where it will. Later, when you finish your draft, you can see whether the new strategy works better than the old or whether it would be best to go back to your former strategy.

It may also happen, however, that while writing your rough draft you run into a difficulty that prevents you from moving forward. For example, you want to tell the story of something that happened to you but aren't certain whether you should be using the pronoun *I* so often. If you turn to the essays in Section 2 to see how authors of narrations handle this problem, you will find that it's no problem at all: for an account of a personal experience, it's perfectly acceptable to say *I* as often as you need to. Or, while trying to describe someone you think is quite a character, you find you've been writing for pages, but your draft seems flat and doesn't begin to express how lively and funny your friend really is. If you look through the introduction to Section 3, you will come across the advice that descriptions need lots of factual, concrete detail, and the selections in this section give further proof of this. You suddenly realize that just such detail is what's missing from your draft. Reading, then, is helpful because it enables you to see how other writers successfully dealt with problems similar to yours.

Reading while Revising

Once you have completed your first draft, it is crucial that you set it aside and give yourself a rest. Then you can come back to it with some freshness and some objectivity. When you do, resist the temptation to plunge immediately into a second draft: mere changes are not necessarily improvements. Try to tackle your writing problems systematically. It's better to reread and analyze carefully what you have written, perhaps using the six basic questions you apply to other people's essays to criticize your own.

One way to begin the revision process is to make an outline of your first draft—not as you meant it to be, but as it actually came out. What does your outline tell you about the strategy you have used? Does it suit your purpose? Perhaps you meant to compare your two grandmothers, but you have not clearly shown their similarities and differences. Consequently, your draft is not one unified essay in comparison and contrast, but two descriptive essays under one roof. Or perhaps you set out to write about your grandmothers, but did not have a definite purpose in mind. Outlining your rough draft helps you see that, despite some differences in looks and habits, both grandmothers are essentially alike in all the ways that matter. This gives you both a point to make and a strategy for making it: comparison and contrast.

Even if you are satisfied with the overall strategy of your draft, an outline can still help you make improvements. Perhaps your directions for preparing a pizza leave out an important step in the process—adding oregano to the tomato sauce, for example. Or perhaps your classification essay on types of college students is confused because you create overlapping categories—computer majors, athletes, and foreign students (a computer major could, of course, be a foreign student, an athlete, or both). You may uncover a flaw in your organization and strategy, such as lack of coherence in an argument or of parallelism in a comparison and contrast.

Now is the time to discover these problems and fix them. Return to the appropriate section in *Subject and Strategy*. Review the introductory discussion; reread one or more of the essays; look over the interview with the student writer—possibly he or she had the same problems you are having, and the interview will suggest ways to solve them.

Finally, if you find yourself dissatisfied with specific elements of your draft, look at several essays to see how other writers have dealt with the particular situation you are confronting. For example, if you don't like the way your essay starts, find some beginnings you think are particularly effective; if your paragraphs don't seem to flow into one another, examine how various writers use transitions; if your essay seems too general, examine the way other writers include details and examples to substantiate their ideas. Analytical reading can provide you with any number of solutions to the problems you may have with your own writing.

Two Model Student Essays

An Expository Essay in Progress

Keith Eldred, while a first-year student at the University of Vermont, was assigned to write an essay using the strategy of definition; he was able to choose whatever topic he wished. Keith began by reading the introduction and all the essays in the definition section of this text. Then, because he had been recently introduced to the Hindu concept of the *mantra*, he decided he would like to explore this concept as it pertained to the secular world. Having made this decision, he began to generate some notes that would help to get him started writing. These notes provided him with several examples of what he intended to call "secular mantras"; a dictionary definition of the word *mantra*; and the idea that a good starting point for his rough draft might be the story of "The Little Engine That Could."

counting ten when angry
Dunkin' Donuts commercial—"Gotta make the donuts!"
"Little Engine That Could" (possible beginning)

Mantra—"a mystical formula of invocation or incantation" (Webster's)
"Let's Go Celtics" → action because crowd wants players to say it to
   self
swearing (not always a mantra)
John McEnroe—"Get serious!"
"Come on, come on" (at traffic light)
"Geronimo" "Ouch!"
Hindu mythology

After mulling over his list, Keith began to organize his ideas with
the following scratch outline:

1. begin with story of "Little Engine That Could"
2. talk about the magic of secular mantras
3. dictionary definition and Hindu connections
4. examples of individuals using mantras
5. crowd chants as mantras—Celtics
6. conclusion—talk about how you can't get through the day without
   using mantras

Based on this outline, as well as on what he had learned through
his reading about definition as a writing strategy, Keith came up
with the following rough draft.

Secular Mantras: Magic Words

Remember "The Little Engine That Could"? That's
the story about the tiny locomotive that pulled the
train over the mountain when the big locomotives
wouldn't. Remember how the Little Engine strained and
chugged, "I think I can--I think I can--I think I
can" until she reached the top of the mountain? That's
a perfect example of a secular mantra in action.
   A secular mantra (pronounced man-truh) is any
word or group of words that helps a person use his
energy. The key word there is "helps"--repeating a
secular mantra doesn't <u>create</u> energy; it just makes it
easier to channel a given amount. The Little Engine,
for instance, obviously had the strength to pull the

train up the mountain; apparently, she could have done it without saying a word. But we all know she wouldn't have been able to, any more than any one of us would be able to sky-dive the first time without yelling, "Geronimo" or not say "Ouch" if we touched a hot stove. Some words and phrases simply have a certain magic that makes a job easier or that makes us feel better when we repeat them. Those are secular mantras.

It is because of their magical quality that these expressions are called "secular mantras" in the first place. A mantra (Sanskrit for "sacred counsel") is literally "a mystical formula of invocation or incantation" used in Hinduism (Webster's). According to Hindu mythology, Manu, lawgiver and progenitor of mankind, created the first language by teaching men the thought-forms of objects and substances. "VAM," for example, is the thought-form of what we call "water." Mantras, groups of these ancient words, can summon any object or deity if they are miraculously revealed to a seer and properly repeated silently or vocally. Hindus use divine mantras to communicate with gods, acquire superhuman powers, and cure diseases, and for many other purposes. Hence, everyday words that a person concentrates on to help him accomplish tasks or cope with stress act as secular mantras.

All sorts of people use all sorts of secular mantras for all sorts of reasons. A father counts to 10 before saying anything when his son brings the car home dented. A tennis player faults and chides himself, "Get serious!" A frustrated mother pacing with her wailing baby mutters, "You'll have your own kids someday." A college student writhing before an exam instructs himself not to panic. A freshly spanked child glares at his mother's back and repeatedly promises himself never to speak to her again. Secular mantras are everywhere.

Usually, we use secular mantras to make ourselves walk faster or keep silent or do some other act. But we can also use them to influence the actions of other

persons. Say, for instance, the Boston Celtics are
behind in the final minutes of a game. 10,000 fans who
want them to win scream, "Let's go, Celtics!" The
Celtics are roused and win by 20 points. Chalk up the
victory to the fans' secular mantra, which transferred
their energy to the men on the court.
 If you're not convinced of the power of secular
mantras, try to complete a day without using any.
Don't mutter anything to force yourself out of bed.
Don't utter a sound when the water in the shower is
cold. Don't grumble when the traffic lights are long.
Don't speak to the TV when it's slow warming up. And
don't be surprised if you have an unusually long,
painful, frustrating day.

In class Keith read his paper aloud, and other students had an
opportunity to ask him questions about secular mantras. As a result
of this class conference, Keith had a good idea of what he needed
to do in subsequent drafts, and he made the following notes to
himself so that he wouldn't forget:

> get more examples, especially from everyday experiences
> class thought Celtics example didn't work—expand or cut
> be more specific in my definition of secular mantra—maybe tell what
>   secular mantras are *not*
> make use of "The Little Engine That Could" example in the body of the
>   paper
> get new conclusion—present conclusion doesn't follow from paper
> explain how mantras might work and why they are important
> don't eliminate background information about mantras

In subsequent drafts, Keith worked on each of the areas he had
listed. While doing so, he found it helpful to reread particular portions of the essays on definition. Several of these led him to new
insights about how to accomplish the changes he wanted to make.
He found that, as he revised his paper, he needed to make yet
other changes that he had not anticipated. For example, when he
made his definition more specific, he found that he needed to do
some reorganization (moving the background information on man-

tras to a position later in the paper) and to develop a new paragraph. By the deadline, Keith had completed the following final draft. To help you see more clearly what he retained from his rough draft, those portions are underlined. Marginal annotations point to the revisions he has made and comment on the overall structure of the paper.

Secular Mantras

Introductory Example (from first draft)

Remember "The Little Engine That Could"? That's the story about the tiny locomotive that hauled the train over the mountain when the big, rugged locomotives wouldn't. Remember how the Little Engine strained and heaved and chugged, "I think I can—— I think I can——I think I can" until she reached the top of the mountain? That's a perfect example of a secular mantra in action.

Formal Definition (revised)

You probably have used a secular mantra——pronounce it "mantruh"—— already today. It's any word or group of words that helps you use your energy when you consciously repeat it

Controlling Sentence (new)

to yourself. You must understand two things about secular mantras to be able to recognize one.

Qualifier No. 1 (new)

First of all, a secular mantra is not simply any word or phrase you say to yourself. It must help you use your energy. Thus, "I wish I were home" is not a secular mantra if you just think the words. But the sentence is a secular mantra if. walking home on a cold day, you repeat it each time you take a step, willing your feet to move in a fast rhythm. By the same token, every swear word you mutter to bear down on a job is a secular mantra, while every one you unthinkingly repeat is simple profanity.

Qualifier No. 2 (slightly revised)

Secondly, secular mantras only help you use your energy. They don't create energy. The Little Engine, for instance, obviously had enough power to pull the train up the mountainside--she could have done it without a peep. But we all know that puffing "I think I can" somehow made her job easier, just like, say, chanting "left-right-left" makes it easier for us to march in step. Any such word or phrase that magically seems to help you perform an action when you purposefully utter it is a secular mantra.

In fact, it is to highlight this apparent magic that I dubbed these expressions with so odd a title as "secular mantras."

Historical Definition of *Mantra* (slightly revised)

"Mantra" means "sacred counsel" in Sanskrit. The term refers to a "mystical formula of invocation or incantation" used in Hinduism (Webster's). According to Hindu mythology, the god Manu created the first language by teaching humans the thought-form of every object and substance. "VAM," for example, was what he told them to call the stuff we call "water." But men altered or forgot most of Manu's thought-forms.

Followers of Hinduism believe mantras, groups of these ancient words revealed anew by gods to seers, can summon specific objects or deities if they are properly repeated, silently or vocally. Hindus repeat mantras to gain superhuman powers, cure diseases, and for many other purposes. Sideshow fakirs chant "AUM" ("I agree" or "I accept") to become immune to pain when lying on beds of nails.

Definition of Secular (expanded)

Our "mantras" are "secular" because, unlike Hindus, we do not attribute them to gods. Instead, we borrow them from tradition or invent them to fit a situation, as the Little Engine did. They work not by divine power but because they help us, in a way, to govern transmissions along our central nervous systems.

Explanation (new)

Secular mantras give our brains a sort of dual signal-boosting and signal-damping capacity. The act of repeating them pushes messages, or impulses, with extra force along our nerves or interferes with incoming messages we would rather ignore. We can then perform actions more easily or cope with stress that might keep us from functioning the way we want to. We may even accomplish both tasks at once. A sky-diver might yell

Example (elaborated)

"Geronimo," for example, both to louden the signals telling his legs to jump and to drown out the ones warning him he's dizzy or scared.

More Examples (new)   Any one of us can use any words
in this way to help himself do any
task. A father might count to ten to
keep from bellowing when Junior
brings the car home dented. A tennis
player who faults may chide himself
"Get serious!" as he swings, to
concentrate harder on directing the
ball. A sleepy mother pacing with her
wailing baby can make her chore less
painful by muttering, "You'll have
kids someday." Chanting "Grease
Personal Example   Cartridge" always cools my temper
(new)   because doing that once kept me from
exploding at my father when we were
working on a meddlesome Buick.

Revised Conclusion   You probably have favorite
(more positive)   secular mantras already. Think about
it. How about those phrases you
mumble to force yourself from your
warm bed on chilly mornings? And
those words you chant to ease your
impatience when the traffic lights
are endless. And the reminders you
mutter so you'll remember to buy
bread at the store. You know what I'm
talking about. And you must see how
much less painful and frustrating
your life is because of those magic
words and phrases.

"Secular Mantras" is a fine essay of definition. Keith Eldred provides a clear explanation of the concept, offers numerous examples
to illustrate it, and suggests how mantras work and how we use
them. More importantly, the notes and the two drafts of Keith's
paper show how writing is accomplished. By reading analytically—both his own writing and the writing of others more experienced than he—Keith has discovered the requirements of the

strategy and how best to achieve them. Then an honest and thorough appraisal of his rough draft has led to thoughtful revisions, resulting in a stronger and more effective piece of writing.

An Argumentative Essay

Betty Platt's paper grew out of her reading the essays in Section 11. Her assignment was to write an argument and, like Keith, she was free to choose her own topic. She knew from past experience that in order to write a good essay, she would have to write on a topic she cared about. She also knew that she should allow herself a reasonable amount of time to find such a topic and gather her ideas. Betty, a socially conscious nontraditional student, was personally troubled by hearing and reading about homelessness, and she decided to write about the plight of these people. She saw this paper, then, as an opportunity to become more informed about the issue and articulate her own position on it.

Betty began by brainstorming about the topic. She made lists of all the ideas, facts, issues, arguments, opposing arguments, and refutations that came to mind as a result of her own reflections on the topic. She then went to the library to find additional information and was successful in locating several helpful articles. Once she was confident that she had enough information to begin writing she made a rough outline of an organizational pattern she felt would work well for her. Keeping this pattern in mind, Betty wrote a first draft of her essay, then went back and examined it carefully, assessing how it could be improved.

Betty was writing this particular essay in the second half of the semester after she had read and written a number of essays and had learned the importance of such matters as good paragraphing, unity, and sound organization. In working out her thinking on the issue of homelessness she realized that a historical or chronological organizational pattern would best suit her purpose and rearranged her discussion of popular explanations for homelessness accordingly. She also found places where phrases and even whole sentences could be added to make her meaning clearer. She repositioned some sentences, added some key transitions, and rewrote her concluding paragraphs to make them forceful as well as more persuasive.

As you read Betty's final draft notice how she assesses each of the causes of homelessness, uses specific information and statistics to support her thesis and purpose, and how she has used the MLA in-text citation system to acknowledge her sources. Finally, notice how she uses her opening paragraph to establish a context for the essay and her last three paragraphs to identify what she considers the real problem and call her readers to action.

The "Housed" or the Homeless: With Which Group Does the Problem Lie?

Why are there so many people living in shelters, in their cars, and on the streets of one of the world's richest countries? Perhaps more importantly, what is the obligation of society to provide for the most basic needs of its members? It was not until the late 1970s that people living on the street began to be visible in public places, and in the 80s, citizens started to address some of the problems. For a time, "helping the homeless" became a cause célèbre. National fund raising events like Hands Across America took place. New shelters opened and existing shelters expanded. Churches and service organizations rallied, and people who wanted to help found themselves serving soup and muffins at the soup kitchen. Governments at all levels implemented or improved services for the homeless or provided money for such services. But by the end of the decade, weariness and frustration set in—the problems of the homeless weren't getting better. Public opinion in many places has now turned against the homeless and the sympathy and good will homeless people once enjoyed is waning. This new callousness makes life on the streets even more difficult for those who have no other home.

To understand why so many adults and children are without something as basic as safe housing, it is useful to look back a few years. In the 1960s, Lyndon Johnson's Great Society promised relief and hope to millions of poor Americans. In those prosperous

economic years the new social programs did make people
better off. By the mid–70s, for example, only a
minority of the elderly continued to live in poverty,
that is, below the official federal poverty line. It
began to seem that the homelessness that had existed
in greater or lesser degrees since the Great
Depression would finally be eliminated. The oil crisis
of the early 1970s, however, caused high inflation,
and increasing unemployment cut away at the gains of
the previous decades. Further economic distress late
in the '70s eroded the ledge of safety to which many
low–income people had been clinging, and the number of
homeless people began to grow. When recession struck
again in 1982, thousands of men, women, and families
became homeless and, for the first time, easily found
in major cities and small towns across the country.

Of course, the vast number of people without
homes, conservatively estimated at 300,000, cannot be
attributed solely to the performance of the economy.
Perhaps in response to economic conditions or perhaps
as the result of the ascendance of a conservative
ideology in American politics in the 1980s, federal
policymakers, under the direction and leadership of
the administration, tore apart the programs that
served people with little or no income. Cash benefits
to thousands of disabled persons, families with
children, and veterans were arbitrarily cut off,
leaving them few alternatives for survival. Housing
subsidies for these same impoverished groups were also
reduced drastically. In 1981 such subsidies amounted
to $32 billion. Within eight years, this amount had
been reduced to $9 billion. These draconian cuts
accelerated the deterioration of existing public
housing complexes because little money was provided
for even routine maintenance, and virtually no new
public housing units were constructed. Ironically,
housing subsidies for wealthier Americans, in the form
of property tax and mortgage interest deductions,

survived. In 1990, this foregone revenue cost the government $34 billion (Dreier, Appelbaum 18).

Another explanation is given for the increase in the number of homeless people by housing specialist Peter Salins, who believes it is "mainly due . . . to an increase in the number of dysfunctional people" (qtd. in Landers 182). Salins argues that serious mental problems, alcohol and drug abuse, an increasing prison population, and the breakdown of the black family contribute to the dysfunction and create "a swamp of pathology" from which it is difficult to escape. It is not a lack of affordable housing that keeps people homeless, Salins believes, but the inability of these dysfunctional people to maintain themselves and their housing.

The large population of mentally ill people who are homeless is often considered to be the consequence of the Community Mental Health Act of 1963. In seeking a more humane alternative to long-term institutional care for mentally ill persons in psychiatric hospitals, a policy was adopted that required the release of those patients who would be able to live in the community with support from a local mental health center. The Act called for the creation of hundreds of community mental health centers, but fewer than half the number planned were ever opened. Many suppose that the lack of local services left mentally ill people without support, leading, eventually, to homelessness. However, author James Wright points out that "deinstitutionalization" was largely accomplished by the late 1970s and cannot be a significant "contributing factor to the rise of homelessness in the 1980s" (qtd. in Landers 183).

Whether or not the emptying of state mental hospitals caused so many mentally ill people to become homeless, their disabilities prevented them from working. Therefore, many former patients received a small monthly disability check from the Social Security Administration. But, in the effort to cut

government expenditures, the Reagan administration
decided that thousands of recipients were no longer
disabled "enough" and eliminated their benefits.
Without this source of income, many of the mentally
ill simply had no money to pay for housing and were
left to fend for themselves on the street.

In discussing "dysfunctional people," Peter
Salins refers also to those who suffer alcohol and
drug addiction. Among those who have studied
homelessness, there is general agreement that about
one-third of homeless people abuse drugs and alcohol.
In a society that glamorizes the use of alcohol and
offers drugs as the rational response to a host of
problems, we should not be surprised at the scope of
usage among street people. What is less clear than the
number of homeless people with substance abuse
problems is whether it is the cause or effect of their
homelessness. By some it is argued that the behavior
resulting from abuse of alcohol or drugs costs people
their jobs, and without a source of income, their
housing. Others maintain that the harsh reality of
living on the street leads people to numb themselves
with alcohol or drugs just to get through long days
and cold nights. Thirty or forty years ago alcoholics
on the margins of society could find housing in old
run-down hotels where they rented rooms for next to
nothing. But as the urban renewal and gentrification
projects of the 1960s and 1970s claimed these old
buildings for grander purposes, the poor tenants were
displaced. Replacement housing was seldom built, and
these people, too, were forced to live on the streets.

Both the housing shortage explanation and the
dysfunctional person explanation have flaws. Among
those who advance the housing shortage idea, there is
a tendency to ignore the serious problems of some
homeless people that make it difficult for them to
live independently without support services. On the
other hand, the "dysfunctional person" thinking tends
to blame the homeless for their situation or to view

the problems as insurmountable. Either accounting of
the extraordinarily large problem of homelessness
illustrates the failure of society to make the comfort
and safety of even its weakest members a priority.
These members have been pushed into the margins of
society against their will and without regard for
their best interest. Society has a duty to correct
this inequity. As Peter Marin writes in "Helping and
Hating the Homeless," society owes those who are
involuntarily marginalized "whatever it takes for them
to regain their place in the social order" (48).

But what will it take for these marginalized
citizens to regain their place in the social order?
Perhaps the homeless themselves are better able to
propose a solution than the hundreds of "experts" who
have designed the answers so far. In a survey in
southeastern Vermont in 1988, homeless people were
asked what it would take for them to overcome the
state of homelessness. Their responses were realistic
and modest. Most said they would like to have a job
that would allow them to support themselves; a clean,
quiet place to live where they could go and turn the
lock every night; a treatment program; and
intervention from outside (Ruth 64). These solutions
seem eminently sensible.

Dr. David Ruth, author of the Vermont research,
expanding on an idea of Robert Bierstedt, explains
that society—we in "Group A"—study the social
problems experienced by the homeless in "Group B" to
try to solve the serious social problem of the latter
group. Dr. Ruth continues,

> Upon reflection, however, it seems more likely
> the cause of our social problems is to be found
> not in Group B but in Group A. It is, after all,
> Group A who allows the social problems to exist
> and who enacts and embraces policies that
> maintain the continuing existence of that social
> problem (71).

If Dr. Ruth is correct, it would seem that the problem of homelessness is of our own making. And it is, therefore, our obligation to correct the problem. By almost any measure, the programs and services for homeless people have not been very successful in eliminating homelessness. But we cannot abandon the homeless to the streets and their own devices because our plans have failed. It is past time to find out from homeless people themselves how they can "regain their place in the social order," and then society must do "whatever it takes" to enable that change. Morally, we can do no less.

Works Cited

Dreier, Peter and Richard Appelbaum. "The Housing Crisis Meets the Nineties." Tikkun 5.5 (1990): 15–18+.

Landers, Robert K. "Why Homeless Need More Than Shelter." Editorial Research Reports 30 Mar. 1990: 174–187.

Marin, Peter. "Helping and Hating the Homeless: The Struggle at the Margins of America." Harper's Magazine Jan. 1987: 39–44+.

Ruth, David N., Christine Nolan and Edgar Sather. The World of the Homeless, Brattleboro, Vermont: Initial Report. Unpublished, 1990.

1
Four Writers on Writing

Like any other craft, writing involves basic skills that can be learned, as well as more sophisticated techniques that can be refined and then passed from one practitioner to another. Some of the most important lessons a student writer encounters may come from the shared experiences of other writers: suggestions, advice, cautions, corrections, encouragement. This section brings together a group of essays in which writers discuss their individual habits, difficulties, and judgments, and at the same time express the joy that writing has given them and the hard work it can entail. These writers deal with the full range of the writing process—from freeing the imagination in journal entries to correcting punctuation errors for the final draft—and the advice they offer is pertinent and sound. The skills and techniques presented here can help you as you set out in your writing course to exert a greater measure of control over your writing and, in the process, to become more confident in how best to achieve your goals.

Freewriting

Peter Elbow

Peter Elbow was born in New York in 1935, and received degrees from Williams College, Exeter College, Oxford, and Brandeis University. A well-known writing teacher, Elbow is currently a professor of English at the University of Massachusetts at Amherst. Previously he taught at the State University of New York at Stony Brook, the Massachusetts Institute of Technology, Franconia College, and Evergreen State College. He is best known for his innovative books Writing without Teachers, Writing with Power, Embracing Contraries, *and* What Is English?

In "Freewriting," taken from Writing without Teachers, *Elbow explains an exercise for writers that he helped popularize in American colleges and universities.*

The most effective way I know to improve your writing is to do freewriting exercises regularly. At least three times a week. They are sometimes called "automatic writing," "babbling," or "jabbering" exercises. The idea is simply to write for ten minutes (later on, perhaps fifteen or twenty). Don't stop for anything. Go quickly without rushing. Never stop to look back, to cross something out, to wonder how to spell something, to wonder what word or thought to use, or to think about what you are doing. If you can't think of a word or a spelling, just use a squiggle or else write, "I can't think of it." Just put down something. The easiest thing is just to put down whatever is in your mind. If you get stuck it's fine to write "I can't think what to say, I can't think what to say" as many times as you want; or repeat the last word you wrote over and over again; or anything else. The only requirement is that you *never* stop.

What happens to a freewriting exercise is important. It must be a piece of writing which, even if someone reads it, doesn't send any ripples back to you. It is like writing something and putting it in a bottle in the sea. The teacherless class helps your writing by providing maximum feedback. Freewritings help you by providing no feedback at all. When I assign one, I invite the writer to let me read it. But also tell him to keep it if he prefers. I read it quickly and make no comments at all and I do not speak with him about it. The main thing is that a freewriting must never be evaluated in any way; in fact there must be no discussion or comment at all.

Here is an example of a fairly coherent exercise (sometimes they are very incoherent, which is fine): 3

> I think I'll write what's on my mind, but the only thing on my mind right now is what to write for ten minutes. I've never done this before and I'm not prepared in any way—the sky is cloudy today, how's that? now I'm afraid I won't be able to think of what to write when I get to the end of the sentence—well, here I am at the end of the sentence— here I am again, again, again, again, at least I'm still writing—Now I ask is there some reason to be happy that I'm still writing—ah yes! Here comes the question again—What am I getting out of this? What point is there in it? It's almost obscene to always ask it but I seem to question everything that way and I was gonna say something else pertaining to that but I got so busy writing down the first part that I forgot what I was leading into. This is kind of fun oh don't stop writing—cars and trucks speeding by somewhere out the window, pens clittering across people's papers. The sky is cloudy—is it symbolic that I should be mentioning it? Huh? I dunno. Maybe I should try colors, blue, red, dirty words—wait a minute—no can't do that, orange, yellow, arm tired, green pink violet magenta lavender red brown black green—now that I can't think of any more colors—just about done—relief? maybe.

Freewriting may seem crazy but actually it makes simple sense. Think of the difference between speaking and writing. Writing has the advantage of permitting more editing. But that's its downfall too. Almost everybody interposes a massive and complicated series of editings between the time words start to be born into consciousness and when they finally come off the end of the pencil or typewriter onto the page. This is partly because schooling makes us obsessed with the "mistakes" we make in writing. Many people are constantly thinking about spelling and grammar as they try to write. I am always thinking about the awkwardness, wordiness, and general mushiness of my natural verbal product as I try to write down words.

But it's not just "mistakes" or "bad writing" we edit as we write. 4 We also edit unacceptable thoughts and feelings, as we do in speaking. In writing there is more time to do it so the editing is heavier: when speaking, there's someone right there waiting for a reply and he'll get bored or think we're crazy if we don't come out with *something.* Most of the time in speaking, we settle for the catch-as-catch-can way in which the words tumble out. In writing, however, there's a chance to try to get them right. But the opportunity to get them right is a terrible burden: you can work for two hours trying to get a paragraph "right" and discover it's not right at all. And then give up.

Editing, *in itself,* is not the problem. Editing is usually necessary 5 if we want to end up with something satisfactory. The problem is that editing goes on *at the same time* as producing. The editor is, as it were, constantly looking over the shoulder of the producer and constantly fiddling with what he's doing while he's in the middle of trying to do it. No wonder the producer gets nervous, jumpy, inhibited, and finally can't be coherent. It's an unnecessary burden to try to think of words and also worry at the same time whether they're the right words.

The main thing about freewriting is that it is *nonediting.* It is an 6 exercise in bringing together the process of producing words and putting them down on the page. Practiced regularly, it undoes the ingrained habit of editing at the same time you are trying to produce. It will make writing less blocked because words will come more easily. You will use up more paper, but chew up fewer pencils.

Next time you write, notice how often you stop yourself from 7 writing down something you were going to write down. Or else cross it out after it's written. "Naturally," you say, "it wasn't any good." But think for a moment about the occasions when you spoke well. Seldom was it because you first got the beginning just right. Usually it was a matter of a halting or even garbled beginning, but you kept going and your speech finally became coherent and even powerful. There is a lesson here for writing: trying to get the beginning just right is a formula for failure—and probably a secret tactic to make yourself give up writing. Make some words, whatever they are, and then grab hold of that line and reel in as hard as you can. Afterwards you can throw away lousy beginnings and make new ones. This is the quickest way to get into good writing.

The habit of compulsive, premature editing doesn't just make 8 writing hard. It also makes writing dead. Your voice is damped out by all the interruptions, changes, and hesitations between the consciousness and the page. In your natural way of producing words there is a sound, a texture, a rhythm—a voice—which is the main source of power in your writing. I don't know how it works, but this voice is the force that will make a reader listen to you, the energy that drives the meanings through his thick skull. Maybe you don't *like* your voice; maybe people have made fun of it. But it's the only voice you've got. It's your only source of power. You better get back into it, no matter what you think of it. If you keep writing in it, it may change into something you like better. But if you abandon it, you'll likely never have a voice and never be heard.

Freewritings are vacuums. Gradually you will begin to carry over 9 into your regular writing some of the voice, force, and connectedness that creep into those vacuums.

Questions for Study and Discussion

1. What, according to Elbow, is the purpose of freewriting? Have you ever tried it? If so, what was your experience with it?
2. What does Elbow recommend writers to do during a freewriting exercise?
3. How should freewriting be evaluated?
4. What is the difference between speaking and writing? Why is the difference important to Elbow?
5. What is the author's attitude toward mistakes and editing? What does Elbow mean when he says freewriting is "nonediting" (paragraph 6)?
6. What does Elbow see in paragraph 9 as the connection between freewriting and regular writing?

Starting to Write: Some Practical Advice
William Zinsser

*Born in New York City in 1922, William Zinsser was ed-
ucated at Princeton University. He has worked for the* New
York Herald Tribune, *has taught at Yale University, and
from 1979 to 1987 was general editor of the Book-of-the-Month
Club. Zinsser's books include* The City Dwellers, Pop Goes
America, Spring Training, *and three popular books on writing:* On Writing Well, Writing *with a Word Processor,
and* Writing to Learn.

The following selection is from On Writing Well, *a book
that grew out of Zinsser's experience as a writer and teacher.
In it he offers "some practical advice" to the beginning writer.*

Few people realize how badly they write. Nobody has shown 1
them how much excess or murkiness has crept into their style and
how it obstructs what they are trying to say. If you give me an
article that runs to eight pages and I tell you to cut it to four, you'll
howl and say it can't be done. Then you'll go home and do it, and
it will be infinitely better. After that comes the hard part: cutting
it to three.

The point is that you have to strip down your writing before you 2
can build it back up. You must know what the essential tools are
and what job they were designed to do. If I may labor the metaphor
of carpentry, it is first necessary to be able to saw wood neatly and
to drive nails. Later you can bevel the edges or add elegant finials,
if that's your taste. But you can never forget that you are practicing
a craft that is based on certain principles. If the nails are weak,
your house will collapse. If your verbs are weak and your syntax
is rickety, your sentences will fall apart.

I'll admit that various nonfiction writers, like Tom Wolfe and 3
Norman Mailer, have built some remarkable houses. But these are
writers who spent years learning their craft, and when at last they
raised their fanciful turrets and hanging gardens, to the surprise

36

of all of us who never dreamed of such ornamentation, they knew what they were doing. Nobody becomes Tom Wolfe overnight, not even Tom Wolfe.

First, then, learn to hammer in the nails, and if what you build 4 is sturdy and serviceable, take satisfaction in its plain strength.

But you will be impatient to find a "style"—to embellish the 5 plain words so that readers will recognize you as someone special. You will reach for gaudy similes and tinseled adjectives, as if "style" were something you could buy in a style store at the mall and drape onto your words in bright decorator colors. (Decorator colors are the colors that decorators come in.) There is no style store. Style is organic to the person doing the writing, as much a part of him as his hair, or, if he is bald, his lack of it. Trying to add style is like adding a toupee. At first glance the formerly bald man looks young and even handsome. But at second glance—and with a toupee there is always a second glance—he doesn't look quite right. The problem is not that he doesn't look well groomed; he does, and we can only admire the wigmaker's almost perfect skill. The point is that he doesn't look like himself.

This is the problem of the writer who sets out deliberately to 6 garnish his prose. You lose whatever it is that makes you unique. The reader will usually notice if you are putting on airs. He wants the person who is talking to him to sound genuine. Therefore a fundamental rule is: Be yourself.

No rule, however, is harder to follow. It requires writers to do 7 two things which by their metabolism are impossible. They must relax and they must have confidence.

Telling a writer to relax is like telling a man to relax while being 8 prodded for a possible hernia, and as for confidence, he is a bundle of anxieties. See how stiffly he sits, glaring at the paper or the screen that awaits his words. See how often he gets up to look for something to eat. A writer will do anything to avoid the act of writing. I can testify from my newspaper days that the number of trips made to the water cooler per reporter-hour far exceeds the body's need for fluids.

What can be done to put the writer out of these miseries? Un- 9 fortunately, no cure has yet been found. I can only offer the consoling thought that you are not alone. Some days will go better than others; some will go so badly that you will despair of ever writing again. We have all had many of these days and will have many more.

Still, it would be nice to keep the bad days to a minimum, which 10 brings me back to the matter of trying to relax.

The average writer (as I said earlier) sets out to commit an act 11 of literature. He thinks his article must be of a certain length or it won't seem important. He thinks how august it will look in print. He thinks of all the people who will read it. He thinks it must have the solid weight of authority. He thinks that its style must dazzle. No wonder he tightens: he is so busy thinking of his awesome responsibility to the finished article that he can't even start. Yet he vows to be worthy of the task, and, casting about for heavy phrases that would never occur to him if he weren't trying so hard to make an impression, he plunges in.

Paragraph 1 is a disaster—a tissue of ponderous generalities that 12 seem to have come out of a machine. No *person* could have written them. Paragraph 2 isn't much better. But Paragraph 3 begins to have a somewhat human quality, and by Paragraph 4 the writer begins to sound like himself. He has started to relax. It's amazing how often an editor can simply throw away the first three or four paragraphs of an article and start with the paragraph where the writer begins to sound like himself. Not only are the first few paragraphs hopelessly impersonal and ornate; they also don't really say anything. They are a self-conscious attempt at a fancy introduction, and none is necessary.

A writer is obviously at his most natural and relaxed when he 13 writes in the first person. Writing is a personal transaction between two people, conducted on paper, and the transaction will go well to the extent that it retains its humanity. Therefore I urge people to write in the first person—to use "I" and "me" and "we" and "us." They usually put up a fight.

"Who am I to say what *I* think?" they ask. "Or what *I* feel?" 14

"Who are you *not* to say what you think?" I reply. "There's only 15 one you. Nobody else thinks or feels in exactly the same way."

"But no one cares about my opinions," they say. "It would make 16 me feel conspicuous."

"They'll care if you tell them something interesting," I say, "and 17 tell them in words that come naturally."

Nevertheless, getting writers to use "I" is seldom easy. They 18 think they must somehow earn the right to reveal their emotions or their deepest thoughts. Or that it's egotistical. Or that it's un-dignified—a fear that hobbles the academic world. Hence the pro-fessorial use of "one" ("One finds oneself not wholly in accord with Dr. Maltby's view of the human condition") and of the im-personal "it is" ("It is to be hoped that Professor Felt's essay will find the wider audience it most assuredly deserves"). I don't want to meet "one"—he's a boring guy. I want a professor with a pas-sion for his subject to tell me why it fascinates *him*.

I realize that there are vast regions of writing where "I" is not allowed. Newspapers don't want "I" in their news stories; many magazines don't want it in their articles; businesses and institutions don't want it in the annual reports and pamphlets that they send so profusely into the American home. Colleges don't want "I" in their term papers or dissertations, and English teachers in ele-mentary and high schools have been taught to discourage any first-person pronoun except the literary "we" ("We see in Melville's symbolic use of the white whale . . ."). Many of these prohibitions are valid. Newspaper articles should consist of news, reported ob-jectively. And I sympathize with teachers who don't want to give students an easy escape into opinion—"I think Hamlet was stu-pid"—before the students have grappled with the discipline of assessing a work on its merits and on external sources. "I" can be a self-indulgence and a cop-out.

Still, we have become a society fearful of revealing who we are. We have bred a national language of impersonality. The institu-tions that seek our support by sending us their brochures tend to sound remarkably alike, though surely all of them—hospitals, schools, libraries, museums, zoos—were founded and are still sus-tained by men and women with different dreams and visions. Where are these people? It's hard to glimpse them among all the passive sentences that say "initiatives were undertaken" and "priorities have been identified."

Even when "I" is not permitted, it's still possible to convey a sense of I-ness. James Reston, for instance, doesn't use "I" in his columns; yet I have a good idea of what kind of person he is, and I could say the same of other essayists and reporters. Good writers are always visible just behind their words. If you aren't allowed to use "I," at least think "I" while you write, or write the first draft in the first person and then take the "I"'s out. It will warm up your impersonal style.

Style, of course, is tied to the psyche, and writing has deep 22 psychological roots. The reasons why we express ourselves as we do, or fail to express ourselves because of "writer's block," are buried partly in the subconscious mind. There are as many different kinds of writer's block as there are kinds of writers, and I have no intention of trying to untangle them here. This is a short book, and my name isn't Sigmund Freud.

But I've noticed a new reason for avoiding "I" that runs even 23 deeper than what is not allowed or what is undignified. Americans are suddenly unwilling to go out on a limb. A generation ago our leaders told us where they stood and what they believed. Today they perform the most strenuous verbal feats to escape this fate. Watch them wriggle through TV interviews without committing themselves on a single issue. I remember President Ford trying to assure a group of visiting businessmen that his fiscal policies would work. He said: "We see nothing but increasingly brighter clouds every month." I took this to mean that the clouds were still fairly dark. Ford's sentence, however, was just misty enough to say nothing and still sedate his constituents.

Later administrations brought no relief. Defense Secretary Cas- 24 per Weinberger, assessing a Polish crisis in 1984, said: "There's continuing ground for serious concern and the situation remains serious. The longer it remains serious, the more ground there is for serious concern." President Bush, taking a stand on assault rifles in 1989, said: "There are various groups that think you can ban certain kinds of guns. I am not in that mode. I am in the mode of being deeply concerned."

But my all-time champ is Elliot Richardson, who held four major 25 cabinet positions in the 1970s—attorney general and secretary of defense, commerce and HEW. It's hard to know even where to begin picking from his vast trove of equivocal statements, but consider this one: "And yet, on balance, affirmative action has, I think, been a qualified success." A thirteen-word sentence with five hedging words. I give it first prize as the most wishy-washy sentence in recent public discourse, though a close rival would be Richardson's analysis of how to ease boredom among assembly-line workers: "And so, at last, I come to the one firm conviction that I mentioned at the beginning: it is that the subject is too new for final judgments."

That's a firm conviction? Leaders who bob and weave like aging boxers don't inspire confidence—or deserve it. The same thing is true of writers. Sell yourself, and your subject will exert its own appeal. Believe in your own identity and your own opinions. Proceed with confidence, generating it by pure will-power. Writing is an act of ego, and you might as well admit it. Use its energy to keep yourself going.

26

Questions for Study and Discussion

1. Zinsser says that writers too seldom write in the first-person narrative. Why, according to the author, is this so?
2. Why are many writers "a bundle of anxieties" when they first sit down to write? How do you feel when getting started on an essay?
3. In paragraph 6, Zinsser says that one of the fundamental rules to good writing is to "be yourself." Why do writers find such simple advice so difficult to follow? What assistance does the author offer to help writers follow this rule?
4. How does the "metaphor of carpentry" in paragraph 2 help Zinsser talk about writing? Identify several other metaphors used by the author and explain how each one works in the context of the essay as a whole. (Glossary: *Figures of Speech*)
5. Carefully reread paragraphs 1 through 5, this time circling all of Zinsser's verbs. How can you characterize the verbs? How does the author's choice of verbs add to his essay?
6. What is the purpose of Zinsser's use of dialogue in paragraphs 14 through 17? Is it effective? Why, or why not?
7. Zinsser argues that "you have to strip down your writing before you can build it back up" (2). Do you agree? Explain your experience with having to "strip down" your writing.

The Maker's Eye: Revising Your Own Manuscripts

Donald M. Murray

Donald M. Murray is a writer, who for many years taught writing at the University of New Hampshire. He served as an editor at Time *and won the Pulitzer Prize in 1954 for editorials that appeared in the* Boston Globe. *Murray's published works include novels, short stories, poetry, and sourcebooks for teachers of writing, like* A Writer Teaches Writing *and* Learning by Teaching, *where he explores aspects of the writing process.* Write to Learn, *a textbook for college composition courses, is based on the author's belief that writers learn to write by writing, by taking a piece of writing through the whole process, from invention to revision.*

In the following essay, first published in a different form in The Writer *(October 1973), Murray discusses the importance of revision to the work of a writer.*

When students complete a first draft, they consider the job of 1
writing done—and their teachers too often agree. When professional writers complete a first draft, they usually feel that they are
at the start of the writing process. When a draft is completed, the
job of writing can begin.

That difference in attitude is the difference between amateur and 2
professional, inexperience and experience, journeyman and craftsman. Peter F. Drucker, the prolific business writer, calls his first
draft "the zero draft"—after that he can start counting. Most writers share the feeling that the first draft, and all of those which
follow, are opportunities to discover what they have to say and
how best they can say it.

To produce a progression of drafts, each of which says more and 3
says it more clearly, the writer has to develop a special kind of
reading skill. In school we are taught to decode what appears on
the page as finished writing. Writers, however, face a different

category of possibility and responsibility when they read their own drafts. To them the words on the page are never finished. Each can be changed and rearranged, can set off a chain reaction of confusion or clarified meaning. This is a different kind of reading which is possibly more difficult and certainly more exciting.

Writers must learn to be their own best enemy. They must accept the criticism of others and be suspicious of it; they must accept the praise of others and be even more suspicious of it. Writers cannot depend on others. They must detach themselves from their own pages so that they can apply both their caring and their craft to their own work.

Such detachment is not easy. Science fiction writer Ray Bradbury supposedly puts each manuscript away for a year to the day and then rereads it as a stranger. Not many writers have the discipline or the time to do this. We must read when our judgment may be at its worst, when we are close to the euphoric moment of creation.

Then the writer, counsels novelist Nancy Hale, "should be critical of everything that seems to him most delightful in his style. He should excise what he most admires, because he wouldn't thus admire it if he weren't . . . in a sense protecting it from criticism." John Ciardi, the poet, adds, "The last act of the writing must be to become one's own reader. It is, I suppose, a schizophrenic process, to begin passionately and to end critically, to begin hot and to end cold; and, more important, to be passion-hot and critic-cold at the same time."

Most people think that the principal problem is that writers are too proud of what they have written. Actually, a greater problem for most professional writers is one shared by the majority of students. They are overly critical, think everything is dreadful, tear up page after page, never complete a draft, see the task as hopeless.

The writer must learn to read critically but constructively, to cut what is bad, to reveal what is good. Eleanor Estes, the children's book author, explains: "The writer must survey his work critically, cooly, as though he were a stranger to it. He must be willing to prune, expertly and hard-heartedly. At the end of each revision, a manuscript may look . . . worked over, torn apart, pinned together, added to, deleted from, words changed and words changed back. Yet the book must maintain its original freshness and spontaneity."

Most readers underestimate the amount of rewriting it usually 9 takes to produce spontaneous reading. This is a great disadvantage to the student writer, who sees only a finished product and never watches the craftsman who takes the necessary step back, studies the work carefully, returns to the task, steps back, returns, steps back, again and again. Anthony Burgess, one of the most prolific writers in the English-speaking world, admits, "I might revise a page twenty times." Roald Dahl, the popular children's writer, states, "By the time I'm nearing the end of a story, the first part will have been reread and altered and corrected at least 150 times. . . . Good writing is essentially rewriting. I am positive of this."

Rewriting isn't virtuous. It isn't something that ought to be done. 10 It is simply something that most writers find they have to do to discover what they have to say and how to say it. It is a condition of the writer's life.

There are, however, a few writers who do little formal rewriting, 11 primarily because they have the capacity and experience to create and review a large number of invisible drafts in their minds before they approach the page. And some writers slowly produce finished pages, performing all the tasks of revision simultaneously, page by page, rather than draft by draft. But it is still possible to see the sequence followed by most writers most of the time in rereading their own work.

Most writers scan their drafts first, reading as quickly as possible 12 to catch the larger problems of subject and form, then move in closer and closer as they read and write, reread and rewrite.

The first thing writers look for in their drafts is *information.* They 13 know that a good piece of writing is built from specific, accurate, and interesting information. The writer must have an abundance of information from which to construct a readable piece of writing.

Next writers look for *meaning* in the information. The specifics 14 must build to a pattern of significance. Each piece of specific information must carry the reader toward meaning.

Writers reading their own drafts are aware of *audience.* They put 15 themselves in the reader's situation and make sure that they deliver information which a reader wants to know or needs to know in a manner which is easily digested. Writers try to be sure that they anticipate and answer the questions a critical reader will ask when reading the piece of writing.

Writers make sure that the *form* is appropriate to the subject and the audience. Form, or genre, is the vehicle which carries meaning to the reader, but form cannot be selected until the writer has adequate information to discover its significance and an audience which needs or wants that meaning. 16

Once writers are sure the form is appropriate, they must then look at the *structure,* the order of what they have written. Good writing is built on a solid framework of logic, argument, narrative, or motivation which runs through the entire piece of writing and holds it together. This is the time when many writers find it most effective to outline as a way of visualizing the hidden spine by which the piece of writing is supported. 17

The element on which writers may spend a majority of their time is *development.* Each section of a piece of writing must be adequately developed. It must give readers enough information so that they are satisfied. How much information is enough? That's as difficult as asking how much garlic belongs in a salad. It must be done to taste, but most beginning writers underdevelop, underestimating the reader's hunger for information. 18

As writers solve development problems, they often have to consider questions of *dimension.* There must be a pleasing and effective proportion among all the parts of the piece of writing. There is a continual process of subtracting and adding to keep the piece of writing in balance. 19

Finally, writers have to listen to their own voices. *Voice* is the force which drives a piece of writing forward. It is an expression of the writer's authority and concern. It is what is between the words on the page, what glues the piece of writing together. A good piece of writing is always marked by a consistent, individual voice. 20

As writers read and reread, write and rewrite, they move closer and closer to the page until they are doing line-by-line editing. Writers read their own pages with infinite care. Each sentence, each line, each clause, each phrase, each word, each mark of punctuation, each section of white space between the type has to contribute to the clarification of meaning. 21

Slowly the writer moves from word to word, looking through 22 language to see the subject. As a word is changed, cut, or added, as a construction is rearranged, all the words used before that moment and all those that follow that moment must be considered and reconsidered.

Writers often read aloud at this stage of the editing process, 23 muttering or whispering to themselves, calling on the ear's experience with language. Does this sound right—or that? Writers edit, shifting back and forth from eye to page to ear to page. I find I must do this careful editing in short runs, no more than fifteen or twenty minutes at a stretch, or I become too kind with myself. I begin to see what I hope is on the page, not what actually is on the page.

This sounds tedious if you haven't done it, but actually it is fun. 24 Making something right is immensely satisfying, for writers begin to learn what they are writing about by writing. Language leads them to meaning, and there is the joy of discovery, of understanding, of making meaning clear as the writer employs the technical skills of language.

Words have double meanings, even triple and quadruple mean- 25 ings. Each word has its own potential for connotation and denotation. And when writers rub one word against the other, they are often rewarded with a sudden insight, an unexpected clarification.

The maker's eye moves back and forth from word to phrase to 26 sentence to paragraph to sentence to phrase to word. The maker's eye sees the need for variety and balance, for a firmer structure, for a more appropriate form. It peers into the interior of the paragraph, looking for coherence, unity, and emphasis, which make meaning clear.

I learned something about this process when my first bifocals 27 were prescribed. I had ordered a larger section of the reading portion of the glass because of my work, but even so, I could not contain my eyes within this new limit of vision. And I still find myself taking off my glasses and bending my nose towards the page, for my eyes unconsciously flick back and forth across the page, back to another page, forward to still another, as I try to see each evolving line in relation to every other line.

When does this process end? Most writers agree with the great 28 Russian writer Tolstoy, who said, "I scarcely ever reread my published writings, if by chance I come across a page, it always strikes me: all this must be rewritten; this is how I should have written it."

The maker's eye is never satisfied, for each word has the potential to ignite new meaning. This article has been twice written all the way through the writing process, and it was published four years ago. Now it is to be republished in a book. The editors make a few small suggestions, and then I read it with my maker's eye. Now it has been re-edited, re-revised, re-read, re-re-edited, for each piece of writing to the writer is full of potential and alternatives. 29

A piece of writing is never finished. It is delivered to a deadline, torn out of the typewriter on demand, sent off with a sense of accomplishment and shame and pride and frustration. If only there were a couple more days, time for just another run at it, perhaps then . . . 30

Questions for Study and Discussion

1. Why does Murray see revision as such an important element in the process of writing? What is his purpose in writing this essay?
2. What, according to the author, are the eight things a writer must be conscious of in the process of revision? Describe the process you generally go through when you revise your writing.
3. What does Murray mean when he says, "Writers must learn to be their own best enemy" (paragraph 4)? Is this true for other tasks, as well?
4. What does Murray gain from frequently quoting professional writers? What seems to be the common message from these professionals?
5. How do professional writers view first drafts? Why is it important for students to adopt a similar attitude?
6. What does Murray see as the connection between reading and writing? How does reading help the writer?
7. When, according to Murray, does revision end? Why do you suppose he concludes his essay in mid-sentence?

The Qualities of
Good Writing
Jacqueline Berke

*Jacqueline Berke teaches writing at Drew University in New
Jersey. Her textbook* Twenty Questions for the Writer *approaches the writing process from the standpoint of basic questions writers need to ask themselves when writing.*

*In this selection from the second edition of her text, Berke
looks at those qualities of good writing that make it "pungent,
vital, moving, memorable."*

Even before you set out, you come prepared by instinct and 1
intuition to make certain judgments about what is "good." Take
the following familiar sentence, for example: "I know not what
course others may take, but as for me, give me liberty or give me
death." Do you suppose this thought of Patrick Henry's would
have come ringing down through the centuries if he had expressed
this sentiment not in one tight, rhythmical sentence but as follows:

> It would be difficult, if not impossible, to predict on the basis of my
> limited information as to the predilections of the public, what the citizenry at large will regard as action commensurate with the present provocation, but after arduous consideration I personally feel so intensely
> and irrevocably committed to the position of social, political, and economic independence, that rather than submit to foreign and despotic
> control which is anathema to me, I will make the ultimate sacrifice of
> which humanity is capable—under the aegis of personal honor, ideological conviction, and existential commitment, I will sacrifice my own
> mortal existence.

How does this rambling, "high-flown" paraphrase measure up 2
to the bold "Give me liberty or give me death"? Who will deny
that something is "happening" in Patrick Henry's rousing challenge that not only fails to happen in the paraphrase but is actually

negated there? Would you bear with this long-winded, pompous speaker to the end? If you were to judge this statement strictly on its rhetoric (its choice and arrangement of words), you might aptly call it more boring than brave. Perhaps a plainer version will work better:

> Liberty is a very important thing for a person to have. Most people— at least the people I've talked to or that other people have told me about—know this and therefore are very anxious to preserve their liberty. Of course I can't be absolutely sure about what other folks are going to do in this present crisis, what with all these threats and everything, but I've made up my mind that I'm going to fight because liberty is really a very important thing to me; at least that's the way I feel about it.

This flat, "homely" prose, weighted down with what Flaubert 3 called "fatty deposits," is grammatical enough. As in the pompous paraphrase, every verb agrees with its subject, every comma is in its proper place; nonetheless it lacks the qualities that make a statement—of one sentence or one hundred pages—pungent, vital, moving, memorable.

Let us isolate these qualities and describe them briefly. . . . The 4 first quality of good writing is *economy*. In an appropriately slender volume entitled *The Elements of Style,* authors William Strunk and E. B. White stated concisely the case for economy: "A sentence should contain no unnecessary words, a paragraph no unnecessary sentences, for the same reason that a drawing should have no unnecessary lines and a machine no unnecessary parts. This requires not that the writer make all his sentences short or that he avoid all detail . . . but that every word tell." In other words, economical writing is *efficient* and *aesthetically satisfying*. While it makes a minimum demand on the energy and patience of readers, it returns to them a maximum of sharply compressed meaning. You should accept this as your basic responsibility as a writer: that you inflict no unnecessary words on your readers—just as a dentist inflicts no unnecessary pain, a lawyer no unnecessary risk. Economical writing avoids strain and at the same time promotes pleasure by producing a sense of form and right proportion, a sense of words that fit the ideas that they embody—with not a line of "deadwood" to dull the reader's attention, not an extra, useless phrase to clog the free flow of ideas, one following swiftly and clearly upon another.

Another basic quality of good writing is *simplicity*. Here again this does not require that you make all your sentences primerlike or that you reduce complexities to bare bone, but rather that you avoid embellishment or embroidery. The natural, unpretentious style is best. But, paradoxically, simplicity or naturalness does not come naturally. By the time we are old enough to write, most of us have grown so self-conscious that we stiffen, sometimes to the point of rigidity, when we are called upon to make a statement in speech or in writing. It is easy to offer the kindly advice "Be yourself," but many people do not feel like themselves when they take a pencil in hand or sit down at a typewriter. Thus during the early days of the Second World War, when air raids were feared in New York City, and blackouts were instituted, an anonymous writer— probably a young civil service worker at City Hall—produced and distributed to stores throughout the city the following poster:

> Illumination
> is Required
> to be
> Extinguished
> on These Premises
> After Nightfall

What this meant, of course, was simply "Lights Out After Dark"; but apparently that direct imperative—clear and to the point—did not sound "official" enough; so the writer resorted to long Latinate words and involved syntax (note the awkward passives "*is* Required" and "*to be* Extinguished") to establish a tone of dignity and authority. In contrast, how beautifully simple are the words of the translators of the King James Version of the Bible, who felt no need for flourish, flamboyance, or grandiloquence. The Lord did not loftily or bombastically proclaim that universal illumination was required to be instantaneously installed. Simply but majestically "God said, Let there be light: and there was light. . . . And God called the light Day, and the darkness he called Night."

Most memorable declarations have been spare and direct. Abraham Lincoln and John Kennedy seemed to "speak to each other across the span of a century," notes French author André Maurois, for both men embodied noble themes in eloquently simple terms. Said Lincoln in his second Inaugural Address: "With malice towards none, with charity for all, with firmness in the right as God gives us the right, let us strive on to finish the work we are in. . . ." One hundred years later President Kennedy made his Inaugural dedication: "With a good conscience our only sure reward, with history the final judge of our deeds, let us go forth to lead the land we love. . . ."

A third fundamental element of good writing is *clarity*. Some people question whether it is always possible to be clear; after all, certain ideas are inherently complicated and inescapably difficult. True enough. But the responsible writer recognizes that writing should not add to the complications nor increase the difficulty; it should not set up an additional roadblock to understanding. Indeed, the German philosopher Wittgenstein went so far as to say that "whatever can be said can be said clearly." If you understand your own idea and want to convey it to others, you are obliged to render it in clear, orderly, readable, understandable prose—else why bother writing in the first place? Actually, obscure writers are usually confused, uncertain of what they want to say or what they mean; they have not yet completed that process of thinking through and reasoning into the heart of the subject.

Suffice it to say here that whatever the topic, whatever the occasion, expository writing should be readable, informative, and, wherever possible, engaging. At its best it may even be poetic, as Nikos Kazantzakis suggests in *Zorba the Greek*, where he draws an analogy between good prose and a beautiful landscape:

> To my mind the Cretan countryside resembled good prose, carefully ordered, sober, free from superfluous ornament, powerful and restrained. It expressed all that was necessary with the greatest economy. It had no flippancy nor artifice about it. It said what it had to say with a manly austerity. But between the severe lines one could discern an unexpected sensitiveness and tenderness; in the sheltered hollows the lemon and orange trees perfumed the air, and from the vastness of the sea emanated an inexhaustible poetry.

Even in technical writing, where the range of styles is necessarily 10
limited (and poetry is neither possible nor appropriate), you must
always be aware of "the reader over your shoulder." Take such
topics as how to follow postal regulations for overseas mail, how
to change oil in an engine, how to produce aspirin from salicylic
acid. Here are technical expository descriptions that defy a memorable turn of phrase; here is writing that is of necessity cut and
dried, dispassionate, and bloodless. But it need not be difficult,
tedious, confusing, or dull to those who want to find out about
mailing letters, changing oil, or making aspirin. Those who seek
such information should have reasonably easy access to it, which
means that written instructions should be clear, simple, spare, direct, and most of all, *human:* for no matter how technical a subject,
all writing is done *for* human beings *by* human beings. Writing, in
other words, like language itself, is a strictly human enterprise.
Machines may stamp letters, measure oil, and convert acids, but
only human beings talk and write about these procedures so that
other human beings may better understand them. It is always appropriate, therefore, to be human in one's statement.

Part of this humanity must stem from your sense of who your 11
readers are. You must assume a "rhetorical stance." Indeed this
is a fundamental principle of rhetoric: *nothing should ever be written
in a vacuum.* You should identify your audience, hypothetical or
real, so that you may speak to them in an appropriate voice. A
student, for example, should never "just write," without visualizing a definite group of readers—fellow students, perhaps, or the
educated community at large (intelligent nonspecialists). Without
such definite readers in mind, you cannot assume a suitable and
appropriate relationship to your material, your purpose, and your
audience. A proper rhetorical stance, in other words, requires that
you have an active sense of the following:

1. Who you are as a writer.
2. Who your readers are.
3. Why you are addressing them and on what occasion.
4. Your relationship to your subject matter.
5. How you want your readers to relate to the subject matter.

Questions for Study and Discussion

1. What, according to Berke, are the qualities of good writing? Would you make any additions to or subtractions from her list?
2. What does Berke mean by *simplicity*? Why do you suppose much writing is not simple?
3. What features do memorable declarations share? Can you add any examples to the ones that Berke talks about in paragraph 7?
4. Why is it important to "always be aware of 'the reader over your shoulder'" (10), no matter what type of writing you are doing? How does a writer identify his or her audience?
5. How can a writer make technical writing "human"? How does technical writing differ from other types of writing?
6. What is a rhetorical stance? What, according to Berke, does a proper rhetorical stance require?

2
Narration

What Is Narration?

We all love a good story. We're interested to discover "what happened." The tremendous popularity of current fiction and biography speaks to our avid interest in stories. And, knowing of our interest in stories, many writers and speakers use stories to advantage. A science writer, for example, wishing to make the point that many important scientific discoveries have been made by accident, could tell the story of how Sir Alexander Fleming happened to discover penicillin one day when he saw that a bit of mold that had fallen from a culture plate in his laboratory had destroyed bacteria around it. Or a minister, in writing a sermon about charity, could illustrate and emphasize the point that charity should not always be measured in monetary terms by telling the story of the old woman who spent hours every week visiting hospital patients. Or a politician or after-dinner speaker, taking a cue from comedians, could engage the audience by starting off with a humorous story, either true or fictitious.

Whenever you recount an event, or tell a story or anecdote to illustrate an idea, you are using *narration*. In its broadest sense, narration includes all writing that provides an account of an event or a series of events. Although you are already very familiar with narratives, you probably, like the rest of us, associate narration with novels and short fiction. But narration is effective and useful in nonfiction writing as well. A good narrative essay provides a meaningful account of some significant event—anything from the history of America's involvement in Vietnam to a personal experience that gave you new insight about yourself or others.

A good narrative essay has four essential features. The first is *context:* the writer makes clear when the action happened, where it happened, and to whom. The second is *point of view:* the writer establishes and maintains a consistent relationship to the action, either as a participant or as a reporter simply looking on. The third is *selection of detail:* the writer carefully chooses what to include, focusing on those actions and details that are most important to the story while merely mentioning or actually eliminating others. The fourth is *organization:* the writer organizes the events of the narrative into an appropriate sequence, often a strict chronology with a clear beginning, middle, and end. As you read the selections in this chapter, watch for these features and for how each author uses them to tell his or her story.

Why Do Writers Use Narration?

People have been telling stories since the dawn of time and for purposes that have apparently changed very little over the millennia. Perhaps the most basic of these purposes is to entertain. Children love to tell stories and to have stories told to them, and even adults never seem to outgrow their taste for a well-told narrative. People read novels and biographies and watch dramatized stories on television, at the movies, and in the theater, all for the same reason: to be entertained. Certainly, Jean Shepherd's "Lost at C," a narrative you will find in the following pages, is richly entertaining. But as you will see, even this essay does more than entertain, for narration has other purposes as well.

Another of those purposes is to report—to give the facts, to tell what happened. Journalists and historians, in reporting events of the near and more distant past, provide us with information that we can use in our own ways, perhaps to form an opinion about a current issue or to understand why the world is as it is. A biographer gives us another person's life as a document of an individual past but also, perhaps, as a portrait of more general human po-

tential. Scientists recount their experiments so that we may judge for ourselves whether their conclusions are to be believed. We often expect such narratives to be objective, to "stick to the facts," or at least to make clear the difference between facts and opinions.

Perhaps the most important purpose of narration is to instruct. A story may represent a straightforward moral, or it may make a more subtle point about ourselves and the world we live in. In "A Crime of Compassion," for example, Barbara Huttmann tells a story to try and persuade us to take a specific side on an important public issue. Langston Hughes, on the other hand, in "Salvation," finds an equally important significance in the story he tells of his early childhood experiences in church.

Narration, then, can be put to several purposes at once. The goal of the best storytellers is to report on what happened in such a way that the reader is entertained and at the same time comes to a new understanding of a larger issue.

What to Look for in Reading a Narrative Essay

First, make sure that you can follow the events of the narrative, that you understand what's happening. Then, define the writer's purpose and how the various features of the narrative work together to support this purpose.

Consider, for example, the following paragraph from Willie Morris's "On a Commuter Train":

One afternoon in late August, as the summer's sun streamed into the [railroad] car and made little jumping shadows on the windows, I sat gazing out at the tenement-dwellers, who were themselves looking out of their windows from the gray crumbling buildings along the tracks of upper Manhattan. As we crossed into the Bronx, the train unexpectedly slowed down for a few miles. Suddenly from out of my window I saw a large crowd near the tracks, held back by two policemen. Then, on the other side from my window, I saw a sight I would never be able to forget: a little boy almost severed in halves, lying at an incredible angle near the track. The ground was covered with blood, and the boy's eyes were opened wide, strained and disbelieving in his sudden oblivion. A policeman stood next to him, his arms folded, staring straight ahead at

the windows of our train. In the orange glow of late afternoon the policemen, the crowd, the corpse of the boy were for a brief moment im-
mobile, motionless, a small tableau to violence and death in the city.
Behind me, in the next row of seats, there was a game of bridge. I heard
one of the four men say as he looked out at the sight, "God, that's
horrible." Another said, in a whisper, "Terrible, terrible." There was a
momentary silence, punctuated only by the clicking of the wheels on
the track. Then, after the pause, I heard the first man say: "Two hearts."

Clearly, few readers would have difficulty understanding what
happens here. This is partly because the narrative is so brief and
partly because the events are so memorable. More important,
though, is the fact that Morris has used the four essential features
of narration and has used them effectively. First, he establishes a
clear context for his narrative from the very beginning. He tells
when the action happened: "One afternoon in late August." He
tells where: on the railroad where it crosses from Manhattan into
the Bronx. And he tells who it happened to: the passengers on the
train, including himself. Next, Morris establishes a first-person
point of view (he uses the first-person pronoun *I*) because he is
reporting his own experience, and his point of view allows readers
to take in the events of the narrative directly, as if through his eyes
and ears. He also chooses his details carefully and well. He provides just enough information about the train, the passengers, and
the accident so that readers know what they need to know without
being overwhelmed or bored. He does not bother with needless
data such as the name of the railroad or the precise time; yet he
gives significant attention to the boy's corpse and to the other passengers' reactions, placing the emphasis squarely on these aspects
of his story. Every detail is there for a purpose. Finally, Morris
organizes his story chronologically, so that the events follow each
other as they actually occurred. Notice his use of well-placed words
and phrases such as *suddenly, then, momentary silence,* and *after the
pause* to make transitions between events and clearly indicate how
long each event lasted.

Morris's purpose in telling this story is to make a point. He
doesn't state his point directly, but it comes out in the closing
sentences where he reports the bridge players' reactions to the
grisly sight of the dead boy's corpse: first, "God, that's horrible,"

and "Terrible, terrible"; then, "Two hearts." Morris does not tell his readers what to think of this, and different readers will probably respond in different ways. Some will conclude that the bridge players were unmoved by the boy's death, that they were so callous that they could return to their bridge game after only a "momentary silence." Others may feel that despite everything, even a tragedy such as the death of the boy, life goes on—that it *must* go on— and that the bridge players were not insensitive, merely coping in a typical way with one of life's shocks. You might draw a quite different conclusion of your own. Morris's essay is not a puzzle with a single "right" answer, but an opportunity to broaden your experience and discover your own values and beliefs.

Morris might have told his story from the third-person point of view, as if he were not a participant in the action but merely a reporter of it. Doing so would have cost him some of the immediacy and authority he achieves—it's hard to dispute the facts as he states them, since he was there—but the relative impersonality, the "distance," of third-person point of view has its advantages too. Consider, for example, the following paragraph by William Allen White, from an obituary for his daughter. Again it's a young person who has died and, of course, White was writing from firsthand experience just as Morris was. But he chooses instead to write in the third person:

> The last hour of her life was typical of its happiness. She came home from a day's work at school, topped off by a hard grind with the copy on the High School Annual, and felt that a ride would refresh her. She climbed into her khakis, chattering to her mother about the work she was doing, and hurried to get her horse and be out on the dirt roads for the country air and the radiant green fields of the spring. As she rode through the town on an easy gallop she kept waving at passersby. She knew everyone in town. For a decade the little figure with the long pig-tail and the red hair ribbon has been familiar on the streets of Emporia, and she got in the way of speaking to those who nodded at her. She passed the Kerrs, walking the horse, in front of the Normal Library, and waved at them; passed another friend a few hundred feet further on, and waved at her. The horse was walking and, as she turned into North Merchant street she took off her cowboy hat, and the horse swung into a lope. She passed the Tripletts and waved her cowboy hat at them,

still moving gaily north on Merchant street. A Gazette carrier passed— a High School boy friend—and she waved at him, but with her bridle hand: the horse veered quickly, plunged into the parking lot where the low-hanging limb faced her, and, while she still looked back waving, the blow came. But she did not fall from the horse, she slipped off, dazed a bit, staggered and fell in a faint. She never quite recovered consciousness.

White's third-person point of view keeps the focus squarely on his young daughter and her activities. He himself never appears, never comments, never states his feelings. This objectivity—the psychological distance he sets between himself and his subject— might at first seem strange, even inappropriate, in so personal a narrative. But by presenting the girl in this way, White hopes to make the reader mourn her death as he did. His love for his daughter comes through without his having to assert it, and by keeping his distance he prevents any possibility that sorrow for his daughter will be diluted by sympathy for himself.

Note also that, unlike Morris, White states the point of his story explicitly, indeed in the first sentence: his daughter was a happy little girl. It's this sentence that determines what events he will report, how he will arrange them, and how much detail he will supply about each.

Writing a Narrative Essay

Once you have decided upon the story you want to tell and have determined your purpose, you should keep in mind the basic features of narration and use them when planning, writing, and revising your narrative essay. How you use those features will depend on the story you have to tell and your purpose for telling it.

1. Purpose

Right from the beginning, ask yourself *why* you are telling your story. Your purpose in writing will influence which events and details you include and which you leave out. Suppose, for example, you choose to write about how you learned to ride a bicycle. If you mean mainly to entertain, you will probably include a number of unusual and amusing incidents, unique to your experience. If your purpose is mainly to report or inform, it will make more sense to concentrate on the kinds of details that are common to most people's experience. (However, if your purpose is to tell your readers step-by-step how to ride a bicycle, you should use process analysis and not narration.)

The most successful narrative essays, however, often do more than entertain or inform. Readers will more than likely expect your story to have a point; certainly, you will not be happy if your story is dismissed as essentially "pointless." As you prepare to write, then, look for some significance in the story you want to tell—some broader, more instructive points it may make about the ways of the world. Learning to ride a bicycle may not suggest such points, and it may therefore not be a very good subject for an essay. However, the subject does have possibilities. Here's one: learning to master a difficult, even dangerous, but definitely useful skill like riding a bike is an important experience to have early in life. Here's another: learning to ride a bicycle requires you to acquire and use some basic physics, such as the laws of gravity and the behavior of a gyroscope. Maybe you can think of others. If, however, your story seems pointless even to you, perhaps you can find another, more interesting story to tell.

2. Context

Early in your essay, often in the first paragraph or two, you should establish the context, or setting, of your story—the world within which its action took place:

When it happened—morning, afternoon, 11:37 on the dot.
Where it happened—in the street, at Wendy's, in Pocatello, Idaho.
To whom it happened—to me, to my father, to the waitress, to Teri Hopper.

Without a clear context, your readers can easily get confused or even completely lost.

3. Point of View

You should consider what point of view to take in your narrative. Did you take part in the action? If so, it will seem most natural for you to use the first-person point of view. On the other hand, if you weren't there at all and must rely on other sources for your information, you will probably choose the third-person point of view without even thinking about it. However, if you were a witness to part or all of what happened but not a participant, then you will need to choose between the more immediate and subjective quality of the first person and the more distanced, objective effect of the third person. Whichever you choose, you should maintain that same point of view throughout your narrative, as Willie Morris and William Allen White did in theirs.

4. Selection of Events and Details

When writing your essay, you should include enough detail about the action and its context so that your readers can understand what is going on. In addition, you will want to select and emphasize events and details that serve your purpose. Nonetheless, you should not get so carried away with details that your readers become confused or bored by an excess of information. In good storytelling, deciding what to include is as important as deciding what to leave out.

5. Organization

Storytellers tend to follow an old rule: "Begin at the beginning and go on till you come to the end; then stop." Chronological organization is natural in narration, because it is a reconstruction of the original order of events; it is also easiest for the writer to manage and the reader to understand. However, some narratives are organized using a technique common in movies and the theater called *flashback:* the writer may begin midway through the story with an important or exciting event, then use flashbacks to fill in what happened earlier. Whatever the organization, words and phrases like *for a month, afterward,* and *three days earlier* are examples of devices that will help you and your reader keep the sequence of events straight.

It may help you in organizing to jot down a scratch outline before tackling the first draft of your narrative. Here's an outline of the Willie Morris selection—not by him, of course, but still a useful model:

Narration about an accident on the train line.

> Point: the way the bridge players responded to the boy's death.
>
> Context: commuter train, leaving Manhattan, afternoon, late August.
>
> 1. I'm riding along, looking at the tenements.
> 2. The train slows, I see a crowd out my window.
> 3. I look out the opposite window, see boy killed by train. Lots of detail.
> 4. Bridge players' first comments—quote them.
> 5. Bridge players resume their game as if accident hadn't happened.

Such an outline can remind you of your point, your organization, and the emphasis you want when you write your first draft.

6. *A Few More Pointers*

VERB TENSE   Most narratives are in the past tense, and this is logical: they recount events that have already happened, even if very recently. But writers sometimes like to use the present tense to create an effect of intense immediacy, as if the events were happening as you read about them. The essay by Andrew Kauser, "Challenging My Fears," is an example of the use of present-tense narrative.

NARRATIVE TIME   The number of words or pages you devote to an event does not usually correspond to the number of minutes or hours the event took to happen. You may require several pages to recount an important or complex quarter of an hour, but then pass over years in a sentence or two. Length has to do not with chronological time but with the amount of detail you include, and that's a function of the amount of emphasis you want to give.

TRANSITIONAL WORDS   Words like *next, then,* or *and* are useful, as they help you to carry your readers smoothly through the sequence of events that makes up your narrative. But inexperienced writers sometimes repeat these words needlessly, and this makes their writing style wordy and tiresome. Use these conventional transitions when you really need them, but when you don't—when your readers can follow your story without them—leave them out.

Challenging My Fears

Andrew Kauser

Andrew Kauser was born in Montreal, Canada, where he grew up and still makes his home. While a student at the University of Vermont he majored in recreation management. An avid biker, Andrew has made several bicycle tours through Europe. As a youngster, he often went on weekend-long flying trips with his father, who is a pilot, and these experiences instilled in him a passion for flying and a desire to get his own pilot's license one day.

In the following essay, Andrew narrates how he felt as he took that most important step in becoming a licensed pilot, the first solo flight. Some day Andrew hopes to further his interest in flying, perhaps even combining that interest with his career goals in the recreation management field.

Cedars Airport, just off the western tip of Montreal, is about a 1 half-hour drive from my house. Today's drive is boring as usual except for the chill which runs up the back of my legs because of the cold breeze entering through the rusted floorboards. I peer through the dew-covered windshield to see the leaves changing color. Winter is on its way.

Finally, I arrive at the airport; while my instructor waits, I do 2 my aircraft check. I curse as I touch the steely cold parts of the aircraft. Even though the discomfort is great, I do my check slowly. Hurrying could make me miss a potential problem. It is better to find a problem on the ground instead of in the air. The check takes about fifteen minutes, and by this time my fingertips are white. Everything appears to be in order so now it is time to start up.

My instructor and I climb into the cockpit of the airplane and 3 strap ourselves in. The plane has been out all night, and it is just as cold inside as it is outside. My back shivers as I sit in the seat, and the controls are painfully cold to the touch. The plane starts without a hint of trouble, and in one continuous motion I taxi onto the runway. At full throttle we begin to increase our speed down the runway. In a matter of seconds we leave the ground. The winds are calm and the visibility is endless. It's a beautiful day to fly.

The object of today's lesson is to practice taking off and landing. The first "touch and go" is so smooth that I surprise both myself and my instructor. Unfortunately, my next two attempts are more like "smash and goes." I land once more; this time it is not as jarring as my last two, and my instructor gives me the O.K. to do a circuit alone. We taxi to the hangar and he gets out.

Confined in the small cockpit with my seatbelt strapped around me as tightly as it will go, I look out the window and watch my human security blanket walking back toward the hangars. The calm feeling with which I began the day quickly disappears. I feel like a soldier being sent to the front lines. I begin to feel smothered by the enclosed cockpit. My stomach tightens around the breakfast I ate and squeezes out my last breath. I gulp for air, and my breathing becomes irregular. My mind still functions, though, and I begin to taxi toward the runway.

It is a long taxi, and I have ample time to think about what I am about to do. I remember the time when my father had to land on a football field when his engine quit. My eyes scan the instruments quickly in hope of finding something comforting in all the dials. My hands are still feeling quite cool. I reach out and pull the lever for cabin heat. A rush of warm air saturated with the smell of the engine fills the cockpit. This allows me some comfort and my mind begins to wander. The radio crackles and breaks my train of thought. A student pilot in the air with his instructor announces that he is on final approach for landing. While still taxiing, I look through the Plexiglas windscreen to watch him land. The plane hits hard and bounces right back into the air from which it came. It comes down again and, as though on springs, leaps back into the air. Once again it comes down and this time stays.

At the parking area off the runway, I close the throttle and bring the plane to a stop. I check the instruments and request clearance for take-off from the tower. While I wait I try to calm down.

Now hold your breath and count to ten. Look, the chances of dying in a car accident are twenty times greater, I think to myself. Somehow that wasn't very comforting. The radio crackles, and I exhale quickly. Permission is granted.

I taxi onto the runway and come to a stop. I mentally list my 9
options, but they are very few. One is to get up the courage to
challenge my fears; the other, to turn the plane around and shamefully go back to the hangar. Well, the choices are limited, but
the ultimate decision seems fairly obvious. I reach out and push
the throttle into the full open position. The engine roars to life.
The decision to go has been made. The plane screams down the
runway, and at fifty-five knots I pull back on the controls. In one
clean movement, the plane and I leave the ground.

The noise of the engine is the only thing I can hear as the air 10
pressure begins to clog my ears. My mind still racing, I check my
instruments. The winds are still calm, and the plane cuts through
the air without a hint of trouble. Warm gas-laden air streams
through the vents as the sun streaks into the cockpit through the
passenger window, and I begin to feel quite hot. At seven hundred
feet above the ground, I turn left, check for any traffic, and continue
climbing. At twelve hundred feet, I turn left onto the downwind
portion of the circuit which is parallel to the runway.

This is a longer stretch, and I take a moment to gaze down at 11
the ground below. The view is simply amazing. The trees are all
rich bright colors, and I can see for miles. Then it hits me. I'm
flying alone. It's great, almost tranquil, no instructor yelling things
into my ear, just the machine and myself. A calm feeling begins
to come over me, and I start to enjoy the flight. I check my instruments again and start to descend as I turn left.

Turning onto the final approach, I announce my intentions on 12
the radio. The nice feeling of calm leaves me just as quickly as it
came. What is there to worry about, Andrew? All you have to do
is land the airplane, preferably on the runway. My heart starts to
pound quickly, almost to the beat of the motor. Where is my instructor? Why am I alone?

Lower the nose, Andrew, don't lose speed. Give it some more 13
power, maintain your glidepath, that's it. Bank a little to the left,
that's it, now you're doing it, just a little further. My ears begin
to pop as the pressure on them decreases and the motor gets quieter as I start to decrease power. The plane passes over the thresh-
old of the runway, and I begin to raise the nose. The wheels utter
a squeal as they touch down, but the impact quickly sends the
plane back into the air. The wheels hit again and this time they

stay down. A few seconds later my nose wheel touches down, and I roll to a stop.

Back at the hangar, I climb out of the plane and shudder as the cool air hits me again. A smile comes across my face, and it persists. I told myself that I would just be cool about it and not try to show any emotion but it isn't going to work. I can't stop smiling as my instructor congratulates me. I smile because I know that I was successful in challenging and overcoming my fear. 14

Interview with Andrew Kauser

Your narration is chronological. Did you consider other patterns of organization?

I didn't think much about patterns other than chronological. For the most part, I felt I had no choice but to write it that way. I did have difficulty in beginning the narrative because I wasn't sure whether I wanted to write it in the past or the present tense. I made many attempts at different beginnings, from describing waking up on the morning of my flight to describing how I spent my summer flying. Once I found a beginning that I liked, it was relatively easy to write the rest of the essay because I just wrote about the events in the order that they happened. The beginning solved my tense problem as well.

Why did you feel your narration was worth telling? What was your purpose?

The experience I had with flying was fresh in my mind, and at the time it seemed to be the most interesting thing that had happened to me recently. The purpose of the narrative was to share my experience of flying with the class. When I used to fly with my dad, I was afraid of flying because I didn't know how to operate the plane. In a way, it was a challenge to myself to find out how to fly. I guess I just wanted to tell the readers that you don't get anywhere by just sitting around being afraid.

You don't use any dialogue, or do you?

In paragraph 12 of the narration I do use dialogue—dialogue without quotation marks, however. It is a kind of interior monologue in which I hear my instructor talking to me. I tried other ways of writing the paragraph, but it really didn't come off as well. This passage was very easy for me to write because it was exactly what I was thinking when I was up there.

In writing the essay, what gave you the most trouble? How did you go about solving the problem(s)?

I ran into two problems. The first problem, as I said, was in starting the essay. I knew what I wanted to write about and pretty much what I wanted to say, but I couldn't find a proper beginning for the narrative. I made many attempts at an introduction, but none of them really worked. Finally, I cut a lot of material out that I didn't need and made my beginning much shorter. The second problem I had was trying to make the audience grasp what I was talking about. The first time I read my essay to the class, their reaction was that I didn't use enough detail and so they really didn't feel as though they were there with me. I consequently included many more details when I read the essay, and they were able to understand the experience better.

How important was it for you to set a context for the essay?

Context is very important in anything that you write, but especially in a narrative. The experience I recount in my essay took place in a specific time and place. It wouldn't have been the same narrative if it had taken place in some other city or country. Basically, the narrative is specific to that situation, and it wouldn't be credible to me in another situation.

Coming to an Awareness of Language

Malcolm X

Malcolm X, leader of the Black Muslims, was shot and killed at the age of thirty-nine on February 21, 1965, as he addressed an afternoon rally in Harlem. In his short lifetime, Malcolm X rose from a life on the streets to become one of the most controversial and articulate spokesmen for blacks in the 1960s. With Alex Haley, later the author of Roots, *Malcolm X wrote* The Autobiography of Malcolm X.

In the following chapter from his book, Malcolm X explains how his frustration at being unable to express his ideas led to his determination to master the skills of reading and writing while he was serving time in a federal prison.

I've never been one for inaction. Everything I've ever felt strongly about, I've done something about. I guess that's why, unable to do anything else, I soon began writing to people I had known in the hustling world, such as Sammy the Pimp, John Hughes, the gambling house owner, the thief Jumpsteady, and several dope peddlers. I wrote them all about Allah and Islam and Mr. Elijah Muhammad. I had no idea where most of them lived. I addressed their letters in care of the Harlem or Roxbury bars and clubs where I'd known them.

I never got a single reply. The average hustler and criminal was too uneducated to write a letter. I have known many slick, sharp-looking hustlers, who would have you think they had an interest in Wall Street; privately, they would get someone else to read a letter if they received one. Besides, neither would I have replied to anyone writing me something as wild as "the white man is the devil."

What certainly went on the Harlem and Roxbury wires was that Detroit Red was going crazy in stir, or else he was trying some hype to shake up the warden's office.

During the years that I stayed in the Norfolk Prison Colony,

never did any official directly say anything to me about those letters, although, of course, they all passed through the prison censorship. I'm sure, however, they monitored what I wrote to add
to the files which every state and federal prison keeps on the
conversion of Negro inmates by the teachings of Mr. Elijah
Muhammad.

But at that time, I felt that the real reason was that the white 5
man knew that he was the devil.

Later on, I even wrote to the Mayor of Boston, to the Governor 6
of Massachusetts, and to Harry S. Truman. They never answered;
they probably never even saw my letters. I handscratched to them
how the white man's society was responsible for the black man's
condition in this wilderness of North America.

It was because of my letters that I happened to stumble upon 7
starting to acquire some kind of a homemade education.

I became increasingly frustrated at not being able to express what 8
I wanted to convey in letters that I wrote, especially those to Mr.
Elijah Muhammad. In the street, I had been the most articulate
hustler out there—I had commanded attention when I said something. But now, trying to write simple English, I not only wasn't
articulate, I wasn't even functional. How would I sound writing
in slang, the way I would *say* it, something such as, "Look, daddy,
let me pull your coat about a cat. Elijah Muhammad—"

Many who today hear me somewhere in person, or on television, 9
or those who read something I've said, will think I went to school
far beyond the eighth grade. This impression is due entirely to my
prison studies.

It had really begun back in the Charlestown Prison, when Bimbi 10
first made me feel envy of his stock of knowledge. Bimbi had always
taken charge of any conversation he was in, and I had tried to
emulate him. But every book I picked up had few sentences which
didn't contain anywhere from one to nearly all of the words that
might as well have been in Chinese. When I just skipped those
words, of course, I really ended up with little idea of what the book
said. So I had come to the Norfolk Prison Colony still going through
only book-reading motions. Pretty soon, I would have quit even
these motions, unless I had received the motivation that I did.

I saw that the best thing I could do was get hold of a dictionary— 11
to study, to learn some words. I was lucky enough to reason also

that I should try to improve my penmanship. It was sad. I couldn't even write in a straight line. It was both ideas together that moved me to request a dictionary along with some tablets and pencils from the Norfolk Prison Colony school.

I spent two days just riffling uncertainly through the dictionary's 12 pages. I'd never realized so many words existed! I didn't know *which* words I needed to learn. Finally, just to start some kind of action, I began copying.

In my slow, painstaking, ragged handwriting, I copied into my 13 tablet everything printed on that first page, down to the punctuation marks.

I believe it took me a day. Then, aloud, I read back, to myself, 14 everything I'd written on the tablet. Over and over, aloud, to myself, I read my own handwriting.

I woke up the next morning, thinking about those words—im- 15 mensely proud to realize that not only had I written so much at one time, but I'd written words that I never knew were in the world. Moreover, with a little effort, I also could remember what many of these words meant. I reviewed the words whose meanings I didn't remember. Funny thing, from the dictionary first page right now, that "aardvark" springs to my mind. The dictionary had a picture of it, à long-tailed, long-eared, burrowing African mammal, which lives off termites caught by sticking out its tongue as an anteater does for ants.

I was so fascinated that I went on—I copied the dictionary's next 16 page. And the same experience came when I studied that. With every succeeding page, I also learned of people and places and events from history. Actually the dictionary is like a miniature encyclopedia. Finally the dictionary's A section had filled a whole tablet—and I went on into the B's. That was the way I started copying what eventually became the entire dictionary. It went a lot faster after so much practice helped me to pick up handwriting speed. Between what I wrote in my tablet, and writing letters, during the rest of my time in prison I would guess I wrote a million words.

I suppose it was inevitable that as my word-base broadened, I 17 could for the first time pick up a book and read and now begin to understand what the book was saying. Anyone who has read a great deal can imagine the new world that opened. Let me tell you something: from then until I left that prison, in every free moment I had, if I was not reading in the library, I was reading on my bunk. You couldn't have gotten me out of books with a wedge. Between Mr. Muhammad's teachings, my correspondence, my vistors . . . and my reading of books, months passed without my even thinking about being imprisoned. In fact, up to then, I never had been so truly free in my life.

Questions on Subject

1. Exactly what inspired Malcolm X to "acquire some kind of home-made education"?
2. What are the "Harlem and Roxbury wires" Malcolm X refers to in paragraph 3? Who is Detroit Red?
3. In paragraph 8, Malcolm X refers to the difference between being "articulate" and being "functional" in his speaking and writing. What is the distinction he makes? In your opinion is it a valid one? Why or why not?
4. Malcolm X offers two possible reasons for the warden's keeping track of Negroes' conversion to Muhammadanism. One he states directly; one he implies. What are those two assertions, and what is their effect on the reader?
5. What did Malcolm X hope to learn by copying the dictionary? What unexpected discovery did he make?
6. What is the meaning of *free* as Malcolm X uses it in his final sentence?

Questions on Strategy

1. Malcolm X narrates his experiences as a prisoner in the first person. Why is the first person particularly appropriate?
2. In his opening paragraph, Malcolm X refers to himself as a man of action and conviction. What details does he include to support this assertion?
3. In the opening paragraph, the author presents a list of the names of people he wrote to. How does this list help to establish the context of the story? In what ways is it appropriate?
4. What point is Malcolm X trying to make with his narration? Is it stated directly, or is it implied?

5. Malcolm X makes several references to Muhammad throughout his essay. What effect do these repetitions have on the reader? In what way do they add to the narration?

Questions on Diction and Vocabulary

1. Although Malcolm X taught himself to be articulate, we can still "hear" the voice of the inner city. Cite examples of his diction that help him to maintain a streetwise sound.
2. Malcolm X took great care to copy the dictionary cover to cover. The painstaking nature of this work is apparent in his writing. Cite examples of his choice of phrasing that enable you to feel the almost plodding care he brings to any task.
3. Refer to your desk dictionary to determine the meanings of the following words as they are used in this selection: *hustler* (paragraph 2), *slick* (2), *hype* (3), *frustrated* (8), *articulate* (8), *functional* (8), *emulate* (10), *inevitable* (17).

Writing Suggestions

1. Using Malcolm X's essay as a model, write a story about some goal you have set and achieved in which you were motivated by a strong inner conflict. What was the nature of your conflict? What feeling did it arouse in you, and how did it help you to accomplish your goal?
2. Malcolm X expresses his anger at the white man, but he never asks the reader to feel sorry for him. Tell a story in which you describe your own anger at some injustice to you or someone you know. How can you convey your sense of anger without resorting to a "whining" plea for sympathy?

The Last Flogging

Frederick Douglass

Frederick Douglass (1817–1895) was born into slavery in Maryland. As a young boy, he decided that his only hope of freedom was to learn to read and write. Disguised as a sailor, he escaped from his oppressors. His autobiography, Narrative of the Life of Frederick Douglass, an American Slave *(1845), recounts his experiences as a slave. Douglass also gained fame as a defender not only of the rights of African-Americans but of women as well. His friendship with radical abolitionist John Brown, his tenure as a United States marshall, and his appointment as recorder of deeds for the District of Columbia further attest to the breadth of his experience and the height of his accomplishments.*

In the following excerpt from his autobiography, Douglass narrates the startling consequences of his decision not to tolerate any further abuse at the hands of his oppressors.

Sleep does not always come to the relief of the weary in body, 1 and broken in spirit; especially is it so when past troubles only foreshadow coming disasters. My last hope had been extinguished. My master who I did not venture to hope would protect me *as a man*, had now refused to protect me *as his property*, and had cast me back, covered with reproaches and bruises, into the hands of one who was a stranger to that mercy which is the soul of the religion he professed. May the reader never know what it is to spend such a night as to me was that which heralded my return to the den of horrors from which I had made a temporary escape.

I remained—sleep I did not—all night at St. Michaels, and in 2 the morning (Saturday) I started off, obedient to the order of Master Thomas, feeling that I had no friend on earth, and doubting if I had one in heaven. I reached Covey's about nine o'clock, and just as I stepped into the field, before I had reached the house, true to his snakish habits, Covey darted out at me from a fence-corner, in which he had secreted himself for the purpose of securing me. He was provided with a cowskin and a rope, and he evidently intended to tie me up, and wreak his vengeance on me to the fullest extent. I should have been an easy prey had he succeeded in getting his hands upon me, for I had taken no refreshment since noon on Friday, and this, with the other trying circumstances, had greatly reduced my strength. I, however, darted back into the woods before the ferocious hound could reach me, and buried myself in a thicket, where he lost sight of me. The cornfield afforded me shelter in getting to the woods. But for the tall corn, Covey would have overtaken me, and made me his captive. He was much chagrined that he did not, and gave up the chase very reluctantly, as I could see by his angry movements, as he returned to the house.

For a little time I was clear of Covey and his lash. I was in the wood, buried in its somber gloom and hushed in its solemn silence, hidden from human eyes, shut in with nature and with nature's God, and absent from all human contrivances. Here was a good place to pray, to pray for help, for deliverance—a prayer I had often made before. But how could I pray? Covey could pray—Capt. Auld could pray. I would fain pray; but doubts arising, partly from my neglect of the means of grace and partly from the sham religion which everywhere prevailed there was awakened in my mind a distrust of all religion and the conviction that prayers were unavailing and delusive.

Life in itself had almost become burdensome to me. All my outward relations were against me. I must stay here and starve, or go home to Covey's and have my flesh torn to pieces and my spirit humbled under his cruel lash. These were the alternatives before me. The day was long and irksome. I was weak from the toils of the previous day and from want of food and sleep, and I had been so little concerned about my appearance that I had not yet washed the blood from my garments. I was an object of horror, even to myself. Life in Baltimore, when most oppressive, was a paradise to this. What had I done, what had my parents done, that such a life as this should be mine? That day, in the woods, I would have exchanged my manhood for the brutehood of an ox.

Night came. I was still in the woods, and still unresolved what to do. Hunger had not yet pinched me to the point of going home, and I laid myself down in the leaves to rest, for I had been watching for hunters all day, but not being molested by them during the day, I expected no disturbance from them during the night. I had come to the conclusion that Covey relied upon hunger to drive me home, and in this I was quite correct, for he made no effort to catch me after the morning.

During the night I heard the step of a man in the woods. He was coming toward the place where I lay. A person lying still in the woods in the daytime has the advantage over one walking, and this advantage is much greater at night. I was not able to engage in a physical struggle, and I had recourse to the common resort of the weak. I hid myself in the leaves to prevent discovery. But as the night rambler in the woods drew nearer I found him to be a friend, not an enemy, a slave of Mr. William Groomes of Easton, and kindhearted fellow named "Sandy." Sandy lived that year with Mr. Kemp, about four miles from St. Michaels. He, like myself, had been hired out, but unlike myself had not been hired out to be broken. He was the husband of a free woman who lived in the lower part of Poppie Neck, and he was now on his way through the woods to see her and to spend the Sabbath with her. 6

As soon as I had ascertained that the disturber of my solitude was not an enemy, but the good-hearted Sandy,—a man as famous among the slaves of the neighborhood for his own good nature as for his good sense—I came out from my hiding-place and made myself known to him. I explained the circumstances of the past two days, which had driven me to the woods, and he deeply compassionated my distress. It was a bold thing for him to shelter me, and I could not ask him to do so, for had I been found in his hut he would have suffered the penalty of thirty-nine lashes on his bare back, if not something worse. But Sandy was too generous to permit the fear of punishment to prevent his relieving a brother bondman from hunger and exposure, and therefore, on his own motion, I accompanied him home to his wife—for the house and lot were hers, as she was a free woman. It was about midnight, but his wife was called up, a fire was made, some Indian meal was soon mixed with salt and water, and an ash cake was baked in a hurry, to relieve my hunger. Sandy's wife was not behind him in kindness; both seemed to esteem it a privilege to succor me, for although I was hated by Covey and by my master, I was loved by the colored people, because they thought I was hated for my 7 knowledge, and persecuted because I was feared. I was the only slave in that region who could read or write. There had been one other man, belonging to Mr. Hugh Hamilton, who could read, but he, poor fellow, had, shortly after coming into the neighborhood, been sold off to the far south. I saw him in the cart, to be carried to Easton for sale, ironed and pinioned like a yearling for the slaughter. My knowledge was now the pride of my brother slaves, and no doubt Sandy felt on that account something of the general interest in me. The supper was soon ready, and though over the sea I have since feasted with honorables, lord mayors and aldermen, my supper on ash cake and cold water, with Sandy, was the meal of all my life most sweet to my taste and now most vivid to my memory.

Supper over, Sandy and I went into a discussion of what was 8 possible for me, under the perils and hardships which overshadowed my path. The question was, must I go back to Covey, or must I attempt to run away? Upon a careful survey the latter was found to be impossible, for I was on a narrow neck of land, every avenue from which would bring me in sight of pursuers. There was Chesapeake Bay to the right, and "Pot-pie" River to the left, and St. Michaels and its neighborhood occupied the only space through which there was any retreat.

I found Sandy an odd adviser. He was not only a religious man, 9 but he professed to believe in a system for which I have no name. He was a genuine African, and had inherited some of the so-called magical powers said to be possessed by the eastern nations. He told me that he could help me, that in those very woods there was an herb which in the morning might be found, possessing all the powers required for my protection (I put his words in my own language), and that if I would take his advice he would procure me the root of the herb of which he spoke. He told me, further, that if I would take that root and wear it on my right side it would be impossible for Covey to strike me a blow, and that, with this root about my person, no white man could whip me. He said he had carried it for years, and that he had fully tested its virtues. He had never received a blow from a slaveholder since he carried it, and he never expected to receive one, for he meant always to carry that root for protection. He knew Covey well, for Mrs. Covey was the daughter of Mrs. Kemp, and he (Sandy) had heard of the bar-

barous treatment to which I had been subjected, and he wanted
to do something for me.

Now all this talk about the root was to me very absurd and 10
ridiculous, if not positively sinful. I at first rejected the idea that
the simple carrying a root on my right side (a root, by the way,
over which I walked every time I went into the woods) could possess any such magic power as he ascribed to it, and I was, therefore,
not disposed to cumber my pocket with it. I had a positive aversion
to all pretenders to "divination." It was beneath one of my intelligence to countenance such dealings with the devil as this power
implied. But with all my learning—it was really precious little—
Sandy was more than a match for me. "My book-learning," he
said, "had not kept Covey off me" (a powerful argument just then),
and he entreated me, with flashing eyes, to try this. If it did me
no good it could do me no harm, and it would cost me nothing
any way. Sandy was so earnest and so confident of the good qualities of this weed that, to please him, I was induced to take it. He
had been to me the good Samaritan, and had, almost providen-
tially, found me and helped me when I could not help myself; how
did I know but that the hand of the Lord was in it? With thoughts
of this sort I took the roots from Sandy and put them in my right-
hand pocket.

This was of course Sunday morning. Sandy now urged me to 11
go home with all speed, and to walk up bravely to the house, as
though nothing had happened. I saw in Sandy, with all his superstition, too deep an insight into human nature not to have some
respect for his advice, and perhaps, too, a slight gleam or shadow
of his superstition had fallen on me. At any rate, I started off toward
Covey's, as directed. Having, the previous night, poured my griefs
into Sandy's ears and enlisted him in my behalf, having made his
wife a sharer in my sorrows, and having also become well refreshed
by sleep and food, I moved off quite courageously toward the
dreaded Covey's. Singularly enough, just as I entered the yard-
gate I met him and his wife on their way to church, dressed in
their Sunday best, and looking as smiling as angels. His manner
perfectly astonished me. There was something really benignant in
his countenance. He spoke to me as never before, told me that the
pigs had got into the lot and he wished me to go to drive them out,
inquired how I was, and seemed an altered man. This extraordi-

nary conduct really made me begin to think that Sandy's herb had more virtue in it than I, in my pride, had been willing to allow, and, had the day been other than Sunday, I should have attributed Covey's altered manner solely to the power of the root. I suspected, however, that the Sabbath, not the root, was the real explanation of the change. His religion hindered him from breaking the Sabbath, but not from breaking my skin on any other day than Sunday. He had more respect for the day than for the man for whom the day was mercifully given, for while he would cut and slash my body during the week, he would on Sunday teach me the value of my soul, and the way of life and salvation by Jesus Christ.

All went well with me till Monday morning, and then, whether 12 the root had lost its virtue, or whether my tormentor had gone deeper into the black art than I had (as was sometimes said of him), or whether he had obtained a special indulgence for his faithful Sunday's worship, it is not necessary for me to know or to inform the reader; but this much I may say, the pious and benignant smile which graced the face of Covey on Sunday wholly disappeared on Monday.

Long before daylight I was called up to go feed, rub, and curry 13 the horses. I obeyed the call, as I should have done had it been made at an earlier hour, for I had brought to my mind a firm resolve during that Sunday's reflection to obey every order, however unreasonable, if it were possible, and if Mr. Covey should then undertake to beat me to defend and protect myself to the best of my ability. My religious views on the subject of resisting my master had suffered a serious shock by the savage persecution to which I had been subjected, and my hands were no longer tied by my religion. Master Thomas's indifference had severed the last link. I had backslidden from this point in the slaves' religious creed, and I soon had occasion to make my fallen state known to my Sunday-pious brother, Covey.

While I was obeying his order to feed and get the horses ready 14 for the field, and when I was in the act of going up the stable-loft, for the purpose of throwing down some blades, Covey sneaked into the stable, in his peculiar way, and seizing me suddenly by the leg, he brought me to the stable-floor, giving my newly-mended body a terrible jar. I now forgot all about my roots, and remembered my pledge to stand up in my own defense. The brute was skillfully endeavoring to get a slipknot on my legs, before I could draw up my feet. As soon as I found what he was up to, I gave a sudden spring (my two days' rest had been of much service to me) and by that means, no doubt, he was able to bring me to the floor so heavily. He was defeated in his plan of tying me. While down, he seemed to think that he had me very securely in his power. He little thought he was—as the rowdies say—in for a rough and tumble fight, but such was the fact. Whence came the daring spirit necessary to grapple with a man who, eight-and-forty hours before, could, with his slightest word, have made me tremble like a leaf in a storm, I do not know; at any rate, I was resolved to fight, and what was better still, I actually was hard at it. The fighting madness had come upon me, and I found my strong fingers firmly attached to the throat of the tyrant, as heedless of consequences, at the moment, as if we stood as equals before the law. The very color of the man was forgotten. I felt supple as a cat, and was ready for him at every turn. Every blow of his was parried, thought I dealt no blows in return. I was strictly on the defensive, preventing him from injuring me, rather than trying to injure him. I flung him on the ground several times when he meant to have hurled me there. I held him so firmly by the throat that his blood followed my nails. He held me, and I held him.

All was fair thus far, and the contest was about equal. My re- 15 sistance was entirely unexpected and Covey was taken all aback by it. He trembled in every limb. "Are you going to resist, you scoundrel?" said he. To which I returned a polite "Yes, sir," steadily gazing my interrogator in the eye, to meet the first approach or dawning of the blow which I expected my answer would call forth. But the conflict did not long remain equal. Covey soon cried lustily for help, not that I was obtaining any marked advantage over him, or was injuring him, but because he was gaining none over me, and was not able, single-handed, to conquer me. He called for his cousin Hughes to come to his assistance, and now the scene was changed. I was compelled to give blows, as well as to parry them, and since I was in any case to suffer for resistance, I felt (as the musty proverb goes) that I might as well be hanged for an old sheep as a lamb. I was still defensive toward Covey, but aggressive toward Hughes, on whom, at first approach, I dealt a blow which fairly sickened him. He went off, bending over with pain, and manifesting no disposition to come again within my reach. The poor fellow was in the act of trying to catch and tie my right hand, and while flattering himself with success, I gave him the kick which sent him staggering away in pain, at the same time that I held Covey with a firm hand.

Taken completely by surprise, Covey seemed to have lost his 16 usual strength and coolness. He was frightened, and stood puffing and blowing, seemingly unable to command words or blows. When he saw that Hughes was standing half bent with pain, his courage quite gone, the cowardly tyrant asked if I meant to persist in my resistance. I told him I did mean to resist, come what might, that I had been treated like a brute during the last six months, and that I should stand it no longer. With that he gave me a shake, and attempted to drag me toward a stick of wood that was lying just outside the stable-door. He meant to knock me down with it, but, just as he leaned over to get the stick, I seized him with both hands, by the collar, and with a vigorous and sudden snatch brought my assailant harmlessly, his full length, on the not over-clean ground, for we were now in the cowyard. He had selected the place for the fight, and it was but right that he should have all the advantages of his own selection.

By this time Bill, the hired man, came home. He had been to 17 Mr. Helmsley's to spend Sunday with his nominal wife. Covey and I had been skirmishing from before daybreak till now. The sun was shooting his beams almost over the eastern woods, and we were still at it. I could not see where the matter was to terminate. He evidently was afraid to let me go, lest I should again make off to the woods, otherwise he would probably have obtained arms from the house to frighten me. Holding me, he called upon Bill to assist him. The scene had something comic about it. Bill, who knew precisely what Covey wished him to do, affected ignorance, and pretended he did not know what to do. "What shall I do, Master Covey?" said Bill. "Take hold of him! Take hold of him!" cried Covey. With a toss of his head, peculiar to Bill, he said: "Indeed, Master Covey, I want to go to work." "This is your work," said Covey, "take hold of him." Bill replied, with spirit, "My master hired me here to work, and not to help you whip Frederick." It was my turn to speak. "Bill," said I, "don't put your hands on me." To which he replied, "My God, Frederick, I ain't goin' to tech ye"; and Bill walked off, leaving Covey and myself to settle our differences as best we might.

But my present advantage was threatened when I saw Caroline 18 (the slave woman of Covey) coming to the cowyard to milk, for she was a powerful woman, and could have mastered me easily, exhausted as I was.

As soon as she came near, Covey attempted to rally her to his 19 aid. Strangely and fortunately, Caroline was in no humor to take a hand in any such sport. We were all in open rebellion that morning. Caroline answered the command of her master to "take hold of me," precisely as Bill had done, but in her it was at far greater peril, for she was the slave of Covey, and he could do what he pleased with her. It was not so with Bill, and Bill knew it. Samuel Harris, to whom Bill belonged, did not allow his slaves to be beaten unless they were guilty of some crime which the law would punish. But poor Caroline, like myself, was at the mercy of the merciless Covey, nor did she escape the dire effects of her refusal: he gave her several sharp blows.

At length (two hours had elapsed) the contest was given over. 20 Letting go of me, puffing and blowing at a great rate, Covey said, "Now, you scoundrel, go to your work; I would not have whipped you half so hard if you had not resisted." The fact was, he had not whipped me at all. He had not, in all the scuffle, drawn a single drop of blood from me. I had drawn blood from him, and should even without this satisfaction have been victorious, because my aim had not been to injure him, but to prevent his injuring me.

During the whole six months that I lived with Covey after this 21 transaction, he never again laid the weight of his finger on me in anger. He would occasionally say he did not want to get hold of me again—a declaration which I had no difficulty in believing— and I had a secret feeling which answered, "You had better not wish to get hold of me again, for you will be likely to come off worse in a second fight than you did in the first."

This battle with Mr. Covey, undignified as it was and as I fear 22 my narration of it is, was the turning-point in my "life as a slave." It rekindled in my breast the smouldering embers of liberty. It brought up my Baltimore dreams and revived a sense of my own manhood. I was a changed being after that fight. I was nothing before—I was a man now. It recalled to life my crushed self-respect, and my self-confidence, and inspired me with a renewed determination to be a free man. A man without force is without the essential dignity of humanity. Human nature is so constituted, that it cannot honor a helpless man, though it can pity him, and even this it cannot do long if signs of power do not arise.

He only can understand the effect of this combat on my spirit, 23 who has himself incurred something, or hazarded something, in repelling the unjust and cruel aggressions of a tyrant. Covey was a tyrant and a cowardly one withal. After resisting him, I felt as I had never felt before. It was a resurrection from the dark and pestiferous tomb of slavery, to the heaven of comparative freedom. I was no longer a servile coward, trembling under the frown of a brother worm of the dust, but my long-cowed spirit was roused to an attitude of independence. I had reached the point at which I was *not afraid to die*. This spirit made me a freeman in *fact*, though I still remained a slave in *form*. When a slave cannot be flogged, he is more than half free. He has a domain as broad as his own manly heart to defend, and he is really "a power on earth." From this time until my escape from slavery, I was never fairly whipped. Several attempts were made, but they were always unsuccessful. Bruised I did get, but the instance I have described was the end of the brutification to which slavery had subjected me.

The reader may like to know why, after I had so grievously 24 offended Mr. Covey, he did not have me taken in hand by the authorities; indeed, why the law of Maryland, which assigned hanging to the slave who resisted his master, was not put in force against me; at any rate why I was not taken up, as was usual in such cases, and publicly whipped as an example to other slaves, and as a means of deterring me from again committing the same offence. I confess that the easy manner in which I got off was always a surprise to me, and even now I cannot fully explain the cause, though the probability is that Covey was ashamed to have it known that he had been mastered by a boy of sixteen. He enjoyed the unbounded and very valuable reputation of being a first-rate overseer and Negro-breaker, and by means of his reputation he was able to procure his hands at very trifling compensation and with very great ease. His interest and his pride would mutually suggest the wisdom of passing the matter by in silence. The story that he had undertaken to whip a lad and had been resisted would of itself be damaging to him in the estimation of slaveholders.

It is perhaps not altogether creditable to my natural temper that 25 after the conflict with Mr. Covey I did, at times, purposely aim to provoke him to an attack, by refusing to keep with the other hands in the field, but I could never bully him to another battle. I was determined on doing him serious damage if he ever again attempted to lay violent hands on me.

> Hereditary bondmen, know ye not
> Who would be free, themselves must strike the blow?

Questions on Subject

1. Douglass says he "cannot pray." Why not?
2. In paragraph 10, Douglass condemns his friend's belief in the power of the root. On what ground does he disdain it? How does he finally reconcile those feelings with his attitude toward Sandy? What does Douglass mean when he says he never fought, he just defended himself?
3. At what exact moment did Douglass seem to make the decision not to be flogged?
4. We do not learn Douglass's age until the end of the story. What was your reaction to the fact that he was just sixteen years old on the day of his last flogging? What if anything prepared you for this revelation? Explain.
5. In his last sentence, Douglass explains that "I was determined on doing him serious damage if he ever again attempted to lay violent hands on me." In what way might this confession help to explain Covey's new behavior? In what way, if any, might the "superstition" have contributed to Douglass's attitude?

Questions on Strategy

1. What kinds of details does Douglass use to establish the context of his story?
2. In paragraphs 19–23, Douglass includes the following sentences: "We were all in open rebellion that morning." (19) "The fact was,

he had not whipped me at all." (20) "I had reached the point at which I was *not afraid to die*." (23) Explain what these sentences have in common, and how each functions in the context of the paragraph in which it appears.

3. Douglass writes in lengthy detailed paragraphs. What is the effect of this style on the reader?

4. How has Douglass organized his story? (Glossary: *Organization*)

5. Make a list of the adjectives Douglass uses to describe himself and Covey. Based on this list, and without using the same words, write a short description of the two men. How are they similar? How are they different?

Questions on Diction and Vocabulary

1. In paragraph 10, Douglass says he had "precious little" education. Cite examples of his diction to show the level of education Douglass had obtained by the time he wrote his autobiography. (Glossary: *Diction*)

2. Cite examples of Douglass's diction that offer clues as to the period in history in which this piece was written.

3. Refer to your desk dictionary to determine the meanings of the following words as they are used in this selection: *foreshadow* (paragraph 1), *wreak* (2), *thicket* (2), *contrivances* (3), *fain* (3), *irksome* (4), *pinched* (5), *succor* (7), *cumber* (10), *benignant* (11), *curry* (13), *grapple* (14), *supple* (14), *parried* (14), *skirmishing* (17), *dire* (19), *scuffle* (20), *pestiferous* (23).

Writing Suggestions

1. Write an essay in which you expand on the following sentence taken from paragraph 22 of Douglass's essay: "Human nature is so constituted, that it cannot honor a helpless man, though it can pity him, and even this it cannot do long if signs of power do not arise."

2. Using Douglass's essay as a model, write an essay in which you describe the day you first felt like an adult. What kind of evidence will you need to include and what kind of tone will you set for your story? To answer these questions it will be necessary for you to decide who your audience is. If you are writing for your peers you might even want to make your story humorous.

Lost at C

Jean Shepherd

Actor, radio announcer, humorist, and writer, Jean Shepherd was born in 1929 in Chicago. As an actor he has had four solo shows and has appeared in off-Broadway plays. As an announcer he has worked for radio stations in Cincinnati, Philadelphia, and New York. Shepherd has been a regular columnist for the Village Voice *and* Car and Driver *and has contributed prize-winning fiction to* Playboy. *His books include* In God We Trust: All Others Pay Cash, Wanda Hickey's Night of Golden Memories and Other Disasters, The Ferrari in the Bedroom, *and* The Phantom of the Open Hearth.*

In the following narrative essay from his book A Fistful of Fig Newtons, *Shepherd takes us along as he relives a not-so-easily-forgotten algebra class that he took his freshman year in high school. In telling his story, Shepherd displays his considerable talent for evoking a sense of drama, pathos, and humor.*

Miss Snyder stood at the blackboard and hurled the first harpoon   1
of the season: "You freshmen who are with us today are already
enrolled for the courses you will be required to take. Here are your
program cards." She dealt out 3 × 5-inch blue cards, which were
handed back to the freshmen. Each card was neatly lined into eight
periods, and after each period was the name of a teacher, a subject,
and a classroom. One period was labeled LUNCH, another
STUDY, and so on. Every minute of my day was laid out for me.
So much for my dreams of freedom.

"Freshmen, this is your first day in high school. You are no   2
longer in grade school. If you work hard, you will do well. If you
don't you will regret it. You are here to learn. You are not here to
play. Remember this and remember it well: *What you do here will
follow you all through life.*" She paused dramatically. In the hushed

silence, I could hear Rukowski wheezing ahead of me. None of this, of course, affected him. Anyone who could block the way he could block would have no trouble getting through life.

"Your first class will begin in five minutes. Any questions?" No 3 one raised a hand.

I sat there, pawing in the chute, anxious to begin my glorious 4 career of learning. No more would I fake my way. A new era was about to begin. The bell rang. The starting gate slammed open.

I had thundered a couple of hundred feet through the hall with 5 the mob before it hit me that I had no idea where the hell I was supposed to go. As the crowd surged around me, I struggled to read my program card. All I could make out was Room 127. I had only a minute to make it, so I battled my way down a flight of stairs. Then: 101, 105, 109, 112, 117—127, just in time. Already the classroom was three-quarters filled. Ahead of me, running interference, was Rukowski, trying his luck at this course, I later learned, for the third time in as many semesters. Getting his shoulder into it, he bulled his way through the door, buffeting aside a herd of spindly little freshmen. It was Schwartz, good old Schwartz, and Flick and Chester and Helen Weathers. My old gang! Even poor old Zynzmeister. Whatever it was, I would not have to go through it alone.

"Hi, Schwartz!" 6

Schwartz smiled wanly. And Helen Weathers giggled—until she 7 saw, at the same moment I did, a tall, square man standing motionless at the blackboard. He had a grim blue jaw and short, kinky black crew-cut hair. His eyes were tiny ball bearings behind glasses with thick black rims. He wore a dark, boxy suit that looked like it was made of black sandpaper. The bell rang and the door closed behind us. I joined the crowd around his desk who were putting registration cards into a box. I did likewise.

"All right. Settle down. Let's get organized." The man's voice 8 had a cutting rasp to it, like a steel file working on concrete. "We sit alphabetically in this class. A's up here in front to my right. Get going."

I trudged behind Schwartz and Helen Weathers toward the dim 9 recesses in the back of the classroom. Well, at least I'd be among friends. It was about a quarter of a mile to the front of the room, but I sat bolt upright in my seat, my iron determination intact. No more faking it.

"Class, my name is Mr. Pittinger." He was the first male teacher 10 I had ever had. Warren G. Harding was peopled entirely by motherly ladies like Mrs. Bailey and Miss Shields. Mr. Pittinger was a whole new ball game. And I still had no idea what he taught. I would soon find out.

"If you work in this class, you'll have no trouble. If you don't, 11 I promise you nothing."

I leaned forward at my desk, scribbling madly in my notebook: 12 *class my name is mr. pittinger if you work you will have no trouble if you dont i promise you nothing . . .*

I figured if you wrote everything down there'd be no trouble. 13 Every classroom of my life had been filled with girls on the Honor Roll who endlessly wrote in mysterious notebooks, even when nothing seemed to be going on. I never knew what the hell they were writing, so I took no chances. I figured I'd write everything.

"Braaghk." Mr. Pittinger cleared his gravelly throat. 14

braaaghk, I scribbled, *brummph*. You never know, I thought, it 15 might appear on the exam.

He turned, picked up a piece of chalk, and began to scrawl huge 16 block letters on the blackboard.

A-L—the chalk squeaked decisively—G-E-B-R-A. I copied each 17 letter exactly as he'd written it.

"That is the subject of this course," he barked. 18

Algebra? What the hell is that? 19

"Algebra is the mathematics of abstract numbers." 20

I gulped as I wrote this down. 21

"I will now illustrate." 22

Pittinger printed a huge Y on the blackboard and below it an 23 enormous X. I doggedly followed suit in my notebook. He then put equal signs next to the X and the Y.

"If Y equals five and X equals two, what does the following 24 mean?"

He wrote out: $X + Y = ?$ 25

Black fear seized my vitals. How could you add Xs and Ys? I 26 had enough trouble with nines and sevens!

Already the crowd in front of the room were waving their hands 27 to answer Pittinger's question. The class wasn't thirty seconds old and I was already six weeks behind. I sank lower in my seat, a faint buzzing in my ears. Instinctively I began to weave. I knew it was all over. Out of the corner of my eye I saw that Schwartz, next to me, had hunched lower and begun to emit a high, thin whimpering sound. Helen Weathers had flung up a thin spray of sweat. Chester's skin had changed to the color of the cupboards in the back of the room. And from behind me I could hear the faint, steady click of Zynzmeister's rosary.

Second by second, minute by minute, eon by eon that first algebra class droned on. I couldn't catch another word that was said, and by the time Mr. Pittinger wrote the second equation on the board, I was bobbing and weaving like a cobra and sending out high-voltage thought rays. A tiny molten knot of stark terror hissed and simmered in the pit of my stomach. I realized that for the first time in my school life, I had run into something that was completely opaque and unlearnable, and there was no way to fake it.

Don't call on me, Don't call on me, Don't call on me . . .

That night I ate my meatloaf and red cabbage in sober silence as the family yapped on, still living back in the days when I was known to all of them as the smartest little son of a bitch to ever set foot on Cleveland Street.

"Boy, look at the stuff kids study these days," the old man said with wonder as he hefted my algebra textbook in his bowling hand and riffled through the pages.

"What's all this X and Y stuff?" he asked.

"Yeah, well, it ain't much," I muttered as coolly as I could, trying to recapture some of the old élan.

"Whaddaya mean, ain't much?" His eyes glowed with pride at the idea that his kid has mastered algebra in only one day.

"Abstract mathematics, that's all it is."

The old man knew he'd been totally outclassed. Even my mother stopped stirring the gravy for a few seconds. My kid brother continued to pound away at the little bbs of Ovaltine that floated around on the top of his milk.

That night sleep did not come easily. In fact, it was only the first of many storm-tossed nights to come as, algebra class by algebra class, my terror grew. All my other subjects—history, English, social studies—were a total breeze. My years of experience in fakery came into full flower. In social studies, for example, the more you hoked it up, the better the grades. On those rare occasions when asked a question, I would stand slowly, with an open yet troubled look playing over my thoughtful countenance.

"Mr. Harris, sir," I would drawl hesitantly, as though attempting 38 to unravel the perplexity of the ages, "I guess it depends on how you view it—objectively, which, naturally, is too simple, or subjectively, in which case many factors such as a changing environment must be taken into consideration, and . . ." I would trail off.

Mr. Harris, with a snort of pleasure, would bellow: "RIGHT! 39 There are many diverse elements, which . . ." After which he was good for at least a forty-minute solo.

History was more of the same, and English was almost embar- 40 rassingly easy as, day after day, Miss McCullough preened and congratulated herself before our class. All she needed was a little ass-kissing and there was no limit to her applause. I often felt she regretted that an A+ was the highest grade she could hand out to one who loved her as sincerely and selflessly as I did.

Every morning at eight-thirty-five, however, was another story. 41 I marched with leaden feet and quaking bowels into Mr. Pittinger's torture chamber. By the sixth week I knew, without the shadow of a doubt, that after all these years of dodging and grinning, I was going to fail. Fail! No B, no gentleman's C—Fail. F. The big one: my own Scarlet Letter. Branded on my forehead—F, for Fuckup.

There was no question whatever. True, Pittinger had not yet 42 been able to catch me out in the open, since I was using every trick of the trade. But I knew that one day, inevitably, the icy hand of truth would rip off my shoddy façade and expose me for all the world to see.

Pittinger was of the new school, meaning he believed that kids, 43 theoretically motivated by an insatiable thirst for knowledge, would devour algebra in large chunks, making the final examination only a formality. He graded on performance in class and total grasp of the subject, capped off at the end of the term with an exam of brain-crushing difficulty from which he had the option of excusing those who rated A+ on classroom performance. Since I had no classroom performance, my doom was sealed.

Schwartz, too, had noticeably shrunken. Even fat Helen had 44 developed deep hollows under her eyes, while Chester had almost completely disappeared. And Zynzmeister had taken to nibbling Communion wafers in class.

Christmas came and went in tortured gaiety. My kid brother played happily with his Terry and the Pirates Dragon Lady Detector as I looked on with the sad indulgence of a withered old man whose youth had passed. As for my own presents, what good did it do to have a new first baseman's mitt when my life was over? How innocent they are, I thought as I watched my family trim the tree and scurry about wrapping packages. Before long, they will know. They will loathe me. I will be driven from this warm circle. It was about this time that I began to fear—or perhaps hope—that I would never live to be twenty-one, that I would die of some exotic debilitating disease. Then they'd be sorry. This fantasy alternated with an even better fantasy that if I did reach twenty-one, I would be blind and hobble about with a white cane. Then they'd really be sorry.

Not that I'd given up without a struggle. For weeks, in the privacy of my cell at home, safe from prying eyes, I continued trying to actually learn something about algebra. After a brief mental pep rally—This is simple. If Esther Jane Alberry can understand it, any fool can do it. All you gotta do is think. THINK! Reason it out!—I would sit down and open my textbook. Within minutes, I would break out in a clammy sweat and sink into a funk of nonunderstanding, a state so naked in its despair and self-contempt that it was soon replaced by a mood of defiant truculence. Schwartz and I took to laughing contemptuously at those boobs and brown-noses up front who took it all so seriously.

The first hints of spring began to appear. Birds twittered, buds unfurled. But men on death row are impervious to such intimations of life quickening and reborn. The only sign of the new season that I noticed was Mr. Pittinger changing from a heavy scratchy black suit into a lighter-weight scratchy black suit.

"Well, it won't be long. You gonna get a job this summer?" my old man asked me one day as he bent over the hood of the Olds, giving the fourth-hand paint job its ritual spring coat of Simonize.

"Maybe. I dunno," I muttered. It wouldn't be long, indeed. Then he'd know. Everybody would know that I knew less about algebra than Ralph, Mrs. Gammie's big Airedale, who liked to pee on my mother's irises.

Mr. Pittinger had informed us that the final exam, covering a 50
year's work in algebra, would be given on Friday of the following
week. One more week of stardom on Cleveland Street. Ever since
my devastating rejoinder at the dinner table about abstract mathematics, my stock had been the hottest in the neighborhood. My
opinions were solicited on financial matters, world affairs, even
the infield problems of the Chicago White Sox. The bigger they
are, the harder they fall. Even Ralph would have more respect than
I deserved. At least he didn't pretend to be anything but what he
was—a copious and talented pee-er.

Wednesday, two days before the end, arrived like any other 51
spring day. A faint breeze drifted from the south, bringing with it
hints of long summer afternoons to come, of swung bats, of nights
in the lilac bushes. But not for such as me. I stumped into algebra
class feeling distinctly like the last soul aboard the *Titanic* as she
was about to plunge to the bottom. The smart-asses were already
in their seats, laughing merrily, the goddamn A's and B's and C's
and even the M's. I took my seat in the back, among the rest of
the condemned. Schwartz sat down sullenly and began his usual
moan. Helen Weathers squatted toadlike, drenched in sweat. The
class began, Pittinger's chalk squeaked, hands waved. The sun
filtered in through the venetian blinds. A tennis ball pocked back
and forth over a net somewhere. Faintly, the high clear voices of
the girls' glee club sang, "Can you bake a cherry pie, charming
Billy?" Birds twittered.

My knot of fear, by now an old friend, sputtered in my gut. In 52
the past week, it had grown to roughly the size of a two-dollar
watermelon. True, I had avoided being called on even once the
entire year, but it was a hollow victory and I knew it. Minute after
minute inched slowly by as I ducked and dodged, Pittinger firing
question after question at the class. Glancing at my Pluto watch,
which I had been given for Christmas, I noted with deep relief that
less than two minutes remained before the bell.

It was then that I made my fatal mistake, the mistake that all 53
guerrilla fighters eventually make—I lost my concentration. For
years, every fiber of my being, every instant in every class, had
been directed solely at survival. On this fateful Wednesday, lulled
by the sun, by the gentle sound of the tennis ball, by the steady
drone of Pittinger's voice, by the fact that there were just two min-

utes to go, my mind slowly drifted off into a golden haze. A tiny mote of dust floated down through a slanting ray of sunshine. I watched it in its slow, undulating flight, like some microscopic silver bird.

"You're the apple of my eye, darling Billy . . . I can bake a cherry pie . . ." 54

A rich maple syrup warmth filled my being. Out of the faint distance, I heard a deadly rasp, the faint honking of disaster. 55

For a stunned split second, I thought I'd been jabbed with an electric cattle prod. Pittinger's voice, loud and commanding, was pronouncing my name. He was calling on ME! Oh, my God! With a goddamn minute to go, he had nailed me. I heard Schwartz bleat a high, quavering cry, a primal scream. I knew what it meant: If they got him, the greatest master of them all, there's no hope for ANY of us! 56

As I stood slowly at my seat, frantically bidding for time, I saw a great puddle forming around Helen Weathers. It wasn't all sweat. Chester had sunk to the floor beneath his desk, and behind me Zynzmeister's beads were clattering so loudly I could hardly hear his Hail Marys. 57

"Come to the board, please. Give us the value of C in this equation." 58

In a stupor of wrenching fear, I felt my legs clumping up the aisle. On all sides the blank faces stared. At the board—totally unfamiliar territory to me—I stared at the first equation I had ever seen up close. It was well over a yard and a half long, lacerated by mysterious crooked lines and fractions in parentheses, with miniature twos and threes hovering above the whole thing like tiny barnacles. Xs and Ys were jumbled in crazy abandon. At the very end of this unholy mess was a tiny equal sign. And on the other side of the equal sign was a zero. Zero! All this crap adds up to nothing! Jesus Christ! My mind reeled at the very sight of this barbed-wire entanglement of mysterious symbols. 59

Pittinger stood to one side, arms folded, wearing an expression that said, At last I've nailed the little bastard! He had been playing with me all the time. He knew! 60

I glanced back at the class. It was one of the truly educational moments of my life. The entire mob, including Schwartz, Chester, and even Zynzmeister, were grinning happily, licking their chops 61

with joyous expectation of my imminent crucifixion. I learned then
that when true disaster strikes, we have no friends. And there's
nothing a phony loves more in this world than to see another
phony get what's coming to him.

"The value of C, please," rapped Pittinger. 62

The equation blurred before my eyes. The value of C. Where the 63
hell was it? What did a C look like, anyway? Or an A or a B, for
that matter. I had forgotten the alphabet.

"C, please." 64

I spotted a single letter C buried deep in the writhing melange 65
of Ys and Xs and umlauts and plus signs, brackets, and God knows
what all. One tiny C. A torrent of sweat raged down my spinal
column. My jockey shorts were soaked and sodden with the sweat
and stink of execution. Being a true guerrilla from years of the
alphabetical ghetto, I showed no outward sign of panic, my face
stony: unyielding. You live by the gun, you die by the gun.

"C, please." Pittinger moodily scratched at his granite chin with 66
thumb and forefinger, his blue beard rasping nastily.

"Oh my darling Billy boy, you're the apple of my eye . . ." 67

Somewhere birds twittered on, tennis racquet met tennis ball. 68
My moment had finally arrived.

Now, I have to explain that for years I had been the leader of 69
the atheistic free-thinkers of Warren G. Harding School, scoffers
all at the Sunday School miracles taught at the Presbyterian church:
unbelievers.

That miracle stuff is for old ladies, all that walking on water and 70
birds flying around with loaves of bread in their beaks. Who can
believe that crap?

Now, I am not so sure. Ever since that day in Pittinger's algebra 71
class I have had an uneasy suspicion that maybe something mysterious is going on somewhere.

As I stood and stonily gazed at the enigmatic Egyptian hiero- 72
glyphics of that fateful equation, from somewhere, someplace beyond the blue horizon, it came to me, out of the mist. I heard my
voice say clearly, firmly, with decision:

"C . . . is equal to three." 73

Pittinger staggered back; his glasses jolted down to the tip of his 74
nose.

"How the hell did you know?!" he bellowed hoarsely, his snap-on 75 bow tie popping loose in the excitement.

The class was in an uproar. I caught a glimpse of Schwartz, his 76 face pale with shock. I had caught one on the fat part of the bat. It was a true miracle. I had walked on water.

Instantly, the old instincts took over. In a cool, level voice I an- 77 swered Pittinger's rhetorical question.

"Sir, I used empirical means." 78

He paled visibly and clung to the chalk trough for support. On 79 cue, the bell rang out. The class was over. With a swiftness born of long experience, I was out of the room even before the echo of the bell had ceased. The guerrilla's code is always hit and run. A legend had been born.

That afternoon, as I sauntered home from school, feeling at least 80 twelve and a half feet tall, Schwartz skulked next to me, silent, moody, kicking at passing frogs. I rubbed salt deep into his wound and sprinkled a little pepper on for good measure. Across the street, admiring clusters of girls pointed out the Algebra King as he strolled by. I heard Eileen Akers's silvery voice clearly: "There he goes. He doesn't say much in class, but when he does he makes it count." I nodded coolly toward my fans. A ripple of applause went up. I autographed a few algebra books and walked on, tall and straight in the sun. Deep down I knew that this was but a fleeting moment of glory, that when I faced the blue book exam it would be all over, but I enjoyed it while I had it.

With the benign air of a baron bestowing largess upon a wretched 81 serf, I offered to buy Schwartz a Fudgesicle at the Igloo. He refused with a snarl.

"Why, Schwartz, what seems to be troubling you?" I asked with 82 irony, vigorously working the salt shaker.

"You phony son of a bitch. You know what you can do with 83 your goddamn Fudgesicle."

"Me, a phony? Why would you say an unkind thing like that?" 84

He spat viciously into a tulip bed. "You phony bastard. You 85 studied!"

Inevitably, those of us who are gifted must leave those less for- 86 tunate behind in the race of life. I knew that, and Schwartz knew it. Once again I had lapped him and was moving away from the field, if only for a moment.

The next morning, Thursday, I swaggered into algebra class with 87 head high. Even Jack Morton, the biggest smart-ass in the class, said hello as I walked in. Mr. Pittinger, his eyes glowing with admiration, smiled warmly at me.

"Hi, Pit," I said with a casual flip of the hand. We abstract math- 88 ematicians have an unspoken bond. Naturally, I was not called on during that period. After all, I had proved myself beyond any doubt.

After class, beaming at me with the intimacy of a fellow quadratic 89 equation zealot, Mr. Pittinger asked me to stay on for a few moments.

"All my life I have heard about the born mathematical genius. 90 It is a well-documented thing. They come along once in a while, but I never thought I'd meet one, least of all in a class of mine. Did you always have this ability?"

"Well . . ." I smiled modestly. 91

"Look, it would be pointless for you to waste time on our little 92 test tomorrow. Would you help me grade the papers instead?"

"Gosh, Pit, I was looking forward to taking it, but if you really 93 need me, I'll be glad to help." It was a master stroke.

"I'd appreciate it. I need somebody who really knows his stuff, 94 and most of these kids are faking it."

The following afternoon, together, we graded the papers of my 95 peers. I hate to tell you what, in all honesty, I had to do to Schwartz when I marked his pitiful travesty. I showed no mercy. After all, algebra is an absolute science and there can be no margin for kindness in matters of the mind.

Questions on Subject

1. What do you think is the point of Shepherd's narrative? What, if anything, makes the narrative more than a funny story about the narrator and his friends and their experiences in algebra class?
2. What do you know of the narrator from the story he tells? What do you learn of his appearance? His personality?
3. What kind of teacher was Mr. Pittinger? What does the narrator mean when he says that Pittinger is of the "new school" (paragraph 43)? What are the narrator and his friends afraid of? Pittinger? Algebra? Both? Something else?

4. What is the "alphabetical ghetto" in Pittinger's classroom? In your opinion, do such ghettos exist in real classrooms? Explain.
5. How did the narrator take his "moment of glory" in algebra class? How did he know that he should enjoy the "triumph" while he had it?

Questions on Strategy

1. Like all good storytellers, Shepherd establishes a clear context in his narrative, indicating who, what, when, where, and why. What are the answers to these five questions, and where is this information provided?
2. In paragraph 7, Shepherd introduces the reader to Mr. Pittinger by describing him. How much does Shepherd tell us about Pittinger? How effective do you find this verbal picture? Identify another paragraph in which Shepherd uses description. What does it have in common with paragraph 7? Explain.
3. Identify several passages in this essay that are particularly humorous. What do you find funny about them? What techniques or devices does Shepherd use to capture the humor of each situation?
4. How does Shepherd organize his narrative? Could he have organized his essay in another way? What would have been gained or lost had he opted to do so? Explain. (Glossary: *Organization*)

Questions on Diction and Vocabulary

1. Identify four similes or metaphors that Shepherd uses in his essay. Explain what is being compared to what in each one. Collectively, what do they add to the narrative? (Glossary: *Figures of Speech*)
2. Dialogue is extremely useful in narration because it allows the writer to have the characters speak for themselves. In doing so, the characters reveal things about themselves and their situation. Comment on the differences in diction between Pittinger's speech and the narrator's speech. (Glossary: *Diction*)
3. What is the tone of Shepherd's essay? How does his choice of words throughout the essay help to establish this tone? (Glossary: *Tone*)
4. Refer to your desk dictionary to determine the meanings of the following words as they are used in this selection: *élan* (paragraph 33),

funk (46), *truculence* (46), *impervious* (47), *copious* (50), *enigmatic* (72), *largess* (81), *irony* (82), *zealot* (89), *travesty* (95).

Writing Assignments

1. Write a narrative of a humorous incident that happened to you or that you witnessed. As in Shepherd's essay, the humor may derive from the juxtaposition of a funny action with a serious setting.
2. Each of us can tell of an experience that has been unusually significant for us. Think about your past, identify one experience that has been especially important for you, and write an essay about it. In preparing to write your narrative, you may find it helpful to ask such questions as: Why is the experience important for me? What details are necessary for me to re-create the experience in an interesting and engaging way? How can my narrative of the experience be most effectively organized? What point of view will work best?

Salvation

Langston Hughes

*Born in Joplin, Missouri, Langston Hughes (1902–1967)
wrote poetry, fiction, and drama and regularly contributed a
column to the* New York Post. *An important figure in the
Harlem Renaissance, he is best known for* Weary Blues, The
Negro Mother, Shakespeare in Harlem, *and* Ask Your
Mama, *collections of poetry that reflect his racial pride, his
familiarity with the traditions of African Americans, and his
knowledge of jazz rhythms.*

In this selection taken from his autobiography, The Big Sea,
*Hughes narrates his experiences at a church revival meeting
he attended when he was twelve years old.*

I was saved from sin when I was going on thirteen. But not really ¹
saved. It happened like this. There was a big revival at my Auntie
Reed's church. Every night for weeks there had been much preach-
ing, singing, praying, and shouting, and some very hardened sinners had been brought to Christ, and the membership of the church
had grown by leaps and bounds. Then just before the revival
ended, they held a special meeting for children, "to bring the
young lambs to the fold." My aunt spoke of it for days ahead. That
night I was escorted to the front row and placed on the mourners'
bench with all the other young sinners, who had not yet been
brought to Jesus.

My aunt told me that when you were saved you saw a light, ²
and something happened to you inside! And Jesus came into your
life! And God was with you from then on! She said you could see
and hear and feel Jesus in your soul. I believed her. I have heard
a great many old people say the same thing and it seemed to me
they ought to know. So I sat there calmly in the hot, crowded
church, waiting for Jesus to come to me.

The preacher preached a wonderful rhythmical sermon, all ³
moans and shouts and lonely cries and dire pictures of hell, and

then he sang a song about the ninety and nine safe in the fold, but one little lamb was left out in the cold. Then he said: "Won't you come? Won't you come to Jesus? Young lambs, won't you come?" And he held out his arms to all us young sinners there on the mourners' bench. And the little girls cried. And some of them jumped up and went to Jesus right away. But most of us just sat there.

A great many old people came and knelt around us and prayed, 4 old women with jet-black faces and braided hair, old men with work-gnarled hands. And the church sang a song about the lower lights are burning, some poor sinners to be saved. And the whole building rocked with prayer and song.

Still I kept waiting to *see* Jesus. 5

Finally all the young people had gone to the altar and were 6 saved, but one boy and me. He was a rounder's son named Westley. Westley and I were surrounded by sisters and deacons praying. It was very hot in the church, and getting late now. Finally Westley said to me in a whisper: "God damn! I'm tired o' sitting here. Let's get up and be saved." So he got up and was saved.

Then I was left all alone on the mourners' bench. My aunt came 7 and knelt at my knees and cried, while prayers and songs swirled all around me in the little church. The whole congregation prayed for me alone, in a mighty wail of moans and voices. And I kept waiting serenely for Jesus, waiting, waiting—but he didn't come. I wanted to see him, but nothing happened to me. Nothing! I wanted something to happen to me, but nothing happened.

I heard the songs and the minister saying: "Why don't you come? 8 My dear child, why don't you come to Jesus? Jesus is waiting for you. He wants you. Why don't you come? Sister Reed, what is this child's name?"

"Langston," my aunt sobbed. 9

"Langston, why don't you come? Why don't you come and be 10 saved? Oh, Lamb of God! Why don't you come?"

Now it was really getting late. I began to be ashamed of myself, 11 holding everything up so long. I began to wonder what God thought about Westley, who certainly hadn't seen Jesus either, but who was now sitting proudly on the platform, swinging his knickerbockered legs and grinning down at me, surrounded by deacons and old women on their knees praying. God had not struck Westley dead for taking his name in vain or for lying in the temple. So I decided that maybe to save further trouble, I'd better lie, too, and say that Jesus had come, and get up and be saved.

So I got up. 12

Suddenly the whole room broke into a sea of shouting, as they 13 saw me rise. Waves of rejoicing swept the place. Women leaped in the air. My aunt threw her arms around me. The minister took me by the hand and led me to the platform.

When things quieted down, in a hushed silence, punctuated by 14 a few ecstatic "Amens," all the new young lambs were blessed in the name of God. Then joyous singing filled the room.

That night, for the last time in my life but one—for I was a big 15 boy twelve years old—I cried. I cried, in bed alone, and couldn't stop. I buried my head under the quilts, but my aunt heard me. She woke up and told my uncle I was crying because the Holy Ghost had come into my life, and because I had seen Jesus. But I was really crying because I couldn't bear to tell her that I had lied, that I had deceived everybody in the church, that I hadn't seen Jesus, and that now I didn't believe there was a Jesus any more, since he didn't come to help me.

Questions on Subject

1. Why does the young Langston expect to be saved at the revival meeting? Once the children are in church, what appeals are made to them to encourage them to seek salvation?
2. Trace the various pressures working on Hughes that lead to his decision to "get up and be saved" (paragraph 11). What important realization finally convinces him to lie about being saved?
3. Even though Hughes's account of the events at the revival is at points humorous, the experience was nonetheless painful for him. Why does he cry on the night of his "salvation"? Why does his aunt think he is crying? What significance is there in the disparity between their views?

Questions on Strategy

1. What paradox or apparent contradiction does Hughes present in the first two sentences of the narrative? Why do you suppose he uses this device? (Glossary: *Paradox*)

2. What is the function of the third sentence, "It happened like this"?
3. Hughes consciously varies the structure and length of his sentences to create different effects. What effect does he create through the short sentences in paragraphs 2 and 3 and the long sentence that concludes the final paragraph? How do the short, one-sentence paragraphs aid the author in telling his story?
4. Although Hughes tells most of his story himself, he allows Auntie Reed, the minister, and Westley to speak for themselves. What does Hughes gain by having his characters speak for themselves?

Questions on Diction and Vocabulary

1. How does Hughes's choice of words help to establish a realistic atmosphere for a religious revival meeting? Does he use any traditional religious figures of speech? (Glossary: *Figures of Speech*)
2. Why does Hughes italicize the word *see* in paragraph 5? What do you think he means by *see*? What do you think his aunt means by *see* (2)? Explain.
3. Refer to your desk dictionary to determine the meanings of the following words as they are used in this selection: *dire* (paragraph 3), *gnarled* (4), *vain* (11), *punctuated* (14), *ecstatic* (14).

Writing Assignments

1. Like the young Langston Hughes, we sometimes find ourselves in situations in which, for the sake of conformity, we do things or act in ways we do not believe in. Consider one such experience you have had. What is it about human nature that makes us occasionally act in ways that contradict our inner feelings? Write an essay in which you explore that experience.
2. Any narrative requires that the writer gather information concerning a particular incident from his or her own experience or from other reliable sources. Interview a member of your class so as to obtain enough information to write a brief narrative about an interesting event in that person's life. Write your narrative in the third-person point of view.

A Crime of Compassion

Barbara Huttmann

Barbara Huttmann, a nurse, a teacher, and a writer, was born in Oakland, California, in 1935. Her intense interest in the patients' rights issue is expressed in her two books, The Patient's Advocate *and* Code Blue: A Nurse's True-Life Story. *Currently, she is associate director of nursing services at Children's Hospital of San Francisco.*

In the following essay, which first appeared in Newsweek *in 1983, Huttmann narrates the final months in the life of Mac, one of her favorite patients. Her story is an emotional plea for new legislation that would give terminally ill patients the right to die with dignity.*

"Murderer," a man shouted. "God help patients who get *you* for a nurse." 1

"What gives you the right to play God?" another one asked. 2

It was the Phil Donahue Show where the guest is a fatted calf 3 and the audience a 200-strong flock of vultures hungering to pick at the bones. I had told them about Mac, one of my favorite cancer patients. "We resuscitated him 52 times in just one month. I refused to resuscitate him again. I simply sat there and held his hand while he died."

There wasn't time to explain that Mac was a young, witty, macho 4 cop who walked into the hospital with 32 pounds of attack equipment, looking as if he could single-handedly protect the whole city, if not the entire state. "Can't get rid of this cough," he said. Otherwise, he felt great.

Before the day was over, tests confirmed that he had lung cancer. 5 And before the year was over, I loved him, his wife, Maura, and their three kids as if they were my own. All the nurses loved him. And we all battled his disease for six months without ever giving death a thought. Six months isn't such a long time in the whole scheme of things, but it was long enough to see him lose his youth, his wit, his macho, his hair, his bowel and bladder control, his sense of taste and smell, and his ability to do the slightest thing for himself. It was also long enough to watch Maura's transformation from a young woman into a haggard, beaten old lady.

When Mac had wasted away to a 60-pound skeleton kept alive   6
by liquid food we poured down a tube, i.v. solutions we dripped into his veins, and oxygen we piped to a mask on his face, he begged us: "Mercy . . . for God's sake, please just let me go."

The first time he stopped breathing, the nurse pushed the button   7
that calls a "code blue" throughout the hospital and sends a team rushing to resuscitate the patient. Each time he stopped breathing, sometimes two or three times in one day, the code team came again. The doctors and technicians worked their miracles and walked away. The nurses stayed to wipe the saliva that drooled from his mouth, irrigate the big craters of bedsores that covered his hips, suction the lung fluids that threatened to drown him, clean the feces that burned his skin like lye, pour the liquid food down the tube attached to his stomach, put pillows between his knees to ease the bone-on-bone pain, turn him every hour to keep the bedsores from getting worse, and change his gown and linen every two hours to keep him from being soaked in perspiration.

At night I went home and tried to scrub away the smell of de-   8
caying flesh that seemed woven into the fabric of my uniform. It was in my hair, the upholstery of my car—there was no washing it away. And every night I prayed that Mac would die, that his agonized eyes would never again plead with me to let him die.

Every morning I asked his doctor for a "no-code" order. Without   9
that order, we had to resuscitate every patient who stopped breathing. His doctor was one of several who believe we must extend life as long as we have the means and knowledge to do it. To not do it is to be liable for negligence, at least in the eyes of many people, including some nurses. I thought about what it would be like to stand before a judge, accused of murder, if Mac stopped breathing and I didn't call a code.

And after the fifty-second code, when Mac was still lucid enough   10
to beg for death again, and Maura was crumbled in my arms again, and when no amount of pain medication stilled his moaning and agony, I wondered about a spiritual judge. Was all this misery and

suffering supposed to be building character or infusing us all with the sense of humility that comes from impotence?

Had we, the whole medical community, become so arrogant that 11 we believed in the illusion of salvation through science? Had we become so self-righteous that we thought meddling in God's work was our duty, our moral imperative and our legal obligation? Did we really believe that we had the right to force "life" on a suffering man who had begged for the right to die?

Such questions haunted me more than ever early one morning 12 when Maura went home to change her clothes and I was bathing Mac. He had been still for so long, I thought he at last had the blessed relief of coma. Then he opened his eyes and moaned, "Pain . . . no more . . . Barbara . . . do something . . . God, let me go."

The desperation in his eyes and voice riddled me with guilt. "I'll 13 stop," I told him as I injected the pain medication.

I sat on the bed and held Mac's hands in mine. He pressed his 14 bony fingers against my hand and muttered, "Thanks." Then there was one soft sigh and I felt his hands go cold in mine. "Mac?" I whispered, as I waited for his chest to rise and fall again.

A clutch of panic banded my chest, drew my finger to the code 15 button, urged me to do something, anything . . . but sit there alone with death. I kept one finger on the button, without pressing it, as a waxen pallor slowly transformed his face from person to empty shell. Nothing I've ever done in my 47 years has taken so much effort as it took *not* to press that code button.

Eventually, when I was as sure as I could be that the code team 16 would fail to bring him back, I entered the legal twilight zone and pushed the button. The team tried. And while they were trying, Maura walked into the room and shrieked, "No . . . don't let them do this to him . . . for God's sake . . . please, no more."

Cradling her in my arms was like cradling myself, Mac, and all 17 those patients and nurses who had been in this place before, who do the best they can in a death-denying society.

So a TV audience accused me of murder. Perhaps I am guilty. 18 If a doctor had written a no-code order, which is the only *legal* alternative, would he have felt any less guilty? Until there is legislation making it a criminal act to code a patient who has requested the right to die, we will all of us risk the same fate as Mac. For whatever reason, we developed the means to prolong life, and now we are forced to use it. We do not have the right to die.

Questions on Subject

1. Why did people in the audience at the Phil Donahue Show call Huttmann a "murderer" (paragraph 1)? Is there any sense in which their accusation is justified?
2. Why, according to Huttmann, do some doctors refuse to give a "no-code" order?
3. What made Huttmann's decision not to press the code button so difficult? Why didn't she stop resuscitation efforts earlier? Why did she finally decide not to press the button?
4. What does Huttmann mean when she calls America "a death-denying society" (17)? Do you agree with her characterization? Why, or why not?
5. Huttmann concludes her essay with the statement, "We do not have the right to die" (18). What does this mean? Is she overstating the situation, or telling the simple truth?

Questions on Strategy

1. A good narrative frequently has an attention-grabbing opening and a thought-provoking closing. Explain how this is true of Huttmann's essay. (Glossary: *Beginnings/Endings*)
2. What part do the questions in paragraphs 10 and 11 play in the overall narration? Why are they important to Huttmann's strategy? (Glossary: *Rhetorical Question*)
3. Effective narrations use strong verbs—verbs that contribute significantly to the actions and feelings of a story. Carefully examine the verbs that Huttmann uses to tell Mac's story. What do the verbs contribute to the narrative?
4. Huttmann's narrative covers a period of six months. In paragraphs 4 through 6, she tells us about the first five months of Mac's illness; in paragraphs 7 through 10, the sixth month; and in paragraphs 11 through 17, the final morning. In what ways do Huttmann's selection of detail and use of time reflect her reason for telling her story? Explain.
5. Huttmann believes that new legislation is needed to cover the "coding" of patients who have requested the right to die. How does she attempt to persuade readers to her position? Do you find her presentation persuasive? Why, or why not?

Questions on Diction and Vocabulary

1. Huttmann calls each successful resuscitation of Mac a "miracle" (7). What attitude does she express with this word? (Glossary: *Attitude*)
2. The right-to-die issue is indeed an emotional one. Discuss how Huttmann uses connotation to involve readers emotionally in Mac's case and in the issue in general. (Glossary: *Connotation/ Denotation*)
3. Refer to your desk dictionary to determine the meanings of the following words as they are used in this selection: *resuscitate* (paragraph 3), *irrigate* (7), *lucid* (10), *imperative* (11), *waxen* (15), *pallor* (15).

Writing Assignments

1. Huttmann says, "Nothing I've ever done in my 47 years has taken so much effort as it took *not* to press that code button" (15). Narrate an episode in which you have had to make an important and difficult decision. Be careful to show your readers why the incident was significant for you and why it was hard to arrive at your decision.
2. Select a controversial issue—such as the death penalty, school prayer, military service, or welfare—in which the law and morality seem to you to be in conflict. Write an essay in which you explain the nature of that conflict and attempt to resolve the issue convincingly. Be sure to include enough information to justify your opinions.

Writing Suggestions for Narration

1. Narrate an experience that gave you a new awareness of yourself. Use enough telling detail in your narrative to allow your reader to visualize that experience and understand its significance for you. You may find the following suggestions helpful in choosing an experience to narrate in the first person.
   a. my greatest success
   b. my biggest failure
   c. my most embarrassing moment
   d. my happiest moment
   e. my first truly frightening experience
   f. an experience that turned my hero or idol into an ordinary person
   g. an experience that turned an ordinary person I know into a hero
2. Sometimes the little, insignificant, seemingly trivial experiences in our daily lives can provide the material for entertaining personal narratives—narratives that reveal something about ourselves and the world we live in. Select one of the following experiences, or one of your own choosing, and write an essay in which you narrate that experience and its significance for you.
   a. having your name misspelled and/or mispronounced
   b. being confused with another person in your family
   c. rushing to keep an appointment, only to find that you are a day early or a day late
   d. dialing the wrong telephone number more than once
   e. moving to avoid someone who is moving to avoid you and bumping into that person

      f. sleeping through the alarm clock
     g. not being able to find a parking space
     h. getting "ripped off" by a vending machine
3. Write an essay in which you report what happened at one of the following:
     a. the visit of a state or national figure to your campus
     b. a dormitory meeting
     c. a current event of local, state, or national significance
     d. an important sports event
     e. the current research of one of your professors
     f. a campus demonstration or gathering

3
Description

What Is Description?

Description is conveying, through words alone, the perceptions of our senses. We see, hear, smell, taste, and feel; and through description we try to re-create those sensations in order to share them with others. Some sensations are so basic that they almost precede thought: the color and dazzle of aerial fireworks, the crunch of snow underfoot, the savory aroma of fried onion rings, the tartness of lemonade, the soothing coolness of suntan lotion on burning skin, the pleasant tiredness of leg muscles after a brisk run. Other perceptions appeal more directly to the mind, like the intricate architecture of a spider web or the elaborate complexity of a piece of music. All are the province of description.

It is often said that to describe is to paint a verbal picture—of a thing, a place, a person. The comparison is helpful because it suggests some truths. Both description and painting seek to transform fleeting perceptions into something lasting through the use of a foreign medium, words in the case of description, oils or watercolors in the case of painting. Although the original perception may have taken place in a flash, both description and painting are created bit by bit, word by word, or brushstroke by brushstroke. But the comparison goes only so far. We grasp a painting at a single glance (though appreciation may take longer); but we take in a description only piece by piece, or word by word, just as the writer created it. And, of course, a picture is purely visual, while description may draw on all of our sense perceptions.

There are essentially two types of description—objective and subjective. *Objective description* is as factual as possible, emphasizing the actual qualities of the subject being described, while subordinating the writer's personal responses. For example, a holdup victim would try to give authorities a precise, objective description of the criminal, uncolored by emotional responses, so that positive identification could be made—and so that an innocent person would not be arrested by mistake. *Subjective* or *impressionistic description*, on the other hand, conveys the writer's personal view or impression of the object, often in language rich in modifiers and figures of speech. A food critic describing a memorable meal would inevitably write about it impressionistically, using colorful or highly subjective language; there are, in fact, relatively few words in English to describe objectively the subtleties of smell and taste. Most subjects, however, lend themselves to both objective and subjective description, depending on your purpose. You could write, for example, that you had "exactly four weeks" to finish a history term paper (objective), or that you had "all the time in the world" or "an outrageously short amount of time" (subjective). Each description can be accurate and useful in its own way.

Why Do Writers Use Description?

Description, especially when it is impressionistic and original, can give pleasure, and so one of a writer's purposes in using description may be to entertain. When Jim Tassé in "Trailcheck" describes the scenery he observes and the sensations he experiences while taking the first run of the day on the ski slope where he works, he paints a vivid word-picture that allows us to share in his ecstasy.

Description can also be used to inform—to provide readers with specific data. You may need to describe the results of a chemical reaction for a lab report; the style of a Renaissance painting for an art history term paper; the physical capabilities and limitations of a stroke patient for a case study; or the acting of Jodie Foster in a movie you want your friends to see. Such descriptions will sometimes be scientifically objective, sometimes intensely impression-istic, depending on the subject itself and the information you want to communicate about it.

Another important use of description is to create a mood or atmosphere, or even to convey your own views—to develop a *dominant impression*. In "My Father, the Prince," Phyllis Theroux creates a loving, full-length portrait of a man she wants us to know and like; she builds this impression with such carefully chosen details as that he "wore penny loafers on business trips" and "a Mouseketeer hat to pick up my brother on his first movie date." In "The Shack" the Canadian novelist Margaret Laurence creates a dominant impression of comfort and familiarity in her description of her favorite place to write. Each of the descriptions in this chapter, whether entertaining, informative, or both, is distinguished by the strong dominant impression the writer wishes to create.

Although descriptive writing can stand alone, and often does, it is also used with other types of writing. In a narrative, for ex-ample, descriptions provide the context for the story—the back-ground and setting—and make the characters come alive for us. Description may also help to define a word like *giraffe* or *windmill*, or to clarify the steps of a process such as diagnosing an illness or making butter. Wherever it is used, and for whatever purpose, good description makes writing more vivid and more specific.

What to Look for in Reading a Description

First, allow the words of the description to build up a mental image for you. Try to see in your mind's eye what the writer ac-tually saw; try to hear or smell or taste or feel what the writer's words suggest. Put together the jigsaw puzzle of words and details into a complete picture. Then, define the dominant impression the writer creates.

Consider, for example, this paragraph by writer Roger Angell, in which he describes a baseball:

It weighs just over five ounces and measures between 2.86 and 2.94 inches in diameter. It is made of a composition-cork nucleus encased in two thin layers of rubber, one black and one red, surrounded by 121 yards of tightly wrapped blue-gray wool yarn, 45 yards of white wool yarn, 53 more yards of blue-gray wool yarn, 150 yards of fine cotton yarn, a coat of rubber cement, and a cowhide (formerly horsehide) exterior, which is held together with 216 slightly raised red cotton stitches. Printed certifications, endorsements, and outdoor advertising spherically attest to its authenticity. Like most institutions, it is considered inferior in its present form to its ancient archetypes, and in this case the complaint is probably justified; on occasion in recent years it has actually been known to come apart under the demands of its brief but rigorous active career. Baseballs are assembled and hand-stitched in Taiwan (before this year the work was done in Haiti, and before 1973 in Chicopee, Massachusetts), and contemporary pitchers claim that there is a tangible variation in the size and feel of the balls that now come into play in a single game; a true peewee is treasured by hurlers, and its departure from the premises, by fair means or foul, is secretly mourned. But never mind: any baseball is beautiful. No other small package comes as close to the ideal in design and utility. It is a perfect object for a man's hand. Pick it up and it instantly suggests its purpose; it is meant to be thrown a considerable distance—thrown hard and with precision. Its feel and heft are the beginning of the sport's critical dimensions; if it were a fraction of an inch larger or smaller, a few centigrams heavier or lighter, the game of baseball would be utterly different. Hold a baseball in your hand. As it happens, this one is not brand-new. Here, just to one side of the curved surgical welt of stitches, there is a pale-green grass smudge, darkening on one edge almost to black—the mark of an old infield play, a tough grounder now lost in memory. Feel the ball, turn it over in your hand; hold it across the seam or the other way, with the seam just to the side of your middle finger. Speculation stirs. You want to get outdoors and throw this spare and sensual object to somebody or, at the very least, watch somebody else throw it.

The first thing you probably noticed here is the amount of detail Angell provides about something as seemingly simple as a baseball. But perhaps you noticed, as well, that he leaves out some facts that most readers would find unnecessary—the pattern of the stitches, for example, and the color of the cowhide cover. In forming your mental picture of a baseball, you probably supplied that information from your own experience.

Is Angell's description objective or impressionistic? Actually, it is both. The author begins objectively and tells us not only about a baseball's obvious features—its weight, diameter, covering, stitching, and endorsements—but also about its innards. About halfway through, however, he changes his approach. Starting with the sentence "But never mind: any baseball is beautiful," Angell puts the greatest emphasis on his own attitudes and opinions. This part of his description is impressionistic and highly personal; who else, for example, would say of a baseball that "no other small package comes as close to the ideal in design and utility"?

Does the description create a unified, dominant impression? At first you might think not, because of the sudden switch from objective to impressionistic detail. Yet by the end of the description it's clear that Angell sees a baseball as something of rare perfection, deserving a kind of reverence. And the factual information with which he begins contributes to this impression: anything so complex, made with such extraordinary care and precision, may indeed be called "beautiful."

Angell's description can stand by itself, as it does here. In fact, however, he wrote it to appear at the beginning of a 400-page book about baseball called *Five Seasons*. He chose this description as his starting point because, as he says immediately afterward, "Thinking of the ball and its attributes seems to refresh our appreciation of this game." Certainly, the sort of freshness and enthusiasm Angell reveals in his description can lead readers to an appreciation of any subject, familiar or not.

Writing a Descriptive Essay

You should begin by fixing the subject of your description firmly in your mind. If it's an inanimate object, get it and keep it handy as you work on your essay; if it's a place, go there and spend some time taking in the sights, sounds, and smells; if it's a person, dig out old photographs and letters, or try to make a visit. Observe, observe, observe, and make notes of your sense impressions. If you must work from memory—if, for example, you are describing your great-grandmother—try to "observe" with your mind's eye, to conjure up the half-forgotten face, the quirky way of talking, the special walk. If you must rely on others' writing (for example, to describe Pompeii before the eruption of Vesuvius), try to put together your own picture from the pieces you find in your sources. Without vivid perceptions of your own to work from, you can hardly create a detailed, accurate description.

The way you develop your perceptions will depend, first, on your purpose for writing the description and the audience you are writing for.

1. Purpose

Why you are writing will influence the kinds of descriptive details you use and the way you use them. Let's say, for example, that you want to describe the emergency room of your local hospital. If your purpose is mainly to entertain, then you might want to create an atmosphere of looming, intricate technology as in a mad scientist's laboratory, or of controlled chaos as in the operating room on *M*A*S*H*. If you mean mainly to inform your readers, however, you will use a more objective approach, relying on factual descriptions of individual staff members and pieces of emergency equipment, as well as explaining the functions of each.

2. Audience

Whom do you expect to read your essay? What do they know, and what do they want to learn from you? If you are describing the hospital emergency room for an audience of medical professionals, you will only need to mention a nuclear magnetic resonance scanner for them to know what it looks like and what it does. A less specialized audience, however, will appreciate a more detailed discussion. In addition, the general audience will be more receptive to impressionistic description and to details such as the staff's uniforms and the strong antiseptic smell; the professional readers will consider such things obvious or irrelevant.

3. Gathering Details

Once you have considered your purpose and your audience, writing a description requires that you gather a great many details about your subject, more, in fact, than you are likely to use. Like a reporter at the scene of an accident, you will write notes about what you see and hear directly; but you may also need to list details that you remember or that you have learned from other sources.

When collecting descriptive details, it's easy to forget to use *all* your senses. Sight is so important to us that we tend to pay attention only to what we can see, and inexperienced writers often rely almost completely on visual detail. While making observations of an emergency room, you would by all means take notes about the medical equipment, the blank white walls, the unnaturally brilliant lighting, and the brisk, efficient movements of the medical staff. But don't stop there. Keep your ears open for the hiss of trolley tires on linoleum and the odd, mechanical noises that interrupt the emergency room hush; sniff the hospital smell; touch the starched sheets on the stretchers and the cold stainless steel that seems to be everywhere. Your observations, and the notes you make about them, will give you the details you need when you write your description.

4. *Creating a Dominant Impression*

From the catalog of details that you have collected, select those that will be most helpful in developing a dominant impression. Suppose that you wish to create a dominant impression of the hospital emergency room as a place of great tension. You will then naturally choose details to reinforce that sense of tension: the worried looks on the faces of a man and woman sitting in the corner, the quick movements of the medical staff as they tend a patient on a wheeled stretcher, the urgent whisperings of two interns out in the hallway, the incessant paging of Dr. Thomas. A dominant impression of the emergency room's sterility, however, will call for different details: the smell of disinfectant, the spotless white uniforms of the staff members, the stainless steel tables and chairs, the gleaming instruments a nurse hands to the physician. Building an effective and convincing dominant impression depends on the selection of such details.

Of course, it is equally important to omit any details that conflict with the dominant impression. Perhaps there was an orderly lounging in a corner, chewing gum and reading a magazine, who did not feel the tension of the emergency room; perhaps a room's sterility was marred by several used Styrofoam coffee cups left on a corner table. Deciding what details to include and exclude is up to you.

5. *Organization*

A photographer can capture a large, complicated scene with the press of a button. The writer has to put descriptive details down on paper one at a time. It's not enough to decide which details to include and which to leave out; you also need to arrange your chosen details in a particular order, one that serves your purpose and is easy for the reader to follow.

Visual details, for example, may be presented as if your eyes are moving from left to right, from bottom to top, from far to near, or the reverse of any of these. A description of an emergency room could begin at the entrance, move through the waiting area, pass the registration desk, and proceed into the treatment cubicles. A description of a restaurant kitchen might conjure up the smells and sounds that escape through the swinging doors even before moving on to the first glimpse inside.

Other patterns of organization include moving from the general to the specific, from smallest to largest, from least important to most important, or from the usual to the unusual. Roger Angell's description of a baseball moves from the objective to the impressionistic and subjective. In any case, keep in mind that the very last details you present will probably stay in the reader's mind the longest, and that the very first details will also have special force; those in the middle of your description, though they will have their effect, may not have the same impact as those before and after them.

Before you begin your first draft, you may find it useful to sketch out a scratch outline of your description. Here's a sample of such an outline for the Angell excerpt:

Description of a baseball.
  Dominant impression: a baseball is a perfectly beautiful thing.
  Objective details: weight, size, manufacture.
  Impressions: perfectly suited for its purpose—if it were different, the game would be different—describe a used baseball, how it looks, how to hold it.

Such an outline can remind you of the dominant impression you want to create and suggest which specific details may be most useful to you.

6. Being Specific

Inexperienced writers often believe that adjectives and adverbs are the basis for effective descriptions. They're right in a sense, but not wholly so: while strong adjectives and adverbs are crucial, description also depends on well-chosen nouns and verbs. *Vehicle* is not nearly so descriptive as something more specific—*jeep, snowmobile,* or *Honda Civic*. Why write *see* when what you mean is *glance, stare, spy, gaze, peek, examine,* or *witness?* The more specific and strong you make your nouns and verbs, the more lively and interesting your descriptions will be.

Trailcheck

James C. Tassé

Born in Worcester, Massachusetts, Jim Tassé majored in English and religion while at the University of Vermont. He hopes eventually to teach, perhaps at the college level, but his more immediate interests include biking and singing with a rock band. As his essay "Trailcheck" suggests, Jim is also an enthusiastic skier; his experience working on a ski patrol during winter breaks provides him with the subject for a striking description.

At a quarter to eight in the morning, the sharp cold of the mid-winter night still hangs in the air of Smuggler's Notch. At the base of Madonna Mountain, we stamp our feet and turn up our collars while waiting for Dan to get the chair lift running. Trailcheck always begins with this cold, sleepy wait—but it can continue in many different ways. The ski patrol has to make this first run every morning to assess the trail conditions before the mountain opens—and you never know what to expect on top of the Mad Dog, Madonna Mountain. Sometimes we take our first run down the sweet, light powder that fell the night before; sometimes we have to ski the rock-hard boilerplate ice that formed when yesterday's mush froze. But there's always the cold—the dank, bleary cold of 8 A.M. in January.

I adjust my first-aid belt and heft my backpack up a little higher, cinch it tight. I shiver, and pull my hat down a bit lower. I am sleepy, cold, impatient. Dan's finally got the lift running, and the first two patrollers, Ken and Chuck, get on. Three more chairs get filled, and then there's me. Looks like I'm riding up alone. The chair lift jars me a little more awake as it hits the back of my boots. I sit down and am scooped into the air.

It's a cold ride up, and I snuggle my chin deep into my parka. The bumps of the chair going over the lift tower rollers help keep me awake. Trees piled high and heavy with snow move silently past. Every so often, in sudden randomness, a branch lets go a slide and the air fills with snowdust as the avalanche crashes from branch to branch, finally landing with a soft thud on the ground. Snow dances in the air with kaleidoscopic colors, shining in the early daylight. I imagine what it would have been like on the mountain on a similar day three hundred years ago. A day like this would have been just as beautiful, or maybe even more—the silent mountain, all trees and cold and sunshine, with no men and no lifts. I think of days when the fog rolls out of the Notch, and the wind blows cold and damp, and the trees are close and dark in the mist, and I try to imagine how terrifyingly wild the mountain would have been centuries ago, before the white man came and installed the chair lift that takes me to the top so easily. I think how difficult it would have been to climb through the thick untamed forest that bristles out of the mountain's flanks, and I am glad that I don't have to walk up Madonna this sleepy-eyed morning.

I watch the woods pass, looking for the trails of small animals   4 scrolled around the trees. Skiing should be nice with all the new snow. Arriving at the top, I throw up the safety bar, tip my skis up, make contact, stand, ski clear of the lift. The view from the mountaintop is incredible. I can see over to the slopes of Stowe, where another patrol is running trailcheck just as we are. Across the state, Mt. Washington hangs above the horizon like a mirage. Back towards Burlington, I can see the frozen lake sprawling like a white desert.

I toss my backpack full of lunch and books to Marty, who's going   5 into the patrol shack to get the stove fired up. I stretch my legs a little as we share some small talk, waiting for the mountain captain to say we can go on down. Tighten my boots. Finally Ken's radio crackles out the word, and I pull down my goggles and pole forward.

Wake up! The first run of the day. Trailcheck. Today the run is   6 heaven—eight inches of light dry powder. My turns are relaxed giant slaloms that leave neat S's in the snow behind me. No need to worry about ice or rocks—the snow covers everything with an airy cushion that we float on, fly on, our skis barely on the ground. We split up at the first intersection, and I bear to the left, down into the Glades. My skis gently hiss as they break the powder, splitting the snow like a boat on calm water. I blast through deep drifts of snow, sending gouts and geysers of snow up around me. The air sparkles with snow, breaking the light into tiny flecks of color.

What a day! Some mornings I ride up in fifteen-below-zero cold, 7 only to ski down icy hardpack on which no new snow has fallen for days. There are rocks and other hazards to be noted and later marked with bamboo poles so skiers don't hit them. Fallen branches must be cleared from the trail. On days like that, when the snow is lousy and I have to worry about rocks gouging the bottoms of my skis, trailcheck is work—cold, necessary work done too early in the morning. But when the run is like it is today, that suffering is worthwhile.

I yelp with pleasure as I launch myself off a knoll and gently 8 land in the soft whiteness, blasting down a chute of untracked powder that empties out into a flatter run. I can hear the other patrollers whooping and yelling with me in the distance. Turns are effortless; a tiny shift of weight and the skis respond like wings. I come over the next pitch, moving fast, and my skis hit an unseen patch of ice, my tails slide, too late to get the edge in, POOF! I tumble into the snow in an explosion of snowdust. For a second I lie panting. Then I wallow in ecstasy, scooping handfuls of powder over myself, the sweet light snow tingling in the air. After a moment I hop up and continue down, sluicing more S-turns on the whipped-cream powder.

Reaching the patrol room, I click off my skis and stamp the snow 9 from myself. No longer do I feel the night's cold breath in the air— just the sting of the melting snow on my face. Ken looks at me as I drip and glisten over my trail report, and asks: "Good run, Jim?"

I grin at him and say, "Beau-ti-ful!" 10

Interview with James C. Tassé

Do you enjoy writing?

Yes, I've always been interested in writing, though it's something I always feel I'm not doing well enough. What I like most is turning phrases, putting things into my own words. And I use writing to get a handle on what I know. Sometimes it's papers for my professors, sometimes it's just ramblings in my journal—I'll get some munchies out and start jotting something down.

What do you least enjoy about writing? What is hardest for you?

Clarity, I guess. Like I said, I'm hardly ever satisfied with anything I've written, and I always think I could make it better by doing another draft. And the more drafts you do, the more challenging it gets, because the work you do seems to be finer and finer. You're looking for rough spots to polish, and as a piece gets better and you find more and more good about it, the rough spots become hidden even more. So each draft becomes more of a challenge, but I'm always eager to get at it.

Show me a rough spot and what you did about it.

Okay. Here's the first draft of paragraph 3, about riding up the chair lift.

The ride up gives one a chance to do some serious thinking. You're barely awake, and your first question is usually, "What the hell am I doing here?" But when you see the sun racing between tree branches piled high with snow, and bathing Mt. Mansfield in early morning coral light—you let that question slide. There is great beauty to a mountain in the morning in the winter, and the patrol is always the first to see it. Inevitably I wonder what the mountain would've been like had it remained as it was a hundred years ago: silent, cold, all trees and animals—a lonely, dangerous place for a man to be. But we've changed this mountain. . . .

And it goes on. If you look at the final version, you'll see that I made a lot of changes. Now the subject doesn't shift around from *one* to *you* to *I* to *we*. And instead of saying that the mountain is beautiful, I tried to show how beautiful it was.

Anything else?

Paragraph 7 is new. My instructor suggested it; he said it wasn't clear what trailcheck is for, and by telling about the hazards we sometimes have to deal with I could make that day's run seem even more perfect. I didn't have to add this but it seemed worth trying, and I liked the result. I like to get feedback from a reader. It helps me to have things like this pointed out.

We've talked about how you finish a writing project. How do you get started?

That depends. For descriptive pieces especially, the smallest thing can become a topic to work with. I like to try and capture the feeling of a scene or moment, and though I try to use original descriptions, I feel that I need work on new turns of phrases. Sometimes for practice I'll take a notebook down to Church Street and try to sum up a character, a scene or image in one or two sentences. Really briefly, but precisely. It's fun when it works, but it takes practice to make description work well all the time.

How do you prepare? Do you take notes, or make an outline?

I guess I'm unorthodox, the way I work. When I start on a piece of writing, I start to put it together in my mind, get an idea of its shape, even start finding words. Sometimes if it isn't shaping up, I'll drop it for a while and come back to it, and sometimes something will click and I'll see what I have to do. Then I'll start on a draft. I've never been a person to use outlines or anything like that, or very rarely.

Then it's the first rough draft, not notes or an outline, that's your raw material?

That's right.

Some African Birds

Isak Dinesen

Karen Dinesen was born in Denmark in 1885. In 1914 she went to Kenya with her husband, a Swedish baron, to manage their coffee plantation. Following their divorce, Dinesen remained at the plantation, managing it alone until it failed in 1931. She then returned to Denmark, where she died in 1962. While in Africa, Dinesen took the first name of Isak and began to write in English (the language of whites in Kenya). One of her best-known works is Seven Gothic Tales *(1934), a volume of stories. The motion picture* Out of Africa *was based on her book of the same name in which she reminisces about her years in Africa.*

The following essay from Out of Africa *describes the beautiful birds who made their homes in the area around Dinesen's Kenyan home.*

Just at the beginning of the long rains, in the last week of March, 1
or the first week of April, I have heard the nightingale in the woods of Africa. Not the full song: a few notes only,—the opening bars of the concerto, a rehearsal, suddenly stopped and again begun. It was as if, in the solitude of the dripping woods, some one was, in a tree, tuning a small cello. It was, however, the same melody, and the same abundance and sweetness, as were soon to fill the forests of Europe, from Sicily to Elsinore.

We had the black and white storks in Africa, the birds that build 2
their nests upon the thatched village roofs of Northern Europe. They look less imposing in Africa than they do there, for here they had such tall and ponderous birds as the Marabout and the Secretary Bird to be compared to. The storks have got other habits in Africa than in Europe, where they live as in married couples and are symbols of domestic happiness. Here they are seen together in big flights, as in clubs. They are called locust-birds in Africa, and follow along when the locusts come upon the land, living high

on them. They fly over the plains, too, where there is a grass-fire on, circling just in front of the advancing line of small leaping flames, high up in the scintillating rainbow-coloured air, and the grey smoke, on watch for the mice and snakes that run from the fire. The storks have a gay time in Africa. But their real life is not here, and when the winds of spring bring back thoughts of mating and nesting, their hearts are turned towards the North, they remember old times and places and fly off, two and two, and are shortly after wading in the cold bogs of their birth-places.

Out on the plains, in the beginning of the rains, where the vast 3 stretches of burnt grass begin to show fresh green sprouting, there are many hundred plovers. The plains always have a maritime air, the open horizon recalls the Sea and the long Sea-sands, the wandering wind is the same, the charred grass has a saline smell, and when the grass is long it runs in waves all over the land. When the white carnation flowers on the plains you remember the chopping white-specked waves all around you as you are tacking up the Sund. Out on the plains the plovers likewise take on the appearance of Sea-birds, and behave like Sea-birds on a beach, legging it, on the closing grass, as fast as they can for a short time, and then rising before your horse with high shrill shrieks, so that the light sky is all alive with wings and birds' voices.

The Crested Cranes, which come on to the newly rolled and 4 planted maize-land, to steal the maize out of the ground, make up for the robbery by being birds of good omen, announcing the rain; and also by dancing to us. When the tall birds are together in large numbers, it is a fine sight to see them spread their wings and dance. There is much style in the dance, and a little affectation, for why, when they can fly, do they jump up and down as if they were held on to the earth by magnetism? The whole ballet has a sacred look, like some ritual dance; perhaps the cranes are making an attempt to join Heaven and earth like the winged angels walking up and down Jacob's Ladder. With their delicate pale grey colouring, the little black velvet skull-cap and the fan-shaped crown, the cranes have all the air of light, spirited frescoes. When, after they dance, they lift and go away, to keep up the sacred tone of the show they give out, by the wings or the voice, a clear ringing note, as if a group of church bells had taken to the wing and were sailing off.

You can hear them a long way away, even after the birds them-selves have become invisible in the sky: a chime from the clouds.

The Greater Hornbill was another visitor to the farm, and came there to eat the fruits of the Cape-Chestnut tree. They are very strange birds. It is an adventure or an experience to meet them, not altogether pleasant, for they look exceedingly knowing. One morning before sunrise I was woken up by a loud jabbering outside the house, and when I walked out on the terrace I saw forty-one Hornbills sitting in the trees on the lawn. There they looked less like birds than like some fantastic articles of finery set on the trees here and there by a child. Black they all were, with the sweet, noble black of Africa, deep darkness absorbed through an age, like old soot, that makes you feel that for elegance, vigour and vivacity, no colour rivals black. All the Hornbills were talking together in the merriest mood, but with choice deportment, like a party of inheritors after a funeral. The morning air was as clear as crystal, the sombre party was bathing in freshness and purity, and, behind the trees and the birds, the sun came up, a dull red ball. You wonder what sort of a day you are to get after such an early morning.

The Flamingoes are the most delicately coloured of all the African birds, pink and red like a flying twig of an Oleander bush. They have incredibly long legs and bizarre and recherché curves of their necks and bodies, as if from some exquisite traditional prudery they were making all attitudes and movements in life as difficult as possible.

I once travelled from Port Said to Marseilles in a French boat that had on board a consignment of a hundred and fifty Flamingoes, which were going to the *Jardin D'Acclimatation* in Marseilles. They were kept in large dirty cases with canvas sides, ten in each, stand-ing up close to one another. The keeper, who was taking the birds over, told me that he was counting on losing twenty per cent of them on a trip. They were not made for that sort of life, in rough weather they lost their balance, their legs broke, and the other birds in the cage trampled on them. At night when the wind was high in the Mediterranean and the ship came down in the waves with a thump, at each wave I heard, in the dark, the Flamingoes shriek. Every morning, I saw the keeper taking out one or two dead birds, and throwing them overboard. The noble wader of the Nile, the sister of the lotus, which floats over the landscape like a stray cloud of sunset, had become a slack cluster of pink and red feathers with a pair of long, thin sticks attached to it. The dead birds floated on the water for a short time, knocking up and down in the wake of the ship before they sank.

Questions on Subject

1. According to Dinesen, how do the lives of storks in Africa differ from those in England?
2. What dominant impression of Africa do you get from Dinesen's description? (Glossary: *Dominant Impression*)
3. What does Dinesen mean when she says that the Greater Hornbill is "not altogether pleasant, for they look exceedingly knowing?"
4. In your own words, what is the meaning of the last sentence in paragraph 5?

Questions on Strategy

1. Is Dinesen's description objective or subjective or both? Cite examples from the text to support your answer.
2. Dinesen does not limit her description to the many varieties of birds she saw in Africa. What else does she describe, and how do these other descriptions add to her essay?
3. What kinds of details does Dinesen use in her description of the birds? Does she use the same kinds of details from bird to bird, or do the details vary? Did you find her description complete enough or were there other kinds of details you thought she ought to have included?
4. Dinesen's concluding paragraph is radically different in tone and content from the paragraphs that precede it. (Glossary: *Tone*) Why do you think she has included this paragraph? What would have been gained or lost had she left it out?

Questions on Diction and Vocabulary

1. Does Dinesen use any words that are unfamiliar to you? What effect does her use of these words have on you? Why do you suppose she includes them?

2. Dinesen uses many figures of speech in her descriptions (Glossary: *Figures of Speech*). Cite examples of these figures of speech and explain what each one adds to her description.
3. Refer to your desk dictionary to determine the meanings of the following words as they are used in this selection: *scintillating* (paragraph 2), *bogs* (2), *maritime* (3), *saline* (3), *affectation* (4), *frescoes* (4), *jabbering* (5), *deportment* (5), *recherché* (6).

Writing Suggestions

1. Describe your neighborhood as Dinesen does, except instead of describing the wildlife, describe the people you see there everyday. What kinds of details will you need to include? Will you include the same kinds of detail for each person or will it vary depending on the person and the impression of that person you wish to convey?
2. Dinesen concludes her essay with a comment on the shocking fate of some of the birds she has come to admire and respect. Choose a group you admire or respect which has been subject to a loss of dignity or respect. Begin as Dinesen does with a description of what makes that person a worthy object of your respect, and then describe the injustice or the indignity to which they have been subjected. What kinds of detail will you have to include to make the conclusion of your essay particularly powerful?

The Shack

Margaret Laurence

Margaret Laurence is a Canadian writer. The Otonabee River, described in the following selection from her nonfiction work The Heart of a Stranger *(1976), also figures prominently in her novel* The Diviners. *In the following essay, Laurence conveys to her reader the sights and sounds of one of her favorite places to write.*

The most loved place, for me, in this country has in fact been 1 many places. It has changed throughout the years, as I and my circumstances have changed. I haven't really lost any of the best places from the past, though. I may no longer inhabit them, but they inhabit me, portions of memory, presences in the mind. One such place was my family's summer cottage at Clear Lake in Riding Mountain National Park, Manitoba. It was known to us simply as The Lake. Before the government piers and the sturdy log staircases down to the shore were put in, we used to slither with an exhilarating sense of peril down the steep homemade branch and dirt shelf-steps, through the stands of thin tall spruce and birch trees slender and graceful as girls, passing moss-hairy fallen logs and the white promise of wild strawberry blossoms, until we reached the sand and the hard bright pebbles of the beach at the edge of the cold spring-fed lake where at nights the loons still cried eerily, before too much humanshriek made them move away north.

My best place at the moment is very different, although I guess 2 it has some of the attributes of that long-ago place. It is a small cedar cabin on the Otonabee River in southern Ontario. I've lived three summers there, writing, birdwatching, riverwatching. I sometimes feel sorry for the people in speedboats who spend their weekends zinging up and down the river at about a million miles an hour. For all they're able to see, the riverbanks might just as well be green concrete and the river itself flowing with molten plastic.

Before sunup, I'm wakened by birdvoices and, I may say, bird- 3
feet clattering and thumping on the cabin roof. Cursing only
slightly, I get up *temporarily*, for the pre-dawn ritual of lighting a
small fire in the old brick woodstove (mornings are chilly here,
even in summer) and looking out at the early river. The waters
have a lovely spooky quality at this hour, entirely mist-covered, a
secret meeting of river and sky.

By the time I get up to stay, the mist has vanished and the river 4
is a clear ale-brown, shining with sun. I drink my coffee and sit
looking out to the opposite shore, where the giant maples are
splendidly green now and will be trees of flame in the fall of the
year. Oak and ash stand among the maples, and the grey skeletons
of the dead elms, gauntly beautiful even in death. At the very edge
of the river, the willows are everywhere, water-related trees, magic
trees, pale green in early summer, silvergreen in late summer,
greengold in autumn.

I begin work, and everytime I lift my eyes from the page and 5
glance outside, it is to see some marvel or other. The joyous dance-
like flight of the swallows. The orange-black flash of the orioles
who nest across the river. The amazing takeoff of a red-winged
blackbird, revealing like a swiftly unfolded fan the hidden scarlet
in those dark wings. The flittering of the goldfinches, who always
travel in domestic pairs, he gorgeous in black-patterned yellow
feathers, she (alas) drabber in greenish grey-yellow.

A pair of great blue herons have their huge unwieldy nest about 6
half a mile upriver, and although they are very shy, occasionally
through the open door I hear a sudden approaching rush of air
(yes, you can *hear* it) and look up quickly to see the magnificent
unhurried sweep of those powerful wings. The only other birds
which can move me so much are the Canada geese in their autumn
migration flight, their far-off wilderness voices the harbinger of
winter.

Many boats ply these waterways, and all of them are given men- 7
tal gradings of merit or lack of it, by me. Standing low in the estimation of all of us along this stretch of the river are some of the
big yachts, whose ego-tripping skippers don't have the courtesy
to slow down in cottage areas and whose violent wakes scour out
our shorelines. Ranking highest in my good books are the silent
unpolluting canoes and rowboats, and next to them, the small out-

board motorboats put-putting along and carrying patient fisher-
men, and the homemade houseboats, unspeedy and somehow
cosy-looking, decorated lovingly with painted birds or flowers or
gaudy abstract splodges.

In the quiet of afternoon, if no boats are around, I look out and 8
see the half-moon leap of a fish, carp or muskie, so instantaneous
that one has the impression of having seen not a fish but an arc
of light.

The day moves on, and about four o'clock Linda and Susan from 9
the nearby farm arrive. I call them the Girls of the Pony Express.
Accompanied by dogs and laughter, they ride their horses into my
yard, kindly bringing my mail from the rural route postbox up the
road. For several summers it was Old Jack who used to drive his
battered Volkswagen up to fetch the mail. He was one of the best
neighbours and most remarkable men I've ever known. As a boy
of eighteen, he had homesteaded a hundred miles north of Regina.
Later, he'd been a skilled toolmaker with Ford. He'd travelled to
South America and done many amazing things. He was a man
whose life had taught him a lot of wisdom. After his much-loved
wife died, he moved out here to the river, spending as short a
winter as possible in Peterborough, and getting back into his cottage the first of anyone in the spring, when the river was still in
flood and he could only get in and out, hazardously, by boat. I
used to go out in his boat with him, late afternoons, and we would
dawdle along the river, looking at the forest stretches and the open
rolling farmlands and vast old barns, and at the smaller things
closeby, the heavy luxuriance of ferns at the water's rim, the dozens
of snapping turtles with unblinking eyes, all sizes and generations
of the turtle tribe, sunning themselves on the fallen logs in the
river. One summer, Old Jack's eighty-fourth, he spent some time
planting maple saplings on his property. A year later, when I saw
him dying, it seemed to me he'd meant those trees as a kind of
legacy, a declaration of faith. Those of us along the river, here,
won't forget him, nor what he stood for.

After work, I go out walking and weed-inspecting. Weeds and 10
wildflowers impress me as much as any cultivated plant. I've heard
that in a year when the milkweed is plentiful, the Monarch butterflies will also be plentiful. This year the light pinkish milkweed
flowers stand thick and tall, and sure enough, here are the dozens

of Monarch butterflies, fluttering like dusky orange-gold angels all over the place. I can't identify as many plants as I'd like, but I'm learning. Chickweed, the ragged-leafed lambs' quarters, the purple-and-white wild phlox with its expensive-smelling free perfume, the pink and mauve wild asters, the two-toned yellow of the tiny butter-and-eggs flowers, the burnt orange of devil's paintbrush, the staunch nobility of the huge purple thistles, and, almost best of all, that long stalk covered with clusters of miniature creamy blossoms which I finally tracked down in my wildflower book—this incomparable plant bears the armorial name of the Great Mullein of the Figwort Family. It may not be the absolute prettiest of our wildflowers, but it certainly has the most stunning pedigree.

It is night now, and there are no lights except those of our few cottages. At sunset, an hour or so ago, I watched the sun's last flickers touching the rippling river, making it look as though some underwater world had lighted all its candles down there. Now it is dark. Dinner over, I turn out the electric lights in the cabin so I can see the stars. The black skydome (or perhaps skydom, like kingdom) is alive and alight. 11

Tomorrow the weekend will begin, and friends will arrive. We'll talk all day and probably half the night, and that will be good. But for now, I'm content to be alone, because loneliness is something that doesn't exist here. 12

Questions on Subject

1. Why does Laurence feel sorry for the weekenders?
2. Laurence devotes a large portion of her description to Old Jack. What exactly does he stand for in the context of her description?
3. In your own words, how does Laurence "grade" the boats on the river?
4. Why do you think the weeds and wildflowers impress Laurence? What, if anything, might they have in common with Old Jack?
5. What is the meaning of Laurence's last sentence?

Questions on Strategy

1. Why does Laurence title her essay "The Shack"? Would another title have worked better? Explain. (Glossary: *Title*)

2. Comment on the effectiveness of Laurence's opening paragraph. Why do you suppose she has chosen to begin her essay this way? (Glossary: *Beginnings*)
3. Laurence uses several sentence fragments in paragraph 5. What, if anything, do they add to her description?
4. What details does Laurence use to create her dominant impression? (Glossary: *Dominant Impression*)
5. How has Laurence organized her essay? (Glossary: *Organization*)

Questions on Diction and Vocabulary

1. Laurence uses parentheses throughout her essay. What kind of information is contained in the parentheses?
2. Does Laurence rely more heavily on adjectives, verbs, or nouns in her description? Explain what insights this gives you about writing descriptions.
3. Cite examples of some of the words Laurence has created herself, and explain in what way they add to her description.
4. Refer to your desk dictionary to determine the meanings of the following words as they are used in this selection: *slither* (paragraph 1), *molten* (2), *gauntly* (4), *drabber* (5), *harbinger* (6), *ply* (7), *gaudy* (7), *dawdle* (9), *mauve* (10), *staunch* (10), *armorial* (10).

Writing Suggestions

1. Write a descriptive essay of a place you either like or dislike. Be sure to describe the particular features of the place, the people you encounter there, and what kinds of things happen there.
2. Write a descriptive essay in which you describe what you value most in life, whether it be family, solitude, your work, a special friend, or a combination of things. Along with telling details about that thing or person, be sure to include your reasons for valuing it, him, or her above everything (or everyone) else.

"State-of-the-Art Car": The Ferrari Testarossa

Joyce Carol Oates

Novelist, essayist, and short story writer, Joyce Carol Oates was born in 1938 in Lockport, New York. After receiving her B.A. from Syracuse University and her M.A. in English from the University of Wisconsin, she taught English and creative writing at the University of Detroit and the University of Windsor (Ontario, Canada). She later became an English professor and writer-in-residence at Princeton University. Today, Oates lives near Princeton University. Her first collection of short stories By the North Gate *(1963), published when she was only twenty-five, received rave reviews in which she was compared to William Faulkner. Among her many works of fiction and nonfiction are:* Expensive People *(1968),* Unholy Loves *(1979),* Angel of Light *(1981),* Solstice *(1985), and* On Boxing *(1987). Her books on literary criticism include* The Edge of Impossibility *(1971),* The Poetry of D. H. Lawrence *(1973), and* New Heaven, New Earth *(1974).*

In the following essay, Oates describes with abandon the aesthetic, philosophical, and physical pleasures of the Testarossa, a premiere high-performance automobile made by Ferrari.

Speak of the Ferrari Testarossa to men who know cars and observe their immediate visceral response: the virtual dilation of their eyes in sudden focused *interest*. The Testarossa!—that domestic rocket of a sports car, sleek, low-slung, aggressively wide; startlingly beautiful even in the eyes of non–car aficionados; so spectacular a presence on the road that—as I can personally testify— heads turn, faces break into childlike smiles in its wake. As one observer has noted, the Testarossa drives "civilians" crazy.

Like a very few special cars, the Ferrari Testarossa is in fact a meta-car, a poetic metaphor or trope: an *object* raised to the level

135

of a near-spiritual *value*. Of course it has a use—as a Steinway concert grand or a Thoroughbred racing horse has a use—but its significance hovers above and around mere use. What can one say about a street car (as opposed to a racing car) capable of traveling 177 effortless miles per hour?—accelerating, as it does, again without effort, from 0 mph to 60 mph in 5 seconds, 107 mph in 13.3 seconds? A car that sells for approximately $104,000—if you can get one? (The current waiting period is twelve months and will probably get longer). There are said to be no more than 450 Testarossas in private ownership in the United States; only about three hundred models are made by Ferrari yearly. So popular has the model become, due in part to its much-publicized presence in the television series *Miami Vice* (in which, indeed, fast cars provide a sort of subtextual commentary on the men who drive them), that a line of child-sized motorized "Testarossas" is now being marketed—which extravagant toys range in price from $3,500 to $13,000. (Toys bought by parents who don't want to feel guilty, as one Ferrari dealer remarked.)

For all its high-tech styling, its racing-car image, the Ferrari Testarossa is a remarkably easy car to drive: its accelerative powers are first unnerving, then dangerously seductive. You think you are traveling at about 60 miles per hour when in fact you are moving toward 100 miles per hour (with your radar detector—"standard issue for this model"—in operation). In the luxury-leather seats, low, of course, and accommodatingly wide, you have the vertiginous impression of being somehow below the surface of the very pavement, skimming, flying, *rocketing* past vehicles moving at ordinary speeds; as if in a dream, or an "action" film. (Indeed, viewed through the discreetly tinted windshield of a Testarossa, the world, so swiftly passing, looks subtly altered: less assertive in its dimensions, rather more like "background.") Such speeds are heady, intoxicating, clearly addictive: if you are moving at 120 mph so smoothly, why not 130 mph? why not 160 mph? why not the limit—if, indeed, there is a limit? "Gusty/Emotions on wet roads on autumn nights" acquire a new significance in a car of such unabashed romance. What godly maniacal power: you have only to depress the accelerator of the Ferrari Testarossa and you're at the horizon. Or beyond. 3

The mystique of high-performance cars has always intrigued me 4 with its very opacity. Is it lodged sheerly in speed?—mechanical ingenuity?—the "art" of a finely tuned beautifully styled vehicle (as the mere physical fact of a Steinway piano constitutes "art")?—the adrenal thrill of courting death? Has it primarily to do with display (that of male game fowl, for instance)? Or with masculine prowess of a fairly obvious sort? (Power being, as the cultural critic Henry Kissinger once observed, the ultimate aphrodisiac.)

Or is it bound up with the phenomenon of what the American economist Thorstein Veblen so wittily analyzed as "conspicuous consumption" in his classic *Theory of the Leisure Class* (1899)—Veblen's theory being that the consumption of material goods is determined not by the inherent value of goods but by the social standing derived from their consumption. (Veblen noted how in our capitalistic-democratic society there is an endless "dynamics" of style as the wealthiest class ceaselessly strives to distinguish itself from the rest of society and its habits of consumption trickle down to lower levels.)

Men who work with high-performance cars, however, are likely to value them as ends in themselves: they have no time for theory, being so caught up, so mesmerized, in practice. To say that certain cars at certain times determine the "state-of-the-art" is to say that such machinery, on its most refined levels, constitutes a serious and speculative and ever-changing (improving?) art. The Ferrari Testarossa is not a *car* in the generic sense in which, say, a Honda Accord—which my husband and I own—is a *car*. (For one thing, the Accord has about 90 horsepower; the Testarossa 380.) Each Ferarri is more or less unique, possessed of its own mysterious personality; its peculiar ghost-in-the-machine. "It's a good car," I am told, with typical understatement, by a Testarossa owner named Bill Kontes, "—a *good* car." He pauses, and adds, "But not an antique. This is a car you can actually drive."

(Though it's so precious—the lipstick-red model in particular such an attention-getter—that you dare not park it in any marginally public place. Meta-cars arouse emotions at all points of the spectrum.)

Bill Kontes, in partnership with John Melniczuk, owns and operates Checkered Flag Cars in Vineland, New Jersey—a dealership of such choice content (high-performance exotic cars, "vintage" classics, others) as to make it a veritable Phillips Collection amid its larger rivals in the prestige car market. It was by way of their hospitality that I was invited to test-drive the Ferrari Testarossa for *Quality*, though my only qualifications would seem to have been that I knew how to drive a car. (Not known to Mr. Kontes and Mr. Melniczuk was the ambiguous fact that I did once own, in racier days, a sports car of a fairly modest species—a Fiat Spider also in audacious lipstick-red. I recall that it was always stalling. That it gave up, so to speak, along a melancholy stretch of interstate highway in the approximate vicinity of Gary, Indiana, emitting actual flames from its exhaust. That the garage owner to whose garage it was ignominiously towed stared at it and said contemptuously, "A pile of junk!" That we sold it soon afterward and never bought another "sports" car again.)

It was along a semideserted stretch of South Jersey road that Mr. 9
Kontes turned the Ferrari Testarossa over to me, gallantly, and surely bravely: and conscious of the enormity of the undertaking— a sense, very nearly, that the honor of "woman writerhood" might be here at stake, a colossal blunder or actual catastrophe reflecting not only upon the luckless perpetrator but upon an entire generation and gender—I courageously drove the car, and, encouraged by Mr. Kontes, and by the mysterious powers of the radar detector to detect the presence of uniformed and sanctioned enforcers of the law (which law, I fully understand, *is* for our own good and in the best and necessary interests of the commonwealth), I did in fact accelerate through all five gears to a speed rather beyond one I'd anticipated: though not to 120 mph, which was Mr. Kontes's fairly casual speed a few minutes previously. (This particular Testarossa, new to Vineland, had been driven at 160 mph by Mr. Melniczuk the other day, along a predawn stretch of highway presumably sanctioned by the radar detector. To drive behind the Testarossa, as I also did, and watch it—suddenly—ease away toward the horizon is an eerie sight: if you don't look closely you're likely to be startled into asking, Where did it go?)

But the surprise of the Testarossa, *pace Miami Vice* and the hyped- 10
up media image, is that it is an easy, even comfortable car to drive: user-friendly, as the newly coined cliché would have it. It reminded me not at all of the tricky little Spider I'd quite come to hate by the time of our parting but, oddly, of the unnerving but fiercely exhilarating experience of being behind the controls—so to

speak—of a two-seater open-cockpit plane. (My father flew sporty airplanes years ago, and my childhood is punctured with images of flight: the wind-ravaged open-cockpit belonged to a former navy bomber recycled for suburban airfield use.) As the Testarossa was accelerated I felt that visceral sense of an irresistibly gathering and somehow condensing power—"speed" being in fact a mere distillation or side effect of power—and, within it, contained by it, an oddly humble sense of human smallness, frailty. One of the perhaps unexamined impulses behind high-speed racing must be not the mere "courting" of death but, on a more primary level, its actual pre-experience; its taste.

But what have such thoughts to do with driving a splendid red 11 Ferrari Testarossa in the environs of Vineland, New Jersey, one near-perfect autumn day, an afternoon shading romantically into dusk? Quite beyond, or apart from, the phenomenal machinery in which Bill Kontes and I were privileged to ride I was acutely conscious of the spectacle we and it presented to others' eyes. Never have I seen so many heads turn!—so much staring!—*smiling*! While the black Testarossa may very well resemble, as one commentator has noted, Darth Vader's personal warship, the lipstick-red model evokes smiles of pleasure, envy, awe—most pointedly in young men, of course, but also in older, even elderly women. Like royalty, the Testarossa seems to bestow a gratuitous benison upon its spectators. Merely to watch it pass is to feel singled out, if, perhaps, rather suddenly drab and anonymous. My thoughts drifted onto the pomp of kings and queens and maharajahs, the legendary excesses of the Gilded Age of Morgan, Carnegie, Rockefeller, Mellon, Armour, McCormick, et al.—Edith Rockefeller McCormick, just to give one small example, served her dinner guests on china consisting of over a thousand pieces containing 11,000 ounces of gold—the Hope Diamond, and Liz Taylor's diamonds, and the vision of Mark Twain, in impeccably dazzling white, strolling on Fifth Avenue while inwardly chafing at his increasing lack of privacy. If one is on public display one is of course obliged not to be conscious of it; driving a $104,000 car means being equal to the car in dignity and style. Otherwise the public aspect of the performance is contaminated: we are left with merely conspicuous consumption, an embarrassment in such times of economic trepidation and worldwide hunger.

Still, it's the one incontrovertible truth about the Ferrari Testa- 12
rossa: no matter who is behind the wheel people stare, and they
stare in admiration. Which might not otherwise be the case.

Questions on Subject

1. Early in her essay Oates says the Testarossa has a "near-spiritual
   value." Where in her essay does she support this claim?
2. Oates asks several questions in paragraph 4. How does she answer
   them? How would you answer them?
3. In your own words, what is the "conspicuous consumption" Oates
   refers to in paragraph 5? According to Oates, how does the driver
   of the Testarossa escape this label?
4. In what way do high-performance cars become "ends in themselves"? (6)
5. In what way was "woman writerhood" at stake for Oates?
6. What was the "surprise of the Testarossa"?

Questions on Strategy

1. What is Oates's purpose in writing this essay? Where is it stated?
   (Glossary: *Purpose*)
2. In what way do the first three paragraphs of Oates's description
   serve as an introduction to the rest of her essay? (Glossary:
   Beginnings)
3. Throughout her essay, Oates uses parenthetical expressions. What
   sort of comments does she typically make in parentheses? Why do
   you think she does so?
4. Make a list of the qualities Oates assigns to drivers and spectators
   of the Testarossa. How does she distinguish between the two?
   What is the effect of this contrast she draws for her readers?
5. In what way do Oates's references to members of royalty, Mark
   Twain, and other rich and famous people function in the context
   of her description?

Questions on Diction and Vocabulary

1. Oates manages to create an impression of speed and power in her
   description. What kinds of words does she use to create this

impression? Does she rely more heavily on verbs or on adjectives? Cite examples of her diction to support your answer.

2. Refer to your desk dictionary to determine the meanings of the following words as they are used in this selection: *visceral* (paragraph 1), *vertiginous* (3), *opacity* (4), *inherent* (5), *mesmerized* (6), *audacious* (8), *ignominiously* (8), *perpetrator* (9), *eerie* (9), *environs* (11), *evokes* (11), *gratuitous* (11), *trepidation* (11), *incontrovertible* (12).

Writing Suggestions

1. Write a short descriptive essay about your own or your family's car in which you evoke all the emotions you experience when you drive it. (Your challenge may be even greater if your car is ordinary rather than spectacular.) What kinds of verbs or adjectives will you use to describe something that is not wonderful or exciting?

2. Write an essay in which you describe the greatest thrill of your life. Then, just to make the assignment more challenging, make your description objective rather than subjective. Which version of the experience do you prefer? Why?

Remembering Rachel
Bob Hines

Bob Hines is a retired national wildlife artist who recently illustrated the fiftieth anniversary edition of Rachel Carson's Under the Sea Wind, *published in April 1991. Hines now lives in Arlington, Virginia.*

In the following essay from Yankee Magazine, *Hines reminisces about his sixteen-year friendship with Rachel Carson, during which time he witnessed her love of the natural world and her growing concern for its safety.*

It was mid-July in 1948 when we first met. I had just been hired 1
as an artist for the U.S. Fish and Wildlife Service. When I was offered the job, I had been told I'd be supervised by a woman, and having done odd jobs for hard-to-please housewives during the Depression, I was apprehensive. I was working at my drawing board when a slender, attractive lady walked in. She came directly to me, greeted me with a firm handclasp, and said, "Welcome to the Fish and Wildlife Service. I'm Rachel Carson."

The door to Rachel's office—an uncluttered space with photos 2
of a seascape and a large ghost crab—was always open. As editorial chief of the Service, it was her job to review manuscripts, help authors, write speeches for congressmen and government officials, and write articles for our "Conservation in Action" booklets. Her prose was so beautiful that it was intimidating: When Rachel asked a staff writer to add some new material to an article she had written, he returned it after two weeks, saying it was impossible.

Rachel was a quiet woman. She told none of us at the Service 3
when she sent her book, *The Sea Around Us* to a publisher. But one day she came to my office and motioned for me to follow her. She hurried to a public phone booth in the main corridor, pushed me inside, and crowded in to sit on my lap. She shut the door to ensure privacy and then told me that her book had been selected for the Book of the Month Club. Her eyes were large and wet and her

laugh was almost a giggle—the only time I ever heard such a sound from her.

I enjoyed sharing in her triumph and was pleased when she ₄ asked me to illustrate *The Edge of the Sea*. Although it was first conceived as a seashore guide, Rachel wanted it to be more. She wanted readers to share the sensation of wading with her through tide pools, clambering over barnacle-encrusted rocks, probing into seaweed jungles. "I can't possibly write, 'This is a blue crab,' or 'That is a sea urchin,' as though it is a catalog," she told me. "There is so much to tell—the marvel of survival under the pounding of waves and flow of tides, the relations of one species to another, how they live, and where, and why. I have to be me—I want people to understand the beauty and complexity of the sea and enjoy the pleasure such knowledge brings."

To do this, Rachel traveled the Atlantic coast from Maine to Flor- ₅ ida to study the sea life left onshore between high and low tides. She wanted to see all her subjects—including the pelagic species wave-tossed by storms and tides—in their own habitat. She in- sisted that the drawings be made in the same way. So during the summer of 1951, we headed north to Boothbay Harbor—Rachel with her microscope and writing materials, I with sketch pads and pencils, and Rachel's mother, Maria, with her love of nature. We rented a seashore cottage just north of town with boulders stretch- ing from the front porch to the ocean. It was there my education in marine biology began.

I was a flatlander from Ohio with no knowledge of the sea, and ₆ Rachel opened a new world to me: tunicates, hydroids, sponges, sea squirts, a few small starfish. Normally straightforward, now and then she'd note that a certain crab looked like a certain ac- quaintance of ours, and we'd laugh as the waves splashed our calves.

Every day, while Mrs. Carson kept house, Rachel led me along ₇ the shore to collect live specimens to study and draw. Every night without exception, after we'd finished, we carried the specimens back to the exact spots where we found them and released them. Rachel was adamant about this; her reverence for all living things— plant or animal—would accept no other way.

We went often to Pemaquid Point. Mrs. Carson would bring ₈ table scraps to feed the gulls while Rachel and I set off toward the tide pools within sight of the lighthouse. Rachel always went first to the largest tide pool to check on what the most recent high tide had brought. Once it looked like a starfish convention—14 had been washed in overnight. We found sea gooseberries, little glass-clear comb jellies, that came in on one tide and left on the next, and a floating plank that was home to a gooseneck barnacle colony, waving sets of feathery feet that combed food from the incoming tide. Sometimes Rachel made notes, but she didn't need them—she remembered everything.

The colors in the pools were bright and varied. The dark blue   9
horse mussel shells, green sea urchins, sea slugs, sponges, anemones, and seaweed contrasted sharply with the pink caroline algae. Crabs and brittle stars clambered about, and sometimes blennies, tiny little fish, flopped vigorously at our approach. Rachel observed the color and movement and tried to explain the life in those small rock-bound communities to me. I had difficulty with the scientific names, and in exasperation I called them all "wee beasts," which made her chuckle.

Maine coastal waters are never warm, and the tide pools were   10
often frigid, yet Rachel never hesitated to enter. Clad only in light-weight clothing and tennis shoes, she waded into the hip-deep water and became so engrossed in her research that she paid no attention to the time or how chilled she became. One cloudy day even her determination failed, and when she started to climb out of a pool, she was so numb she nearly fell back in. I splashed in beside her, picked her up, and carried her to the car. Mrs. Carson wrapped her in a blanket and asked me to drive home.

The next summer the three of us were back in New England at   11
Woods Hole, Massachusetts, where we had access to modern research facilities, world-famous scientists, and thousands of jars of marine specimens preserved in formaldehyde. Many students and technicians went out of their way to help Rachel with her project.

The cottage she rented there was set back from the ocean, up a   12
narrow dirt road through second-growth timber. It was light and airy. Though she was busy with her work, she answered all requests for testimonials and autographs and even found time to review Ernest Hemingway's *The Old Man and the Sea*. She complained when requests were blunt and unaccompanied by return postage, but she continued to labor long into the nights.

Twice we went out after dark to a world vastly different than it 13
appeared in the day. The beams of our flashlights showed crabs
of all sizes, feeding with a freedom unknown in the sunlight. Small
fish came up close and were pinned in the glare of our torches.
The sea walnut, a comb jelly with a glasslike body too fragile to
be netted, was easily guided into openmouth jars.

When Rachel decided I had enough sketches to finish later, I 14
returned to Washington, while she and her mother stayed at
Woods Hole. Rachel brought her mother home early that fall. Mrs.
Carson's health was poor, and Rachel's own strength was ebbing,
though she refused to show it. She was eager to go south to the
sand beaches of the mid-Atlantic states and the coral reefs of Florida, but she needed more rest now. The book had to be postponed,
but it was eventually published in 1955.

We saw less of each other after Rachel resigned her government 15
job to write full-time. But we talked frequently on the phone, and
I was pleased when she asked one day if I would drive her to West
Southport, Maine, during the summer of 1959.

We left her Silver Spring, Maryland, home around 8:30 in the 16
morning. Rachel sat beside me; her eight-year-old nephew, Roger,
and her black cat, Jeffie, were in the back. She was eager to get to
her cottage in Maine where many of the frustrations of recent
months could be forgotten. As we drove north, she seemed happy,
but somewhere around New Jersey her talk turned grim as she
turned to the subject of insecticides. When I expressed surprise
that she, a marine biologist, was interested in the subject, she said
she had proposed a magazine article about it in 1945, but was
turned down.

"There are so many proven facts," she said, "so much new data, 17
and tragically, so much wildlife dying and human health endangered that we simply must act—and act fast. For a long time, I
didn't feel that a book would explain the many problems or that
I could write it. But when no one else really told the story, I knew
I had to try—it has become the biggest challenge I've ever met."

She told me about checking on the stories of poisonings from 18
spraying and how she had documented them. She knew she could
write the terrible tale. She also knew what would happen to her
if she did.

"Of course," she said, "when the facts are known, the chemical 19 companies and very likely farmers and agriculture experts will deny most of them and will ask, 'What does a marine biologist know about poisons?' I only hope I'm strong enough to meet their charges, for goodness knows I have the data to prove the truth."

That was the last time I saw Rachel Carson. As she predicted, 20 when *Silent Spring* was published in 1962, it was both praised and denounced worldwide. She was showered with awards. Congressional committees sought her testimony, the White House sent an invitation, the Democratic National Committee named her to a post.

But as her fame grew, her health faltered. She was confined to 21 bed and a wheelchair. I spoke to her once more by telephone. Her voice was slurred, and she assured me that she was *not* drunk, but under sedation. It was the only time in the 16 years I knew her that she ever spoke openly of her illness. I told her I loved her and that the whole world was waiting for her to recover. In April 1964 she died of cancer at the age of 56.

Rachel's name lives on in the Rachel Carson National Wildlife 22 Refuge, a chain of saltwater marshes on the coast of her beloved Maine. I remember a walk we took in such a place, one day when we'd heard that a moose had been seen nearby. We never found the moose, but there were many birds. In 45 minutes we saw 31 species: warblers, thrushes, sandpipers, woodpeckers, and a hawk. I wished we had seen or heard a veery; its song appealed to her more than any other.

When *Silent Spring* was finally completed, Rachel wrote to a 23 friend: ". . . I could never again listen happily to a thrush song if I had not done all that I could. And last night the thoughts of all the birds and other creatures and all the loveliness that is in nature came to me with such a surge of deep happiness, that now I had done what I could—I had been able to complete it—now it had its own life. . . ."

Questions on Subject

1. Why, according to Hines, was Rachel Carson intent on seeing her subjects in their own habitat?
2. How would you describe public reaction to *Silent Spring*?

3. The last time Hines spoke to Carson something significant happened. What was it? How do you explain it?
4. Hines does not account for the lapse of five years between Hines's last phone call to Carson and her death. How would you explain it?
5. In what way is the Rachel Carson National Wildlife Refuge a fitting tribute to Rachel Carson?

Questions on Strategy

1. What is Hines's purpose in writing his essay? (Glossary: *Purpose*)
2. What are some of the details Hines includes to create the impression of the intimacy that existed between him and Carson? (Glossary: *Dominant Impression*)
3. Hines includes the names of many sea creatures in his description of Rachel Carson. Why do you think he has done this? What if anything does it add to his description?
4. What foreshadowing of Carson's illness does Hines offer?
5. Hines reveals many of Carson's personal qualities—some directly, others indirectly. Cite examples of each, and explain how they work to enhance his description of Carson the person.
6. Hines ends his essay with a long quotation from Rachel Carson. Why do you suppose he chose to do this? What is the effect on the reader? (Glossary: *Endings*)

Questions on Diction and Vocabulary

1. In what ways can Hines's diction be said to mirror the qualities he describes in Rachel Carson?
2. Refer to your desk dictionary to determine the meanings of the following words as they are used in this selection: *apprehensive* (paragraph 1), *intimidating* (2), *adamant* (7), *tide pools* (8), *anemones* (9), *clambered* (9), *clad* (10), *endangered* (17).

Writing Assignments

1. Perhaps you share Rachel Carson's concern for the environment. Like her you may realize that one way to engender that concern

in others is to awaken in them an appreciation for that environment by revealing its wonders. Choose an aspect of the environment that you feel is endangered and for which you have a particular concern: for example, the seacoast, rivers, wetlands, mountains, deeryards, or something else. Write a descriptive essay in which you acquaint readers with aspects of nature in your chosen place with which they may not be familiar.

2. Write a descriptive essay about your garden or a favorite park in which you include all the sights, sounds, and smells you encounter there. Choose your diction carefully to reflect the emotions you feel when you are working in your garden or relaxing in the park.

My Father, the Prince

Phyllis Theroux

Phyllis Theroux was born in San Francisco in 1939. A graduate of Manhattanville College, she has worked as a secretary, a school teacher, and a legal researcher. As a writer she has been a frequent contributor to the "Hers" column in the New York Times *as well as to* Reader's Digest, *the* Washington Post, *and* McCall's. *In 1980, Theroux published her first book,* California and Other States of Grace: A Memoir. *She followed this collection with two others,* Peripheral Visions *and* Night Lights: Bedtime Stories for Parents in the Dark.

"My Father, the Prince" is taken from her second book, Peripheral Visions, *a collection of autobiographical essays. In describing her father and his special gift to her, Theroux also probes the crucial relationship that exists between all fathers and daughters.*

Fathers. They say that a woman seeks—in love, marriage, or any 1 male-female relationship of real heft—to approximate the father she had, the father she didn't have but wanted, or the father minus the attributes that caused her mother to leave him for good and sufficient reason. In the winnowing-out process that precedes deep commitment to a new man, the daughter subconsciously throws up the wheat of her father's virtues along with the chaff of his faults, and her decision to commit is strongly influenced by that first experience of male companionship.

I think they're right. 2

We all know that men consider their mothers when they choose 3 a woman for themselves, but fathers have traditionally been considered mere linkage in the rosary of wombs that produce progeny from one decade to the next. Accessories to the fact, off-campus providers, fathers are six o'clock visitors to the nursery tended by all-powerful mothers.

149

One can scarcely overestimate the influence that mothers have 4
upon their sons. But fathers have yet to be properly weighed in
as determinative factors in the lives of their daughters. To my way
of thinking, this is a terrible oversight.

In a grayer, more small-minded period of my life, I used to in- 5
wardly gripe at the inaccuracy of the Cinderella story. Cinderella
does not go from ashes to amethysts. In real life the brooms and
the dustpans materialize after the wedding, whereupon she
spends forever after staring out the window wondering where her
father—the real prince in her life—has gone.

Of course, women are now rewriting that old script, and this is 6
an age in which we are forming piano-moving companies, hiking
up telephone poles, and swimming along with Jacques Cousteau.
But I live with a little woman, aged seven, who recently gave me
to understand that liberation is an acquired taste and no substitute
for gut feeling.

"What's this?" I asked as she handed me a crayon drawing of 7
a little girl next to what looked like a giant lollipop.

"Me," she answered. (There was a crown drawn on the little 8
girl's head.)

"And what are you doing?" I pursued, searching the drawing 9
for some evidence of a plot line.

"Nothing," she said matter-of-factly. "Just standing by the bus 10
stop waiting for the prince."

I put the drawing aside, looked at my matter-of-fact daughter, 11
and thought with chagrin, "Aren't we all!" Spoiled or despoiled
by the first prince in our life, we understand, either way, what it
means to be born to the purple. No, Cinderella did not accidentally
fall for royalty. Her dear departed father had given her an early
taste for it. My father did the same.

He was a tall, crooked-toothed, curly-haired man, who smelled 12
of Lucky Strikes and St. Johns Bay Rum shaving lotion. He was
the only father who wore penny loafers on business trips, a Mouseketeer hat to pick up my brother on his first movie date, and
had the delicious gall to invite the richest girl in my class (she had
her own pool but an exclusive number of invitations) to come on
over to the house ("When you're free, of course") and watch our
lawn sprinklers.

"Sometimes we get them going in opposite directions to each 13
other," he said dryly, "and it's terribly amusing."

The richest girl in the class laughed nervously, I choked back 14
my borrowed triumph, and savored the fact that once again my
father had effectively punched out the opposition on my behalf.
He had a gift for it.

Yet, unlike other men blessed with a quick wit and a rare natural 15
electricity of being, my father was oddly incapable of parlaying his
gifts to his own long-range advantage.

As I grew older and more able to observe him objectively in group 16
situations, I noticed that in a room full of peers he would usually
back up against the mantel and go into a sort of social receivership
that did not jibe with my understanding of him. It made me impatient. He was far and away the largest talent in the room, and
it seemed a terrible waste to give over the floor to anyone else. Yet
he consistently passed up opportunities to reveal himself in public,
and it was many years before I realized that my wonderful father
was *shy*.

I was thunderstruck. Is Douglas Fairbanks, Jr., shy? Does Cary 17
Grant falter? Should my father have anything in the world to hesitate over?

It was one thing to be a pudgy, preadolescent girl trying to make 18
it in a class full of gazelles, but quite another thing to be that little
girl's handsome father, who at various crucial junctures had told
her that all she had to do in order to succeed was to take this step,
or that action, and—for heaven's sake—was the world such a difficult nut to crack after all? Of course not!

If there was any one thing that my father did for me when I was 19
growing up it was to give me the promise that ahead of me was
dry land—a bright, marshless territory, without chuckholes or
traps, where one day I would walk easily and as befitting my talents. The fact that I didn't know what my talents were did not put
my father off in the slightest. He knew potential when he saw it.

Thus it was, when he came upon me one afternoon sobbing out 20
my unsuccesses into a wet pillow, that he sat down on the bed
and, like a strong, omniscient archangel, assured me that my grief
was only a temporary setback.

Oh, very temporary! Why he couldn't think of any other little 21 girl who was so talented, so predestined to succeed in every department as I was. "And don't forget," he added with a smile, "that we can trace our ancestry right back to Pepin the Stupid!"[1]

That last piece of news turned out to be true, but whether he 22 believed the rest of his words or not I don't know. He was, after all, gazing down upon a disheveled ten-year-old who was too embarrassed to shift her gum from one cheek to the other.

But I listened to him carefully, and by the time he had finished 23 talking I really did understand that someday I would live among rational beings, and walk with kind, unvindictive people who, by virtue of their maturity and mine, would take no pleasure in cruelty and would welcome my presence among them as an asset. It was only a question of time before I came ripping out of my cocoon, a free-flying butterfly that would skim triumphantly over the meadow of my choice. I cannot say that my father was completely wrong.

Time has passed. Choices have been made. I am no longer a 24 preteen in a net formal who secretly hoped that all the other girls at the Father-Daughter Dance were eating their hearts out. My father's crooked front tooth was replaced several years ago by a nice, straight, shiny one. He has passed through the hospital several times. There are grandchildren. I sometimes think that it is not the same between us, or perhaps it never was what I thought.

One's memory is selective, and I admit that it's to my advantage 25 to recall only those moments when my father rose to the occasion and parted another Red Sea of Impossibility[2] and elbowed me across. Yet these moments really did happen and I am not the same because of them.

There are some people, my father is one of them, who carry the 26 flint that lights other people's torches. They get them all excited about the possibilities of an idea, the "can-do" potential of one's own being.

That was my father's gift to me, and whatever psychic wounds 27 remain to be thrashed out between us are still lying on the floor of my unconscious, waiting for deep therapy to uncover. The fact

[1] A medieval French ruler.
[2] Refers to the miraculous parting of the actual Red Sea by Moses during the Israelites' escape from Egypt (Exodus 21–29).

is that I am closer to my mother. But they say that a daughter carries around the infection of her father for life.

They are right.

28

Questions on Subject

1. What does Theroux mean by her title, "My Father, the Prince"? In what way was her father a prince?
2. How does the Cinderella story fit into Theroux's description? What point is she making with the anecdote about her daughter's drawing?
3. What was Theroux's father's special "gift" to her? What does this gift have to do with his ability to "punch out the opposition" (paragraph 14), as well as his shyness?
4. Has Theroux's view of her father changed over the years? If so, how?

Questions on Strategy

1. Theroux's description of her father doesn't actually begin until paragraph 12. What function or functions do paragraphs 1–11 serve? (Glossary: *Beginnings*)
2. Two paragraphs in the essay—the second and the last—are linked in several interesting ways. What function do they serve in the overall context?
3. Theroux tells us very little about her father's physical appearance. How, then, does she actually describe him? Do you feel that you know what he is like?
4. Theroux's essay is drawn from her own experience and observations, yet she writes: "They say that . . ." (1); "We all know that . . ." (3); "One can scarcely overestimate . . ." (4); and, again, "But they say that . . ." (27). Why do you suppose Theroux chooses not to limit herself to the first-person *I*, particularly at the beginning and the end?

Questions on Diction and Vocabulary

1. Theroux makes effective use of figurative language in this essay. For example, she says "the daughter subconsciously throws up the

wheat of her father's virtues along with the chaff of his faults" (1), and she refers to herself as a "pudgy, preadolescent girl trying to make it in a class full of gazelles" (18). Locate several other figures of speech and comment on their contributions to this essay. (Glossary: *Figures of Speech*)

2. Refer to your desk dictionary to determine the meanings of the following words as they are used in this selection: *heft* (paragraph 1), *amethysts* (5), *chagrin* (11), *despoiled* (11), *gall* (12), *parlaying* (15), *receivership* (16), *omniscient* (20), *psychic* (27).

Writing Assignments

1. In an essay, describe your mother, your father, or another adult who has been an important influence in your life. Use your description not only to create a portrait of the person, but also to clarify your relationship and its effect on you. In selecting details for your description, keep in mind that personality traits can be just as important, if not more so, than physical characteristics.

2. Using library sources, write a descriptive essay about a person you have never met, perhaps a present-day celebrity or a historical figure. Whether your description is objective or impressionistic, try to create a dominant impression of your subject.

Writing Suggestions for Description

1. Most description is predominantly visual; that is, it appeals to our sense of sight. Good description, however, often goes beyond the visual; it appeals as well to one or more of the other senses—hearing, smelling, tasting, and touching. One way to heighten your awareness of these other senses is purposefully to deemphasize the visual impressions you receive. For example, while standing on a busy street corner, sitting in a classroom, or shopping in a supermarket, carefully note what you hear, smell, taste, or feel. (It may actually help to close your eyes to eliminate visual distraction as you carry out this experiment.) Use these sense impressions to write a brief description of the street corner, the classroom, or the supermarket.

2. Select one of the following topics, and write an objective description of it. Remember that your task in writing objective description is to inform the reader about the object, not to convey to the reader the mood or feeling that the object evokes in you.

   a. a pine tree
   b. a personal computer
   c. a bake shop
   d. a dictionary
   e. a fast-food restaurant
   f. a football field
   g. the layout of your campus
   h. a stereo system
   i. a houseplant
   j. your room

3. Writers of description often rely on factual information to give substance and interest to their writing. Using facts, statistics, or other information found in standard reference works in your college library (encyclopedias, dictionaries, almanacs, atlases, biographical dictionaries, or yearbooks), write an essay of several paragraphs

describing one of the people, places, or things from the following list. Be sure that you focus your description, that you have a purpose for your description, and that you present your facts in an interesting manner.

a. the Statue of Liberty
b. the telephone
c. Sandra Day O'Connor
d. Niagara Falls
e. the Great Wall of China
f. Michael Jordan
g. Bonnie Raitt
h. the Tower of London
i. the sun
j. Disney World
k. Princess Diana
l. Julia Roberts
m. Hillary Clinton

4. Select one of the following places and write a multiparagraph description that captures your subjective sense impressions of that particular place.

a. a busy downtown intersection
b. a bakery
c. an auction
d. a factory
e. a service station
f. a zoo
g. a cafeteria
h. a farmers' market
i. a concert hall
j. a locker room
k. a bank
l. a library

4
Illustration

What Is Illustration?

Illustration is the use of examples—facts, anecdotes, samples, and many other kinds of specific information—to make a generalization more vivid, understandable, or persuasive. Here are a few typical generalizations:

The films coming out of Hollywood place too much emphasis on violence.

Modern art is characterized by the fragmentation of form, composition, color, and image.

Americans are a pain-conscious people who would rather get rid of pain than seek and cure its root causes.

Each of these statements is very broad and vague, even open to challenge. Yet each point could be strengthened and made meaningful through illustration. The first assertion could be given depth and impact with detailed examples taken from actual movies. The second, though puzzling to readers who have not seen much modern art, could be clarified with descriptions of specific paintings and sculptures. And the third claim could be supported with examples of situations and even specific cases in which Americans have gone to the drugstore instead of to the doctor.

Writing that consists wholly of generalizations strung together page after page can be extremely difficult to read. Good writers recognize this fact and try to provide just the right kind and number of examples to make their ideas clear or understandable, interesting, and convincing. In fact, illustration is so useful and versatile a writing strategy that it may be found in all kinds of writing; there is hardly an essay in this book that does not use examples in one way or another.

An example may be anything from a statistic to a story; it may be stated in a few words or go on for several pages. What is required of an example is that it be closely *relevant* to the idea or generalization it is meant to illustrate. While a statistic showing how much of a particular drug Americans purchased in a given year might be interesting, a statistic showing that over the past ten years painkiller sales have increased more rapidly than the population would be relevant to the idea that Americans are a pain-conscious people, and so could be used as an example to support the author's assertion.

To be most effective, an example should be *representative*. The story it tells or the fact it presents should be typical of many others that readers are sure to think of. Figures showing how many people use aspirin, and what for, would be representative, since aspirin is the most widely used painkiller in America. Statistics about a newly discovered and highly specialized barbiturate might well show a tremendous increase in its use, but the example would be unrepresentative and, therefore, less persuasive.

Why Do Writers Use Illustration?

Illustrating a point with examples seems to be a basic strategy of human communication—and serves several purposes for writers. First, examples are used to make writing more vivid or entertaining. An essay about television bloopers will be dull and pointless without some examples of on-screen blunders—"tips of the slongue," as one writer calls them. A more serious essay on the danger of drunken driving will gain in impact if it is illustrated with descriptions of the victims' shattered lives and the grief and outrage of their family and friends.

Writers also use illustration to explain or clarify their ideas. In

Illustration • 159

an essay on political leadership, the assertion "Successful leaders are often a product of their times" will certainly require further explanation. Such explanation could very effectively be provided through examples: Franklin Roosevelt in 1932, Winston Churchill in 1940, and Charles de Gaulle in 1958 all rose to power because their people were looking for leadership in a national crisis, as did Lenin, Hitler, and Mussolini. In her essay "Does Affirmative Action Really Work?" later in this section, Rachel Flick Wildavsky presents a number of case studies to help her arrive at an answer to the question she asks in the title to her essay.

Examples like Wildavsky's also demonstrate another important function of illustration: to support a generalization and make it more convincing. James Thurber, in "Courtship through the Ages," uses examples from the animal kingdom to illustrate the "sorrowful lengths to which all males must go to arouse the interest of a lady." And in "Elvira's Story," Flora Mancuso Edwards provides an extended, detailed example to support her point that the poor "live miserable and know not why."

What to Look for in Reading an Essay of Illustration

First, try to discover what general point the author is making; then, determine how the author has presented examples to develop that point. Sometimes you will find the point stated early on to introduce the examples. At other times you may have to look further for the generalization.

Consider this brief discussion by George Orwell:

> The other night a barmaid informed me that if you pour beer into a damp glass it goes flat much more quickly. She added that to dip your mustache into your beer also turns it flat. I immediately accepted this without further inquiry; in fact, as soon as I got home I clipped my mustache, which I had forgotten to do for some days.
>
> Only later did it strike me that this was probably one of those superstitions which are able to keep alive because they have the air of being scientific truths. In my notebook I have a long list of fallacies which were taught to me in my childhood, in each case not as an old wives'

tale but as a scientific fact. I can't give the whole list, but here are a few hardy favorites: that a swan can break your leg with a blow of its wing; that if you cut yourself between the thumb and forefinger you get lock-jaw; that powdered glass is poisonous; that if you wash your hands in the water eggs have been boiled in (why anyone should do this is a mystery) you will get warts; that bulls become infuriated at the sight of red; that sulphur in a dog's drinking water acts as a tonic.

And so on and so forth. Almost everyone carries some or other of these beliefs into adult life. I have met someone of over thirty who still retained the second of the beliefs I have listed above. As for the third, it is still so widespread that in India, for instance, people are constantly trying to poison one another with powdered glass, with disappointing results.

Not until the third paragraph does Orwell make his generalization: "Almost everyone carries some or other of these beliefs into adult life." Already in paragraphs 1 and 2, Orwell has illustrated such beliefs by referring to numerous examples: first, those told him by the barmaid and, then, a further list of "hardy favorites." These help explain and clarify what Orwell means when he talks about superstitions "that have the air of being scientific truths." Following his generalization Orwell offers two more specific cases: an adult who believes that a cut on the hand causes lockjaw, and people in India who believe that powdered glass is poisonous. Here, again, is a group of examples (obvious even without the telltale phrase *for instance* in the last sentence); but these are offered to support the generalization and persuade readers that it is true, rather than to explain what the generalization means. So Orwell has used two sets of examples for two different purposes in the space of three short paragraphs.

You may even conclude that Orwell has yet another purpose in mind with this collection of examples—to entertain. Certainly the superstitions he lists are particularly silly, even funny: at the end he sketches in the would-be Indian poisoners with dry humor, and in the first paragraph he even makes fun of himself for accepting a barmaid as an expert on the science of beer foam and mustaches. Orwell's point is no deep insight into the human condition but an amused observation about how silly people can be. It's through his examples that he creates his humorous tone.

Illustration • 161

Are Orwell's examples good ones? Certainly. They serve his purposes, and each is relevant to the generalization it develops. Most readers would also agree that the examples are representative. The superstitions he mentions are typical of pseudoscientific "laws" familiar to all (that lightning never strikes twice in the same place, that handling toads causes warts); and his two final examples bring to mind other adults, even sensible ones, who believe such nonsense.

Are there enough examples? Orwell provides plenty to explain what he means by "superstitions which . . . have the air of being scientific truths." For his concluding generalization, however, he supplies only two examples. Are these enough to support his claim that "almost everyone" believes superstitions such as these? Here, readers will make their own judgments, and opinions may differ. Those who disagree with Orwell may well feel that two examples are not sufficient to prove his point.

Sometimes, however, just one example will do, if it is representative and if the writer develops it well. Here is such an example by basketball all-star Bill Russell from his autobiographical *Second Wind:*

> Every champion athlete has a moment when everything goes so perfectly for him he slips into a gear that he didn't know was there. It's easy to spot that perfect moment in a sport like track. I remember watching the 1968 Olympics in Mexico City, where the world record in the long jump was just under 27 feet. Then Bob Beamon flew down the chute and leaped out over the pit in a majestic jump that I have seen replayed many times. There was an awed silence when the announcer said that Beamon's jump measured 29 feet 2¼ inches. Generally world records are broken by fractions of inches, but Beamon had exceeded the existing record by more than two feet. On learning what he had done, Beamon slumped down on the ground and cried. To all those who saw it, this was an unforgettable moment in sport. Most viewers' image of Beamon ends with the picture of him weeping on the ground, but in fact he got up and took some more jumps that day. I like to think that he did so because he had jumped for so long at his best that *even then* he didn't know what might come out of him. At the end of that day he wanted to be absolutely sure that he'd had his perfect day.

Few readers have been world-class athletes and known that "extra gear" Russell describes, so he illustrates what he means with a single, extended example—in this case an anecdote that gives substance to the idea he wants us to understand.

Writing an Essay Using Illustration

Begin by thinking of ideas and generalizations about your topic that you can make clearer and more persuasive by illustrating them in your writing with facts, anecdotes, or other specifics. Most important, of course, is your main point, the central generalization that you will develop in your essay. But also be alert for other statements or references that may gain from illustration—as Orwell did in writing about superstition. Those that are already clear and uncontroversial, that your readers will understand and immediately agree with, can stand on their own as you pass along quickly to your next point; belaboring the obvious wastes your time and energy, as well as your readers'. Often, however, you will find that examples add clarity, color, and weight to what you want to say.

1. Gathering Examples

Before beginning to write, bring together as many examples as you can think of that are related to your subject, more even than you can possibly use. Then you will be able to choose the strongest and most representative for your essay, not merely the first that come to mind. This abundance of materials will also make it less likely that you will have to stop in mid-draft and hunt for further examples, losing the thread of your ideas. In addition, the more examples you gather, the more you are likely to learn about your subject.

What kinds of examples you look for and where you look for them will depend, of course, on your subject and the point you want to make about it. If you plan to write about all the quirky, fascinating individuals who make up your family, you can gather your examples without leaving your room: descriptions of their habits and clothing, stories about their strange adventures, facts

Illustration • 163

about their backgrounds, quotations from their talk. If, however, you are writing an essay on book censorship in American public schools, you will need to go to the library and read many sources there to supply yourself with examples. Your essay might well include accounts drawn from newspapers; statistics published by librarians' or teachers' professional organizations; court transcripts and judicial opinions on censorship; and interviews with school board members, parents, book publishers, even the authors whose work has been pulled off library shelves or kept out of the classroom. The range of sources and the variety of examples are limited only by your own imagination and the time you can spend on research.

2. Testing Examples

First, make sure that your examples are, in fact, relevant. Do they concern the points you want to make, or the ideas you want to clarify? If not, then they aren't really examples at all. Suppose the main point of your planned essay is that book censorship has spread throughout American public education. A newspaper story about the banning of *Catcher in the Rye* and *The Merchant of Venice* from the local high school's English curriculum would clearly be relevant, since it concerns book censorship at a public school. But the fact that James Joyce's novel *Ulysses* was first banned as obscene and then vindicated in a famous trial, although an important case of censorship, has nothing to do with books in public schools. Consequently, it is not relevant to your essay.

Next, determine which of your examples are most representative. If, while working on the censorship paper, you have found a dozen quiet administrative hearings and orderly court cases reported, but only one sensational incident where books were actually burned in a school parking lot, the latter, however dramatic, is clearly not a representative example. You might want to mention the book-burning in your essay, but you could not present it as typical of how censorship is handled.

What if your examples do not support your point? Perhaps you have missed some important information and need to look further. But perhaps the problem is with the point itself. For example, you intend your censorship paper to illustrate the following generalization: "Book censorship has spread throughout American public education." However, you have not found very many examples in which specific books were actually censored or banned outright. Although many attempts at censorship have been made, most were ultimately prevented or overturned in the courts. You might then have to revise your original generalization: "Although there have been many well-publicized attempts to censor books in public schools, actual censorship is comparatively rare."

3. Organization

It is important to arrange your examples in an order that serves your purpose, is easy for readers to follow, and will have maximum effect. Some possible patterns of organization include chronological order and spatial order, as well as moving from the simplest example to the most difficult, from the least to the most controversial, or from the least to the most important. If your examples are fairly brief, similar to each other, and equally important, you may hit upon an order that "feels right" to you, as George Orwell did in his paragraphs about superstitions.

Before starting the first draft, it may help you to work out your pattern of organization in a scratch outline, using only enough words so that you will be able to tell which example each entry refers to. Here's a scratch outline of the Orwell selection:

Examples of common superstitions.
    Generalization: some superstitions are carried into adult life
        because they seem like scientific truths.
    what turns beer flat—I believed a barmaid
    swan's wing
    lockjaw—some adults still believe it
    powdered glass—Indians still believe this one
    bulls see red
    sulphur & water a tonic for dogs

You could add another line, right after "generalization," to remind yourself of your pattern of organization, perhaps "order: increasing importance." Such an outline can help you keep track of which examples you mean to use and your order of presentation.

Diets—Do They Work?

Eleanor DeLisa

Originally from New York City, Eleanor DeLisa attends California State University, Long Beach. After surviving many northeastern winters, Eleanor is now enjoying life as a student in southern California. She is an education major and plans to become an English teacher at the middle school level. In this essay, Eleanor presents many examples to explain why fad diets are so popular and yet fail to fulfill their promise.

Americans are obsessed with thinness. A recent article in *Time* reported on a *Better Homes and Gardens* study that showed "nearly 90 percent of Americans think that they weigh too much." According to a Gallup poll, approximately "31 percent of American women ages 19 to 39 diet at least once a month, and 16 percent of them consider themselves to be perpetual dieters" (Toulexis 54). It seems as if almost all Americans consider themselves in need of some type of diet. One of the most alluring characteristics of diets is that they promise quick weight loss. But in the long term nearly everyone who goes on some type of a diet risks failure. Another survey on the results of dieting showed that "two-thirds of people who lose weight gain it all back, and then some, within a few years. After seven years, only 2 percent can still flaunt svelter selves" (Toulexis 55).

Most quick weight-loss schemes fall into two categories, fasting and crash dieting. Both of these methods will in fact allow people to lose pounds, but will they allow them to keep the weight off? Also, such programs can be dangerous if continued for a long period of time. Although there is a technical difference between fasting and starving, metabolically the human body can't tell the difference. If a person fasts, the body has to rely on producing energy from its own resources. In order to conserve fuel, the body then lowers its metabolism. A few days of fasting may produce lost pounds on the scale, but it's not the fat loss most dieters aim for.

It's mainly water loss, which is almost immediately regained once the fast is broken. Moreover, the longer the fast continues, the greater the serious risk to the body's protein reserves. There is also a greater risk of gaining even more weight after coming off a fast because the body will still function at a lower metabolic rate, allowing a more rapid weight gain on fewer calories. Many people believe that a one-or-two-day fast helps reduce the appetite. While this is true, repeated fasting can permanently alter the body's base metabolic rate.

The other major quick weight-loss scheme, crash dieting, is no 3 better than its counterpart. Most crash diets promise quick weight loss by limiting the amount of food eaten. They also tend to emphasize certain food groups, while excluding others. The Beverly Hills Diet, for example, requires only fresh fruits during the first two or three weeks of the regimen. Because diets do restrict food, it is very important to maintain good nutrition. Crash diets do not. If a person eats too many foods from one food group and doesn't eat any from another, the body will not be able to function correctly. The infamous Last Chance Diet, with its emphasis on liquid protein, led to numerous heart attacks and over sixty deaths among users. The Scarsdale Diet, an enormously popular diet from a decade ago, is another prime example. Neither medically sound nor nutritionally safe, this diet results in a rapid and dangerous drop in weight caused by fluid and protein loss. The diet permits only limited amounts of bread and cereal, allows no dairy products, and results in carbohydrate and calcium deficiencies. Protein, niacin, and vitamins A and C intake far exceeds the recommended daily amount. Meat is also emphasized to the exclusion of other foods, making the diet high in cholesterol. In spite of the fact that this and other diets like it can destroy a person's health, people actually follow these diets to shed their excess pounds.

It is obvious from even this cursory examination of the negative 4 effects of fad dieting that the "get-thin-quick" schemes offer little more than empty promises. The key to real weight loss is not dieting. The best results come from a long-term weight-control plan. Weight control is commonsense eating—foods high in nutrition and low in fat and sugar—in conjunction with an exercise program. The weight-control method can't offer fast results, but it can be successful where diets fail. Here's why.

Losing weight is a slow process. Given an adequate period of time, along with a sensible eating and exercise plan, the body will naturally start to slim down. Eating a well-balanced diet with foods from the four food groups gives the body all the essentials it needs. The high amounts of fiber in these foods make the stomach feel full and satisfied. When the body receives the nutrients it needs, it functions better as well. Studies show that depression, migraine headaches, and lethargy are triggered by certain nutritional deficiencies. Once these deficiencies are eliminated, the ailments tend to disappear.

Most fad diets don't advocate exercise, but "working out" is an essential ingredient in the weight-control program. Exercise tones up the body and gives people more energy and life. Moderate exercise such as walking can rev-up the metabolism and help the body burn calories more efficiently. Regular exercise has the additional benefit of increasing over time the body's base metabolic rate, so that more food may be eaten with no weight gain.

Fad dieting as practiced in the 1980s just doesn't work. Fasting and crash dieting in particular often do more harm than good in terms of nutrition and general well-being. A weight-control program, however, offers success where diets fail. When overweight people forsake the lure of quick weight loss and understand all the negative aspects of dieting, they will look to weight control for the solution to their health problem.

Works Cited

Farley, Dixie. "Eating Disorders: When Thinness Becomes an Obsession." *FDA Consumer* May 1986.

"Is Fasting Safe for Quick Weight Loss?" *Glamour* Mar. 1987.

Toulexis, Anastasia. "Dieting: The Losing Game." *Time* 20 Jan. 1986.

Interview with Eleanor DeLisa

How did you happen to come up with diets as a topic?

I had originally wanted to do a paper on starvation—I was interested in the famine in Africa. While researching this topic in the library, I discovered an abundance of material on anorexia nervosa and, on a broader scale, dieting. The topic itself is a good one because diets and weight control interest a great many people nowadays because of the recent drive to promote better health awareness and because people are more conscious of their appearance.

So diets turned out to be a subject that was more interesting to you?

Yes, it was a subject I felt more comfortable with. Besides, a lot of my friends were talking about quick and easy ways to lose those extra pounds, and I always had my suspicions.

Well, what do you mean by "suspicions"?

It just seemed to me that if these diets really worked, why were people constantly looking for new ones. I also wondered if these diets posed any special risks, especially when I saw the crazy regimens that other students were on.

Let's get back to the examples. How did you come up with them?

Actually, that wasn't so hard. I started with the *Reader's Guide to Periodical Literature*. I also thought it was wise to use a variety of magazines, ranging from women's magazines, such as *Glamour*, to popular newsmagazines such as *Time* and *U.S. News and World Report*. I did a lot of reading before I selected the examples that seemed best suited to illustrate what I wanted to say.

As you were writing this paper did you share your drafts with other students in the class?

Yes. In total, I probably wrote five or six different versions of this essay. I shared them with members of the class, and they were extremely helpful. I remember one student's questions in particular, because she really got me to focus on the problems with fad diets. The students also helped me to see where I needed examples to explain what I was talking about. The very first draft that I wrote is completely different from the one I handed in.

So, while you needed a number of drafts to get your essay right, the assignment went smoothly for the most part?

Well, not exactly. I had a difficult time writing the essay, mainly because the subject itself is very popular and there was a lot of information and material to sift through and organize. I also had a problem with audience. It always seemed as if I was writing an article for a women's magazine even though I was trying to gear it toward a more general college audience.

Elvira's Story

Flora Mancuso Edwards

> *Flora Mancuso Edwards has been the president of Middlesex County College in Edison, New Jersey, since 1986. Prior to coming to Middlesex County College, Edwards was president of Hostos Community College of the City University of New York. She earned her B.A., M.A., and Ph.D. in Romance languages and linguistics from New York University. She also taught at Columbia University, New York City Community College, and LaGuardia Community College, where she was an academic dean.*
>
> *In "Elvira's Story," first published in 1978, Edwards uses a single extended example to explain the particular plight of the laboring poor.*

Over 150 years ago the English historian Thomas Carlyle had 1 this to say about Victorian society:

> It is not to die, or even to die of hunger, that makes a man wretched; many men have died; all men must die. . . . But it is to live miserable we know not why; to work sore and yet gain nothing; to be heartworn, weary, yet isolated, unrelated, girt in with a cold, universal Laissez-faire.[1]

There are over 4 million people in the United States today who 2 still live miserable and know not why, who still "work sore and yet gain nothing." They are our laboring poor.

Elvira Ramirez is just one example of those who must sell their 3 labor so cheaply that the necessities of life are just barely met. Elvira is a soft-spoken, cheerful, well-mannered woman who works in a

---

[1] Quoted in Robert Hunter, *Poverty*, ed. Peter d'A. Jones (New York: Macmillan, 1904; Harper & Row, 1965), p. 1 [Author's note]. *Laissez-faire:* loosely translated, this French expression means "let-things-be."

luxurious East Side beauty salon doing shampoos and manicures. Her average day is filled by serving New York's well-to-do matrons who spend spring in New York, winter in Miami, and summer on Cape Cod. Elvira listens sympathetically to their problems in getting "reliable help" or to their last-minute preparations for a child's wedding in Switzerland.

For her services and good company she receives $0.25 to $0.50   4 from each one and occasionally $1.00 from a more generous customer. These tips bring up her total salary of $90.00 to approximately $110.00 a week. On this salary, Elvira supports herself, her son, a teen-age daughter, and her mother in a one-bedroom apartment in the Nathan Strauss Housing Projects in the Chelsea section on Manhattan's West Side.

Her apartment is on the third floor of a building whose elevators   5 are as offensive as they are nonfunctioning. Elvira, her mother, her daughter, and her son all used to sleep in one room, but now the boy is older and has inherited the sofa in the living room, which doubles as his bedroom. The apartment has no closets, and there is little room even for the metal Woolworth's wardrobes. The kitchen is so small that there is no place for a table, so when the family must eat together, the sofa is moved and a table set up in the living room.

Elvira receives no health insurance from her job, nor does she   6 receive a vacation or overtime pay. Her mother is only sixty and neither blind nor technically disabled, so she receives no social security or public assistance. Elvira's income—marginal as it may be—is too high for Medicaid, so Elvira works fourteen to sixteen hours a day, six days a week, and prays that no one will get sick. But, because the windows of the third-floor apartment keep getting broken, New York's winter always seems to take its toll in doctor bills, which each year are increasingly hard to pay.

When Elvira was hospitalized several years ago, the Department   7 of Social Services came to her rescue. But it did not take long for Elvira to realize that the benefits came at a high price.

No, the welfare is all waiting with the children crying, waiting outside the office for hours in the freezing cold, sick hungry waiting all day in the clinic, waiting to be looked down on, insulted, and humiliated. No, I'm not earning much more—but it's better than waiting.

God willing, I don't get sick again.[2]

Elvira has no savings and therefore cannot move to larger quar-   8
ters. As it is, rent is her biggest expenditure. Her hopes?

Maybe I go back to the Island[3] when Michele finish school. You know, I guess I didn't do so bad after all. Michele finish fourth in her class. Now she goes to Harpur College. She got a scholarship, you know. I thought when she finish high school she would get a job and help out, but maybe it's better like this. Now she'll be somebody. . . . You know, like a teacher or a nurse or something. That's the most important thing—the kids. Sure I work hard—but the kids—they're going to be something.

Am I poor? No, not really. Really poor people take the welfare. Most of the time we manage to get by.[4]

Elvira receives no benefits, no medical coverage, no public assis-   9
tance. She earns $6,000 a year before taxes. She works harder and longer than most people and earns considerably less. She eats little meat and indulges herself in no luxuries. She does not own a car, goes on no vacations, eats in few restaurants, and buys a minimum of clothing.

Elvira's job is similar to almost one-third of all the jobs in New   10
York, and Elvira is one of 600,000 New Yorkers who live below the poverty line and struggle on day by day, eking out a marginal existence in New York, one of the richest cities in the world.

On a national level, over 4.5 million people (not counting rural   11
sharecroppers) are employed full time and are still poor. In almost half of these families, two people work full time in order to reap the bitter rewards of poverty and want.

---

[2] Personal interviews conducted between May and December 1973 [Author's note].

[3] Puerto Rico, her birthplace.

[4] See note 2.

Questions on Subject

1. Who is Elvira Ramirez? How does she earn her living? What distinguishes her position from that of middle-class laborers?
2. What is Elvira Ramirez's attitude toward welfare?
3. What is the relevance of Edwards's quotation from Carlyle (paragraph 1)? What does it add to her essay?
4. What hope, if any, does Edwards offer that the "laboring poor" can be helped?

Questions on Strategy

1. What is Edwards's purpose in this essay? How does the extended example of Elvira Ramirez serve that purpose? (Glossary: *Purpose*)
2. Edwards points up several ironies in Elvira's situation and attitude. What are they, and where do you find them? Is her use of irony effective? (Glossary: *Irony*)
3. Is the treatment of Elvira's situation objective or subjective? Why do you think so? (Glossary: *Objective/Subjective*)

Questions on Diction and Vocabulary

1. What details of Elvira's speech, as quoted in paragraphs 7 and 8, reveal her not to be a native speaker of English? Why do you think Edwards did not silently correct Elvira's mistakes?
2. What details in the quotation from Carlyle indicate that this is not contemporary American prose? Pay attention not only to the diction but to how the sentences are composed.
3. Refer to your dictionary to determine the meanings of the following words as they are used in this selection: *Laissez-faire* (paragraph 1), *marginal* (6), *eking* (10), *sharecroppers* (11).

Writing Assignments

1. When asked if she is poor, Elvira Ramirez says "no, not really. Really poor people take the welfare. Most of the time we manage to get by." Yet Flora Mancuso Edwards has chosen Elvira as a prime example of the "laboring poor." Obviously, they have different

views of the same situation, different definitions of the word *poor*. Consider how psychological factors such as pride, self-respect, and control over one's life, as well as employment, income, and the cost of living, affect different people's views of what poverty is and who the poor are. Write an essay illustrating some common definitions of poverty.

2. Gather examples from your personal experience or your reading and write an essay illustrating one of the following generalizations:

   a. Being involved in politics is/isn't a very rewarding experience.

   b. Most products do/don't live up to the claims of their advertisements.

   c. You are what you say.

   d. Nature works in mysterious ways.

   e. Television teaches us as many bad things as good.

My Grandmother, the Bag Lady

Patsy Neal

> *Patsy Neal teaches physical education and is the volleyball coach at Montreal-Anderson College in North Carolina. The following essay first appeared in the* My Turn *column in* Newsweek *in 1985.*
>
> *In her essay, Neal describes the way in which her own grandmother has come to resemble the homeless, not because she has no place to live, but because age and illness have forced her into a nursing home where she had to relinquish her most cherished possessions and her sense of independence.*

1. Almost all of us have seen pictures of old, homeless ladies, moving about the streets of big cities with everything they own stuffed into a bag or a paper sack.

2. My grandmother is 89 years old, and a few weeks ago I realized with a jolt that she, too, had become one of them. Before I go any further, I had best explain that I did not see my grandmother's picture on TV. I discovered her plight during a face-to-face visit at my mother's house—in a beautiful, comfortable, safe, middle-class environment with good china on the table and turkey and chicken on the stove.

3. My grandmother's condition saddened me beyond words, for an 89 year old should not have to carry around everything she owns in a bag. It's enough to be 89, without the added burden of packing the last fragments of your existence into a space big enough to accommodate only the minutest of treasures.

4. Becoming a bag lady was not something that happened to her overnight. My grandmother has been in a nursing home these last several years; at first going back to her own home for short visits, then less frequently as she became older and less mobile.

5. No matter how short these visits were, her greatest pleasure came from walking slowly around her home, touching every item lovingly and spending hours browsing through drawers and clos-

175

ets. Then, I did not understand her need to search out all her belongings.

As she spent longer days and months at the nursing home, I 6 could not help noticing other things. She began to hide her possessions under the mattress, in her closet, under the cushion of her chair, in every conceivable, reachable space. And she began to think that people were "stealing" from her.

Unsteady: When a walker became necessary, my mother took the 7 time to make a bag that could be attached to it, so that my grandmother could carry things around while keeping her hands on the walker. I had not paid much attention to this bag until we went to the nursing home to take her home with us for our traditional Christmas Eve sharing of gifts.

As we left, my grandmother took her long, unsteady walk down 8 the hallway, balancing herself with her walker, laboriously moving it ahead, one step at a time, until finally we were at the car outside. Once she was safely seated, I picked up her walker to put it in the back. I could barely lift it. Then I noticed that the bag attached to it was bulging. Something clicked, but it still wasn't complete enough to grasp.

At home in my mother's house, I was asked to get some pho- 9 tographs from my grandmother's purse. Lifting her pocketbook, I was surprised again at the weight and bulk. I watched as my mother pulled out an alarm clock, a flashlight, a small radio, thread, needles, pieces of sewing, a book and other items that seemed to have no reason for being in a pocketbook.

I looked at my grandmother, sitting bent over in her chair, rum- 10 maging through the bag on the walker, slowly pulling out one item and then another, and lovingly putting it back. I looked down at her purse with all its disconnected contents and remembered her visits to her home, rummaging through drawers and through closets.

"Oh, Lord," I thought with sudden insight. "That walker and 11 that purse are her home now."

I began to understand that over the years my grandmother's 12 space for living had diminished like melting butter—from endless fields and miles of freedom as a child and young mother to, with age, the constrictions of a house, then a small room in a nursing home and finally to the tightly clutched handbag and the bag on her walker.

When the family sent her to a nursing home, it was the toughest 13 decision it had ever had to make. We all thought she would be secure there; we would no longer have to worry about whether she had taken her medicine, or left her stove on, or was alone at night.

But we hadn't fully understood her needs. Security for my grand- 14 mother was not in the warm room at the nursing home, with 24-hour attendants to keep her safe and well fed, nor in the family who visited and took her to visit in their homes. In her mind her security was tied to those things she could call her own—and over the years those possessions had dwindled away like sand dropping through an hourglass: first her car, sold when her eyes became bad and she couldn't drive; then some furnishings she didn't really need. Later it was the dogs she had trouble taking care of. And finally it would be her home when it became evident that she could never leave the nursing home again. But as her space and mobility dwindled, so did her control over her life.

Dignity: I looked at my grandmother again, sitting so alone before 15 me, hair totally gray, limbs and joints swollen by arthritis, at the hearing aid that could no longer help her hear, and the glasses too thick but so inadequate in helping her to see . . . and yet there was such dignity about her. A dignity I could not understand.

The next day, after my grandmother had been taken back to the 16 nursing home and my mother was picking up in her room, she found a small scrap of paper my grandmother had scribbled these words on:

"It is 1:30 tonight and I had to get up and go to the bathroom. 17 I cannot go back to sleep. But I looked in on Margaret and she is sleeping *so* good, and Patsy is sleeping too."

With that note, I finally understood, and my 89-year-old bag- 18 lady grandmother changed from an almost helpless invalid to a courageous, caring individual still very much in control of her environment.

What intense loneliness she must have felt as she scribbled that 19 small note on that small piece of paper with the small bag on her walker and her small purse next to her. Yet she chose to experience it alone rather than wake either of us from much-needed sleep. Out of her own great need, she chose to meet our needs.

As I held that tiny note, and cried inside, I wondered if she 20 dreamed of younger years and more treasured possessions and a bigger world when she went back to sleep that night. I certainly hoped so.

Questions on Subject

1. List the steps Neal's grandmother went through as she passed from independent woman to bag lady.
2. Neal was at first horrified to think that her grandmother's walker and purse were her home (paragraph 11). What caused her to change her mind?
3. What wish does Neal have for her grandmother? Is her wish realistic? Explain.
4. In your opinion, is Neal's grandmother really a "bag lady"? Why or why not?

Questions on Strategy

1. Neal's discussion of her grandmother's plight depends on one major generalization. What is that generalization, and how well does it serve as a basis for her example?
2. Neal's account is highly subjective, yet she expects her reader to understand that her grandmother's situation is typical of many people her age. What kinds of detail does Neal use to establish the universality of her grandmother's situation?
3. How has Neal organized her essay? (Glossary: *Organization*)
4. How does paragraph 13 function in the context of Neal's essay? Would her illustration have been weakened in any way had she left it out? Explain.
5. Neal's grandmother is "silent" until the end of the essay. Why do you suppose Neal waited until then to have her grandmother "speak"?

Questions on Diction and Vocabulary

1. What is the effect of Neal's repeated use of the word *small* in paragraph 19?

2. Neal uses two metaphors in her illustration. Locate those metaphors and comment on the appropriateness and effectiveness of each.
3. Refer to your desk dictionary to determine the meanings of the following words as they are used in this selection: *jolt* (paragraph 2), *browsing* (5), *laboriously* (8), *rummaging* (10), *dwindled* (14), *invalid* (18).

Writing Suggestions

1. Dependence on others and a sense of isolation seem to be inevitable aspects of growing old in our culture. Where once the elderly grew old and died at home among family, it is becoming more common for aging parents and grandparents to move into nursing homes where they can receive the medical and personal attention that modern families are increasingly unable to give. But it could be argued that modern culture creates this same sense of isolation and abandonment among other groups as well. Write an essay in which you examine some causes other than age that lead to a sense of isolation from the community in which you live. Illustrate your essay with specific examples.
2. Using Neal's essay as a model, write a first-person account of your perception of one of your grandparents. What hardships do they endure, what pleasures? Include clear examples of the ways in which they have embraced old age.

Does Affirmative Action Really Work?
Rachel Flick Wildavsky

> *Rachel Flick Wildavsky was born in Seattle, Washington, in October 1958 and graduated from the University of Chicago in 1980. Before joining* Reader's Digest *in 1989, Wildavsky worked as a speechwriter for U.S. Senator Paul Trible and as a special assistant in the White House Office of Planning and Evaluation under President Reagan, developing program proposals on poverty, welfare, and social issues. From 1985 to 1989 she covered the White House, Capitol Hill, and the financial markets for the* New York Post. *Based in* Reader's Digest's *Washington bureau, Wildavsky reports on major national and international issues for the magazine. In 1991 she received the "Article of the Year" award from* Reader's Digest. *Wildavsky's articles have also appeared in the* Wall Street Journal, *the* New Republic, Harper's, *and* New York Magazine.*
>
> *In the following essay, which first appeared in the August 1991 issue of* Reader's Digest, *Wildavsky uses a series of well-developed examples to discuss the success—or lack of success—of affirmative action, first established in the mid-1960s.*

Its intent was to ensure that every American would have an equal chance at education and jobs. But affirmative action has moved from "color-blind hiring" to the pointed consideration of race. Those passed over have responded with anger and bitterness.

The dissatisfaction, however, goes beyond those who feel they have been deprived of a job, a promotion or admission to a university. While many minority Americans continue to support affirmative action, others are uneasy about it. Some doubt the policy's success; some are even convinced it does great long-term harm. Here is a sampling of their experiences.

The Musician

Detroit is more than 75-percent black, but in 1988 the Detroit 3 Symphony Orchestra employed only one black musician. For years, two black Michigan state legislators had berated the DSO for this imbalance. In 1988 they lowered the boom: hire more blacks, the legislators said, or forfeit nearly $1.3 million in state funding.

Suddenly all eyes were on Rick Robinson, a 25-year-old black 4 bassist then touring with the orchestra as a substitute. Making him full-time would save the funding.

But there was a problem: Detroit hired by "blind" audition, a 5 process adopted in the 1960s to prevent discrimination. Candidates performed behind a screen and were judged by their music alone. If the orchestra ran Robinson through the blind process, he might not win. So the members of the orchestra voted to waive union rules and offer Robinson the job without an audition.

Robinson disliked the idea of "representing the race." He knew 6 life had often been cruelly unfair to blacks, but he had been raised outside Detroit by middle-class parents and had never experienced discrimination. He had invested his pride not in his race but in his achievements. He feared that taking the offer would prompt a backlash from whites and devalue black players who had won their jobs in the normal, competitive way. But, needing work, the young bassist agonized—and said yes.

Across the country, black musicians lashed out at an action they 7 said discredited them all. Michael Morgan, black assistant conductor of the Chicago Symphony Orchestra, predicted that with this type of hiring "people will lose confidence in why they were brought on." Protested Owen Young, a black cellist in Pittsburgh, "Who wants to win a job just because he's black?"

In the Detroit Symphony, some musicians greeted Robinson's 8 hiring apprehensively. Was he there to perform or to make a point? And while most, black and white, concentrated their anger on the two legislators, Robinson was left feeling "compromised having taken the job."

Today Robinson believes in his heart he cannot stay with the 9 Detroit Symphony. As a professional, he longs to win a blind audition "with the best orchestra I can." He also knows he'll never feel easy with his position. "I think I deserved the job," he says, "but I don't feel I received it 100-percent honestly."

The Engineer

"Why do we have to stand here in the sun while the other chil- 10
dren eat inside with their parents?"
The summer heat was sweltering outside the little restaurant. 11
But Willie and Rosa Wilson, embarrassed, had had no answer for
their son David other than "colored is not supposed to go in there."
Jim Crow was the law in postwar Loris, S.C., and their education
had not prepared them with sophisticated explanations. David's
parents had left school in the third grade, when poverty forced
them into the grinding labor of sharecropping.
The unanswerable mystery of segregation left a mark on young 12
Wilson—a mark of doubt. Maybe, he feared, black people were
not as smart as white people. *If I can't share a hot-dog stand or a
schoolroom with a white child, there might be a reason.*
This doubt ended forever when Wilson joined the Army in 1963. 13
For the first time he could match wits with whites on an even
footing. He received telecommunications instruction in fully integrated classrooms. "I realized that I was scoring just as well as
Caucasian people," he recalls. "So I said to myself, they are no
better. From that day on, I never questioned my ability to compete
with anybody."
After the Army, Wilson worked his way up through a series of 14
jobs in the defense industry. He earned a technical degree in elec-
tronics, plus a college degree and a master's, both in electrical
engineering.
Today he is an electrical engineer for IBM in Poughkeepsie, N.Y. 15
In 1985 Wilson started a program that tutors blacks and Hispanics
in math and science. Three years later, IBM agreed to fund the
project.
Wilson, 49, thinks often about what he wants for those kids— 16
and for his own two sons as well. Always, he stops short of concluding that affirmative action should end. He remembers segregation and fears that without a special policy it would come back.
"It's like a medication," he says. "A person takes it and feels better

and thinks he's okay without it. But when he stops taking it, he goes back downhill."

Yet when Wilson reflects on his own life, he is glad he had no 17 help from affirmative action. Had the Army offered him a boost to compensate for the disadvantages in his past, the lesson he learned there "would not have been the same. I would still think there must be a secret; I would still have had that doubt. But there was no special advantage, and it really was the turning point for me."

The Businessman

James Lowry first benefited from affirmative action in the eighth 18 grade in 1952. The son of postal workers, he was recruited to become one of the first black students admitted to Francis W. Parker, an elite private school in Chicago.

Whatever awkwardness Lowry felt when he first mingled with 19 his affluent white classmates is now far behind him. Today he is president and CEO of James H. Lowry & Associates, a 25-person consulting firm. And Lowry gives much of the credit to affirmative action. After Francis W. Parker, he says, the policy helped admit him to Grinnell College, to graduate school at the University of Pittsburgh, into his first crucial consulting job and an advanced program at Harvard University.

In college, Lowry ran several businesses, including a coin laun- 20 dry, a flower concession and a sandwich service. But years would pass before he considered an entrepreneurial career. A year in Tanzania on a fellowship, five years with the Peace Corps and his graduate degree would come first.

Then in 1968, Lowry took a job with a not-for-profit corporation 21 in New York City's Bedford-Stuyvesant ghetto. The spectacle of the government giving money to blacks unprepared to earn or manage it convinced Lowry that what blacks really needed was to learn to contribute economically.

Later that year McKinsey & Co., a prestigious international con- 22 sulting firm under federal pressure to hire black professionals, recruited Lowry. The match was good, for him and the firm.

Still, Lowry knows that affirmative-action hirees have floun- 23 dered elsewhere. The policy has left white bosses dissatisfied and minority employees stuck beneath a "glass ceiling" above which they are seldom promoted. As a business consultant, Lowry has seen many such situations close up, and he holds both blacks and whites responsible.

Whites—fearful of lawsuits—are to blame for failing to criticize 24 unsatisfactory black employees. All employees need constructive criticism to know what their bosses want. And Lowry blames some black employees for too often failing to "produce on time, take stuff home, do those things necessary to win."

Lowry, now 52, thinks tough overseas competition is radically 25 altering American business. If minority workers are to survive the change, he says, there will have to be fewer lawsuits so bosses can demand high performance of all their employees, including blacks. And young blacks must aggressively seek to meet employers' needs.

However, Lowry believes affirmative action must remain. "Rac- 26 ism is not as bad as when I was coming up," he says. And one reason is that affirmative action helped blacks move into every job and profession.

Lowry adds that there will always be those who will attach a 27 stigma to people hired under affirmative action. His reaction: "So be it. Take the opportunity. And then, so you can look yourself in the mirror, do the best you can."

The Firefighter

"You'll never get in, because you're Chinese." Those were the 28 words Roland Lee heard from his father when he sought to join the San Francisco Fire Department in 1971.

As a Chinese-American, Lee's father knew real racial prejudice 29 in the 1930s and '40s. But Roland, born in 1948, had a different experience. There had been occasional fights with whites who called him names, but he had never felt that discrimination blocked his ambitions. So, while attending San Francisco State University, Lee took the fire department's employment test. In 1974 he was hired—one of the first Asians on the force.

Lee's first years were as great as he had hoped. He remembers 30 his excitement when he first saved a life. He relished the foxhole camaraderie, the horsing around, the underlying trust. "What made it so good," he says, "was mostly the people."

But that began to change in 1978, when the San Francisco Black 31 Firefighters Association—eventually joined by groups representing Hispanics, women and Asians—started challenging the department's entrance and promotion exams. They claimed minorities scored poorly because the tests measured technical knowledge and "rote memory" instead of "job related" skills like leadership. As a result of the challenges, promotions in the fire department currently are determined not by highest test scores but by the courts. The promotions are carefully balanced by race.

The department had been hiring by affirmative action since 1971, 32 and that policy had ruffled feathers. But promoting by affirmative action affected opportunities for men who knew one another and worked together, and that had a toxic effect on life in the firehouses.

Today race-based promotions have left white firefighters with 33 little chance of upward mobility. As a result, Lee says, many are angry. Some whites won't even speak to minority firefighters.

Even among minorities, relations soured. The groups challeng- 34 ing the promotional tests made the "discriminatory environment" of the department part of their suit. To build this case, Black Firefighters Association members were told to report racial harassment. In 1988 some 300 such charges were filed covering the period from 1981 through '87. Even those eventually exonerated felt their morale unstrung and their careers threatened. Lee himself was the victim of a baseless charge of sexual harassment. "Such allegations can mess up somebody's reputation forever," he says.

In June 1988 Lee was among those promoted by the court. He 35 believes he deserved the move, yet can't fully enjoy it. He says, "It's like, here's your new job, but we're tying all this other garbage onto it."

Lee is faced with a dilemma. He recalls his father's plight and 36 wants the fire department to be integrated. But affirmative action? "I don't know if there's any ultimate justification for it," he says.

The Minister

Buster Soaries was rushing to catch a plane. The year was 1975, 37
and at 24 he was already national field director of Jesse Jackson's
Operation PUSH. Committed to helping his fellow blacks, Soaries
was absorbed in Jackson's brand of affirmative action.

As he headed for the door of his East Orange, N.J., apartment, 38
the phone rang. His father, just hospitalized for minor surgery,
had suffered a complication. At 48, he was dead.

For the next six months, Soaries did what his father no longer 39
could: pay bills, run his mother's house, be a "dad" for his eight-
year-old sister. In doing so, he came to understand the lessons of
his father's life—and the limitations of his own work.

One week before he died, Soaries's father had reviewed the fam- 40
ily's finances with Buster and given him detailed written instructions. Everything was in perfect order. Now he marveled at his
father's foresight. "I realized the values Dad gave me were the
basis of success," Soaries says. "That with discipline, you can prosper in any circumstances; and without it, the best of circumstances
won't help you."

As a boy, he had chafed at his parents' strict moral code. Yet he 41
also bristled when his father was denied service in a diner. By high
school in the late 1960s, Soaries was swept up in the nation's racial
turmoil.

In 1973 he landed at PUSH, which was using boycotts to pressure 42
businesses to employ blacks. Initially excited, Soaries soon saw
PUSH's weaknesses. Some companies left town instead of signing
"agreements" under duress—a net loss for everyone. When others
did sign, the agreements couldn't create black workers to do the
jobs.

Soaries's discomfort increased on visits to housing projects, 43
where he saw undisciplined children and disrespect for property.
Thus when his father's death raised "life-size questions," Soaries
was ready. He left PUSH to found the New Jersey Leadership
Institute, which taught minority kids the skills and personal habits
of a working life. He was ordained in 1977 and now heads the First
Baptist Church of Lincoln Gardens in Somerset, N.J.

Last year, President Bush met with Soaries and other black lead- 44
ers to discuss a bill that would tighten affirmative-action laws. Soar-

ies made some others angry when he told the President: "In our community, we have a 50-percent school dropout rate. This bill won't change that."

Says Soaries today: "When people are afraid to vote because of 45 crime and when more teen-age girls than married women are having babies, affirmative action is no longer the way to save black America." His brow furrows in anger. "I don't know how we got this far off track with this talk about affirmative action. I really don't."

Questions on Subject

1. According to Wildavsky, what are the chief drawbacks of affirmative action?
2. Why did Rick Robinson dislike the idea of "representing the race"?
3. What alternatives to affirmative action do its opponents suggest?
4. According to David Wilson, why must affirmative action, however flawed, remain in effect?
5. What is the "glass ceiling" Wildavsky mentions in paragraph 23?
6. In your own words, explain the argument used by the San Francisco Black Firefighters Association to challenge the entrance and promotion exams of the San Francisco Fire Department.

Questions on Strategy

1. Wildavsky identifies several ironies in the practice of affirmative action. What are those ironies, and how crucial are they to her argument?
2. Wildavsky draws her examples of the way affirmative action has failed from ordinary people in all walks of life. In what way, if any, does her choice of examples strengthen her argument? Are her examples sufficient to make her point?
3. Identify several of the transitional phrases Wildavsky uses throughout her essay and discuss in what ways they serve to unify her examples. (Glossary: *Transitions*)
4. What is Wildavsky's purpose in writing this essay? (Glossary: *Purpose*) How do you know?
5. Wildavsky ends her essay with an anecdote about President George

Bush. What is striking about this reference, and in what way, if any, does it serve to strengthen her argument? (Glossary: *Endings*)

Questions on Diction and Vocabulary

1. After reading this selection how would you characterize Wildavsky's position on affirmative action? Cite examples of her diction to support your answer.
2. Refer to your desk dictionary to determine the meanings of the following words as they are used in this selection: *berated* (paragraph 3), *waive* (5), *sharecropping* (11), *boost* (17), *affluent* (19), *crucial* (19), *concession* (20), *entrepreneurial* (20), *floundered* (23), *camaraderie* (30), *rote* (31).

Writing Suggestions

1. Write an essay in which you use examples from your own experience, observation, or reading to support the necessity of affirmative action.
2. In paragraph 32, Wildavsky points out the subtle distinction between hiring by affirmative action and promoting by affirmative action. In a short essay of your own, develop the distinction Wildavsky makes.

Courtship through the Ages

James Thurber

James Thurber (1894–1961), writer and cartoonist, has been one of America's favorite and most prolific humorists for more than fifty years. Most of his early essays, short stories, and line drawings appeared in the New Yorker *after he joined its editorial staff in 1925. Some of his books include* Is Sex Necessary? *(1929, with E. B. White),* The Thurber Carnival *(1945), and* Alarms and Diversions *(1957).*

In the following essay, first published in My World—And Welcome to It, *Thurber makes a masterful use of absurd and ironic examples to poke fun at the mating rituals of humans and animals alike.*

Surely nothing in the astonishing scheme of life can have nonplussed Nature so much as the fact that none of the females of any of the species she created really cared very much for the male, as such. For the past ten million years Nature has been busily inventing ways to make the male attractive to the female, but the whole business of courtship, from the marine annelids up to man, still lumbers heavily along, like a complicated musical comedy. I have been reading the sad and absorbing story in Volume 6 (Code to Dama) of the *Encyclopaedia Britannica*. In this volume you can learn all about cricket, cotton, costume designing, crocodiles, crown jewels, and Coleridge, but none of these subjects is so interesting as the Courtship of Animals, which recounts the sorrowful lengths to which all males must go to arouse the interest of a lady.

We all know, I think, that Nature gave man whiskers and a mustache with the quaint idea in mind that these would prove attractive to the female. We all know that, far from attracting her, whiskers and mustaches only made her nervous and gloomy, so that man had to go in for somersaults, tilting with lances, and performing feats of parlor magic to win her attention; he also had to bring her candy, flowers, and the furs of animals. It is common knowledge that in spite of all these "love displays" the male is constantly being turned down, insulted, or thrown out of the house. It is rather comforting, then, to discover that the peacock, for all his gorgeous plumage, does not have a particularly easy time in courtship; none of the males in the world do. The first peahen, it turned out, was only faintly stirred by her suitor's beautiful train. She would often go quietly to sleep while he was whisking it around. The *Britannica* tells us that the peacock actually had to learn a certain little trick to wake her up and revive her interest: he had to learn to vibrate his quills so as to make a rustling sound. In ancient times man himself, observing the ways of the peacock, probably tried vibrating his whiskers to make a rustling sound; if so, it didn't get him anywhere. He had to go in for something else; so, among other things, he went in for gifts. It is not unlikely that he got this idea from certain flies and birds who were making no headway at all with rustling sounds.

One of the flies of the family Empidae, who had tried everything, 3 finally hit on something pretty special. He contrived to make a glistening transparent balloon which was even larger than himself. Into this he would put sweetmeats and tidbits and he would carry the whole elaborate envelope through the air to the lady of his choice. This amused her for a time, but she finally got bored with it. She demanded silly little colorful presents, something that you couldn't eat but that would look nice around the house. So the male Empis had to go around gathering flower petals and pieces of bright paper to put into his balloon. On a courtship flight a male Empis cuts quite a figure now, but he can hardly be said to be happy. He never knows how soon the female will demand heavier presents, such as Roman coins and gold collar buttons. It seems probable that one day the courtship of the Empidae will fall down, as man's occasionally does, of its own weight.

The bowerbird is another creature that spends so much time 4 courting the female that he never gets any work done. If all the male bowerbirds became nervous wrecks within the next ten or fifteen years, it would not surprise me. The female bowerbird insists that a playground be built for her with a specially constructed bower at the entrance. This bower is much more elaborate than an ordinary nest and is harder to build; it costs a lot more, too. The female will not come to the playground until the male has filled it up with a great many gifts: silvery leaves, red leaves, rose petals, shells, beads, berries, bones, dice, buttons, cigar bands, Christmas seals, and the Lord knows what else. When the female finally condescends to visit the playground, she is in a coy and silly mood and has to be chased in and out of the bower and up and down the playground before she will quit giggling and stand still long enough even to shake hands. The male bird is, of course, pretty well done in before the chase starts, because he has worn himself out hunting for eyeglass lenses and begonia blossoms. I imagine that many a bowerbird, after chasing a female for two or three hours, says the hell with it and goes home to bed. Next day, of course, he telephones someone else and the same trying ritual is gone through with again. A male bowerbird is as exhausted as a night-club habitué before he is out of his twenties.

The male fiddler crab has a somewhat easier time, but it can 5 hardly be said that he is sitting pretty. He has one enormously large and powerful claw, usually brilliantly colored, and you might suppose that all he had to do was reach out and grab some passing cutie. The very earliest fiddler crabs may have tried this, but, if so, they got slapped for their pains. A female fiddler crab will not tolerate any caveman stuff; she never has and she doesn't intend to start now. To attract a female, a fiddler crab has to stand on tiptoe and brandish his claw in the air. If any female in the neighborhood is interested—and you'd be surprised how many are not—she comes over and engages him in light badinage, for which he is not in the mood. As many as a hundred females may pass the time of day with him and go on about their business. By nightfall of an average courting day, a fiddler crab who has been standing on tiptoe for eight or ten hours waving a heavy claw in the air is in pretty sad shape. As in the case of the male of all species, however, he gets out of bed next morning, dashes some water on his face, and tries again.

The next time you encounter a male web-spinning spider, stop 6 and reflect that he is too busy worrying about his love life to have any desire to bite you. Male web-spinning spiders have a tougher life than any other males in the animal kingdom. This is because the female web-spinning spiders have very poor eyesight. If a male lands on a female's web, she kills him before he has time to lay down his cane and gloves, mistaking him for a fly or a bumblebee who has tumbled into her trap. Before the species figured out what to do about this, millions of males were murdered by ladies they called on. It is the nature of spiders to perform a little dance in front of the female, but before a male spinner could get near enough for the female to see who he was and what he was up to, she would lash out at him with a flat-iron or a pair of garden shears. One night, nobody knows when, a very bright male spinner lay awake worrying about calling on a lady who had been killing suitors right and left. It came to him that this business of dancing as a love display wasn't getting anybody anywhere except the grave. He decided to go in for web-twitching, or strand-vibrating. The next day he tried it on one of the nearsighted girls. Instead of dropping in on her suddenly, he stayed outside the web and began monkeying with one of its strands. He twitched it up and down and in and out with such a lilting rhythm that the female was charmed. The serenade worked beautifully; the female let him live. The *Britannica*'s spider-watchers, however, report that this system is not always successful. Once in a while, even now, a female will fire three bullets into a suitor or run him through with a kitchen knife. She keeps threatening him from the moment he strikes the first low notes on the outside strings, but usually by the time he has got up to the high notes played around the center of the web, he is going to town and she spares his life.

Even the butterfly, as handsome a fellow as he is, can't always 7 win a mate merely by fluttering around and showing off. Many butterflies have to have scent scales on their wings. Hepialus carries a powder puff in a perfumed pouch. He throws perfume at the ladies when they pass. The male tree cricket, Oecanthus, goes Hepialus one better by carrying a tiny bottle of wine with him and giving drinks to such doxies as he has designs on. One of the male snails throws darts to entertain the girls. So it goes, through the long list of animals, from the bristle worm and his rudimentary dance steps to man and his gift of diamonds and sapphires. The goldeneye drake raises a jet of water with his feet as he flies over a lake; Hepialus has his powder puff, Oecanthus his wine bottle, man his etchings. It is a bright and melancholy story, the age-old desire of the male for the female, the age-old desire of the female to be amused and entertained. Of all the creatures on earth, the only males who could be figured as putting any irony into their courtship are the grebes and certain other diving birds. Every now and then a courting grebe slips quietly down to the bottom of a lake and then, with a mighty "Whoosh!" pops out suddenly a few feet from his girl friend, splashing water all over her. She seems to be persuaded that this is a purely loving display, but I like to think that the grebe always has a faint hope of drowning her or scaring her to death.

I will close this investigation into the mournful burdens of the 8
male with *Britannica's* story about a certain Argus pheasant. It appears that the Argus displays himself in front of a female who stands perfectly still without moving a feather. . . . The male Argus the *Britannica* tells about was confined in a cage with a female of another species, a female who kept moving around, emptying ashtrays and fussing with lampshades all the time the male was showing off his talents. Finally, in disgust, he stalked away and began displaying in front of his water trough. He reminds me of a certain male (*Homo sapiens*) of my acquaintance who one night after dinner asked his wife to put down her detective magazine so that he could read a poem of which he was very fond. She sat quietly enough until he was well into the middle of the thing, intoning with great ardor and intensity. Then suddenly there came a sharp, disconcerting *slap!* It turned out that all during the male's display, the female had been intent on a circling mosquito and had finally trapped it between the palms of her hands. The male in this case did not stalk away and display in front of a water trough; he went over to Tim's and had a flock of drinks and recited the poem to the fellas. I am sure they all told bitter stories of their own about how their displays had been interrupted by females. I am also sure that they all ended up singing "Honey, Honey, Bless Your Heart."

Questions on Subject

1. All kidding aside, what are some of the "love displays" common to both men and animals?
2. How are females' reactions to male overtures similar among species? Can you think of other traits they have in common?
3. Which species has a "tougher life than any other males in the an-

imal kingdom"? Why is this so? Of the species Thurber names, which seems to have the easiest time courting females? Explain your answer.

Questions on Strategy

1. What is the thesis of Thurber's essay? Where is it stated? Thurber is, of course, known for his witty writing. Do you think he intends his thesis to be serious? How do you know? (Glossary: *Thesis*)
2. Thurber uses several lengthy examples of animal behavior to show the many ways nature has come up with to make males attractive to females. What figure of speech does Thurber use throughout his essay to remind us that these rules apply to humans as well? Is this device effective? Explain your answer using examples from the text. (Glossary: *Figures of Speech*)
3. Review the essay, and identify the topic sentences in each paragraph. What do they have in common? How do they work to achieve unity in this essay? (Glossary: *Unity*)
4. Reread the concluding sentence in each of Thurber's paragraphs. What do the sentences have in common? How do they work to illustrate his point?
5. Thurber mixes fact and fiction to achieve humor in his essay. For example, in paragraph 7, Thurber describes how many butterflies have scent scales on their wings but the male tree cricket goes him one better by carrying "a tiny bottle of wine with him." Find other examples of his mixing fact and fiction to achieve humor in the essay. What does this technique add to the essay?

Questions on Diction and Vocabulary

1. Thurber takes delight at making fun of men's foolishness as they show off for their ladies, but he is also commiserating with them. Cite examples from the text of the words Thurber uses that show he also feels sorry for his hapless comrades.
2. Refer to your desk dictionary to determine the meaning of the following words as they are used in this selection: *nonplussed* (paragraph 1), *lumbers* (1), *quaint* (2), *coy* (4), *badinage* (5), *doxies* (7).

Writing Assignments

1. Write an essay offering the point of view opposite from that of Thurber's essay. That is, explain the ways females traditionally have been frustrated in their efforts to attract males.
2. Thurber is telling us that the animal kingdom supplies many helpful insights into our own behavior. What other areas of human behavior can you illustrate using examples from the world of insects, mammals, or reptiles? The possibilities cover the same range as human behavior: work habits, parenting habits, couples' behavior, and shopping habits are just a few.

Writing Suggestions for Illustration

1. Write an essay on one of the following statements, using examples to illustrate your ideas. You should be able to draw your examples primarily from personal experience and firsthand observation. As you plan your essay, consider whether you will want to use a series of short examples or one or more extended examples.
   a. Fads never go out of style.
   b. Television has produced a number of "classic" programs.
   c. Every college campus has its own slang terms.
   d. Making excuses sometimes seems like a national pastime.
   e. A liberal arts education can have many practical applications.
   f. College students are not often given credit for the community volunteer work that they do.
   g. Clothes make the person.
   h. All good teachers have certain traits in common.
   i. Graffiti can tell us a good deal about our life and times.
   j. There are a number of simple strategies one can use to relax.
2. Write an essay on one of the following statements using examples to illustrate your ideas. Draw your examples from as many sources as necessary: your reading, the media, interviews, conversations, lectures, and whatever else may be helpful. As you plan your essay, consider whether you will want to use a series of short examples or one or more extended examples.
   a. Much has been (*or* should still be) done to eliminate barriers for the physically handicapped.
   b. Nature's oddities are numerous.
   c. Throughout history dire predictions have been made about the end of the world.

d. The past predictions of science fiction are today's realities.
e. Boxing should be outlawed.
f. The world has seen no absence of wars since World War II.
g. The Japanese have developed many innovative management strategies.
h. A great work of art may come out of an artist's most difficult period.
i. The misjudgments and mistakes of our presidents can be useful lessons in leadership.
j. Genius is 10 percent talent and 90 percent hard work.
k. Drugs have taken an economic toll on American business.
l. Democracy is enjoying a renewed interest in countries outside of the United States.

5
Process Analysis

What Is Process Analysis?

A process is a series of actions or stages that follow one another in a specific, unchanging order and lead to a particular end. People have invented many processes, like assembling pickup trucks or making bread; others occur naturally, like the decay of uranium or the development of a fetus in its mother's womb. All are processes because, if each step occurs correctly and in the right order, the results will be predictable: a completed pickup will roll off the assembly line, and a fully formed baby will be born. Process analysis involves separating such an event or operation or cycle of development into distinct steps, describing each step precisely, and arranging it in its proper order.

Whenever you explain how plants create oxygen, tell how to make ice cream, or merely give directions to your house, you are using process analysis. Each year thousands of books and magazine articles tell us how to make home repairs, how to lose weight and get physically fit, how to improve our memories, how to play better tennis, how to manage our money; they try to satisfy our curiosity about how television shows are made, how plants grow, how jet planes work, and how monkeys, bees, or whales mate. People simply want to know how things work and how to do things for themselves, so it's not surprising that process analysis is one of the most widespread and popular forms of writing today.

199

Process analysis resembles narration, because both strategies present a series of events occurring over time. But a narration is the story of how things happened in a particular way during one particular period of time; process analysis relates how things always happen (or always should happen) in essentially the same way time after time.

Why Do Writers Use Process Analysis?

There are essentially two reasons for writing a process analysis. One is to provide a reader with the necessary directions to achieve a desired result; this kind of writing is called, naturally enough, *directional process analysis.* The directions may be as short and simple as the instructions on a frozen-food package ("Heat over a low flame for 45 minutes, stir, and serve") or as long and complex as the operator's manual for a mainframe computer. But all directions have the same purpose: to guide the reader through a series of steps, resulting in a particular goal. William Peterson's "I Bet You Can" and Maxine Kumin's "Building Fence," later in this section, are examples of directional process analysis.

Informational process analysis, however, deals not with processes that readers want to perform for themselves, but with processes that readers are curious about or would like to understand: how presidents are elected, how soil is eroded, how an elevator works, how the brain functions. Alexander Petrunkevitch's "The Spider and the Wasp," later in this section, analyzes a natural process that fascinates readers because it is so unlike anything they will experience on their own.

What to Look for in Reading a Process Analysis

First, decide whether the process analysis is directional or informational—whether it describes something you can do or something you can only observe. Then, as you read, try to "see" the process with your mind's eye. If it is directional, imagine yourself following the directions; if it is informative, try to visualize the process as the author describes it.

Consider, for example, Bernard Gladstone's piece about building a fire in a fireplace, taken from *The New York Times Complete Manual of Home Repair:*

> Though "experts" differ as to the best technique to follow when building a fire, one generally accepted method consists of first laying a generous amount of crumpled newspaper on the hearth between the andirons. Kindling wood is then spread generously over this layer of newspaper and one of the thickest logs is placed across the back of the andirons. This should be as close to the back of the fireplace as possible, but not quite touching it. A second log is then placed an inch or so in front of this, and a few additional sticks of kindling are laid across these two. A third log is then placed on top to form a sort of pyramid with air space between all logs so that flames can lick freely up between them.
>
> A mistake frequently made is in building the fire too far forward so that the rear wall of the fireplace does not get properly heated. A heated back wall helps increase the draft and tends to suck smoke and flames rearward with less chance of sparks or smoke spurting out into the room.
>
> Another common mistake often made by the inexperienced firetender is to try to build a fire with only one or two logs, instead of using at least three. A single log is difficult to ignite properly, and even two logs do not provide an efficient bed with adequate fuel-burning capacity.
>
> Use of too many logs, on the other hand, is also a common fault and can prove hazardous. Building too big a fire can create more smoke and draft than the chimney can safely handle, increasing the possibility of sparks or smoke being thrown out into the room. For best results, the homeowner should start with three medium-size logs as described above, then add additional logs as needed if the fire is to be kept burning.

In the very first sentence, Gladstone indicates what process he is going to describe: a generally accepted method for building a fire. Even a reader who never wants to build a fire—who doesn't have a fireplace—can quickly see that this is a "how-to" discussion, a directional process analysis. Gladstone takes his readers through six steps which, if followed to the letter, will result in a wood-and-paper structure that will light at the touch of a match and stay lit. Each step is described in a sentence or less, but Gladstone provides enough specific detail so that his directions will be clear, easy to understand, and easy to follow. The process analysis is over in a paragraph.

Even so, Gladstone goes on, describing three mistakes that people often make when building a fire. Note that anyone who follows Gladstone's six steps exactly could not possibly make any of these mistakes; but the writer recognizes that many of us are careless about following directions. Having told us what to do, he reinforces his instructions by telling us what *not* to do, as well.

Here's another process analysis, in which Alan Devoe explains what happens to an animal when it goes into hibernation. The selection is from *Lives Around Us:*

The woodchuck's hibernation usually starts about the middle of September. For weeks he has been foraging with increased appetite among the clover blossoms and has grown heavy and slow-moving. Now, with the coming of mid-September, apples and corn and yarrow tops have become less plentiful, and the nights are cool. The woodchuck moves with slower gait, and emerges less and less frequently for feeding trips. Layers of fat have accumulated around his chest and shoulders, and there is thick fat in the axils of his legs. He has extended his summer burrow to a length of nearly thirty feet, and has fashioned a deep nest-chamber at the end of it, far below the level of the frost. He has carried in, usually, a little hay. He is ready for the Long Sleep.

When the temperature of the September days falls below 50 degrees or so, the woodchuck becomes too drowsy to come forth from his burrow in the chilly dusk to forage. He remains in the deep nest-chamber, lethargic, hardly moving. Gradually, with the passing of hours or days, his coarse-furred body curls into a semicircle, like a foetus, nose-tip touching tail. The small legs are tucked in, the handlike clawed forefeet folded. The woodchuck has become a compact ball. Presently the temperature of his body begins to fall.

In normal life the woodchuck's temperature, though fluctuant, averages about 97 degrees. Now, as he lies tight-curled in a ball with the winter sleep stealing over him, this body heat drops ten degrees, twenty degrees, thirty. Finally, by the time the snow is on the ground and the woodchuck's winter dormancy has become complete, his temperature is only 38 or 40. With the falling of the body heat there is a slowing of his heartbeat and his respiration. In normal life he breathes thirty or forty times each minute; when he is excited, as many as a hundred times.

Now he breathes slower and slower—ten times a minute, five times a minute, once a minute, and at last only ten or twelve times in an hour. His heartbeat is a twentieth of normal. He has entered fully into the oblivion of hibernation.

The process Devoe describes is natural to woodchucks but not to humans, so obviously he cannot be giving instructions. Rather, he has created an informational process analysis to help us understand what happens during the remarkable process of hibernation. As Devoe's analysis reveals, hibernation is not a series of well-defined steps but a long, slow change from the activity of late summer to the immobility of a deep winter's sleep. The woodchuck does not suddenly stop feeding, nor do his temperature, pulse, and rate of respiration plummet at once. Using transitional expressions and time markers, Devoe shows us that this process lasts for weeks, even months. He connects the progress of hibernation with changes in the weather because the woodchuck's body responds to the dropping temperature as autumn sets in rather than to the passage of specific periods of time.

Writing a Process Analysis Essay

In a process analysis, always aim for precision and clarity. Few things are more frustrating to readers of directions than an unclear or misplaced step that prevents them from achieving the result you have promised. The same sort of error in an informational process analysis will cause misunderstanding and confusion. Whatever your purpose, process analysis requires a systematic, logical approach.

1. Dividing the Process into Steps

As much as possible, make each step a simple and well-defined action, preferably a single action. To guide yourself in doing so, write up a scratch outline listing the steps. Here, for example, is an outline of Bernard Gladstone's directions for building a fire.

Process analysis of building a fire in a fireplace
Directional
1. put down crumpled newspaper

2. lay kindling
3. place back log near rear wall but not touching
4. place front log an inch forward
5. bridge logs with kindling
6. place third log on top of kindling bridge

Next, check your outline to make sure that the steps are in the right order and that none has been omitted. Then analyze your outline more carefully. Are any steps so complex that they need to be described in some detail—or perhaps divided into more steps? Will you need to explain the purpose of a certain step because the reason for it is not obvious? Especially in an informational process analysis, it may happen that two steps take place at the same time; perhaps they are performed by different people or different parts of the body. Does your outline make this clear? (One solution is to assign both steps the same number but label one of them "A" and the other "B.") When you feel certain that the steps of the process are complete and correct, ask yourself two more questions. Will the reader need any other information to understand the process—definitions of unusual terms, for example, or descriptions of special equipment? Should you anticipate common mistakes or misunderstandings and discuss them, as Gladstone does? If so, be sure to add an appropriate note or two to your scratch outline as a reminder.

2. Testing Your Process Analysis

After finishing a first draft of your essay, have someone else read it. If you are writing a directional process analysis, ask your reader to follow the instructions and then to tell you whether he or she was able to understand each step and perform it satisfactorily. Was the desired result achieved? Did the fire burn well, the computer program run, the lasagna taste good? If not, examine your process analysis step by step, looking for errors and omissions that would explain the unsatisfactory result (no kindling wood, perhaps, or a loop in the program, or too much garlic).

For an informational process analysis, it may be a bit trickier to make sure that your reader really understands. Test your reader's comprehension by asking a few questions. If there seems to be any confusion, try rereading what you have written with an objective eye. Sometimes an especially intricate or otherwise difficult step can be made clear by rewriting it in everyday language; sometimes a recognizable comparison or analogy will help, especially if you are analyzing a scientific or otherwise unfamiliar process. (For example, American readers might better understand the British game of rugby if it was compared with American football; nonspecialists might grasp the circulation of the blood more easily through an analogy between the cardiovascular system and domestic plumbing. See Sections 6 and 7 for discussions of *comparison and contrast* and *analogy*.) Again, try to pin down the specific cause of any misunderstanding, the step or steps that are confusing your reader. Keep on revising until he or she can demonstrate a clear understanding of what you've tried to say.

3. Using Transitional Words

Transitional words and phrases such as *then, next, after doing this,* and *during the summer months* can both emphasize and clarify the sequence of steps in your process analysis. The same is true of sequence markers like *first, second, third,* and so on. The Devoe piece uses such words effectively to make it clear which stages in the process of hibernation are simultaneous and which are not; Gladstone includes an occasional *first* or *then* to alert us to shifts from one step to the next. But both writers are careful not to overuse these words, and so should you be. Transitions are a resource of language, but they should not be used routinely.

I Bet You Can

William Peterson

Bill Peterson grew up in New Hartford, New York. After completing a business major at the University of Vermont, he entered the music business and now works as a booking agent. He had extensive experience organizing campus concerts for the UVM Student Association. Bill is also an avid juggler, and he enjoys teaching others the craft. In "I Bet You Can," he shares with us, step by step, the basics of how to juggle. Try it.

Have you ever seen Michael Davis on television? He's a standup comic and a juggler. His antics got me interested in learning how to juggle. Several years ago after watching his act on "Saturday Night Live" I went out to my garage and started to experiment with some tennis balls. At first I felt helpless after tossing and chasing the balls for what seemed like countless hours. However, I actually did start to learn how to juggle. To my surprise I discovered that juggling is much easier than it had at first appeared. If you'd like to learn how to juggle, I recommend that you find some tennis balls or lacrosse balls and continue reading.

Step one is the simple toss. Stand erect and hold one ball in your right hand. Carefully toss the ball up to approximately an inch above your head and to about half an arm's length in front of you. The ball should arch from your right hand across to your left. This step should now be repeated, starting with your left hand and tossing to your right. Be sure that the ball reaches the same height and distance from you and is not simply passed from your left hand to your right. Keep tossing the ball back and forth until you have become thoroughly disgusted with this step. If you have practiced this toss enough we can now call this step "the perfect toss." If it is not quite perfect, then you have not become disgusted enough with the step. We'll assume that you've perfected it. Now you're ready to take a little breather and move on.

Step two is the toss and return. Get back on your feet and this 3
time hold a ball in each hand. Take a deep breath and make a
perfect toss with the ball in your right hand. As that ball reaches
its peak make another perfect toss with the ball in your left hand.
The second ball should end up passing under the first one and
reaching approximately the same height. When the second ball
peaks you should be grabbing—or already have grabbed, depending on timing—the first ball. The second ball should then
gently drop into your awaiting right hand. If it was not that easy,
then don't worry about the "gently" bit. Most people do not
achieve perfection at first. Step two is the key factor in becoming
a good juggler and should be practiced at least five times as much
as step one.

Don't deceive yourself after a few successful completions. This 4
maneuver really must be perfected before step three can be ap-
proached. As a way to improve dexterity, you should try several
tosses and returns starting with your left hand. Let's call step two
"the exchange." You're now ready for another well-deserved
breather before you proceed.

Ready or not, here it goes. Step three is merely a continuum of 5
"the exchange" with the addition of a third ball. Don't worry if
you are confused—I will explain. Get back up again and now hold
two balls in your right hand and one in your left. Make a perfect
toss with one of the balls in your right hand and then an exchange
with the one in your left hand. The ball coming from your left hand
should now be exchanged with the, as of now, unused ball in your
right hand. This process should be continued until you find yourself reaching under nearby chairs for bouncing tennis balls. It is
true that many persons' backs and legs become sore when learning
how to juggle because they've been picking up balls that they've
inadvertently tossed around the room. Try practicing over a bed;
you won't have to reach down so far. Don't get too upset if things
aren't going well, you're probably keeping the same pace as everyone else at this stage. You're certainly doing better than I was
because you've had me as a teacher.

Don't worry, this teacher is not going to leave you stranded with 6
hours of repetition of the basic steps. I am sure that you have
already run into some basic problems. I will now try to relate some

of my beginners' troubles and some of the best solutions you can try for them.

Problem one, you are getting nowhere after the simple toss. This 7 requires a basic improvement of hand to eye coordination. Solution one is to just go back and practice the simple toss again and again. Unfortunately, this becomes quite boring. Solution two is not as tedious and involves quite a bit of skill. Try juggling two balls in one hand. Some people show me this when I ask them if they can juggle—they're not fooling anyone. Real juggling is what you're here to learn. First try circular juggling in one hand. This involves tosses similar to "the perfect toss." They differ in that the balls go half as far towards the opposite hand, are tossed and grabbed by the same hand, and end up making their own circles (as opposed to going up and down in upside down V-s like exchanges). Then try juggling the balls in the same line style—I think this is harder. You have to keep two balls traveling in their own vertical paths (the balls should go as high as they do in a "perfect toss") with only one hand. I think this is harder than the circular style because my hands normally tend to make little circles when I juggle.

Problem two, you can make exchanges but you just can't accom- 8 plish step three. The best solution to this is to just continue practicing step two, but now add a twist. As soon as the first ball is caught by the left hand in our step two, throw it back up in another perfect toss for another exchange. Continue this and increase speed up to the point where two balls just don't seem like enough. You should now be ready to add the third ball and accomplish what you couldn't before—real Michael Davis kind of juggling.

Problem three, you have become the "runaway juggler." This 9 means you can successfully achieve numerous exchanges but you're always chasing after balls tossed too far in front of you. The first solution is to stand in front of a wall. This causes you to end up catching a couple of balls bouncing off the wall or else you'll end up consciously keeping your tosses in closer to your body. The second solution is to put your back up against a wall. This will tend to make you toss in closer to yourself because you will be restricted to keeping your back up against the wall. This solution can work but more often than not you'll find yourself watching balls fly across the room in front of you! I've told you about the back on the wall method because some people find it effective. As you can tell, I don't.

Step 1 Step 2 Step 3

  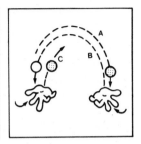

Juggling is a simple three-step process. Following my routine is 10 the easiest way to get from being a spastic ball chaser to an accomplished juggler. Patience and coordination are really not required. The only requirements are a few tennis balls, the ability to follow some basic instructions, and the time to have some fun.

Interview with William Peterson

What made you do a paper on juggling?

Well, I've been juggling for almost ten years, and in that time I've taught many people how to juggle. It's very easy to teach another person, especially one-on-one. All I need is a set of tennis balls. It's just something that comes easily to most people once they are shown how to do it. And my friends tell me that I'm pretty successful at showing others just how to do it. As a result, I thought I'd try to explain the process on paper.

Did you start with a process analysis paper in mind?

In all honesty, I'd done a speech on juggling before writing this essay. In class, I discovered that the neat three-step process fit perfectly into the process analysis category. It's a natural. I started by making a thorough outline of the process. That made the rough draft relatively easy.

I hear you actually gave your essay to some friends to have them test your directions. What happened?

Yes, I gave it to people who had never tried juggling to see if there were any "bugs" or unclear sections in my instructions. This helped me a lot as a writer because they told me where certain things were not clear or outright confusing. This enabled me to go back and revise, knowing exactly what the problem was.

Did any part give you trouble, Bill?

I had trouble with paragraph 2, the explanation of the simple toss. In my rough draft I just couldn't get detailed enough. See what I mean:

> Step one is the simple toss. Stand erect and hold one object (we'll call it a ball from now on) in your most adroit hand (we'll say the right). Toss the ball into the air to approximately an inch above your head and to about half an arm's length in front of you. The ball should take an arched path traveling from your right hand to your left. This step should now be repeated using your left hand first and returning it to your right hand. Repeat this until completely proficient. We'll now call this action the "perfect toss." Take a breather and then move on.

After several drafts, I finally felt satisfied. You can see my final version in paragraph 2.

How to Say Nothing in 500 Words

Paul Roberts

Paul Roberts (1917–1967) was a linguist, a teacher, and a writer. His books on writing, including English Syntax *(1954) and* Patterns of English *(1956), have helped generations of high school and college students to become better writers.*

"How to Say Nothing in 500 Words" is taken from his best-known book, Understanding English *(1958). Although written over thirty years ago, the essay is still relevant for student writers today. Good writing, Roberts tells us, is not simply a matter of filling up a page; rather, the words have to hold the reader's interest and they must say something. In this essay, the author uses lively prose and a step-by-step process to guide the student from the blank page to the finished essay. His bag of writing tricks is good advice to anyone who wants to write well.*

Nothing about Something

It's Friday afternoon, and you have almost survived another 1 week of classes. You are just looking forward dreamily to the week end when the English instructor says: "For Monday you will turn in a five-hundred word composition on college football."

Well, that puts a good big hole in the weekend. You don't have 2 any strong views on college football one way or the other. You get rather excited during the season and go to all the home games and find it rather more fun than not. On the other hand, the class has been reading Robert Hutchins in the anthology and perhaps Shaw's "Eighty-Yard Run," and from the class discussion you have got the idea that the instructor thinks college football is for the birds. You are no fool, you. You can figure out what side to take.

After dinner you get out the portable typewriter that you got for 3
high school graduation. You might as well get it over with and
enjoy Saturday and Sunday. Five hundred words is about two
double-spaced pages with normal margins. You put in a sheet of
paper, think up a title, and you're off:

Why College Football Should Be Abolished

College football should be abolished because it's bad for the school
and also bad for the players. The players are so busy practicing that
they don't have any time for their studies.

This, you feel, is a mighty good start. The only trouble is that 4
it's only thirty-two words. You still have four hundred and sixty-
eight to go, and you've pretty well exhausted the subject. It comes
to you that you do your best thinking in the morning, so you put
away the typewriter and go to the movies. But the next morning
you have to do your washing and some math problems, and in
the afternoon you go to the game. The English instructor turns up
too, and you wonder if you've taken the right side after all. Saturday night you have a date, and Sunday morning you have to go
to church. (You shouldn't let English assignments interfere with
your religion.) What with one thing and another, it's ten o'clock
Sunday night before you get out the typewriter again. You make
a pot of coffee and start to fill out your views on college football.
Put a little meat on the bones.

Why College Football Should Be Abolished

In my opinion, it seems to me that college football should be abolished. The reason why I think this to be true is because I feel that football
is bad for the colleges in nearly every respect. As Robert Hutchins says
in his article in our anthology in which he discusses college football, it
would be better if the colleges had race horses and had races with one
another, because then the horses would not have to attend classes. I
firmly agree with Mr. Hutchins on this point, and I am sure that many
other students would agree too.

One reason why it seems to me that college football is bad is that it
has become too commercial. In the olden times when people played
football just for the fun of it, maybe college football was all right, but

they do not play football just for the fun of it now as they used to in the old days. Nowadays college football is what you might call a big business. Maybe this is not true at all schools, and I don't think it is especially true here at State, but certainly this is the case at most colleges and universities in America nowadays, as Mr. Hutchins points out in his very interesting article. Actually the coaches and alumni go around to the high schools and offer the high school stars large salaries to come to their colleges and play football for them. There was one case where a high school star was offered a convertible if he would play football for a certain college.

Another reason for abolishing college football is that it is bad for the players. They do not have time to get a college education, because they are so busy playing football. A football player has to practice every afternoon from three to six, and then he is so tired that he can't concentrate on his studies. He just feels like dropping off to sleep after dinner, and then the next day he goes to his classes without having studied and maybe he fails the test.

(Good ripe stuff so far, but you're still a hundred and fifty-one words from home. One more push.)

Also I think college football is bad for the colleges and the universities because not very many students get to participate in it. Out of a college of ten thousand students only seventy-five or a hundred play football, if that many. Football is what you might call a spectator sport. That means that most people go to watch it but do not play it themselves.

(Four hundred and fifteen. Well, you still have the conclusion, and when you retype it, you can make the margins a little wider.)

These are the reasons why I agree with Mr. Hutchins that college football should be abolished in American colleges and universities.

On Monday you turn it in, moderately hopeful, and on Friday ₅ it comes back marked "weak in content" and sporting a big "D."

This essay is exaggerated a little, not much. The English instruc- ₆ tor will recognize it as reasonably typical of what an assignment on college football will bring in. He knows that nearly half of the class will contrive in five hundred words to say that college football

is too commercial and bad for the players. Most of the other half
will inform him that college football builds character and prepares
one for life and brings prestige to the school. As he reads paper
after paper all saying the same thing in almost the same words,
all bloodless, five hundred words dripping out of nothing, he wonders how he allowed himself to get trapped into teaching English
when he might have had a happy and interesting life as an elec-
trician or a confidence man.

Well, you may ask, what can you do about it? The subject is one 7
on which you have few convictions and little information. Can you
be expected to make a dull subject interesting? As a matter of fact,
this is precisely what you are expected to do. This is the writer's
essential task. All subjects, except sex, are dull until somebody
makes them interesting. The writer's job is to find the argument,
the approach, the angle, the wording that will take the reader with
him. This is seldom easy, and it is particularly hard in subjects that
have been much discussed: College Football, Fraternities, Popular
Music, Is Chivalry Dead?, and the like. You will feel that there is
nothing you can do with such subjects except repeat the old bromides. But there are some things you can do which will make your
papers, if not throbbingly alive, at least less insufferably tedious
than they might otherwise be.

Avoid the Obvious Content

Say the assignment is college football. Say that you've decided 8
to be against it. Begin by putting down the arguments that come
to your mind: it is too commercial, it takes the students' minds off
their studies, it is hard on the players, it makes the university a
kind of circus instead of an intellectual center, for most schools it
is financially ruinous. Can you think of any more arguments just
off hand? All right. Now when you write your paper, *make sure
that you don't use any of the material on this list.* If these are the points
that leap to your mind, they will leap to everyone else's too, and
whether you get a "C" or a "D" may depend on whether the
instructor reads your paper early when he is fresh and tolerant or
late, when the sentence "In my opinion, college football has be-

come too commercial," inexorably repeated, has brought him to the brink of lunacy.

Be against college football for some reason or reasons of your 9 own. If they are keen and perceptive ones, that's splendid. But even if they are trivial or foolish or indefensible, you are still ahead so long as they are not everybody else's reasons too. Be against it because the colleges don't spend enough money on it to make it worthwhile, because it is bad for the characters of the spectators, because the players are forced to attend classes, because the football stars hog all the beautiful women, because it competes with baseball and is therefore un-American and possibly Communist inspired. There are lots of more or less unused reasons for being against college football.

Sometimes it is a good idea to sum up and dispose of the trite 10 and conventional points before going on to your own. This has the advantage of indicating to the reader that you are going to be neither trite nor conventional. Something like this:

> We are often told that college football should be abolished because it has become too commercial or because it is bad for the players. These arguments are no doubt very cogent, but they don't really go to the heart of the matter.

Then you go to the heart of the matter.

Take the Less Usual Side

One rather simple way of getting interest into your paper is to 11 take the side of the argument that most of the citizens will want to avoid. If the assignment is an essay on dogs, you can, if you choose, explain that dogs are faithful and lovable companions, intelligent, useful as guardians of the house and protectors of children, indispensable in police work—in short, when all is said and done, man's best friends. Or you can suggest that those big brown eyes conceal, more often than not, a vacuity of mind and an inconstancy of purpose; that the dogs you have known most intimately have been mangy, ill-tempered brutes, incapable of instruction; and that only your nobility of mind and fear of arrest prevent you from kicking the flea-ridden animals when you pass them on the street.

Naturally, personal convictions will sometimes dictate your ap- 12 proach. If the assigned subject is "Is Methodism Rewarding to the Individual?" and you are a pious Methodist, you have really no choice. But few assigned subjects, if any, will fall in this category. Most of them will lie in broad areas of discussion with much to be said on both sides. They are intellectual exercises and it is legitimate to argue now one way and now another, as debaters do in similar circumstances. Always take the side that looks to you hardest, least defensible. It will almost always turn out to be easier to write interestingly on that side.

This general advice applies where you have a choice of subjects. 13 If you are to choose among "The Value of Fraternities" and "My Favorite High School Teacher" and "What I Think about Beetles," by all means plump for the beetles. By the time the instructor gets to your paper, he will be up to his ears in tedious tales about the French teacher at Bloombury High and assertions about how fraternities build character and prepare one for life. Your views on beetles, whatever they are, are bound to be a refreshing change.

Don't worry too much about figuring out what the instructor 14 thinks about the subject so that you can cuddle up with him. Chances are his views are no stronger than yours. If he does have convictions and you oppose them, his problem is to keep from grading you higher than you deserve in order to show he is not biased. This doesn't mean that you should always cantankerously dissent from what the instructor says; that gets tiresome too. And if the subject assigned is "My Pet Peeve," do not begin, "My pet peeve is the English instructor who assigns papers on 'my pet peeve.' " This was still funny during the War of 1812, but it has sort of lost its edge since then. It is in general good manners to avoid personalities.

Slip out of Abstraction

If you will study the essay on college football . . . you will per- 15 ceive that one reason for its appalling dullness is that it never gets down to particulars. It is just a series of not very glittering generalities: "football is bad for the colleges," "it has become too commercial," "football is a big business," "it is bad for the players," and so on. Such round phrases thudding against the reader's brain are unlikely to convince him, though they may well render him unconscious.

If you want the reader to believe that college football is bad for 16 the players, you have to do more than say so. You have to display the evil. Take your roommate, Alfred Simkins, the second-string center. Picture poor old Alfy coming home from football practice every evening, bruised and aching, agonizingly tired, scarcely able to shovel the mashed potatoes into his mouth. Let us see him staggering up to the room, getting out his econ textbook, peering desperately at it with his good eye, falling asleep and failing the test in the morning. Let us share his unbearable tension as Saturday draws near. Will he fail, be demoted, lose his monthly allowance, be forced to return to the coal mines? And if he succeeds, what will be his reward? Perhaps a slight ripple of applause when the third-string center replaces him, a moment of elation in the locker room if the team wins, of despair if it loses. What will he look back on when he graduates from college? Toil and torn ligaments. And what will be his future? He is not good enough for pro football, and he is too obscure and weak in econ to succeed in stocks and bonds. College football is tearing the heart from Alfy Simkins and, when it finishes with him, will callously toss aside the shattered hulk.

This is no doubt a weak enough argument for the abolition of 17 college football, but it is a sight better than saying, in three or four variations, that college football (in your opinion) is bad for the players.

Look at the work of any professional writer and notice how con- 18 stantly he is moving from the generality, the abstract statement, to the concrete example, the facts and figures, the illustration. If he is writing on juvenile delinquency, he does not just tell you that juveniles are (it seems to him) delinquent and that (in his opinion) something should be done about it. He shows you juveniles being delinquent, tearing up movie theatres in Buffalo, stabbing high school principals in Dallas, smoking marijuana in Palo Alto. And more than likely he is moving toward some specific remedy, not just a general wringing of the hands.

It is no doubt possible to be *too* concrete, too illustrative or an- 19
ecdotal, but few inexperienced writers err this way. For most the
soundest advice is to be seeking always for the picture, to be always
turning general remarks into seeable examples. Don't say, "Sororities teach girls the social graces." Say, "Sorority life teaches a
girl how to carry on a conversation while pouring tea, without
sloshing the tea into the saucer." Don't say, "I like certain kinds
of popular music very much." Say, "Whenever I hear Gerber
Spinklittle play 'Mississippi Man' on the trombone, my socks creep
up my ankles."

Get Rid of Obvious Padding

The student toiling away at his weekly English theme is too often 20
tormented by a figure: five hundred words. How, he asks himself,
is he to achieve this staggering total? Obviously by never using
one word when he can somehow work in ten.

He is therefore seldom content with a plain statement like "Fast 21
driving is dangerous." This has only four words in it. He takes
thought, and the sentence becomes:

In my opinion, fast driving is dangerous.

Better, but he can do better still:

In my opinion, fast driving would seem to be rather dangerous.

If he is really adept, it may come out:

In my humble opinion, though I do not claim to be an expert on this
complicated subject, fast driving, in most circumstances, would seem
to be rather dangerous in many respects, or at least so it would seem
to me.

Thus four words have been turned into forty, and not an iota of
content has been added.

Now this is a way to go about reaching five hundred words, and 22
if you are content with a "D" grade, it is as good a way as any.

But if you aim higher, you must work differently. Instead of stuffing your sentences with straw, you must try steadily to get rid of the padding, to make your sentences lean and tough. If you are really working at it, your first draft will greatly exceed the required total, and then you will work it down, thus:

> It is thought in some quarters that fraternities do not contribute as much as might be expected to campus life.

> Some people think that fraternities contribute little to campus life.

> The average doctor who practices in small towns or in the country must toil night and day to heal the sick.

> Most country doctors work long hours.

> When I was a little girl, I suffered from shyness and embarrassment in the presence of others.

> I was a shy little girl.

> It is absolutely necessary for the person employed as a marine fireman to give the matter of steam pressure his undivided attention at all times.

> The fireman has to keep his eye on the steam gauge.

You may ask how you can arrive at five hundred words at this rate. Simply. You dig up more real content. Instead of taking a couple of obvious points off the surface of the topic and then circling warily around them for six paragraphs, you work in and explore, figure out the details. You illustrate. You say that fast driving is dangerous, and then you prove it. How long does it take to stop a car at forty and at eighty? How far can you see at night? What happens when a tire blows? What happens in a head-on collision at fifty miles an hour? Pretty soon your paper will be full of broken glass and blood and headless torsos, and reaching five hundred words will not really be a problem.

Call a Fool a Fool

Some of the padding in freshman themes is to be blamed not on anxiety about the word minimum but on excessive timidity. The student writes, "In my opinion, the principal of my high school acted in ways that I believe every unbiased person would have to call foolish." This isn't exactly what he means. What he means is, "My high school principal was a fool." If he was a fool, call him a fool. Hedging the thing about with "in-my-opinion's" and "it-seems-to-me's" and "as-I-see-it's" and "at-least-from-my-point-of-view's" gains you nothing. Delete these phrases whenever they creep into your paper.

The student's tendency to hedge stems from a modesty that in 25 other circumstances would be commendable. He is, he realizes, young and inexperienced, and he half suspects that he is dopey and fuzzy-minded beyond the average. Probably only too true. But it doesn't help to announce your incompetence six times in every paragraph. Decide what you want to say and say it as vigorously as possible, without apology and in plain words.

Linguistic diffidence can take various forms. One is what we call 26 *euphemism.* This is the tendency to call a spade "a certain garden implement" or women's underwear "unmentionables." It is stronger in some eras than others and in some people than others but it always operates more or less in subjects that are touchy or taboo: death, sex, madness, and so on. Thus we shrink from saying "He died last night" but say instead "passed away," "left us," "joined his Maker," "went to his reward." Or we try to take off the tension with a lighter cliché: "kicked the bucket," "cashed in his chips," "handed in his dinner pail." We have found all sorts of ways to avoid saying *mad:* "mentally ill," "touched," "not quite right upstairs," "feeble-minded," "innocent," "simple," "off his trolley," "not in his right mind." Even such a now plain word as *insane* began as a euphemism with the meaning "not healthy."

Modern science, particularly psychology, contributes many 27 polysyllables in which we can wrap our thoughts and blunt their force. To many writers there is no such thing as a bad schoolboy. Schoolboys are maladjusted or unoriented or misunderstood or in need of guidance or lacking in continued success toward satisfactory integration of the personality as a social unit, but they are never bad. Psychology no doubt makes us better men or women, more sympathetic and tolerant, but it doesn't make writing any easier. Had Shakespeare been confronted with psychology, "To be or not to be" might have come out, "To continue as a social unit or not to do so. That is the personality problem. Whether 'tis a better sign of integration at the conscious level to display a psychic tolerance toward the maladjustments and repressions induced by one's lack of orientation in one's environment or—" But Hamlet would never have finished the soliloquy.

Writing in the modern world, you cannot altogether avoid modern jargon. Nor, in an effort to get away from euphemism, should you salt your paper with four-letter words. But you can do much if you will mount guard against those roundabout phrases, those echoing polysyllables that tend to slip into your writing to rob it of its crispness and force. 28

Beware of the Pat Expression

Other things being equal, avoid phrases like "other things being equal." Those sentences that come to you whole, or in two or three doughy lumps, are sure to be bad sentences. They are no creation of yours but pieces of common thought floating in the community soup. 29

Pat expressions are hard, often impossible, to avoid, because they come too easily to be noticed and seem too necessary to be dispensed with. No writer avoids them altogether, but good writers avoid them more often than poor writers. 30

By "pat expressions" we mean such tags as "to all practical intents and purposes," "the pure and simple truth," "from where I sit," "the time of his life," "to the ends of the earth," "in the twinkling of an eye," "as sure as you're born," "over my dead body," "under cover of darkness," "took the easy way out," "when all is said and done," "told him time and time again," "parted the best of friends," "stand up and be counted," "gave him the best years of her life," "worked her fingers to the bone." Like other clichés, these expressions were once forceful. Now we should use them only when we can't possibly think of anything else. 31

Some pat expressions stand like a wall between the writer and thought. Such a one is "the American way of life." Many student writers feel that when they have said that something accords with the American way of life or does not they have exhausted the 32 subject. Actually, they have stopped at the highest level of abstraction. The American way of life is the complicated set of bonds between a hundred and eighty million ways. All of us know this when we think about it, but the tag phrase too often keeps us from thinking about it.

So with many another phrase dear to the politician: "this great ³³ land of ours," "the man in the street," "our national heritage." These may prove our patriotism or give a clue to our political beliefs, but otherwise they add nothing to the paper except words.

Colorful Words

The writer builds with words, and no builder uses a raw material ³⁴ more slippery and elusive and treacherous. A writer's work is a constant struggle to get the right word in the right place, to find that particular word that will convey his meaning exactly, that will persuade the reader or soothe him or startle or amuse him. He never succeeds altogether—sometimes he feels that he scarcely succeeds at all—but such successes as he has are what make the thing worth doing.

There is no book of rules for this game. One progresses through ³⁵ everlasting experiment on the basis of ever-widening experience. There are few useful generalizations that one can make about words as words, but there are perhaps a few.

Some words are what we call "colorful." By this we mean that ³⁶ they are calculated to produce a picture or induce an emotion. They are dressy instead of plain, specific instead of general, loud instead of soft. Thus, in place of "Her heart beat," we may write "Her heart *pounded, throbbed, fluttered, danced.*" Instead of "He sat in his chair," we may say, "He *lounged, sprawled, coiled.*" Instead of "It was hot," we may say, "It was *blistering, sultry, muggy, suffocating, steamy, wilting.*"

However, it should not be supposed that the fancy word is always better. Often it is as well to write "Her heart beat" or "It was ³⁷ hot" if that is all it did or all it was. Ages differ in how they like their prose. The nineteenth century liked it rich and smoky. The twentieth has usually preferred it lean and cool. The twentieth-century writer, like all writers, is forever seeking the exact word, but he is wary of sounding feverish. He tends to pitch it low, to understate it, to throw it away. He knows that if he gets too colorful, the audience is likely to giggle.

See how this strikes you: "As the rich, golden glow of the sunset 38 died away along the eternal western hills, Angela's limpid blue eyes looked softly and trustingly into Montague's flashing brown ones, and her heart pounded like a drum in time with the joyous song surging in her soul." Some people like that sort of thing, but most modern readers would say, "Good grief," and turn on the television.

Colored Words

Some words we would call not so much colorful as colored— 39 that is, loaded with associations, good or bad. All words—except perhaps structure words—have associations of some sort. We have said that the meaning of a word is the sum of the contexts in which it occurs. When we hear a word, we hear with it an echo of all the situations in which we have heard it before.

In some words, these echoes are obvious and discussable. The 40 word *mother*, for example, has, for most people, agreeable associations. When you hear *mother* you probably think of home, safety, love, food, and various other pleasant things. If one writes, "She was like a mother to me," he gets an effect which he would not get in "She was like an aunt to me." The advertiser makes use of the associations of *mother* by working it in when he talks about his product. The politician works it in when he talks about himself.

So also with such words as *home, liberty, fireside, contentment,* 41 *patriot, tenderness, sacrifice, childlike, manly, bluff, limpid.* All of these words are loaded with favorable associations that would be rather hard to indicate in a straightforward definition. There is more than a literal difference between "They sat around the fireside" and "They sat around the stove." They might have been equally warm and happy around the stove, but *fireside* suggests leisure, grace, quiet tradition, congenial company, and *stove* does not.

Conversely, some words have bad associations. *Mother* suggests 42 pleasant things, but *mother-in-law* does not. Many mothers-in-law are heroically lovable and some mothers drink gin all day and beat their children insensible, but these facts of life are beside the point. The thing is that *mother* sounds good and *mother-in-law* does not.

Or consider the word *intellectual*. This would seem to be a com- 43 plimentary term, but in point of fact it is not, for it has picked up associations of impracticality and ineffectuality and general dopiness. So also with such words as *liberal, reactionary, Communist, Socialist, capitalist, radical, schoolteacher, truck driver, undertaker, operator, salesman, huckster, speculator*. These convey meanings on the literal level, but beyond that—sometimes, in some places—they convey contempt on the part of the speaker.

The question of whether to use loaded words or not depends 44 on what is being written. The scientist, the scholar, try to avoid them; for the poet, the advertising writer, the public speaker, they are standard equipment. But every writer should take care that they do not substitute for thought. If you write, "Anyone who thinks that is nothing but a Socialist (or Communist or capitalist)" you have said nothing except that you don't like people who think that, and such remarks are effective only with the most naïve readers. It is always a bad mistake to think your readers more naïve than they really are.

Colorless Words

But probably most student writers come to grief not with words 45 that are colorful or those that are colored but with those that have no color at all. A pet example is *nice*, a word we would find it hard to dispense with in casual conversation but which is no longer capable of adding much to a description. Colorless words are those of such general meaning that in a particular sentence they mean nothing. Slang adjectives, like *cool* ("That's real cool") tend to explode all over the language. They are applied to everything, lose their original force, and quickly die.

Beware also of nouns of very general meaning, like *circumstances,* 46 *cases, instances, aspects, factors, relationships, attitudes, eventualities,* etc. In most circumstances you will find that those cases of writing which contain too many instances of words like these will in this and other aspects have factors leading to unsatisfactory relationships with the reader resulting in unfavorable attitudes on his part and perhaps other eventualities, like a grade of "D." Notice also what "etc." means. It means "I'd like to make this list longer, but I can't think of any more examples."

Questions on Subject

1. According to Roberts, what is the job of the writer? Why, in particular, is it difficult for college students to do this job well? Discuss how your college experience leads you to agree or disagree with Roberts.
2. The author offers several "tricks" of good writing in his essay. What are they? Do you find some of them more useful than others? Explain.
3. If, according to Roberts, a good writer never uses unnecessary words, what then are the legitimate ways a student can reach the goal of a 500-word essay?
4. How has modern psychology made it more difficult to write well?

Questions on Strategy

1. Make a scratch outline of Roberts's essay. What are the similarities between his organization of material and the process analyses he outlines for students? Explain. (Glossary: *Organization*)
2. Roberts's writing style is clearly well suited to his student audience. How would you describe his writing style? What are some of the ways he uses humor, diction, and illustration to make the process analyses easy to follow? (Glossary: *Diction; Illustration*)
3. What kind of information does the title of Roberts's essay lead you to expect? Does the author deliver what he promises in the title? Why do you think he chose this title?

Questions on Diction and Vocabulary

1. Roberts wrote this essay over thirty years ago. Is there anything in his diction that gives this away, or does his writing sound contemporary? Choose examples from the text to support your answer. (Glossary: *Diction*)
2. Refer to your desk dictionary to determine the meanings of the

following words as they are used in this selection: *contrive* (paragraph 6), *bromides* (7), *tedious* (7), *inexorably* (8), *trite* (10), *cogent* (10), *vacuity* (11), *cantankerously* (14), *iota* (21), *diffidence* (26), *soliloquy* (27).

Writing Assignments

1. Pick up a copy of your college newspaper and find an article that uses the dull, limp writing Roberts talks about. Using an editor's eye (almost everyone can edit other people's writing), rewrite the article eliminating unnecessary words, substituting colorful verbs and adjectives for dull ones, and perhaps even shifting the focus of the article to make it more interesting. Then consider how you can edit your own writing in this way.
2. In paragraph 16, Roberts explains how a brief but good essay on college football might be written. He obeys the first rule of good writing—show don't tell. Thus, instead of a dry lump of words, his essay uses humor, exaggeration, and particulars to breathe life into the football player. Review Roberts's tricks for good writing, choose one of the dull topics he suggests or one of your own, and, following the steps he lays out in his essay, write a 500-word process analysis.

Building Fence
Maxine Kumin

Maxine Kumin was born in 1925, and earned a B.A. at Radcliffe College. Kumin lived outside Boston while she wrote and raised her family of three children. In 1976 she and her husband moved to New Hampshire. Their farm there—with its horses, sheep, and vegetable garden—inspires much of Kumin's writing, which is as ample and diverse as the garden she keeps. Although her main love is poetry, Kumin has also written children's books, four novels, a collection of short stories, and two volumes of essays—most recently In Deep *(1987), from which the following selection is taken. Among her eight books of poetry are* Up Country, *which won the Pulitzer Prize in 1973, her selected poems,* Our Ground Time Here Will Be Brief *(1982), and* The Long Approach *(1985).*

In the following selection, Kumin reveals not only the technique needed to erect a fence, but the sentiment and attitudes that compel such an undertaking.

When I look left or right, I yearn for pastures with daisies and   1
black-eyed Susans, hawkweed and Indian paintbrush visible at the far
edges. Fields someone has paid attention to. The terrain is too hilly
for mechanized equipment except for our ancient Gravely walk-behind
rotary mower and the jackhammer-heavy weed whacker. It is the surprise of clearings come upon in the midst of tangled, second-growth
forest. These New England upland pastures are like a secret garden,
like the impulse toward a poem. Every dip and scarp is engraved now
on my brainpan.

Making fences presupposes not only pastures but a storehouse   2
of diligence. When you start from a tangle of sumac and blackberry,
every reclaimed square yard seems more precious than an acre of
riverbottom land. For a dozen years we've been pushing back the
forest, clearing, seeding, and sustaining what now adds up to four-

227

teen up-and-down acres of the once two hundred-odd that nurtured a dairy herd between the two world wars.

Building the fence itself is an imperfect science. Despite actual 3 measurements, you have to yield to the contours of the land. Post holes are soul destroyers. Technology hasn't done much for the fence line on a hill farm. Even if you hire a neighbor's tractor with auger attachment, at least half the holes will have to be handcrafted as you ease them this side or that of expectation. Stones annoy, rocks impede, boulders break your heart as you tunnel down at a slant, hunting in vain for the earth bottom. If obdurate ledge or obstinate pudding stone does not require acts of faith and leaps of imagination, here and there you can count on a slope too steep for machinery to navigate. The gasoline-powered two-man auger is more adaptable, but even that ingenious tool will not maneuver between stump and bedrock with the same agility as the old manual clamshell tool.

Setting the posts exacts more faith from the dogged fence- 4 pilgrim. Somehow there is never enough dirt in the pile you took out, even after you've placed a ring of stones in the bottom of the hole to brace the post. Even with a ring of stones stomped in nearly at the top for further support, your supply of loose dirt has vanished. You end up digging part of a second hole to make enough friable earth to hold the first pole solid. Clearly, you do not come out even.

You've set 225 posts, roughly ten feet apart. From an appropriate 5 distance, if you squint, it's merely a toothpick stockade, inconclusive and raw-looking. You long to get on with it, to establish the feeling of fence, the ethos of enclosure.

The best part of building the fence is tacking up the string that 6 denotes where the line of top boards means to be. You go around importantly to do this light work, trailing your ball of twine, wearing your apron of nails. You measure with your fold-up rule fifty-two inches from the ground—but where exactly *is* the ground? This mound, this declivity, this solitary flat patch? You tap in a nail, pull the string taut from the previous post, catch it with a few easy twists around, and so on. String stands in for wood, a notion, a suggestion of what's to come. Foreshadowing, you could call it.

Because this is New England, the fence travels uphill and down; 7 only little bits of it are on the level. Although string lightheartedly imitates the contours of the land, boards have to be held in place, the angle of cut defined by pencil. Invariably, both ends of the boards want cutting. The eye wants readjustments despite the ruler. Sometimes bottom boards catch on hummocks, outcroppings, or earth bulges which must be shoveled out or the board rearranged. But let's say you've tacked up your whole top line for the day, you've stepped back, eyeballed and readjusted it. Oh, the hammering home! The joy and vigor of sending nails through hemlock into the treated four-by-four uprights. Such satisfying whacks, such permanence, such vengeance against the mass bustications of horses and heifers through the puny electric wire of yore. Visions of acres and acres of fences, field after field tamed, groomed, boarded in; that is the meaning of gluttony.

Finishing the fence—painting, staining, or applying preservative—requires the same constancy as the slow crafting of it. You put in your two hours a day, rejoice when rain interrupts the schedule and your Calvinist soul is permitted to tackle some other chore. Cleaning tack, for example, provides a pleasurable monotony compared to the servitude of the four-inch roller and the can of Noxious Mixture. In our case, it's composed of one-third diesel oil, one-third used crankcase oil, and one-third creosote. You are properly garbed to apply this Grade C syrup, wearing cast-off overalls, a battered felt hat, decayed boots, and thick neoprene gloves. You stand almost an arm's length away from the fence in order to get enough leverage so the mixture will penetrate wood grain—here tough, there smooth, here cracked and warty, there slick as a duck's feather. You invent methods for relieving the dreary sameness of the job. On one course you begin left to right, top to bottom, back to front. On the next you reverse the order. Sometimes you do all the undersides first, or all the backs. Sometimes you spring ahead, lavishly staining all the front-facing boards just to admire the dark wood lines dancing against the hummocky terrain of these young—yea, virginal—fields. The process gets you in the shoulder blades, later in the knees. You spatter freckles of the stuff on your protected body. Your protective eyeglasses are now freckled with iridescent dots. The stench of the mix permeates your hair, your gloved hands, becomes a way of life. You can no longer gain a new day without putting in your two hours staining board fences.

More compelling than tobacco or alcohol, that addictive odor of char, of disinfectant, of grease pits. The horses follow you along the fence line, curious, but even the fresh-faced filly keeps a respectful distance from you and your repellent mixture.

A year later you sit atop the remnants of a six-foot-wide stone 9 wall unearthed along the perimeter of number two field and look across to the remarkable pear tree that stands alone in the third and newest field. Behind you, the first field; behind it, the barn. Between fields, hedgerow and hickory trees, red pine and hemlock. An intermittent brook further defines the boundary between number one and number two. A tributary meanders at the foot of number three. Beyond, a lifetime of second-growth woodland awaits. In your mind's eye, an infinity of fenced fields recedes but never vanishes. And all the livestock of a lifetime safely graze.

Questions on Subject

1. Why is reclaimed land more precious to Kumin than riverbottom land?
2. In what ways is building a fence an "imperfect science"?
3. What does Kumin mean in paragraph 3 when she says that post holes will have to be handcrafted "as you ease them this side and that of expectation"?
4. In paragraph 6 Kumin describes "the meaning of gluttony." What is she referring to and what does she mean by her statement? What other kinds of forces compel people to build fences according to Kumin?
5. Explain Kumin's use of the phrase, "the Calvinist soul," in paragraph 8.
6. How is Kumin able to relieve the "dreariness" of fence painting? What makes this distasteful task compelling for her?

Questions on Strategy

1. What are the several different tasks Kumin describes? For which of them has she included a process analysis?
2. Does Kumin intend her process analysis to instruct or to explain or both? How do you know?

3. How has Kumin organized her essay? (Glossary: *Organization*)
4. Kumin's essay reveals as much about the author as it does about the many tasks she describes. Select details from the essay that are telling aspects of the author's nature.
5. What is the tone of Kumin's essay? Does it remain the same throughout the essay? Explain. (Glossary: *Tone*)

Questions on Diction and Vocabulary

1. Cite details of Kumin's diction that you found unexpected or challenging, and explain what they add to her essay.
2. Kumin makes effective use of figurative language. For example, she says "Stones annoy, rocks impede, boulders break your heart" (3), "the fence travels uphill and down; . . . string lightheartedly imitates the contours of the land" (7), and "this Grade C syrup" (8). Locate other figures of speech and comment on their contribution to this essay.
3. Refer to your dictionary to determine the meanings of the following words as they are used in this selection: *scarp* (paragraph 1), *diligence* (2), *auger* (3), *impede* (3), *obdurate* (3), *obstinate* (3), *ingenious* (3), *friable* (4), *squint* (5), *ethos* (5), *denotes* (6), *declivity* (6), *hummocks* (7), *bustications* (7), *puny* (7), *warty* (8), *repellent* (8).

Writing Suggestions

1. Kumin describes the technique she uses to relieve the boredom of fence painting. Recall a job you find boring or tedious, and describe the steps you take to add variety and interest to an otherwise impossible task. For example, you might write about cleaning your room, mowing the lawn, paying your bills, or grocery shopping.
2. Kumin writes about the need people have to build fences. Almost all of us feel a need to "fence off" our territory, whether it be acres of land or our side of a dormitory room. Write an essay in which you include not only a process analysis of some territorial activity you have experienced, but the feelings that compel that activity.

Going to the Gym

Anna Quindlen

> *Columnist Anna Quindlen was born in 1952. She began her newspaper writing career at the New York Post after graduating from Barnard College. Later she worked for the New York Times, writing the column "About New York," a series of vignettes about New York City neighborhoods and culture. Quindlen became deputy metropolitan editor when she was thirty-one and soon began writing the column "Life in the Thirties." Here she reflected on the inner thoughts and doubts that arise in the attempt to balance a career with the demands of marriage and motherhood. The best of these essays were collected in her book* Living Out Loud *(1988). Quindlen has also been a frequent contributor to the "Hers" column of the* Times *and currently writes the "Private and Public" column for the* Times, *in which she interprets global issues on a personal level. In 1992 she was awarded a Pulitzer Prize for her column. Quindlen is also the author of a novel,* Object Lessons.*
>
> *In the following essay, Quindlen takes a lighthearted look at the reasons and rewards for her interest in "working out."*

For most of my life I have pursued a policy toward my body that 1
could best be characterized as benign neglect. From the time I could
remember until the time I was 15 it looked one way, and from the
time I was 15 until I was 30 it looked another way. Then in the
space of two years, I had two children and more weight changes
than Ted Kennedy, and my body headed south without me.

This is how I began to work out. I work out for a very simple 2
reason, and it is not because it makes me feel invigorated and
refreshed. The people who say that exercise is important because
it makes you feel wonderful are the same people who say a mink
coat is nice because it keeps you warm. Show me a woman who
wears a mink coat to keep warm and who exercises because it feels

good and I'll show you Jane Fonda. I wear a mink coat because it is a mink coat, and I work out so that my husband will not gasp when he runs into me in the bathroom and run off with an 18-year-old who looks as good out of her clothes as in them. It's as simple as that.

So I go to this gym three times a week, and here is how it works. First I go into the locker room. On the wall is an extremely large photograph of a person named Terri Jones wearing what I can only assume is meant to be a bathing suit. The caption above her body says Slim Strong and Sexy. It is accurate. I check to make sure no one else is in the locker room, then I take my clothes off. As soon as I've done this, one of two people will enter the locker room: either an 18-year-old who looks as good out of her clothes as in them who spontaneously confides in me that she is having an affair with a young lawyer whose wife has really gone to seed since she had her two kids, or a 50-year-old woman who has had nine children, weighs 105 and has abdominal muscles you could bounce a quarter off and who says she can't understand why, maybe it's her metabolism, but she can eat anything she wants, including a pint of Frusen Glädjé Swiss chocolate almond candy ice cream, and never gain a pound. So then I go out and exercise.

I do Nautilus. It is a series of fierce looking machines, each designed, according to this book I have, to exercise some distinct muscle group, which all happen in my case never to have been exercised before. Nautilus was allegedly invented by Arthur Jones, husband of the aforementioned slim and strong and sexy Terri, who is his 17th wife or something like that. But I think anyone who comes upon a Nautilus machine suddenly will agree with me that its prototype was clearly invented at some time in history when torture was considered a reasonable alternative to diplomacy. Over each machine is a little drawing of a human body—not mine, of course—with a certain muscle group inked in red. This is so you can recognize immediately the muscle group that is on fire during the time you are using the machine.

There is actually supposed to be a good reason to do Nautilus, and it is supposed to be that it results in toning without bulk. That is, you will look like a dancer, not a defensive lineman. That may be compelling for Terri Jones, but I chose it because it takes me only a little more than a half hour—or what I like to think of as the time an average person burning calories at an average rate would need to read "Where the Wild Things Are," "Good Night Moon" and "The Cat in the Hat" twice—to finish all the machines. It is also not social, like aerobics classes, and will not hold you up to widespread ridicule, like running. I feel about exercise the same way that I feel about a few other things: that there is nothing wrong with it if it is done in private by consenting adults.

Actually, there are some of the Nautilus machines I even like.   6
Call it old-fashioned machisma, but I get a kick out of building biceps. This is a throwback to all those times when my brothers would flex their arms and a mound of muscle would appear, and I would flex mine and nothing would happen, and they'd laugh and go off somewhere to smoke cigarettes and look at dirty pictures. There's a machine to exercise the inner thigh muscles that bears such a remarkable resemblance to a delivery room apparatus that every time I get into it I think someone is going to yell push and I will have another baby. I feel comfortable with that one. On the other hand, there is another machine on which I am supposed to lift a weight straight up in the air and the most I ever manage is squinching my face up until I look like an infant with bad gas. My instructor explained to me that this is because women have no upper body strength, which probably explains why I've always found it somewhat difficult to carry a toddler and an infant up four flights of stairs with a diaper bag over one shoulder while holding a Big Wheel.

Anyhow, the great thing about working out is that I have met   7
a lot of very nice men. This would be a lot more important if I weren't married and the mother of two. But of course if I was single and looking to meet someone, I would never meet anyone except married men and psychopaths. (This is Murphy's Other Law, named after a Doreen Murphy, who in 1981 had a record 11 bad relationships in one year.) The men I have met seem to really get a kick out of the fact that I work out, not unlike the kick that most of us get out of hearing very small children try to say words like hippopotamus or chauvinist. As one of the men at my gym said, "Most of the people here are guys or women who are uh well hmm umm. . . ."

"In good shape," I said.   8

"I wouldn't have put it like that," he answered.   9

Because I go to the gym at the same time on the same days, I 10
actually see the same men over and over again. One or two of them
are high school students, which I find truly remarkable. When I
was in high school, it was a big deal if a guy had shoulders, never
mind muscles. So when I'm finished I go back into the locker room
and take a shower. The 18-year-old is usually in there, and sometimes she'll say something like, "Oh, that's what stretch marks
look like." Then I put on my clothes and go home by the route
that does not pass Dunkin' Donuts. The bottom line is that I really
hate to exercise but I have found on balance that this working out
is all worth it. One day we were walking down the street and one
of the guys from my gym—it was actually one of the high school
guys, the one with the great pecs—walked by and said, "How ya
doing?" My husband said, "Who the hell is that guy?" and I knew
that Nautilus had already made a big difference in my life.

Questions on Subject

1. According to Quindlen, what is the "real" reason people work out?
   Do you agree or disagree?
2. What is the "Nautilus" weight system? What is its chief benefit
   over other systems supposed to be? Why does Quindlen like it?
3. What myth about female strength does Quindlen debunk? How
   does she do it?
4. What makes "working out" worth it for Quindlen?

Questions on Strategy

1. Who are the different people Quindlen encounters at the gym?
   How do these different types function in the context of her essay?
   (Glossary: *Classification*)
2. At what point in her essay does Quindlen reveal the process analysis she will describe? What kind of process analysis is it?
3. Quindlen includes a great deal of information that has no direct
   relevance to her subject. Cite examples of this additional information, and explain why you think she includes it.
4. Paragraph 3 of Quindlen's essay is comprised almost entirely of
   one sentence. What kind of information does she include in this

sentence? Why do you suppose Quindlen chose to present this information in this way?

5. Locate and identify the transitional phrases Quindlen uses to move from one step of her process analysis to another. How well do these phrases work? (Glossary: *Transitions*)

Questions on Diction and Vocabulary

1. Describe the tone of this essay. How does Quindlen establish this tone? In what way is Quindlen's tone appropriate to her audience and subject? (Glossary: *Tone*)

2. Refer to your dictionary to determine the meanings of the following words as they are used in this selection: *benign* (paragraph 1), *invigorated* (2), *distinct* (4), *prototype* (4), *apparatus* (6), *psychopaths* (7).

Writing Suggestions

1. One reason for the popularity of Anna Quindlen's column "Life in the Thirties" was her ability to write about her own life in a way that made it possible for readers her age to identify on a personal level with the various emotions and issues she faced. In an essay of your own, offer a process analysis you and your peers can identify with, such as preparing to write a term paper, working up the courage to call someone for a date, or applying for a job. Remember to include the kind of details that reveal not only the essential process, but the attitudes and emotions that accompany it.

2. Almost everyone knows someone who is a devoted disciple of America's "fitness craze." Write an essay about the habits of someone you know (perhaps yourself), who has made keeping fit a way of life.

The Spider and the Wasp

Alexander Petrunkevitch

Alexander Petrunkevitch (1875–1964), a Russian-born zo-ologist, was a leading authority on spiders. He published his first important work, The Index Catalogue of Spiders of North, Central, and South America, *in 1911. In addition to his scientific research, Petrunkevitch was widely recognized for his accomplished translations of English and Russian poetry.*

In this essay, first published in 1952 in Scientific Amer-ican, *Petrunkevitch describes the way in which the "intelli-gence" of digger wasps is pitted against the "instincts" of tarantula spiders.*

In the feeding and safeguarding of their progeny insects and spiders exhibit some interesting analogies to reasoning and some crass examples of blind instinct. The case I propose to describe here is that of the tarantula spiders and their arch-enemy, the dig-ger wasps of the genus Pepsis. It is a classic example of what looks like intelligence pitted against instinct—a strange situation in which the victim, though fully able to defend itself, submits un-wittingly to its destruction.

Most tarantulas live in the tropics, but several species occur in the temperate zone and a few are common in the southern U.S. Some varieties are large and have powerful fangs with which they can inflict a deep wound. These formidable looking spiders do not, however, attack man; you can hold one in your hand, if you are gentle, without being bitten. Their bite is dangerous only to insects and small mammals such as mice; for man it is no worse than a hornet's sting.

Tarantulas customarily live in deep cylindrical burrows, from which they emerge at dusk and into which they retire at dawn. Mature males wander about after dark in search of females and occasionally stray into houses. After mating, the male dies in a few weeks, but a female lives much longer and can mate several years in succession. In a Paris museum is a tropical specimen which is said to have been living in captivity for 25 years.

A fertilized female tarantula lays from 200 to 400 eggs at a time; thus it is possible for a single tarantula to produce several thousand young. She takes no care of them beyond weaving a cocoon of silk to enclose the eggs. After they hatch, the young walk away, find convenient places in which to dig their burrows and spend the rest of their lives in solitude. The eyesight of tarantulas is poor, being limited to a sensing of change in the intensity of light and to the perception of moving objects. They apparently have little or no sense of hearing, for a hungry tarantula will pay no attention to a loudly chirping cricket placed in its cage unless the insect happens to touch one of its legs. 4

But all spiders, and especially hairy ones, have an extremely delicate sense of touch. Laboratory experiments prove that tarantulas can distinguish three types of touch: pressure against the body wall, stroking of the body hair, and riffling of certain very fine hairs on the legs called trichobothria. Pressure against the body, by the finger or the end of a pencil, causes the tarantula to move off slowly for a short distance. The touch excites no defensive response unless the approach is from above where the spider can see the motion, in which case it rises on its hind legs, lifts its front legs, opens its fangs and holds this threatening posture as long as the object continues to move. 5

The entire body of a tarantula, especially its legs, is thickly clothed with hair. Some of it is short and woolly, some long and stiff. Touching this body hair produces one of two distinct reactions. When the spider is hungry, it responds with an immediate and swift attack. At the touch of a cricket's antennae the tarantula seizes the insect so swiftly that a motion picture taken at the rate of 64 frames per second shows only the result and not the process of capture. But when the spider is not hungry, the stimulation of its hairs merely causes it to shake the touched limb. An insect can walk under its hairy belly unharmed. 6

The trichobothria, very fine hairs growing from disclike membranes on the legs, are sensitive only to air movement. A light breeze makes them vibrate slowly, without disturbing the common hair. When one blows gently on the trichobothria, the tarantula 7 reacts with a quick jerk of its four front legs. If the front and hind legs are stimulated at the same time, the spider makes a sudden jump. This reaction is quite independent of the state of its appetite.

These three tactile responses—to pressure on the body wall, to 8 moving of the common hair, and to flexing of the trichobothria— are so different from one another that there is no possibility of confusing them. They serve the tarantula adequately for most of its needs and enable it to avoid most annoyances and dangers. But they fail the spider completely when it meets its deadly enemy, the digger wasp Pepsis.

These solitary wasps are beautiful and formidable creatures. 9 Most species are either a deep shiny blue all over, or deep blue with rusty wings. The largest have a wing span of about four inches. They live on nectar. When excited, they give off a pungent odor—a warning that they are ready to attack. The sting is much worse than that of a bee or common wasp, and the pain and swelling last longer. In the adult stage the wasp lives only a few months. The female produces but a few eggs, one at a time at intervals of two or three days. For each egg the mother must provide one adult tarantula, alive but paralyzed. The mother wasp attaches the egg to the paralyzed spider's abdomen. Upon hatching from the egg, the larva is many hundreds of times smaller than its living but helpless victim. It eats no other food and drinks no water. By the time it has finished its single Gargantuan meal and become ready for wasphood, nothing remains of the tarantula but its indigestible chitinous skeleton.

The mother wasp goes tarantula-hunting when the egg in her 10 ovary is almost ready to be laid. Flying low over the ground late on a sunny afternoon, the wasp looks for its victim or for the mouth of a tarantula burrow, a round hole edged by a bit of silk. The sex of the spider makes no difference, but the mother is highly discriminating as to species. Each species of Pepsis requires a certain species of tarantula, and the wasp will not attack the wrong species. In a cage with a tarantula which is not its normal prey, the wasp avoids the spider and is usually killed by it in the night.

Yet when a wasp finds the correct species, it is the other way 11 about. To identify the species the wasp apparently must explore the spider with her antennae. The tarantula shows an amazing tolerance to this exploration. The wasp crawls under it and walks over it without evoking any hostile response. The molestation is so great and so persistent that the tarantula often rises on all eight legs, as if it were on stilts. It may stand this way for several minutes. Meanwhile the wasp, having satisfied itself that the victim is of the right species, moves off a few inches to dig the spider's grave. Working vigorously with legs and jaws, it excavates a hole 8 to 10 inches deep with a diameter slightly larger than the spider's girth. Now and again the wasp pops out of the hole to make sure that the spider is still there.

When the grave is finished, the wasp returns to the tarantula to 12 complete her ghastly enterprise. First she feels it all over once more with her antennae. Then her behavior becomes more aggressive. She bends her abdomen, protruding her sting, and searches for the soft membrane at the point where the spider's legs join its body—the only spot where she can penetrate the horny skeleton. From time to time, as the exasperated spider slowly shifts ground, the wasp turns on her back and slides along with the aid of her wings, trying to get under the tarantula for a shot at the vital spot. During all this maneuvering, which can last for several minutes, the tarantula makes no move to save itself. Finally the wasp corners it against some obstruction and grasps one of its legs in her powerful jaws. Now at last the harassed spider tries a desperate but vain defense. The two contestants roll over and over on the ground. It is a terrifying sight and the outcome is always the same. The wasp finally manages to thrust her sting into the soft spot and holds it there for a few seconds while she pumps in the poison. Almost immediately the tarantula falls paralyzed on its back. Its legs stop twitching; its heart stops beating. Yet it is not dead, as is shown by the fact that if taken from the wasp it can be restored to some sensitivity by being kept in a moist chamber for several months.

After paralyzing the tarantula, the wasp cleans herself by drag- 13 ging her body along the ground and rubbing her feet, sucks the drop of blood oozing from the wound in the spider's abdomen, then grabs a leg of the flabby, helpless animal in her jaws and drags it down to the bottom of the grave. She stays there for many minutes, sometimes for several hours, and what she does all that time in the dark we do not know. Eventually she lays her egg and attaches it to the side of the spider's abdomen with a sticky secretion. Then she emerges, fills the grave with soil carried bit by bit in her jaws, and finally tramples the ground all around to hide any trace of the grave from prowlers. Then she flies away, leaving her descendant safely started in life.

In all this the behavior of the wasp evidently is qualitatively 14 different from that of the spider. The wasp acts like an intelligent animal. This is not to say that instinct plays no part or that she reasons as man does. But her actions are to the point; they are not automatic and can be modified to fit the situation. We do not know for certain how she identifies the tarantula—probably it is by some olfactory or chemo-tactile sense—but she does it purposefully and does not blindly tackle a wrong species.

On the other hand, the tarantula's behavior shows only con- 15 fusion. Evidently the wasp's pawing gives it no pleasure, for it tries to move away. That the wasp is not simulating sexual stimulation is certain because male and female tarantulas react in the same way to its advances. That the spider is not anesthetized by some odorless secretion is easily shown by blowing lightly at the tarantula and making it jump suddenly. What, then, makes the tarantula behave as stupidly as it does?

No clear, simple answer is available. Possibly the stimulation by 16 the wasp's antennae is masked by a heavier pressure on the spider's body, so that it reacts as when prodded by a pencil. But the explanation may be much more complex. Initiative in attack is not in the nature of tarantulas; most species fight only when cornered so that escape is impossible. Their inherited patterns of behavior apparently prompt them to avoid problems rather than attack them. For example, spiders always weave their webs in three dimensions, and when a spider finds that there is insufficient space to attach certain threads in the third dimension, it leaves the place and seeks another, instead of finishing the web in a single plane. This urge to escape seems to arise under all circumstances, in all phases of life, and to take the place of reasoning. For a spider to change the pattern of its web is as impossible as for an inexperienced man to build a bridge across a chasm obstructing his way.

In a way the instinctive urge to escape is not only easier but often 17 more efficient than reasoning. The tarantula does exactly what is most efficient in all cases except in an encounter with a ruthless and determined attacker dependent for the existence of her own species on killing as many tarantulas as she can lay eggs. Perhaps in this case the spider follows its usual pattern of trying to escape, instead of seizing and killing the wasp, because it is not aware of its danger. In any case, the survival of the tarantula species as a whole is protected by the fact that the spider is much more fertile than the wasp.

Questions on Subject

1. What is Petrunkevitch's purpose in this essay? Where is his purpose revealed? (Glossary: *Purpose*)
2. Petrunkevitch contrasts the behavior of the tarantula with that of the wasp. What significant differences does he note? How are these differences related to his overall purpose in the essay?
3. Briefly describe the process that the mother wasp follows in hunting a tarantula.

Questions on Strategy

1. Petrunkevitch describes the way the wasp hunts the tarantula in order to use it as food for its young. How is the author's description of this process related to his overall purpose in the essay?
2. How has Petrunkevitch organized his essay? You may find it helpful to outline the essay in answering this question. (Glossary: *Organization*)
3. In paragraphs 10–13, Petrunkevitch describes what happens when the wasp encounters the tarantula. How has the author organized this process analysis? What transitional or linking devices has he used to give coherence to his description of the process? (Glossary: *Transitions*)

Questions on Diction and Vocabulary

1. Identify some examples in the text of informal or colloquial expressions (for example, "pitted against" [1]) and impressionistic words and phrases (for example, "ghastly enterprise" [12]), which, while

not appropriate in a technical report, engage the nonscientific reader. What specifically do they add to Petrunkevitch's essay?

2. Refer to your desk dictionary to determine the meanings of the following words as they are used in this selection: *progeny* (paragraph 1), *crass* (1), *unwittingly* (1), *fangs* (2), *riffling* (5), *tactile* (8), *qualitatively* (14).

Writing Assignments

1. Using Petrunkevitch's essay as a model, write an essay in which you describe and explain a recurring natural process—for example, seed germination, bird migration, pollination, hibernation, an eclipse, or digestion.

2. In his essay, Petrunkevitch closely examines the interdependent relationship between the tarantula and the digger wasp. What other interdependent relationships do you know about in your own experience of the natural world? Write an essay in which you explore one of these relationships. What do such relationships seem to tell us about life itself?

Writing Suggestions for Process Analysis

1. Write a directional process analysis on one of the following topics:
   a. how to make chocolate-chip cookies
   b. how to adjust brakes on a bicycle
   c. how to change a tire
   d. how to give a permanent
   e. how to use the memory function on a calculator
   f. how to add, drop, or change a course
   g. how to play a specific card game
   h. how to wash a sweater
   i. how to develop film
   j. how to make a pizza
   k. how to make a long-distance call from a phone booth and charge it to your home phone
   l. how to do batik dyeing
   m. how to select a major course of study
   n. how to winterize a car
   o. how to rent an apartment
   p. how to develop confidence
   q. how to operate a small business
   r. how to run for a student government office
   s. how to do a magic trick
2. Write an informational process analysis on one of the following topics:
   a. how your heart functions
   b. how a United States president is elected
   c. how ice cream is made

d. how a hurricane forms
e. how hailstones are formed
f. how a volcano erupts
g. how the circulatory system works
h. how a camera works
i. how photosynthesis takes place
j. how an atomic bomb works
k. how fertilizer is made
l. how a refrigerator works
m. how water evaporates
n. how flowers bloom
o. how a recession occurs
p. how an automobile is made
q. how a bill becomes law in your state
r. how a caterpillar becomes a butterfly
s. how the judicial appeals process works
t. how a video camera works

6
Comparison and Contrast

What Are Comparison and Contrast?

A *comparison* presents two or more objects, considers them together, and shows in what ways they are alike; a *contrast* shows how the objects differ. These two perspectives, apparently in opposition to each other, actually work so often in conjunction that they are commonly considered a single strategy, called *comparison and contrast* or simply *comparison* for short.

Comparison and contrast are so much a part of daily life that people are often not aware of using them. Whenever you make a choice—what to wear, where to eat, what college to attend, what career to pursue—you implicitly use comparison and contrast to arrive at your decision. Consider an easy choice, like picking what shirt or blouse to wear for the day. You probably have a fair number to choose from, neatly stowed in a drawer. All are comparable in certain ways—they all fit you, they are all clean and ready to wear, and they all reflect your taste in clothes. But they also contrast with each other. Some have short sleeves, others have long; some are lightweight, others are warm; some are plain white or pale blue, others are in bright colors and patterns; one is a DisneyWorld T-shirt, another a sweatshirt stenciled "Property of Tampa Bay Rowdies." Eventually, you select from among them the shirt that suits your purpose, that fits where you are going, who you will see, and the weather you will be passing through on the way. You make your choice by comparing and contrasting the items in your wardrobe, even though you may not consciously realize exactly what you are doing.

The strategy of comparison and contrast works best when the objects under discussion belong to the same class or general category of things: four makes of car, for example, or two candidates for the Senate. (See Section 8, "Division and Classification," for a fuller discussion of classes.) Such objects are said to be comparable, or to have a strong *basis for comparison*. (A special form of comparison called *analogy* reveals likenesses between objects that belong to different classes and seem to have little in common, such as *life* and *a lottery*. But, because analogy has a different kind of effect on readers and calls for a different kind of thought in writers, it is discussed separately in Section 7.)

Once a basis for comparison has been established, an effective comparison and contrast does not dwell on obvious similarities and differences; rather, it tells readers something significant that they do not already know. As a rule, therefore, writers tend to emphasize either the contrast between obviously similar objects or the comparison between objects usually thought to be quite different. For example, although an essay about Minneapolis and St. Paul might begin by showing why they are called the Twin Cities, it would likely give more attention to the contrasts that reveal how much the two communities differ. On the other hand, a consumer magazine might mention the contrasting claims made for a dozen different brands of frozen dinners, but the purpose of the article would be to demonstrate that, under all the packaging, the products are very much the same.

Why Do Writers Use Comparison and Contrast?

Comparison and contrast can serve a number of writing purposes. One of these is to inform, to point out similarities or differences that are interesting in themselves. Bruce Catton's essay "Grant and Lee: A Study in Contrasts," which appears later in this section, is primarily informative. A writer may also seek to emphasize the particular qualities of two types of people by comparing and contrasting them, as Lance Morrow does in "Busybody and

Crybaby." Another use of comparison and contrast is to explain the unfamiliar in terms of the familiar; yet another is to evaluate, to show that an object is not only different from but better than others of its kind, whether kitchen appliances or tennis players. Finally, comparison and contrast can be used in various ways to make a persuasive point. Student writer Barbara Bowman does this in her essay "Guns and Cameras," setting up a comparison between hunting and photography to show that there is an alternative to killing animals for sport.

What to Look for in Reading an Essay of Comparison and Contrast

First, determine what objects are being compared and the basis of comparison; then consider why and how the comparisons are made. Sometimes the subjects of the comparison will be clear from the beginning, as in Catton's "Grant and Lee: A Study in Contrasts." At other times you may be well into your reading before you even realize that the author is using comparison and contrast. In the following selection from *Why They Behave Like Russians* by John Fischer, the author declares his subject and strategy in the first sentence:

The Ukrainians are the Texans of Russia. They believe they can fight, drink, ride, sing, and make love better than anybody else in the world, and if pressed will admit it. Their country, too, was a borderland—that's what "Ukraine" means—and like Texas it was originally settled by outlaws, horse thieves, land-hungry farmers, and people who hadn't made a go of it somewhere else. Some of these hard cases banded together, long ago, to raise hell and livestock. They called themselves Cossacks, and they would have felt right at home in any Western movie. Even today the Ukrainians cherish a wistful tradition of horsemanship, although most of them would feel as uncomfortable in a saddle as any Dallas banker. They still like to wear knee-high boots and big, furry hats, made of gray or black Persian lamb, which are the local equivalent of the Stetson.

Even the country looks a good deal like Texas—flat, dry prairie, shading off in the south to semidesert. Through the middle runs a strip of dark, rich soil, the Chernozom Belt, which is almost identical with the black waxy soil of central Texas. It grows the best wheat in the Soviet Union. The Ukraine is also famous for its cattle, sheep, and cotton, and—again like Texas—it has been in the throes of an industrial boom for the last twenty years. On all other people the Ukrainians look with a sort of kindly pity. They might have thought up for their own use the old Western rule of etiquette: "Never ask a man where he comes from. If he's a Texan, he'll tell you; if he's not, don't embarrass him."

It is immediately clear that these paragraphs compare the Soviet region of the Ukraine with the state of Texas and the people of the Ukraine with Texans. Close attention to the writer's methods reveals further information.

What is Fischer's basis of comparison? Both objects are members of the same class or general category, *geographic regions and their people.*

What is the purpose of this comparison? Fischer helps us understand an unfamiliar region, the Ukraine, by comparing it with a more familiar one, Texas.

What comparisons does he make? There are almost too many points of comparison to count—six in the second sentence alone—but they can be summed up in this way: paragraph 1 compares the self-image of Ukrainians with that of Texans, the early history of each group, and their current life-style; paragraph 2 compares the geography of the two regions and ends with a comparison of Ukrainian and Texan attitudes toward the rest of the world. Often the comparisons are explicit, as when Fischer says, "Even the country looks a good deal like Texas—flat, dry prairie, shading off in the south to semidesert." Sometimes, however, the comparison may be implicit, taking for granted what readers already know. In the second sentence, Fischer suggests that Ukrainians "believe they can fight, drink, ride, sing, and make love better than anybody else . . ."; he assumes that his readers know Texan mythology well enough to spot his implied comparison.

How does Fischer organize his comparison? He uses a pattern called *point-by-point comparison.* He starts by comparing both objects in terms of a particular point, then moves on to a second point and compares both objects, then moves on to a third point, and so on.

The other way to organize a comparison is called *block comparison*. In this pattern the information about one object is gathered into a block, which is set against a block of comparable information about the second object. Here is an example of block comparison, from "There are 00 Trees in Russia" by Otto Friedrich:

> There is an essential difference between a news story, as understood by a newspaperman or a wire-service writer, and a newsmagazine story. The chief purpose of the conventional news story is to tell what happened. It starts with the most important information and continues into increasingly inconsequential details, not only because the reader may not read beyond the first paragraph, but because an editor working on galley proofs a few minutes before press time likes to be able to cut freely from the end of the story.
>
> A newsmagazine is very different. It is written to be read consecutively from beginning to end, and each of its stories is designed, following the critical theories of Edgar Allan Poe, to create one emotional effect. The news, what happened that week, may be told in the beginning, the middle, or the end; for the purpose is not to throw information at the reader but to seduce him into reading the whole story, and into accepting the dramatic (and often political) point being made.

A quick reading of Friedrich's paragraphs shows that his objects of comparison are a newspaper story and a newsmagazine story; both of these certainly belong to the same class. But what is Friedrich's purpose? First of all, he offers information about particular journalistic practices his readers may not be aware of. He also uses his comparison for emphasis, to strengthen a reader's sense of each kind of news story by contrasting it with the other. He may even have a further purpose in mind: to persuade his reader that newsmagazine stories tend to be more biased than the standard newspaper story.

Each pattern of comparison, point-by-point and block, has its own advantages and disadvantages. Point-by-point comparison allows the reader to grasp fairly easily the specific points of comparison the author is making; it may be harder, though, to pull together the details and form a distinct impression of what each object is like. The block comparison, on the other hand, guarantees that each object will receive a more unified discussion; however, the points of comparison between the different objects may be less clear. (These two patterns of organization are discussed more fully on pages 254–255.)

Writing an Essay of Comparison and Contrast

As you choose your objects of comparison and contrast, keep in mind the requirements of this writing strategy. These requirements, along with your purpose for using the strategy, will guide you as you plan, write, and revise your essay.

1. Objects

Remember that the objects of your comparison should be in the same class or general category—that you should be able to define a clear basis for comparison. (There are any number of possible classes, such as particular types of persons, places, and things, as well as occupations, activities, philosophies, points in history, even concepts and internal qualities.) Remember also that, if the similarities and differences between the objects are all simply obvious, the reader of the essay is certain to be bored.

2. Purpose

Suppose you choose to compare and contrast solar energy with wind energy. It is clear that both are members of the same class, *energy*, so there is a basis for comparing them; there also seem to be enough interesting differences to make a comparison and contrast possible. But before going any further, you must ask yourself *why* you want to compare and contrast these particular objects. Do you want to inform, to emphasize, to explain, to evaluate, to persuade? Do you have more than one purpose? Whatever your purpose, it will influence the content and organization of your comparison.

Comparing and contrasting solar and wind energy, you will certainly provide information; but more than likely you will also want to evaluate—to determine whether one or the other or both is a practical means of producing significant amounts of energy. You may also want to persuade your readers that one technology is superior to the other.

3. Points of Comparison

What qualities and features of your chosen objects do you want to base your comparison on? At this stage, if you don't yet know very much about the objects of your comparison, you may only be able to guess. Perhaps wind energy means no more to you than an image of giant windmills lined up on a California ridge, and solar energy brings to mind only the odd-looking glassy roof on a Colorado ski lodge. Even so, list possible points of comparison that will be relevant to your objects and your purpose. For example:

cost
convenience
efficiency
environmental impact

Of course, as you learn more about your objects and think about what you are learning, you may want to change some of these points or add new ones. But meanwhile a tentative list will help you by suggesting the kind of information you need to gather for your comparison and contrast.

4. Gathering Information

For some comparisons you will find the information you need in your own head; for others you will have to search for that information in books, magazines, and newspapers. Let your tentative points of comparison be your guide, but remain alert for other points you may not have thought of. For example, you may find that maintenance requirements are an important factor in considering energy systems and so want to add that point to your list:

cost
convenience
efficiency
maintenance
environmental impact

5. *Organization*

Remember that there are two patterns for structuring a comparison and contrast: block and point-by-point. Once you have gathered the necessary information, you should decide which pattern will serve your purpose best. It may help you to jot down a scratch outline before beginning your draft.

Block organization works best when the two objects of comparison are relatively simple, when the points of comparison are rather general and few in number, and when the amount of information you have to present is not great. As a scratch outline indicates, block organization makes for a unified discussion of each object, which can help your readers absorb the information you have to give them:

> *Solar energy*
>   Cost
>   Efficiency
>   Convenience
>   Maintenance
>   Environmental impact
> *Wind energy*
>   Cost
>   Efficiency
>   Convenience
>   Maintenance
>   Environmental impact

If your essay will be more than two or three pages long, however, block organization may be a poor choice. By the time your readers come to your discussion of the cost of wind energy, they may well have forgotten what you had to say about solar energy costs several pages earlier and have to flip back and forth to grasp the comparison. If such difficulties are possible, you would do better to use point-by-point organization, in which comparisons are made immediately as each point is raised:

> *Cost*
>   Solar energy
>   Wind energy

Efficiency
  Solar energy
  Wind energy
Convenience
  Solar energy
  Wind energy
Maintenance
  Solar energy
  Wind energy
Environmental impact
  Solar energy
  Wind energy

6. Drawing a Conclusion

Only after you have gathered your information and made your comparisons are you really ready to decide what your conclusion should be. Perhaps, for example, your comparison shows that solar and wind energy are both feasible, with solar energy having a slight edge on most points. Then, if your purpose has been evaluation, you might conclude, "Both solar energy and wind energy are practical alternatives to conventional energy sources." If you wish to convince your readers that one of the technologies is superior to the other, your comparison will support a more persuasive conclusion: "While both solar and wind energy are practical technologies, solar energy now seems the better investment."

Guns and Cameras

Barbara Bowman

A studio art major from Pittsburgh, Pennsylvania, Barbara Bowman has a special interest in photography. She was particularly pleased, therefore, with her internship as a photographer's assistant at Vermont's Shelburne Museum; she may even make a career of museum work. In her writing courses, Barbara has discovered many similarities between the writing process and the process that an artist follows. Her essay "Guns and Cameras," however, explores similarities of another kind: those between hunting with a gun and hunting with a camera.

With a growing number of animals heading toward extinction, and with the idea of protecting such animals on game reserves increasing in popularity, photographic safaris are replacing hunting safaris. This may seem odd because of the obvious differences between guns and cameras. Shooting is aggressive, photography is passive; shooting eliminates, photography preserves. However, some hunters are willing to trade their guns for cameras because of similarities in the way the equipment is used, as well as in the relationship among equipment, user, and "prey."

The hunter has a deep interest in the apparatus he uses to kill his prey. He carries various types of guns, different kinds of ammunition, and special sights and telescopes to increase his chances of success. He knows the mechanics of his guns and understands how and why they work. This fascination with the hardware of his sport is practical—it helps him achieve his goal—but it frequently becomes an end, almost a hobby in itself.

Not until the very end of the long process of stalking an animal does a game hunter use his gun. First he enters into the animal's world. He studies his prey, its habitat, its daily habits, its watering holes and feeding areas, its migration patterns, its enemies and allies, its diet and food chain. Eventually the hunter himself becomes animal-like, instinctively sensing the habits and moves of

256

his prey. Of course, this instinct gives the hunter a better chance of killing the animal; he knows where and when he will get the best shot. But it gives him more than that. Hunting is not just pulling the trigger and killing the prey. Much of it is a multifaceted and ritualistic identification with nature.

After the kill, the hunter can do a number of things with his 4 trophy. He can sell the meat or eat it himself. He can hang the animal's head on the wall, or lay its hide on the floor or even sell these objects. But any of these uses is a luxury, and its cost is high. An animal has been destroyed; a life has been eliminated.

Like the hunter, the photographer has a great interest in the 5 tools he uses. He carries various types of cameras, lenses, and film to help him get the picture he wants. He understands the way cameras work, the uses of telephoto and micro lenses, and often the technical procedures of printing and developing. Of course, the time and interest a photographer invests in these mechanical aspects of his art allow him to capture and produce the image he wants. But as with the hunter, these mechanics can and often do become fascinating in themselves.

The wildlife photographer also needs to stalk his "prey" with 6 knowledge and skill in order to get an accurate "shot." Like the hunter, he has to understand the animal's patterns, characteristics, and habitat, must become animal-like, in order to succeed; and like the hunter's, his pursuit is much more prolonged and complicated than the shot itself. The stalking processes are almost identical and give many of the same satisfactions.

The successful photographer also has something tangible to 7 show for his efforts. A still picture of an animal can be displayed in a home, a gallery, a shop; it can be printed in a publication, as a postcard, or as a poster. In fact, a single photograph can be used in all these ways at once, can in fact be reproduced countless times. And despite all these ways of using his "trophies," the photographer continues to preserve his prey.

Photography is obviously the less violent and to me the more 8 acceptable method for obtaining a trophy of a wild animal. We no longer need to hunt in order to feed or clothe ourselves, and hunting for "sport" seems to be barbaric. Luckily, the excitement of pursuing an animal, learning its habits and patterns, outsmarting it on its own level, and finally "getting" it can all be done with a camera. So why use guns?

Interview with Barbara Bowman

Tell me something about yourself.

Photography is a big part of my life right now. I'm a studio art major, and this summer I'll be an intern with the local weekly newspaper, their only staff photographer. So you can see why my bias is toward cameras instead of guns.

How did you think of comparing them?

I was reading a photography book and it mentioned a safari in Africa that used cameras instead of guns. I thought that was very interesting, so I thought I'd use it for a writing subject. I don't know that much about guns, but there's a guy in my English class who's a big hunter—he wrote a paper for the class about hunting— so I asked him about it. I could tell from what he said that he got the same gratification from it that a nature photographer would. Other people I know who hunt do it mostly for the meat and for the adventure of stalking the prey. So that's how I got what I needed to know about hunting. Photography I knew lots about already, of course.

Why did you use block comparison?

Well, the first draft was a point-by-point comparison, and it was very bumpy, shifting back and forth between the hunter and the photographer, and I thought it was probably confusing. As I kept developing the paper, it just made more sense to switch to block comparison. Unfortunately, this meant that I had to throw out some paragraphs in the first draft that I liked. That's hard for me— to throw out some writing that seems different and new—but it wasn't fitting right, so I had to make the cuts.

Did you make any other large-scale changes as you revised?

Nothing in particular, but each time I revised I threw things out that I didn't need, and now the essay is only half as long as it used to be. For example, here's a sentence from the next-to-last draft: "Guns kill, cameras don't; guns use ammunition, cameras use film; shooting eliminates, photography preserves." Everybody knows this, and the first and last parts say the same thing. I liked the last part, the way the words go together, so I kept that, but I cut out the rest. I did a lot of that.

You use your comparison to support a particular point of view.

I don't like the idea of killing things for sport. I can see the hunter's argument that you've got to keep the animals' numbers under control, but I still would rather they weren't shot to death. That was the point of the comparison right from the first draft.

Two Ways of Seeing a River

Mark Twain

Mark Twain (1835–1910), the pen name of Samuel L. Clemens, was born in Mississippi and raised in Hannibal, Missouri. He created Huckleberry Finn *(1884),* Tom Sawyer *(1876),* The Prince and the Pauper *(1882), and* A Connecticut Yankee in King Arthur's Court *(1889), among other classics. One of America's most popular writers, Twain is generally regarded as the most important practitioner of the realistic school of writing, a style that emphasizes observable details.*

The following passage is taken from Life on the Mississippi *(1883), Twain's study of that great river and his account of his early experiences learning to be a river steamboat pilot. As you read the passage, notice how Twain makes use of figurative language in offering two quite different ways of seeing the Mississippi River.*

Now when I had mastered the language of this water and had 1 come to know every trifling feature that bordered the great river as familiarly as I knew the letters of the alphabet, I had made a valuable acquisition. But I had lost something, too. I had lost something which could never be restored to me while I lived. All the grace, the beauty, the poetry, had gone out of the majestic river! I still kept in mind a certain wonderful sunset which I witnessed when steamboating was new to me. A broad expanse of the river was turned to blood; in the middle distance the red hue brightened into gold, through which a solitary log came floating, black and conspicuous; in one place a long, slanting mark lay sparkling upon the water; in another the surface was broken by boiling, tumbling rings that were as many-tinted as an opal; where the ruddy flush was faintest was a smooth spot that was covered with graceful circles and radiating lines, ever so delicately traced; the shore on our left was densely wooded, and the somber shadow that fell from this forest was broken in one place by a long, ruffled trail that shone like silver; and high above the forest wall a clean-stemmed dead tree waved a single leafy bough that glowed like a flame in the unobstructed splendor that was flowing from the sun. There were graceful curves, reflected images, woody heights, soft distances, and over the whole scene, far and near, the dissolving lights drifted steadily, enriching it every passing moment with new marvels of coloring.

I stood like one bewitched. I drank it in, in a speechless rapture. 2 The world was new to me and I had never seen anything like this at home. But as I have said, a day came when I began to cease from noting the glories and the charms which the moon and the sun and the twilight wrought upon the river's face; another day came when I ceased altogether to note them. Then, if that sunset scene had been repeated, I should have looked upon it without rapture and should have commented upon it inwardly after this fashion: "This sun means that we are going to have wind tomorrow; that floating log means that the river is rising, small thanks to it; that slanting mark on the water refers to a bluff reef which is going to kill somebody's steamboat one of these nights, if it keeps on stretching out like that; those tumbling 'boils' show a dissolving bar and a changing channel there; the lines and circles in the slick water over yonder are a warning that that troublesome place is shoaling up dangerously; that silver streak in the shadow of the forest is the 'break' from a new snag and he has located himself in the very best place he could have found to fish for steamboats; that tall dead tree, with a single living branch, is not going to last long, and then how is a body ever going to get through this blind place at night without the friendly old landmark?"

No, the romance and beauty were all gone from the river. All 3 the value any feature of it had for me now was the amount of usefulness it could furnish toward compassing the safe piloting of a steamboat. Since those days, I have pitied doctors from my heart. What does the lovely flush in a beauty's cheek mean to a doctor but a "break" that ripples above some deadly disease? Are not all her visible charms sown thick with what are to him the signs and symbols of hidden decay? Does he ever see her beauty at all, or doesn't he simply view her professionally and comment upon her unwholesome condition all to himself? And doesn't he sometimes wonder whether he has gained most or lost most by learning his trade?

Questions on Subject

1. What two attitudes toward the Mississippi River does Twain discuss? What was his first attitude toward the river? His second? What brought about the change? (Glossary: *Attitude*)
2. What points of contrast does Twain refer to in his two ways of seeing the river?
3. What point does Twain make in this selection regarding the difference between appearance and reality, between romance and practicality? What role does knowledge play in Twain's inability to see the river as he once did?
4. Now that he has learned the trade of steamboating, does Twain feel he has "gained most or lost most"?

Questions on Strategy

1. What method of organization does Twain use in this selection? What alternative methods might he have used? What would have been gained or lost? (Glossary: *Organization*)
2. Explain the analogy that Twain uses in paragraph 3. What is his purpose in using the analogy? (Glossary: *Analogy*)
3. Reread Twain's conclusion. How effective do you find it? (Glossary: *Beginnings/Endings*)
4. What is Twain's tone in this essay? (Glossary: *Tone*)

Questions on Diction and Vocabulary

1. Twain uses a number of similes and metaphors in this passage. Identify three of each, and explain what is being compared in each case. (Glossary: *Figures of Speech*)
2. What effect do the italicized words have in each of the following quotations from this selection? How do these words contribute to Twain's description?
   a. "ever so *delicately* traced" (paragraph 1)
   b. "shadow that *fell* from this forest" (1)

c. "*wrought* upon the river's face" (2)
d. "show a *dissolving* bar" (2)
e. "to get through this *blind* place at night" (2)
f. "lovely *flush* in a beauty's cheek" (3)
3. Refer to your desk dictionary to determine the meanings of the following words as they are used in this selection: *acquisition* (paragraph 1), *hue* (1), *opal* (1), *rapture* (2), *romance* (3).

Writing Assignments

1. Write an essay modeled on Twain's in which you offer your two different views of a particular scene, event, or issue. Describe how you once regarded your subject, and then describe how you now view the subject. For example, you might wish to present the way you once viewed your hometown or high school, and the way you now view it. Be sure that you consider both your purpose in writing and the manner in which you conclude your essay.
2. Write an essay in which you use comparison and/or contrast to help you describe one of the following places or another place of your choice:
   a. a place of worship
   b. a fast-food restaurant
   c. your dormitory
   d. your college library
   e. your favorite place on campus
   f. your college student center
   g. your hometown

Neat People versus Sloppy People

Suzanne Britt

Born in Winston-Salem, North Carolina, Suzanne Britt now makes her home in Raleigh. She graduated from Salem College and Washington University, where she received her M.A. in English. A freelance writer, Britt has a regular column in North Carolina Gardens & Homes. *Her work appears from time to time in the* New York Times, Newsweek, *and the* Boston Globe. *Her essays have been collected in two books,* People Are Dull and Crunchy like Carrots *and* Show and Tell. *Currently she teaches English at Meredith College in North Carolina and continues to write.*

In the following essay taken from Show and Tell, *Britt takes a humorous look at the differences between neat and sloppy people by giving us some serious insights about several important personality traits.*

I've finally figured out the difference between neat people and 1 sloppy people. The distinction is, as always, moral. Neat people are lazier and meaner than sloppy people.

Sloppy people, you see, are not really sloppy. Their sloppiness 2 is merely the unfortunate consequence of their extreme moral rectitude. Sloppy people carry in their mind's eye a heavenly vision, a precise plan, that is so stupendous, so perfect, it can't be achieved in this world or the next.

Sloppy people live in Never-Never Land. Someday is their mé- 3 tier. Someday they are planning to alphabetize all their books and set up home catalogs. Someday they will go through their wardrobes and mark certain items for tentative mending and certain items for passing on to relatives of similar shape and size. Someday sloppy people will make family scrapbooks into which they will put newspaper clippings, postcards, locks of hair, and the dried corsage from their senior prom. Someday they will file everything on the surface of their desks, including the cash receipts from coffee purchases at the snack shop. Someday they will sit down and read all the back issues of *The New Yorker.*

For all these noble reasons and more, sloppy people never get 4 neat. They aim too high and wide. They save everything, planning someday to file, order, and straighten out the world. But while these ambitious plans take clearer and clearer shape in their heads, the books spill from the shelves onto the floor, the clothes pile up in the hamper and closet, the family mementos accumulate in every drawer, the surface of the desk is buried under mounds of paper and the unread magazines threaten to reach the ceiling.

Sloppy people can't bear to part with anything. They give loving 5 attention to every detail. When sloppy people say they're going to tackle the surface of the desk, they really mean it. Not a paper will go unturned; not a rubber band will go unboxed. Four hours or two weeks into the excavation, the desk looks exactly the same, primarily because the sloppy person is meticulously creating new piles of papers with new headings and scrupulously stopping to read all the old book catalogs before he throws them away. A neat person would just bulldoze the desk.

Neat people are bums and clods at heart. They have cavalier 6 attitudes toward possessions, including family heirlooms. Everything is just another dust-catcher to them. If anything collects dust, it's got to go and that's that. Neat people will toy with the idea of throwing the children out of the house just to cut down on the clutter.

Neat people don't care about process. They like results. What 7 they want to do is get the whole thing over with so they can sit down and watch the rasslin' on TV. Neat people operate on two unvarying principles: never handle any item twice, and throw everything away.

The only thing messy in a neat person's house is the trash can. 8 The minute something comes to a neat person's hand, he will look at it, try to decide if it has immediate use and, finding none, throw it in the trash.

Neat people are especially vicious with mail. They never go 9 through their mail unless they are standing directly over a trash can. If the trash can is beside the mailbox, even better. All ads, catalogs, pleas for charitable contributions, church bulletins and money-saving coupons go straight into the trash can without being opened. All letters from home, postcards from Europe, bills and paychecks are opened, immediately responded to, then dropped in the trash can. Neat people keep their receipts only for tax purposes. That's it. No sentimental salvaging of birthday cards or the last letter a dying relative ever wrote. Into the trash it goes.

Neat people place neatness above everything, even economics. They are incredibly wasteful. Neat people throw away several toys every time they walk through the den. I knew a neat person once who threw away a perfectly good dish drainer because it had mold on it. The drainer was too much trouble to wash. And neat people sell their furniture when they move. They will sell a La-Z-Boy recliner while you are reclining in it. 10

Neat people are no good to borrow from. Neat people buy everything in expensive little single portions. They get their flour and sugar in two-pound bags. They wouldn't consider clipping a coupon, saving a leftover, reusing plastic nondairy whipped cream containers or rinsing off tin foil and draping it over the unmoldy dish drainer. You can never borrow a neat person's newspaper to see what's playing at the movies. Neat people have the paper all wadded up and in the trash by 7:05 A.M. 11

Neat people cut a clean swath through the organic as well as the inorganic world. People, animals, and things are all one to them. They are so insensitive. After they've finished with the pantry, the medicine cabinet, and the attic, they will throw out the red geranium (too many leaves), sell the dog (too many fleas), and send the children off to boarding school (too many scuffmarks on the hardwood floors). 12

Questions on Subject

1. Why do you suppose Britt characterizes the distinction between sloppy and neat people as a "moral" one? What is she really poking fun at with this reference?
2. In your own words, what is the "heavenly vision," the "precise plan," Britt refers to in paragraph 2? How does Britt use this idea to explain why sloppy people can never be neat?
3. Choose one sentence in Britt's essay that best sums up her idea of a neat person.

4. Exaggeration, as Britt uses it, is only effective if it departs from some shared idea of the truth. What commonly understood ideas about sloppy and neat people does Britt rely on? Do you agree with here? Why or why not?

Questions on Strategy

1. Note Britt's use of transitions as she moves from trait to trait. How well does she use transitions to achieve unity in her essay? Explain. (Glossary: *Transitions*)
2. Britt uses a block system of contrast. Why do you suppose she has chosen this strategy? What would have been gained or lost had she used a point-by-point system of contrast?
3. One of the ways Britt achieves a sense of the ridiculous in her essay is to switch the attributes of sloppy and neat people. Cite examples of this technique and discuss the ways in which it adds to her essay. What does it reveal to the reader about her purpose in writing this essay? (Glossary: *Purpose*)
4. Britt uses a block system of contrast to point out the differences between sloppy and neat people. Make a side-by-side list of the traits of sloppy and neat people; now see if you can determine any ways in which they may be similar. Why do you suppose Britt does not include some of the ways in which they are the same?

Questions on Diction and Vocabulary

1. Cite examples of Britt's diction that indicate her change of tone when she is talking about either sloppy or neat people. (Glossary: *Tone*)
2. Refer to your desk dictionary to determine the meanings of the following words as they are used in this selection: *rectitude* (paragraph 2), *stupendous* (2), *tentative* (3), *excavation* (5), *meticulously* (5), *scrupulously* (5), *heirlooms* (6), *vicious* (9), *salvaging* (9), *swath* (12).

Writing Suggestions

1. Write an essay in which you describe yourself as either sloppy or neat. In what ways does your behavior compare or contrast with the traits Britt offers?

2. Compare and contrast two personality traits that are typically seen as opposites such as stingy and generous, serious and silly, emotional and rational, responsible and flighty, or choose two of your own. Remember that to be convincing you will have to base your analysis on a germ of truth even if you are speaking tongue-in-cheek.

Busybody and Crybaby

Lance Morrow

Lance Morrow was born in 1935 in Lewisburg, Pennsylvania, and graduated from Harvard. He began his writing career as a reporter for the Washington Star, *and then in 1965 he moved to* Time *magazine where he was at one time a senior writer. His essays for* Time *earned him a National Magazine Award in 1981 and have been collected and published as* Fishing in the Tiber. *He has also published two books,* America: A Rediscovery *and* The Chief, *a memoir of his father Hugh Morrow, who was also a journalist.*

In the following selection, which first appeared in the August 12, 1991, issue of Time, *Morrow discusses the way in which a growing intolerance and irresponsibility are combining to undermine the very foundation of our culture.*

The busybody and the crybaby are getting to be the most conspicuous children on the American playground.

The busybody is the bully with the ayatullah shine in his eyes, gauleiter of correctness, who barges around telling the other kids that they cannot smoke, be fat, drink booze, wear furs, eat meat or otherwise nonconform to the new tribal rules now taking shape.

The crybaby, on the other hand, is the abject, manipulative little devil with the lawyer and, so to speak, the actionable diaper rash. He is a mayor of Washington, arrested (and captured on videotape) as he smokes crack in a hotel room with a woman not his wife. He pronounces himself a victim—of the woman, of white injustice, of the universe. Whatever.

Both these types, the one overactive and the other overpassive, are fashioning some odd new malformations of American character. The busybodies have begun to infect American society with a nasty intolerance—a zeal to police the private lives of others and hammer them into standard forms. In Freudian terms, the busybodies might be the superego of the American personality, the

overbearing wardens. The crybabies are the messy id, all blubbering need and a virtually infantile irresponsibility. Hard pressed
in between is the ego that is supposed to be healthy, tolerant and
intelligent. It all adds up to what the *Economist* perceptively calls
"a decadent puritanism within America: an odd combination of
ducking responsibility and telling everyone else what to do."

Zealotry of either kind—the puritan's need to regiment others 5
or the victim's passion for blaming everyone except himself—tends
to produce a depressing civic stupidity. Each trait has about it the
immobility of addiction. Victims become addicted to being victims:
they derive identity, innocence and a kind of devious power from
sheer, defaulting helplessness. On the other side, the candle-
snuffers of behavioral and political correctness enact their paradox,
accomplishing intolerance in the name of tolerance, regimentation
in the name of betterment.

The spectacle of the two moral defectives of the schoolyard jump- 6
ing up and down on the social contract is evidence that America
is not entirely a society of grownups. A drama in Encino, Calif.: a
lawyer named Kenneth Shild built a basketball court in his yard,
60 feet from the bedroom window of a neighbor, Michael Rubin,
also a lawyer. The bouncing of the basketball produced a "per-
cussion noise that was highly annoying," according to Rubin, who
asked Shild and his son to stop playing. Shild refused, and Rubin,
knowing that his rights allowed him to take action to stop a nui-
sance, sprayed water from his garden hose onto the neighbor's
basketball court. Suit and countersuit. Rubin's restraining order
limiting the hours of the day during which the Shilds could play
was overturned by an appeals-court judge. Each side seeks more
than $100,000 in punitive damages. Shild argues mental stress.
Rubin claims that his property has been devalued.

Fish gotta swim. Locusts devour the countryside. Lawyers sue. 7
For all the American plague of overlitigation, lawyers also act as a
kind of priesthood in the rituals of American faith. Most religions
preach a philosophical endurance of the imperfections of the
world. Suffering must be borne. Americans did not come to the
New World to live like that. They operate on a pushy, querulous
assumption of perfectibility on earth ("the pursuit of happiness"—
their own personal happiness). That expectation, which can make
Americans charming and unreasonable and shallow, is part of their

formula for success. But it has led Americans into absurdities and discontents that others who know life better might never think of. The frontiersman's self-sufficiency and stoicism in the face of pain belong now in some wax museum of lost American self-images.

Each approach, that of busybody or crybaby, is selfish, and each 8 poisons the sense of common cause. The sheer stupidity of each seeps into public discourse and politics. *Idiot* in the original Greek meant someone who cared nothing for issues of public life. The pollster Peter Hart asked some young people in a focus group to name qualities that make America special. Silence. Then one young man said, "Cable TV." Asked how to encourage more young people to vote, a young woman replied, "Pay them."

In her book *Rights Talk*, Mary Ann Glendon of Harvard Law 9 School argues that the nation's legal language on rights is highly developed, but the language of responsibility is meager: "A tendency to frame nearly every social controversy in terms of a clash of rights (a woman's right to her own body vs. a fetus's right to life) impedes compromise, mutual understanding, and the discovery of common ground."

But of course deciding about abortion is not easy. Compromise 10 and common ground are difficult to find on many issues. The American social contract is fluid, rapidly changing, postmodernist, just as the American gene and culture pool is turbulently new every day. Life improvises rich dilemmas, but they fly by like commercial breaks, hallucinatory, riveting, half-noticed. What is the moral authority behind a social contract so vivid and illegible? Only the zealously asserted styles of the new tribes (do this, don't do this, look a certain way, think a certain way, and that will make you all right).

When old coherences break down, civilities and tolerances fall 11 away as well. So does an ideal of self-reliance and inner autonomy and responsibility. The new tribes, strident and anxious and dogmatic, push forward to impose a new order. Yet they seem curiously faddish, unserious: youth culture unites with hypochondria and a childish sense of entitlement. Long ago, Carry Nation actually thought the U.S. would be better off if everyone stopped drinking. The busybodies today worry not about their society but about themselves—they imagine that they would be beautiful and virtuous and live forever, if only you would put out that cigar.

Questions on Subject

1. Define *busybody* and *crybaby* as Morrow uses them in his essay.
2. Busybodies and crybabies are polar opposites, yet they share many qualities. What are these qualities, and what single effect have they had on American culture, according to Morrow?
3. What does Morrow say is the "paradox" of the busybodies?
4. What basic assumption seems to be unique to Americans? What does Morrow say is the flaw in this assumption?
5. According to Morrow, what is significant in the fact that America's legal language is heavy on the concept of "rights" and light on the concept of "responsibility"?

Questions on Strategy

1. In the opening sentence of his essay, Morrow introduces an analogy. What is that analogy and how well does it suit Morrow's subject? (Glossary: *Analogy*)
2. Make a brief outline of Morrow's essay. How has he organized his specific points of comparison and contrast?
3. What exactly is Morrow's thesis? Is it stated or implied? (Glossary: *Thesis*)
4. Explain the function of paragraph 6 in the context of Morrow's essay. In what way does it contribute to his thesis? Explain.

Questions on Diction and Vocabulary

1. Morrow uses several quotes in his essay. What do they have in common? Why do you suppose he has included them? How do they strengthen his essay?
2. Morrow uses highly-charged language in his essay. For example, "ayatullah shine in his eyes" (paragraph 2), "all blubbering need and a virtually infantile irresponsibility" (4), "civic stupidity" (5). Cite other examples of his use of such language and explain its effect on the reader.

3. Refer to your desk dictionary to determine the meanings of the following words as they are used in this selection: *gauleiter* (paragraph 2), *abject* (3), *decadent* (4), *zealotry* (5), *querulous* (7), *stoicism* (7), *seeps* (8), *clash* (9), *strident* (11), *faddish* (11).

Writing Suggestions

1. In an essay, expand on Morrow's reference to the word *idiot*, which, in the original Greek, was intended to mean someone who cared nothing for issues of public life. How do modern "idiots" compare or differ from their Greek counterparts? When framing your answer, consider the ways in which modern idiots share the qualities of the "crybabies" and the "busybodies" Morrow describes.
2. Our government contends that driving a car is a privilege, not a right. Thus we must pass both a written and a road test before we get behind the wheel of a car. Not everyone agrees with the government's position. Some argue that in a mobile society, where employment may be available only at a great distance from home, a license becomes a necessity and should not be subject to forfeiture. Therefore it follows, they reason, that any infractions of rules of the road should be punished in some other manner. Write an essay in which you defend or attack this line of reasoning.

Grant and Lee: A Study in Contrasts
Bruce Catton

Bruce Catton (1899–1978) was born in Petoskey, Michigan, and attended Oberlin College. Early in his career, Catton worked as a reporter for various newspapers, among them the Cleveland Plain Dealer. *Having an interest in history, Catton became a leading authority on the Civil War and published a number of books on this subject. These include* Mr. Lincoln's Army, Glory Road, A Stillness at Appomattox, This Hallowed Ground, The Coming Fury, Never Call Retreat, *and* Gettysburg: The Final Fury. *Catton was awarded both the Pulitzer Prize and the National Book Award in 1954.*

The following selection was included in The American Story, *a collection of historical essays edited by Earl Schenk Miers. In it Catton considers "two great Americans, Grant and Lee—very different, yet under everything very much alike."*

When Ulysses S. Grant and Robert E. Lee met in the parlor of 1
a modest house at Appomattox Court House, Virginia, on April
9, 1865, to work out the terms for the surrender of Lee's Army of
Northern Virginia, a great chapter in American life came to a close,
and a great new chapter began.

These men were bringing the Civil War to its virtual finish. To 2
be sure, other armies had yet to surrender, and for a few days the
fugitive Confederate government would struggle desperately and
vainly, trying to find some way to go on living now that its chief
support was gone. But in effect it was all over when Grant and
Lee signed the papers. And the little room where they wrote out
the terms was the scene of one of the poignant, dramatic contrasts
in American history.

They were two strong men, these oddly different generals, and 3
they represented the strengths of two conflicting currents that,
through them, had come into final collision.

Back of Robert E. Lee was the notion that the old aristocratic 4
concept might somehow survive and be dominant in American life.
Lee was tidewater Virginia, and in his background were family, 5
culture, and tradition . . . the age of chivalry transplanted to a New
World which was making its own legends and its own myths. He
embodied a way of life that had come down through the age of
knighthood and the English country squire. America was a land
that was beginning all over again, dedicated to nothing much more
complicated than the rather hazy belief that all men had equal
rights and should have an equal chance in the world. In such a
land Lee stood for the feeling that it was somehow of advantage
to human society to have a pronounced inequality in the social
structure. There should be a leisure class, backed by ownership of
land; in turn, society itself should be keyed to the land as the chief
source of wealth and influence. It would bring forth (according to
this ideal) a class of men with a strong sense of obligation to the
community; men who lived not to gain advantage for themselves,
but to meet the solemn obligations which had been laid on them
by the very fact that they were privileged. From them the country
would get its leadership; to them it could look for the higher
values—of thought, of conduct, of personal deportment—to give
it strength and virtue.

Lee embodied the noblest elements of this aristocratic ideal. 6
Through him, the landed nobility justified itself. For four years,
the Southern states had fought a desperate war to uphold the ideals
for which Lee stood. In the end, it almost seemed as if the Confederacy fought for Lee; as if he himself was the Confederacy . . .
the best thing that the way of life for which the Confederacy stood
could ever have to offer. He had passed into legend before Appomattox. Thousands of tired, underfed, poorly clothed Confederate soldiers, long since past the simple enthusiasm of the early
days of the struggle, somehow considered Lee the symbol of everything for which they had been willing to die. But they could not
quite put this feeling into words. If the Lost Cause, sanctified by
so much heroism and so many deaths, had a living justification,
its justification was General Lee.

Grant, the son of a tanner on the Western frontier, was every- 7
thing Lee was not. He had come up the hard way and embodied
nothing in particular except the eternal toughness and sinewy fiber

of the men who grew up beyond the mountains. He was one of a body of men who owed reverence and obeisance to no one, who were self-reliant to a fault, who cared hardly anything for the past but who had a sharp eye for the future.

These frontier men were the precise opposite of the tidewater 8 aristocrats. Back of them, in the great surge that had taken people over the Alleghenies and into the opening Western country, there was a deep, implicit dissatisfaction with a past that had settled into grooves. They stood for democracy, not from any reasoned conclusion about the proper ordering of human society, but simply because they had grown up in the middle of democracy and knew how it worked. Their society might have privileges, but they would be privileges each man had won for himself. Forms and patterns meant nothing. No man was born to anything, except perhaps to a chance to show how far he could rise. Life was competition.

Yet along with this feeling had come a deep sense of belonging 9 to a national community. The Westerner who developed a farm, opened a shop, or set up in business as a trader, could hope to prosper only as his own community prospered—and his community ran from the Atlantic to the Pacific and from Canada down to Mexico. If the land was settled, with towns and highways and accessible markets, he could better himself. He saw his fate in terms of the nation's own destiny. As its horizons expanded, so did his. He had, in other words, an acute dollars-and-cents stake in the continued growth and development of his country.

And that, perhaps, is where the contrast between Grant and Lee 10 becomes most striking. The Virginia aristocrat, inevitably, saw himself in relation to his own region. He lived in a static society which could endure almost anything except change. Instinctively, his first loyalty would go to the locality in which that society existed. He would fight to the limit of endurance to defend it, because in defending it he was defending everything that gave his own life its deepest meaning.

The Westerner, on the other hand, would fight with an equal 11 tenacity for the broader concept of society. He fought so because everything he lived by was tied to growth, expansion, and a constantly widening horizon. What he lived by would survive or fall with the nation itself. He could not possibly stand by unmoved in the face of an attempt to destroy the Union. He would combat it with everything he had, because he could only see it as an effort to cut the ground out from under his feet.

So Grant and Lee were in complete contrast, representing two 12 diametrically opposed elements in American life. Grant was the modern man emerging; beyond him, ready to come on the stage, was the great age of steel and machinery, of crowded cities and a restless burgeoning vitality. Lee might have ridden down from the old age of chivalry, lance in hand, silken banner fluttering over his head. Each man was the perfect champion of his cause, drawing both his strengths and his weaknesses from the people he led.

Yet it was not all contrast, after all. Different as they were—in 13 background, in personality, in underlying aspiration—these two great soldiers had much in common. Under everything else, they were marvelous fighters. Furthermore, their fighting qualities were really very much alike.

Each man had, to begin with, the great virtue of utter tenacity 14 and fidelity. Grant fought his way down the Mississippi Valley in spite of acute personal discouragement and profound military handicaps. Lee hung on in the trenches at Petersburg after hope itself had died. In each man there was an indomitable quality . . . the born fighter's refusal to give up as long as he can still remain on his feet and lift his two fists.

Daring and resourcefulness they had, too; the ability to think 15 faster and move faster than the enemy. These were the qualities which gave Lee the dazzling campaigns of Second Manassas and Chancellorsville and won Vicksburg for Grant.

Lastly, and perhaps greatest of all, there was the ability, at the 16 end, to turn quickly from war to peace once the fighting was over. Out of the way these two men behaved at Appomattox came the possibility of a peace of reconciliation. It was a possibility not wholly realized, in the years to come, but which did, in the end, help the two sections to become one nation again . . . after a war whose bitterness might have seemed to make such a reunion wholly impossible. No part of either man's life became him more than the part he played in their brief meeting in the McLean house at Appomattox. Their behavior there put all succeeding generations of Americans in their debt. Two great Americans, Grant and Lee—very different, yet under everything very much alike. Their encounter at Appomattox was one of the great moments of American history.

Questions on Subject

1. In paragraphs 10 through 12, Catton discusses what he considers to be the most striking contrast between Grant and Lee. What is that difference?
2. List the similarities that Catton sees between Grant and Lee. Which similarity does Catton feel is most important? Why?
3. What attitudes and ideas does Catton describe to support his view that tidewater Virginia was a throwback to the "age of chivalry" (paragraph 5)?
4. Catton says that Grant was "the modern man emerging" (12). How does he support that statement? Do you agree?

Questions on Strategy

1. What would have been lost had Catton compared Grant and Lee before contrasting them? Would anything have been gained?
2. How does Catton organize the body of his essay (3–16)? You may find it helpful in answering this question to summarize the point of comparison in each paragraph and label it as being concerned with Lee, Grant, or both. (Glossary: *Organization*)
3. Catton has carefully made clear transitions between paragraphs. For each paragraph, identify the transitional devices he uses. How do they help your reading? (Glossary: *Transitions*)

Questions on Diction and Vocabulary

1. Identify at least two metaphors that Catton uses, and explain what each contributes to his comparison. (Glossary: *Figures of Speech*)
2. Refer to your desk dictionary to determine the meanings of the following words as they are used in this selection: *poignant* (paragraph 2), *chivalry* (5), *sanctified* (6), *sinewy* (7), *obeisance* (7), *tidewater* (8), *tenacity* (11), *aspiration* (13).

Writing Assignments

1. Select one of the following topics for an essay of comparison and contrast. In selecting your topic, you should consider (a) what your purpose will be, (b) whether you will emphasize similarities or differences, (c) what specific points you will discuss, and (d) what organizational pattern will best suit your purpose. As you plan your essay, consider whether the objects of your comparison can be discussed as representatives of particular types, the way Catton does with Grant and Lee.
   a. two actors or actresses
   b. two friends or roommates
   c. two books by the same author
   d. two paintings
   e. two popular campus hangouts
   f. two musical groups
2. Compare and contrast two famous people whose careers have at some point crossed in a dramatic or decisive way: John F. Kennedy and Richard Nixon, for example, or Ernest Hemingway and F. Scott Fitzgerald, or Sir Thomas More and Henry VIII, or Franklin Roosevelt and Winston Churchill.

Writing Suggestions for Comparison and Contrast

1. Write an essay in which you compare and/or contrast two objects, persons, or events to show at least one of the following:
   a. their important differences
   b. their significant similarities
   c. their relative value
   d. their distinctive qualities
2. Select a topic from the list that follows. Write an essay using comparison and/or contrast as your primary means of development. Be sure that your essay has a definite purpose and a clear direction.
   a. two methods of dieting
   b. two television situation comedies
   c. two types of summer employment
   d. two people who display different attitudes toward responsibility
   e. two restaurants
   f. two courses in the same subject area
   g. two friends who exemplify different life-styles
   h. two network television or local news programs
   i. two professional quarterbacks
   j. two ways of studying for an exam
   k. two rooms in which you have classes
   l. two of your favorite magazines
   m. two attitudes toward death
   n. two ways to heat a home
3. Use one of the following "before and after" situations as the basis for an essay of comparison and/or contrast:

    a. before and after an examination
    b. before and after seeing a movie
    c. before and after reading an important book
    d. before and after dieting
    e. before and after a long trip

4. The following poems attempt to capture the essence of a moment
of poetic truth in baseball and basketball, respectively. After reading the two poems, write an essay in which you compare and
contrast the subjects and/or the way the poets have treated them.

THE BASE STEALER

Poised between going on and back, pulled
Both ways taut like a tightrope-walker,
Fingertips pointing the opposites,
Now bouncing tiptoe like a dropped ball
Or a kid skipping rope, come on, come on,
Running a scattering of steps sidewise,
How he teeters, skitters, tingles, teases,
Taunts them, hovers like an ecstatic bird,
He's only flirting, crowd him, crowd him,
Delicate, delicate, delicate, delicate—now!

                            Robert Francis

FOUL SHOT

With two 60's stuck on the scoreboard
And two seconds hanging on the clock,
The solemn boy in the center of eyes,
Squeezed by silence,
Seeks out the line with his feet,
Soothes his hands along his uniform,
Gently drums the ball against the floor,
Then measures the waiting net,

Raises the ball on his right hand,
Balances it with his left,
Calms it with fingertips,
Breathes,
Crouches,

Waits,
And then through a stretching of stillness,
Nudges it upward.

The ball
Slides up and out,
Lands,
Leans,
Wobbles,
Wavers,
Hesitates,
Exasperates,
Plays it coy
Until every face begs with unsounding screams—
And then

    And then
        And then,
Right before ROAR-UP,
Dives down and through.

Edwin A. Hoey

7
Analogy

What Is Analogy?

When a subject is unobservable, complex, or abstract—when it is so generally unfamiliar that readers may have trouble understanding it—*analogy* can be most effective. Analogy is really a special form of comparison. By pointing out the certain similarities between a difficult subject and a more familiar or concrete subject, writers can help their readers achieve a firmer grasp of the difficult subject. Unlike a true comparison, though, which analyzes items that belong to the same class—breeds of dogs or types of engines—analogy pairs things from different classes, things that have nothing in common except through the imagination of the writer. In addition, whereas comparison seeks to illuminate specific features of both subjects, the primary purpose of analogy is to clarify the one subject that is complex or unfamiliar. For example, an exploration of the similarities (and differences) between short stories and novels—two forms of fiction—would constitute a logical comparison: short stories and novels belong to the same class, and your purpose would be to learn something about both. If, however, your purpose was to explain the craft of fiction writing, you might note its similarities to the craft of carpentry. Then, you would be drawing an analogy, because the two subjects clearly belong to different classes. Carpentry is the more concrete subject and the one more people will have direct experience with. If you use your imagination, you will easily see many ways the tangible work of the carpenter can be used to help readers understand the more abstract work of the novelist. Depending on its purpose, an analogy can be made in one or two paragraphs to clarify a particular aspect of the larger topic being discussed; or it can provide the organizational strategy for an entire essay.

Why Do Writers Use Analogy?

The more difficult the subject matter, the more likely a writer is to use an analogy. Natural scientists, social scientists, and theologians or philosophers frequently find analogies essential, particularly for an audience of general readers. Such writers use analogies in an effort to make a new, abstract, or complex topic understandable to people who might otherwise have trouble grasping it.

Writers may also use analogy as they would an example: to illustrate an idea that seems surprising or that might take considerable time to explain in another way. The parables of the New Testament of the Bible are a good example. These brief, straightforward narratives illustrate concepts or situations that are not immediately within human experience. Consider the following passage from the Gospel of Luke:

> Another time, the tax-gatherers and other bad characters were all crowding in to listen to him; and the Pharisees and the doctors of the law began grumbling among themselves: "This fellow," they said, "welcomes sinners and eats with them." [Jesus] answered them with this parable: "If one of you has a hundred sheep and loses one of them, does he not leave the ninety-nine in the open pasture and go after the missing one until he has found it? How delighted he is then! He lifts it on to his shoulders, and home he goes to call his friends and neighbors together. 'Rejoice with me!' he cries. 'I have found my lost sheep.' In the same way, I tell you, there will be greater joy in heaven over one sinner who repents than over ninety-nine righteous people who do not need to repent."

Here Jesus uses the analogy of the lost sheep and the sinner to illustrate his ultimate precept. You'll find another illustrative analogy in "The Ducks on Corrigan's Pond" by student writer Hesterly Goodson.

Finally, analogy can help writers give force or structure to persuasive writing, as in "Kill 'Em! Crush 'Em! Eat 'Em Raw!," where former pro linebacker John McMurtry protests the violence of football by drawing an analogy between the way the game is played and the way war is waged. Analogies should not, however, serve as one's only evidence in a logical argument. The power of the analogy may be impressive, but an analogy alone does not prove anything. Remember: By suggesting similarities between things, analogies are useful to explain, to illustrate, and to simplify; but an analogy will never serve to prove a point.

What to Look for in Reading an Analogy

First, determine the two items involved in the analogy—the one that is being explained and the one that is helping in the explanation. (The second of these should be familiar to you, or at least simple enough for you to follow easily.) Then, because the purpose of an analogy is to clarify, see how the comparison makes it easier for you to understand the item being explained.

Observe in the following example from *The Mysterious Sky* how Lester Del Rey explains the functions of the earth's atmosphere (a subject that people have difficulty with because they can't "see" it) by referring to an ordinary window.

The atmosphere of Earth acts like any window in serving two very important functions. It lets light in and it permits us to look out. It also serves as a shield to keep out dangerous or uncomfortable things. A normal glazed window lets us keep our houses warm by keeping out cold air, and it prevents rain, dirt, and unwelcome insects and animals from coming in. As we have already seen, Earth's atmospheric window also helps to keep our planet at a comfortable temperature by holding back radiated heat and protecting us from dangerous levels of ultraviolet light.

Lately, we have discovered that space is full of a great many very dangerous things against which our atmosphere guards us. It is not a perfect shield, and sometimes one of these dangerous objects does get through. There is even some evidence that a few of these messengers from space contain life, though this has by no means been proved yet.

You'll notice that Del Rey's analogy establishes no *direct* relationship between the earth's atmosphere and a window. The analogy is effective precisely because it enables the reader to "visualize" something that is unobservable by comparing it to something quite different from it, but familiar and concrete.

The following passage from A. M. Winchester's *Biology and Its Relation to Mankind* also explains something unobservable by drawing an analogy with something concrete.

> An analogy might help us to remember the principle of diffusion. Suppose we had a hundred blindfolded people tightly bunched in one corner of a large gymnasium and held in this corner by a surrounding rope. These people could move to a certain extent, but would be so crowded that they could not move freely about with one another. These we might compare to the crystal of dye with its molecules in the solid state. Now suppose that the rope was cut and the people were told to walk and keep walking. Those at the outer edge of the bunch could not move inward, but they could begin walking outward. As they moved out those farther in could begin walking. There would be frequent collisions at first among the congestion of the newly loosed people, but each time they collided they would turn and move in a different direction. Those that moved outward from the greater concentration of people would travel farther without collisions. When they hit the walls they would turn and go in a different direction. In the course of time there would be a gradual dispersion of people until they would be about equally spaced in the room and would remain that way even though they continued walking and bumping. If we think of the particles of a dissolved substance in place of the people and the energy of heat as the force which keeps them moving, we have a rough impression of what happens in diffusion.

The purpose of Winchester's analogy is to explain the principle of diffusion. His subjects are clearly from different classes, the first (a hundred blindfolded people) more readily visualized than the second (molecules of dye). At first, roped into the corner of a large gymnasium, the blindfolded people Winchester conjures up are analogous to the undissolved molecules in a crystal of dye. Both are tightly packed and barely able to move. When Winchester cuts the rope and turns the blindfolded people loose in the gymnasium, they gradually become equally dispersed throughout the room. This, the writer suggests, is roughly how molecules of a dissolved dye crystal diffuse in a liquid when they are heated. Winchester's vivid analogy makes the process of diffusion clear even to a child.

An analogy can also help a writer address an abstract issue. In the following paragraphs from *Living with Nuclear Weapons*, the Harvard Nuclear Study Group raises the questions, "What is the balance between American and Soviet nuclear arsenals? Who is ahead?"

> When the question is asked in this manner, it might appear easy to give a definitive and objective answer. Unfortunately, this is not the case. No definitive answer is possible.
>
> This can best be understood by way of an analogy. Comparing the nuclear arsenals of the superpowers is like comparing the strengths of two football teams. Each team may be stronger in some departments: one in running, the other in passing; one in special teams, the other in placekicking. Specialists try to predict the winner by comparing, for example, one side's aerial attack with the other side's pass defense. This is a better comparison than contrasting the quarterbacks or the receivers. But the accuracy of such complicated predictions cannot be known until the game is over.
>
> Similarly, as long as nuclear peace is maintained, it is impossible to measure the complex balance between two nuclear arsenals with any certainty. Given this fortunate uncertainty, different individuals can hold very different beliefs about the nuclear balance. Such differences are usually not about what numbers of weapons exist in the arsenals of the two superpowers, but about how to interpret the differences between the arsenals and the importance of certain kinds of nuclear advantages and disadvantages.

The authors want to explain why "No definitive answer is possible," and they find the best way to do so is to provide an analogy. Thus, they liken any comparison of American and Soviet nuclear arsenals (an abstraction) to a comparison of the strengths of two football teams (a familiar activity—in fact, one is reminded of the pre-game predictions of commentators and coaches on "NFL Today"). No matter how detailed the analyses of two teams' strengths and weaknesses, the accuracy of any predictions cannot be verified until after the game is played. So it is with the question of nuclear arsenals. In the absence of nuclear war, there are bound to be different and equally justifiable interpretations of each country's nuclear advantages and disadvantages. The authors' analogy helps them make their point neatly and concisely.

Writing an Essay of Analogy

If you find yourself trying to explain a subject that the average reader will have trouble seeing clearly—something that is unfamiliar, perhaps, or complex or intangible or simply hard to understand—you should consider the possibility of using an analogy. Are you talking about a single object, a group of objects, a process, an activity? What is your range of possibilities for analogies? Then, your most important task is to use your imagination. Sometimes an analogy will occur almost naturally; John McMurtry's comparison of football violence and war is such an analogy, as is Lester Del Rey's analogy between the earth's atmosphere and a window. At other times, however, you may have to work to create the analogy, as A. M. Winchester does when he compares diffusion with the movement of blindfolded people.

As you organize and write your essay, the usefulness of your analogy will depend on the points of comparison you can discover and how well these points help both to clarify and explain the topic of your essay.

1. Evaluating the Situation

First of all, make sure the topic you are explaining warrants the use of analogy. Is it unobservable or abstract or so complicated that it cannot be explained more directly? Is your analogy functional and not merely decorative? An analogy can seem silly if the topic of discussion is readily understandable. Equally important is ascertaining that the analogy you come up with will, indeed, make things clearer and more meaningful to your readers: explaining the U.S. banking system by comparing it to the process of photosynthesis will be more confusing than helpful. Finally, remember that an analogy requires the items being compared to belong to different classes. You can't draw an analogy between a colony of ants and a hive of bees, for example, although you can compare and contrast the two. But to explain an ant colony by pointing out its similarities to a battalion of soldiers is certainly to create an analogy.

2. Listing Similarities

Once you feel confident that the items of your analogy are suitable, brainstorm a list of ways in which they can be seen as similar. Sometimes, in order to generate similarities, it's useful to put your analogy in the form of a question: How is writing an essay like following a road map? How is wrestling like ballet? How is poverty like a nightmare? Ultimately, you'll have to eliminate any similarities that seem irrelevant or that stretch logic to a ridiculous extreme. After all, the two are from different classes and, therefore, are essentially unlike one another. There is bound to be a breaking point beyond which the differences begin to outweigh the similarities and, consequently, destroy the analogy. Be careful that the similarities you discover are reasonable and also relevant to your central explanation.

3. Organization

Like a comparison and contrast, an analogy is most commonly arranged according to one of two patterns: block or point-by-point. (See pages 254–255 in Section 6 for a full explanation of these two patterns.) Before you begin to draft, you will probably want to jot down a scratch outline that shows which pattern you will use to develop your analogy and in which order you will present the various points of similarity. For example, Lester Del Rey's passage about the earth's atmosphere is organized in the block pattern, as a scratch outline shows:

Analogy: window and Earth's atmosphere.
  Window is like a shield.
    Temperature
    Protection

Atmosphere is like a shield.
Temperature
Protection

Of course, an analogy can be pushed further than Del Rey's and may include many more points of similarity.

4. Developing Your Analogy

Be sure to announce your analogy directly, probably at the beginning of your essay. Then, even though your readers are already knowledgeable about it, don't slight your development of the familiar subject. It is common, in fact, for the familiar subject of the analogy to be discussed at greater length than the less familiar: you've already seen that, after his detailed description of blindfolded people dispersing throughout a gymnasium, A. M. Winchester needs only to suggest the similarity with diffusion for his explanation to be clear. Whether or not your analogy follows this relatively lopsided format will depend on what you are trying to help your reader understand. But without a thorough, concrete presentation of the familiar subject, a meaningful comparison to the unfamiliar subject is almost impossible.

As you develop the two subjects of your analogy, be careful that you mark the points of the comparison with appropriate words and phrases (such as *like, in the same way, similarly, compared to,* and *corresponds*). Try not to overuse such pointers, but make sure your reader can see the similarities that are central to your explanation.

5. The Limits of Analogy

Analogies are useful to help a reader visualize unobservable phenomena and understand complicated situations. They can provide a fresh viewpoint on a subject or serve to illustrate a particular idea. But they cannot be considered conclusive evidence. Therefore, the thrust of an argument should never be based on an analogy. It may be possible to see the two subjects of the analogy as similar in important ways; however, don't forget that there will always be significant differences, which must eventually strain a reader's belief.

The Ducks on Corrigan's Pond

Hesterly Goodson

Hesterly Goodson was born in Burlington, Vermont, but grew up in Stowe, where she still lives. An English major when she wrote the following essay, Hesterly now teaches composition herself. When she's not busy with her teaching, Hesterly enjoys skiing and rock climbing in Vermont's Green Mountains. In her essay "The Ducks on Corrigan's Pond," Hesterly uses an analogy to help explain the way she feels about her hometown and the people who live there.

I used to see them every morning from the school bus. They were decoys—three wooden mallards, anchored to the bottom. I watched them move across the surface of the pond. On windy days they were blown toward the reeds, where they stopped and leaned against their tethers. On calmer days they floated in the center, bobbing and changing their position in relation to one another. I never understood why they were there, for they never drew other ducks to the pond—they just turned in the breeze and weathered.

Driving by the other day, I noticed that the reeds had grown and the ducks were gone. No one was around, so I got out of my car and circled the pond to search for them. I found them anchored on the far side, water-heavy and stripped of their paint, but floating still. I could see their age in the cracks and the moss on their backs. As I sat on the bank and watched them bobbing purposelessly, my thoughts turned to the past, to growing up in this town.

I remembered the summers I spent riding my bike on the hot sidewalk under the storefront awnings on Main Street. Mr. Adams always waved from his egg truck, and I always waved back. Mrs. Wilkins was usually in her garden. I remembered the candy counter at Lackey's, the Reverend Hall, the Junior Prom. I remembered, also, every Memorial Day when I marched in the high school band down Maple Street. A few people stood on the sidewalk to watch, but most just fell in behind as we turned down Old Cemetery Road. Every year we went the same route, wore the same uniforms, played the same songs. We were always impatient to be done, to have the rest of the day off. But the veterans led the march, and they were old and walked slowly. We listened to the speech that we knew by heart, and watched while the old men stood as straight as they could when the guns were fired.

Somehow, I felt like one of those decoys on the pond. I was 4 floating on the surface, yet anchored to the mud on the bottom. I wanted to escape the smallness here. I wanted more. When Andy Lockwood proposed marriage to me in the first grade, I accepted. When Heather Adams proposed that we run away in the sixth grade, I also accepted. Not until I was twenty, however, did I really leave. I took my car, my clothes, and four hundred dollars, and I escaped with my first serious boyfriend.

In those days, I felt such contempt for my friends who stayed. 5 Beth had Scott's child, and Laura had twins. Will worked in his father's store, and Larry worked the family farm. Ann and Dean were married, Bobby drove the school bus, Randy fixed the streets. Like the ducks, they were anchored here. They seemed mindlessly content to repeat their parents' lives, and I couldn't understand why they stayed.

But the longer I was away, the more I began to understand. 6 They stayed for the same reason that eventually brought me back: they needed the comfort of the familiar, the security of every-day ritual. They wanted to raise their children the way they had been raised because they found satisfaction in the regularity of life here.

I finally saw what I had missed before—that the ducks are here 7 because they have to be, but the people are here by choice. Once I thought the people were as mindless as the ducks. Going away made me recognize that they are not. The ducks were anchored by someone else; the people have anchored themselves. I've come back—back home—because I realize that I need Lackey's store and the Memorial Day parade. I need this town and the security of my past.

Interview with Hesterly Goodson

How did you hit on the analogy between the decoys and the townspeople?

The essay is about feelings that I had had for a long time and wanted to write about. I started with a different analogy, though. Near the highway I pass along every day, there's a rock that dangles from a string tied to the limb of an elm tree—maybe it has to do with the wind, or it's someone's idea of art—and its flat side catches the sun when you drive by. I thought that would make for an effective analogy, how I felt tied to Vermont and could turn like the rock to see all those vistas but not really be able to go anywhere. But being suspended like that had a real negative connotation for me. Then I drove by the duck decoys and they seemed to be a way of describing what I felt. I didn't have anything handy to write with at the time, but all the way home I was thinking about it. Even sentences—I had "written" the entire opening before I actually started a draft.

So it all actually happened.

Yes, it actually happened. I've no idea what the man's name was—it wasn't actually Corrigan—this old man who lived in a trailer across the street and actually moved the decoys around. It just struck me as odd when I was a little kid. The decoys were exactly what I was looking for to write the paper: anchored, able to move around a little bit on the surface. When I moved away I was homesick the entire time, I wanted to come back and I couldn't put into words why, and I didn't understand being tied to a place.

Once you had your object and the opening, did the rest come easily?

The essay went through about four drafts. I started out on a couple of different tacks and had to change them. For example, I first included the old man who had moved the ducks around, but my analogy would have made me provide something or someone to move the people around; I didn't want to do that because they were there by choice. So I cut out the old man. I wanted to include the Memorial Day parade, but I wasn't sure where, so I tried a couple of different ways. I moved paragraphs around—that kind of thing. And there were a lot of smaller revisions. But I'd say that I had the overall content and shape about right in the first draft.

Why an analogy?

It helped me to objectify my feelings, and maybe clarify them. Making a comparison between the townspeople and the decoys, listing points they did and didn't have in common, helped me to think. I don't think I could have written about these feelings in a different way. I might have done it as a narration, but I don't think it would have been as effective and I don't think it would have made my emotions and thoughts as clear to the reader.

You sound as though you like to write.

Writing is a way of dealing with a strong emotion, at least for me. For instance, last summer I drove by an auction on a country road and I stopped and went in. All the possessions were being auctioned off. The family wasn't there, but their personal things were being sold—I saw photographs being pulled out of their albums—and I felt so strongly that I needed to write about it to help vent the emotions. I write to communicate too, of course, and I'd like to be a writer—some fiction, some nonfiction. I do some writing at least every other day, but I don't usually finish it; who has time?

The World House

Martin Luther King, Jr.

Martin Luther King, Jr. (1929–1968), was the son of a Baptist minister. Ordained at the age of eighteen, King went on to study at Morehouse College, Crozer Theological Seminary, Boston University, and Chicago Theological Seminary. He came to prominence in 1955 in Montgomery, Alabama, when he led a successful boycott against the city's segregated bus system. The first president of the Southern Christian Leadership Conference, King became the leading spokesman for the civil rights movement during the 1950s and 1960s. He also championed women's rights and protested the Vietnam War. In 1964 he was awarded the Nobel Peace Prize for his policy of massive but nonviolent resistance to racial injustice. King was assassinated in April of 1968 after he spoke at a rally in Memphis, Tennessee.

In the following essay, King expands on the idea of racial harmony to include the ways in which everyone must learn to coexist for the good of the planet.

Some years ago a famous novelist died. Among his papers was found a list of suggested plots for future stories, the most prominently underscored being this one: "A widely separated family inherits a house in which they have to live together." This is the great new problem of mankind. We have inherited a large house, a great "world house" in which we have to live together—black and white, Easterner and Westerner, Gentile and Jew, Catholic and Protestant, Moslem and Hindu—a family unduly separated in ideas, culture and interest, who, because we can never again live apart, must learn somehow to live with each other in peace.

However deeply American Negroes are caught in the struggle to be at last at home in our homeland of the United States, we cannot ignore the larger world house in which we are also dwellers. Equality with whites will not solve the problems of either whites or Negroes if it means equality in a world society stricken by poverty and in a universe doomed to extinction by war.

All inhabitants of the globe are now neighbors. This worldwide 3
neighborhood has been brought into being largely as a result of the modern scientific and technological revolutions. The world of today is vastly different from the world of just one hundred years ago. A century ago Thomas Edison had not yet invented the incandescent lamp to bring light to many dark places of the earth. The Wright brothers had not yet invented that fascinating mechanical bird that would spread its gigantic wings across the skies and soon dwarf distance and place time in the service of man. Einstein had not yet challenged an axiom and the theory of relativity had not yet been posited.

Human beings, searching a century ago as now for better understanding, had no television, no radios, no telephones and no 4
motion pictures through which to communicate. Medical science had not yet discovered the wonder drugs to end many dread plagues and diseases. One hundred years ago military men had not yet developed the terrifying weapons of warfare that we know today—not the bomber, an airborne fortress raining down death; nor napalm, that burner of all things and flesh in its path. A century ago there were no skyscraping buildings to kiss the stars and no gargantuan bridges to span the waters. Science had not yet peered into the unfathomable ranges of interstellar space, nor had it penetrated oceanic depths. All these new inventions, these new ideas, these sometimes fascinating and sometimes frightening developments came later. Most of them have come within the past sixty years, sometimes with agonizing slowness, more characteristically with bewildering speed, but always with enormous significance for our future.

The years ahead will see a continuation of the same dramatic 5
developments. Physical science will carve new highways through the stratosphere. In a few years astronauts and cosmonauts will probably walk comfortably across the uncertain pathways of the moon. In two or three years it will be possible, because of the new supersonic jets, to fly from New York to London in two and one-half hours. In the years ahead medical science will greatly prolong the lives of men by finding a cure for cancer and deadly heart ailments. Automation and cybernation will make it possible for

working people to have undreamed-of amounts of leisure time. All this is a dazzling picture of the furniture, the workshop, the spacious rooms, the new decorations and the architectural pattern of the large world house in which we are living.

Along with the scientific and technolgical revolution, we have 6 also witnessed a worldwide freedom revolution over the last few decades. The present upsurge of the Negro people of the United States grows out of a deep and passionate determination to make freedom and equality a reality "here" and "now." In one sense the civil rights movement in the United States is a special American phenomenon which must be understood in the light of American history and dealt with in terms of the American situation. But on another and more important level, what is happening in the United States today is a significant part of a world development.

We live in a day, said the philosopher Alfred North Whitehead, 7 "when civilization is shifting its basic outlook; a major turning point in history where the presuppositions on which society is structured are being analyzed, sharply challenged, and profoundly changed." What we are seeing now is a freedom explosion, the realization of "an idea whose time has come," to use Victor Hugo's phrase. The deep rumbling of discontent that we hear today is the thunder of disinherited masses, rising from dungeons of oppression to the bright hills of freedom. In one majestic chorus the rising masses are singing, in the words of our freedom song, "Ain't gonna let nobody turn us around." All over the world like a fever, freedom is spreading in the widest liberation movement in history. The great masses of people are determined to end the exploitation of their races and lands. They are awake and moving toward their goal like a tidal wave. You can hear them rumbling in every village street, on the docks, in the houses, among the students, in the churches and at political meetings. For several centuries the direction of history flowed from the nations and societies of Western Europe out into the rest of the world in "conquests" of various sorts. That period, the era of colonialism, is at an end. East is moving West. The earth is being redistributed. Yes, we are "shifting our basic outlooks."

These developments should not surprise any student of history. 8 Oppressed people cannot remain oppressed forever. The yearning for freedom eventually manifests itself. The Bible tells the thrilling story of how Moses stood in Pharaoh's court centuries ago and cried, "Let my people go." This was an opening chapter in a continuing story. The present struggle in the United States is a later chapter in the same story. Something within has reminded the Negro of his birthright of freedom, and something without has reminded him that it can be gained. Consciously or unconsciously, he has been caught up by the spirit of the times, and with his black brothers of Africa and his brown and yellow brothers in Asia, South America and the Caribbean, the United States Negro is moving with a sense of great urgency toward the promised land of racial justice.

Nothing could be more tragic than for men to live in these revolutionary times and fail to achieve the new attitudes and the new mental outlooks that the new situation demands. In Washington Irving's familiar story of Rip Van Winkle, the one thing that we usually remember is that Rip slept twenty years. There is another important point, however, that is almost always overlooked. It was the sign on the inn in the little town on the Hudson from which Rip departed and scaled the mountain for his long sleep. When he went up, the sign had a picture of King George III of England. When he came down, twenty years later, the sign had a picture of George Washington. As he looked at the picture of the first President of the United States, Rip was confused, flustered and lost. He knew not who Washington was. The most striking thing about this story is not that Rip slept twenty years, but that he slept through a revolution that would alter the course of human history. 9

One of the great liabilities of history is that all too many people fail to remain awake through great periods of social change. Every society has its protectors of the status quo and its fraternities of the indifferent who are notorious for sleeping through revolutions. But today our very survival depends on our ability to stay awake, to adjust to new ideas, to remain vigilant and to face the challenge of change. The large house in which we live demands that we transform this worldwide neighborhood into a worldwide brotherhood. Together we must learn to live as brothers or together we will be forced to perish as fools. 10

We must work passionately and indefatigably to bridge the gulf between our scientific progress and our moral progress. One of the great problems of mankind is that we suffer from a poverty of the spirit which stands in glaring contrast to our scientific and 11 technological abundance. The richer we have become materially, the poorer we have become morally and spiritually.

Every man lives in two realms, the internal and the external. 12 The internal is that realm of spiritual ends expressed in art, literature, morals and religion. The external is that complex of devices, techniques, mechanisms and instrumentalities by means of which we live. Our problem today is that we have allowed the internal to become lost in the external. We have allowed the means by which we live to outdistance the ends for which we live. So much of modern life can be summarized in that suggestive phrase of Thoreau: "Improved means to an unimproved end." This is the serious predicament, the deep and haunting problem, confronting modern man. Enlarged material powers spell enlarged peril if there is not proportionate growth of the soul. When the external of man's nature subjugates the internal, dark storm clouds begin to form.

Western civilization is particularly vulnerable at this moment, 13 for our material abundance has brought us neither peace of mind nor serenity of spirit. An Asian writer has portrayed our dilemma in candid terms:

> You call your thousand material devices "labor-saving machinery," yet you are forever "busy." With the multiplying of your machinery you grow increasingly fatigued, anxious, nervous, dissatisfied. Whatever you have, you want more; and wherever you are you want to go somewhere else . . . your devices are neither time-saving nor soul-saving machinery. They are so many sharp spurs which urge you on to invent more machinery and to do more business.

This tells us something about our civilization that cannot be cast aside as a prejudiced charge by an Eastern thinker who is jealous of Western prosperity. We cannot escape the indictment.

This does not mean that we must turn back the clock of scientific 14 progress. No one can overlook the wonders that science has wrought for our lives. The automobile will not abdicate in favor of the horse and buggy, or the train in favor of the stagecoach, or the tractor in favor of the hand plow, or the scientific method in favor of ignorance and superstition. But our moral and spiritual "lag" must be redeemed. When scientific power outruns moral power, we end up with guided missiles and misguided men. When we foolishly minimize the internal of our lives and maximize the external, we sign the warrant for our own day of doom.

Our hope for creative living in this world house that we have 15
inherited lies in our ability to reestablish the moral ends of our
lives in personal character and social justice. Without this spiritual
and moral reawakening we shall destroy ourselves in the misuse
of our own instruments.

Questions on Subject

1. According to King, why is "equality" for African-Americans not
   the solution to their problems?
2. King was writing in the 1960s of several future events. Which of
   his prophecies have come to pass, which have not? Can you name
   any modern development that King never even thought to
   anticipate?
3. In what way does King think the civil rights movement is a "significant part of a world development"? What is the "freedom explosion" he refers to in paragraph 7?
4. According to King, what is the "liability of history"? What, if anything, does he expect his readers to do?

Questions on Strategy

1. Explain the analogy that King has set up to explain the new global
   reality. How effective is his analogy? In what way is it appropriate
   to his subject?
2. In his opening sentence, King refers to an author without naming
   him. Why do you suppose he has chosen to do this?
3. King quotes several famous thinkers to make his point. Cite examples of these quotes and explain how they work to strengthen
   his argument.
4. King has organized his argument using a deductive system of organization. In what way does this choice of organization suit his
   argument? What would have been gained or lost had he organized
   his argument using inductive reasoning? (Glossary: *Deductive* and
   Inductive)
5. Identify King's use of parallelism, and explain how it works to
   enhance his meaning. (Glossary: *Parallelism*)

Questions on Diction and Vocabulary

1. Who does King intend for his audience? Cite examples of his diction that led you to your conclusion.
2. King alternates between the use of the pronoun "we" and the pronoun "you." Is his use of these two pronouns arbitrary or can you discover a difference in tone or intended meaning in the instances when he uses one or the other of them?
3. Note King's use of the words *family* (paragraph 1), *dwellers* (2), *neighbors* (3), *furniture* (5), *brothers* (8), and *brotherhood* (10). What kinds of connotations does each of these words have for you and how do they help further King's purpose in his essay? (Glossary: *Connotation*)
4. Refer to your desk dictionary to determine the meanings of the following words as they are used in this selection: *stricken* (paragraph 2), *extinction* (2), *incandescent* (3), *axiom* (3), *gargantuan* (4), *peered* (4), *cybernation* (5), *exploitation* (7), *rumbling* (7), *urgency* (8), *flustered* (9), *vigilant* (10), *indefatigably* (11), *predicament* (12), *subjugates* (12), *indictment* (13), *wrought* (14).

Writing Suggestions

1. Write an essay in which you argue for or against Thoreau's notion of "improved means to an unimproved end."
2. Analogies are particularly useful for writers trying to describe something very large or something very small. For example, King has used a single family home to help his reader understand a problem that is quite literally as big as the world. Create an analogy of your own to describe something very large.

The Attic of the Brain

Lewis Thomas

Physician, administrator, teacher, and writer, Lewis Thomas was born in 1913 in New York and attended Princeton and the Harvard Medical School. A former president of the Memorial Sloan-Kettering Cancer Center, Lewis began his writing career in 1971 with a series of essays for the New England Journal of Medicine. *The best of them were collected in his book* The Lives of a Cell: Notes of a Biology Watcher, *winner of a National Book Award in 1974. Three other collections have followed:* The Medusa and the Snail: More Notes of a Biology Watcher, Late Night Thoughts on Listening to Mahler's Ninth Symphony, *and* Etcetera, Etcetera.

In the following essay, taken from Late Night Thoughts, *Lewis cautions against the irreverent and ill-advised intrusion into the unconscious by using the analogy of the attic to explain complexities and mysteries of the human brain.*

My parents' house had an attic, the darkest and strangest part 1
of the building, reachable only by placing a stepladder beneath the
trapdoor and filled with unidentifiable articles too important to be
thrown out with the trash but no longer suitable to have at hand.
This mysterious space was the memory of the place. After many
years all the things deposited in it became, one by one, lost to
consciousness. But they were still there, we knew, safely and comfortably stored in the tissues of the house.

These days most of us live in smaller, more modern houses or 2
in apartments, and attics have vanished. Even the deep closets in
which we used to pile things up for temporary forgetting are rarely
designed into new homes.

Everything now is out in the open, openly acknowledged and 3
displayed, and whenever we grow tired of a memory, an old chair,
a trunkful of old letters, they are carted off to the dump for burning.

This has seemed a healthier way to live, except maybe for the 4 smoke—everything out to be looked at, nothing strange hidden under the roof, nothing forgotten because of no place left in impenetrable darkness to forget. Openness is the new life-style, no undisclosed belongings, no private secrets. Candor is the rule in architecture. The house is a machine for living, and what kind of a machine would hide away its worn-out, obsolescent parts?

But it is in our nature as human beings to clutter, and we hanker 5 for places set aside, reserved for storage. We tend to accumulate and outgrow possessions at the same time, and it is an endlessly discomforting mental task to keep sorting out the ones to get rid of. We might, we think, remember them later and find a use for them, and if they are gone for good, off to the dump, this is a source of nervousness. I think it may be one of the reasons we drum our fingers so much these days.

We might take a lesson here from what has been learned about 6 our brains in this century. We thought we discovered, first off, the attic, although its existence has been mentioned from time to time by all the people we used to call great writers. What we really found was the trapdoor and a stepladder, and off we clambered, shining flashlights into the corners, vacuuming the dust out of bureau drawers, puzzling over the names of objects, tossing them down to the floor below, and finally paying around fifty dollars an hour to have them carted off for burning.

After several generations of this new way of doing things we 7 took up openness and candor with the febrile intensity of a new religion, everything laid out in full view, and as in the design of our new houses it seemed a healthier way to live, except maybe again for smoke.

And now, I think, we have a new kind of worry. There is no 8 place for functionless, untidy, inexplicable notions, no dark comfortable parts of the mind to hide away the things we'd like to keep but at the same time forget. The attic is still there, but with the trapdoor always open and the stepladder in place we are always in and out of it, flashing lights around, naming everything, unmystified.

I have an earnest proposal for psychiatry, a novel set of thera- 9 peutic rules, although I know it means waiting in line.

Bring back the old attic. Give new instructions to the patients 10 who are made nervous by our times, including me, to make a conscious effort to hide a reasonable proportion of thought. It would have to be a gradual process, considering how far we have come in the other direction talking, talking all the way. Perhaps only one or two thoughts should be repressed each day, at the outset. The easiest, gentlest way might be to start with dreams, first by forbidding the patient to mention any dream, much less to recount its details, then encouraging the outright forgetting that there was a dream at all, remembering nothing beyond the vague sense that during sleep there had been the familiar sound of something shifting and sliding, up under the roof.

We might, in this way, regain the kind of spontaneity and zest 11 for ideas, things popping into the mind, uncontrollable and ungovernable thoughts, the feel that this notion is somehow connected unaccountably with that one. We could come again into possession of real memory, the kind of memory that can come from jumbled forgotten furniture, old photographs, fragments of music.

It has been one of the great errors of our time to think that by 12 thinking about thinking, and then talking about it, we could possibly straighten out and tidy up our minds. There is no delusion more damaging than to get the idea in your head that you understand the functioning of your own brain. Once you acquire such a notion, you run the danger of moving in to take charge, guiding your thoughts, shepherding your mind from place to place, *controlling* it, making lists of regulations. The human mind is not meant to be governed, certainly not by any book of rules yet written; it is supposed to run itself, and we are obliged to follow it along, trying to keep up with it as best we can. It is all very well to be aware of your awareness, even proud of it, but never try to operate it. You are not up to the job.

I leave it to the analysts to work out the techniques for doing 13 what now needs doing. They are presumably the professionals most familiar with the route, and all they have to do is turn back and go the other way, session by session, step by step. It takes a certain amount of hard swallowing and a lot of revised jargon, and I have great sympathy for their plight, but it is time to reverse course.

If after all, as seems to be true, we are endowed with unconscious 14 minds in our brains, these should be regarded as normal structures, installed wherever they are for a purpose. I am not sure what they are built to contain, but as a biologist, impressed by the usefulness of everything alive, I would take it for granted that they are useful, probably indispensable organs of thought. It cannot be a bad thing to own one, but I would no more think of meddling with it than trying to exorcise my liver, an equally mysterious apparatus. Until we know a lot more, it would be wise, as we have learned from other fields in medicine, to let them be, above all not to interfere. Maybe, even—and this is the notion I wish to suggest to my psychiatric friends—to stock them up, put more things into them, make *use* of them. Forget whatever you feel like forgetting. From time to time, practice *not* being open, discover new things *not* to talk about, learn reserve, hold the tongue. But above all, develop the human talent for forgetting words, phrases, whole unwelcome sentences, all experiences involving wincing. If we should ever lose the loss of memory, we might lose as well that most attractive of signals ever flashed from the human face, the blush. If we should give away the capacity for embarrassment, the touch of fingertips might be the next to go, and then the suddenness of laughter, the unaccountable sure sense of something gone wrong, and, finally, the marvelous conviction that being human is the best thing to be.

Attempting to operate one's own mind, powered by such a magical instrument as the human brain, strikes me as rather like using the world's biggest computer to add columns of figures, or towing a Rolls-Royce with a nylon rope. 15

I have tried to think of a name for the new professional activity, but each time I think of a good one I forget it before I can get it written down. Psychorepression is the only one I've hung on to, but I can't guess at the fee schedule. 16

Questions on Subject

1. To what does Thomas liken psychoanalysis?
2. What is Thomas's proposal for psychiatry? What does he want us to get back? Why?
3. How does Thomas define "real memory" (paragraph 11)? How is it associated with the "blush" he refers to in paragraph 14?
4. What does Thomas say is the danger in imagining we can control our brains? Do you agree? Why or why not?

5. What exactly does Thomas mean when he says operating one's own mind is like "towing a Rolls-Royce with a nylon rope"?

Questions on Strategy

1. Explain the analogy Thomas uses to discuss the unconscious. Is it effective?
2. How has Thomas organized his essay? (Glossary: *Organization*) What one sentence provides the unifying idea for his essay? (Glossary: *Thesis*)
3. Point out a few of the specific examples Thomas uses to compare the human brain to an attic. Explain in what way these examples contribute to your understanding of the subject.
4. Although the use of analogy is a powerful strategy in an argument, it alone cannot "prove" a position. What other kinds of evidence does Thomas use to support his argument?

Questions on Diction and Vocabulary

1. In addition to the analogy of the attic, Thomas uses other figures of speech in his essay. Identify them and explain in what way each of them contributes to the overall effectiveness of his essay. (Glossary: *Figures of Speech*)
2. Does Thomas intend for his essay to be taken seriously? How do you know? Cite examples of his diction to support your answer.
3. Refer to your desk dictionary to determine the meanings of the following words as they are used in this selection: *candor* (paragraph 4), *obsolescent* (4), *hanker* (5), *clambered* (6), *febrile* (7), *repressed* (10), *vague* (10), *spontaneity* (11), *delusion* (12), *jargon* (13), *meddling* (14), *exorcise* (14), *apparatus* (14), *wincing* (14), *blush* (14).

Writing Suggestions

1. Write an essay in which you develop an analogy to explain some abstract notion of interest to you such as mathematics, faith, friendship, commitment, jealousy, infatuation, or music.
2. For one week, use your journal to keep track of the times you find yourself or others you know with "everything looked at, noth-

ing . . . hidden under the roof." Also record the times you gave into the need for "private secrets." What, if anything, did the events in each group have in common? What feelings do you associate with those moments? Do you find yourself hankering "for places set aside"? At the end of the week, write about your findings in an essay. In what way did your research support Thomas's essay?

Kill 'Em! Crush 'Em!
Eat 'Em Raw!

John McMurtry

John McMurtry was born in 1939 in Toronto, Canada, and received his B.A. at the University of Toronto, where he was a linebacker on the football team. He then played briefly for the Calgary Stampeders of the Canadian Football League before completing a Ph.D. in philosophy at the University of London. Since 1970 he has taught social and political philosophy at the University of Guelph in Canada and has written The Structure of Marx's World-View.

The following essay appeared in the Canadian newsmagazine Maclean's *in 1971, when protests against the Vietnam War were at their peak. Accordingly, McMurtry makes an analogy between football and war to argue against the violence of the sport.*

A few months ago my neck got a hard crick in it. I couldn't turn my head; to look left or right I'd have to turn my whole body. But I'd had cricks in my neck since I started playing grade-school football and hockey, so I just ignored it. Then I began to notice that when I reached for any sort of large book (which I do pretty often as a philosophy teacher at the University of Guelph) I had trouble lifting it with one hand. I was losing the strength in my left arm, and I had such a steady pain in my back I often had to stretch out on the floor of the room I was in to relieve the pressure.

A few weeks later I mentioned to my brother, an orthopedic surgeon, that I'd lost the power in my arm since my neck began to hurt. Twenty-four hours later I was in a Toronto hospital not sure whether I might end up with a wasted upper limb. Apparently the steady pounding I had received playing college and professional football in the late Fifties and early Sixties had driven my head into my backbone so that the discs had crumpled together at the neck—"acute herniation"—and had cut the nerves to my left arm like a pinched telephone wire (without nerve stimulation, of course, the muscles atrophy, leaving the arm crippled). So I spent my Christmas holidays in the hospital in heavy traction and much of the next three months with my neck in a brace. Today most of the pain has gone, and I've recovered most of the strength in my arm. But from time to time I still have to don the brace, and surgery remains a possibility.

Not much of this will surprise anyone who knows football. It is 3 a sport in which body wreckage is one of the leading conventions. A few days after I went into hospital for that crick in my neck, another brother, an outstanding football player in college, was undergoing spinal surgery in the same hospital two floors above me. In his case it was a lower, more massive herniation, which every now and again buckled him so that he was unable to lift himself off his back for days at a time. By the time he entered the hospital for surgery he had already spent several months in bed. The operation was successful, but, as in all such cases, it will take him a year to recover fully.

These aren't isolated experiences. Just about anybody who has 4 ever played football for any length of time, in high school, college or one of the professional leagues, has suffered for it later physically.

Indeed, it is arguable that body shattering is the very *point* of 5 football, as killing and maiming are of war. (In the United States, for example, the game results in 15 to 20 deaths a year and about 50,000 major operations on knees alone.) To grasp some of the more conspicuous similarities between football and war, it is instructive to listen to the imperatives most frequently issued to the players by their coaches, teammates and fans. "Hurt 'em!" "Level 'em!" "Kill 'em!" "Take 'em apart!" Or watch for the plays that are most enthusiastically applauded by the fans. Where someone is "smeared," "knocked silly," "creamed," "nailed," "broken in two," or even "crucified." (One of my coaches when I played corner linebacker with the Calgary Stampeders in 1961 elaborated, often very inventively, on this language of destruction: admonishing us to "unjoin" the opponent, "make 'im remember you" and "stomp 'im like a bug.") Just as in hockey, where a fight will bring fans to their feet more often than a skillful play, so in football the mouth waters most of all for the really crippling block or tackle. For the kill. Thus the good teams are "hungry," the best players are "mean," and "casualties" are as much a part of the game as they are of a war. The family resemblance between football and war is, indeed, 6 striking. Their languages are similar: "field general," "long bomb," "blitz," "take a shot," "front line," "pursuit," "good hit," "the draft" and so on. Their principles and practices are alike: mass hysteria, the art of intimidation, absolute command and total obedience, territorial aggression, censorship, inflated insignia and propaganda, blackboard maneuvers and strategies, drills, uniforms, formations, marching bands and training camps. And the virtues they celebrate are almost identical: hyper-aggressiveness, coolness under fire and suicidal bravery. All this has been implicitly recognized by such jock-loving Americans as media stars General Patton and President Nixon, who have talked about war as a football game. Patton wanted to make his Second World War tank men look like football players. And Nixon, as we know, was fond of comparing attacks on Vietnam to football plays and drawing coachly diagrams on a blackboard for TV war fans.

One difference between war and football, though, is that there 7 is little or no protest against football. Perhaps the most extraordinary thing about the game is that the systematic infliction of injuries excites in people not concern, as would be the case if they were sustained at, say, a rock festival, but a collective rejoicing and euphoria. Players and fans alike revel in the spectacle of a combatant felled into semiconsciousness, "blindsided," "clotheslined" or "decapitated." I can remember, in fact, being chided by a coach in pro ball for not "getting my hat" injuriously into a player who was already lying helpless on the ground. (On another occasion, after the Stampeders had traded the celebrated Joe Kapp to BC, we were playing the Lions in Vancouver and Kapp was forced on one play to run with the ball. He was coming "down the chute," his bad knee wobbling uncertainly, so I simply dropped on him like a blanket. After I returned to the bench I was reproved for not exploiting the opportunity to unhinge his bad knee.)

After every game, of course, the papers are full of reports on the 8 day's injuries, a sort of post-battle "body count," and the respective teams go to work with doctors and trainers, tape, whirlpool baths, cortisone and morphine to patch and deaden the wounds before the next game. Then the whole drama is reenacted—injured athletes held together by adhesive, braces and drugs—and the days following it are filled with even more feverish activity to put on the show yet again at the end of the next week. (I remember being so taped up in college that I earned the nickname "mummy.") The team that survives this merry-go-round spectacle of skilled masochism with the fewest incapacitating injuries usually wins. It is a sort of victory by ordeal: "We hurt them more than they hurt us."

My own initiation into this brutal circus was typical. I loved the 9 game from the moment I could run with a ball. Played shoeless on a green open field with no one keeping score and in a spirit of reckless abandon and laughter, it's a very different sport. Almost no one gets hurt and it's rugged, open and exciting (it still is for me). But then, like everything else, it starts to be regulated and institutionalized by adult authorities. And the fun is over.

So it was as I began the long march through organized football. 10 Now there was a coach and elders to make it clear by their behavior that beating other people was the only thing to celebrate and that trying to shake someone up every play was the only thing to be really proud of. Now there were severe rule enforcers, audiences, formally recorded victors and losers, and heavy equipment to permit crippling bodily moves and collisions (according to one American survey, more than 80% of all football injuries occur to fully equipped players). And now there was the official "given" that the only way to keep playing was to wear suffocating armor, to play to defeat, to follow orders silently and to renounce spontaneity for joyless drill. The game had been, in short, ruined. But because I loved to play and play skillfully, I stayed. And progressively and inexorably, as I moved through high school, college and pro leagues, my body was dismantled. Piece by piece.

I started off with torn ligaments in my knee at 13. Then, as the 11 organization and the competition increased, the injuries came faster and harder. Broken nose (three times), broken jaw (fractured in the first half and dismissed as a "bad wisdom tooth," so I played with it for the rest of the game), ripped knee ligaments again. Torn ligaments in one ankle and a fracture in the other (which I remember feeling relieved about because it meant I could honorably stop drill-blocking a 270-pound defensive end). Repeated rib fractures and cartilage tears (usually carried, again, through the remainder of the game). More dislocations of the left shoulder than I can remember (the last one I played with because, as the Calgary Stampeder doctor said, it "couldn't be damaged any more"). Occasional broken or dislocated fingers and toes. Chronically hurt lower back (I still can't lift with it or change a tire without worrying about folding). Separated right shoulder (as with many other injuries, like badly bruised hips and legs, needled with morphine for the games). And so on. The last pro game I played—against the Winnipeg Blue Bombers in the Western finals in 1961—I had a recently dislocated left shoulder, a more recently wrenched right shoulder and a chronic pain centre in one leg. I was so tied up with soreness I couldn't drive my car to the airport. But it never occurred to me or anyone else that I miss a play as a corner linebacker.

By the end of my football career, I had learned that physical 12 injury—giving it and taking it—is the real currency of the sport. And that in the final analysis the "winner" is the man who can hit to kill even if only half his limbs are working. In brief, a warrior game with a warrior ethos into which (like almost everyone else I played with) my original boyish enthusiasm had been relentlessly taunted and conditioned.

In thinking back on how all this happened, though, I can pick 13 out no villains. As with the social system as a whole, the game has a life of its own. Everyone grows up inside it, accepts it and fulfills its dictates as obediently as helots. Far from ever questioning the principles of the activity, people simply concentrate on executing these principles more aggressively than anybody around them. The result is a group of people who, as the leagues become of a higher and higher class, are progressively insensitive to the possibility that things could be otherwise. Thus, in football, anyone who might question the wisdom or enjoyment of putting on heavy equipment on a hot day and running full speed at someone else with the intention of knocking him senseless would be regarded simply as not really a devoted athlete and probably "chicken." The choice is made straightforward. Either you, too, do your very utmost to efficiently smash and be smashed, or you admit incompetence or cowardice and quit. Since neither of these admissions is very pleasant, people generally keep any doubts they have to themselves and carry on.

Of course, it would be a mistake to suppose that there is more blind acceptance of brutal practices in organized football than elsewhere. On the contrary, a recent Harvard study has approvingly argued that football's characteristics of "impersonal acceptance of inflicted injury," an overriding "organization goal," the "ability to turn oneself on and off" and being, above all, "out to win" are of "inestimable value" to big corporations. Clearly, our sort of football is no sicker than the rest of our society. Even its organized destruction of physical well-being is not anomalous. A very large part of our wealth, work and time is, after all, spent in systematically destroying and harming human life. Manufacturing, selling and using weapons that tear opponents to pieces. Making ever bigger and faster predator-named cars with which to kill and injure one another by the million every year. And devoting our very lives to outgunning one another for power in an ever more destructive rat race. Yet all these practices are accepted without question by most people, even zealously defended and honored. Competitive, organized injuring is integral to our way of life, and football is simply one of the more intelligible mirrors of the whole process: a sort of colorful morality play showing us how exciting and rewarding it is to Smash Thy Neighbor.

Now it is fashionable to rationalize our collaboration in all this by arguing that, well, man *likes* to fight and injure his fellows and such games as football should be encouraged to discharge this original-sin urge into less harmful channels than, say, war. Public-show football, this line goes, plays the same sort of cathartic role as Aristotle said stage tragedy does: without real blood (or not much), it releases players and audience from unhealthy feelings stored up inside them.

As an ex-player in this seasonal coast-to-coast drama, I see little to recommend such a view. What organized football did to me was make me *suppress* my natural urges and re-express them in an alienating, vicious form. Spontaneous desires for free bodily exuberance and fraternization with competitors were shamed and forced under ("If it ain't hurtin' it ain't helpin' ") and in their place were demanded armored mechanical moves and cool hatred of all opposition. Endless authoritarian drill and dressing-room harangues (ever wonder why competing teams can't prepare for a game in the same dressing room?) were the kinds of mechanisms employed to reconstruct joyful energies into mean and alien shapes. I am quite certain that everyone else around me was being similarly forced into this heavily equipped military precision and angry antagonism, because there was always a mutinous attitude about full-dress practices, and everybody (the pros included) had to concentrate incredibly hard for days to whip themselves into just one hour's hostility a week against another club. The players never speak of these things, of course, because everyone is so anxious to appear tough.

The claim that men like seriously to battle one another to some 17 sort of finish is a myth. It only endures because it wears one of the oldest and most propagandized of masks—the romantic combatant. I sometimes wonder whether the violence all around us doesn't depend for its survival on the existence and preservation of this tough-guy disguise.

As for the effect of organized football on the spectator, the fan 18 is not released from supposed feelings of violent aggression by watching his athletic heroes perform it so much as encouraged in the view that people-smashing is an admirable mode of self-expression. The most savage attackers, after all, are, by general agreement, the most efficient and worthy players of all (the biggest applause I ever received as a football player occurred when I ran over people or slammed them so hard they couldn't get up). Such circumstances can hardly be said to lessen the spectators' martial tendencies. Indeed it seems likely that the whole show just further develops and titillates the North American addiction for violent self-assertion. . . . Perhaps, as well, it helps explain why the greater the zeal of U.S. political leaders as football fans (Johnson, Nixon, Agnew), the more enthusiastic the commitment to hardline politics. At any rate there seems to be a strong correlation between people who relish tough football and people who relish intimidating and beating the hell out of commies, hippies, protest marchers and other opposition groups.

Watching well-advertised strong men knock other people 19 around, make them hurt, is in the end like other tastes. It does not weaken with feeding and variation in form. It grows.

I got out of football in 1962. I had asked to be traded after Calgary 20 had offered me a $25-a-week-plus-commissions off-season job as a clothing-store salesman. ("Dear Mr. Finks:" I wrote. [Jim Finks was then the Stampeders' general manager.] "Somehow I do not think the dialectical subtleties of Hegel, Marx and Plato would be suitably oriented amidst the environmental stimuli of jockey shorts and herringbone suits. I hope you make a profitable sale or trade of my contract to the East.") So the Stampeders traded me to Montreal. In a preseason intersquad game with the Alouettes I ripped the cartilages in my ribs on the hardest block I'd ever thrown. I had trouble breathing and I had to shufflewalk with my torso on a tilt. The doctor in the local hospital said three weeks rest, the coach said scrimmage in two days. Three days later I was back home reading philosophy.

Questions on Subject

1. What is McMurtry's thesis in this essay, and where is it stated? (Glossary: *Thesis*)
2. In his opening paragraph, McMurtry mentions that he is a teacher of philosophy at a university. How did knowing this influence your response to the essay? How important is it that McMurtry played professional football himself? Why do you think so?
3. Why did McMurtry continue to play football for so long, in spite of his many injuries? What made him finally leave the game?
4. Where does McMurtry make specific connections between football and other areas of life? What conclusions does he draw from such connections? Do you find his conclusions justified? Why, or why not?
5. Where does McMurtry place the blame for violence in football?

Questions on Strategy

1. In paragraphs 5 through 8, McMurtry draws an extended analogy between football and war. What points of direct comparison does he suggest? Can you add other elements that football and war have in common? How does the analogy affect your understanding of the game?

2. How does McMurtry try to persuade you to accept his position? What do you see as the strengths and weaknesses of his central argument? (Glossary: *Argument*)
3. Why does McMurtry describe his football injuries in such vivid detail? What effect do these descriptions have on your response to his essay?
4. Why does McMurtry bring up the argument that football "releases players and audience from unhealthy feelings stored up inside them" (15) without real bloodshed? How does he counter this argument?
5. What is the effect of such short sentences and fragments as "For the kill" (5); "And the fun is over" (9); "Piece by piece" (10); and "It grows" (19)?

Questions on Diction and Vocabulary

1. What is the connotative value of the italicized words or phrases in each of the following excerpts from the essay? (Glossary: *Connotation*)
   a. "*body wreckage* is one of the leading conventions" (paragraph 3)
   b. "*body shattering* is the very point of football" (5)
   c. "the *family* resemblance between football and war" (6)
   d. "*merry-go-round* spectacle of *skilled masochism*" (8)
   e. "my own initiation into this *brutal circus*" (9)
   f. "only way to keep playing was to wear *suffocating armor*" (10)
   g. "my body was *dismantled*" (10)
   h. "*predator-named* cars with which to kill" (14)
2. Refer to your desk dictionary to determine the meanings of the following words as they are used in this selection: *euphoria* (paragraph 7), *inexorably* (10), *helots* (13), *anomalous* (14), *cathartic* (15), *exuberance* (16), *harangues* (16), *martial* (18), *titillates* (18).

Writing Assignments

1. Write a short essay in which you use an analogy to help you describe a game or explain how it is played. Select one of the games listed below or one of your own choice.

a. rugby	c. lacrosse	e. bridge
b. cribbage	d. Monopoly	f. boxing

g. wrestling   i. bowling   k. competitive
h. gymnastics   j. poker   swimming

2. Should athletics be a part of college life? How do intercollegiate varsity sports benefit a college? What do intramural sports contribute? What are the drawbacks or dangers of each? Do the benefits outweigh the costs, or not? Write an essay in which you deal with one or more of these questions.

Writing Suggestions for Analogy

1. Select one of the following general subjects, narrow it to a more specific topic, and then use an analogy to develop that topic. For example, if you choose astronomy as your subject, you might develop the topic of recent discoveries by astronomers; to do so, you could compare astronomers with explorers who are charting unknown territories. You may find it helpful before making your final selection to consider two or three topics and the possible analogies you could use.
   a. political scandal
   b. procrastination
   c. the drug problem
   d. a well-organized business
   e. a natural disaster
   f. the CIA
   g. travel to the moon or the planets
   h. sale of foreign products in the United States
   i. competition in school
   j. a successful parent, teacher, or coach
   k. foreign policy
   l. capitalism
   m. starting a new course of study
   n. religion in your life
   o. a handicap or a disabling disease
   p. punctuation marks
   q. astrology
   r. reconciling differences

    s. surgery
    t. poverty and/or starvation
    u. selecting an elective course
    v. power of the media
    w. an ecosystem
    x. dormitory life
    y. breaking off a relationship
    z. playing a sport

2. Creating analogies can be an interesting way of clarifying for your-self concepts that you are trying to master. Select a topic from one of the courses that you are taking this semester, particularly a topic that you are still working to understand. Try to find an analogy that will help make that topic more meaningful to you. Then write an essay in which you use the analogy to explain the topic to a reader who has never studied the subject matter in detail.

8
Division and Classification

What Are Division and Classification?

Like comparison and contrast, division and classification are separate yet closely related mental operations. Division involves breaking down a single large unit into smaller subunits, or separating a group of items into discrete categories. For example, a state government can be divided into its various branches and even further into departments or agencies; the whole pool of registered voters in the United States can be divided among political affiliations—Democrat, Republican, Independent, and so forth. Classification, on the other hand, entails sorting individual items and placing them into established categories: a boxer is classified with other boxers according to weight, a movie is placed in a particular rating category, a library book is shelved according to an elaborate system of subject codes, and a voter is categorized with others in his or her political party. Division, then, takes apart, whereas classification groups together. But even though the two processes can operate separately, the activity of dividing and classifying is more often circular.

Another example may help clarify how division and classification work hand in hand. Suppose a sociologist wants to determine whether the socioeconomic status of the people in a particular neighborhood has any influence on their voting behavior. Having decided on her purpose, the sociologist chooses as her subject the fifteen families living on Maple Street. Her goal then becomes to group these families in a way that will be relevant to her purpose. She immediately knows that she wants to divide the neighborhood in two ways—(1) according to socioeconomic status (low-income earners, middle-income earners, and high-income earners) and (2) according to voting behavior (voters and nonvoters). However, her process of division won't be complete until she can classify individual families into her various groupings.

In confidential interviews with each family, the sociologist learns first its income and then whether or not any member of the household has voted in a state or federal election during the last four years. Based on this information, she begins to classify each family according to her established categories and at the same time to divide the neighborhood into the subclasses crucial to her study. Her work leads her to construct a diagram of her divisions/classifications (see page 323). This diagram allows the sociologist to visualize her division and classification system and its essential components: *subject, basis* or *principle of division; subclasses* or *categories;* and *conclusion.* It is clear that her ultimate conclusion depends on her ability to work back and forth between the potential divisions or subclasses and the actual families to be classified.

Why Do Writers Use Division and Classification?

As the work of the Maple Street sociologist shows, division and classification are used primarily to demonstrate a particular point about the subject under discussion. In a paper about the emphasis a television network places on reaching various audiences, you could begin by dividing prime-time programing into suitable subclasses: shows primarily for adults, shows for families, shows for children, and so forth. You could then classify each of that network's individual programs into one of these categories. Ultimately, you would want to analyze how the programs are divided among the various categories; in this way you could make a point about which audiences the network works hardest to reach.

Classification and division can also help to explain a broadly complicated subject by reducing it to its more manageable parts. In an essay later in this section, for example, Bruce A. Baldwin

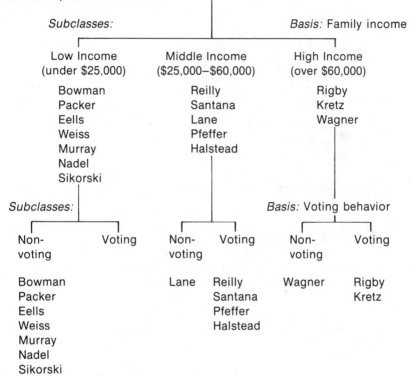

Subject: The 15 families on Maple Street

Purpose: To group the families according to socioeconomic status and voting behavior in order to study the relationship between the two.

Subclasses:

Basis: Family income

Low Income (under $25,000)	Middle Income ($25,000–$60,000)	High Income (over $60,000)
Bowman	Reilly	Rigby
Packer	Santana	Kretz
Eells	Lane	Wagner
Weiss	Pfeffer	
Murray	Halstead	
Nadel		
Sikorski		

Subclasses:

Basis: Voting behavior

Non-voting	Voting	Non-voting	Voting	Non-voting	Voting
Bowman		Lane	Reilly	Wagner	Rigby
Packer			Santana		Kretz
Eells			Pfeffer		
Weiss			Halstead		
Murray					
Nadel					
Sikorski					

Conclusion: On Maple Street there seems to be a relationship between socioeconomic status and voting behavior: the low-income families are nonvoters.

focuses his discussion on identifying and classifying experiences that lead to our being manipulated into workable categories.

Another purpose of division and classification can be to help writers and readers make choices. A voter may classify politicians on the basis of their attitudes toward nuclear energy or abortion; *Consumer Reports* classifies refrigerators on the basis of capacity, energy efficiency, repair record, freezer size, and warranty; high school seniors classify colleges and universities on the basis of the programs available at each. In such cases, division and classification have an absolutely practical end—making a decision about whom to vote for, which refrigerator to buy, and where to apply for admission to college.

Finally, division and classification can serve as a basic organizational strategy, one that is particularly helpful in informal essays. As you'll see later in this section, Russell Baker's system of classification in "The Plot against People" is hardly scientific; but his three categories of inanimate objects (those that break down, those that get lost, and those that don't work) create a clear and logical structure for his tongue-in-cheek musings.

What to Look for in Reading an Essay of Division and Classification

First, be sure that you understand the writer's classification system; pay particular attention to the principle of division, the specific categories or subclasses, and how individual items can be grouped. Then, see how the writer's system of dividing and classifying helps to clarify the subject for you.

Consider, for example, the following passage from E. B. White's "Here Is New York," in which he discusses New Yorkers and their city:

> There are roughly three New Yorks. There is, first, the New York of the man or woman who was born here, who takes the city for granted and accepts its size and its turbulence as natural and inevitable. Second, there is the New York of the commuter—the city that is devoured by locusts each day and spat out each night. Third, there is the New York of the person who was born somewhere else and came to New York in quest of something. Of these three trembling cities the greatest is the last—the city of final destination, the city that is a goal. It is this third city that accounts for New York's highstrung disposition, its poetical deportment, its dedication to the arts, and its incomparable achieve-

ments. Commuters give the city its tidal restlessness; natives give it solidarity and continuity; but the settlers give it passion. And whether it is a farmer arriving from Italy to set up a small grocery store in a slum, or a young girl arriving from a small town in Mississippi to escape the indignity of being observed by her neighbors, or a boy arriving from the Corn Belt with a manuscript in his suitcase and a pain in his heart, it makes no difference: each embraces New York with the intense excitement of first love, each absorbs New York with the fresh eyes of an adventurer, each generates heat and light to dwarf the Consolidated Edison Company.

In his opening sentences, White suggests a principle for dividing the population of New York, establishing his three categories on the basis of a person's relation to the city. There is the New York of the native, the New York of the worker who commutes to the city, and the New York of the immigrant. (White's only specific examples belong to his third grouping; it is easy to see, however, where any individual would be classified.) The purpose and result of White's divisions are clear and effective: they help him make a point about the characteristics of New York City, its restlessness, its solidarity, and its passion.

Division and classification can also make it considerably easier for you to follow a writer's ideas. In the following paragraphs from *Rhetorical Models for Effective Writing*, a text for college composition courses, note how J. Karl Nicholas and James R. Nicholl use this strategy to organize their discussion of prose writing:

Prose writing may be divided into three types based on the effect the writing is supposed to have on its audience. The first, *narrative-descriptive writing*, strives to make readers see and feel as it presents a scene or series of actions witnessed or imagined by the writer. Travelogs, news accounts, short stories, and novels are examples of narrative-descriptive writing.

The second kind of writing is called *exposition*. In expository writing the writer presumes that readers do not know some piece of information and therefore seeks to explain it. Textbooks, essays and reports, instruction manuals, and legal documents furnish examples of expository writing. It is the most common type of writing in both school and work situations.

The third type of writing is *argumentation,* in which the writer presumes that readers already hold an opinion concerning the subject matter. It is not the purpose of argumentation to add new information (although this is sometimes necessary), but to discuss known information in a way that will persuade readers to change their minds about it, adopting the writer's opinion on the matter. Advertisements, scholarly and scientific treatises, debates, congressional speeches, and editorials offer examples of this kind of writing.

It is important that you understand these divisions . . . because they will help you answer the most important question that will confront you as a writer: What is my purpose in writing? If you want to make your audience see, you will write in a narrative-descriptive mode and use narrative-descriptive techniques. If you want to inform, to educate, to add to the reader's fund of information, then you will write expositorily, using expository techniques. And if you want to change the minds of your readers, you will write persuasively, using the techniques of argumentation.

Nicholas and Nicholl divide prose writing into three basic types: narrative–descriptive writing, exposition, and argumentation. In the first sentence, they announce that their basis of division is "the effect the writing is supposed to have on its audience." The authors then briefly describe each type of subclass of writing and classify individual examples accordingly. The value of their system of division and classification is clear in the final paragraph: understanding the three types of prose writing will help a writer determine the purpose suitable to a particular task and the techniques suitable to a particular purpose. Readers of this passage are given practical information to help them make a decision; the organizational strategy helps make that information absolutely clear.

Writing an Essay of Division and Classification

Begin by making certain that your subject, in fact, represents a single, coherent entity. In order to do so, you will have to set definite limits for yourself and then stick to them. For example, the sociologist whose purpose was to survey relationships between family income and voting patterns limited her study to residents of Maple Street. Including a family from Oak Street would upset the established system and, consequently, suggest the need to set new limits. Similarly, if you take as your subject for classification the student body at your school, you obviously cannot include students who are visiting from somewhere else, unless you first redefine your subject.

As you redefine your essay of classification, pay particular attention to your purpose, the divisions of your subject, your organization, and your conclusion. Your further process of planning and writing will depend on your purpose and on how that purpose leads you to divide your subject.

1. Purpose

The principle you use to divide your subject into classes or categories depends on your larger purpose for writing. It is crucial, then, that you determine a clear purpose for your division and classification before you begin to examine your subject in detail. For example, a study of the student body at your school might have any number of purposes: to discover how much time your classmates spend in the library during a week, to explain how financial aid is distributed among majors, to discuss the types of movies that are most popular on campus, to describe styles of dorm-room decor. The categories into which you divide the student body will vary according to your chosen purpose.

2. Dividing Your Subject

In many cases, once you have decided on a subject and determined a purpose, your principle of division will be obvious. The sociologist studying voting patterns on Maple Street could immediately divide her topic into three standard socioeconomic classes and into voters or nonvoters. Her important task was then to classify families according to these divisions. In a study of how much time students spend in the library, you might just as readily divide your subject into categories: for example, those who spend less than one hour a week, those who spend between one and four hours, and those who spend more than four hours. You would then use these categories as your basis for classifying various individuals.

Just make certain, first, that your principle of division is appropriate to your purpose. In determining financial aid distribution you might consider family income, academic major, or athletic participation; but obviously you would not consider dancing ability or brand of toothpaste. Second, make sure that the categories you come up with are consistent and mutually exclusive. For example, trying to work with the classes *men, women,* and *athletes* would only be confusing, because *athletes* could include *men* or *women*. Rather, the student body could be divided into *male athletes, female athletes, male nonathletes,* and *female nonathletes*. Third, make sure your categories are complete and that they will account for all the members of your subject class. In dividing the student body according to place of birth, it would be inaccurate to consider only home states; such a division could never account for foreign students or citizens born outside of the country. A diagram (such as the one of families on Maple Street) can often help you determine whether or not your classes are consistent, mutually exclusive, and complete.

For some subjects and purposes, however, appropriate divisions will not be immediately apparent. In fact, your most challenging task can often be the creation of interesting and accurate classes based on careful observation. Dividing dorm rooms according to style of decor, for example, will require some canvassing before a system of classification becomes clear. Once you have developed a system, though, you can easily classify individual rooms: *homey, spartan, childish, contemporary, cluttered,* and so on. The effect of many informal essays depends on the writer's ability to establish clever yet useful divisions and classifications that might not otherwise be noticed by the reader.

3. Organization

Essays of division and classification, when sensibly planned, can generally be organized with little trouble; the essay's chief divisions will reflect the classes into which the subject itself has been divided. A scratch outline can help you see those divisions and plan your order of presentation. For example, here is an outline of the preceding passage from Nicholas and Nicholl's *Rhetorical Models for Effective Writing:*

Three types of writing
1. Narrative–descriptive to make readers see and feel examples
2. Expository to explain examples
3. Argumentative to persuade examples

Such an outline clearly reveals the essay's overall structure.

4. Stating Your Conclusion

Your purpose for writing will determine the kinds of conclusions you reach. For example, a study of the student body might show that 67 percent of all male athletes receive financial aid, compared with 46 percent of all female athletes, 45 percent of all male nonathletes, and 44 percent of all female nonathletes. These facts could provide a conclusion in themselves, or they might be the basis for a more controversial assertion about your school's athletic program. A study of dorm-room decor might conclude with the observation that juniors and seniors tend to have more elaborate rooms than first-year students. Your conclusions will depend on the way you work back and forth between the various classes you establish and the individual objects available for you to classify.

How Loud? How Good?
How Much? How Pretty!

Gerald Cleary

> *Gerry Cleary graduated with a B.S. in mathematics from the University of Vermont in 1986, and later attended law school at Cornell University. He grew up in Burlington, Vermont, but spent his last two years of high school in West Germany as a military dependent. During that time, Gerry sold stereo equipment at a large Post Exchange. In this essay, Gerry has fun classifying the different types of customers he dealt with during his time on the job.*

As stereo equipment gets better and prices go down, stereo systems are becoming household necessities rather than luxuries. People are buying stereos by the thousands. During my year as a stereo salesman, I witnessed this boom firsthand. I dealt with hundreds of customers, and it didn't take long for me to learn that people buy stereos for different reasons. Eventually, though, I was able to divide all the stereo buyers into four basic categories: the looks buyer, the wattage buyer, the price buyer, and the quality buyer.

The looks buyer cannot be bothered with the question of how her stereo will sound. Her only concern is how the stereo *looks*, making her the buyer least respected by the stereo salesperson. The looks buyer has an irresistible attraction to flashing lights, knobs, switches, and frivolous features. Even the loudspeakers are chosen on the basis of appearance—the looks buyer always removes the grill to make sure a couple of knobs are present. Enjoyment for her is watching the output meters flash on her amplifier, or playing with her cassette deck's remote control. No matter what component she is shopping for, the looks buyer always decides on the flashiest, exclaiming, "Wait 'til my friends see this!"

Slightly more respected is the wattage buyer, who is most easily identified by his trademark question: "How many watts does it put out?" He will not settle for less than 100 watts from his amp, and his speakers must be able to handle all this power. He is interested only in the volume level his stereo can produce, for the wattage buyer always turns it up loud—so loud that most would find it painful. The wattage buyer genuinely enjoys his music— either soul or heavy metal—at this volume. He is actually proud of his stereo's ability to put out deafening noise. As a result, the wattage buyer becomes as well-known to his neighbors as he is to the salesperson. His competitive nature makes him especially obvious as he pays for his new system, telling his friend, "Man, this is gonna blow Jones's stereo away!"

In this money-conscious world, the price buyer has the under- 4 standing, if not the respect, of the salesperson. Often, she is ashamed of her budget limitations and will try to disguise herself as one of the other types of buyers, asking, "What's the loudest receiver I can buy for $200?" Or, "What's the best turntable for under $150?" It is always obvious that price is the price buyer's greatest worry—she doesn't really want the "loudest" or the "best." The price buyer can be spotted looking over the sale items, or staring open-mouthed at the price tag of an expensive unit. After asking the salesperson where the best deal in the store can be found, she cringes at the standard reply: "You usually get what you pay for." But the price buyer still picks the cheapest model, telling her friends, "You won't believe the deal I got on this!"

Only one category remains: the quality buyer. He is the buyer 5 most respected by the salesperson, although he is often not even in the store to buy—he may simply want to listen to the new compact-disc player tested in his latest issue of *High Fidelity*. The quality buyer never buys on impulse; he has already read about and listened to any piece of equipment he finally buys. But along with high quality comes high price. The quality buyer can often be seen fingering the price tag of that noise reduction unit he just has to own but can't yet afford. He never considers a cheaper model, preferring to wait until he can afford the high standard of quality he demands. The quality buyer shuns salespeople, believing that he knows more than them anyway. Asking him "May I help you?" is the greatest insult of all.

Recognizing the kind of buyer I was dealing with helped me 6 steer her to the right corner of the store. I took looks buyers to the visually dazzling working displays, and wattage buyers into the soundproof speaker rooms. I directed price buyers to the sale items, and left quality buyers alone. By the end of the year, I was able to identify the type of buyer almost instantly. My expertise paid off, making me the most successful salesperson in the store.

Interview with Gerald Cleary

Do you enjoy writing?

Yes, I enjoy writing, even though I don't think I have as much natural ability as a writer as some people have. I thought I was a natural writer until I took this class. Being a math major, this was the only writing class I took and probably the main thing I learned from this class was that writing is a lot of work and there is a lot of learning involved. It's not all just natural ability. I found out that I just can't write a paper in one or two drafts; I have to sit down, and it takes me several drafts, several revisions, until I get what I want, what I'm going to be satisfied with. So although I enjoy writing, like I think almost everyone does, it takes me a lot of work and a lot of revising to get it to the point where I'm satisfied with it.

Can you give us an example of some revising you did for this paper?

One of the things I spent the most time working on and did the most revisions of was the introduction to the paper. I think it's probably always a problem with division and classification, a problem of how to get the reader into your actual divisions and get going on them. How do you prepare readers for the divisions that they're about to read about? In my first draft I went out of my way trying to explain how I came up with the classifications and why I was going to do it. I went on about how I had the job for a year and had helped hundreds of customers. I began to notice that each customer seemed to belong to one of four general categories. I felt that in that rough draft of my introduction I was really going out of my way to explain where the categories came from and why I was going to write about them. I had a couple [of] people read my rough draft during class and it really didn't work for any of them. By the time I came up with the final introduction, I realized that I wanted to keep the introduction short. I didn't need to go out of my way to explain as I did in that first draft, so I kept the introductory paragraph very brief. Simply, I told readers that I was a stereo salesman and I was able to divide the buyers up into four categories. I thought that's all the readers needed to get them hooked on my essay.

What's the purpose of the paper and of the classification?

Well, I guess it's kind of hard for me to put my finger on the purpose, and this is the thing I struggled with when I was in the outlining stage. I really think the purpose of the paper is to entertain. I think that what I tried to do is talk about buyers in general. I think these buyers aren't just stereo buyers—they're buyers of almost every high-priced product. Buyers are buyers. You have the same thing for cars, for furniture, for virtually anything. What I wanted to do was to let readers see a little part of themselves and their buying behavior. Depending on what they're looking for, they've probably been "looks buyers" at some times and "quality buyers" at others. It was my hope that people would learn something about themselves or laugh at themselves or be entertained when reading the essay. I think mainly the point of the paper is to entertain and to show us something about ourselves.

How did you find the topic and decide on classification?

Well, part of it was just a process of elimination. I could have narrated my experiences as a stereo salesman, but I had already written a narration. Narration comes most naturally to me. I also could have done this as an argument paper, arguing that the best way to buy a stereo is to buy quality. I could have then poked fun at the other reasons people have for buying. But I thought that was too obvious. I think division and classification just kind of suggested itself. I didn't decide that I was going to have four groups, I just started writing down groups and these were the main four. It's really hard to break something up into perfect groups.

So what I tried to do was just get the four main groups and concentrate on them.

How did you organize the four categories?

Deciding what order to put the four categories in was one of the hardest things I had to deal with. At first I was going to do it in order of least common to most common, but that wasn't really working out. At that point I knew I wanted to have something in my essay about the respect that the stereo salesperson has for each buyer. So I decided to have the respect element run through each of the four groups and put them in order of the respect—from least to most—that they received from the salesperson.

How did you come up with your title?

I'm still not really happy with the title. I came up with it during a class exercise. I wrote down a list of about ten titles for this piece, and we passed them around the classroom. Other students selected this title as the one that jumped out at them—the one that grabbed their interest most and would make them want to read my essay. But the title still doesn't sit right with me, and I think somewhere out there is a better title for this paper. So I guess sometimes you're never really satisfied with some aspect of an essay, even at the very end. Which reminds me that I do feel there's still room for another revision of this paper and that it still could be a better paper with more time and work on it. But then there are deadlines.

Stand Up for Yourself

Bruce A. Baldwin

*Bruce A. Baldwin was born in Milton, Pennsylvania, in
1943. He studied at Pennsylvania State University, the University of Florida, and Arizona State University, where he
earned his Ph.D. in psychology. He taught for several years
at ASU. Today, Baldwin is a practicing psychologist and head
of Direction Dynamics, a group which specializes in life-style
management. In addition to his practice, Baldwin has written
more than one hundred articles and a book entitled* It's All in
Your Head, *which deals with the successful management of
one's personal and professional life.*

In the following essay, taken from Beyond the Cornucopia
Kids, *Baldwin suggests ways we can identify our weaknesses
in order to avoid being manipulated by others.*

At a store, five-year-old Sam spots a toy truck. His mother knows 1
the ritual:

"Can I have this truck?" 2

"Not now." 3

Sam bursts into tears. "You *never* let me have anything!" he cries. 4
"Mrs. Brown bought Tommy a truck."

"Oh, all right," his mother says. "Just this once." 5

Sam is used to getting things his way. He has learned to use 6
emotional pressure to manipulate his mother. Because Sam's maneuvers work so well, his manipulative behavior is reinforced—
and will be used again.

If a child of five can manipulate others by discovering their vul- 7
nerabilities, think what a savvy adult can do! This is the way it
works:

Locating an emotional vulnerability, often by trial and error, the 8
manipulator exploits that knowledge to arouse our emotions and
create internal pressure. We lose objectivity and make decisions to
appease the one who has created the pressure—rather than do
what is right. Then we feel used.

But if we can recognize and reduce our weaknesses, we will feel 9
more in control, and our relationships will improve.

To help you close up the chinks in *your* emotional armor, con- 10
sider the following list of vulnerabilities.

1. *You feel guilty.* Inducing guilt is the most common form of ma- 11
nipulation. Martyrs are masters of this kind of emotional blackmail.

2. *You fear conflict or anger.* Many nonassertive men and women agree 12
to almost anything to avoid a fight. Sometimes a person's early
family life was so filled with parental conflict that he or she learned
to abhor differences of any kind. Other parents so carefully hide
conflict that their children grow up with an unrealistic idea of a
"good relationship."

3. *You consistently fall for a "hard luck" story.* Some people become 13
expert at the game of "woe is me." They "hook" others into taking
care of them. When confronted by this kind of manipulator, ask
yourself: "Is this person playing on my emotions? How should I
respond to help him help himself?"

   Tears are also a favorite ploy. Children can turn tears off and 14
on like a faucet and use them selectively on the parent who is
most vulnerable. (Don't forget that some adults can cry on demand
too.)

4. *You fall for flattery.* When little Johnny is about to be punished, he 15
professes undying love for his parents with bear hugs and sloppy
kisses. His parents melt, and Johnny gets off scot-free. Similar
cons are used in adult relationships. Flattery distorts your perception and makes you want to please.

5. *You fear disapproval.* It's surprising how many otherwise bright and 16
insightful people can't stand the thought of not being liked by
someone. So they give in. These unrealistic adults have never
learned that the price of their need for approval is self-respect—
and the respect of others.

6. *You feel insecure in your role.* In a defined role (as parent, manager 17
or supervisor) you have been given responsibilities, prerogatives
and boundaries. Another person, usually one who makes an unfair or unwarranted demand, makes accusations ("You don't like
me!") or threats ("I'm going to report you to your supervisor!").
The recipient of the threats becomes insecure in the assigned defined role and gives in.

7. *You can't stand silence.* Here a manipulator's responses are formal, [18] monosyllabic. As time passes, feelings of rejection grow within you. To deal with this power play, avoid participating: pressure the pouter to end the game by going about your business as usual.

8. *You're afraid to be different.* At work here is a feeling that if you're [19] different, you're somehow wrong. Two facts should be considered, however. First, what everyone else is doing isn't necessarily right. Second, when your major frame of reference is other people, you lose the capacity to define and live by your own values.

How do you reduce your vulnerabilities? Begin by thinking about [20] occasions when you gave in to others or felt used. What feelings were dominant? What did others say or do to arouse those emotions? Who in particular arouses such feelings?

Once you pinpoint situations, people and feelings that influence [21] your decisions, you can use two strategies to avoid being manipulated. The best is to resolve the underlying issue that makes you vulnerable. For example, you can define your role in a given situation so that no one can make you insecure. Or you can decide what you owe yourself so that others can't make you feel "selfish."

Even if you can't completely stifle your vulnerability, you can [22] still resist manipulation. Define the feelings that lead to your exploitation, and then use them as cues to be cautious. For instance, if you are susceptible to guilt, *any* feelings of guilt should make you wary. Do what is right to avoid being manipulated in spite of your feelings.

By outmaneuvering your manipulators, you regain control, and [23] your decisions reflect what's right for you. This feels good, and others learn to respect you. It's interesting that those who are easily manipulated are well-liked but not respected. By working through your emotional weak spots, you create a basis for respect *and* approval.

Questions on Subject

1. According to Baldwin, what is the underlying cause of our susceptibility to manipulation?
2. What does Baldwin say is the most common form of manipulation? Why do you suppose this is true?

3. What two strategies does Baldwin suggest to avoid manipulation?
4. How can our emotions help us avoid manipulation?

Questions on Strategy

1. List the divisions or categories Baldwin establishes. Are they clear and mutually exclusive?
2. Baldwin opens his essay with an extended example. Describe the example and explain how well it serves as an effective opening for his purpose. (Glossary: *Beginnings*)
3. Baldwin has organized his essay into a series of short paragraphs, many of which are only one sentence long. What effect does this strategy have on the overall tone of his essay? How well does it suit his purpose? (Glossary: *Purpose*)
4. Although he does not develop them in his essay, Baldwin suggests other subjects that could also be divided into groups. Locate those subjects in his essay, and construct a system of division of your own for each of them.

Questions on Diction and Vocabulary

1. Baldwin uses clear, simple language to make his point. Cite other characteristics of Baldwin's diction, and discuss how his choice of words shows who he intends for his audience. (Glossary: *Audience*)
2. Why do you suppose Baldwin has chosen to use the pronoun "you" throughout his essay? How did you react to its use? Explain.
3. Refer to your desk dictionary to determine the meanings of the following words as they are used in this selection: *manipulate* (paragraph 6), *savvy* (7), *vulnerability* (8), *exploits* (8), *appease* (8), *chinks* (10), *martyrs* (11), *flattery* (15), *prerogatives* (17), *pouter* (18), *stifle* (22), *wary* (22).

Writing Suggestions

1. Take Baldwin's suggestion and for one week keep track of the situations, feelings, and people that lead to your being manipulated. Did your experiences fall into Baldwin's categories, or did you discover additional ones?

2. Choose a social-psychological situation other than feeling manipulated, such as feeling envy, feeling rejected, or feeling empowered. Now develop a system of classification that accounts for the different kinds of people or situations that cause you to feel that way.

The Plot against People

Russell Baker

> *Born in Virginia in 1925, Russell Baker graduated from Johns Hopkins University in 1947 and began his career as a newspaper reporter with the* Baltimore Sun. *He joined the* New York Times *in 1954; after eight years with its Washington bureau covering national politics, he began writing his syndicated "Observer" column, which is now published four times a week. In 1979, he was awarded the Pulitzer Prize, journalism's highest award, for his column. Baker's books include* An American in Washington, No Cause for Panic, Poor Russell's Almanac, So This Is Depravity, *and the autobiographical* Growing Up, *which won a Pulitzer in 1983, and* The Good Times.*
>
> *In the following essay, which first appeared in the* New York Times *in 1968, Baker humorously classifies inanimate objects according to the method they use "to resist man and ultimately to defeat him."*

Inanimate objects are classified scientifically into three major categories—those that break down, those that get lost, and those that don't work. 1

The goal of all inanimate objects is to resist man and ultimately to defeat him, and the three major classifications are based on the method each object uses to achieve its purpose. As a general rule, any object capable of breaking down at the moment when it is most needed will do so. The automobile is typical of the category. 2

With the cunning peculiar to its breed, the automobile never breaks down while entering a filling station which has a large staff of idle mechanics. It waits until it reaches a downtown intersection in the middle of the rush hour, or until it is fully loaded with family and luggage on the Ohio Turnpike. Thus it creates maximum inconvenience, frustration, and irritability, thereby reducing its owner's lifespan. 3

Washing machines, garbage disposals, lawn mowers, furnaces, 4

TV sets, tape recorders, slide projectors—all are in league with the automobile to take their turn at breaking down whenever life threatens to flow smoothly for their enemies.

Many inanimate objects, of course, find it extremely difficult to break down. Pliers, for example, and gloves and keys are almost totally incapable of breaking down. Therefore, they have had to evolve a different technique for resisting man.

They get lost. Science has still not solved the mystery of how they do it, and no man has ever caught one of them in the act. The most plausible theory is that they have developed a secret method of locomotion which they are able to conceal from human eyes.

It is not uncommon for a pair of pliers to climb all the way from the cellar to the attic in its single-minded determination to raise its owner's blood pressure. Keys have been known to burrow three feet under mattresses. Women's purses, despite their great weight, frequently travel through six or seven rooms to find hiding space under a couch.

Scientists have been struck by the fact that things that break down virtually never get lost, while things that get lost hardly ever break down. A furnace, for example, will invariably break down at the depth of the first winter cold wave, but it will never get lost. A woman's purse hardly ever breaks down; it almost invariably chooses to get lost.

Some persons believe this constitutes evidence that inanimate objects are not entirely hostile to man. After all, they point out, a furnace could infuriate a man even more thoroughly by getting lost than by breaking down, just as a glove could upset him far more by breaking down than by getting lost.

Not everyone agrees, however, that this indicates a conciliatory attitude. Many say it merely proves that furnaces, gloves and pliers are incredibly stupid.

The third class of objects—those that don't work—is the most curious of all. These include such objects as barometers, car clocks, cigarette lighters, flashlights and toy-train locomotives. It is inaccurate, of course, to say that they *never* work. They work once, usually for the first few hours after being brought home, and then quit. Thereafter, they never work again.

In fact, it is widely assumed that they are built for the purpose of not working. Some people have reached advanced ages without ever seeing some of these objects—barometers, for example—in working order.

Science is utterly baffled by the entire category. There are many 13 theories about it. The most interesting holds that the things that don't work have attained the highest state possible for an inanimate object, the state to which things that break down and things that get lost can still only aspire.

They have truly defeated man by conditioning him never to ex- 14 pect anything of them. When his cigarette lighter won't light or his flashlight fails to illuminate, it does not raise his blood pressure. Objects that don't work have given man the only peace he receives from inanimate society.

Questions on Subject

1. Into what three broad categories does Baker classify inanimate objects? How do you suppose he arrived at these particular categories? In what other ways might inanimate objects be classified?
2. What is the relationship between objects that break down and objects that get lost?
3. According to Baker, what is the highest possible state an inanimate object can reach? What does he mean when he says, "Objects that don't work have given man the only peace he receives from inanimate society" (paragraph 14)?
4. Explain the meaning of Baker's title. Why does he use the word *plot?*

Questions on Strategy

1. How does Baker make it clear at the beginning of the essay that his approach to the subject is humorous? How does he succeed in being more than simply silly? Point to several passages to illustrate your answer.
2. How does Baker organize his essay? Why do you think he waits until the conclusion to discuss objects "that don't work"? (Glossary: *Organization*)
3. How does paragraph 5 act as a transition? (Glossary: *Transitions*)
4. What is the relationship between paragraphs 6 and 7? Where else

does Baker use examples, as he does in paragraph 7? For what purposes does he use them? (Glossary: *Examples*)
5. Baker personifies inanimate objects in his essay. What is the effect of his doing so? Identify several specific examples of personification. (Glossary: *Figures of Speech*)

Questions on Diction and Vocabulary

1. How would you describe Baker's tone? Point to specific words and phrases to explain your answer. (Glossary: *Tone*)
2. How would you describe Baker's attitude toward inanimate objects? How does his diction help reveal his attitude? (Glossary: *Diction*)
3. Refer to your desk dictionary to determine the meanings of the following words as they are used in this selection: *cunning* (paragraph 3), *league* (4), *plausible* (6), *conciliatory* (10), *baffled* (13).

Writing Assignments

1. Using Baker's essay as a model, create a system of classification for one of the following topics. Then write an essay like Baker's, classifying objects within that system.
   a. cars
   b. friends
   c. recreational activities
   d. sports
   e. drivers
   f. students
   g. music
   h. pet peeves
2. Most of us have had frustrating experiences with mechanical objects that seem to have perverse minds of their own. Write a narrative recounting one such experience—with a vending machine, a television set, an automobile, a computer, a pay telephone, a typewriter, or any other such object. Be sure to establish a clear context for your essay.

Teenagers: Managing Stress

David Elkind

Born in Detroit, Michigan, in 1931, and educated at UCLA, David Elkind is currently a professor of child psychology at Tufts University. His books on this topic include Children and Adolescence; Exploitation in Middle-Class Delinquency; A Sympathetic Understanding of the Child; *and* The Hurried Child: Growing Up Too Fast, Too Soon.

In the following selection from All Grown Up and No Place to Go, *Elkind classifies the different kinds of stress that teenagers suffer as a result of social pressures.*

Most situations that produce psychological stress involve some 1
sort of conflict between self and society. So long as we satisfy a
social demand at the expense of a personal need, or vice versa,
the social or personal demand for action is a psychological stress.
If, for example, we stay home from work because of a personal
problem, we create a new demand (for an explanation, for made-
up time) at our place of work. On the other hand, if we devote too
much time to the demands of work, we create new demands on
the part of family. If we don't manage our energy budgets well,
we create more stress than is necessary.

The major task of psychological stress management is to find 2
ways to balance and coordinate the demands that come from within
with those that come from without. This is where a healthy sense
of self and identity comes in. An integrated sense of identity . . .
means bringing together into a working whole a set of attitudes,
values, and habits that can serve both self and society. The attainment of such a sense of identity is accompanied by a feeling of self-
esteem, of liking and respecting oneself and being liked and respected by others.

More than anything else, the attainment of a healthy sense of 3
identity and a feeling of self-esteem gives young people a perspective, a way of looking at themselves and others, which enables

them to manage the majority of stress situations. Young people with high self-esteem look at situations from a single perspective that includes both themselves and others. They look at situations from the standpoint of what it means to their self-respect and to the respect others have for them. This integrated perspective enables them to manage the major types of stress efficiently and with a minimum expenditure of energy and personal distress.

The Three Stress Situations

There are three major types of stress situation that all of us encounter. One of these occurs when the potential stress is both foreseeable and avoidable. This is a *Type A* stress situation. If we are thinking about going on a roller coaster or seeing a horror movie, the stress is both foreseeable and avoidable. We may choose to expose ourselves to the stress if we find such controlled danger situations exciting or stimulating. Likewise if we know that a particular neighborhood or park is dangerous at night, the danger is both foreseeable and avoidable, and we do avoid it, unless we are looking for trouble.

The situation becomes more complicated when the foreseeable and avoidable danger is one for which there is much social approval and support, even though it entails much personal risk. Becoming a soldier in times of war is an example of this more complicated Type A danger. The young person who enlists wins social approval at the risk of personal harm. On the other hand, the young person who refuses to become a soldier protects himself or herself from danger at the cost of social disapproval.

Teenagers are often caught in this more difficult type of situation. If the peer group uses alcohol or drugs, for example, there is considerable pressure on the young person to participate. But such participation often puts the teenager at risk with parents and teachers, and also with respect to themselves. They may not like the image of themselves as drinkers or drug abusers. It is at this point that a sense of identity and a positive feeling of self-esteem stand the teenager in good stead.

A young person with a healthy sense of identity will weigh the danger to his or her hard-won feeling of self-esteem against the feelings associated with the loss of peer approval. When the teenager looks at the situation from this perspective, the choice is easy to make. By weighing the laboriously arrived-at feeling of self-esteem against the momentary approval of a transient peer group, the teenager with an integrated sense of self is able to avoid potentially stressful situations. It should be said, too, that the young person's ability to foresee and avoid is both an intellectual and an emotional achievement. The teenager must be able to foresee events . . . but also to place sufficient value upon his or her self-esteem and self-respect to avoid situations that would jeopardize these feelings.

A second type of stress situation involves those demands which 8 are neither foreseeable nor avoidable. These are *Type B* stress situations. Accidents are of this type, as when a youngster is hit by a baseball while watching a game, or when a teenager who happens to be at a place in school where a fight breaks out gets hurt even though he was not involved. The sudden, unexpected death of a loved one is another example of a stress that is both unforeseeable and unavoidable. Divorce of parents is unthinkable for many teenagers and therefore also unforeseeable and unavoidable.

Type B stress situations usually make the greatest demands upon 9 young people. . . . With this type of stress teenagers have to deal with the attitudes of their friends and teachers at the same time that they are struggling with their own feelings. Such stress situations put demands upon young people both from within and from without. A youngster who has been handicapped by an accident, like the teenager who has to deal with divorce, has to adjust to new ways of relating to others as well as new ways of thinking about himself or herself.

Again, the young person with a strong sense of identity and a 10 feeling of self-esteem has the best chance of managing these stress situations as well as they can be managed. In the case of divorce, for example, the teenager who incorporates other people's perspectives with his or her own is able to deal with the situation better than other teenagers who lack this perspective. For example, one young man, who went on to win honors at an Ivy League school, told his father when he and the mother divorced, "You are entitled to live your own life and to find happiness too."

This integrated perspective also helps young people deal with 11 the death of a loved one. If it was an elderly grandparent who had been suffering great pain, the young person can see that from the perspective of the grandparent dying may have been preferable to living a life of agony with no hope of recovery. As one teenager told me with regard to his grandfather who had just died, "He was in such pain, he was so doped up he couldn't really recognize me. I loved him so much I just couldn't stand to see him that way." By enabling the young person to see death from the perspective of others, including that of the person who is dying, the young person is able to mourn the loss but also to get on with life.

The third type of stress situation is one in which the potential 12 stress is foreseeable but not avoidable. This is a *Type C* stress situation. A teenager who has stayed out later than he or she was supposed to foresees an unavoidable storm at home. Likewise, exams are foreseeable but unavoidable stress situations. Being required to spend time with relatives one does not like is another stress situation that the teenager can foresee but not avoid. These are but a few examples of situations the teenager might wish to avoid but must learn to accept as inevitable.

To young people who have attained a solid sense of self and 13 identity, foreseeable and unavoidable stress situations are manageable, again, because of self-esteem and the integrated perspective. They look at the situation from the perspective of themselves as well as that of the other people involved and try to prepare accordingly. They may decide, as one young man of my acquaintance did, that "with my folks, honesty is the best policy. I get into less trouble if I tell the truth than if I make up stories." In the case of visiting relatives they do not like, integrated teenagers see it from the perspective of what it means to others, such as their parents. And with respect to stress situations like exams, because they want to maintain their self-esteem, they prepare for the exam so that they will make a good showing for themselves as well as for others.

It is important to say, too, that integrated teenagers come in any 14 and all personality types. Some are introverted and shy, others are extroverted and fun-loving. Some are preoccupied with intellectual concerns, others primarily with matters of the heart. Despite this diversity, they all share the prime characteristics of the integrated teenager: a set of attitudes, values, and habits that enable the young person to serve self and society, and a strong sense of self-esteem.

To be sure, life is complex and varied. Even the most integrated 15 teenager, of whatever personality type, may occasionally be so overwhelmed by stress that he or she loses the integrated perspective and suffers bouts of low self-esteem. We need to remember that teenagers are new at the game of stress management and have just acquired the skills they need for this purpose. Nonetheless, the general principle holds true. The more integrated the teenager is with respect to self and identity, the better prepared he or she is to manage the basic stress situations.

Questions on Subject

1. Elkind distinguishes among three types of stressful situations—Types A, B, and C. What are the two variables on which Elkind bases Types A, B, and C situations? How does he use these variables to develop the categories?
2. According to Elkind, what is the cause of most stress? How does stress management work to relieve stress?
3. The author repeatedly uses the phrase "integrated perspective." What does he mean by it?
4. Teenagers are the focus of Elkind's essay. In your opinion, do the ideas he presents apply only to young people? Explain.

Questions on Strategy

1. Reread the essay paying particular attention to the author's discussion of the three types of stressful situations. How does Elkind organize each paragraph in this section? What organizational features do the paragraphs have in common? How does this organization help your understanding of the essay? (Glossary: *Organization*)
2. Elkind uses examples to clarify each type of stressful situation. Do you find these examples helpful? Why, or why not? (Glossary: *Examples*)
3. Reread the concluding sentence of each paragraph in the essay.

How are these sentences alike? How do they work together to move the author's argument along?
4. Has Elkind designated three categories that do not overlap? Can you think of any categories he has left out? Following the model on page 323, make a diagram in which you classify the three categories of stress discussed in this essay.

Questions on Diction and Vocabulary

1. Is Elkind's tone emotional, angry, defensive, or passive? How does his choice of words create that tone? What other elements of the essay contribute to the tone? (Glossary: *Tone*)
2. Cite several examples of Elkind's use of psychology jargon in the essay. Does he define these terms? Do you find these words helpful or confusing?
3. Refer to your desk dictionary to determine the meanings of the following words as they are used in this selection: *integrated* (paragraph 3), *expenditure* (3), *stead* (6), *laboriously* (7), *transient* (7), *introverted* (14), *extroverted* (14), *bouts* (15).

Writing Assignments

1. Think about some of the stressful situations you have dealt with and consider how they might fit into Elkind's three categories. List several examples of stressful situations in your life for each type of stress, and then determine which type you experience more often than the others. Discuss your findings in an essay.
2. Using the model on page 323, construct a diagram in which you categorize your friendships with other people. Then, in an essay, discuss why you are closer to some friends and how these friendships differ from mere acquaintances.

Teaching Types

M. Stephen Arnold

> *A longtime classroom observer, M. Stephen Arnold explains to college students that the rigors of the college experience are at least as challenging as the "real world," if not more so. To help students meet the challenge more successfully, Arnold describes the different teaching styles students will encounter among the more than forty professors they will have as teachers during their college career.*

Four years, forty professors, and about two *thousand* hours of 1
class time. Add on the time spent scheduling your time, time spent
getting advice and counseling and buying books, the eons spent
registering—or standing in interminable lines waiting for what
seems like forever to register for classes you already know are
canceled or closed or a figment of someone's imagination. Plus
some time to study. Most colleges figure this adds up to around
a forty-hour work week. Yet, three hours per week per class mul-
tiplied by five classes equals a minimum of thirty hours of class
time each week. Add on that amount or more of study time to
prepare for those classes—again, what most colleges figure—and
the weekly total comes out somewhat closer to sixty hours. And
add on a few more hours to your weekly schedule, since no college
I know of figures in travel time between classes. Not time spent
commuting, mind you, but time spent traveling in the middle of
your work day from class to class, from library to lecture hall to
lab to gym and back again. Imagine the workplace in the "real"
world that demanded all its employees get up every ninety minutes, leave what they were doing, move to a new location (often
after traveling a considerable distance outside), and begin a new
and often totally unrelated project. Handling these sorts of demands is a major part of what higher education is about.

So the next time someone tells you that you're escaping the 2
"real" world by staying in school, feel free to call their bluff and

compare schedules. Ask them about their coffee breaks, for instance. How they're written into a contract, spelled out in black and white. And if they're not, well, all the better, since that means that there's money enough changing hands so that contractual coffee breaks seem silly. The fact of the matter is that the demands of college are in most ways greater than the demands of "real life." That's why prospective employers respect a college degree. They figure if you can put up with school, you can put up with anything, since college life is like real life only more condensed and exaggerated and harder to control. For instance, instead of reaping the customary rewards in return for your work, you pay for the privilege: somewhere between $5,000 and $15,000 a year. And don't be deceived if you're getting help from either Uncle Sam or First National Dad. You'll simply pay back later and in different, often uncomfortable ways. So you're paying somewhere around $200 to $400 a week. Hard to believe while sitting in a freshman writing course. And these figures don't include fun. Or even a roof over your head and something warm in your belly. So college is something like the "real" world. Only worse. No secretary, no perks, no weekends in Bermuda. And no money. And this, too, is something of its point. When you're finished, people know you've had the moxy to stick it out, to serve your time.

But even jail doesn't quite serve as an appropriate analogy, since 3 there's no warden to help you serve your time. Ergo the dismal and somewhat trite thought that disciplining yourself to the many demands of college—and not just the academic demands—is also a part of college. Though that sheepskin does announce time served, it also announces time served successfully. It does not say that you understand quantum mechanics, macro-economics, or Shakespeare. But it does say that you managed to put up with a lot of stuff and that you shoveled your way clear of it all without wigging out. And, to those who have shoveled away in an institute of higher learning, that diploma means even more than time and money spent.

It also means over forty professors, give or take a few teaching 4 assistants, visiting part-time lecturers, and stray neanderthals. And a close relationship with each. Close enough to pass the course, at least. Which is exactly the point. Forty-odd bosses is more bosses than most workers meet in a lifetime. And it's guaranteed that they'll provide plenty of practice in putting up with them as you court them on their own terms. Forty professors, forty different sets of terms. Each and every one of them dedicated and devoted. Your job is to discover to what and to whom.

It's a sad fact that the interests and devotions of college only imitate similar interests in the "real" world. Imitate, and, if the professors do their jobs well, exaggerate. That's why it's called "higher" education. It's "higher" than the absolutely pragmatic learning found elsewhere. It's also high-minded, high-toned, high-test, high-pressure, high-principled, high-priced, high-brow, and most of all high-falutin'. Everything about it is kept hyperbolically overcharged. That's why the professors are so open to caricature. Except it's not really caricature as you realize when you return to the "real" world and find everything and everybody a trifle bland and boring. These people and the world they've created are different, an over-blown exaggeration meant to impress, meant to make a mark on you. It's a theatrical land of Platonic forms, real essences, absolute zeros, moral imperatives, where everyone is tremendously dedicated yet no two to the same ideals.

This helps explain the difficulty you can encounter when you try to describe what you're learning in school. It's not a "thing," or a "what" that you can easily describe. It's not even exactly learning. It's more an "exposure," in all the senses of that word. You are at once revealed, set forth, put in your place, opened to influences, and unprotected. This is why the adventure stories that college graduates share about academia are rarely about thermophysical properties or the Magna Carta, but rather they are about the experience of college itself and, most often, about the more memorable men and women of learning they've encountered. What follows are some typical examples from my own experience. I believe they also ring true in a general way, and, however silly some of them seemed at the time, I don't believe I'd give up any.

Early on, I ran into the classic absent-minded professor. Though he didn't invent "flubber" as Fred MacMurray did in the classic movie of the same name nor ignore the attentions of Kate Hepburn as Cary Grant did in *Bringing Up Baby*, he did wear the same clothes for fifteen straight weeks. Or, as we in the class began to conjecture (the scholarly mind at work on a problem befitting its level of expertise), perhaps he simply—and more hygienically—had row after row of identical ragged tweed jackets, salamander-striped shirts, and opera buffa plaid pantaloons, which he carefully rotated for consistent wear and tear. The class eventually became somewhat protective of his farcical behavior. We worried that one day, while walking and reading in the manner that typifies this stereotype, he would trip over his own feet and fall headlong into the path of a train. We had found out (by employing the scientific method and observing) that he sensibly didn't trust himself to drive. Instead, he took the train three miles to his home nearby. Our investigation was prompted by the unlaced combat boots he affected since they seemed somewhat awkward and clumsy and therefore dangerous. In a like manner, his oratory left the class feeling awkward, bemused, somewhat concerned and perhaps a little in danger. Most often he would simply read from his notes, and, though he read aloud, he left the distinct impression that he was absolutely unaware of his audience. Yet he knew all the students by name and by their achievements or lack thereof. And we also found out that this professor of introductory history, who taught what was basically a civics class, was also teaching himself calculus and trigonometry because, as he put it, "I've forgotten most of it, and what I haven't forgotten is new since I learned it. And I need to keep up with my students." A strange man, unquestionably absent-minded, yet also unforgettable.

Before you leave college, odds are you'll also run into a professor of another extreme—and rarely is the Aristotelian mean between the extremes seen in school. This teacher is on top of everything, with a ready answer no matter what the question, often able even to predict the question, or at least come up with a question—any question just so the class continues to move along—this sort of teacher can be most exasperating. Rarely will you find this individual involved in the "hard" sciences—not enough room to move. Instead, this type likes to throw a blinding light on the gray areas of the humanities, to neaten up some of the abiding questions of the ages. This sort can lecture volubly without notes, without a text, and often without even a class (a word of warning, avoid office hours with teachers of this ilk, since even casual conferences can turn into colloquia). Generally, you can recognize this kind of teacher by your own newfound desire to take down every word uttered in class and your subsequent inability, also newfound, to make sense of those notes later. The range of allusion in such classes can be literally stunning, even painful. But then normal folk don't always see those clearcut connections between, say, Nixon's foreign policies and Ptolemy's inability to account for retrograde planetary motion. Or the necessary causal relation between the Wobblies and Elvis Presley. You can, if you dare, imagine this sort of teacher—or more properly, lecturer since that's all they actually do—at home, in bed, making the important connections between Russia's Red Army and family planning.

You can easily spot such lecturers. No matter the occasion, the ⁹ weather, the fashion, or their gender, they wear gray tweed, made from material as stiff as their classroom manner, evidently some sort of spun steel. Their gray hair is thinning, sucked inward, one imagines, to feed the ravenous gray matter within. They're given to innumerable handouts, generally of their own device, and in these reams of indecipherable xerography they often condense their own lecture material in ways that seemingly make perfect sense yet invariably prompt questions that can only be answered by more handouts and further lectures creating a veritable black hole where the average undergraduate's time and space and energy are warped beyond human understanding. To add insult to injury, they're the first to insist that some absolutely huge area of expertise can conveniently be reduced to "just three essential points," the third of which, try as you might to get them to it during class, will only come up on the final exam.

The lecturer's shadowy double is the "discusser." In contrast to ¹⁰ the lecturer, whose answers inundate you from a font of wisdom, the discusser only answers questions with questions: You ask, "When did Elizabeth abdicate?" The discusser answers "What do you mean by abdicate?" It's as if the discusser were trapped in an endless logical fallacy of the complex question sort: "When did you stop beating your wife?" If it escalates far enough, it starts to resemble a scene from a grade B terror movie, with the student in a Peter Lorre–like role, all sweaty, eyes rolling nervously, stuttering and halting, sliding on and off the track: "Regardless of Elizabeth the Queen's, I mean Queen Elizabeth's, though she wouldn't be Queen if she abdicated, regardless of her sex life, her sexual wants before or after her marriage, or her impending marriage, what was the date, that is, the time of her leaving the throne?" And the discusser, as cool as Sidney Greenstreet, responding: "But *was* Elizabeth ever really Queen if by Queen you mean ruler of all she surveys?" And the student is left to flounder like a fish.

You can easily spot and avoid the discusser, if you so choose 11 (such choices make up your real education and they're invariably parenthetical), since the discussers avoid "limiting" themselves with comprehensible course descriptions, eschew the "rigidity" of syllabi, and often do away with common textbooks, assignments, and exams. Instead, they favor oral reports, the aforementioned handouts, and small group discussions, and they're often seen shifting the furniture around in their classrooms to accommodate those reports and group activities. Tests and grading and such are decided on by consensus. Some say the bell curve was invented expressly for discussers or at least what little hard evidence there is suggests that a conference may have been held at which one of the topics may have been "student assessment," and its outcome may have been grading on the curve. Such terminology is typical of the discusser, at least as long as such terms remain flexible enough to admit virtually any definition.

And therein lies another opportunity for learning, since the dis- 12 cusser's own remarkable elasticity often can be manipulated to your own advantage. Dragging a "red herring" through everything you say and do in class, for instance, allows you enough lateral movement so that you can sidestep "facts" in favor of "issues." For instance, if the class is considering the symbiotic relation between agrarian producers and entrepreneurial merchants, you might want to bring up the "issue" of gender. Or if the class is studying the sonnet form you might well relate that form "in the obvious ways" to death as a rite of passage.

Late in my academic career, I served time in a class led by a 13 mindless boob. She combined the agonies of a foreign exchange teaching assistant with the pretentiousness of a Dean of Student Affairs (perhaps it is that very title that forces such deans to act like they know the comings and goings of all their students). An indecipherable accent of unknown origin made her seem to be, at least at first, a mercy case like the absent-minded professor. We struggled to understand, but it was like listening to rapid and random dialings around on late-night talk radio. Her lectures were mostly static, interspersed with vocals which faded in and out and were, every so often, mysteriously punctuated by inexplicable enthusiasm and seeming clarity. We could make nothing of it. Yet initially this person seemed sympathetic, and might even have been so had not certain students become convinced that they were obligated to learn in her class. When pressed to teach them, she turned with fury on the class as a whole. Most of us wilted, as we should have. A foolhardy few pressed farther only to find themselves faced down at last. The lesson here is simple. Tenure is a stacked deck. It beats a full house every time.

Don't be deceived by seeming mindlessness in faculty though. The fiftieth run-through of a set-piece on the "macro vs. micro in applied economics" can create some remarkable aberrations, aka "anecdotes." And these sorts of asides sometimes serve a function other than filling time. Sometimes they electrify the inside track to a particular discipline, illuminating what life would be like on Wall Street or in the physics lab or in Silicon Valley. Finding a use for such anecdotes (other than as a moment to turn the page in your notebook) can be one of the more fruitful academic lessons. After a particularly brutal session of kvetching about the inanities of a particular professor, a friend of mine pointed out that even this nitwit had something to offer—he provided valuable advice on how not to act and what not to learn. 14

But don't be deceived by Mr. Nice Guy, or rather Dr. Nice Guy, either. More insidious than the most mindless of professors, Dr. Nice Guy often turns out to be your worst enemy, though he'll tell you again and again how he's only interested in your welfare, your education. My particular Nice Guy cultivated a whiny sort of "I'm not good enough for you" persona, and, as it turned out, when the chips were down and I needed a recommendation, he was right. His classroom demeanor was likewise all fumbled apologies for not being properly prepared, yet he could talk the socks off a corpse. His classes invariably ran overtime, the more students he could keep late, the longer the better. The material itself seemed substantial, yet when our final papers produced the same sort of substance, its worth plummeted. These papers were, of course, the result of uncounted hours of toil in the wearying dungeons of the college library, wading through puddles of dust that could choke a horse. Knowledge gleaned from a tome that had stood untouched and gathering filth for fifty or sixty years would be, ipso 15 facto, worthwhile, if we could but "execute" it in the proper way, "execution," as he said, being everything. So true.

College, of course, is more than making the best of a bad situ- 16 ation. It's also making the best of a banal situation. And sometimes even luxuriating in a good situation. And a baccalaureate, to those who have one, means more than a good word for a spelling bee. The shared experience it represents has little to do with any specific curriculum, as more and more and more law schools and graduate business schools and even engineering firms are willing to admit. Rather, that diploma means you have met many potential disasters on the enemy's home turf. You have done more than dabbled. You have worked your way onto sacred ground, within the stronghold of a "discipline," no matter which, and you have returned unscathed with a passing grade.

Questions on Subject

1. According to Arnold in what way is college life like "real life"?
2. What does Arnold say is the significance of a college diploma? In what way is jail not an appropriate analogy for time served in school? (Glossary: *Analogy*)
3. Why does the college atmosphere subject college professors to caricature?
4. According to Arnold, why is it difficult to describe what you learn in school?
5. Which of the types of professors does Arnold seem to prefer? least prefer? Explain.

Questions on Strategy

1. How has Arnold organized his essay? (Glossary: *Organization*) What is the purpose of paragraphs 1 through 3? How are they related to paragraph 4?
2. Name the different types of professors Arnold distinguishes. Is his system of division complete? What additions, if any, would you make to his categories of teachers?
3. Instead of including several examples of each type of teacher, Arnold draws his portraits using a single example. How effective is

this strategy? In what way might a series of examples have strengthened or weakened his essay? (Glossary: *Illustration*) Explain.

4. Who do you think is Arnold's intended audience? (Glossary: *Audience*)

Questions on Diction and Vocabulary

1. What does Arnold mean by his use of the term the "real world" (paragraph 1)?

2. How would you describe Arnold's tone in this essay? (Glossary: *Tone*) How does his diction establish that tone? Do you find the tone appropriate for Arnold's subject and purpose? Explain.

3. Refer to your desk dictionary to determine the meanings of the following words as they are used in this selection: *figment* (paragraph 1), *ergo* (3), *caricature* (5), *bland* (5), *conjecture* (7), *farcical* (7), *bemused* (7), *volubly* (8), *allusion* (8), *retrograde* (8), *inundate* (10), *eschew* (11), *lateral* (12), *symbiotic* (12), *foolhardy* (13), *aberrations* (14), *inanities* (14), *nitwit* (14), *turf* (16).

Writing Suggestions

1. Write a short essay in which you describe Arnold's teaching style. Does his teaching style fall into one of the categories he creates, or will you have to designate another one for him? Be sure to cite examples of his diction and other evidence to support your written portrait.

2. In an essay discuss the various student types found at your school. First determine your purpose. Do you wish to point out the different approaches students have to learning? Perhaps you want to discuss the various reasons students have for attending college. Or will your survey describe the different ways students finance their college career?

Writing Suggestions for Division and Classification

1. To write a meaningful paper of classification, you must analyze a body of unorganized material, arranging it for a particular purpose. For example, in order to identify for a buyer the most economical cars currently on the market, you might initially determine which cars can be purchased for under $10,000, which cost between $10,000 and $15,000, and which cost more than $15,000. Then, using a second basis of selection—fuel economy—you could determine which cars have the best gas mileage within each price range. A different purpose would result in a different classification. For example, you might initially want to determine which cars on the market comfortably accommodate a family of six. Next, using a second principle of selection—price—you could determine which vehicles might be purchased for under $10,000. Such a classification would identify for a buyer all six-passenger cars available for under $10,000.

   Select one of the following subjects, and write a paper of classification. Be sure that your purpose is clearly explained and that your bases of selection are chosen and ordered in accordance with your purpose.
   a. attitudes toward physical fitness
   b. contemporary American music
   c. reading materials
   d. reasons for going to college
   e. attitudes toward the religious or spiritual side of life
   f. choosing a hobby
   g. television comedies

  h. college professors
  i. local restaurants
  j. choosing a career
  k. college courses
  l. recreational activities
  m. ways of financing a college education
  n. parties or other social events
2. We sometimes resist classifying other people because it can seem like "pigeonholing" or stereotyping individuals unfairly. In an essay, compare and contrast two or more ways of classifying people—at least one that you would call legitimate and one that you would call misleading. What conclusions can you draw about the difference between useful classifications and damaging stereotypes?

9
Definition

What Is Definition?

A definition explains the meaning of a word or phrase, as every-one who has ever used a dictionary knows. Words need to be defined because their sounds and spelling hardly ever indicate ex-actly what they are intended to mean. A word like *draft* can refer to a current of air, conscription, a ship's depth in the water, a bank check, or the first attempt at a piece of writing. It's amazing that this jumble of apparently unrelated meanings can all belong to one simple set of letters and sounds; but, then, words are abstract sym-bols and represent a large and complex world of things and ideas. We can only communicate with each other properly when we agree on a definition for the words we use. To assure such agreement, writers have a variety of techniques at their disposal.

A *formal definition* explains the meaning of a word by assigning it to a class and then differentiating it from other members of that class.

TERM		CLASS	DIFFERENTIATION
Music	is	sound	made by voices or instruments and characterized by melody, harmony, or rhythm.

Note how crucial the differentiation is here: there are many sounds—from the roar of a passing jet airplane to the fizz of soda in a glass—that must be excluded for the definition to be precise and useful. Dictionary entries often follow the class–differentiation pattern of the formal definition.

A *synonymous definition* explains a word by pairing it with another word of similar but perhaps more limited meaning.

> Music is melody.

Synonymous definition can never be as precise as formal definition, because few words share exactly the same meaning. But, particularly when the word being defined is reasonably familiar and somewhat broad, a well-chosen synonym can provide readers with a surer sense of its meaning in context. Occasionally, a synonymous definition may even be metaphorical.

A *negative definition* explains a word by saying what it does not mean.

> Music is not silence, and it is not noise.

Such a definition must obviously be incomplete: there are sounds which are neither silence nor noise and yet are not music—quiet conversation, for example. But specifying what something is *not* may often help to clarify other statements about what it *is*.

An *etymological definition* also seldom stands alone, but by tracing a word's origins it helps readers understand its meaning.

> Music is descended from the Greek word *mousikē*, meaning literally "the art of the Muse."

The Muses, according to Greek mythology, were deities and the sources of inspiration in the arts. Thus, the etymology suggests why we think of music as an art and as the product of inspiration. Etymological definitions can often reveal surprising sources that suggest new ways of looking at ideas or objects.

A *stipulative definition* is a definition invented by a writer to convey a special or unexpected sense of an existing and often familiar word.

Music is a language, but a language of the intangible, a kind of soul-language.—*Edward MacDowell*

Music is the arithmetic of sounds.—*Claude Debussy*

Although these two examples seem to disagree with each other, and perhaps also with your idea of what music is, note that neither is arbitrary. (That is, neither assigns to the word *music* a completely foreign meaning, as Humpty-Dumpty did in *Through the Looking-Glass* when he defined *glory* as "a nice knock-down argument.") The stipulative definitions by MacDowell and Debussy help explain each composer's conception of the subject and can lead, of course, to further elaboration. Stipulative definitions almost always provide the basis for a more complex discussion.

Sometimes a word, or the idea it stands for, requires more than a sentence of explanation. Such a longer definition—called, naturally enough, *extended definition*—may go on for a paragraph, a page, an essay, or even an entire book. It may employ any of the techniques mentioned already in this chapter, as well as the various strategies discussed throughout the text. An extended definition of music might provide *examples,* ranging from African drumming to a Bach fugue to a Bruce Springsteen song, in order to develop a fuller and more vivid sense of what music is. A writer might *describe* music in detail by showing its characteristic features, or explain the *process* of composing music, or *compare and contrast* music with language (according to MacDowell's stipulative definition) or arithmetic (according to Debussy's). Any of these strategies, and others too, will help to make the meaning of a writer's words and ideas clear.

Why Do Writers Use Definition?

Since most readers have dictionaries, it might seem that writers would hardly ever have to define their terms. In fact, they seldom do, even when using an unusual word like *tergiversation*, which few readers will have in their active vocabularies; if readers don't know it, the reasoning goes, let them look it up. But there are times when a definition is really necessary. One is when a writer uses a word so specialized, or so new, that it simply won't be in the dictionaries; another is when a writer must use a number of unfamiliar technical terms within only a few sentences. Also, when a word has several different meanings or may mean different things to different people, authors will often state exactly the sense in which they are using the word. In each of these cases, definition serves the purpose of achieving clarity.

But writers also use definition, particularly extended definition, to explain the essential nature of the things and ideas they write about. Such writing goes beyond answering the question, "What does _____ mean?" to tackle the much broader and deeper question, "What is _____?" And while this may be the primary object of such a definition, an author may also go further and use extended definition to make a persuasive point. That's what Ellen Goodman does in "The Company Man" and Jo Goodwin Parker does in "What Is Poverty?" later in this section.

What to Look for in Reading an Extended Definition

First, determine what word or idea the definition is about—what subject it seeks to explain. Sometimes the title will tell you, as with "What Is Poverty?" and "Best Friends"; at other times you may have to read further into the essay. Then, consider the writer's purpose, and pay attention to the strategies and techniques the writer uses to develop the definition.

The subject of the following extended definition by Robert Keith Miller is clear, if not from the title ("Discrimination Is a Virtue"), then from the second sentence.

> We have a word in English which means "the ability to tell differences." That word is *discrimination*. But within the last twenty years, this word has been so frequently misused that an entire generation has grown up believing that "discrimination" means "racism." People are always proclaiming that "discrimination" is something that should be done away with. Should that ever happen, it would prove to be our undoing.
>
> Discrimination means discernment; it means the ability to perceive the truth, to use good judgment and to profit accordingly. "The Oxford

English Dictionary" traces this understanding of the word back to 1648 and demonstrates that for the next 300 years, "discrimination" was a virtue, not a vice. Thus, when a character in a nineteenth-century novel makes a happy marriage, Dickens has another character remark, "It does credit to your discrimination that you should have found such a very excellent young woman."

Of course, "the ability to tell differences" assumes that differences exist, and this is unsettling for a culture obsessed with the notion of equality. The contemporary belief that discrimination is a vice stems from the compound "discriminate against." What we need to remember, however, is that some things deserve to be judged harshly: we should not leave our kingdoms to the selfish and the wicked.

Discrimination is wrong only when someone or something is discriminated against because of prejudice. But to use the word in this sense, as so many people do, is to destroy its true meaning. If you discriminate against something because of general preconceptions rather than particular insights, then you are not discriminating—bias has clouded the clarity of vision which discrimination demands.

The subject of Miller's extended definition is, of course, the word *discrimination*. His purpose, however, is less immediately obvious. At first it appears that he wants only to explain what the word *discrimination* means. But by the third sentence he is distinguishing what it does *not* mean, and at the end it's clear he's trying to persuade readers to use the word correctly, and thus discriminate more sharply and more justly themselves.

Miller begins with a very brief formal definition of discrimination: "the ability [class] to tell differences" [differentiation]. He then offers a negative definition (discrimination is not racism) and a synonymous definition (discrimination is discernment). Next he cites the entry in a great historical dictionary of English to support his claim and quotes an example to illustrate his definition. He concludes by contrasting the word *discrimination* with the compound "discriminate against." Each of these techniques helps make the case that the most precise meaning of discrimination is in direct opposition to its common usage today.

For an analysis of another extended definition, consult the discussion of Laurence Perrine's "Paradox," pp. 6–8.

Writing an Essay of Extended Definition

Whatever your subject, make sure you have a clear sense of your purpose. Why are you writing a definition? If it's only to explain what a word or phrase means, you'll probably run out of things to say in a few sentences—or find that a good dictionary has already said them for you. An effective extended definition should attempt to explain the essential nature of a thing or an idea, whether photosynthesis or spring fever or Republicanism or prison or common sense. You have at least a general idea of what your subject means to you, as well as a sense of the audience you are writing your definition for and the impact you want your definition to achieve. These will guide you as you plan and draft your essay.

1. Considering the Nature of Your Subject

Certain subjects, like Republicanism and discrimination, lend themselves to different interpretations depending on the writer's point of view. While readers may agree in general about what such subjects mean, there will be much disagreement over particulars— and, therefore, room for you to propose and defend your own definitions. A subject like photosynthesis, though, is a specific natural process, so all definitions of it must agree very closely on particulars—even though your general approach to the definition may be quite original. In preparing to define a specific subject like photosynthesis, your preparations will include some reading and note-taking to make sure that you've got your facts right. If your subject is more general or subjective, there may be fewer facts to look for; but it is wise to take your readers' probable views into account, and possibly the views of other writers on the subject— not necessarily to change your own definition, but to present it more effectively to your audience.

2. Considering Your Audience

What do your readers know? If you're an economics major in an undergraduate writing course, you can safely assume that you know your subject better than your readers do and so will have to explain even very basic terms and ideas. If, however, you're writing a paper for your course in econometrics, your most important reader—the one who grades your paper—won't even slow down at your references to *monetary aggregates* and *Philips Curves*, provided, of course, that you obviously know what you mean.

3. *Choosing a Technique or Techniques of Definition*

The choices you make depend on your subject and your readers. Photosynthesis, for example, is a natural process, so a good choice of strategy in defining it would be a process analysis; readers who know little about biology may better understand photosynthesis if you draw an analogy with the eating and breathing of human beings. Common sense is an abstract concept, so its meaning could certainly be illustrated with concrete examples; in addition, its special nature would emerge more sharply through comparison and contrast with other ways of thinking. To define a salt marsh, you might choose a typical marsh and describe it. To define economic inflation or a particular disease, you might discuss causes and effects. Only two requirements limit your choice of definition strategy: the strategy must be appropriate to your subject, and it must help you explain your subject's essential nature.

Many inexperienced writers believe that any extended definition, no matter what the subject, should begin with a formal "dictionary" definition, or at least introduce one before the essay has proceeded very far. This is not necessarily so; you will find that most of the following essays include no such formal definition. Assume that your readers have dictionaries and know how to use them. If, however, you think your readers do require a short, formal definition at some point, don't simply quote from a dictionary. Unless you have some very good reason for doing otherwise, put the definition into your own words, words that suit your approach and the probable readers of your essay. (Certainly, nonscientists would be baffled by an essay that began, "The dictionary defines photosynthesis as 'the process by which chlorophyll-containing cells in green plants convert incident light to chemical energy and synthesize organic compounds from inorganic compounds, especially carbohydrates from carbon dioxide and water, with the simultaneous release of oxygen.' ") There's another advantage to using your own words: you won't have to write "The dictionary defines . . ." or "According to Webster's . . ."; stock phrases like these almost immediately put the reader's mind to sleep.

4. Developing Your Strategy

The various strategies for extended definition are discussed fully in sections of their own; if you need to, look up the strategy you have chosen and review the suggestions there on gathering and organizing information and ideas for your essay.

Best Friends

Howard Solomon, Jr.

A native of New York City, Howard Solomon now lives in Lincoln, Vermont. He studied in France as part of the AFS program in high school and he majored in French at the University of Vermont. Howard's other interests include foreign affairs, languages, photography, and cycling; in his wildest dreams, he imagines becoming an international lawyer. For the following essay, Howard began by interviewing students in his dormitory, collecting information and opinions that he eventually brought together with his own experiences to develop a definition of "best friends."

Best friends, even when they are not a part of our day-to-day lives, are essential to our well-being. They supply the companionship, help, security, and love that we all need. It is not easy to put into words exactly what a best friend is, because the matter is so personal. From time to time, however, we may think about our best friends—who they are, what characteristics they share, and why they are so important to us—in order to gain a better understanding of ourselves and our relationships.

I recently asked several people for their opinions on the subject, beginning with the qualities they valued in their own best friends. They all agreed on three traits: reciprocity, honesty, and love. Reciprocity means that one can always rely on a best friend in times of need. A favor doesn't necessarily have to be returned; but best friends will return it anyway, because they want to. Best friends are willing to help each other for the sake of helping and not just for personal gain. One woman said that life seemed more secure because she knew her best friend was there if she ever needed help.

Honesty in a best friendship is the sharing of feelings openly and without reserve. The people I interviewed said they could rely on their best friends as confidants: they could share problems with their best friends and ask for advice. They also felt that, even if best friends were critical of each other, they would never be hurtful or spiteful.

Love is probably the most important quality of a best friend relationship, according to the people I interviewed. They very much prized the affection and enjoyment they felt in the company of their best friends. One man described it as a "gut reaction," and all said it was a different feeling from being with other friends. Private jokes, looks, and gestures create personal communication between best friends that is at a very high level—many times one person knows what the other is thinking without anything being said. The specifics differ, but most everyone I talked to agreed that a special feeling exists, which is best described as love. 4

I next asked who could be a best friend and who could not. My sources all felt it was impossible for parents, other relatives, and people of the opposite sex (especially husbands or wives) to be best friends. One woman said such people were "too inhibitive." Personally, I disagree—I have two best friends who are women. However, I may be an exception, and most best friends may fit the above requirements. There could be a good reason for this, too: most of the people I interviewed felt that their best friends were not demanding, while relatives and partners of the opposite sex can be very demanding. 5

To the question of how many best friends one can have, some in my sample responded that it is possible to have several best friends, although very few people can do so; others said it was possible to have only a very few best friends; and still others felt they could have just one—that single friend who is most outstanding. It was interesting to see how ideas varied on this question. Although best friends may be no less special for one person than another, people do define the concept differently. 6

Regarding how long it takes to become best friends and how long the relationship lasts, all were in agreement. "It is a long hard process which takes a lot of time," one woman explained. "It isn't something that can happen overnight," suggested another. One man said, "You usually know the person very well before you consider him your best friend. In fact you know everything about him, his bad points as well as his good points, so there is little likelihood you can come into conflict with him." In addition, every- 7 one thought that once a person has become a best friend, he or she remains so for the rest of one's life.

During the course of the interviews I discovered one important 8 and unexpected difference between men and women regarding the qualities of their best friends. The men all said that a best friend usually possessed one quality that stood out above all others—an easygoing manner or humor or sympathy, for example. One of them told me that he looked not for loyalty but for honesty, for someone who was truthful, because it was so rare to find this quality in anyone. The women I surveyed, however, all responded that they looked for a well-rounded person who had many good qualities. One said that a person who had just one good quality and not several would be "too boring to associate with." Does this difference hold true beyond my sample? If so, it means that men and women have quite different definitions of their best friends.

I have always wondered why my own best friends were so im- 9 portant to me; but it wasn't until recently that something happened to make me really understand my relationship with my best friends. My father died, and this was a crisis for me. Most of my friends gave me their condolences. But my best friends did more than that: they actually supported me. They called long distance to see how I was and what I needed, to try and help me work out my problems or simply to talk. Two of my best friends even took time from their spring break and, along with two other best friends, attended my father's memorial service; none of my other friends came. Since then, these are the only people who have continued to worry about me and talk to me about my father. I know that, whenever I need someone, they will be there and willing to help me. I know also that, whenever they need help, I will be ready to do the same for them.

Yet, I don't value my best friends so much just for what they do 10 for me. I simply enjoy their company more than anyone else's. We talk, joke, play sports, and do all kinds of things when we are together. I never feel ill at ease, even after we've been apart for a while. However, the most important thing for me about best friends is the knowledge that I am never alone, that there are others in the world who care about my well-being as much as I do about theirs. Surely this is a comforting feeling for everyone.

Interview with Howard Solomon, Jr.

How did you hit on the idea of defining what a best friend is?

A friend of mine had become a best friend—we're like brothers almost—and I was trying to figure out what had happened, what was the difference. So I decided to explore what was on my mind. Of course, I shared the paper with the other students in my class, because that's what we do, but I think I was really writing for myself, not for them.

How did you feel about getting feedback from your classmates?

The first time I had to read a paper, I was afraid and embarrassed because I didn't know how it was going to be received, so I got someone to read it aloud for me. Everybody liked the paper, so the next time it was better. The other students showed me I was doing better than I thought I was, and that helped my confidence.

Friendship is a very personal topic, but I see that you've gone beyond your own opinions and experiences.

In fact, the first drafts didn't have anything personal in them at all. I've not written a personal paper since maybe sixth grade— my high school teachers made me show evidence for what I had to say, and my opinion wasn't evidence. The teacher would tell me that I wasn't an authority. So even though I was writing on a very personal kind of topic, I still kept thinking that I wasn't an authority. Fortunately, my college writing teacher told me that sometimes teachers are wrong and that on certain subjects like this you can write from your own experiences and beliefs. But that didn't come in until a late draft.

What led you to interview other people about their ideas of best friendship?

The first draft I wrote was nothing. I tried to get a start with the dictionary definition, but it didn't help—it just put into two words what really needs hundreds of words to explain, and the words it used had to be defined, too. My teacher suggested I might get going better if I talked about my topic with other people. I decided to make it semiformal, so I made up a list of a few specific questions—five questions—and went to about a dozen people I knew and asked them. Questions like, "What qualities do your best friends have?" and "What are some of the things they've done for you?" And I took notes on the answers. I was surprised when so many of them agreed. It isn't a scientific sampling, but the results helped get me started.

So the hard part of the paper was past.

Not exactly! Doing this paper showed me that writing isn't all that easy. Boy, I went through so many copies—adding some things, taking out some things, reorganizing. At one point half the paper was a definition of *friends*, so I could contrast them with *best friends*. That wasn't necessary. Then, I've said that the personal stuff came in late. In fact, my father died after I'd begun writing the paper, so that paragraph came in almost last of all. On the next-to-last draft everything was there, but it was put together in a sort of random way—not completely random, one idea would lead to the next and then the next, but there was a lot of circling around. My teacher pointed this out and suggested I outline what I'd written and work on the outline. So I tried it and I saw what the problem was and what I had to do. It was just a matter of getting things into the right order, and finally everything clicked into place.

The Company Man

Ellen Goodman

Ellen Goodman was born in Boston in 1941. After gradu-
ating cum laude from Radcliffe College in 1963, she worked
as a reporter and researcher for Newsweek. *In 1967, she*
began working at the Boston Globe *and, since 1974, has been*
a full-time columnist. Her regular column, "At Large," is
syndicated by the Washington Post *Writer's Group and ap-*
pears in nearly four hundred newspapers across the country.
In addition, her writing has appeared in McCall's, Harper's
Bazaar, *and* Family Circle, *and her commentaries have been*
broadcast on radio and television. In 1979, Goodman published
Close to Home, *a collection of her columns; several other*
collections have appeared since then, including At Large,
Keeping in Touch, *and* Making Sense.

In "The Company Man," taken from Close to Home,
Goodman defines the "workaholic" by offering a poignant case-
in-point example.

He worked himself to death, finally and precisely, at 3:00 A.M.   1
Sunday morning.

The obituary didn't say that, of course. It said that he died of a   2
coronary thrombosis—I think that was it—but everyone among
his friends and acquaintances knew it instantly. He was a perfect
Type A, a workaholic, a classic, they said to each other and shook
their heads—and thought for five or ten minutes about the way
they lived.

This man who worked himself to death finally and precisely at   3
3:00 A.M. Sunday morning—on his day off—was fifty-one years
old and a vice-president. He was, however, one of six vice-pres-
idents, and one of three who might conceivably—if the president
died or retired soon enough—have moved to the top spot. Phil
knew that.

He worked six days a week, five of them until eight or nine at   4 night, during a time when his own company had begun the four-day week for everyone but the executives. He worked like the Important People. He had no outside "extracurricular interests," unless, of course, you think about a monthly golf game that way. To Phil, it was work. He always ate egg salad sandwiches at his desk. He was, of course, overweight, by 20 or 25 pounds. He thought it was okay, though, because he didn't smoke.

On Saturdays, Phil wore a sports jacket to the office instead of 5 a suit, because it was the weekend.

He had a lot of people working for him, maybe sixty, and most 6 of them liked him most of the time. Three of them will be seriously considered for his job. The obituary didn't mention that.

But it did list his "survivors" quite accurately. He is survived by 7 his wife, Helen, forty-eight years old, a good woman of no par-ticular marketable skills, who worked in an office before marrying and mothering. She had, according to her daughter, given up trying to compete with his work years ago, when the children were small. A company friend said, "I know how much you will miss him." And she answered, "I already have."

"Missing him all these years," she must have given up part of 8 herself which had cared too much for the man. She would be "well taken care of."

His "dearly beloved" eldest of the "dearly beloved" children is 9 a hard-working executive in a manufacturing firm down South. In the day and a half before the funeral, he went around the neigh-borhood researching his father, asking the neighbors what he was like. They were embarrassed.

His second child is a girl, who is twenty-four and newly married. 10 She lives near her mother and they are close, but whenever she was alone with her father, in a car driving somewhere, they had nothing to say to each other.

The youngest is twenty, a boy, a high-school graduate who has 11 spent the last couple of years, like a lot of his friends, doing enough odd jobs to stay in grass and food. He was the one who tried to grab at his father, and tried to mean enough to him to keep the man at home. He was his father's favorite. Over the last two years, Phil stayed up nights worrying about the boy.

The boy once said, "My father and I only board here." 12

At the funeral, the sixty-year-old company president told the 13 forty-eight-year-old widow that the fifty-one-year-old deceased had meant much to the company and would be missed and would be hard to replace. The widow didn't look him in the eye. She was afraid he would read her bitterness and, after all, she would need him to straighten out the finances—the stock options and all that.

Phil was overweight and nervous and worked too hard. If he wasn't at the office, he was worried about it. Phil was a Type A, a heart-attack natural. You could have picked him out in a minute from a lineup. 14

So when he finally worked himself to death, at precisely 3:00 A.M. Sunday morning, no one was really surprised. 15

By 5:00 P.M. the afternoon of the funeral, the company president had begun, discreetly of course, with care and taste, to make inquiries about his replacement. One of three men. He asked around: "Who's been working the hardest?" 16

Questions on Subject

1. In paragraph 4, Goodman says that Phil worked like "Important People." What does she mean?
2. Why did Phil's son go around the neighborhood researching his father? What is ironic about this? What significance do you see in the fact that Phil's son is an executive in a manufacturing plant down South? (Glossary: *Irony*)
3. In your own words, explain the meaning of paragraph 11.
4. Do you think Phil's problems were all his own? Does Goodman suggest that the "system" may, in part, also be responsible for Phil's untimely end? Explain.

Questions on Strategy

1. What is Goodman's purpose in this essay? Goodman's tone is unemotional. Why is that tone especially fitting for her purpose? (Glossary: *Purpose; Tone*)
2. In your own words, give a brief definition of *workaholic* based on the information that Goodman provides in this essay. What information, if any, has the author failed to provide?

3. What significance do you see in the statement "I think that was it" (paragraph 2)?
4. In paragraphs 1, 3, and 15, Goodman tells us the precise time of Phil's death. Why do you suppose this is an important fact for Goodman? Why do you think she repeats the information?
5. Comment on the effectiveness of Goodman's last sentence. (Glossary: *Beginnings/Endings*)

Questions on Diction and Vocabulary

1. Why does the author place the phrase "dearly beloved" in quotation marks in paragraph 9?
2. Refer to your desk dictionary to determine the meanings of the following words as they are used in this selection: *coronary thrombosis* (paragraph 2), *workaholic* (2), *conceivably* (3), *obituary* (6), *marketable* (7), *deceased* (13), *discreetly* (16).

Writing Assignments

1. The procrastinator—the type of person who continually puts off responsibilities and jobs—is very different from the workaholic. Write an essay, modeled on Goodman's if you like, that attempts to use an extended example to define this interesting personality type.
2. One issue that Goodman does not raise is how a person becomes a workaholic. Write an essay in which you speculate about some reasons for such an addiction. How might workaholism be avoided? Or should it be?

Ambition

Perri Klass

Perri Klass is a pediatrician, a mother of two, and the author of four books, including A Not Entirely Benign Procedure: Four Years as a Medical Student *and* Other Women's Children. *In the following essay from the June 1990 issue of* Self, *Klass confesses her admiration of ambition as the necessary impetus to our dreams and our success. However, she advises us to tread cautiously because ambition has an ugly side too. We must be willing to understand what ambition is at its worst and its best and be ready to ask just "how much is too much?"*

In college, my friend Beth was very ambitious, not only for herself but for her friends. She was interested in foreign relations, in travel, in going to law school. "I plan to be secretary of state someday," she would say matter-of-factly. One mutual friend was studying literature, planning to go to graduate school; he would be the chairman of the Yale English department. Another friend was interested in political journalism and would someday edit *Time* magazine. I was a biology major, which was a problem: Beth's best friend from childhood was also studying biology, and Beth had already decided *she* would win the Nobel Prize. This was resolved by my interest in writing fiction. I would win *that* Nobel, while her other friend would win for science.

It was a joke; we were all smart-ass college freshmen, pretending the world was ours for the asking. But it was not entirely a joke. We were *smart* college freshmen, and why should we limit our ambitions?

I've always liked ambitious people, and many of my closest friends have had grandiose dreams. I like such people, not because I am desperate to be buddies with a future secretary of state but because I find ambitious people entertaining, interesting to talk to, fun to watch. And, of course, I like such people because I am ambitious myself, and I would rather not feel apologetic about it.

Ambition has gotten bad press. Back in the seventeenth century, 4
Spinoza thought ambition and lust were "nothing but species of
madness, although they are not enumerated among diseases." Especially in women, ambition has often been seen as a profoundly
dislikable quality; the word "ambitious" linked to a "career
woman" suggested that she was ruthless, hard as nails, clawing
her way to success on top of the bleeding bodies of her friends.

Then, in the late Seventies and the Eighties, ambition became 5
desirable, as books with titles like *How to Stomp Your Way to Success*
became bestsellers. It was still a nasty sort of attribute, but nasty
attributes were good because they helped you look out for number
one.

But what I mean by ambition is dreaming big dreams, putting 6
no limits on your expectations and your hopes. I don't really like
very specific, attainable ambitions, the kind you learn to set in the
career-strategy course taught by the author of *How to Stomp Your
Way to Success*. I like big ambitions that suggest that the world could
open up at any time, with work and luck and determination. The
next book could hit it big. The next research project could lead to
something fantastic. The next bright idea could change history.

Of course, eventually you have to stop being a freshman in col- 7
lege. You limit your ambitions and become more realistic, wiser
about your potential, your abilities, the number of things your life
can hold. Sometimes you get close to something you wanted to
do, only to find it looks better from far away. Back when I was a
freshman, to tell the truth, I wanted to be Jane Goodall, go into
the jungle to study monkeys and learn things no one had ever
dreamed of. This ambition was based on an interest in biology and
several *National Geographic* television specials; it turned out that
wasn't enough of a basis for a life. There were a number of other
early ambitions that didn't pan out either. I was not fated to live
a wild, adventurous life, to travel alone to all the most exotic parts
of the world, to leave behind a string of broken hearts. Oh well,
you have to grow up, at least a little.

One of the worst things ambition can do is tell you you're a 8
failure. The world is full of measuring tapes, books and articles to
tell you where you should be at your age, after so-and-so many
years of doing what you do.

Almost all of us have to deal with the tremendous success of 9 friends (or enemies), with those who somehow started out where we did but are now way in front. My college-alumni magazine arrives every two months without fail, so I can find out who graduated two years *after* I did but is now running a groundbreaking clinic at a major university hospital (and I'm only just finishing my residency!). Who is restoring a fabulous mansion in a highly desirable town by the sea. Who got promoted yet again, due to natural brilliance and industry.

I read an article recently about how one's twenties are the decade   10
for deciding on a career and finishing your training, and the thirties are for consolidating your success and rising within your chosen job (and here I am in my thirties, not even sure what I want to do yet!). With all these external yardsticks, the last thing anyone needs is an internal voice as well, whispering irritably that you were supposed to do it better, get further and that all you've actually accomplished is mush, since you haven't met your own goals.

The world is full of disappointed people. Some of them probably   11
never had much ambition to start with; they sat back and waited for something good and feel cheated because it never happened. Some of them had very set, specific ambitions and, for one reason or another, never got what they wanted. Others got what they wanted but found it wasn't exactly what they'd expected it to be. Disappointed ambition provides fodder for both drama and melodrama: aspiring athletes (who coulda been contenders), aspiring dancers (all they ever needed was the music and the mirror).

The world is also full of people so ambitious, so consumed by   12
drive and overdrive that nothing they pass on the way to success has any value at all. Life becomes one long exercise in delayed gratification; everything you do, you're doing only because it will one day get you where you want to be. Medical training is an excellent example of delayed gratification. You spend years in medical school doing things with no obvious relationship to your future as a doctor, and then you spend years in residency, living life on a miserable schedule, staying up all night and slogging through the day, telling yourself that one day all this will be over. It's what you have to do to become a doctor, but it's a lousy model for life in general. There's nothing wrong with a little delayed gratification every now and then, but a job you do only because of where it will get you—and not because you like it—means a life of mut-

tering to yourself, "Someday this will be over." This is bad for the disposition.

As you grow up, your ambitions may come into conflict. Most 13 prominently nowadays, we have to hear about Women Torn Between Family and Career, about women who make it to the top only to realize they left their ovaries behind. Part of growing up, of course, is realizing that there is only so much room in one life, whether you are male or female. You can do one thing wholeheartedly and single-mindedly and give up some other things. Or you can be greedy and grab for something new without wanting to give up what you already have. This leads to a chaotic and crowded life in which you are always late, always overdue, always behind, but rarely bored. Even so, you have to come to terms with limitations; you cannot crowd your life with occupations and then expect to do each one as well as you might if it were all you had to do. I realize this when I race out of the hospital, offending a senior doctor who had offered to explain something to me, only to arrive late at the day-care center, annoying the people who have been taking care of my daughter.

People consumed by ambition, living with ambition, get to be a 14 little humorless, a little one-sided. On the other hand, people who completely abrogate their ambition aren't all fun and games either. I've met a certain number of women whose ambitions are no longer for themselves at all; their lives are now dedicated to their offspring. I hope my children grow up to be nice people, smart people, people who use good grammar; and I hope they grow up to find things they love to do, and do well. But my ambitions are still for *me*.

Of course, I try to be mature about it all. I don't assign my friends 15 Nobel Prizes or top government posts. I don't pretend that there is room in my life for any and every kind of ambition I can imagine. Instead, I say piously that all I want are three things: I want to write as well as I can, I want to have a family and I want to be a good pediatrician. And then, of course, a voice inside whispers . . . to write a bestseller, to have ten children, to do stunning medical research. Fame and fortune, it whispers, fame and fortune. Even though I'm not a college freshman anymore, I'm glad to find that little voice still there, whispering sweet nothings in my ear.

Questions on Subject

1. According to Klass, ambition has traditionally been regarded as a "nasty attribute." Why? Do you agree?
2. Why does Klass prefer ambitious people to unambitious people?
3. What are the different kinds of ambition Klass defines? Which type does she prefer? Why?
4. Why does Klass think it is necessary to limit our ambition as we grow older?
5. How does Klass define "delayed gratification"? What are its benefits? Its deficits? In what way is medical training a perfect example of delayed gratification?
6. In her concluding paragraph, Klass admits to being "glad" for the vestige of outrageous ambition that still haunts her. Does this contradict her earlier assertion that ambition has to be limited? Explain.

Questions on Strategy

1. Klass opens her essay with several examples. Why do you suppose she does this? How effective is this strategy? (Glossary: *Beginnings*)
2. What is Klass's purpose in writing this essay? (Glossary: *Purpose*)
3. Prepare a brief outline of Klass's essay. How has she organized her essay? What kinds of information does she include in each of her paragraphs? (Glossary: *Organization*)
4. What audience is Klass writing for? How can you tell? (Glossary: *Audience*)
5. Klass's essay includes a number of different strategies and techniques of definition. Point out as many of these strategies as you can, and discuss what each contributes to her essay.

Questions on Diction and Vocabulary

1. What do phrases such as "smart-ass college freshmen" (2), "I would rather not feel apologetic about it" (3), "Oh well, you have to grow up" (7), and "This is bad for the disposition" (12) contribute to the overall tone of Klass's essay? (Glossary: *Tone*)
2. Refer to your desk dictionary to determine the meanings of the following words as they are used in this selection: *grandiose* (paragraph 3), *ruthless* (4), *consumed* (12), *abrogate* (14).

Writing Suggestions

1. Klass defines ambition as "dreaming big dreams, putting no limits on your expectations and your hopes." Is that what ambition means to you? If so, develop that definition into an essay of your own. If not, develop your own definition of the word "ambition," being sure to offer evidence from your own experiences and observations to support your definition.

2. Ambition is an abstract term, open to interpretation, yet any definition of it must still be supported with credible evidence. Write an essay in which you define one of the following abstract terms. Following Klass's example, include in your definition of the word a definition of what it is "not."

choice	honesty
peace	discrimination
patriotism	morality
civil disobedience	responsibility
censorship	rights

What Is Poverty?

Jo Goodwin Parker

All we know about Jo Goodwin Parker is that when George Henderson, a professor at the University of Oklahoma, was preparing his 1971 book, America's Other Children: Public Schools Outside Suburbia, *the following essay was mailed to him from West Virginia under Parker's name. Henderson included Parker's essay in his book, and according to him, her piece was an unpublished speech, given in Deland, Florida, on December 27, 1965. Perhaps she is, as her essay says, one of the rural poor who eke out a hardscrabble living just beyond view of America's middle-class majority; or perhaps she is a spokesperson for them, writing not from her own experience but from long and sympathetic observation. In either case, her definition of poverty is so detailed and forceful as to convey, even to those who have never known it, the nature of poverty.*

You ask me what is poverty? Listen to me. Here I am, dirty, smelly, and with no "proper" underwear on and with the stench of my rotting teeth near you. I will tell you. Listen to me. Listen without pity. I cannot use your pity. Listen with understanding. Put yourself in my dirty, worn out, ill-fitting shoes, and hear me.

Poverty is getting up every morning from a dirt- and illness-stained mattress. The sheets have long since been used for diapers. Poverty is living in a smell that never leaves. This is a smell of urine, sour milk, and spoiling food sometimes joined with the strong smell of long-cooked onions. Onions are cheap. If you have smelled this smell, you did not know how it came. It is the smell of the outdoor privy. It is the smell of young children who cannot walk the long dark way in the night. It is the smell of the mattresses where years of "accidents" have happened. It is the smell of the milk which has gone sour because the refrigerator long has not worked, and it costs money to get it fixed. It is the smell of rotting garbage. I could bury it, but where is the shovel? Shovels cost money.

Poverty is being tired. I have always been tired. They told me 3 at the hospital when the last baby came that I had chronic anemia caused from poor diet, a bad case of worms, and that I needed a corrective operation. I listened politely—the poor are always polite. The poor always listen. They don't say that there is no money for iron pills, or better food, or worm medicine. The idea of an operation is frightening and costs so much that, if I had dared, I would have laughed. Who takes care of my children? Recovery from an operation takes a long time. I have three children. When I left them with "Granny" the last time I had a job, I came home to find the baby covered with fly specks, and a diaper that had not been changed since I left. When the dried diaper came off, bits of my baby's flesh came with it. My other child was playing with a sharp bit of broken glass, and my oldest was playing alone at the edge of a lake. I made twenty-two dollars a week, and a good nursery school costs twenty dollars a week for three children. I quit my job.

Poverty is dirt. You say in your clean clothes coming from your 4 clean house, "Anybody can be clean." Let me explain about housekeeping with no money. For breakfast I give my children grits with no oleo or cornbread without eggs and oleo. This does not use up many dishes. What dishes there are, I wash in cold water and with no soap. Even the cheapest soap has to be saved for the baby's diapers. Look at my hands, so cracked and red. Once I saved for two months to buy a jar of Vaseline for my hands and the baby's diaper rash. When I had saved enough, I went to buy it and the price had gone up two cents. The baby and I suffered on. I have to decide every day if I can bear to put my cracked, sore hands into the cold water and strong soap. But you ask, why not hot water? Fuel costs money. If you have a wood fire it costs money. If you burn electricity, it costs money. Hot water is a luxury. I do not have luxuries. I know you will be surprised when I tell you how young I am. I look so much older. My back has been bent over the wash tubs for so long, I cannot remember when I ever did anything else. Every night I wash every stitch my school age child has on and just hope her clothes will be dry by morning.

Poverty is staying up all night on cold nights to watch the fire, 5 knowing one spark on the newspaper covering the walls means your sleeping children die in flames. In summer poverty is watching gnats and flies devour your baby's tears when he cries. The screens are torn and you pay so little rent you know they will never be fixed. Poverty means insects in your food, in your nose, in your eyes, and crawling over you when you sleep. Poverty is hoping it never rains because diapers won't dry when it rains and soon you are using newspapers. Poverty is seeing your children forever with runny noses. Paper handkerchiefs cost money and all your rags you need for other things. Even more costly are antihistamines. Poverty is cooking without food and cleaning without soap.

Poverty is asking for help. Have you ever had to ask for help, 6 knowing your children will suffer unless you get it? Think about asking for a loan from a relative, if this is the only way you can imagine asking for help. I will tell you how it feels. You find out where the office is that you are supposed to visit. You circle that block four or five times. Thinking of your children, you go in. Everyone is very busy. Finally, someone comes out and you tell her that you need help. That never is the person you need to see. You go see another person, and after spilling the whole shame of your poverty all over the desk between you, you find that this isn't the right office after all—you must repeat the whole process, and it never is any easier at the next place.

You have asked for help, and after all it has a cost. You are again 7 told to wait. You are told why, but you don't really hear because of the red cloud of shame and the rising black cloud of despair.

Poverty is remembering. It is remembering quitting school in 8 junior high because "nice" children had been so cruel about my clothes and my smell. The attendance officer came. My mother told him I was pregnant. I wasn't but she thought that I could get a job and help out. I had jobs off and on, but never long enough to learn anything. Mostly I remember being married. I was so young then. I am still young. For a time, we had all the things you have. There was a little house in another town, with hot water and everything. Then my husband lost his job. There was unemployment insurance for a while and what few jobs I could get. Soon, all our nice things were repossessed and we moved back here. I was pregnant then. This house didn't look so bad when we first moved in. Every week it gets worse. Nothing is ever fixed. We now had no money. There were a few odd jobs for my husband, but everything went for food then, as it does now. I don't know how we lived through three years and three babies, but we did. I'll tell you something, after the last baby I destroyed my marriage. It had been a good one, but could you keep on bringing children in this dirt? Did you ever think how much it costs for any kind of birth control? I knew my husband was leaving the day he left, but there were no good-byes between us. I hope he has been able to climb out of this mess somewhere. He never could hope with us to drag him down.

That's when I asked for help. When I got it, you know how much 9 it was? It was, and is, seventy-eight dollars a month for the four of us; that is all I ever can get. Now you know why there is no soap, no needles and thread, no hot water, no aspirin, no worm medicine, no hand cream, no shampoo. None of these things forever and ever and ever. So that you can see clearly, I pay twenty dollars a month rent, and most of the rest goes for food. For grits and cornmeal, and rice and milk and beans. I try my best to use only the minimum electricity. If I use more, there is that much less for food.

Poverty is looking into a black future. Your children won't play 10 with my boys. They will turn to other boys who steal to get what they want. I can already see them behind the bars of their prison instead of behind the bars of my poverty. Or they will turn to the freedom of alcohol or drugs, and find themselves enslaved. And my daughter? At best, there is for her a life like mine.

But you say to me, there are schools. Yes, there are schools. My 11 children have no extra books, no magazines, no extra pencils, or crayons, or paper and the most important of all, they do not have health. They have worms, they have infections, they have pinkeye all summer. They do not sleep well on the floor, or with me in my one bed. They do not suffer from hunger, my seventy-eight dollars keeps us alive, but they do suffer from malnutrition. Oh yes, I do remember what I was taught about health in school. It doesn't do much good. In some places there is a surplus commodities program. Not here. The county said it cost too much. There is a school lunch program. But I have two children who will already be damaged by the time they get to school.

But, you say to me, there are health clinics. Yes, there are health 12 clinics and they are in the towns. I live out here eight miles from town. I can walk that far (even if it is sixteen miles both ways), but can my little children? My neighbor will take me when he goes; but he expects to get paid, *one way or another*. I bet you know my neighbor. He is that large man who spends his time at the gas station, the barbershop, and the corner store complaining about the government spending money on the immoral mothers of illegitimate children.

Poverty is an acid that drips on pride until all pride is worn away. 13 Poverty is a chisel that chips on honor until honor is worn away. Some of you say that you would do *something* in my situation, and maybe you would, for the first week or the first month, but for year after year after year?

Even the poor can dream. A dream of a time when there is 14 money. Money for the right kinds of food, for worm medicine, for iron pills, for toothbrushes, for hand cream, for a hammer and nails and a bit of screening, for a shovel, for a bit of paint, for some sheeting, for needles and thread. Money to pay *in money* for a trip to town. And, oh, money for hot water and money for soap. A dream of when asking for help does not eat away the last bit of pride. When the office you visit is as nice as the offices of other governmental agencies, when there are enough workers to help you quickly, when workers do not quit in defeat and despair. When you have to tell your story to only one person, and that person can send you for other help and you don't have to prove your poverty over and over and over again.

I have come out of my despair to tell you this. Remember I did 15 not come from another place or another time. Others like me are all around you. Look at us with an angry heart, anger that will help you help me. Anger that will let you tell of me. The poor are always silent. Can you be silent too?

Questions on Subject

1. Why did Parker not have the operation that was recommended for her? Why did she quit her job?
2. In Parker's view, what makes asking for help such a difficult and painful experience? What compels her to do so anyway?

3. Why did Parker's husband leave her? How does she justify her attitude toward his leaving? (Glossary: *Attitude*)
4. In paragraph 12, Parker says the following about a neighbor giving her a ride to the nearest health clinic: "My neighbor will take me when he goes; but he expects to get paid, *one way or another.* I bet you know my neighbor." What is she implying in these sentences and in the rest of the paragraph?
5. What are the chances that the dreams described in paragraph 14 will come true? What do you think Parker would say?

Questions on Strategy

1. What is Parker's purpose in defining poverty as she does? (Glossary: *Purpose*) Why has she cast her essay in the form of an extended definition?
2. What techniques of definition does Parker use? What is missing that you would expect to find in a more general and impersonal definition of poverty? Why does Parker leave such information out?
3. How would you characterize Parker's tone and her style? How do you respond to her presentation? Point to specific examples as support for your view. (Glossary: *Style; Tone*)
4. Parker repeats words and phrases throughout this essay. Choose some typical examples and explain how they work. What do they accomplish? (Glossary: *Coherence*)

Questions on Diction and Vocabulary

1. Although her essay is written for the most part in simple, straightforward language, Parker does make use of an occasional striking figure of speech. Identify three such figures of speech—you might begin with those in paragraph 13—and explain their effect on the reader. (Glossary: *Figures of Speech*)
2. In paragraph 10, Parker makes a paradoxical statement. Identify the statement and explain why it is paradoxical. (Glossary: *Paradox*)
3. Refer to your desk dictionary to determine the meanings of the following words as they are used in this selection: *chronic* (paragraph 3), *anemia* (3), *grits* (4), *oleo* (4), *antihistamines* (5).

Writing Assignments

1. Using Parker's essay as a model, write an extended definition of a general topic from the firsthand perspective of an expert. Choose as your subject a particular environment (suburbia, the inner city, a frat house) or way of living (children of divorce, the physically handicapped, the working student).
2. Write an essay of your own defining poverty. You may wish to gather statistical data on the problem as it exists today in the United States and abroad, or draw exclusively on personal observations and experiences.

Why I Want a Wife

Judy Brady

Born in San Francisco in 1937, Judy Brady studied painting at the University of Iowa and received her B.F.A. in 1962. The mother of two daughters, she is currently a political activist and freelance reporter who writes on subjects ranging from abortion to union-organizing to the role of women in society.

In the following essay, which first appeared in Ms. *magazine in 1971, Brady gives the reasons she wants a wife and in the process defines the "perfect" wife. She uses satire and wit to ridicule the unrealistic expectations of a wife.*

I belong to that classification of people known as wives. I am A 1 Wife. And, not altogether incidentally, I am a mother.

Not too long ago a male friend of mine appeared on the scene 2 fresh from a recent divorce. He had one child, who is, of course, with his ex-wife. He is obviously looking for another wife. As I thought about him while I was ironing one evening, it suddenly occurred to me that I, too, would like to have a wife. Why do I want a wife?

I would like to go back to school so that I can become econom- 3 ically independent, support myself, and, if need be, support those dependent upon me. I want a wife who will work and send me to school. And while I am going to school I want a wife to take care of my children. I want a wife to keep track of the children's doctor and dentist appointments. And to keep track of mine, too. I want a wife to make sure my children eat properly and are kept clean. I want a wife who will wash the children's clothes and keep them mended. I want a wife who is a good nurturant attendant to my children, who arranges for their schooling, makes sure that they have an adequate social life with their peers, takes them to the park, the zoo, etc. I want a wife who takes care of the children when they are sick, a wife who arranges to be around when the children need special care, because, of course, I cannot miss classes at school. My wife must arrange to lose time at work and not lose the job. It may mean a small cut in my wife's income from time to time, but I guess I can tolerate that. Needless to say, my wife will arrange and pay for the care of the children while my wife is working.

I want a wife who will take care of *my* physical needs. I want a   4 wife who will keep my house clean. A wife who will pick up after me. I want a wife who will keep my clothes clean, ironed, mended, replaced when need be, and who will see to it that my personal things are kept in their proper place so that I can find what I need the minute I need it. I want a wife who cooks the meals, a wife who is a *good* cook. I want a wife who will plan the menus, do the necessary grocery shopping, prepare the meals, serve them pleas- antly, and then do the cleaning up while I do my studying. I want a wife who will care for me when I am sick and sympathize with my pain and loss of time from school. I want a wife to go along when our family takes a vacation so that someone can continue to care for me and my children when I need a rest and change of scene.

I want a wife who will not bother me with rambling complaints   5 about a wife's duties. But I want a wife who will listen to me when I feel the need to explain a rather difficult point I have come across in my course of studies. And I want a wife who will type my papers for me when I have written them.

I want a wife who will take care of the details of my social life.   6 When my wife and I are invited out by my friends, I want a wife who will take care of the babysitting arrangements. When I meet people at school that I like and want to entertain, I want a wife who will have the house clean, will prepare a special meal, serve it to me and my friends, and not interrupt when I talk about the things that interest me and my friends. I want a wife who will have arranged that the children are fed and ready for bed before my guests arrive so that the children do not bother us. I want a wife who takes care of the needs of my guests so that they feel com- fortable, who makes sure that they have an ashtray, that they are passed the hors d'oeuvres, that they are offered a second helping of the food, that their wine glasses are replenished when necessary, that their coffee is served to them as they like it. And I want a wife who knows that sometimes I need a night out by myself.

I want a wife who is sensitive to my sexual needs, a wife who 7
makes love passionately and eagerly when I feel like it, a wife who makes sure that I am satisfied. And, of course, I want a wife who will not demand sexual attention when I am not in the mood for it. I want a wife who assumes the complete responsibility for birth control, because I do not want more children. I want a wife who will remain sexually faithful to me so that I do not have to clutter up my intellectual life with jealousies. And I want a wife who understands that *my* sexual needs may entail more than strict adherence to monogamy. I must, after all, be able to relate to people as fully as possible.

If, by chance, I find another person more suitable as a wife than 8
the wife I already have, I want the liberty to replace my present wife with another one. Naturally, I will expect a fresh, new life; my wife will take the children and be solely responsible for them so that I am left free.

When I am through with school and have a job, I want my wife 9
to quit working and remain at home so that my wife can more fully and completely take care of a wife's duties.

My God, who *wouldn't* want a wife? 10

Questions on Subject

1. Does Brady really want a wife? What is the point of her essay? Where does it become clear?
2. What kinds of tasks does Brady assign to her description of a wife? What kinds of activities has she left out? What is the effect of the omissions?
3. Brady's list not only describes a perfect wife; indirectly it also describes the man who would want to marry her. What are the qualities of the man who expects a wife to behave the way Brady's "wife" does?
4. Is Brady's description of a wife's duties realistic? That is, does the wife she describes actually exist? Would anybody want to be the wife Brady wants?

Questions on Strategy

1. Brady never writes "A wife is . . ." yet her essay is an extended definition. How does she go about defining her subject?
2. How does Brady use parallelism in her essay? Is it effective? Why, or why not? (Glossary: *Parallelism*)
3. Reread Brady's essay. What pattern does she use to arrange the list of services she assigns to her "wife"?
4. What is the relation between the question that ends paragraph 2 and the question that concludes the essay? What function do these two questions serve?

Questions on Diction and Vocabulary

1. Comment on Brady's use of italics in her essay. What do the different italicized words have in common?
2. Would you describe Brady's tone as resentful, resigned, hopeful, or something else? Choose particular words and phrases from the essay to explain your answer.
3. Refer to your desk dictionary to determine the meanings of the following words as they are used in this selection: *nurturant* (paragraph 3), *hors d'oeuvres* (6), *replenished* (6), *entail* (7), *monogamy* (7).

Writing Assignments

1. Brady wrote her essay over twenty years ago. How many women do you know today who would fit her definition of a wife? Do you know women who aspire to that definition? How many men do you know who would want the wife Brady describes? In a short essay, answer these questions and discuss any other issues that arose for you as you read Brady's essay.
2. Write a companion piece to Brady's essay entitled "Why I Want a Husband" (or "Girlfriend" or "Boyfriend"). Be sure that you adopt the same perspective Brady uses; for example, "Why I Want a Boyfriend" should be written from the boyfriend's point of view.

Writing Suggestions for Definition

1. Some of the most pressing social issues in American life today are further complicated by imprecise definition of critical terms. Various medical cases, for example, have brought worldwide attention to the legal and medical definitions of the word *death*. Debates continue about the meanings of other controversial words such as:

   a. morality
   b. minority (ethnic)
   c. alcoholism
   d. cheating
   e. pornography
   f. kidnapping
   g. drugs
   h. censorship
   i. remedial
   j. insanity
   k. monopoly (business)
   l. literacy
   m. success
   n. happiness
   o. life
   p. equality

   Select one of these words, and write an essay in which you discuss not only the definition of the term but also the problems associated with defining it.

2. Write an essay in which you define one of the words listed at the top of page 396 by telling not only what it *is* but also what it *is not*. (For example, it has been said that "poetry is that which cannot be expressed in any other way.") Remember, however, that defining by negation does not relieve you of the responsibility of defining the term in other ways as well.

a. intelligence
b. leadership
c. fear
d. patriotism
e. wealth
f. failure
g. family
h. style
i. loyalty
j. selflessness
k. creativity
l. humor

10
Cause and Effect Analysis

What Is Cause and Effect Analysis?

From the time children begin to talk, they exhibit a natural curiosity about the world by asking questions. Such questioning is among the most common of human activities: "Why are babies born?" "Why do people cheat?" "Why can't we find a cure for cancer?" "Why are there homeless and hungry people in America?" "What if grades were abolished in college?" "What if the stock market crashed again?" "What would happen if drunk drivers were given mandatory jail sentences?" "What would happen if the U.S. space program was expanded?" Answering questions like these means engaging in the process of *cause and effect analysis*. Whenever a question asks *why*, answering it will require discovering a *cause* or series of causes for a particular *effect*; whenever a question asks *what if*, its answer will point out the effect or effects that can result from a particular cause. Cause and effect analysis, then, is a way of discovering important relationships between events or circumstances.

You will have frequent opportunity to use cause and effect analysis in the writing you do in college. For example, a history instructor might ask you to explain the causes of the Seven-Day War between Egypt and Israel. In a paper for an American literature course, you might try to determine why *The Adventures of Huckleberry Finn* has sparked so much controversy in a number of schools and communities. On an environmental studies exam, you might have to speculate about the effects acid rain will have on the ecology of northeastern Canada and the United States. Demonstrating an understanding of cause and effect is crucial to the process of learning.

While the ultimate purpose of cause and effect analysis may seem simple—*to know* or *to understand*—determining causes and effects is often a thought-provoking and complex strategy. One reason for this complexity is that some causes are less obvious than others. *Immediate causes* are readily apparent, because they are closest in time to the effect; the immediate cause of a flood, for example, may be the collapse of a dam. However, *remote causes* may be just as important, even though they are not so apparent and perhaps even hidden. The remote (and, in fact, primary) cause of the flood might have been an engineering error or the use of substandard building materials or the failure of personnel to relieve the pressure on the dam caused by unseasonably heavy rains. In many cases it is necessary to look beyond the most immediate causes to discover the true sources of an event.

Furthermore, it may be necessary to trace a *causal chain:* an initial cause may bring about a particular effect, which in turn becomes the immediate cause of a further effect, and so on down to the effect that interests you. Before a computer salesperson approaches an important client about a big sale, she prepares extensively for the meeting (initial cause). Her preparation leads her to impress the client (effect A), which guarantees her the big sale (effect B), which results in her promotion to district sales manager (effect C). The sale she made is the most immediate and the most obvious cause of her promotion; but it is possible to trace the chain back to its more essential cause, her hard work preparing for the meeting.

A second reason for the complexity of this strategy is the difficulty of distinguishing between possible and actual causes, as well as between possible and actual effects. An upset stomach may be caused by spoiled food; but it may also be caused by overeating, by flu, by nervousness, by pregnancy, or by a combination of factors. Similarly, an increase in the cost of electricity may have multiple effects: higher profits for utility companies, fewer sales of electrical appliances, higher prices for other products that depend on electricity in their manufacture, even the development of alternative sources of energy. Making reasonable choices among the various possibilities requires thought and care.

Why Do Writers Use Cause and Effect Analysis?

Writers may use cause and effect analysis for three essential purposes: to inform, to speculate, and to argue. Most commonly, they will want to inform, to help their readers understand some identifiable fact. A state wildlife biologist, for example, might wish to tell the public about the effects severe winter weather has had on the state's deer herd; or in a newsletter a member of Congress might explain to his or her constituency the reasons changes are being made in the Social Security system. In an essay later in this section ("Why Young Women Are More Conservative"), Gloria Steinem uses cause and effect analysis to inform, by exploring the reasons why women, as they grow older, are more interested in the women's rights movement.

Cause and effect analysis may also allow writers to speculate, to consider what might be or what might have been. To satisfy the Board of Trustees, for example, a university treasurer could discuss the impact a raise in tuition will have on the school's budget; a columnist for *People* magazine might speculate about the reasons for a new singer's increasing popularity. Similarly, pollsters are estimating the effects the female vote will have on future elections, and historians are evaluating how the Kennedy presidency will continue to influence American government in the closing decade of this century.

Finally, cause and effect analysis provides an excellent basis from which to argue a given position or point of view. Parents, for example, might argue that the ill effects of curtailing extracurricular activities in their children's high school far outweigh the potential savings. An editorial writer could argue that bringing a professional ball club into the area would have many positive effects on the local economy and on the community as a whole. And educators who think that video games are a cause of delinquency and poor school performance have argued in newspapers and professional journals against the widespread acceptance of such games.

Marie Winn's essay "Television and Family Life" is an excellent example of how cause and effect analysis can provide the basis for an effective argument.

What to Look for in Reading a Cause and Effect Analysis

First, determine whether the author is more interested in the causes or the effects of the action, event, or object under discussion. Then consider how reasonable, effective, and helpful the author's analysis actually seems to be.

One common use of the strategy is for the writer to identify the particular causal agent or circumstance and then discuss the consequences or effects it has had (or may have). In the following passage from his book *The Telephone*, it is clear from the first sentence that John Brooks is primarily concerned with the effects that the telephone has had (or may have had) on modern life.

What has the telephone done to us, or for us, in the hundred years of its existence? A few effects suggest themselves at once. It has saved lives by getting rapid word of illness, injury, or famine from remote places. By joining with the elevator to make possible the multistory residence or office building, it has made possible—for better or worse—the modern city. By bringing about a quantum leap in the speed and ease with which information moves from place to place, it has greatly accelerated the rate of scientific and technological change and growth in industry. Beyond doubt it has crippled if not killed the ancient art of letter writing. It has made living alone possible for persons with normal social impulses; by so doing, it has played a role in one of the greatest social changes of this century, the breakup of the multigenerational household. It has made the waging of war chillingly more efficient than formerly. Perhaps (though not provably) it has prevented wars that might have arisen out of international misunderstanding caused by written communication. Or perhaps—again not provably—by magnifying and extending irrational personal conflicts based on voice contact, it has caused wars. Certainly it has extended the scope of human conflicts, since it impartially disseminates the useful knowledge of scientists and the babble of bores, the affection of the affectionate and the malice of the malicious.

The bulk of Brooks's paragraph is devoted to a catalog that answers the very question he poses in his opening sentence: "What has the telephone done to us, or for us, in the hundred years of its existence?" Notice that even though many of the effects Brooks discusses are verifiable or probable, he is willing to admit that he is speculating about effects that he cannot prove.

Another common use of the strategy is for the writer to describe an important event or problem (effect) and then to examine the possible reasons (causes) for it. For example, different experts might trace the causes of poverty to any or all of the following: poor education, a nonprogressive tax system, declining commitment to social services, inflation, discrimination, or the very welfare system that is designed to help the poor.

A third use of the strategy is for the writer to explore a complex causal chain. In this selection from his book *The Politics of Energy*, Barry Commoner examines the series of malfunctions that led to the near disaster at Three Mile Island nuclear facility in Harrisburg, Pennsylvania.

On March 28, 1979, at 3:53 A.M., a pump at the Harrisburg plant failed. Because the pump failed, the reactor's heat was not drawn off in the heat exchanger and the very hot water in the primary loop overheated. The pressure in the loop increased, opening a release valve that was supposed to counteract such an event. But the valve stuck open and the primary loop system lost so much water (which ended up as a highly radioactive pool, six feet deep, on the floor of the reactor building) that it was unable to carry off all the heat generated within the reactor core. Under these circumstances, the intense heat held within the reactor could, in theory, melt its fuel rods, and the resulting "meltdown" could then carry a hugely radioactive mass through the floor of the reactor. The reactor's emergency cooling system, which is designed to prevent this disaster, was then automatically activated; but when it was, apparently, turned off too soon, some of the fuel rods overheated. This produced a bubble of hydrogen gas at the top of the reactor. (The hydrogen is dissolved in the water in order to react with oxygen that is produced when the intense reactor radiation splits water molecules into their atomic constituents. When heated, the dissolved hydrogen bubbles out of the solution.) This bubble blocked the flow of cooling water so that despite the action of the emergency cooling system the reactor core was again in danger of melting down. Another danger was that the gas might contain enough oxygen to cause an explosion that could rupture the huge containers that surround the reactor and release a deadly cloud of radioactive material into the surrounding countryside. Working desperately, technicians were able to gradually reduce the size of the gas bubble using a special apparatus brought in from the atomic laboratory at Oak Ridge, Tennessee, and the danger of a catastrophic release of radioactive materials subsided. But the sealed-off plant was now so radioactive that no one could enter it for many months—or, according to some observers, for years—without being exposed to a lethal dose of radiation.

Tracing a causal chain, as Commoner does here, is similar to narration: the writer must organize the events sequentially to show clearly how each one leads to the next.

Writing a Cause and Effect Analysis

Begin by selecting a manageable topic for your essay. In making your decision, you will need to consider both the amount of information available to you and the time you have to complete your research and your writing. For a short essay due in two weeks, for example, you might concentrate on what is causing increasing numbers of students in your community to seek part-time jobs; you probably should not, however, try to examine the reasons for the decline of American labor unions. The second topic will clearly require a significant amount of research and a more elaborate presentation; it is really more suitable for a term paper.

What is then necessary for a successful cause and effect analysis is a clear sense of purpose, as well as a careful and objective examination of the topic.

1. Establishing Your Focus

Decide whether your essay will propose causes, talk about effects, or analyze both causes and effects. Any research you do, any questions you ask, will depend on how you wish to concentrate your attention. For example, as a reporter for the school paper, you are writing a story about a fire that destroyed a high-rise apartment building in the neighborhood, killing four people. In doing so, you might focus on the cause of the fire (Was there more than one cause? Was carelessness to blame? Was the fire of suspicious origin?); you might focus on the effects of the fire (How much damage was done to the building? How many people were left homeless? What was the impact on the families of the four victims?); or you might cover both the reasons for this tragic event and its ultimate effects, setting up a sort of causal chain. Such a focus is crucial as you gather information.

2. Determining Your Purpose

Once you begin to draft your essay and as you continue to refine it, make sure your purpose or intention is clear. Do you wish your cause and effect analysis to be primarily informative, speculative, or argumentative? An informative essay allows readers to say, "I learned something from this; I didn't know that the fire was caused by faulty wiring." A speculative essay suggests to readers new possibilities: "That never occurred to me before; the high-rise could indeed be replaced by a professional building." An argumentative essay convinces readers that some sort of action should be taken: "I have to agree; fire inspections should occur more regularly in our neighborhood." Whatever your purpose, be sure to provide the information necessary to carry it through.

3. Avoiding Oversimplification and Errors of Logic

Sound and thoughtful reasoning, while present in all good writing, is central to any analysis of cause and effect. Writers of convincing cause and effect analysis must examine their material objectively and develop their essays carefully, taking into account any potential objections that readers might raise. Therefore, do not jump to conclusions or let your own prejudices interfere with the logic of your interpretation or the completeness of your presentation.

Be sure that you do not oversimplify the cause and effect relationship you are writing about. A good working assumption is that most important matters cannot be traced to a single provable cause; similarly, a cause or set of causes rarely produces a single isolated effect. In order to be believable, your analysis of your topic must demonstrate a thorough understanding of the surrounding circumstances; there is often nothing less convincing than the single-minded determination to show one particular connection. Of course, to achieve coherence, you will want to emphasize the important causes or the most significant effects. But be careful not to lose your reader's trust by insisting on a simple "X leads to Y" relationship.

The other common problem of cause and effect analysis is the error known as the "after this, therefore because of this" fallacy (in Latin, *post hoc ergo propter hoc*). In attempting to discover an explanation for a particular event or circumstance, a writer may point to something that merely preceded it in time, assuming causal connection where none has in fact been proven. If you have dinner out one evening and the next day come down with stomach cramps, you may blame your illness on the restaurant where you ate the night before; but you do so without justification if your only proof is the fact that you ate there beforehand. More evidence would be required to establish a causal relationship. The *post hoc ergo propter hoc* fallacy is often harmlessly foolish ("I failed the exam because I lost my lucky key chain"). It can, however, lead writers into serious errors of judgment and blind them to more reasonable explanations of cause and effect. And, like oversimplification, such mistakes in logic can undercut a reader's confidence. Make sure that the causal relationships you see are, in fact, based on demonstrable evidence and not merely on a temporal connection.

4. Striking a Balanced Tone

Be careful neither to overstate nor to understate your position. Avoid superfluous exaggerations like *"there can be no question"* and *"the evidence speaks for itself."* Such diction is generally annoying and brings into question your confidence in the power of your interpretation. Instead, allow your analysis of the facts to convince readers of the cause and effect relationship you wish to suggest; do not be afraid to admit the possibility of other viewpoints. At the same time no analytical writer convinces by understating or qualifying information with words and phrases such as *perhaps, maybe, I think, sometimes, most often, nearly always,* or *in my opinion.* While it may be your intention to appear reasonable, overusing such words can make you sound unclear or indecisive, and your analysis, therefore, will be less convincing. Present your case forcefully, but do so honestly and sensibly.

Gentrification

Kevin Cunningham

Born in Brooklyn, New York, Kevin Cunningham spent most of his life in Flemington, New Jersey. While enrolled in the mechanical engineering program at the University of Vermont, Kevin shared an apartment near the Burlington waterfront with several other students. There he became interested in the effects that private real estate development—or gentrification—would have on his neighborhood. (Such development is not peculiar to Burlington, Vermont; it is happening in the older sections of cities across the country.) After gathering information for his essay by talking with the various people who live in the neighborhood, Cunningham found it useful to discuss both the causes and the effects of gentrification.

"I went back to Ohio, and my city was gone . . ."

Chrissie Hynde, of the Pretenders

My city is in Vermont, not Ohio, but soon my neighborhood will 1 probably be gone, too. Or maybe it's I that will be gone. My street, Lakeview Terrace, lies unobtrusively in the old northwest part of Burlington and is notable, as its name suggests, for spectacular views of Lake Champlain framed by the Adirondacks. It's not that the neighborhood is going to seed—no, quite the contrary. Recently it has been Discovered, and now it is on the verge of being Gentrified. For some of us who live here, that's bad.

Cities are often assigned human characteristics, one of which is 2 a life-cycle: they have a birth, a youth, a middle age, and an old age. A neighborhood is built and settled by young, vibrant people, proud of their sturdy new homes. Together, residents and houses mature, as families grow larger and extensions get built on. Eventually, though, the neighborhood begins to show its age. Buildings sag a little, houses aren't repainted as quickly, and maintenance

406

slips. The neighborhood may grow poorer, as the young and up-wardly mobile find new jobs and move away, while the older and less successful inhabitants remain.

One of three fates awaits the aging neighborhood. Decay may 3 continue until the neighborhood becomes a slum. It may face urban renewal, with old buildings being razed and ugly, new apartment houses taking their place. Or it may undergo redevelopment, in which government encourages the upgrading of existing housing stock by offering low-interest loans or outright grants; thus, the original character of the neighborhood may be retained or restored, allowing the city to keep part of its identity.

An example of redevelopment at its best is Hoboken, New Jer- 4 sey. In the early 1970s Hoboken was a dying city, with rundown housing and many abandoned buildings. However, low-interest loans enabled some younger residents to begin to refurbish their homes, and soon the area began to show signs of renewed vigor. Even outsiders moved in and rebuilt some of the abandoned houses. Today, whole blocks have been restored, and neighbor-hood life is active again. The city does well too, because property values are higher and so are property taxes. And there, at least for my neighborhood, is the rub.

Lakeview Terrace is a demographic potpourri of students and 5 families, young professionals and elderly retirees, home-owners and renters. It's a quiet street where kids can play safely and the neighbors know each other. Most of the houses are fairly old and look it, but already some redevelopment has begun. Recently, sev-eral old houses were bought by a real estate company, rebuilt, and sold as condominiums; the new residents drive BMWs and keep to themselves. The house where I live is owned by a Young Urban Professional couple—he's an architect—and they have renovated the place to what it must have looked like when it was new. They did a nice job, too. These two kinds of development are the main forms of gentrification, and so far they have done no real harm.

But the city is about to start a major property tax reappraisal. 6 Because of the renovations, the houses on Lakeview Terrace are currently worth more than they used to be; soon there will be a big jump in property taxes. And then a lot of people will be hurt— even dispossessed from their own neighborhood.

Clem is a retired General Electric employee who has lived on 7

Lakeview for over thirty years and who owns his home. About three years ago some condos were built on the lot next door, which didn't please Clem—he says they just don't fit in. But with higher property taxes, it may be Clem that no longer fits in. At the very least, since he's on a fixed income, he will have to make sacrifices in order to stay. Ryan works as a mailman and also owns his Lakeview Terrace home, which is across the street from the houses that were converted into condos: same cause, same effect.

Then there are those of us who rent. As our landlords have to 8 pay higher property taxes, they will naturally raise rents at least as much (and maybe more, if they've spent money on renovations of their own). Some of us won't be able to afford the increase and will have to leave. "Some of us" almost certainly includes me, as well as others who have lived on Lakeview Terrace much longer than I have. In fact, the exodus has already begun, with the people who were displaced by the condo conversions.

Of course, many people would consider what's happening on 9 Lakeview Terrace a genuine improvement in every way, resulting not only in better-looking houses but also in a better class of people. I dispute that. The new people may be more affluent than those they displace, but certainly not "better," not by any standard that counts with me. Gentrification may do wonders for a neighborhood's aesthetics, but it certainly can be hard on its soul.

Interview with Kevin Cunningham

I know that you are a relaxed, fluent talker. Is writing as easy for you?

I don't mind writing at all, but I hate doing rewrites. Actually, I always have trouble getting started, and I can spend a lot of time trying to get the first couple of paragraphs or the first page down, but once I get started I can roar right along to the end. In fact, I need to, because if I stop to think too much about any part I can lose the thread. After I've finished a draft I let it sit and then go back to it, and that's when I can see what works and what doesn't. I enjoy the second draft, because I can see the paper as a whole, but the third draft is just torture. I guess I don't have the patience—

it's like I've done this twice already. But I see that it has to be done again.

So it's the revision that makes writing harder than talking.

That's part of it. But the two tie in. When I write, even if it's on a dry topic, I like to write the way I talk, in a conversational tone. Even recently when I was writing a paper for business, I found myself writing that way. I hate formal, pretentious prose.

But your gentrification essay, when I read it, doesn't "sound" to me quite the same as your conversation.

Yeah, in writing you have to finish your sentences, specify your nouns, make sure you're understood. It has to be more precise. You'll have to fix up this interview if you're really going to print it. [Editor's note: Kevin was right.]

In gathering information for your paper, how did you distinguish between cause and effect and mere coincidence?

You have to know your subject, and you have to be honest. For example, my downstairs neighbors moved out last month because the rent was raised. Somebody who didn't know the situation might say, "See? Gentrification." But that wasn't the reason—it's that heating costs went up. This is New England, and we had a cold winter; gentrification had nothing to do with it. It's something that is just beginning to happen and it's going to have a big effect, but we haven't actually felt many of its effects here yet.

So you are using cause and effect to predict the future.

Is there any other way?

Tell me more about your revisions.

In my first draft, I strung things together almost on a geograph- ical basis, as if I were walking down Lakeview Terrace talking with my neighbors—which is actually one of the things I did. For my second draft, to show my professor, I was just polishing the writing. Then he showed me that the logic wasn't quite there—it jumped around from one idea to another, and I also took some stuff for granted that needed explaining. Also, I used to think of a cause and effect paper as just an explanation of why something happens; but I was writing about a subject that affects me, so part of me wanted to keep it objective and part of me was trying to say what I feel. My professor said, "Look, if you want to say something, just use this as your vehicle for saying it." So I felt much freer when I went back to revise again, because I could say what I wanted to say.

Do you ever use an outline to prevent organization problems, or solve them?

I always make a scratch outline at some point—sometimes before the first draft, sometimes later. When I saw that my logic was off, I made a scratch outline to help me revise. I would probably have saved myself some trouble if I had used it earlier.

It's Time to Stop Playing Indians

Arlene B. Hirschfelder

Born in Chicago in 1943, Arlene Hirschfelder attended Brandeis University and the University of Chicago and did her graduate work in American history and education at Columbia University. Since 1969, she has been on the staff of the Association on American Indian Affairs, and she currently serves as a freelance education consultant in Indian affairs. A prolific writer on the subject of Native Americans, Hirschfelder wrote Happily May I Walk: American Indians and Alaska Natives *which won the Carter G. Woodson Book Award and a Western Heritage Book Award. Her articles have appeared in* Ms., *the* Los Angeles Times, Social Studies, *and* Indian Affairs.*

In the following essay, first published in the Los Angeles Times *in 1987, Hirschfelder argues that the stereotyping of Native Americans is a double-edged sword that trivializes their culture while turning a blind eye to their battle with poverty and discrimination.*

It is predictable. At Halloween, thousands of children trick-or-treat in Indian costumes. At Thanksgiving, thousands of children parade in school pageants wearing plastic headdresses and pseudo-buckskin clothing. Thousands of card shops stock Thanksgiving greeting cards with images of cartoon animals wearing feathered headbands. Thousands of teachers and librarians trim bulletin boards with Anglo-featured, feathered Indian boys and girls. Thousands of gift shops load their shelves with Indian figurines and jewelry.

Fall and winter are also the seasons when hundreds of thousands of sports fans root for professional, college and public school teams with names that summon up Indians—"Braves," "Redskins," "Chiefs." (In New York State, one out of eight junior and senior high school teams call themselves "Indians," "Tomahawks" and the like.) War-whooping team mascots are imprinted on school uniforms, postcards, notebooks, tote bags and car floor mats.

All of this seems innocuous; why make a fuss about it? Because 3 these trappings and holiday symbols offend tens of thousands of other Americans—the Native American people. Because these invented images prevent millions of us from understanding the authentic Indian America, both long ago and today. Because this image-making prevents Indians from being a relevant part of the nation's social fabric.

Halloween costumes mask the reality of high mortality rates, 4 high diabetes rates, high unemployment rates. They hide low average life spans, low per capita incomes and low educational levels. Plastic war bonnets and ersatz buckskin deprive people from knowing the complexity of Native American heritage—that Indians belong to hundreds of nations that have intricate social organizations, governments, languages, religions and sacred rituals, ancient stories, unique arts and music forms.

Thanksgiving school units and plays mask history. They do not 5 tell how Europeans mistreated Wampanoags and other East Coast Indian peoples during the 17th century. Social studies units don't mention that, to many Indians, Thanksgiving is a day of mourning, the beginning of broken promises, land theft, near extinction of their religions and languages at the hands of invading Europeans.

Athletic team nicknames and mascots disguise real people. War- 6 painted, buckskin-clad, feathered characters keep the fictitious Indian circulating on decals, pennants and team clothing. Toy companies mask Indian identity and trivialize sacred beliefs by manufacturing Indian costumes and headdresses, peace pipes and trick-arrow-through-the-head gags that equate Indianness with playtime. Indian figures equipped with arrows, guns and tomahawks give youngsters the harmful message that Indians favor mayhem. Many Indian people can tell about children screaming in fear after being introduced to them.

It is time to consider how these images impede the efforts of 7 Indian parents and communities to raise their children with positive information about their heritage. It is time to get rid of stereotypes that, whether deliberately or inadvertently, denigrate Indian cultures and people.

It is time to bury the Halloween costumes, trick arrows, bulletin- 8 board pin-ups, headdresses and mascots. It has been done before. In the 1970s, after student protests, Marquette University dropped its "Willie Wampum," Stanford University retired its mascot, "Prince Lightfoot," and Eastern Michigan University and Florida State modified their savage-looking mascots to reduce criticism.

It is time to stop playing Indians. It is time to abolish Indian 9 images that sell merchandise. It is time to stop offending Indian people whose lives are all too often filled with economic deprivation, powerlessness, discrimination and gross injustice. This time next year, let's find more appropriate symbols for the holiday and sports seasons.

Questions on Subject

1. In paragraph 3, Hirschfelder asks a question. What is that question, and how does she answer it?
2. How do Halloween costumes mask the "complexity of Native American heritage"?
3. According to Hirschfelder, why do many Native Americans mark Thanksgiving as a day of mourning?
4. What is significant in Hirschfelder's assertion that "many Indian people can tell about children screaming in fear after being introduced to them"?
5. In her concluding paragraph, Hirschfelder suggests we find "more appropriate symbols for the holiday and sports seasons." Do you agree? If so, what alternatives to Indian symbols can you suggest?

Questions on Strategy

1. Is Hirshfelder's purpose in writing her essay to inform, to speculate, or to argue? How do you know? (Glossary: *Purpose*)
2. Hirschfelder's essay is comprised almost entirely of a series of examples. (Glossary: *Examples*) Is this an effective strategy? Why or why not?
3. Discuss how paragraphs 7, 8, and 9 function in the context of Hirschfelder's essay.
4. Hirschfelder never discusses the possible reasons for the trivialization of the Native American culture. Why do you think she considered it unnecessary to do this?

414 • *Arlene B. Hirschfelder*

5. Into what general categories has Hirschfelder divided her examples? (Glossary: *Division and Classification*)

Questions on Diction and Vocabulary

1. What irony arises in the author's use of the word *Indian* throughout her essay?
2. Hirschfelder uses parallelism throughout her essay. Cite examples of this writing strategy, and discuss its effect on the reader. (Glossary: *Parallelism*)
3. Refer to your desk dictionary to determine the meanings of the following words as they are used in this selection: *mascots* (paragraph 2), *innocuous* (3), *relevant* (3), *ersatz* (4), *trivialize* (6), *mayhem* (6), *impede* (7), *inadvertently* (7), *denigrate* (7), *deprivation* (9).

Writing Suggestions

1. From time to time several professional sports teams—namely the Atlanta Braves, Washington Redskins, and the Cleveland Indians—have come under attack by critics who think the teams' names should be changed because they are an insult to Native Americans. Compose a letter to the management of one of these teams in which you discuss your own reactions to a name change.
2. Consider a situation in which you or someone you know has been stereotyped on the basis of age, race, gender, religion, or something else. Using Hirschfelder's essay as a guide, write an essay describing the effects on our culture of this kind of stereotyping.

Why Young Women Are More Conservative

Gloria Steinem

Gloria Steinem is a political activist, editor, lecturer, writer, and one of the country's leading supporters of the women's movement. She was born in Toledo, Ohio, in 1934 and graduated from Smith College in 1956. After college she traveled to India to study and then returned to New York, where she later helped to found two important magazines, New York *and* Ms. *A former editor and writer for* Ms., *Steinem has published important articles in popular magazines and has written* The Thousand Indias, The Beach Book, *and* Outrageous Acts and Everyday Rebellions, *from which the following essay is taken. Her most recent book, the autobiographical* Revolution from Within, *offers startling, personal insights into the women's movement.*

In "Why Young Women Are More Conservative," written in 1979, Steinem explores the reasons why her assumption that college-age women are liberal in their beliefs and open to change was wrong. In the process she discovers that it is older women, women who have married and borne children, who are the active feminists and supporters of the women's rights movement.

If you had asked me a decade or more ago, I certainly would have said the campus was the first place to look for the feminist or any other revolution. I also would have assumed that student-age women, like student-age men, were much more likely to be activist and open to change than their parents. After all, campus revolts have a long and well-publicized tradition, from the students of medieval France, whose "heresy" was suggesting that the university be separate from the church, through the anticolonial student riots of British India; from students who led the cultural revolution of the People's Republic of China, to campus demonstrations against the Shah of Iran. Even in this country, with far less tradition of student activism, the populist movement to end the war in Vietnam was symbolized by campus protests and mistrust of anyone over thirty.

It has taken me many years of traveling as a feminist speaker 2 and organizer to understand that I was wrong about women; at least, about women acting on their own behalf. In activism, as in so many other things, I had been educated to assume that men's cultural pattern was the natural or the only one. If student years were the peak time of rebellion and openness to change for men, then the same must be true for women. In fact, a decade of listening to every kind of women's group—from brown-bag lunchtime lectures organized by office workers to all-night rap sessions at campus women's centers; from housewives' self-help groups to campus rallies—has convinced me that the reverse is more often true. Women may be the one group that grows more radical with age. Though some students are big exceptions to this rule, women in general don't begin to challenge the politics of our own lives until later.

Looking back, I realize that this pattern has been true for my 3 life, too. My college years were full of uncertainties and the personal conservatism that comes from trying to win approval and fit into the proper grown-up and womanly role, whether that means finding a well-to-do man to be supported by or a male radical to support. Nonetheless, I went right on assuming that brave exploring youth and cowardly conservative old age were the norms for everybody, and that I must be just an isolated and guilty accident. Though every generalization based on female culture has many exceptions, and should never be used as a crutch or excuse, I think we might be less hard on ourselves and each other as students, feel better about our potential for change as we grow older— and educate reporters who announce feminism's demise because its red-hot center is not on campus—if we figured out that for most of us as women, the traditional college period is an unrealistic and cautious time. Consider a few of the reasons.

As students, women are probably treated with more equality 4 than we ever will be again. For one thing, we're consumers. The school is only too glad to get the tuitions we pay, or that our families or government grants pay on our behalf. With population rates declining because of women's increased power over childbearing, that money is even more vital to a school's existence. Yet more than most consumers, we're too transient to have much power as a group. If our families are paying our tuition, we may have even less power.

As young women, whether students or not, we're still in the stage most valued by male-dominant cultures: we have our full potential as workers, wives, sex partners, and childbearers.

That means we haven't yet experienced the life events that are most radicalizing for women: entering the paid-labor force and discovering how women are treated there; marrying and finding out that it is not yet an equal partnership; having children and discovering who is responsible for them and who is not; and aging, still a greater penalty for women than for men.

Furthermore, new ambitions nourished by the rebirth of feminism may make young women feel and behave a little like a classical immigrant group. We are determined to prove ourselves, to achieve academic excellence, and to prepare for interesting and successful careers. More noses are kept to more grindstones in an effort to demonstrate newfound abilities, and perhaps to allay suspicions that women still have to have more and better credentials than men. This doesn't leave much time for activism. Indeed, we may not yet know that it is necessary.

In addition, the very progress into previously all-male careers that may be revolutionary for women is seen as conservative and conformist by outside critics. Assuming male radicalism to be the measure of change, they interpret any concern with careers as evidence of "campus conservatism." In fact, "dropping out" may be a departure for men, but "dropping in" is a new thing for women. Progress lies in the direction we have not been.

Like most groups of the newly arrived or awakened, our faith in education and paper degrees also has yet to be shaken. For instance, the percentage of women enrolled in colleges and universities has been increasing at the same time that the percentage of men has been decreasing. Among students entering college in 1978, women *outnumbered* men for the first time. This hope of excelling at the existing game is probably reinforced by the greater cultural pressure on females to be "good girls" and observe somebody else's rules.

Though we may know intellectually that we need to have new 10
games with new rules, we probably haven't quite absorbed such
facts as the high unemployment rate among female Ph.D.s; the
lower average salary among women college graduates of all races
than among counterpart males who graduated from high school
or less; the middle-management ceiling against which even those
eagerly hired new business-school graduates seem to bump their
heads after five or ten years; and the barrier-breaking women in
nontraditional fields who become the first fired when recession
hits. Sadly enough, we may have to personally experience some
of these reality checks before we accept the idea that lawsuits,
activism, and group pressure will have to accompany our individual excellence and crisp new degrees.

Then there is the female guilt trip, student edition. If we're not 11
sailing along as planned, it must be *our* fault. If our mothers didn't
"do anything" with their educations, it must have been *their* fault.
If we can't study as hard as we think we must (because women
still have to be better prepared than men), and have a substantial
personal and sexual life at the same time (because women are supposed to care more about relationships than men do), then we feel
inadequate, as if each of us were individually at fault for a problem
that is actually culture-wide.

I've yet to be on a campus where most women weren't worrying 12
about some aspect of combining marriage, children, and a career.
I've yet to find one where many men were worrying about the
same thing. Yet women will go right on suffering from the double-
role problem and terminal guilt until men are encouraged, pres-
sured, or otherwise forced, individually and collectively, to integrate themselves into the "women's work" of raising children and
homemaking. Until then, and until there are changed job patterns
to allow equal parenthood, children will go right on growing up
with the belief that only women can be loving and nurturing, and
only men can be intellectual or active outside the home. Each half
of the world will go on limiting the full range of its human talent.

Finally, there is the intimate political training that hits women 13
in the teens and early twenties: the countless ways we are still
brainwashed into assuming that women are dependent on men
for our basic identities, both in our work and our personal lives,
much more than vice versa. After all, if we're going to enter a

marriage system that's still legally designed for a person and a half, submit to an economy in which women still average about fifty-nine cents on the dollar earned by men, and work mainly as support staff and assistants, or *co*-directors and *vice*-presidents at best, then we have to be convinced that we are not whole people on our own.

In order to make sure that we will see ourselves as half-people, 14 and thus be addicted to getting our identity from serving others, society tries hard to convert us as young women into "man junkies"; that is, into people who are addicted to regular shots of male-approval and presence, both professionally and personally. We need a man standing next to us, actually and figuratively, whether it's at work, on Saturday night, or throughout life. (If only men realized how little it matters *which* man is standing there, they would understand that this addiction depersonalizes them, too.) Given the danger to a male-dominant system if young women stop internalizing this political message of derived identity, it's no wonder that those who try to kick the addiction—and, worse yet, to help other women do the same—are likely to be regarded as odd or dangerous by everyone from parents to peers.

With all that pressure combined with little experience, it's no 15 wonder that younger women are often less able to support each other. Even young women who espouse feminist goals as individuals may refrain from identifying themselves as "feminist": it's okay to want equal pay for yourself (just one small reform) but it's not okay to want equal pay for women as a group (an economic revolution). Some retreat into individualized career obsessions as a way of avoiding this dangerous discovery of shared experience with women as a group. Others retreat into the safe middle ground of "I'm not a feminist but. . . ." Still others become politically active, but only on issues that are taken seriously by their male counterparts.

The same lesson about the personal conservatism of younger 16 women is taught by the history of feminism. If I hadn't been conned into believing the masculine stereotype of youth as the "natural" time for freedom and rebellion, a time of "sowing wild oats" that actually is made possible by the assurance of power and security later on, I could have figured out the female pattern of activism by looking at women's movements of the past.

In this country, for instance, the nineteenth-century wave of 17 feminism was started by older women who had been through the radicalizing experience of getting married and becoming the legal chattel of their husbands (or the equally radicalizing experience of *not* getting married and being treated as spinsters). Most of them had also worked in the antislavery movement and learned from the political parallels between race and sex. In other countries, that wave was also led by women who were past the point of maximum pressure toward marriageability and conservatism.

Looking at the first decade of this second wave, it's clear that 18 the early feminist activist and consciousness-raising groups of the 1960s were organized by women who had experienced the civil rights movement, or homemakers who had discovered that raising kids and cooking didn't occupy all their talents. While most campuses of the late sixties were still circulating the names of illegal abortionists privately (after all, abortion could damage our marriage value), slightly older women were holding press conferences and speak-outs about the reality of abortions (including their own, even though that often meant confessing to an illegal act) and demanding reform or repeal of antichoice laws. Though rape had been a quiet epidemic on campus for generations, younger women victims were still understandably fearful of speaking up, and campuses encouraged silence in order to retain their reputation for safety with tuition-paying parents. It took many off-campus speak-outs, demonstrations against laws of evidence and police procedures, and testimonies in state legislatures before most student groups began to make demands on campus and local cops for greater rape protection. In fact, "date rape"—the common campus phenomenon of a young woman being raped by someone she knows, perhaps even by several students in a fraternity house—is just now being exposed. Marital rape, a more difficult legal issue, was taken up several years ago. As for battered women and the attendant exposé of husbands and lovers as more statistically dangerous than unknown muggers in the street, that issue still seems to be thought of as a largely noncampus concern, yet at many of the colleges and universities where I've spoken, there has been at least one case within current student memory of a young woman beaten or murdered by a jealous lover.

This cultural pattern of youthful conservatism makes the grow- 19 ing number of older women going back to school very important. They are life examples and pragmatic activists who radicalize women young enough to be their daughters. Now that the median female undergraduate age in this country is twenty-seven because so many older women have returned, the campus is becoming a major place for cross-generational connections.

None of this should denigrate the courageous efforts of young 20 women, especially women on campus, and the many changes they've pioneered. On the contrary, they should be seen as even more remarkable for surviving the conservative pressures, recognizing societal problems they haven't yet fully experienced, and organizing successfully in the midst of a transient student population. Every women's history course, rape hot line, or campus newspaper that is finally covering *all* the news; every feminist professor whose job has been created or tenure saved by student pressure, or male administrator whose consciousness has been permanently changed; every counselor who's stopped guiding women one way and men another; every lawsuit that's been fueled by student energies against unequal athletic funds or graduate school requirements: all those accomplishments are even more impressive when seen against the back-drop of the female pattern of activism.

Finally, it would help to remember that a feminist revolution 21 rarely resembles a masculine-style one—just as a young woman's most radical act toward her mother (that is, connecting as women in order to help each other get some power) doesn't look much like a young man's most radical act toward his father (that is, breaking the father-son connection in order to separate identities or take over existing power).

It's those father-son conflicts at a generational, national level that 22 have often provided the conventional definition of revolution; yet they've gone on for centuries without basically changing the role of the female half of the world. They have also failed to reduce the level of violence in society, since both fathers and sons have included some degree of aggressiveness and superiority to women in their definition of masculinity, thus preserving the anthropological model of dominance.

Furthermore, what current leaders and theoreticians define as 23 revolution is usually little more than taking over the army and the radio stations. Women have much more in mind than that. We have to uproot the sexual caste system that is the most pervasive power structure in society, and that means transforming the patriarchal values of those who run the institutions, whether they are politically the "right" or the "left," the fathers or the sons. This cultural part of the change goes very deep, and is often seen as too intimate, and perhaps too threatening, to be considered as either serious or possible. Only conflicts among men are "serious." Only a takeover of existing institutions is "possible."

That's why the definition of "political," on campus as elsewhere, 24 tends to be limited to who's running for president, who's demonstrating against corporate investments in South Africa, or which is the "moral" side of some conventional revolution, preferably one that is thousands of miles away.

As important as such activities are, they are also the most com- 25 fortable ones when we're young. They provide a sense of virtue without much disruption in the power structure of our daily lives. Even when the most consistent energies on campus are actually concentrated around feminist issues, they may be treated as apolitical and invisible. Asked "What's happening on campus?" a student may reply, "The antinuke movement," even though that resulted in one demonstration of two hours, while student antirape squads have been patrolling the campus every night for two years and women's studies have begun to transform the very textbooks we read.

No wonder reporters and sociologists looking for revolution on 26 campus often miss the depth of feminist change and activity that is really there. Women students themselves may dismiss it as not political and not serious. Certainly, it rarely comes in the masculine sixties style of bombing buildings or burning draft cards. In fact, it goes much deeper than protesting a temporary symptom—say, the draft—and challenges the right of one group to dominate another, which is the disease itself.

Young women have a big task of resisting pressures and chal- 27 lenging definitions. Their increasing success is a miracle of foresight and courage that should make us all proud. But they should know that they, too, may grow more radical with age.

One day, an army of gray-haired women may quietly take over 28 the earth.

Questions on Subject

1. Why did Steinem assume that college-age women would be campus activists? What caused her to question this assumption?
2. What reasons does Steinem give for this lack of activism among young women?
3. Why, according to Steinem, do women grow more radical as they grow older?
4. Why does Steinem consider the changes that have occurred on college campuses—women's studies courses, rape hot lines, more female professors—as impressive accomplishments?
5. In what ways, according to Steinem, is "a feminist revolution" different from "a masculine-style one"?

Questions on Strategy

1. What is the effect of Steinem's opening paragraph? (Glossary: *Beginnings/Endings*)
2. Is this essay's primary focus on finding causes, predicting effects, or both? Explain your answer.
3. What sort of evidence does Steinem present to substantiate her analysis? (Glossary: *Evidence*)
4. How does Steinem organize her cause and effect analysis? Is there a specific order to her list of causes? (Glossary: *Organization*)
5. Who, in your opinion, is Steinem's audience? How do you know? What assumptions does she make about this audience? (Glossary: *Audience*)
6. How did you respond to Steinem's last sentence? Does it work well as a conclusion? Explain. (Glossary: *Beginnings/Endings*)

Questions on Diction and Vocabulary

1. How would you describe the tone of this essay? Cite several examples of words and phrases that you believe help create this tone. (Glossary: *Tone*)
2. Sometimes feminists are criticized for their strident rhetoric and diction. Is there anything strident about Steinem's diction in this essay? Explain. (Glossary: *Diction*)
3. Refer to your desk dictionary to determine the meanings of the

following words as they are used in this selection: *heresy* (paragraph 1), *demise* (3), *espouse* (15), *chattel* (17), *denigrate* (20), *caste* (23).

Writing Assignments

1. Write an essay in which you analyze the state of political and/or social activism on your campus. How active is the student body in general? Do the student leaders represent the views of the majority of students? If not, why not? In your essay, be sure to discuss what you believe are the reasons for the level of activity at your school.
2. Write an essay in which you explain a "mystery" in your own life. It may be a baffling question you once had to solve, a secret you had to keep, or even a current difficulty to which you are still looking for an answer. Be sure to provide all the information, or "clues," necessary, and be careful to establish clear cause and effect relationships.

Television and Family Life
Marie Winn

Marie Winn was born in 1937 in Czechoslovakia and as a child came with her family to settle in New York City. She graduated from Radcliffe College, did graduate work at Columbia University, and then embarked on a career as a writer for and about children. Her articles have appeared in the New York Times Magazine *and the* Village Voice, *and she has written and edited books for children, including* What Shall We Do *and* Allee Galloo, *a collection of songs and singing games.*

The following selection is taken from her 1977 best-seller, The Plug-In Drug: Television, Children, and the Family, *in which Winn examines the effects of television on American parents and their children.*

Home and family life have changed in important ways since the advent of television. The peer group has become television-oriented, and much of the time children spend together is occupied by television viewing. Culture generally has been transformed by television. Therefore it is improper to assign to television the subsidiary role its many apologists (too often members of the television industry) insist it plays. Television is not merely one of a number of important influences upon today's child. Through the changes it has made in family life, television emerges as *the* important influence in children's lives today.

The Quality of Family Life

Television's contribution to family life has been an equivocal one. For while it has, indeed, kept the members of the family from dispersing, it has not served to bring them *together*. By its domination of the time families spend together, it destroys the special quality that distinguishes one family from another, a quality that depends to a great extent on what a family *does*, what special rituals, games, recurrent jokes, familiar songs, and shared activities it accumulates.

"Like the sorcerer of old," writes Urie Bronfenbrenner, "the tele- 3
vision set casts its magic spell, freezing speech and action, turning the living into silent statues so long as the enchantment lasts. The primary danger of the television screen lies not so much in the behavior it produces—although there is danger there—as in the behavior it prevents: the talks, the games, the family festivities and arguments through which much of the child's learning takes place and through which his character is formed. Turning on the television set can turn off the process that transforms children into people."[1]

Yet parents have accepted a television-dominated family life so 4
completely that they cannot see how the medium is involved in whatever problems they might be having. A first-grade teacher reports:

"I have one child in the group who's an only child. I wanted to 5
find out more about her family life because this little girl was quite isolated from the group, didn't make friends, so I talked to her mother. Well, they don't have time to do anything in the evening, the mother said. The parents come home after picking up the child at the baby-sitter's. Then the mother fixes dinner while the child watches TV. Then they have dinner and the child goes to bed. I said to this mother, 'Well, couldn't she help you fix dinner? That would be a nice time for the two of you to talk,' and the mother said, 'Oh, but I'd hate to have her miss "Zoom." It's such a good program!' "

Even when families make efforts to control television, too often 6
its very presence counterbalances the positive features of family life. A writer and mother of two boys aged 3 and 7 described her family's television schedule in the *New York Times:*

We were in the midst of a full-scale War. Every day was a new battle

---

[1] Urie Bronfenbrenner, "Who Cares for America's Children?" Address presented at the Conference of the National Association for the Education of Young Children, 1970.

and every program was a major skirmish. We agreed it was a bad scene all around and were ready to enter diplomatic negotiations. . . . In principle we have agreed on 2½ hours of TV a day, "Sesame Street," "Electric Company" (with dinner gobbled up in between) and two half-hour shows between 7 and 8:30 which enables the grown-ups to eat in peace and prevents the two boys from destroying one another. Their pre-bedtime choice is dreadful, because, as Josh recently admitted, "There's nothing much on I really like." So . . . it's "What's My Line" or "To Tell the Truth." . . . Clearly there is a need for first-rate children's shows at this time. . . .[2]

Consider the "family life" described here: Presumably the father 7 comes home from work during the "Sesame Street"–"Electric Company" stint. The children are either watching television, gobbling their dinner, or both. While the parents eat their dinner in peaceful privacy, the children watch another hour of television. Then there is only a half-hour left before bedtime, just enough time for baths, getting pajamas on, brushing teeth, and so on. The children's evening is regimented with an almost military precision. They watch their favorite programs, and when there is "nothing much on I really like," they watch whatever else is on—because *watching* is the important thing. Their mother does not see anything amiss with watching programs just for the sake of watching; she only wishes there were some first-rate children's shows on at those times.

Without conjuring up memories of the Victorian era with family 8 games and long, leisurely meals, and large families, the question arises: isn't there a better family life available than this dismal, mechanized arrangement of children watching television for however long is allowed them, evening after evening?

Of course, families today still do *special* things together at times: 9 go camping in the summer, go to the zoo on a nice Sunday, take various trips and expeditions. But their *ordinary* daily life together is diminished—that sitting around at the dinner table, that spontaneous taking up of an activity, those little games invented by children on the spur of the moment when there is nothing else to

[2] Eleanor Dienstag, "What Will the Kids Talk About? Proust?" *New York Times*, December 24, 1972.

do, the scribbling, the chatting, and even the quarreling, all the things that form the fabric of a family, that define a childhood. Instead, the children have their regular schedule of television programs and bedtime, and the parents have their peaceful dinner together.

The author of the article in the *Times* notes that "keeping a family 10 sane means mediating between the needs of both children and adults."[3] But surely the needs of adults are being better met than the needs of the children, who are effectively shunted away and rendered untroublesome, while their parents enjoy a life as undemanding as that of any childless couple. In reality, it is those very demands that young children make upon a family that lead to growth, and it is the way parents accede to those demands that builds the relationships upon which the future of the family depends. If the family does not accumulate its backlog of shared experiences, shared *everyday* experiences that occur and recur and change and develop, then it is not likely to survive as anything other than a caretaking institution.

Family Rituals

Ritual is defined by sociologists as "that part of family life that 11 the family likes about itself, is proud of and wants formally to continue."[4] Another text notes that "the development of a ritual by a family is an index of the common interest of its members in the family as a group."[5]

What has happened to family rituals, those regular, dependable, 12 recurrent happenings that gave members of a family a feeling of *belonging* to a home rather than living in it merely for the sake of convenience, those experiences that act as the adhesive of family unity far more than any material advantages?

Mealtime rituals, going-to-bed rituals, illness rituals, holiday rit- 13 uals, how many of these have survived the inroads of the television set?

[3] Ibid.

[4] James H. Bossard and Eleanor S. Boll, *Ritual in Family Living* (Philadelphia: University of Pennsylvania Press, 1950).

[5] Bossard and Boll, *The Sociology of Child Development* (New York: Harper & Row, 1960).

A young woman who grew up near Chicago reminisces about 14
her childhood and gives an idea of the effects of television upon
family rituals:

"As a child I had millions of relatives around—my parents both 15
come from relatively large families. My father had nine brothers
and sisters. And so every holiday there was this great swoop-down
of aunts, uncles, and millions of cousins. I just remember how
wonderful it used to be. These thousands of cousins would come
and everyone would play and ultimately, after dinner, all the
women would be in the front of the house, drinking coffee and
talking, all the men would be in the back of the house, drinking
and smoking, and all the kids would be all over the place, playing
hide and seek. Christmas time was particularly nice because everyone always brought all their toys and games. Our house had a
couple of rooms with go-through closets, so there were always kids
running in a great circle route. I remember it was just wonderful.

"And then all of a sudden one year I remember becoming sud- 16
denly aware of how different everything had become. The kids
were no longer playing Monopoly or Clue or the other games we
used to play together. It was because we had a television set which
had been turned on for a football game. All of that socializing that
had gone on previously had ended. Now everyone was sitting in
front of the television set, on a holiday, at a family party! I remember being stunned by how awful that was. Somehow the television had become more attractive."

As families have come to spend more and more of their time 17
together engaged in the single activity of television watching, those
rituals and pastimes that once gave family life its special quality
have become more and more uncommon. Not since prehistoric
times when cave families hunted, gathered, ate, and slept, with
little time remaining to accumulate a culture of any significance,
have families been reduced to such a sameness.

Real People

It is not only the activities that a family might engage in together 18
that are diminished by the powerful presence of television in the
home. The relationships of the family members to each other are
also affected, in both obvious and subtle ways. The hours that the

young child spends in a one-way relationship with television people, an involvement that allows for no communication or interaction, surely affect his relationships with real-life people.

Studies show the importance of eye-to-eye contact, for instance, 19 in real-life relationships, and indicate that the nature of a person's eye-contact patterns, whether he looks another squarely in the eye or looks to the side or shifts his gaze from side to side, may play a significant role in his success or failure in human relationships.[6] But no eye contact is possible in the child-television relationship, although in certain children's programs people purport to speak directly to the child and the camera fosters this illusion by focusing directly upon the person being filmed. (Mr. Rogers is an example, telling the child "I like you, you're special," etc.) How might such a distortion of real-life relationships affect a child's development of trust, of openness, of an ability to relate well to other *real* people?

Bruno Bettelheim writes: 20

> Children who have been taught, or conditioned, to listen passively most of the day to the warm verbal communications coming from the TV screen, to the deep emotional appeal of the so-called TV personality, are often unable to respond to real persons because they arouse so much less feeling than the skilled actor. Worse, they lose the ability to learn from reality because life experiences are much more complicated than the ones they see on the screen. . . .[7]

A teacher makes a similar observation about her personal view- 21 ing experiences:

"I have trouble mobilizing myself and dealing with real people 22 after watching a few hours of television. It's just hard to make that transition from watching television to a real relationship. I suppose it's because there was no effort necessary while I was watching, and dealing with real people always requires a bit of effort. Imagine, then, how much harder it might be to do the same thing for a small child, particularly one who watches a lot of television every day."

[6] Ralph V. Extine, "Visual Interaction: The Glances of Power and Preference," in *Nonverbal Communication—Reading with Commentaries,* ed. Shirley Weitz (New York: Oxford University Press, 1974).

[7] Bruno Bettelheim, *The Informed Heart* (New York: The Free Press, 1960).

But more obviously damaging to family relationships is the elim- 23
ination of opportunities to talk, and perhaps more important, to
argue, to air grievances, between parents and children and brothers and sisters. Families frequently use television to avoid confronting their problems, problems that will not go away if they are
ignored but will only fester and become less easily resolvable as
time goes on.

A mother reports: 24

"I find myself, with three children, wanting to turn on the TV 25
set when they're fighting. I really have to struggle not to do it
because I feel that's telling them this is the solution to the quarrel—
but it's so tempting that I often do it."

A family therapist discusses the use of television as an avoidance 26
mechanism:

"In a family I know the father comes home from work and turns 27
on the television set. The children come and watch with him and
the wife serves them their meal in front of the set. He then goes
and takes a shower, or works on the car or something. She then
goes and has her own dinner in front of the television set. It's a
symptom of a deeper-rooted problem, sure. But it would help them
all to get rid of the set. It would be far easier to work on what the
symptom really means without the television. The television simply encourages a double avoidance of each other. They'd find out
more quickly what was going on if they weren't able to hide behind
the TV. Things wouldn't necessarily be better, of course, but they
wouldn't be anesthetized."

The decreased opportunities for simple conversation between 28
parents and children in the television-centered home may help
explain an observation made by an emergency room nurse at a
Boston hospital. She reports that parents just seem to sit there these
days when they come in with a sick or seriously injured child,
although talking to the child would distract and comfort him.
"They don't seem to know *how* to talk to their own children at any
length," the nurse observes. Similarly, a television critic writes in
the *New York Times:* "I had just a day ago taken my son to the
emergency ward of a hospital for stitches above his left eye, and
the occasion seemed no more real to me than Maalot or 54th Street,
south-central Los Angeles. There was distance and numbness and

an inability to turn off the total institution. I didn't behave at all; I just watched. . . ."[8]

A number of research studies substantiate the assumption that television interferes with family activities and the formation of family relationships. One survey shows that 78 percent of the respondents indicate no conversation taking place during viewing except at specified times such as commercials. The study notes: "The television atmosphere in most households is one of quiet absorption on the part of family members who are present. The nature of the family social life during a program could be described as 'parallel' rather than interactive, and the set does seem to dominate family life when it is on."[9] Thirty-six percent of the respondents in another study indicated that television viewing was the only family activity participated in during the week.[10]

In a summary of research findings on television's effect on family interactions James Gabardino states: "The early findings suggest that television had a disruptive effect upon interaction and thus presumably human development. . . . It is not unreasonable to ask: 'Is the fact that the average American family during the 1950's came to include two parents, two children and a television set somehow related to the psychosocial characteristics of the young adults of the 1970's?' "[11]

Undermining the Family

In its effect on family relationships, in its facilitation of parental withdrawal from an active role in the socialization of their children, and in its replacement of family rituals and special events, television has played an important role in the disintegration of the American family. But of course it has not been the only contributing factor, perhaps not even the most important one. The steadily ris-

[8] Cyclops, "Watching the World through TV-Colored Glasses," *New York Times*, June 2, 1974.

[9] E. Maccoby, "Television: Its Impact on School Children," *Public Opinion Quarterly*, Vol. 15, 1951.

[10] R. Hamilton and R. Lawless, "Television within the Social Matrix," *Public Opinion Quarterly*, Vol. 20, 1956.

[11] James Gabardino, "A Note on the Effects of Television Viewing," in Urie Bronfenbrenner and Maureen A. Mahoney, *Influences on Human Development*, 2nd ed. (Hinsdale, Illinois: The Dryden Press, 1975).

ing divorce rate, the increase in the number of working mothers, the decline of the extended family, the breakdown of neighborhoods and communities, the growing isolation of the nuclear family—all have seriously affected the family.

As Urie Bronfenbrenner suggests, the sources of family break- 32 down do not come from the family itself, but from the circumstances in which the family finds itself and the way of life imposed upon it by those circumstances. "When those circumstances and the way of life they generate undermine relationships of trust and emotional security between family members, when they make it difficult for parents to care for, educate and enjoy their children, when there is no support or recognition from the outside world for one's role as a parent and when time spent with one's family means frustration of career, personal fulfillment and peace of mind, then the development of the child is adversely affected," he writes.[12]

But while the roots of alienation go deep into the fabric of Amer- 33 ican social history, television's presence in the home fertilizes them, encourages their wild and unchecked growth. Perhaps it is true that America's commitment to the television experience masks a spiritual vacuum, an empty and barren way of life, a desert of materialism. But it is television's dominant role in the family that anesthetizes the family into accepting its unhappy state and prevents it from struggling to better its condition, to improve its relationships, and to regain some of the richness it once possessed.

Others have noted the role of mass media in perpetuating an 34 unsatisfactory *status quo*. Leisure-time activity, writes Irving Howe, "must provide relief from work monotony without making the return to work too unbearable; it must provide amusement without insight and pleasure without disturbance—as distinct from art which gives pleasure through disturbance. Mass culture is thus oriented towards a central aspect of industrial society: the depersonalization of the individual."[13] Similarly, Jacques Ellul rejects the idea that television is a legitimate means of educating the citizen:

[12] Urie Bronfenbrenner, "The Origins of Alienation," *Scientific American*, August, 1974.
[13] Irving Howe, "Notes on Mass Culture," *Politics*, Spring, 1948.

"Education . . . takes place only incidentally. The clouding of his consciousness is paramount. . . ."[14]

And so the American family muddles on, dimly aware that some- 35 thing is amiss but distracted from an understanding of its plight by an endless stream of television images. As family ties grow weaker and vaguer, as children's lives become more separate from their parents', as parents' educational role in their children's lives is taken over by television and schools, family life becomes increasingly more unsatisfying for both parents and children. All that seems to be left is Love, an abstraction that family members *know* is necessary but find great difficulty giving each other because the traditional opportunities for expressing love within the family have been reduced or destroyed.

For contemporary parents, love toward each other has increas- 36 ingly come to mean successful sexual relations, as witnessed by the proliferation of sex manuals and sex therapists. The opportunities for manifesting other forms of love through mutual support, understanding, nurturing, even, to use an unpopular word, *serving* each other, are less and less available as mothers and fathers seek their independent destinies outside the family.

As for love of children, this love is increasingly expressed 37 through supplying material comforts, amusements, and educational opportunities. Parents show their love for their children by sending them to good schools and camps, by providing them with good food and good doctors, by buying them toys, books, games, and a television set of their very own. Parents will even go further and express their love by attending PTA meetings to improve their children's schools, or by joining groups that are acting to improve the quality of their children's television programs.

But this is love at a remove, and it is rarely understood by chil- 38 dren. The more direct forms of parental love require time and patience, steady, dependable, ungrudgingly given time actually spent *with* a child, reading to him, comforting him, playing, joking, and working with him. But even if a parent were eager and willing to demonstrate that sort of direct love to his children today, the opportunities are diminished. What with school and Little League

[14] Jacques Ellul, *The Technological Society* (New York: Alfred A. Knopf, 1964).

and piano lessons and, of course, the inevitable television programs, a day seems to offer just enough time for a good-night kiss.

Questions on Subject

1. What is the central point Winn develops throughout her essay?
   Locate several different places where she states that point (or thesis) directly, in more or less detail. (Glossary: *Thesis*)
2. What does Winn mean when she says, "Television's contribution
   to family life has been an equivocal one" (paragraph 2)? What does
   she point to as television's specific negative effects?
3. According to Winn, family rituals have been undermined by television. What rituals does she mention? Can you think of any other
   family rituals that have been affected?
4. What does Winn mean when she states that television fosters only
   a "one-way relationship" (18)? How are people on television different from "real people"? Why isn't Mr. Rogers a real person?
5. How, according to Winn, is television used by families as a way
   to avoid confronting problems? What examples does she give?
6. Winn knows that television is not the sole cause of "the disintegration of the American family" (31). What other factors does she
   suggest have exerted an influence? How is television related to
   these other factors?

Questions on Strategy

1. Winn believes that "parents have accepted a television-dominated
   family life so completely that they cannot see how the medium is
   involved in whatever problems they might be having" (4). How
   does she support this generalization? Are you convinced?
2. Before talking about the effects of television on family rituals, Winn
   offers several sociological definitions of *ritual* (11). Why do you
   suppose she thought it necessary to define the term? (Glossary:
   Definition)
3. Analyze the effectiveness of the material Winn quotes from various
   sources. Which quotations do you find most interesting and convincing? What other kinds of evidence does she use to document
   the effects television has on the American family? (Glossary:
   Evidence)

4. Briefly describe the causal chain that Winn presents in paragraph 35. Why do you suppose she reserves her discussion of love until paragraphs 35 through 38?
5. How has Winn organized her essay? Do you find the headings helpful in understanding her organization? Why, or why not? (Glossary: *Organization*)

Questions on Diction and Vocabulary

1. Winn italicizes a number of words in her essay, such as in paragraphs 1 and 2. Explain her reason for using italics in several specific instances. Do you find the emphasis particularly effective?
2. Comment on the connotative value of each of the following italicized words. (Glossary: *Connotation/Denotation*)
   a. "will only *fester* and become less easily resolvable" (23)
   b. "television has played an important role in the *disintegration* of the American family" (31)
   c. "while the *roots* of alienation go deep into the *fabric* of American social history, television's presence in the home *fertilizes* them" (33)
   d. "the American family *muddles* on" (35)
   e. "independent *destinies* outside the family" (36)
3. How does Winn's diction make a difference in the tone of her essay? You might contrast Winn's tone with Gloria Steinem's in "Why Young Women Are More Conservative." (Glossary: *Diction; Tone*)
4. Refer to your desk dictionary to determine the meanings of the following words as they are used in this selection: *apologists* (paragraph 1), *equivocal* (2), *conjuring* (8), *spontaneous* (9), *shunted* (10), *accede* (10), *purport* (19), *status quo* (34), *paramount* (34), *proliferation* (36), *ungrudgingly* (38).

Writing Assignments

1. How do you feel about mathematics, English, science, art, or another general area of study? Write an essay discussing the causes and the effects of your attitude toward one of these subjects. What events or relationships in your past have led you to feel the way

you do? How does this attitude determine the kinds of choices you make and other aspects of your behavior?

2. Write an essay in which you discuss the effects of television on you or on American society. You may wish to focus on the specific influences of one of the following aspects of television:
   a. advertising
   b. sports broadcasts
   c. cultural programming
   d. talk shows
   e. cartoons

The Reality of Crime on Campus
Todd S. Purdum

> *Todd S. Purdum is a reporter for the City Hall bureau of
> the* New York Times. *In the following selection he reports
> on campus crime. The apparent increase in crime, especially
> sexual assault, has forced colleges and universities—some-
> times against their will—to deal with the problem by tight-
> ening campus security and raising student awareness.*

A man on a university campus walks up to a woman he has   1
never met and bites her breast in a collegiate fad known as "shark-
ing." Racial brawls break out on campuses from Massachusetts to
Maryland. Four university football players in California gang-rape
a woman. A student rapes and strangles a 19-year-old college freshman in her Pennsylvania dormitory room. Another student mur-
ders two others in a Michigan dormitory with a sawed-off shot-
gun.

These and similar violent incidents at American colleges and   2
universities in recent years have focused sharp attention on an
issue many students, parents and administrators long considered
a contradiction of a sort: crime on campus.

For years, college campuses had an image of being safe, bucolic   3
havens, academic groves where the pursuit of knowledge and the
cultivation of fellowship shut out many of the threats and fears of
everyday life.

No longer. Several well-publicized crimes, a growing number of   4
negligence lawsuits against colleges accused of lax security and a
greater awareness of "date rape," gang rape and other crimes
against women have forced schools to confront the problem in an
unprecedented way. Many have responded with seminars and forums on safety and sexual harassment, added lighting and increased security patrols.

"It's a new era on college campuses, where everybody—stu-   5
dents, faculty, staff—is trying to pay greater attention to it," said

William Schafer, director of the office of student conduct at the University of Colorado at Boulder. "Whereas before, a lot of these issues weren't dealt with very openly, either because people didn't know it was occurring or they didn't want to admit it."

Experts say no comprehensive statistics on campus crime are available. Only a little more than 300 of the nation's 2,100 four-year colleges and universities report data individually through the Federal Bureau of Investigation's voluntary Uniform Crime Reports system. Figures for most institutions, including many of the most prestigious private schools, are blended with local crime statistics—assuming that the schools report the crimes to begin with, and some critics contend many do not, for fear such information will damage their admissions and fund-raising efforts as well as their reputations.

A review of F.B.I. data from 1980 to 1986, the latest period for which statistics are available, shows a negligible increase in violent crimes reported, from about 2,300 on slightly more than 300 campuses in 1980 to about 2,400 crimes on 340 campuses in 1986. The number of crimes in general reported to the F.B.I. peaked in 1981, and the rate then declined until the last half of 1985, when a slight rise began.

"I'd be hard pressed to believe that there is any major increase statistically on campuses," said Daniel P. Keller, director of public safety for the 23,000-student University of Louisville. On the other hand, he said, "There is an increased awareness of crime on campus." Yet he and other college officials are quick to acknowledge that the F.B.I. data are incomplete. "Significant numbers of schools don't report, and the criteria are interpreted differently by different schools," said Mr. Keller, who is also a consultant to other schools. "They're the best thing we have, but they're certainly not by any stretch or means accurate."

Mr. Keller and other experts say many crimes, regardless of where they happen, go unreported, but in the closed environment of the college campus crimes of a sexual nature are under-reported. Victims and attacker often move in the same social circles, and there is a great disincentive to go to the police and press charges.

But officials at Towson State University in Maryland who have conducted surveys of crime on 1,100 campuses for the last two years, say they do detect a rise in violence.

"What we've been finding is there has been some increase in 11
acts of violence, physical and sexual assault, rape and major van-
dalism in the last year," said Jan Sherrill, the school's assistant vice
president of student affairs. "What we don't know, because this
is all self-reported, is just how extensive it is. What we do know
is that most of the facts that are given to us are considered by the
people who are reporting them to us to be lower than what's actually happening."

Mr. Sherrill said assessments of violence varied widely, even 12
among officials on the same campus. For example, he said, Towson's surveys found that while two-thirds of the deans of students
who answered questionnaires said violence on their campus was
under control, two-thirds of residence-hall directors said it was out
of control.

Another problem is that a substantial portion of "campus- 13
related" crimes actually occur off school property, although they
involve students, fraternities and other student organizations.
"It's real difficult to get an accurate portrayal of exactly what is
happening," Mr. Keller said.

What actually is happening falls into two major categories: 14
crimes against students by outsiders and student-on-student
crime.

Crimes committed against students by outsiders who come on 15
campus range from those committed by thieves tempted by stereos,
computers and bicycles to sex offenders drawn by the presence of
large numbers of young women. Urban campuses have long faced
such realities. Increasingly, suburban and even rural schools have
had to recognize that their campuses are no longer the isolated,
protected outposts of a generation ago.

The area around Princeton University in central New Jersey has 16
grown greatly in the last decade. Businesses, attracted by the region's rich academic atmosphere and historic charm, have built
office parks and shopping centers along the Route 1 corridor, a
few miles from the campus in Princeton.

"Any direction you go, you see great, rapid growth," said Jerrold 17
L. Witsil, the school's director of public safety. "That has to mean
there are going to be a lot of new people in the area, and with that
kind of growth and exposure, things are going to change in the
way of crime."

At the same time, Mr. Witsil, former president of the Interna- 18 tional Association of Campus Law Enforcement Administrators, says Princeton is determined to remain "an open environment," without gates locking it off from the surrounding communities and with entrances to dormitories and class buildings kept open. "We'll keep a lid on those who'd want to come on campus for illegal purposes by strengthening patrols and our preventive and aware-ness activities," he said.

Sometimes, awareness comes too late. A year and a half ago, 19 Katherine M. Hawelka, a 19-year-old sophomore, was raped and murdered at Clarkson University in Potsdam, N.Y., a quiet town near the Canadian border. Two campus security guards drove by and saw Ms. Hawelka on the ground with a man about 3:30 A.M., yet did nothing because they thought the couple were engaged in consensual sex. They returned later to find Ms. Hawelka uncon-scious and beaten. She died three days later. The man convicted of murdering her, Brian M. McCarthy, 23, a Potsdam resident, was sentenced to 23 years to life in prison. He was not a Clarkson student and did not know Ms. Hawelka.

Ms. Hawelka's family is suing Clarkson for $550 million, arguing 20 that its guards were negligent. Ms. Hawelka grew up in Syracuse, and her family said they were well aware of the potential dangers in an urban area like that of Syracuse University. "So when Katie went up to Potsdam, I don't think we even saw it in terms of anything like that being possible," said her mother, Terry Con-nelly. "Even a lot of her friends asked, 'How could it happen?'"

Clarkson officials have defended the guards' actions. Potsdam's 21 police chief, Clinton Mattot, agreed, saying the men could not have known a rape was occurring. He said their attitude toward seeing people have sex in public seemed casual, but added: "Mommies and daddies don't stop sex and neither does a college." Others perhaps would argue that the guards' attitude merely reflected society's updated, blasé sexual mores.

At the heart of the second major category—crimes committed 22 by students against other students—is the question of what be-havior a college can legitimately be expected to prevent. In the late 1960's and early 70's, most colleges eliminated the rigid codes of conduct that had governed student life for generations, substitut-ing more general, perhaps permissive standards.

As the nation's mood retreated to conservatism in the 1980's, 23 many states reinstated 21 as the legal drinking age. Schools reacted by getting tougher. Many stopped serving liquor at campus events. In sexual matters, some schools decided that rape was grounds for expulsion.

Students, concerned about sexual harassment and other inci- 24 dents of sexism, also encouraged administrators to take a more active role in student life. "The idea that a college stands in for parents, *in loco parentis,* is today a faded memory," said Ernest L. Boyer, president of the Carnegie Endowment for the Advancement of Teaching, in his book *College,* published last year. "But on many campuses, there is great uncertainty about what should replace it."

Howard and Constance Clery, whose 19-year-old daughter, 25 Jeanne Ann, was raped and murdered in her Lehigh University dorm room in 1986, advocate a return to greater supervision of student life by college officials. The Clerys are suing the school for $25 million, arguing that inadequate campus security led to their daughter's death. Although Miss Clery's dormitory had locking doors, students had propped them open.

Lehigh denies negligence, but the school has since undertaken 26 several major improvements in security, including increasing its security force from 12 to 19; establishing a foot patrol; installing better lighting; locking dorms around the clock instead of only at night, and starting a campus shuttle-bus system during evening hours.

Jeanne Ann Clery was killed by a Lehigh student who had had 27 earlier scrapes with the law. Her parents, besides suing the university, have launched a campaign for legislation, now pending in the Pennsylvania legislature, to require all colleges in the state to disclose to applicants not only their crime statistics for the previous three years but also their policies on student drug and alcohol abusers and admitting convicted felons.

Some administrators see such measures as misguided. "It's real 28 difficult to lock up a university, so to speak," said Mr. Keller of Louisville. "It's an atypical society. It's not like a K-Mart that you can lock up at nine at night and not expect anyone to be in there till nine in the morning. It's a very, very live and vibrant environment that it's very difficult to put an umbrella over."

Sexual assaults by students on students are perhaps the most 29 difficult for schools to confront. They are also the ones most often ignored or hushed up. A 1985 survey of 7,000 American students on 32 campuses by Mary Koss, a professor of psychology at Kent State University in Ohio, found that one in eight women had been raped (date rape included). Moreover, one in every 12 men admitted to having used physical coercion to force, or try to force, a woman to have intercourse.

While experts estimate that up to 90 percent of all rapes in the 30 nation go unreported, they say women are especially reluctant to report rapes by dates or acquaintances. "Schools don't like to air their dirty linen in public, and I think that's understandable," said Dr. Bernice Sandler, executive director of the Association of American Colleges' Project on the Status and Education of Women, in Washington, D.C. "But some don't know the linen is dirty. Often, women are embarrassed. When these things happen, they don't report it."

In a recent study, eight of the nine campus rape-prevention cen- 31 ters in the University of California system said they annually saw a total of about 240 rape victims who had failed to report the assaults to police. In 1986, according to a report by the Commission on California State Government Organization and Economy, as many as 20 acquaintance-rape victims sought help from the rape-prevention center on the Berkeley campus alone.

On college-related gang rape Dr. Sandler's office has docu- 32 mented at least 70 such incidents, often occurring in athletic or fraternity settings. The office has also received reports from several campuses of men publicly biting women's breasts or buttocks, sometimes as part of fraternity initiation rituals, Dr. Sandler said.

Administrators say such violence is often linked to alcohol abuse, 33 an increasing concern since several recent alcohol-related deaths on campuses. "I would say 100 percent of our sexual-assault cases are alcohol-related," said Mr. Schafer of the University of Colorado.

Officials say schools are coping with such problems in varying 34 degrees. After a series of incidents in which women students were either verbally or physically harassed by male students at Princeton last year, the university hired a full-time sexual-harassment counselor, something a number of other schools have already done. All

Princeton's campus security officers have undergone training with
the new counselor.

Dr. Sandler, of the Project on the Status and Education of 35
Women, says it is difficult to know whether sexual assaults are
more frequent than a generation ago. However, in the past such
acts were often written off as youthful rambunctiousness; today,
at a time of heightened awareness of sexism, they are seen as violent crimes.

In California last year, Assemblyman Tom Hayden sponsored a 36
resolution calling on state schools to establish policies for dealing
with sexual assaults and to provide students with statistics on
crime. Although the resolution lacks the force of law, Curtis
Richards, an aide to Mr. Hayden, said it would have "a very strong
impact" because of the Assembly's power over the budget of the
state university system. Mr. Hayden heads the Assembly's sub-
committee on education.

Whether the solution lies in legislation, stricter disciplinary pol- 37
icies, tighter security or some combination of them, the Clerys and
other parents say they are encouraged by educators and students
displaying greater awareness of campus crime.

A recent editorial in the Lehigh student newspaper on the Clery 38
case concluded with these words: "There is no such thing as a safe,
idyllic campus. A college campus, composed of adults from many
different backgrounds, is an extension of the real world. A world
that has good and bad."

Questions on Subject

1. According to Purdum, why are statistics on campus crime una-
   vailable? What factors may be contributing to the apparently increasing incidence of campus crime?
2. What two major categories of campus crime does Purdum distinguish? What types of crimes does he include in each category?
3. What question lies at the heart of student-against-student crimes?
   What, if anything, can colleges and universities do to answer this
   question? What can students do?
4. Which student crimes are the most difficult for students to confront? Why?

5. What role does alcohol play on college campuses?
6. List the security precautions that some schools have initiated in an attempt to deal with campus crimes.

Questions on Strategy

1. What is the effect of Purdum's opening paragraph? How well does it serve as a beginning for his essay? Explain. (Glossary: *Beginnings*)
2. What is Purdum's purpose in writing his essay? Does he wish to inform, to speculate, or to argue? (Glossary: *Purpose*)
3. Construct the causal chain that results in a woman's being reluctant to report a campus rape.
4. In his analysis, Purdum relies heavily on the use of statistics. What different kinds of statistics does he use? Which kind did you find the most convincing? Explain.

Questions on Diction and Vocabulary

1. How does Purdum's diction in paragraphs 19, 20, and 21 suggest the tragedy of Katherine M. Hawelka's death without being sensational? In general, how does his choice of words reflect his training as a news reporter?
2. Refer to your desk dictionary to determine the meanings of the following words as they are used in this selection: *fad* (paragraph 1), *bucolic* (3), *lax* (4), *disincentive* (9), *consensual* (19), *blasé* (21), *mores* (21), *expulsion* (23), *initiation* (32), *coping* (34), *rambunctiousness* (35), *idyllic* (38).

Writing Suggestions

1. Create a causal chain of your own for some action or activity that culminated in community action in your town or your school. For example, a volunteer program in the school, the building of a new firehouse, a neighborhood watch committee, or a summer recreation program. Be sure that the different parts of your chain are authentically related and not *non sequiturs*.
2. Write an essay in which you discuss the safety measures your college has taken to reduce the possibility of campus crime.

Writing Suggestions for Cause and Effect Analysis

1. Write an essay in which you analyze the most significant reasons why you went to college. You may wish to discuss such matters as your family background, your high-school experience, people and events that influenced your decision, and your goals in college as well as in later life.

2. It is interesting to think of ourselves in terms of the influences that have caused us to be who we are. Write an essay in which you discuss two or three of what you consider the most important influences on your life. Following are some areas you may wish to consider in planning and writing your paper:

    a. a parent
    b. a book or movie
    c. a member of the clergy
    d. a teacher
    e. a hero
    f. a friend
    g. a youth organization
    h. a coach
    i. your neighborhood
    j. your ethnic background

3. Decisions often involve cause and effect relationships; that is, a person usually weighs the possible results of an action before deciding to act. Write an essay in which you consider the possible effects that would result from one decision or another in one of the following controversies:

    a. taxing cars on the basis of fuel consumption
    b. reinstituting the military draft
    c. legalizing marijuana
    d. mandatory licensing of handguns
    e. raising the legal drinking age to twenty-one
    f. ending subsidies to tobacco growers

g. abolishing grades for college courses
h. raising the minimum wage
i. mandatory community service (one year) for all eighteen-year-olds
j. banning the use of pesticides on produce
k. requiring an ethics course in college

11
Argumentation

What Is Argument?

The word *argument* probably brings to mind a verbal disagreement of the sort that everyone has at least witnessed, if not participated in directly. Such disputes are occasionally satisfying; you can take pleasure in knowing you have converted someone to your point of view. More often, though, arguments like these are inconclusive and result only in the frustration of realizing that you have failed to make your position understood, or in sputtering anger over your opponent's unreasonable stubbornness. Such dissatisfaction is inevitable, because verbal arguments generally arise spontaneously and so cannot be thoughtfully planned or researched; it is difficult to come up with appropriate evidence on the spur of the moment or to find the language that will make a point hard to deny. Indeed, it is often not until later, in retrospect, that the convincing piece of evidence, the forcefully phrased assertion, finally comes to mind.

Written arguments have much in common with spoken ones: they attempt to convince a reader to agree with a particular point of view, to make a particular decision, to pursue a particular course of action; they involve the presentation of well-chosen evidence and the artful manipulation of language. However, writers of argument have no one around to dispute their words directly, so they must imagine their probable audience in order to predict the sorts of objections that may be raised. This requires that written arguments be much more carefully planned—the writer must settle in advance on a specific, sufficiently detailed assertion (or thesis), rather than grope toward one as in a verbal argument. There is a greater need for organization, for choosing among all the available evidence, for shaping the order of presentation, for determining the strategies of rhetoric, language, and style that will best suit the argument's purpose, its thesis, and its impact on an audience. In the end, however, such work can be far more satisfying than the slap-dash of a spontaneous oral argument.

There are different ways of presenting an argument and appealing to readers, but all of these can be divided into two essential categories: persuasion and logic. A *persuasive argument* relies primarily on appeals to emotion, to the subconscious, even to prejudice. These appeals involve connotative diction, figurative language, analogy, rhythmic patterns of speech, and the establishment of a tone that will encourage a positive response. Examples of such argument are found in the exaggerated claims of advertisers and the speechmaking of political or social activists. A *logical argument*, on the other hand, appeals primarily to the mind, to a reader's intellectual faculties, understanding, and knowledge. Such appeals depend on the reasoned movement from assertion to evidence to conclusion, and on an almost mathematical system of proof and counterproof. Logical argument is commonly found in scientific or philosophical articles, in legal decisions, and in technical proposals.

Most arguments, however, are neither purely logical nor purely persuasive. A well-written newspaper editorial, for example, will rest on a logical arrangement of assertions and evidence, but it will also employ striking diction and other persuasive patterns of language to reinforce its effectiveness. Thus, the kinds of appeals a writer emphasizes depend on the subject, the purpose, and the audience. The strongest arguments, though, will always be those that are logically sound; for college work, you will need to discover an appropriately persuasive tone, but you should give most of your attention to the techniques of logical argument.

Why Do Writers Use Argument?

True arguments are limited to assertions about which there is a legitimate and recognized difference of opinion. It is unlikely that anyone will ever need to convince a reader that falling in love is a rare and intense experience, that crime rates should be reduced, or that computers are changing the world; most everyone would agree with such assertions. But not everyone would agree that women experience love more intensely than men, that reinstating the death penalty will reduce the incidence of crime, or that computers are changing the world for the worse; these assertions are arguable and admit of differing perspectives. Similarly, a leading heart specialist might argue in a popular magazine that too many doctors are advising patients to have pacemakers implanted when they are not necessary; the editorial writer for a small-town newspaper could write urging that a local agency supplying food to poor families be given a larger percentage of the tax budget; in a lengthy and complex book, a foreign policy specialist might attempt to prove that the current administration exhibits no consistent policy in its relationship with other countries and that the Department of State is in need of overhauling. No matter what its forum or its structure, an argument has as its chief purpose the detailed setting forth of a particular point of view and the rebuttal of any opposing views.

Most of the readings in the argument section of *Subject and Strategy* are devoted to three subjects in which there is great concern today and on which there are also strong differences of opinion. While not necessarily always arguing directly with each other, the authors in each subject area present differing views on their topics: Nat Hentoff, Tipper Gore, and Loudon Wainwright show why the question of censorship is not a simple problem of whether to ban or not to ban; Barbara Ehrenreich, Arthur Schlesinger, Jr., TaRessa Stovall, and L. Douglas Wilder present different arguments on the value of diversity and the status of African-Americans in the United States; and Issac Asimov, Charles Krauthammer, Rachel Carson, and Linnea Saukko debate the environmental issues of the day.

In general, writers of argument are interested in explaining aspects of a subject as well as in advocating a particular view. Consequently, argumentation frequently adopts the other rhetorical strategies. In your efforts to argue convincingly, you may find it necessary to define, to compare and contrast, to analyze causes and effects, to classify, to describe, to narrate. Nevertheless, it is the writer's attempt to convince, not explain, that is of primary importance in an argumentative essay.

What to Look for in Reading an Argumentative Essay

First, note whatever persuasive appeals the argument makes: its language and tone, any powerful images it presents, the way it may play on your own prejudices. Not until you move beyond its subjective effects can you consider whether an argument's logic is valid and convincing.

Next, you should determine whether the argument is built on inductive or deductive reasoning. *Inductive reasoning* moves from a set of specific examples to a general statement or principle. As long as the evidence is accurate, pertinent, complete, and sufficient to represent the assertion, the conclusion of an inductive argument can be regarded as valid; if, however, you can spot inaccuracies in the evidence or point to contrary evidence, you have good reason to doubt the assertion as it stands. Inductive reasoning is the most common of argumentative structures.

Deductive reasoning, more formal and complex than inductive, moves from an overall premise, rule, or generalization to a more specific conclusion. Deductive logic follows the pattern of the syllogism, a simple three-part argument consisting of a major premise, a minor premise, and a conclusion. For example, notice how the following syllogism works:

a. All humans are mortal. (*major premise*)
b. Carolann is a human. (*minor premise*)
c. Carolann is mortal. (*conclusion*)

The conclusion here is true because both premises are true and the logic of the syllogism is valid.

Obviously, a syllogism will fail to work if either of the premises is untrue:

a. All living creatures are mammals. (*major premise*)
b. A lobster is a living creature. (*minor premise*)
c. A lobster is a mammal. (*conclusion*)

The problem is immediately apparent. The major premise is obviously false: there are many living creatures that are not mammals, and a lobster happens to be one of them. Consequently, the conclusion is invalid.

Syllogisms, however, can fail in other ways, even if both premises are objectively true. Such failures occur most often when the arguer jumps to a conclusion without taking obvious exceptions into account:

    a. All college students read books. (*major premise*)
    b. Kristin reads books. (*minor premise*)
    c. Kristin is a college student. (*conclusion*)

Both the premises in this syllogism are true, but the syllogism is still invalid because it does not take into account that other people besides college students read books. The problem is in the way the major premise has been interpreted: if the minor premise was instead "Martin is a college student," then the valid conclusion "Martin reads books" would logically follow.

It is fairly easy to see the problems in a deductive argument when its premises and conclusion are rendered in the form of a syllogism. It is often more difficult to see errors in logic when the argument is presented discursively or within the context of a lengthy essay. If you can reduce the argument to its syllogistic form, however, you will have much less difficulty testing its accuracy. Similarly, if you can isolate and examine out of context the evidence provided to support an inductive assertion, you can more readily evaluate the written inductive argument.

Consider the following excerpt from "The Draft: Why the Country Needs It," an article by James Fallows that first appeared in the *Atlantic* magazine:

> The Vietnam draft was unfair racially, economically, educationally. By every one of those measures, the volunteer Army is less representative still. Libertarians argue that military service should be a matter of choice, but the plain fact is that service in the volunteer force is too frequently dictated by economics. Army enlisted ranks E1 through E4, the privates and corporals, the cannon fodder, the ones who will fight and die, are 36 percent black now. By the Army's own projections, they will be 42 percent black in three years. When other "minorities" are taken into account, we will have, for the first time, an army whose

fighting members are mainly "non-majority," or more bluntly, a black and brown army defending a mainly white nation. The military has been an avenue of opportunity of many young blacks. They may well be firstclass fighting men. They do not represent the nation.

Such a selective sharing of the burden has destructive spiritual effects in a nation based on the democratic creed. But its practical implications can be quite as grave. The effect of a fair, representative draft is to hold the public hostage to the consequences of its decisions, much as the children's presence in the public schools focuses parents' attention on the quality of the schools. If the citizens are willing to countenance a decision that means that *someone's* child may die, they may contemplate more deeply if there is the possibility that the child will be theirs. Indeed, I would like to extend this principle even further. Young men of nineteen are rightly suspicious of the congressmen and columnists who urge them to the fore. I wish there were a practical way to resurrect provisions of the amended Selective Service Act of 1940, which raised the draft age to forty-four. Such a gesture might symbolize the desire to offset the historic injustice of the Vietnam draft, as well as suggest the possibility that, when a bellicose columnist recommends dispatching the American forces to Pakistan, he might also realize that he could end up as a gunner in a tank.

Here Fallows presents an inductive argument against the volunteer army and in favor of reinstating a draft. His argument can be summarized as follows:

ASSERTION: The volunteer army is racially and economically unfair.

EVIDENCE: The disproportionate percentage of blacks in the army, and projections which indicate that, within three years of the article's publication, more than half of the army's fighting members will be nonwhite.

CONCLUSION: "Such a selective sharing of the burden has destructive spiritual effects in a nation based on the democratic ideal." Not until there is a fair, representative draft will the powerful majority be held accountable for any decision to go to war.

Fallows's inductive scheme here is, in fact, very effective—the evidence is convincing and the conclusion strong. But his argument also depends on a more complicated deductive syllogism:

a. The democratic ideal requires equal representation in the re-sponsibilities of citizenship. (*major premise*)
b. Military service is a responsibility of citizenship. (*minor premise*)
c. The democratic ideal requires equal representation in military service. (*conclusion*)

In order to attack Fallows's argument, it would be necessary to deny one of these premises.

Fallows also employs a number of more persuasive techniques, including an analogy: "The effect of a fair, representative draft is to hold the public hostage to the consequences of its decisions, much as children's presence in the public schools focuses parents' attention on the quality of the schools." The use of such an analogy proves nothing, but it can force readers to reconsider their view-point and make them more open-minded. The same is true of Fal-lows's almost entirely unserious suggestion about raising the draft age to forty-four. Like most writers, Fallows uses persuasive ar-guments to complement his more important logical ones.

Writing an Argumentative Essay

Begin by determining a topic that interests you and about which there is some significant difference of opinion. As you pursue your research, consider what assertion or assertions you can make about the topic. The more specific this thesis, the more directed your research can become and the more focused your ultimate argument will be. Don't hesitate to modify or even reject an initial thesis as continued research warrants.

Once you feel you have sufficient evidence to make your asser-tion convincing, consider how best to organize your argument for an eventual audience, and how to avoid any flaws of reasoning that could distract that audience from your primary purpose.

1. Taking Account of Your Audience

It is well worth remembering that in no other type of writing is the question of audience more important than in argumentation.

The tone you establish, the type of diction you choose, the evidence you present to support your assertions, and indeed whether you argue inductively or deductively all depend on your audience. If you know beforehand that your readers are likely to be hostile, neutral, complacent, or receptive, you will be able to tailor your argument accordingly.

Somewhere near the beginning of your argument, identify for your audience the topic to be discussed. Explain its importance and, if possible, show your reader that you share a common concern or interest in this issue. You may wish to state your central assertion directly in your first or second paragraph, so that there is no possibility for your reader to be confused about your position. You may, as well, wish to lead off with a particularly striking piece of evidence, to capture your reader's interest. As you proceed with your argument, if there is a good chance that readers will have strong disagreements, then acknowledge the merits of their potential objections and, at the same time, provide a reasonable refutation. Above all, don't get ahead of your readers—the fact that you are convinced of your position doesn't assure that others will agree.

2. Organization

To some extent, your organization will depend on your method of reasoning: inductive, deductive, or a combination of the two. For example, is it necessary to establish a major premise before moving on to discuss a minor premise? Should most of your evidence precede your direct statement of an assertion, or follow it? As you present your primary points, you may find it effective to move from those that are least important to those that are most important, or from those that are most familiar to those that are least familiar. A scratch outline can help; but it is often the case that a writer's most crucial revisions in an argument involve cutting the essay into pieces and shifting these pieces around into a sharper, more coherent order.

3. Presenting Evidence

For each point of your argument, be sure to provide appropriate and sufficient supporting evidence: verifiable facts and statistics, illustrative examples and narratives, or quotations from authorities. Don't overwhelm your reader with evidence, but don't skimp either; it is important to demonstrate your command of the subject by choosing carefully among all the facts at your disposal.

4. Avoiding Logical Fallacies

Any one of several habitual flaws of reasoning may render your argument effectively invalid. Be careful that you don't fall victim to one of these.

A. OVERSIMPLIFICATION A foolishly simple solution to what is clearly a complex problem: *The reason we have inflation today is that OPEC has unreasonably raised the price of oil.*

B. HASTY GENERALIZATION In inductive reasoning, a generalization that is based on too little evidence or on evidence that is not representative: *It was the best movie I saw, and so it should get an Academy Award.*

C. POST HOC ERGO PROPTER HOC "After this, therefore because of this." Confusing chance or coincidence with causation. The fact that one event comes after another does not necessarily mean that the first event caused the second: *After I went to the hockey game, I caught a cold.*

D. BEGGING THE QUESTION Assuming in a premise something that needs to be proven: *Conservation is the only means of meeting the energy crisis; therefore, we should seek out methods to conserve energy.*

E. FALSE ANALOGY Making a misleading analogy between logically connected ideas: *Of course he'll make a fine coach. He was an all-star basketball player.*

F. EITHER/OR THINKING Seeing only two alternatives when there may in fact be other possibilities: *After twenty-five years as a prison warden, either you love your job or you hate it.*

G. NON SEQUITUR "It does not follow." An inference or conclusion

that is not clearly related to the established premises or evidence:
She is a sincere speaker; she must know what she is talking about.

5. Concluding Forcefully

In the conclusion of your essay, be sure to restate your position, at least briefly. Besides persuading your reader to accept your point of view, you may also want to encourage some specific course of action. Above all, your conclusion should not introduce new information that may surprise your reader; it should seem to follow naturally, almost seamlessly, from the series of points that have been carefully established in the body of the essay. Don't overstate your case, but at the same time don't qualify your conclusion with the use of too many words or phrases like *I think, in my opinion, maybe, sometimes,* and *probably.* Rather than rational and sensible, the results of these words can often sound indecisive and fuzzy.

Environmental Education: Toward an Ethic of Stewardship

Don Wynns

Born in Buffalo, New York, Don Wynns now lives in Naples, Florida. Although he majored in English, Don took a number of electives in environmental studies. After completing his graduate studies in journalism, he hopes to combine his interests in writing and the environment by securing a position with an environmental publication. In this essay, Don argues that more environmental education is needed at all levels, if future generations are to solve the problems currently facing the world. To support his points, Don relies on information he discovered in the course of library research; he has documented his essay appropriately whenever he quotes or paraphrases outside sources.

Most Americans today seem to agree that, as a nation, we should follow an ethic of environmental stewardship. We nod our heads complacently and say, yes, we need to conserve our finite natural resources and protect our environment from becoming unfit to live in. Unfortunately, we don't live this way.

Perhaps the United States came closest to living by this ethic in 1973, the year of the Arab oil embargo. The resulting marathon gas lines and soaring heating bills left us no choice but to limit our ravenous consumption of oil and conserve our own natural resources. We had discovered the reality of a finite environment. Apathy, though, soon set in. A mere six years after the embargo, a Gallup poll showed that only half of Americans felt our energy situation was "fairly serious." Incredibly, 33% didn't even realize that the U.S. imports oil! (Miller 258). Today forgetfulness seems to be running rampant. The big auto makers' marketing tests show that people again want big, soft-riding gas-guzzlers, probably because of greater gas supplies and lower prices resulting from the temporary oil glut. And so Detroit, instead of producing cars that get sixty miles per gallon (this would raise a car's price about $800, but the money would be returned to the owner in only fifteen months through fuel savings [Lovins]), has reverted to the 1960 mentality of making large, lower-mileage cars and vans.

Shortsightedness is the rule of the day, and nowhere is this more 3 evident than in Washington. Whether it be zero-budgeting a program for insulating the homes of low-income citizens, an Interior Department that all but invites coal-mining interests to strip-mine public land, or an Environmental Protection Agency which has chosen to ignore the illegal dumping of toxic wastes, our government itself has proven to be at best a weak supporter of the ethic of environmental stewardship. With such a model, no wonder the general public has not acted more responsibly.

This national myopia of the 1980s has occurred despite news- 4 paper exposés and editorials, TV series and specials, environmental magazines and newsletters, and an increase in the number of basic environmental-awareness courses in our universities. Obviously, such publicity has succeeded in raising the environmental consciousness of some; but the message tends to reach a limited audience of people who either already live according to an environmental ethic or sincerely wish to do so. Most of us, however, have remained uncommitted to environmental stewardship of even the lowest order.

Perhaps this is because the stewardship ethic is not presented 5 early enough in our schools, and because what is done is not of adequate quality. There is evidence to support such a belief. In 1974 and 1981, two concerned teachers surveyed all fifty state education agencies, forty-two of which returned both surveys. The responses show that on the average each agency's coordinator for environmental education spent 59% of his or her time working on other projects, such as devising new general science programs (Disinger and Bouquet 19). Between 1974 and 1981, the "decreasing priority for environmental education is lucidly demonstrated by the data evidencing decreasing percentages of staff time for its coordination in the state education agencies"; this results at least partly from the "lack of priority for environmental education within the federal establishment" combined with "state education agencies following federal funding priorities (Disinger and Bouquet 20).

Moreover, the teachers of environmental studies courses in our 6 primary and secondary schools have themselves never had to take environmental studies in college. There is no such thing as a mandatory environmental curriculum for future elementary and high school teachers. In fact, from the peak of environmental awareness on Earth Day in 1970 through late 1979, there was no increase in the number of state universities that offered certifiable majors and minors in environmental education (Trent 15). So youngsters are not receiving the quality of instruction that they should from their teachers. No matter how hard a teacher tries, if he or she is not versed in a subject the students cannot learn it well.

It seems reasonable to infer that without adequate programs in 7 elementary and high schools, few students will understand what an environmental ethic is, much less choose to live by it; fewer still will want to become environmental or natural resources professionals. Even if a high school graduate does aspire to such a career, there is a scarcity of college and university programs offering specialization in environmental science and engineering. In a recent survey of 206 U.S. and Canadian universities, only 48% were found to have a viable curriculum in environmental studies (as opposed to a few scattered courses). And only 11% had such programs leading to a degree (Klee 34). Thus, the options for students seriously interested in scientific research or policy-making are rare indeed.

It is time to fill this void. Universities along with state and local 8 governments must share the responsibility. By renewing their commitment to environmental courses at the introductory and advanced levels and by developing programs for future elementary and high school teachers, universities can help prepare the way. With adequate public funding at all levels, such curricula could lead to better and more numerous courses in the schools, a key to the development of widespread environmental consciousness and responsibility.

As things are, it seems that only some major environmental ca- 9 tastrophe will break through the ignorance and apathy of most people about the environment and its problems. But surely it is better to avert a disaster than to cause one and then learn from it. Thanks to fifteen years of consciousness-raising and hard experience, the foundation exists for better understanding through better education. But we cannot afford to leave it at that. The system can work; whether it will, however, remains to be seen.

Works Cited

Disinger, J., and W. Bouquet. "Environmental Education and State Education Agencies." *Journal of Environmental Education* (Spring 1982).

Klee, G. "The Status of Environmental Studies in U.S. and Canadian Geography Departments." *Journal of Environmental Education* (Winter 1982–83).

Lovins, Hunter. Speech. University of Vermont, 3 Apr. 1984.

Miller, Tyler. *Living in the Environment*. Belmont, CA: Wadsworth, 1982.

Trent, J. "Environmental Education in Our Schools During the 1970's." *Journal of Environmental Education* (Fall 1983).

Interview with Don Wynns

How did you find the topic for your essay?

I'm interested in the environment, and I've taken several environmental courses at the university, though I'm an English major. I was paging through a copy of *Environmental Management* magazine and read an editorial by Robert DeSanto. There was a sentence that struck me: "The concept of environmental stewardship encapsulates the idea that there is a need for (a) the public to better sense our environment and its ecology, (b) the politician to better sense the capacities and limitations of applied science, (c) the scientist to better sense the practical need for applied ecology, and (d) the means by which we can better communicate and instill these sensitivities." That got me started. In fact, I quoted it at the beginning of my first draft.

Was it all easy from there to your final draft?

It was very difficult. There's almost no comparison between my first and last drafts. Along the way I included and then dropped a history of changing American attitudes and use of the land, and I included and dropped a detailed proposal for what the schools should teach. I also finally dropped the quotation that began the whole thing. The shape of the essay changed drastically with each of the six drafts.

What was the problem?

I had lots of problems, but the worst was that I didn't really understand when I started just what an argument is. I made a lot of assertions without any supporting evidence, and I made a lot of proposals without explaining why they should be adopted. My teacher pointed out that what seemed obvious to me would be new and possibly controversial to my readers, and suggested that I share my facts and reasoning with them. For one thing, it's not obvious to many people that we're doing so badly in conserving and protecting the environment, so I had to show that we are, and that we need to do better. And I couldn't just rely on my memory for the facts I needed, so I had to go to the library and do research. While I was at it, I found some articles in the *Journal of Environmental Education* that showed just how bad things are in the schools and educational bureaucracies. So that discussion replaced my specific proposals for a new curriculum—I couldn't defend them anyway, not in a short paper like this.

So this wasn't a research paper from the beginning?

No—I just found that I couldn't write it out of my head. I needed some facts and I didn't have them.

Tell me about your other problems.

Well, I don't think I was clear about my audience—who would read this, and why, and how they would respond—so I had no basis other than my own ideas and opinions for deciding what to put in and what to leave out. All those proposals for reforming school and university curricula might have fitted into a piece for teachers and administrators, but not for general readers, people who are concerned about the environment, or education, or both. And it's people like that that I'd want to reach and persuade.

The State of My Plate

Mundy Wilson-Libby

> *Born in Bennington, Vermont, Mundy Wilson-Libby has lived in Florida, Maryland, and every New England state except Connecticut. She now resides in rural Wakefield, Rhode Island, with her husband, Mark, and her cat, Spades. While at the University of Vermont, Mundy earned a degree in English with a coordinate major in environmental studies. Currently, she is working at Brown University where she earned a master's degree in English. In this essay, Mundy humorously tries to persuade meat eaters to be more tolerant of vegetarians by recounting her own experiences as a vegetarian amongst a family of "non-veggies."*

The holiday that I dread the most is fast approaching. The relatives will gather to gossip and bicker, the house will be filled with the smells of onions, giblets, and allspice, and I will be pursuing trivial conversations in the hopes of avoiding any commentaries upon the state of my plate.

Do not misunderstand me: I am not a scrooge. I enjoy the idea of Thanksgiving—the giving of thanks for blessings received in the past year and the opportunity to share an unhurried day with family and friends. The problem for me is that I am one of those freaky, misunderstood dampers on the party—a vegetarian. Since all traditional Western holidays revolve around food and more specifically around the ham, turkey, lamb, or roast beef and their respective starchy accompaniments, it's no picnic for we "rabbit food" people. The mention of the word *vegetarian* has, on various similar occasions, caused Great-Aunt Bertha to rant and rave for what seems like hours about "those Communist conspirators." Other relations cough or groan or simply stare, change the subject or reminisce about somebody they used to know who was "into that," and some proceed either to demand that I defend my position or try to talk me out of it. That is why I try to avoid the subject at all times, but especially during the holidays.

In years past I have had about as many successes as failures in steering comments about my food toward other topics. Politics and religion are the easiest outs, guaranteed to immerse the family into a heated debate lasting until the loudest shouter has been abandoned amidst empty pie plates, wine corks, and rumpled linen napkins. I prefer, however, to use this tactic as a last resort. Holidays are supposed to be for relaxing.

I can already picture the scenario. As plates, platters, and bowls holding the traditional fixings of the Thanksgiving feast are passed around the table, two or three I transfer immediately from the person on my right to the one on my left. Seldom is this noticed since everyone from Uncle Fred to little Ely is engrossed in what is happening on their own plates. After our traditional secular prayer (supposedly designed to keep the peace) and about five minutes of horse-like chomping mingled with contented moans and groans, my observant Aunt Nancy will usually say something like, "Why M.L., you don't have any turkey or duck on your plate! Let me help you to some."

"Thanks, Nance, but I'm fine," I say, grinding my teeth.

"But how can you have a Thanksgiving meal without turkey? You're not still one of those vegetarians, are you?"

I try an avoidance maneuver. "So Uncle Russ, how's life in Florida?" Not a chance this time. All eyes are on me waiting for the response they do not wish to hear. Why is it such a big deal for my family to swallow that I do not eat meat? I hardly ever encounter such resistance to the way I choose to nourish my body outside of my relatives. They seem to take it as a personal affront, a betrayal, and an undermining of, God forbid, tradition. They want to understand, in a patronizing way. My brother was a vegetarian for ten years until the recent birth of his second child caused his wife to declare she was no longer going to spend her precious time preparing meals of complementary proteins. The relatives gave him a hard time too, but with less vigor. It may have something to do with my being the only female of the younger generation; what will happen when my mother relinquishes the "Dinner Rights"? Tofu turkey, granola stuffing, and yogurt pie for Thanksgiving???

I close my eyes tightly and concentrate on controlling the pitch of my voice. "Do we have to go through this again? I have been a vegetarian through the last six Thanksgivings and I am tired of this new tradition of having a conversation about it every year. You must grasp the idea that I am not crazy, fanatical, unhealthy, or unhappy. I just do not like to eat meat."

Silence. I pray for someone to change the subject.   9

"We're only concerned about you, dear. You're so thin and meat 10 is so good for you."

"Hey, leave her alone," my brother chimes in. "She simply feels 11 that eating meat is unnecessary, irrational, anatomically unsound, unhealthy, unhygienic, uneconomic, unecological, unaesthetic, unkind, and unethical. Right, M.L.? Now let's talk about really important things—like football."

Interview with Mundy Wilson-Libby

How did you find the topic for your essay?

It was November 1985. My mother had just telephoned to finalize our plans for Thanksgiving—immediately I recalled past holidays and the frustration I felt about my relatives' attitudes toward my vegetarianism. All of my writing topics come from my life experiences. I especially enjoy relating everyday types of events from a humorous perspective. Usually when I'm in the midst of writing a piece I'll find several or a dozen other related topics in which I'm interested. I keep a topic notebook—a three-by-five-inch pad— with me at all times so I can jot down my ideas. When I feel like writing and can't think of a topic, I flip through my notebook and one always jumps out at me.

Did any parts of your essay prove more difficult than you had expected? If so, explain the problem and how you resolved it.

Yes, I had a difficult time with the ending. I wanted it to be meaningful but not heavy, and it took a long time to achieve some satisfaction. Actually, I'm still not completely satisfied with it, but I've yet to come up with anything else. I can only rethink a piece so many times before I get frustrated with it and have to move on. I finally decided on this ending after remembering all the arguments my brother and I made to defend our choice of not eating meat. Then I remembered nothing is more important to my brother than football (at least during the winter holidays). I think it made for an ironic resolution because in many ways vegetarianism and football are completely incongruous.

Who is your audience for this essay? What did you want them to do or think as a result of reading your piece?

When I first started it I thought of my family as my audience. Later I realized I was perhaps speaking for and to vegetarians and to meat eaters who have close relationships with "veggies." Then it dawned on me that I was really trying to persuade anyone who is intolerant of other people's different choices and life-styles to be more accepting instead of resistant and antagonistic. I've always found it amazing that when a person makes a decision to improve his or her well-being, people surrounding that person often make it difficult. I hoped that after reading this essay people might think twice about giving anyone—perhaps especially relatives—a hard time about their choices.

How many drafts do you usually write?

Not nearly enough on paper. I do a lot of writing and rewriting in my head before I'm able to put anything on paper. I think it's left over from my sixth-grade teacher who *insisted* we do a lot of thinking before picking up the pen. Lately, I've been doing some freewriting to get loosened up before I allow myself to work on a piece.

What do you enjoy most about writing?

Writing's an outlet for me. By changing the form or style or perspective to suit my topic, I learn things about myself, other people, and the world. And this gives me a fresh outlook on life. Also, I have always expressed myself better in writing than orally. I always feel rushed in conversations whereas when writing I can take time to think things through and to get closer to what I really want to say.

I understand that you had this essay published in the local newspaper just before Thanksgiving. What did that feel like?

Fantastic! I was so surprised and elated that the newspaper published it. It's funny—even though I've had several more articles published in local papers since then, it feels the same every time. I hope I never lose the feeling of "success" because it really helps my confidence—it spurs me on to write more and more.

When Nice People Burn Books

Nat Hentoff

Born in Boston in 1925, Nat Hentoff is a columnist for the Washington Post *and* The Village Voice *and writes for liberal publications such as* The Progressive. *His writings also include more than twenty-five books of fiction and non-fiction. Referring to himself as an "advocacy writer," Hentoff says his interest in civil rights grew out of his interest in jazz and the world it reflects. He has written extensively on such issues as racism, the draft, educational reform, and police spying, earning himself a reputation as a spokesman for the Left.*

In the following essay originally published in The Progressive *(1983), Hentoff argues that totalitarian tendencies to limit free speech and a free press are not confined to the far Right; rather, they are also beginning to appear among groups to the Left. The author expresses his fear of people who claim to champion the cause of civil rights and yet justify censorship when it supports their idea of what is right and good.*

It happened one splendid Sunday morning in a church. Not Jerry Falwell's Baptist sanctuary in Lynchburg, Virginia, but rather the First Unitarian Church in Baltimore. On October 4, 1981, midway through the 11 A.M. service, pernicious ideas were burned at the altar.

As reported by Frank P. L. Somerville, religion editor of the *Baltimore Sun*, "Centuries of Jewish, Christian, Islamic, and Hindu writings were 'expurgated'—because of sections described as 'sexist.'

"Touched off by a candle and consumed in a pot on a table in front of the altar were slips of paper containing 'patriarchal' excerpts from Martin Luther, Thomas Aquinas, the Koran, St. Augustine, St. Ambrose, St. John Chrysostom, the Hindu Code of Manu V, an anonymous Chinese author, and the Old Testament." Also hurled into the purifying fire were works by Kierkegaard and Karl Barth.

The congregation was much exalted: "As the last flame died in 4 the pot, and the organ pealed, there was applause," Somerville wrote.

I reported this news of the singed holy spirit to a group of Amer- 5 ican Civil Liberties Union members in California, and one woman was furious. At me.

"We did the same thing at our church two Sundays ago," she 6 said. "And long past time, too. Don't you understand it's just *symbolic?*"

I told this ACLU member that when the school board in Drake, 7 North Dakota, threw thirty-four copies of Kurt Vonnegut's *Slaughterhouse Five* into the furnace in 1973, it wasn't because the school was low on fuel. That burning was symbolic, too. Indeed, the two pyres—in North Dakota and in Baltimore—were witnessing to the same lack of faith in the free exchange of ideas.

What an inspiring homily for the children attending services at 8 a liberated church: They now know that the way to handle ideas they don't like is to set them on fire.

The stirring ceremony in Baltimore is just one more illustration 9 that the spirit of the First Amendment is not being savaged only by malign forces of the Right, whether private or governmental. Campaigns to purge school libraries, for example, have been conducted by feminists as well as by Phyllis Schlafly. Yet, most liberal watchdogs of our freedom remain fixed on the Right as *the* enemy of free expression.

For a salubrious change, therefore, let us look at what is hap- 10 pening to freedom of speech and press in certain enclaves—some colleges, for instance—where the New Right has no clout at all. Does the pulse of the First Amendment beat more vigorously in these places than where the Yahoos are?

Well, consider what happened when Eldridge Cleaver came to 11 Madison, Wisconsin, last October to savor the exhilarating openness of dialogue at the University of Wisconsin. Cleaver's soul is no longer on ice; it's throbbing instead with a religious conviction

that is currently connected financially, and presumably theologi-
cally, to the Reverend Sun Myung Moon's Unification Church. In
Madison, Cleaver never got to talk about his pilgrim's progress
from the Black Panthers to the wondrously ecumenical Moonies.
In the Humanities Building—*Humanities*—several hundred students and others outraged by Cleaver's apostasy shouted, stamped
their feet, chanted "Sieg Heil," and otherwise prevented him from
being heard.

After ninety minutes of the din, Cleaver wrote on the blackboard, 12
"I regret that the totalitarians have deprived us of our constitutional
rights to free assembly and free speech. Down with communism.
Long live democracy."

And, raising a clenched fist while blowing kisses with his free 13
hand, Cleaver left. Cleaver says he'll try to speak again, but he
doesn't know when.

The University of Wisconsin administration, through Dean of 14
Students Paul Ginsberg, deplored the behavior of the campus totalitarians of the Left, and there was a fiercely denunciatory editorial in the Madison *Capital Times:* "These people lack even the
most primitive appreciation of the Bill of Rights."

It did occur to me, however, that if Eldridge Cleaver had not 15
abandoned his secularist rage at the American Leviathan and had
come to Madison as the still burning spear of black radicalism, the
result might have been quite different if he had been shouted down
that night by young apostles of the New Right. That would have
made news around the country, and there would have been collectively signed letters to the *New York Review of Books* and *The
Nation* warning of the prowling dangers to free speech in the land.
But since Cleaver has long since taken up with bad companions,
there is not much concern among those who used to raise bail for
him as to whether he gets to speak freely or not.

A few years ago, William F. Buckley Jr., invited to be com- 16
mencement speaker at Vassar, was told by student groups that he
not only would be shouted down if he came but might also suffer
some contusions. All too few liberal members of the Vassar faculty
tried to educate their students about the purpose of a university,
and indeed a good many faculty members joined in the protests
against Buckley's coming. He finally decided not to appear because, he told me, he didn't want to spoil the day for the parents.

I saw no letters on behalf of Buckley's free-speech rights in any of the usual liberal forums for such concerns. After all, he had not only taken up with bad companions; he was an original bad companion.

During the current academic year, there were dismaying devel- 17 opments concerning freedom for bad ideas in the college press. The managing editor of *The Daily Lobo,* the University of New Mexico's student newspaper, claimed in an editorial that Scholastic Aptitude Test scores show minority students to be academically inferior. Rather than rebut his facile misinterpretation of what those scores actually show—that class, not race, affects the results—black students and their sympathizers invaded the newspaper's office.

The managing editor prudently resigned, but the protesters were 18 not satisfied. They wanted the head of the editor. The brave Student Publications Board temporarily suspended her, although the chairman of the journalism department had claimed the suspension was a violation of her First Amendment rights. She was finally given her job back, pending a formal hearing, but she decided to quit. The uproar had not abated, and who knew what would happen at her formal hearing before the Student Publications Board?

When it was all over, the chairman of the journalism department 19 observed that the confrontation had actually reinforced respect for First Amendment rights on the University of New Mexico campus because infuriated students now knew they couldn't successfully insist on the firing of an editor because of what had been published.

What about the resignations? Oh, they were free-will offerings. 20

I subscribe to most of the journalism reviews around the country, 21 but I saw no offer of support to those two beleaguered student editors in New Mexico from professional journalists who invoke the First Amendment at almost any public opportunity.

Then there was a free-speech war at Kent State University, as 22 summarized in the November 12, 1982, issue of *National On-Campus Report.* Five student groups at Kent State are vigorously attempting to get the editor of the student newspaper fired. They are: "gay students, black students, the undergraduate and graduate student governments, and a progressive student alliance."

Not a reactionary among them. Most are probably deeply con- 23 cerned with the savaging of the free press in Chile, Uruguay, Guatemala, South Africa, and other such places.

What had this editor at Kent State done to win the enmity of so 24 humanistic a grand alliance? He had written an editorial that said that a gay student group should not have access to student-fee money to sponsor a Hallowe'en dance. Ah, but how had he gone about making his point?

"In opening statements," says the *National On-Campus Report*, 25 "he employed words like 'queer' and 'nigger' to show that prejudice against any group is undesirable." Just like Lenny Bruce. Lenny, walking on stage in a club, peering into the audience, and asking, "Any spics here tonight? Any kikes? Any niggers?"

Do you think Lenny Bruce could get many college bookings 26 today? Or write a column for a college newspaper?

In any case, the rest of the editorial went on to claim that the 27 proper use of student fees was for educational, not social, activities. The editor was not singling out the Kent Gay/Lesbian Foundation. He was opposed to *any* student organization using those fees for dances.

Never mind. He had used impermissible words. Queer. Nigger. 28 And those five influential cadres of students are after his head. The editor says that university officials have assured him, however, that he is protected at Kent State by the First Amendment. If that proves to be the case, those five student groups will surely move to terminate, if not defenestrate, those university officials.

It is difficult to be a disciple of James Madison on campus these 29 days. Take the case of Phyllis Schlafly and Wabash College. The college is a small, well-regarded liberal arts institution in Crawfordsville, Indiana. In the spring of 1981, the college was riven with discord. Some fifty members of the ninety-odd faculty and staff wrote a stiff letter to the Wabash Lecture Series Committee, which had displayed the exceedingly poor taste to invite Schlafly to speak on campus the next year.

The faculty protesters complained that having the Sweetheart of 30 the Right near the Wabash River would be "unfortunate and inappropriate." The dread Schlafly is "an ERA opponent . . . a far-right attorney who travels the country, being highly paid to tell women to stay at home fulfilling traditional roles while sending their sons off to war."

Furthermore, the authors wrote, "The point of view she rep- 31 resents is that of an ever-decreasing minority of American women and men, and is based in sexist mythology which promulgates beliefs inconsistent with those held by liberally educated persons, and this does not merit a forum at Wabash College under the sponsorship of our Lecture Series."

This is an intriguing document by people steeped in the tradi- 32 tions of academic freedom. One of the ways of deciding who gets invited to a campus is the speaker's popularity. If the speaker appeals only to a "decreasing minority of American women and men," she's not worth the fee. So much for Dorothy Day, were she still with us.

And heaven forfend that anyone be invited whose beliefs are 33 "inconsistent with those held by liberally educated persons." Mirror, mirror on the wall. . . .

But do not get the wrong idea about these protesting faculty 34 members: "We subscribe," they emphasized, "to the principles of free speech and free association, of course."

All the same, "it does not enhance our image as an all-male 35 college to endorse a well-known sexist by inviting her to speak on our campus." If Phyllis Schlafly is invited nonetheless, "we intend not to participate in any of the activities surrounding Ms. Schlafly's visit and will urge others to do the same."

The moral of the story: If you don't like certain ideas, boycott 36 them.

The lecture committee responded to the fifty deeply offended 37 faculty members in a most unkind way. The committee told the signers that "William Buckley would endorse your petition. No institution of higher learning, he told us on a visit here, should allow to be heard on its campus any position that it regards as detrimental or 'untrue.'

"Apparently," the committee went on, "error is to be refuted 38 not by rational persuasion, but by censorship."

Phyllis Schlafly did come to Wabash and she generated a great 39 deal of discussion—most of it against her views—among members of the all-male student body. However, some of the wounded faculty took a long time to recover. One of them, a tenured professor, took aside at a social gathering the wife of a member of the lecture committee that had invited Schlafly. Both were in the same feminist group on campus.

The professor cleared her throat, and said to the other woman, 40
"You are going to leave him, aren't you?"

"My husband? Why should I leave him?" 41

"Really, how can you stay married to someone who invited Phyl- 42
lis Schlafly to this campus?"

And really, should such a man even be allowed visitation rights 43
with the children?

Then there is the Ku Klux Klan. As Klan members have learned 44
in recent months, both in Boston and in Washington, their First
Amendment right peaceably to assemble—let alone actually to
speak their minds—can only be exercised if they are prepared to
be punched in the mouth. Klan members get the same reception
that Martin Luther King Jr. and his associates used to receive in
Bull Conner's Birmingham.

As all right-thinking people know, however, the First Amend- 45
ment isn't just for anybody. That presumably is why the administration of the University of Cincinnati has refused this year to
allow the KKK to appear on campus. Bill Wilkerson, the Imperial
Wizard of the particular Klan faction that has been barred from the
University of Cincinnati, says he's going to sue on First Amendment grounds.

Aside from the ACLU's, how many *amicus* briefs do you think 46
the Imperial Wizard is likely to get from liberal organizations devoted to academic freedom?

The Klan also figures in a dismaying case from Vancouver, Wash- 47
ington. There, an all-white jury awarded $1,000 to a black high
school student after he had charged the Battle Ground School District (including Prairie High School) with discrimination. One of
the claims was that the school had discriminated against this young
man by permitting white students to wear Ku Klux Klan costumes
to a Hallowe'en assembly.

Symbolic speech, however, is like spoken or written speech. It 48
is protected under the First Amendment. If the high school administration had originally forbidden the wearing of the Klan costumes to the Hallowe'en assembly, it would have spared itself that
part of the black student's lawsuit, but it would have set a prec-
edent for censoring symbolic speech which would have shrunken
First Amendment protections at Prairie High School.

What should the criteria be for permissible costumes at a Hal- 49
lowe'en assembly? None that injure the feelings of another student? So a Palestinian kid couldn't wear a PLO outfit. Or a Jewish
kid couldn't come as Ariel Sharon, festooned with maps. And
watch out for the wise guy who comes dressed as that all-around
pain-in-the-ass, Tom Paine.

School administrators might say the best approach is to have no 50
costumes at all. That way, there'll be no danger of disruption. But
if there were real danger of physical confrontation in the school
when a student wears a Klan costume, is the school so powerless
that it can't prevent a fight? And indeed, what a compelling opportunity the costumes present to teach about the Klan, to ask
those white kids who wore Klan costumes what they know of the
history of the Klan. To get black and white kids *talking* about what
the Klan represents, in history—and right now.

Such teaching is too late for Prairie High School. After that $1,000 51
award to the black student, the white kids who have been infected
by Klan demonology will circulate their poison only among themselves, intensifying their sickness of spirit. There will be no more
Klan costumes in that school, and so no more Klan costumes to
stimulate class discussion.

By the way, in the trial, one offer of proof that the school district 52
had been guilty of discrimination was a photograph of four white
boys wearing Klan costumes to that Hallowe'en assembly. It's a
rare picture. It was originally printed in the school yearbook but,
with the lawsuit and all, the picture was cut out of each yearbook
before it was distributed.

That's the thing about censorship, whether good liberals or bad 53
companions engage in it. Censorship is like a greased pig. Hard
to confine. You start trying to deal with offensive costumes and
you wind up with a blank space in the yearbook. Isn't that just
like the Klan? Causing decent people to do dumb things.

Questions on Subject

1. Hentoff describes two instances of book burning in the beginning
   of his essay. In what ways did the two book burnings differ? In
   what ways were they similar?

2. One member of a liberated church justified the burning of books at her church by claiming it was only "symbolic." What does Hentoff consider to be the flaw in this reasoning? Explain.

3. In paragraphs 15 and 16, Hentoff refers to "bad companions." What does he mean by this? What type of people is he referring to?

4. The author offers a host of examples of persons and groups to the political Left who have in one way or another denied freedom of speech to people with whom they disagree. Choose one sentence from Hentoff's essay that best sums up the attitude he thinks these acts embody. Explain why you chose it.

5. According to Hentoff, what is "symbolic speech" (48)? How does it compare to spoken or written speech? What is the danger in suppressing symbolic speech?

Questions on Strategy

1. Why does Hentoff refer to Jerry Falwell, St. Augustine, the ACLU, Phyllis Schlafly, William F. Buckley, Tom Paine, and several other people and groups without explaining who they are? Is he simply dropping names? What assumptions does he make about his audience? (Remember, he's writing for readers of *The Progressive*.) What in particular makes Hentoff a convincing advocate for freedom of speech in this case?

2. Hentoff gives numerous examples of left-wing violations of the First Amendment. Are all of his examples necessary? Why, or why not? (Glossary: *Examples*)

3. The author concludes his essay by saying "Isn't that just like the Klan? Causing decent people to do dumb things." Who are the real targets of Hentoff's criticism? What is he saying about them? Why does the author end his essay in this way? (Glossary: *Beginnings/Endings*)

4. Several paragraphs in the essay are only one or two sentences in length. Why do you think Hentoff uses this technique? What is the effect on the reader? Choose several short paragraphs and explain how each one works in the context of the essay. (Glossary: *Paragraph*)

Questions on Diction and Vocabulary

1. The author's diction clearly reveals his attitude toward people from the Left who violate the principles of the First Amendment. In your

opinion, what is Hentoff's attitude toward these people? What words in particular reveal his attitude? (Glossary: *Attitude*)
2. Refer to your desk dictionary to determine the meanings of the following words as they are used in this selection: *pernicious* (paragraph 1), *expurgated* (2), *homily* (8), *salubrious* (10), *apostasy* (11), *secularist* (15), *riven* (29), *promulgates* (31).

Writing Assignments

1. "What should the criteria be for permissible costumes at a Hallowe'en assembly? None that injure the feelings of another student?" Have you ever been "offended" by the appearance of someone who stands in extreme opposition to your beliefs? Do you agree with Hentoff that free expression of this kind prevents more serious consequences? In an essay, present an argument for where you think the line should be drawn (or not drawn) between freedom of expression and censorship of undesirable expression.
2. Hentoff alludes to "the purpose of a university," in relation to students refusing freedom of speech to speakers whose ideas they despise. In a brief essay, discuss Hentoff's idea of the "purpose" of a university. Do you agree? Would you or the people you know be apt to boycott speakers whose views you consider unworthy?

Curbing the Sexploitation Industry

Tipper Gore

> *Born in Washington, D.C., in 1948, Tipper Gore is the co-founder of the Parents' Music Resource Center and the author of* Raising PG Kids in an X-Rated Society (1987), *a book about violence and obscenity in music, television, and film. Her husband is Vice President Albert Gore, Jr.*
>
> *In the following selection from her book, Gore offers a cause and effect analysis of violence in music and film to argue parents' right to screen the music their children listen to. To uphold that right, the author suggests that producers use a labeling system for rock music album covers, similar to the one used for films, to alert parents to objectionable lyrics.*

I can't even count the times in the last three years, since I began 1 to express my concern about violence and sexuality in rock music, that I have been called a prude, a censor, a music hater, even a book burner. So let me be perfectly clear: I detest censorship. I'm not advocating censorship but rather a candid and vigorous debate about the dangers posed for our children by what I call the "sexploitation industry."

We don't need to put a childproof cap on the world, but we do 2 need to remind the nation that children live in it, too, and deserve respect and sensitive treatment.

When I launched this campaign in 1985 . . . I went to the source 3 of the problem, sharing my concerns and proposals with the entertainment industry. Many producers were sympathetic. Some cooperated with my efforts. But others have been overtly hostile, accusing me of censorship and suggesting, unfairly, that my motives are political. This resistance and hostility has convinced me of the need for a two-pronged campaign, with equal effort from the entertainment industry and concerned parents. Entertainment producers must take the first step, by labeling sexually explicit material.

But the industry cannot be expected to solve the problem on its 4 own. Parents should encourage producers to cooperate and praise them when they do. Producers need to know that parents are aware of the issue and are reading their advisory labels. Above all, they need to know that somebody out there cares, that the community at large is not apathetic about the deep and lasting damage being done to our children.

What's at issue is not the occasional sexy rock lyric. What troubles—indeed, outrages—me is far more vicious: a celebration of the most gruesome violence, coupled with the explicit message that sado-masochism is the essence of sex. We're surrounded by examples—in rock lyrics, on television, at the movies and in rental videos. One major TV network recently aired a preview of a soap opera rape scene during a morning game show.

The newest craze in horror movies is something called the "teen slasher" film, and it typically depicts the killing, torture and sexual mutilation of women in sickening detail. Several rock groups now simulate sexual torture and murder during live performances. Others titillate youthful audiences with strippers confined in cages on stage and with half-naked dancers, who often act out sex with band members. Sexual brutality has become the common currency of America's youth culture and with it the pervasive degradation of women.

Why is this graphic violence dangerous? It's especially damaging for young children because they lack the moral judgment of adults. Many children are only dimly aware of the consequences of their actions, and, as parents know, they are excellent mimics. They often imitate violence they see on TV, without necessarily understanding what they are doing or what the consequences might be. One 5-year-old boy from Boston recently got up from watching a teen-slasher film and stabbed a 2-year-old girl with a butcher knife. He didn't mean to kill her (and luckily he did not). He was just imitating the man in the video.

Nor does the danger end as children grow older. National health officials tell us that children younger than teen-agers are apt to react to excessive violence with suicide, satanism, drug and alcohol abuse. Even grown-ups are not immune. One series of studies by researchers at the University of Wisconsin found that men exposed to films in which women are beaten, butchered, maimed and raped were significantly desensitized to the violence. Not only did they express less sympathy for the victims, they even approved of lesser penalties in hypothetical rape trials.

Sado-masochistic pornography is a kind of poison. Like most 9 poisons, it probably cannot be totally eliminated, but it certainly could be labeled for what it is and be kept away from those who are most vulnerable. The largest record companies have agreed to this—in principle at least. In November 1985, the Recording Industry Association of America adopted my proposal to alert parents by having producers either put warning labels on records with explicitly sexual lyrics or display the lyrics on the outside of the record jackets. Since then, some companies have complied in good faith, although others have not complied at all.

This is where we parents must step in. We must let the industry 10 know we're angry. We must press for uniform voluntary compliance with labeling guidelines. And we must take an active interest at home in what our children are watching and listening to. After all, we can hardly expect that the labels or printed lyrics alone will discourage young consumers.

Some parents may want to write to the record companies. Others 11 can give their support to groups like the Parent Teacher Association, which have endorsed the labeling idea. All of us can use our purchasing power. We have more power than we think, and we must use it. For the sake of our children, we simply can't afford to slip back into apathy.

My concern for the health and welfare of children has nothing 12 to do with politics: It is addressed to conservatives and liberals alike. Some civil libertarians believe it is wrong even to raise these questions—just as some conservatives believe that the Government should police popular American culture. I reject both these views. I have no desire to restrain artists or cast a "chill" over popular culture. But I believe parents have First Amendment rights, too.

The fate of the family, the dignity of women, the mental health 13 of children—these concerns belong to everyone. We must protect our children with choice, not censorship. Let's start working in our communities to forge a moral consensus for the 1990's. Children need our help, and we must summon the courage to examine the culture that shapes their lives.

Questions on Subject

1. In the first paragraph of her essay, Gore makes it clear that she is not an advocate of censorship. What is she advocating in the essay?
2. What are the two steps Gore says must be taken to "curb the sexploitation industry"? Who does she seek to enlist in the campaign to curb "sexploitation"?
3. Gore argues that graphic violence is damaging to small children "because they lack the moral judgment of adults." In your own words, explain what you think Gore means by this.
4. Gore describes some of the actions that parents can take to convey to the record industry their anger about violence in contemporary music. Which of these measures do you think would be the most effective? Why?

Questions on Strategy

1. In presenting an argument, writers use rhetorical strategies such as definition, cause and effect, and narration. What rhetorical strategy does Gore use in her argument? How appropriate is it for her particular argument? Would one of the other rhetorical strategies have worked just as well? Explain.
2. Why does the author include so many examples of the results of explicit violence in music and films in her essay? What is your reaction to these examples? (Glossary: *Examples*)
3. Reread the beginning and ending paragraphs of Gore's essay, in which she acknowledges the fierce opposition to her suggestion of labeling rock music album covers. Are these paragraphs necessary? Do they work to strengthen or to weaken her argument? Explain. (Glossary: *Beginnings/Endings*)
4. How has Gore organized the evidence for her argument? Make a scratch outline of the essay. (Glossary: *Organization*)

Questions on Diction and Vocabulary

1. Who is Gore's audience? How do you know? How has the author adapted the tone of her essay to suit her audience? Is her tone angry, resigned, objective, or something else? Select examples of

her diction from the text to support your answer. (Glossary: *Audience; Tone*)

2. In the title of this essay, Gore coins the word *sexploitation*. What effect did this word have on you when you read it for the first time? Did it convey from the start the main idea of the essay or did it mainly serve to attract your attention? Explain.

3. Refer to your desk dictionary to determine the meanings of the following words as they are used in this selection: *prude* (paragraph 1), *candid* (1), *explicit* (3), *apathetic* (4), *sado-masochism* (5), *titillate* (6), *hypothetical* (8), *pornography* (9), *consensus* (13).

Writing Assignments

1. Parents groups have attempted and sometimes succeeded in banning certain books from school libraries. Even books like *Huckleberry Finn* and *Catcher in the Rye* have been labeled by some as unfit for young minds. In a short essay, discuss whether you think Gore is guilty of this type of censorship or if she is merely advocating her right to free expression as put forth in the First Amendment. As you reflect on this issue, consider what Gore sees as the result of her efforts. Can she be accused of censorship if she does not call for the outright banning of rock music? Or is the labeling of someone else's written expression a denial of the First Amendment? You may even consider reading the First Amendment to the U.S. Constitution before you begin writing.

2. Should rock and roll stations be allowed to play any music they want to? Many college radio stations, because they are noncommercial, are free to broadcast whatever they choose, limited only by the school's administrative policies. What are your thoughts on this issue? In a short essay, present your argument for or against unrestrained air time for rock music that includes sexually and violently explicit lyrics.

A Little Banning Is a Dangerous Thing
Loudon Wainwright

Loudon Wainwright is a native New Yorker and a graduate of the University of North Carolina. After leaving the Marine Corps in 1945, Wainwright began a career at Life *magazine, where he worked as a writer, assistant picture editor, articles editor, and, until his retirement, assistant managing editor. He still writes "A View from Here,"* Life's *first and longest-running column, in which he deals with topics as diverse as drug abuse and censorship. In 1986 he wrote* The Great American Magazine: An *Inside* Story of "Life" *based on his long association with the magazine.*

In the following essay originally published in Life *in 1982, Wainwright argues against censorship from a unique perspective. Instead of following the more common argument that defends the First Amendment, Wainwright indulges in a wittily perverse harangue, claiming that the censors simply don't know what they are talking about.*

My own introduction to sex in reading took place about 1935, I think, just when the fertile soil of my young mind was ripe for planting. The exact place it happened (so I've discovered from checking the source in my local library) was the middle of page 249, in a chapter titled "Apples and Ashes," soon after the beginning of Book III of a mildly picaresque novel called *Anthony Adverse.* The boy Anthony, 16, and a well-constructed character named Faith Paleologus ("Her shoulders if one looked carefully were too wide. But so superb was the bosom that rose up to support them. . . .") made it right there in her apartment where he'd gone to take a quick bath, thinking (ho-ho) that she was out.

Faith was Anthony's sitter, sort of, and if author Hervey Allen was just a touch obscure about the details of their moon-drenched meeting, I filled in the gaps. "He was just in time," Allen wrote, "to see the folds of her dress rustle down from her knees into coils at her feet. . . . He stood still, rooted. The faint aroma of her body floated to him. A sudden tide of passion dragged at his legs. . . . He was half blind, and speechless now. All his senses had merged into one feeling. . . . To be supported and yet possessed by an ocean of unknown blue depths below you and to cease to think! Yes, it was something like swimming on a transcendent summer night."

Wow! Praying that my parents wouldn't come home and catch 3 me reading this terrific stuff, I splashed ahead, line after vaguely lubricious line, exhilarated out of my mind at Anthony's good fortune. "After a while he was just drifting in a continuous current of ecstasy that penetrated him as if he were part of the current in which he lay." I still don't understand *that* line, but I sure feel the old surge of depravity. And reading it again, I thank God there was no righteous book banner around at the time to snatch it from me. *Anthony Adverse* doesn't rank as literature, or even required reading, but I'm convinced it served a useful, even educational, purpose for me at the time.

Alert vigilantes of the printed word worked hard to suppress 4 the novel then. The wretched little war to keep the minds of children clean is always going on. In fact, it has heated up considerably since President Reagan came to power, with libraries around the country reporting a threefold increase in demands that various volumes even less ruinous than *Anthony Adverse* be withdrawn. School boards, too, are feeling the cleansing fire of assorted crusaders against dirty words and irreverent expressions of one sort or another. Protesters range from outraged individual parents to teachers to local ministers to such well-organized watchdog outfits as the Gabler family of Texas, Washington's Heritage Foundation and, of course, the Moral Majority.

The victims are fighting back. Writers are leading public "read- 5 ins" of their banned works. One school board case, which actually dates to 1976, has gone all the way to the U.S. Supreme Court. Before the end of the current term, the court is expected to rule on whether or not the First Amendment rights (to free expression) of five students in Island Trees, N.Y., were denied when the board took nine books out of circulation. A far more personal thrust against censorship was made recently by author Studs Terkel. At the news that his book *Working* was in danger of being banned in

Girard, Pa., Terkel went there and standing before the whole school in assembly made his own eloquent case for the book, for the so-called bad language in it and for reading in general. Six weeks later the school board voted unanimously to keep *Working* in the reading program where it had initially been challenged. Presumably they were persuaded, in part at least, that Terkel was *not*, as Kurt Vonnegut wrote in a furious and funny defense of his own *Slaughterhouse-Five*, one of those "sort of ratlike people who enjoy making money from poisoning the minds of young people."

What gets me is the weird presumption that the book banners 6 actually know something about the minds of young people. Vonnegut, among others, suspects that a lot of censors never even get around to reading the books they suppress. And just the briefest scanning of the list of titles currently banned or under threat in various communities calls the banners' credentials to rude question. *The Scarlet Letter, The Great Gatsby, A Farewell to Arms, Huckleberry Finn, The Grapes of Wrath* are a few of the variously seminal works challenged as somehow being dangerous to the stability of impressionable young minds. *Mary Poppins* and *The American Heritage Dictionary* have been under attack, too, the former after protests that its black characters were stereotypes, the latter presumably as a storehouse of words that shouldn't be viewed by innocent eyes, much less defined.

More critically, the censors forget, if they ever knew, many of 7 the needs of childhood. One, obviously, is the need for privacy, for a place to get away from the real world, a place where one is safe from—among other things—difficult or boring adult demands. The world that a reader makes is a perfect secret world. But if its topography is shaped by adults pushing their own hardened views of life, the secret world is spoiled.

Yet the world of the young human mind is by no means a comfy 8 habitat, as much as a lot of interfering adults would like to shape it that way. In *The Uses of Enchantment*, Bruno Bettelheim's book about the great importance of folk and fairy tales to child development, the author writes: "There is a widespread refusal to let children know that the source of much that goes wrong in life is due to our very own natures—the propensity of all men for acting aggressively, asocially, selfishly, out of anger and anxiety. Instead, we want our children to believe that, inherently, all men are good.

But children know that *they* are not always good; and often, even when they are, they would prefer not to be." In the fantasies commonly churned out in the mind of a normal child, whatever that is, bloody acts of revenge and conquest, daredevil assaults and outlandish wooings are common currency. To achieve the bleak, cramped, sanitized, fear-ridden state of many adults takes years of pruning and repression.

Books, as everyone but the censors knows, stimulate growth 9 better than anything—better than sit-coms, better than *Raiders of the Lost Ark,* better than video games. Many books, to be sure, are dreadful heaps of trash. But most of these die quickly in the marketplace or become best-sellers incapable of harming the adults who buy them.

It's often the best books that draw the beadiest attention of the 10 censors. These are the books that really have the most to offer, the news that life is rich and complicated and difficult. Where else, for example, could a young male reader see the isolation of his painful adolescence reflected the way it is in *The Catcher in the Rye,* one of the *most* banned books in American letters. In the guise of fiction, books offer opportunities, choices and plausible models. They light up the whole range of human character and emotion. Each, in its own way, tells the truth and prepares its eager readers for the unknown and unpredictable events of their own lives.

Anthony Adverse, my first banned book, was just a huge potboiler 11 of the period. Still, it tickled my fantasy. And it sharpened my appetite for better stuff, like *Lady Chatterley's Lover.* Actually I didn't read that tender and wonderful book until I was almost 50. I wish I'd read it much sooner while we were both still hot.

Questions on Subject

1. In paragraphs 6 and 7, Wainwright discusses what censors don't know about children. What does he say? What do children know about themselves? Do you agree? Why, or why not?
2. What, according to Wainwright, can books offer children that television and movies cannot?
3. What kind of books draw the most opposition from banners, according to the author?

4. Who are the banners of books? What kind of people are they? What do they want to accomplish?
5. Wainwright claims that reading *Anthony Adverse* "served a useful, even educational, purpose for me at the time" (paragraph 3). What was that purpose? Where is it stated?

Questions on Strategy

1. What is Wainwright's purpose in writing this essay? (Glossary: *Purpose*)
2. The title of this essay is a variation of the popular expression, "A little knowledge is a dangerous thing." What does this expression mean? How does it relate to the title of the essay? Is Wainwright's title a good choice for his essay? Why, or why not?
3. In the first three paragraphs of the essay, Wainwright describes in detail some of the scenes from the novel *Anthony Adverse*. Then, in the last paragraph, he refers to it again as well as to *Lady Chatterley's Lover*, another highly controversial book. The author's references to these books are likely to reinforce the book banners' position that young minds should be kept away from "dirty" books. How did you respond to these paragraphs? Why do you think Wainwright begins and ends his essay in this way? (Glossary: *Beginnings/Endings*)
4. Wainwright quotes only one expert in his essay. Who is that expert? Why is he a reliable authority for the issues raised in the essay?

Questions on Diction and Vocabulary

1. The tone of Wainwright's essay could be described as perverse or mocking. Cite examples of the author's choice of words and phrases that show how he creates this tone. (Glossary: *Tone; Diction*)
2. Refer to your desk dictionary to determine the meanings of the following words as they are used in this selection: *picaresque* (paragraph 1), *lubricious* (3), *ecstasy* (3), *depravity* (3), *vigilantes* (4), *potboiler* (11).

Writing Assignments

1. Bruno Bettelheim has cited the importance of fairy tales to children and chided those who "want our children to believe that, inher-

ently, all men are good. But children know that *they* are not always good; and often, even when they are, they would prefer not to be." Wainwright quotes Bettelheim to support his idea that children understand their nature better than the censors do. In fact, Wainwright argues, by keeping children from the kinds of books that they are drawn to by nature, censors are committing an unnatural act. What is your opinion? Are children wise about the kinds of information they can handle? Keep in mind Wainwright's reference to *Anthony Adverse* and the part it played in his education just when he was "ripe for planting." Did you have a similar experience at a young age? Were such books helpful to you? Discuss your position on this issue in an essay.

2. Wainwright's essay is unusual and entertaining because it focuses on the censors rather than on the books they want to ban. Write an essay in which you respond to Wainwright's argument from the censors' perspective. Try, like Wainwright, to make the argument unusual or unexpected. You may find it helpful to reread Paul Roberts's "How to Say Nothing in 500 Words" (page 211) for tips on making your essay fresh and colorful.

Teach Diversity—with a Smile

Barbara Ehrenreich

Born in 1941, Barbara Ehrenreich graduated from Reed College and earned her Ph.D. in biology from Rockefeller University in 1968. Before beginning her writing career, she taught classes in women's studies at New York University and State University of New York. Since 1982, Ehrenreich has been a fellow of the Institute for Policy Studies in Washington, D.C. Ehrenreich is active in the Democratic Socialists of America and the women's movement, and her writing on women's issues is considered among the most vital and relevant to the feminist cause. Her books include For Her Own Good: 150 Years of the Experts' Advice to Women *(with Deirdre English);* The Hearts of Men: American Dreams and the Flight from Commitment; *and* Re-Making Love: The Feminization of Sex *with Elizabeth Hess and Gloria Jacobs. She is a frequent contributor to* Ms., Mother Jones, Esquire, *and the* New York Times.*

In the following essay, which first appeared in the April 8, 1991, issue of Time, *Ehrenreich argues in favor of cultural diversity and against political correctness.*

Something had to replace the threat of communism, and at last   1
a workable substitute is at hand. "Multiculturalism," as the new
menace is known, has been denounced in the media recently as
the new McCarthyism, the new fundamentalism, even the new
totalitarianism—take your choice. According to its critics, who include a flock of tenured conservative scholars, multiculturalism
aims to toss out what it sees as the Eurocentric bias in education
and replace Plato with Ntozake Shange and traditional math with
the Yoruba number system. And that's just the beginning. The

490

Jacobins of the multiculturalist movement, who are described de-
risively as P.C., or politically correct, are said to have launched a
campus reign of terror against those who slip and innocently say
"freshman" instead of "freshperson," "Indian" instead of "Native
American" or, may the Goddess forgive them, "disabled" instead
of "differently abled."

So you can see what is at stake here: freedom of speech, freedom   2
of thought, Western civilization and a great many professorial
egos. But before we get carried away by the mounting backlash
against multiculturalism, we ought to reflect for a moment on the
system that the P.C. people aim to replace. I know all about it; in
fact it's just about all I *do* know, since I—along with so many
educated white people of my generation—was a victim of
monoculturalism.

American history, as it was taught to us, began with Columbus'   3
"discovery" of an apparently unnamed, unpeopled America, and
moved on to the Pilgrims serving pumpkin pie to a handful of
grateful red-skinned folks. College expanded our horizons with
courses called Humanities or sometimes Civ, which introduced us
to a line of thought that started with Homer, worked its way
through Rabelais and reached a poignant climax in the pensées of
Matthew Arnold. Graduate students wrote dissertations on what
long-dead men had thought of Chaucer's verse or Shakespeare's
dramas; foreign languages meant French or German. If there had
been high technology in ancient China, kingdoms in black Africa
or women anywhere, at any time, doing anything worth noticing,
we did not know it, nor did anyone think to tell us.

Our families and neighborhoods reinforced the dogma of mon-   4
oculturalism. In our heads, most of us '50s teenagers carried
around a social map that was about as useful as the chart that
guided Columbus to the "Indies." There were "Negroes,"
"whites" and "Orientals," the latter meaning Chinese and "Japs."
Of religions, only three were known—Protestant, Catholic and
Jewish—and not much was known about the last two types. The
only remaining human categories were husbands and wives, and
that was all the diversity the monocultural world could handle.
Gays, lesbians, Buddhists, Muslims, Malaysians, Mormons, etc.
were simply off the map.

So I applaud—with one hand, anyway—the multiculturalist goal   5 of preparing us all for a wider world. The other hand is tapping its fingers impatiently, because the critics are right about one thing: when advocates of multiculturalism adopt the haughty stance of political correctness, they quickly descend to silliness or worse. It's obnoxious, for example, to rely on university administrations to enforce P.C. standards of verbal inoffensiveness. Racist, sexist and homophobic thoughts cannot, alas, be abolished by fiat but only by the time-honored methods of persuasion, education and exposure to the other guy's—or, excuse me, woman's—point of view.

And it's silly to mistake verbal purification for genuine social reform. Even after all women are "Ms." and all people are "he or she," women will still earn only 65¢ for every dollar earned by men. Minorities by any other name, such as "people of color," will still bear a hugely disproportionate burden of poverty and discrimination. Disabilities are not just "different abilities" when there are not enough ramps for wheelchairs, signers for the deaf or special classes for the "specially" endowed. With all due respect for the new politesse, actions still speak louder than fashionable phrases. 6

But the worst thing about the P.C. people is that they are such poor advocates for the multicultural cause. No one was ever won over to a broader, more inclusive view of life by being bullied or relentlessly "corrected." Tell a 19-year-old white male that he can't say "girl" when he means "teen-age woman," and he will most likely snicker. This may be the reason why, despite the conservative alarms, P.C.-ness remains a relatively tiny trend. Most campuses have more serious and ancient problems: faculties still top-heavy with white males of the monocultural persuasion; fraternities that harass minorities and women; date rape; alcohol abuse; and tuition that excludes all but the upper fringe of the middle class. 7

So both sides would be well advised to lighten up. The conservatives ought to realize that criticisms of the great books approach to learning do not amount to totalitarianism. And the advocates of multiculturalism need to regain the sense of humor that enabled their predecessors in the struggle to coin the term P.C. years ago—not in arrogance but in self-mockery. 8

Beyond that, both sides should realize that the beneficiaries of multiculturalism are not only the "oppressed peoples" on the stan- 9 dard P.C. list (minorities, gays, etc.). The "unenlightened"—the victims of monoculturalism—are oppressed too, or at least deprived. Our educations, whether at Yale or at State U, were narrow and parochial and left us ill-equipped to navigate a society that truly is multicultural and is becoming more so every day. The culture that we studied was, in fact, *one* culture and, from a world perspective, all too limited and ingrown. Diversity is challenging, but those of us who have seen the alternative know it is also richer, livelier and ultimately more fun.

Questions on Subject

1. What is monoculturalism? Multiculturalism?
2. How would you define the two sides in the multicultural debate? What three major objections to the politically correct position does Ehrenreich give?
3. According to Ehrenreich, what is a major problem with politically correct speech? Why does she believe that the P.C. are poor advocates for the multicultural cause?
4. What exactly does Ehrenreich want the two sides in the multicultural debate to do? How do you know?
5. According to Ehrenreich, what are the benefits of multiculturalism?

Questions on Strategy

1. Who is Ehrenreich's audience? (Glossary: *Audience*) How do you know?
2. Does Ehrenreich intend her essay to persuade or to inform? (Glossary: *Purpose*)
3. Ehrenreich clearly favors cultural diversity. Then what does she gain by her uncompromising attack on the P.C.? What kinds of evidence does she use to maintain the strength of her argument while she seemingly disagrees with an advocate of her cause?
4. Does Ehrenreich rely more on persuasive appeals or logic to make her point? Cite examples of each, and discuss which kind you find more convincing.
5. What kinds of evidence does Ehrenreich use to define mono- and multiculturalism?

Questions on Diction and Vocabulary

1. Ehrenreich makes frequent use of sarcasm and exaggeration in her essay. Cite examples of this strategy. In what ways is her tone appropriate for her subject and audience? (Glossary: *Tone*)
2. What kind of information does Ehrenreich include in the quotations she uses in her essay?
3. Refer to your desk dictionary to determine the meanings of the following words as they are used in this selection: *menace* (paragraph 1), *backlash* (2), *dogma* (4), *haughty* (5), *stance* (5), *purification* (6), *politesse* (6), *advocates* (7), *trend* (7), *arrogance* (8), *parochial* (9).

Writing Suggestions

1. Across the country, college campuses are struggling with the issue of "cultural diversity." Students representing minority groups are insisting not only that schools offer ethnic studies, but that student enrollment be representative of the races and cultures living in the population at large. Write an essay for your college newspaper in which you take a position either for or against this position. Keep in mind that your audience will be an academic one. What kind of evidence will you use? In what ways will your evidence differ from the kinds of evidence you might use for a more general readership?
2. In her argument in favor of cultural diversity, Ehrenreich argues the position of the opposition almost as strongly as she argues her own. Choose a controversial subject of particular interest to you. Then, using Ehrenreich's essay as a model, present the leading arguments on both sides of the issue while still maintaining your point of view.

The Cult of Ethnicity, Good and Bad

Arthur Schlesinger, Jr.

*An active member of the Democratic party, Arthur Schle-
singer, Jr., came to prominence in 1961 when President John
F. Kennedy appointed him as his special assistant for Latin
American affairs.* A Thousand Days *(1965), Schlesinger's
book on Kennedy during his White House years, won a Pulitzer
prize for biography. In addition to being a professor at the City
University of New York, Schlesinger is widely recognized for
his books on American history.*

In the following essay, which first appeared in Time, *Schlesinger argues that the premise upon which our democracy was
founded is being threatened by the steady "tribalization" of
our culture along ethnic lines.*

The history of the world has been in great part the history of   1
the mixing of peoples. Modern communication and transport accelerate mass migrations from one continent to another. Ethnic and
racial diversity is more than ever a salient fact of the age.

But what happens when people of different origins, speaking   2
different languages and professing different religions, inhabit the
same locality and live under the same political sovereignty? Ethnic
and racial conflict—far more than ideological conflict—is the explosive problem of our times.

On every side today ethnicity is breaking up nations. The Soviet   3
Union, India, Yugoslavia, Ethiopia, are all in crisis. Ethnic tensions
disturb and divide Sri Lanka, Burma, Indonesia, Iraq, Cyprus, Ni-
geria, Angola, Lebanon, Guyana, Trinidad—you name it. Even
nations as stable and civilized as Britain and France, Belgium and
Spain, face growing ethnic troubles. Is there any large multiethnic
state that can be made to work?

The answer to that question has been, until recently, the United   4
States. "No other nation," Margaret Thatcher has said, "has so
successfully combined people of different races and nations within

a single culture." How have Americans succeeded in pulling off this almost unprecedented trick?

We have always been a multiethnic country. Hector St. John de Crèvecoeur, who came from France in the 18th century, marveled at the astonishing diversity of the settlers—"a mixture of English, Scotch, Irish, French, Dutch, Germans and Swedes . . . this promiscuous breed." He propounded a famous question: "What then is the American, this new man?" And he gave a famous answer: "Here individuals of all nations are melted into a new race of men." *E pluribus unum.*

The U.S. escaped the divisiveness of a multiethnic society by a brilliant solution: the creation of a brand-new national identity. The point of America was not to preserve old cultures but to forge a new, *American* culture. "By an inter-mixture with our people," President George Washington told Vice President John Adams, immigrants will "get assimilated to our customs, measures and laws: in a word, soon become one people." This was the ideal that a century later Israel Zangwill crystallized in the title of his popular 1908 play *The Melting Pot.* And no institution was more potent in molding Crèvecoeur's "promiscuous breed" into Washington's "one people" than the American public school.

The new American nationality was inescapably English in language, ideas and institutions. The pot did not melt everybody, not even all the white immigrants; deeply bred racism put black Americans, yellow Americans, red Americans and brown Americans well outside the pale. Still, the infusion of other stocks, even of nonwhite stocks, and the experience of the New World reconfigured the British legacy and made the U.S., as we all know, a very different country from Britain.

In the 20th century, new immigration laws altered the composition of the American people, and a cult of ethnicity erupted both among non-Anglo whites and among nonwhite minorities. This had many healthy consequences. The American culture at last began to give shamefully overdue recognition to the achievements of groups subordinated and spurned during the high noon of Anglo dominance, and it began to acknowledge the great swirling world beyond Europe. Americans acquired a more complex and invigorating sense of their world—and of themselves.

But, pressed too far, the cult of ethnicity has unhealthy consequences. It gives rise, for example, to the conception of the U.S. as a nation composed not of individuals making their own choices but of inviolable ethnic and racial groups. It rejects the historic American goals of assimilation and integration. And, in an excess of zeal, well-intentioned people seek to transform our system of education from a means of creating "one people" into a means of promoting, celebrating and perpetuating separate ethnic origins and identities. The balance is shifting from *unum* to *pluribus*.

That is the issue that lies behind the hullabaloo over "multicul- 10 turalism" and "political correctness," the attack on the "Eurocentric" curriculum and the rise of the notion that history and literature should be taught not as disciplines but as therapies whose function is to raise minority self-esteem. Group separatism crystallizes the differences, magnifies tensions, intensifies hostilities. Europe—the unique source of the liberating ideas of democrary, civil liberties and human rights—is portrayed as the root of all evil, and non-European cultures, their own many crimes deleted, are presented as the means of redemption.

I don't want to sound apocalyptic about these developments. 11 Education is always in ferment, and a good thing too. The situation in our universities, I am confident, will soon right itself. But the impact of separatist pressures on our public schools is more troubling. If a Kleagle of the Ku Klux Klan wanted to use the schools to disable and handicap black Americans, he could hardly come up with anything more effective than the "Afrocentric" curriculum. And if separatist tendencies go unchecked, the result can only be the fragmentation, resegregation and tribalization of American life.

I remain optimistic. My impression is that the historic forces 12 driving toward "one people" have not lost their power. The eruption of ethnicity is, I believe, a rather superficial enthusiasm stirred by romantic ideologues on the one hand and by unscrupulous con men on the other: self-appointed spokesmen whose claim to represent their minority groups is carelessly accepted by the media. Most American-born members of minority groups, white or non-white, see themselves primarily as Americans rather than primarily as members of one or another ethnic group. A notable indicator today is the rate of intermarriage across ethnic lines, across religious lines, even (increasingly) across racial lines. "We Americans," said Theodore Roosevelt, "are children of the crucible."

The growing diversity of the American population makes the quest for unifying ideals and a common culture all the more urgent. In a world savagely rent by ethnic and racial antagonisms, the U.S. must continue as an example of how a highly differentiated society holds itself together. 13

Questions on Subject

1. Until recently, how has the United States managed to avoid the conflict of ethnicity?
2. What have been the positive effects of the new "ethnicity"? the negative? What does Schlesinger say are the long-term results of an escalating ethnicity?
3. How does Schlesinger defend the "Eurocentric" curriculum?
4. What forces have precipitated the eruption of ethnicity?
5. In paragraph 11, Schlesinger makes a shocking assertion. What is it, and what does he mean by it?
6. According to Schlesinger, what signs are there that most American-born members of minority groups consider themselves primarily "American" rather than as members of a minority group?

Questions on Strategy

1. What is Schlesinger's thesis, and where is it stated? (Glossary: *Thesis*)
2. Construct the syllogism that provides the framework for Schlesinger's argument. (Glossary: *Syllogism*) In your opinion, is it logical?
3. Schlesinger says the eruption of ethnicity is a "superficial enthusiasm" (paragraph 12). If so, then what do you suppose is his purpose in writing this essay? (Glossary: *Purpose*)
4. Schlesinger makes several strong assertions in his essay. Cite several of those assertions, and discuss what kinds of evidence, if any, he uses to support them. Which kinds of evidence did you find the most convincing? the least convincing? (Glossary: *Evidence*)

Questions on Diction and Vocabulary

1. In paragraph 11, Schlesinger says he doesn't want to sound "apocalyptic." What is his tone in this essay? (Glossary: *Tone*) Is it apocalyptic, resentful, angry, or is it something else?
2. Discuss Schlesinger's use of the term *E pluribus unum* in making his point.
3. Refer to your desk dictionary to determine the meanings of the following words as they are used in this selection: *accelerate* (paragraph 1), *salient* (1), *sovereignty* (2), *ideological* (2), *promiscuous* (5), *propounded* (5), *assimilated* (6), *pale* (7), *infusion* (7), *reconfigured* (7), *spurned* (8), *inviolable* (9), *hullabaloo* (10), *redemption* (10), *apocalyptic* (11), *ferment* (11), *tribalization* (11), *unscrupulous* (12), *crucible* (12), *quest* (13).

Writing Suggestions

1. Write an essay in which you elaborate on Schlesinger's assertion that the public school, more than any other American institution, has contributed to the molding of the American people. What kinds of evidence will you need to introduce to make your argument convincing to your reader?
2. Argue against Schlesinger's central point that an increased ethnicity is threatening the great American melting pot. Perhaps you can begin with the examples of the benefits of diversity that he points out in paragraph 8. Or you could offer evidence to show that Schlesinger is mistaken in his fears and that the melting pot is no better or worse off than it has ever been.

Can Our Son Beat the Odds?

TaRessa Stovall

> TaRessa Stovall has worked as a television producer, a magazine editor, a freelance feature writer, and a public relations consultant. A Seattle native, Stovall earned her B.A. in communications at The Evergreen State College in Olympia, Washington. She served as a speech writer for Health and Human Services Secretary Louis W. Sullivan and has coauthored (with Ray Garrett) a book on health care, Catching Good Health (1986). She has published poetry, had several of her plays produced on the West Coast and in the Midwest, and is currently working on her first novel. "I am pleased to report," said Stovall recently, "that Calvin, named after his wonderful Daddy, made it through the first year of life in very good shape."
>
> In the following essay, which first appeared in USA Weekend in July 1991, Stovall reflects on the problems that she and her husband face in trying to raise a new son to thrive in a hard world.

1   Amid distressing reports about the disadvantages, the dire future, the virtual demise of African-American men, I am becoming the mother of a member of this "endangered" species.

2   As you read this, I will be holding in my arms a newly born boy. While my husband and I face the perplexing challenges of raising a healthy, happy kid—a formidable task for all parents—we also face the statistical improbability of rearing a physically, mentally and psychologically fit black male to adulthood in 21st-century America.

3   By every measure, the odds are against us. Statistics show that our son is more likely to die from anything from infant mortality to urban warfare, less likely to flourish in school, more likely to be the perpetrator or victim of a violent crime, less likely to attend college, more likely to go to prison and more likely to meet a tragic end at an early age than any nonblack person, male or female. Yet

it is impossible to hear his heartbeat, to feel him kicking and growing within me and not believe that he can overcome these odds.

He comes from a family of exceptional men. His father is a successful, responsible black man, committed to his family and able to negotiate the maze of racism with his dignity intact. But this man was brought up nearly 40 years ago in a predominantly black environment in the rural South, part of a loving extended family with ironclad values. Our son will be born in the nation's capital, where black youths destroy their communities and themselves with regularity.

He'll enter the world at a time when separate classrooms are being formed for black boys to counter the damage caused by many teachers' belief that, because of race and sex, these kids have learning disabilities and behavior problems.

Our child could be aided by being born to educated professionals with strong identities and some political savvy. But we don't fool ourselves that this will tip the scales more than a millimeter or two in his favor.

As new parents about to negotiate the intricacies of bonding and potty-training, we must devise strategies to equip our son to thrive in a world that seems to negate the value of his existence. As we teach him to read and reason, we must counter the onslaught of messages that he is a "minority" (definition: "less than") with images of black folks whose achievements have made an impact on the world. We must teach him to stand up and fight for his rights.

Before he learns history in school, he must know that, while he is a descendant of slaves, he is just as likely to bear the blood of African rulers, scientists, artists and scholars.

As we teach him to wear seat belts and look both ways before crossing the street, we must help him mix confidence with caution to navigate the avenues and alleys of his neighborhood, his nation and the world. We'll expose him to methods of self-defense. And we'll hope against hope that he won't be attacked for a few dollars or an item of clothing.

We must find rites of passage to discourage him from defining himself through self-destruction. We hope he'll follow athletic or artistic pursuits instead of joining a gang, find enough pleasure in life to resist the allure of drugs.

The problems are obvious; the solutions are not. We will res- 11
urrect old traditions, like respect for elders and courtesy to women,
and invent new ones. We'll try to balance the propaganda of
"mainstream" culture with Afrocentric affirmations. Anything to
nurture this precious being into a man of courage and character,
love and laughter, purpose and pride.

And despite the mythology likening black men to modern-day 12
dinosaurs, we cannot afford to believe this baby is being born for
naught. His very existence is an affirmation of power; his every
movement is a sign that he is but the latest in a long line of survivors. He is a budding miracle. As Alice Walker wrote, "The nature of this flower is to bloom."

Questions on Subject

1. Where in her essay does Stovall observe that black men have actually lost ground in their fight for survival?
2. How does Stovall explain the fact that although her son will be
   born into an educated, enlightened family, he still faces the same
   odds as a black child born into an impoverished and uneducated
   family?
3. What strategies does Stovall plan to use to balance the "propaganda of 'mainstream' culture" (paragraph 11)? Which do you
   think will be the most effective? the least effective?
4. How many of the dangers Stovall's son faces do you think might
   be shared by young men in the "mainstream" culture she refers
   to? Explain.
5. In what way is the author's son an "affirmation of power"?

Questions on Strategy

1. Stovall asks a question in her title. How does she answer it? How
   would you answer it?
2. Comment on Stovall's use of parallelism in her essay. (Glossary:
   Parallelism) In what way does it strengthen her argument?
3. What is Stovall's purpose in writing this essay? (Glossary: *Purpose*)
   What, if anything, does she expect her reader to do?
4. What do paragraphs 1 and 12 have in common? How well do they

function as a beginning and ending to Stovall's essay? Explain. (Glossary: *Beginnings and Endings*)

Questions on Diction and Vocabulary

1. Comment on Stovall's use of the words *endangered* (1) and *minority* (7). In what way, if any, is her intended use of these words unexpected?
2. Refer to your desk dictionary to determine the meanings of the following words as they are used in this selection: *dire* (paragraph 1), *formidable* (2), *flourish* (3), *perpetrator* (3), *maze* (4), *ironclad* (4), *savvy* (6), *allure* (10), *naught* (12).

Writing Suggestions

1. In her essay, Stovall refers to several strategies she will use to compensate for the deficiencies of the culture in which her son will grow up. However, in most cases she does not identify those deficiencies directly. In an essay of your own, draw a profile of the white culture that Stovall describes by implication.
2. Stovall's insistence that her son will have to be educated in his African heritage could be taken as a rebuttal of the argument Arthur Schlesinger uses in "The Cult of Ethnicity: Good and Bad" that a growing "cult of ethnicity" is unraveling the fabric of the American culture. Write an essay in which you argue either for or against Stovall's point of view as it relates to Schlesinger's argument.

On Our Own: The Black Family

L. Douglas Wilder

L. Douglas Wilder, Democratic governor of Virginia, is the nation's first African-American governor. In 1991, while contemplating a run for the presidency, he announced he "would not object at all" to random drug testing of college students. This statement followed a federal raid of three University of Virginia fraternity houses.

In the following speech, which was reprinted in The Responsive Community *in 1991, Governor Wilder argues that "chastity" offers the best hope for young blacks to break the cycle of poverty, drug abuse, and death that plagues the American black family.*

Each and every day, we in Richmond, Virginia are burning the ¹ proverbial "midnight oil" to ensure that the youth and families of this state and nation are not burned beyond recognition as we enter the 21st Century. But we are no pollyannas. We know that gubernatorial proclamations, speeches, legislation and community involvement are no safety net for the free falling American family.

If we are to be brutally honest—ultimately—the families of this ² state and nation are going to have to do more *themselves* if the family unit is to have any hope of remaining intact and being rejuvenated in the 1990s and the 21st Century.

Recent surveys paint an extraordinarily bleak picture of today, ³ and of what tomorrow may hold for many black families across this nation. We need only look at one statistic with which many of you are probably all too aware: today approximately 1 in 4 young black males in America is behind bars; on parole; or on probation. According to this survey, 23 percent of black men 20 to 29 are under the watchful eye of the criminal justice system, while only 1 in 16 white, and 1 in 10 Hispanic males of the same age group have a similar, disturbing familiarity with the law.

And although an alarming number of young males are having ⁴

extreme difficulty staying clear of the law—and making a future for themselves through long hours of hard, honest work—all too many are having no problem whatsoever making babies. But contrary to what many of today's young people may believe, making babies is no act of manhood. Mere rats and rabbits are more virile than the most virile male in this country—teenagers and young people who insist upon clinging to the self-destructive doctrine of machismo, while forever ignoring the need to grow up.

More than ever, our young people must come to understand that: making mature decisions; making life-long commitments; making structured and loving families—rather than merely making babies; and making the most of the opportunities that *do* exist in every aspect of life; *these* are the actions which constitute the beginning of a passage into manhood; into adulthood.

How are this and future generations of children to re-dig the wells of their forefathers, when so many do not—and will not—know their own fathers; when they have no male role model to which they can look? Of course—given some of the lifestyles of many young fathers in this nation—it's actually *a blessing* that these fathers (and I use that term *only* in the biological sense) are not spending time with their children, lest the child suffer a fate *worse* than having no role model: looking to, and learning from, the *wrong* kind of role model.

And yet, tragically, the *only* male role models that many of our children ever see are those not working real jobs, but pushing and helping to push self-destruction in our neighborhoods. They have the jewelry; the cars; the girls. Some say that they *have* no future. But we know that they do—a future in jail; a future in an early grave.

As unfair as it may be, in light of absentee fathers, the responsibilities of being a parent in many instances fall to the financially and emotionally deserted, single mothers. Nationally, 55.3% of black families with children under 18 are maintained by the mother, many of them living in inner cities, *most of them single, rather than divorced*.

Worse yet, in many of the houses and apartments across this country headed by single, black females, we are witnessing a disturbing double-standard between what is expected of male and female children growing up under the same roof; with the latter often having household chores assigned to them; curfews imposed upon them; and greater expectations for academic success placed upon them; and the former rarely having little discipline; even less responsibility, and much later, *if any*, curfews imposed upon them in the course of daily life. Not surprisingly, as a result of this glaring dichotomy of experience during their formative years—at the same time that many young females are being encouraged to develop at least some of the skills needed to rise to the challenges of the class-room; adulthood; and eventual parenthood; many of their male counterparts have learned nothing more than the ways of the street, and the first names of all too many guards at city lock-up.

With many of our young males being exposed to this kind of 10 absentee parenting—a total lack of discipline and responsibility throughout their formative years—today, black men in inner city neighborhoods are less likely to reach 65 than men in Bangladesh, one of the poorest nations in the world. In 1990, tragically—and senselessly—*violence* is the leading cause of death for blacks be-tween the ages of 15 and 25. Given these statistics, it's no surprise that in many communities—*especially* inner-cities—the black family is teetering near the darkest abyss: self-destruction.

But—as common sense tells us—so much needless pain could 11 be avoided. There are precautions to be taken by the young and by the unmarried, especially for those who know that they are not remotely close to being ready for the unending responsibilities of parenthood.

Above all, if they want to have a future, it is imperative that our 12 young—male and female alike—embrace the *ultimate* precaution—abstinence. For as others have noted, "The *essence* of chastity is the total orientation of one's life *toward a goal*," and—in this instance—that goal must be a life of self-discipline; self-improvement; and an abiding spirit of selflessness—a willingness to work for the com-mon good of family and community alike; to take full advantage of all opportunities which do exist; and to make full use of the freedoms which are rightfully theirs.

If we are to improve the lot of this and future generations— 13 above all—we must constantly encourage our youth and families *to make lasting demands on themselves.*

Questions on Subject

1. How does Wilder describe the typical male role model for young blacks?
2. What is the "double standard" Wilder refers to in paragraph 9?
3. What is the leading cause of death among young black men?
4. How does Wilder define "manhood"?
5. What does Wilder say is the "ultimate precaution"? What is its essence? How does he expect the use of that precaution to save the American black family?

Questions on Strategy

1. What is Wilder's thesis? (Glossary: *Thesis*) Where is it stated?
2. How has Wilder organized his essay? (Glossary: *Organization*) You may find it helpful to outline the essay before answering this question.
3. What different kinds of evidence does Wilder use to support his argument? Does he offer enough evidence for each of his points? Which kinds of evidence did you find the most convincing? (Glossary: *Evidence*) Explain.
4. Who do you suppose Wilder intends for his audience? (Glossary: *Audience*) How do you know?

Questions on Diction and Vocabulary

1. What is the tone of Wilder's essay? (Glossary: *Tone*) In what way is it suitable to his subject and intended audience? Cite examples of his diction to support your answer.
2. Refer to your desk dictionary to determine the meanings of the following words as they are used in this selection: *probation* (paragraph 3), *virile* (4), *curfews* (9), *formative* (10), *teetering* (10), *imperative* (12), *chastity* (12), *abiding* (12).

Writing Suggestions

1. Wilder insists that "chastity" is the best hope the young black male has to help save the American black family. If "chastity" is not the

best answer to the problem, what is? Write an essay in which you agree or disagree with Wilder's argument. Who is your audience? What kinds of evidence will you need to provide to convince your audience?

2. Choose a social problem of significance to you and, as Wilder has done, advocate the single solution that you believe is the most likely to affect change for the better. For example, you might write about crime on your campus, the national budget deficit, political corruption, environmental pollution, or something else. Ask yourself what particular responsibilities arise for you as a writer when you decide to argue for only one solution to a problem.

The Case against Man

Isaac Asimov

> Born in the Soviet Union, Isaac Asimov emigrated to the
> United States in 1923. His death in April 1992 ended a long,
> prolific career as a science-fiction and nonfiction writer. Asi-
> mov was uniquely talented at making a diverse range of topics
> from Shakespeare to atomic physics, history, theories of time,
> the Bible, and detective fiction, not only comprehensible, but
> entertaining to the general reader. Asimov earned three degrees
> at Columbia University and later taught biochemistry at Bos-
> ton University. At the time of his death, he had published more
> than five hundred books.
>
> In the following essay, taken from Science Past–Science
> Future, Asimov warns his readers that the human population
> explosion is endangering all life forms, including our own.

The first mistake is to think of mankind as a thing in itself. It 1
isn't. It is part of an intricate web of life. And we can't think even
of life as a thing in itself. It isn't. It is part of the intricate structure
of a planet bathed by energy from the Sun.

The Earth, in the nearly 5 billion years since it assumed ap- 2
proximately its present form, has undergone a vast evolution.
When it first came into being, it very likely lacked what we would
today call an ocean and an atmosphere. These were formed by the
gradual outward movement of material as the solid interior settled
together.

Nor were ocean, atmosphere, and solid crust independent of 3
each other after formation. There is interaction always: evaporation, condensation, solution, weathering. Far within the solid crust
there are slow, continuing changes, too, of which hot springs, vol-

canoes, and earthquakes are the more noticeable manifestations here on the surface.

Between 2 billion and 3 billion years ago, portions of the surface water, bathed by the energetic radiation from the Sun, developed complicated compounds in organization sufficiently versatile to qualify as what we call "life." Life forms have become more complex and more various ever since. 4

But the life forms are as much part of the structure of the Earth as any inanimate portion is. It is all an inseparable part of a whole. If any animal is isolated totally from other forms of life, then death by starvation will surely follow. If isolated from water, death by dehydration will follow even faster. If isolated from air, whether free or dissolved in water, death by asphyxiation will follow still faster. If isolated from the Sun, animals will survive for a time, but plants would die, and if all plants died, all animals would starve. 5

It works in reverse, too, for the inanimate portion of Earth is shaped and molded by life. The nature of the atmosphere has been changed by plant activity (which adds to the air the free oxygen it could not otherwise retain). The soil is turned by earthworms, while enormous ocean reefs are formed by coral. 6

The entire planet, plus solar energy, is one enormous intricately interrelated system. The entire planet is a life form made up of nonliving portions and a large variety of living portions (as our own body is made up of nonliving crystals in bones and nonliving water in blood, as well as of a large variety of living portions). 7

In fact, we can pursue the analogy. A man is composed of 50 trillion cells of a variety of types, all interrelated and interdependent. Loss of some of those cells, such as those making up an entire leg, will seriously handicap all the rest of the organism: serious damage to a relatively few cells in an organ, such as the heart or kidneys, may end by killing all 50 trillion. 8

In the same way, on a planetary scale, the chopping down of an entire forest may not threaten Earth's life in general, but it will produce serious changes in the life forms of the region and even in the nature of the water runoff and, therefore, in the details of geological structure. A serious decline in the bee population will affect the numbers of those plants that depend on bees for fertilization, then the numbers of those animals that depend on those particular bee-fertilized plants, and so on. 9

Or consider cell growth. Cells in those organs that suffer constant 10 wear and tear—as in the skin or in the intestinal lining—grow and multiply all life long. Other cells, not so exposed, as in nerve and muscle, do not multiply at all in the adult, under any circumstances. Still other organs, ordinarily quiescent, as liver and bone, stand ready to grow if that is necessary to replace damage. When the proper repairs are made, growth stops.

In a much looser and more flexible way, the same is true of the 11 "planet organism" (which we study in the science called ecology). If cougars grow too numerous, the deer they live on are decimated, and some of the cougars die of starvation, so that their "proper number" is restored. If too many cougars die, then the deer multiply with particular rapidity, and cougars multiply quickly in turn, till the additional predators bring down the number of deer again. Barring interference from outside, the eaters and the eaten retain their proper numbers, and both are the better for it. (If the cougars are all killed off, deer would multiply to the point where they destroy the plants they live off, and more would then die of starvation than would have died of cougars.)

The neat economy of growth within an organism such as a 12 human being is sometimes—for what reason, we know not—disrupted, and a group of cells begins growing without limit. This is the dread disease of cancer, and unless that growing group of cells is somehow stopped, the wild growth will throw all the body structure out of true and end by killing the organism itself.

In ecology, the same would happen if, for some reason, one 13 particular type of organism began to multiply without limit, killing its competitors and increasing its own food supply at the expense of that of others. That, too, could end only in the destruction of the larger system—most or all of life and even of certain aspects of the inanimate environment.

And this is exactly what is happening at this moment. For thou- 14 sands of years, the single species Homo sapiens, to which you and I have the dubious honor of belonging, has been increasing in numbers. In the past couple of centuries, the rate of increase has itself increased explosively.

At the time of Julius Caesar, when Earth's human population is 15 estimated to have been 150 million, that population was increasing at a rate such that it would double in 1,000 years if that rate remained steady. Today, with Earth's population estimated at about 4,000 million (26 times what it was in Caesar's time), it is increasing at a rate which, if steady, will cause it to double in 35 years.

The present rate of increase of Earth's swarming human pop- 16 ulation qualifies Homo sapiens as an ecological cancer, which will destroy the ecology just as surely as any ordinary cancer would destroy an organism.

The cure? Just what it is for any cancer. The cancerous growth 17 must somehow be stopped.

Of course, it will be. If we do nothing at all, the growth will 18 stop, as a cancerous growth in a man will stop if nothing is done. The man dies and the cancer dies with him. And, analogously, the ecology will die and man will die with it.

How can the human population explosion be stopped? By raising 19 the deathrate, or by lowering the birthrate. There are no other alternatives. The deathrate will rise spontaneously and finally catastrophically, if we do nothing—and that within a few decades. To make the birthrate fall, somehow (almost *any* how, in fact), is surely preferable, and that is therefore the first order of mankind's business today.

Failing this, mankind would stand at the bar of abstract justice 20 (for there may be no posterity to judge) as the mass murderer of life generally, his own included, and mass disrupter of the intricate planetary development that made life in its present glory possible in the first place.

Am I too pessimistic? Can we allow the present rate of population 21 increase to continue indefinitely, or at least for a good long time? Can we count on science to develop methods for cleaning up as we pollute, for replacing wasted resources with substitutes, for finding new food, new materials, more and better life for our waxing numbers?

Impossible! If the numbers continue to wax at the present rate. 22

Let us begin with a few estimates (admittedly not precise, but 23 in the rough neighborhood of the truth).

The total mass of living objects on Earth is perhaps 20 trillion 24 tons. There is usually a balance between eaters and eaten that is about 1 to 10 in favor of the eaten. There would therefore be about 10 times as much plant life (the eaten) as animal life (the eaters)

on Earth. There is, in other words, just a little under 2 trillion tons
of animal life on Earth.

But this is all the animal life that can exist, given the present 25
quantity of plant life. If more animal life is somehow produced, it
will strip down the plant life, reduce the food supply, and then
enough animals will starve to restore the balance. If one species
of animal life increases in mass, it can only be because other species
correspondingly decrease. For every additional pound of human
flesh on Earth, a pound of some other form of flesh must disappear.

The total mass of humanity now on Earth may be estimated at 26
about 200 million tons, or one ten-thousandth the mass of all animal
life. If mankind increases in numbers ten thousandfold, then Homo
sapiens will be, perforce, the *only* animal species alive on Earth. It
will be a world without elephants or lions, without cats or dogs,
without fish or lobsters, without worms or bugs. What's more, to
support the mass of human life, all the plant world must be put
to service. Only plants edible to man must remain, and only those
plants most concentratedly edible and with minimum waste.

At the present moment, the average density of population of the 27
Earth's land surface is about 73 people per square mile. Increase
that ten thousandfold and the average density will become 730,000
people per square mile, or more than seven times the density of
the workday population of Manhattan. Even if we assume that
mankind will somehow spread itself into vast cities floating on the
ocean surface (or resting on the ocean floor), the average density
of human life at the time when the last nonhuman animal must
be killed would be 310,000 people per square mile over all the
world, land and sea alike, or a little better than three times the
density of modern Manhattan at noon.

We have the vision, then, of high-rise apartments, higher and 28
more thickly spaced than in Manhattan at present, spreading all
over the world, across all the mountains, across the Sahara Desert,
across Antarctica, across all the oceans; all with their load of humanity and with no other form of animal life beside. And on the
roof of all those buildings are the algae farms, with little plant cells
exposed to the Sun so that they might grow rapidly and, without
waste, form protein for all the mighty population of 35 trillion
human beings.

Is that tolerable? Even if science produced all the energy and 29 materials mankind could want, kept them all fed with algae, all educated, all amused—is the planetary high-rise tolerable?

And if it were, can we double the population further in 35 more 30 years? And then double it again in another 35 years? Where will the food come from? What will persuade the algae to multiply faster than the light energy they absorb makes possible? What will speed up the Sun to add the energy to make it possible? And if vast supplies of fusion energy are added to supplement the Sun, how will we get rid of the equally vast supplies of heat that will be produced? And after the icecaps are melted and the oceans boiled into steam, what?

Can we bleed off the mass of humanity to other worlds? Right 31 now, the number of human beings on Earth is increasing by 80 million per year, and each year that number goes up by 1 and a fraction percent. Can we really suppose that we can send 80 million people per year to the Moon, Mars, and elsewhere, and engineer those worlds to support those people? And even so, merely remain in the same place ourselves?

No! Not the most optimistic visionary in the world could hon- 32 estly convince himself that space travel is the solution to our population problem, if the present rate of increase is sustained.

But when will this planetary high-rise culture come about? How 33 long will it take to increase Earth's population to that impossible point at the present doubling rate of once every 35 years? If it will take 1 million years or even 100,000, then, for goodness sake, let's not worry just yet.

Well, we don't have that kind of time. We will reach that dead 34 end in no more than 460 years.

At the rate we are going, without birth control, then even if 35 science serves us in an absolutely ideal way, we will reach the planetary high-rise with no animals but man, with no plants but algae, with no room for even one more person, by A.D. 2430.

And if science serves us in less than an ideal way (as it certainly 36 will), the end will come sooner, much sooner, and mankind will start fading long, long before he is forced to construct that building that will cover all the Earth's surface.

So if birth control *must* come by A.D. 2430 at the very latest, even 37 in an ideal world of advancing science, let it come *now*, in heaven's name, while there are still oak trees in the world and daisies and tigers and butterflies, and while there is still open land and space, and before the cancer called man proves fatal to life and the planet.

Questions on Subject

1. In your own words explain the principle, discussed in paragraph 11, by which nature maintains balance. What could be the catastrophic consequence of this principle for humankind?
2. What does Asimov mean by the "bar of abstract justice" in paragraph 20?
3. According to Asimov, how can the human population explosion be stopped?
4. What is the ratio of eaters to eaten? How is this ratio maintained? How is the human population explosion affecting this balance?
5. In paragraph 29, Asimov asks a question. What is another way the question could be asked?

Questions on Strategy

1. What is the analogy Asimov establishes in paragraph 7? (Glossary: *Analogy*) How well does it work in a discussion of population control? Explain.
2. Asimov begins his essay by introducing views opposing his argument. (Glossary: *Beginnings*) What effect does this have on the reader?
3. In paragraph 16, Asimov compares the human population to a cancer. How effective is this comparison in the context of his argument? In your opinion, is the comparison fair? Explain.
4. Asimov says that long before people are living shoulder-to-shoulder and dining on algae, humanity will have ceased to exist. Why do you suppose he indulges in this exaggeration? What purpose does it serve?
5. Does Asimov argue inductively or deductively? Explain.
6. Asimov relies almost exclusively on the use of statistics for his argument. How effective is this strategy for his subject and purpose? What other kinds of evidence does he rely on to make his argument? (Glossary: *Evidence*) In what way are they more or less effective?

Questions on Diction and Vocabulary

1. In paragraph 21, Asimov asks "Am I too pessimistic?" How would you answer him? What is the overall tone of his essay? (Glossary: *Tone*) Cite examples of his diction to support your answer.
2. Refer to your desk dictionary to determine the meanings of the following words as they are used in this selection: *intricate* (paragraph 1), *versatile* (4), *inanimate* (5), *dehydration* (5), *asphyxiation* (5), *quiescent* (10), *ecology* (11), *decimated* (11), *predators* (11), *dread* (12), *dubious* (14), *swarming* (16), *posterity* (20), *perforce* (26).

Writing Suggestions

1. Write an essay in which you present a statistical argument for the continued nationwide media campaign against drunk driving. How has the campaign affected the death rate? At its present rate, how will it affect the death rate in the future?
2. Asimov relies heavily on the frightening consequences of the human population explosion to make the point that we need to practice birth control. Reread his essay and then rewrite it in your own words, using an entirely different tone. For example, you could try being neutral or satirical. What effect does a change of tone make in the overall impression of the essay?

Saving Nature, But Only for Man

Charles Krauthammer

Charles Krauthammer, who was born in 1950, has a degree in medicine. He has served as chief resident in psychiatry at Harvard Medical School and as an assistant adviser for psychiatric research in the Carter administration. In 1978, at the same time he went to Washington, Krauthammer began writing for the New Republic. *During the 1980 presidential campaign, he was speechwriter for Walter Mondale, the vice-presidential candidate. Later, he joined the staff of the* New Republic.*

In the following essay, originally written for Time, *Krauthammer argues that it is folly to consider any but humanity's best interest when devising an environmental policy.*

Environmental sensitivity is now as required an attitude in polite 1
society as is, say, belief in democracy or aversion to polyester. But
now that everyone from Ted Turner to George Bush, Dow to Exxon
has professed love for Mother Earth, how are we to choose among
the dozens of conflicting proposals, restrictions, projects, regulations and laws advanced in the name of the environment? Clearly
not everything with an environmental claim is worth doing. How
to choose?

There is a simple way. First, distinguish between environmental 2
luxuries and environmental necessities. Luxuries are those things
it would be nice to have if costless. Necessities are those things
we must have regardless. Then apply a rule. Call it the fundamental axiom of sane environmentalism: Combatting ecological
change that directly threatens the health and safety of people is
an environmental necessity. All else is luxury.

For example: preserving the atmosphere—stopping ozone de- 3
pletion and the greenhouse effect—is an environmental necessity.
In April scientists reported that ozone damage is far worse than
previously thought. Ozone depletion not only causes skin cancer

and eye cataracts, it also destroys plankton, the beginning of the food chain atop which we humans sit.

The reality of the greenhouse effect is more speculative, though 4 its possible consequences are far deadlier: melting ice caps, flooded coastlines, disrupted climate, parched plains and, ultimately, empty breadbaskets. The American Midwest feeds the world. Are we prepared to see Iowa acquire Albuquerque's climate? And Siberia acquire Iowa's?

Ozone depletion and the greenhouse effect are human disasters. 5 They happen to occur in the environment. But they are urgent because they directly threaten man. A sane environmentalism, the only kind of environmentalism that will win universal public support, begins by unashamedly declaring that nature is here to serve man. A sane environmentalism is entirely anthropocentric: it enjoins man to preserve nature, but on the grounds of self-preservation.

A sane environmentalism does not sentimentalize the earth. It 6 does not ask people to sacrifice in the name of other creatures. After all, it is hard enough to ask people to sacrifice in the name of other humans. (Think of the chronic public resistance to foreign aid and welfare.) Ask hardworking voters to sacrifice in the name of the snail darter, and, if they are feeling polite, they will give you a shrug.

Of course, this anthropocentrism runs against the grain of a con- 7 temporary environmentalism that indulges in earth worship to the point of idolatry. One scientific theory—Gaia theory—actually claims that Earth is a living organism. This kind of environmentalism likes to consider itself spiritual. It is nothing more than sentimental. It takes, for example, a highly selective view of the benignity of nature. My nature worship stops with the April twister that came through Andover, Kansas, or the May cyclone that killed more than 125,000 Bengalis and left 10 million (!) homeless.

A nonsentimental environmentalism is one founded on Protag- 8 oras' maxim that "Man is the measure of all things." Such a principle helps us through the thicket of environmental argument. Take the current debate raging over oil drilling in a corner of the Alaska National Wildlife Refuge. Environmentalists, mobilizing against a bill working its way through Congress to permit such exploration, argue that we should be conserving energy instead of drilling for it. This is a false either/or proposition. The country does need a sizable energy tax to reduce consumption. But it needs more production too. Government estimates indicate a nearly fifty-fifty chance that under the ANWR lies one of the five largest oil fields ever discovered in America.

We have just come through a war fought in part over oil. Energy 9 dependence costs Americans not just dollars but lives. It is a bizarre sentimentalism that would deny ourselves oil that is peacefully attainable because it risks disrupting the calving grounds of Arctic caribou.

I like the caribou as much as the next man. And I would be rather 10 sorry if their mating patterns are disturbed. But you can't have everything. And if the choice is between the welfare of caribou and reducing an oil dependency that gets people killed in wars, I choose man over caribou every time.

Similarly the spotted owl. I am no enemy of the owl. If it could 11 be preserved at no or little cost, I would agree: the variety of nature is a good, a high aesthetic good. But it is no more than that. And sometimes aesthetic goods have to be sacrificed to the more fundamental ones. If the cost of preserving the spotted owl is the loss of livelihood for 30,000 logging families, I choose family over owl.

The important distinction is between those environmental goods 12 that are fundamental and those that are merely aesthetic. Nature is our ward. It is not our master. It is to be respected and even cultivated. But it is man's world. And when man has to choose between his well-being and that of nature, nature will have to accommodate.

Man should accommodate only when his fate and that of nature 13 are inextricably bound up. The most urgent accommodation must be made when the very integrity of man's habitat—e.g., atmospheric ozone—is threatened. When the threat to man is of a lesser order (say, the pollutants from coal- and oil-fired generators that cause death from disease but not fatal damage to the ecosystem), a more modulated accommodation that balances economic against health concerns is in order. But in either case the principle is the same: protect the environment—because it is man's environment.

The sentimental environmentalists will call this saving nature 14 with a totally wrong frame of mind. Exactly. A sane—a humanistic—environmentalism does it not for nature's sake but for our own.

Questions on Subject

1. According to Krauthammer, why is it difficult for the average person to adopt a consistent environmental position?
2. How does Krauthammer define a "sane environmentalism"? Upon what principle is it founded?
3. What are some of the environmental priorities Krauthammer names? How does he justify them? Do you agree or disagree with his assessments?
4. Why does Krauthammer believe that it is unreasonable to expect humans to make sacrifices for the sake of other creatures?
5. What does Krauthammer say is the problem with modern environmentalism? How is this problem linked to the "Gaia theory"?
6. Under what general circumstances does Krauthammer say people should accommodate nature?

Questions on Strategy

1. Krauthammer divides environmental concerns into two major categories. What are they? Throughout the essay, Krauthammer expresses those two groups in different terms. What are those terms? What other system of classification might he have used? (Glossary: *Division and Classification*)
2. What is Krauthammer's thesis, and where is it stated? (Glossary: *Thesis*)
3. What kinds of evidence does Krauthammer use to support his thesis? Which kinds of evidence did you find the most convincing? (Glossary: *Evidence*) What if anything has Krauthammer overlooked in his argument for a "sane environmentalism"?
4. Krauthammer's essay is a deductive argument; thus it can be presented as a syllogism. What are the major premise, the minor premise, and the conclusion of Krauthammer's argument?

Questions on Diction and Vocabulary

1. Throughout his essay, Krauthammer refers to environmentalists as "sentimental." Locate several places where he uses this word and discuss how it helps make his argument persuasive.

2. How would you describe the overall tone Krauthammer establishes in his argument? (Glossary: *Tone*) In what way, if any, can he be said to fit the definition of an "environmentalist"?

3. Refer to your dictionary to determine the meanings of the following words as they are used in this selection: *axiom* (paragraph 2), *depletion* (3), *urgent* (5), *anthropocentric* (5), *sentimentalize* (6), *chronic* (6), *indulges* (7), *idolatry* (7), *bizarre* (9), *aesthetic* (11), *ward* (12), *inextricably* (13), *modulated* (13).

Writing Suggestions

1. Write an essay in which you discuss Krauthammer's argument that "man is the measure of all things" in light of Isaac Asimov's point (in "The Case Against Man") that it is a mistake to "think of mankind as a thing in itself."

2. The notion that "man is the measure of all things" is also used to justify animal experimentation in medical research. Write an essay in which you argue for or against the use of animals in medical or other types of research.

From "The Obligation to Endure"

Rachel Carson

> *Rachel Carson was a writer and naturalist who believed that the best way to make the physical world real to her readers was to describe creatures in their natural habitat and not as specimens isolated in the laboratory. In her books* The Sea Around Us *(1951),* Under the Sea Wind *(1952), and* The Edge of the Sea *(1955), Carson combines her love of nature with a poetic style that brings the sea world to life. However, it was* Silent Spring *(1962), a gloomy forecast of environmental havoc wreaked by the indiscriminate and widespread use of insecticides, which brought her into prominence. At first dismissed as an alarmist, Carson is now regarded as a pioneer in the modern environmental movement. Carson died in 1964.*
>
> *In this essay, taken from the second chapter of* Silent Spring, *Carson argues that humankind has managed to undo five billion years of nature's good work in the relative space of a heartbeat.*

It took hundreds of millions of years to produce the life that now 1 inhabits the earth—eons of time in which that developing and evolving and diversifying life reached a state of adjustment and balance with its surroundings. The environment, rigorously shaping and directing the life it supported, contained elements that were hostile as well as supporting. Certain rocks gave out dangerous radiation; even within the light of the sun, from which all life draws its energy, there were short-wave radiations with power to injure. Given time—time not in years but in millennia—life adjusts, and a balance has been reached. For time is the essential ingredient; but in the modern world there is no time.

The rapidity of change and the speed with which new situations 2 are created follow the impetuous and heedless pace of man rather than the deliberate pace of nature. Radiation is no longer merely the background radiation of rocks, the bombardment of cosmic rays, the ultraviolet of the sun that have existed before there was any life on earth; radiation is now the unnatural creation of man's tampering with the atom. The chemicals to which life is asked to make its adjustment are no longer merely the calcium and silica and copper and all the rest of the minerals washed out of the rocks and carried in rivers to the sea; they are the synthetic creations of man's inventive mind, brewed in his laboratories, and having no counterparts in nature.

To adjust to these chemicals would require time on the scale that 3 is nature's; it would require not merely the years of a man's life but the life of generations. And even this, were it by some miracle possible, would be futile, for the new chemicals come from our laboratories in an endless stream; almost five hundred annually find their way into actual use in the United States alone. The figure is staggering and its implications are not easily grasped—five hundred new chemicals to which the bodies of men and animals are required somehow to adapt each year, chemicals totally outside the limits of biologic experience.

Among them are many that are used in man's war against nature. 4 Since the mid-1940's over two hundred basic chemicals have been created for use in killing insects, weeds, rodents, and other organisms described in the modern vernacular as "pests"; and they are sold under several thousand different brand names.

These sprays, dusts, and aerosols are now applied almost uni- 5 versally to farms, gardens, forests, and homes—nonselective chemicals that have the power to kill every insect, the "good" and the "bad," to still the song of birds and the leaping of fish in the streams, to coat the leaves with a deadly film, and to linger on in soil—all this though the intended target may be only a few weeds or insects. Can anyone believe it is possible to lay down such a barrage of poisons on the surface of the earth without making it unfit for all life? They should not be called "insecticides," but "biocides."

The whole process of spraying seems caught up in an endless 6 spiral. Since DDT was released for civilian use, a process of escalation has been going on in which ever more toxic materials must be found. This has happened because insects, in a triumphant vindication of Darwin's principle of the survival of the fittest, have evolved super races immune to the particular insecticide used, hence a deadlier one has always to be developed—and then a deadlier one than that. It has happened also because, for reasons to be described later, destructive insects often undergo a "flare-back," or resurgence, after spraying, in numbers greater than before. Thus the chemical war is never won, and all life is caught in its violent crossfire.

Along with the possibility of the extinction of mankind by nuclear war, the central problem of our age has therefore become the contamination of man's total environment with such substances of incredible potential for harm—substances that accumulate in the tissues of plants and animals and even penetrate the germ cells to shatter or alter the very material of heredity upon which the shape of the future depends. 7

Some would-be architects of our future look toward a time when it will be possible to alter the human germ plasm by design. But we may easily be doing so now by inadvertence, for many chemicals, like radiation, bring about gene mutations. It is ironic to think that man might determine his own future by something so seemingly trivial as the choice of an insect spray. 8

All this has been risked—for what? Future historians may well be amazed by our distorted sense of proportion. How could intelligent beings seek to control a few unwanted species by a method that contaminated the entire environment and brought the threat of disease and death even to their own kind? Yet this is precisely what we have done. We have done it, moreover, for reasons that collapse the moment we examine them. We are told that the enormous and expanding use of pesticides is necessary to maintain farm production. Yet is our real problem not one of *overproduction*? Our farms, despite measures to remove acreages from production and to pay farmers *not* to produce, have yielded such a staggering excess of crops that the American taxpayer in 1962 is paying out more than one billion dollars a year as the total carrying cost of the surplus-food storage program. And is the situation helped when one branch of the Agriculture Department tries to reduce production while another states, as it did in 1958, "It is believed generally that reduction of crop acreages under provisions of the Soil Bank will stimulate interest in use of chemicals to obtain maximum production on the land retained in crops." 9

All this is not to say there is no insect problem and no need of 10 control. I am saying, rather, that control must be geared to realities, not to mythical situations, and that the methods employed must be such that they do not destroy us along with the insects.

The problem whose attempted solution has brought such a train 11 of disaster in its wake is an accompaniment of our modern way of life. Long before the age of man, insects inhabited the earth—a group of extraordinarily varied and adaptable beings. Over the course of time since man's advent, a small percentage of the more than half a million species of insects have come into conflict with human welfare in two principal ways: as competitors for the food supply and as carriers of human disease.

Disease-carrying insects become important where human beings 12 are crowded together, especially under conditions where sanitation is poor, as in time of natural disaster or war or in situations of extreme poverty and deprivation. Then control of some sort becomes necessary. It is a sobering fact, however, as we shall presently see, that the method of massive chemical control has had only limited success, and also threatens to worsen the very conditions it is intended to curb.

Under primitive agricultural conditions the farmer had few insect 13 problems. These arose with the intensification of agriculture—the devotion of immense acreages to a single crop. Such a system set the stage for explosive increases in specific insect populations. Single-crop farming does not take advantage of the principles by which nature works; it is agriculture as an engineer might conceive it to be. Nature has introduced great variety into the landscape, but man has displayed a passion for simplifying it. Thus he undoes the built-in checks and balances by which nature holds the species within bounds. One important natural check is a limit on the amount of suitable habitat for each species. Obviously then, an insect that lives on wheat can build up its population to much higher levels on a farm devoted to wheat than on one in which wheat is intermingled with other crops to which the insect is not adapted.

The same thing happens in other situations. A generation or 14 more ago, the towns of large areas of the United States lined their streets with the noble elm tree. Now the beauty they hopefully created is threatened with complete destruction as disease sweeps through the elms, carried by a beetle that would have only limited chance to build up large populations and to spread from tree to tree if the elms were only occasional trees in a richly diversified planting.

Another factor in the modern insect problem is one that must   15
be viewed against a background of geologic and human history: the spreading of thousands of different kinds of organisms from their native homes to invade new territories. This worldwide migration has been studied and graphically described by the British ecologist Charles Elton in his recent book *The Ecology of Invasions*. During the Cretaceous Period, some hundred million years ago, flooding seas cut many land bridges between continents and living things found themselves confined in what Elton calls "colossal separate nature reserves." There, isolated from others of their kind, they developed many new species. When some of the land masses were joined again, about 15 million years ago, these species began to move out into new territories—a movement that is not only still in progress but is now receiving considerable assistance from man.

The importation of plants is the primary agent in the modern   16
spread of species, for animals have almost invariably gone along with the plants, quarantine being a comparatively recent and not completely effective innovation. The United States Office of Plant Introduction alone has introduced almost 200,000 species and varieties of plants from all over the world. Nearly half of the 180 or so major insect enemies of plants in the United States are accidental imports from abroad, and most of them have come as hitchhikers on plants.

In new territory, out of reach of the restraining hand of the nat-   17
ural enemies that kept down its numbers in its native land, an invading plant or animal is able to become enormously abundant. Thus it is no accident that our most troublesome insects are introduced species.

These invasions, both the naturally occurring and those depen-   18
dent on human assistance, are likely to continue indefinitely. Quarantine and massive chemical campaigns are only extremely expensive ways of buying time. We are faced, according to Dr. Elton, "with a life-and-death need not just to find new technological means of suppressing this plant or that animal"; instead we need the basic knowledge of animal populations and their relations to

their surroundings that will "promote an even balance and damp down the explosive power of outbreaks and new invasions."

Much of the necessary knowledge is now available but we do 19 not use it. We train ecologists in our universities and even employ them in our governmental agencies but we seldom take their advice. We allow the chemical death rain to fall as though there were no alternative, whereas in fact there are many, and our ingenuity could soon discover many more if given opportunity.

Have we fallen into a mesmerized state that makes us accept as 20 inevitable that which is inferior or detrimental, as though having lost the will or the vision to demand that which is good? Such thinking, in the words of the ecologist Paul Shepard, "idealizes life with only its head out of water, inches above the limits of toleration of the corruption of its own environment . . . Why should we tolerate a diet of weak poisons, a home in insipid surroundings, a circle of acquaintances who are not quite our enemies, the noise of motors with just enough relief to prevent insanity? Who would want to live in a world which is just not quite fatal?"

Yet such a world is pressed upon us. The crusade to create a 21 chemically sterile, insect-free world seems to have engendered a fanatic zeal on the part of many specialists and most of the so-called control agencies. On every hand there is evidence that those engaged in spraying operations exercise a ruthless power. "The regulatory entomologists . . . function as prosecutor, judge and jury, tax assessor and collector and sheriff to enforce their own orders," said Connecticut entomologist Neely Turner. The most flagrant abuses go unchecked in both state and federal agencies.

It is not my contention that chemical insecticides must never be 22 used. I do contend that we have put poisonous and biologically potent chemicals indiscriminately into the hands of persons largely or wholly ignorant of their potentials for harm. We have subjected enormous numbers of people to contact with these poisons, without their consent and often without their knowledge. If the Bill of Rights contains no guarantee that a citizen shall be secure against lethal poisons distributed either by private individuals or by public officials, it is surely only because our forefathers, despite their considerable wisdom and foresight, could conceive of no such problem.

I contend, furthermore, that we have allowed these chemicals 23 to be used with little or no advance investigation of their effect on soil, water, wildlife, and man himself. Future generations are unlikely to condone our lack of prudent concern for the integrity of the natural world that supports all life.

Questions on Subject

1. What distinction does Carson make between natural and synthetic chemicals in their effect on the balance of nature?
2. What is the "spiral" of spraying that Carson refers to in paragraph 6?
3. Carson suggests that the insect problem might be the result of social conditions. What are those conditions?
4. According to Carson, what is the problem with single-crop farming? How does it relate to the problem of Dutch Elm disease?
5. What are "introduced species"? How do they contribute to the overall imbalance of nature to which Carson refers?
6. In paragraph 19, Carson refers to a possible solution to the ecological imbalance facing our planet. Where in her essay does she suggest what that solution might be?

Questions on Strategy

1. How do the first three paragraphs of Carson's essay serve to introduce her thesis and subject? (Glossary: *Beginnings*) Do you find this an effective opening? Why or why not?
2. Carson asks several questions in paragraph 9. Does she answer them? Why do you suppose she has asked these questions? In what way do they strengthen her essay?
3. Carson includes both persuasive and logical arguments to make her point against the indiscriminate use of insecticides. Cite examples of each, and discuss in what way each of them contributes to the overall effectiveness of her argument.
4. Point out several terms and concepts that Carson defines in her essay. What is her purpose in defining them? (Glossary: *Definition*)
5. Is Carson's argument concerned more with the causes or the effects of widespread pesticide use? (Glossary: *Cause and Effect Analysis*) Explain.

Questions on Diction and Vocabulary

1. Discuss Carson's suggestion that the word *biocide* be used in place of *pesticide* (paragraph 5).
2. Cite several examples of Carson's diction that support her reputation as a lover of the natural world.
3. Refer to your dictionary to determine the meanings of the following words as they are used in this selection: *eons* (paragraph 1), *impetuous* (2), *bombardment* (2), *tampering* (2), *futile* (3), *staggering* (3), *vernacular* (4), *barrage* (5), *escalation* (6), *vindication* (6), *immune* (6), *resurgence* (6), *contamination* (7), *inadvertence* (8), *mutations* (8), *quarantine* (16), *abundant* (17), *ingenuity* (19), *condone* (21), *prudent* (21), *contention* (22).

Writing Suggestions

1. Using Carson's essay as a model, write an essay of your own in which you argue against a prevalent practice in your school or home that could be seen as beneficial in the short run but could prove harmful in the long run. For example: cheating among college students or your parents' ignorance of a younger sibling's drinking problem.
2. Rachel Carson was labeled an "alarmist" thirty years ago when she wrote in *Silent Spring* about the dangers of indiscriminate pesticide use. Write an evaluation of what you think might be the response today if her essay were to appear in print for the first time.

How to Poison the Earth

Linnea Saukko

Born in 1954 in Warren, Ohio, Linnea Saukko received a degree in environmental quality control from Muskingum Area Technical College. For several years she worked as an environmental technician, developing hazardous waste programs and advising on matters of chemical safety for a large corporation. Concerned about the unsafe disposal of toxic waste and wishing to gain better insights on ways to address the problem, she returned to school and earned her B.A. in geology from Ohio State University. Today she lives in Hilliard, Ohio, and works at the Groundwater Division of the Ohio Environmental Protection Division Agency where she supervises and evaluates sites for possible groundwater contamination.

The following essay, written for a freshman writing class, was subsequently chosen from among 1100 entries as one of thirty-one winners of the 1983 Bedford Prize in Student Writing. It was included in Student Writers at Work: The Bedford Prizes. *In her essay, Saukko uses irony and satire to suggest the means by which we can most efficiently ensure the speedy and thorough contamination of the earth's environment.*

Poisoning the earth can be difficult because the earth is always 1
trying to cleanse and renew itself. Keeping this in mind, we should
generate as much waste as possible from substances such as ura-
nium-238, which has a half-life (the time it takes for half of the
substance to decay) of one million years, or plutonium, which has
a half-life of only 0.5 million years but is so toxic that if distributed
evenly, ten·pounds of it could kill every person on the earth. Because the United States generates about eighteen tons of plutonium
per year, it is about the best substance for long-term poisoning of
the earth. It would help if we would build more nuclear power
plants because each one generates only 500 pounds of plutonium

each year. Of course, we must include persistent toxic chemicals such as polychlorinated biphenyl (PCB) and dichlorodiphenyl trichloroethane (DDT) to make sure we have enough toxins to poison the earth from the core to the outer atmosphere. First, we must develop many different ways of putting the waste from these nuclear and chemical substances in, on, and around the earth.

Putting these substances in the earth is a most important step in the poisoning process. With deep-well injection we can ensure that the earth is poisoned all the way to the core. Deep-well injection involves drilling a hole that is a few thousand feet deep and injecting toxic substances at extremely high pressures so they will penetrate deep into the earth. According to the Environmental Protection Agency (EPA), there are about 360 such deep injection wells in the United States. We cannot forget the groundwater aquifers that are closer to the surface. These must also be contaminated. This is easily done by shallow-well injection, which operates on the same principle as deep-well injection, only closer to the surface. The groundwater that has been injected with toxins will spread the contamination beneath the earth. The EPA estimates that there are approximately 500,000 shallow injection wells in the United States.

Burying the toxins in the earth is the next best method. The toxins from landfills, dumps, and lagoons slowly seep into the earth, guaranteeing that contamination will last a long time. Because the EPA estimates there are only about 50,000 of these dumps in the United States, they should be located in areas where they will leak to the surrounding ground and surface water.

Applying pesticides and other poisons on the earth is another part of the poisoning process. This is good for coating the earth's surface so that the poisons will be absorbed by plants, will seep into the ground, and will run off into surface water.

Surface water is very important to contaminate because it will transport the poisons to places that cannot be contaminated directly. Lakes are good for long-term storage of pollutants while they release some of their contamination to rivers. The only trouble with rivers is that they act as a natural cleansing system for the earth. No matter how much poison is dumped into them, they will try to transport it away to reach the ocean eventually.

The ocean is very hard to contaminate because it has such a large volume and a natural buffering capacity that tends to neutralize some of the contamination. So in addition to the pollution from rivers, we must use the ocean as a dumping place for as many toxins as possible. The ocean currents will help transport the pollution to places that cannot otherwise be reached.

Now make sure that the air around the earth is very polluted. 7 Combustion and evaporation are major mechanisms for doing this. We must continuously pollute because the wind will disperse the toxins while rain washes them from the air. But this is good because a few lakes are stripped of all living animals each year from acid rain. Because the lower atmosphere can cleanse itself fairly easily, we must explode nuclear test bombs that shoot radioactive particles high into the upper atmosphere where they will circle the earth for years. Gravity must pull some of the particles to earth, so we must continue exploding these bombs.

So it is that easy. Just be sure to generate as many poisonous 8 substances as possible and be sure they are distributed in, on, and around the entire earth at a greater rate than it can cleanse itself. By following these easy steps we can guarantee the poisoning of the earth.

Questions on Subject

1. According to Saukko, why is it difficult to poison the earth?
2. Saukko divides the means of poisoning the earth into three major categories. (Glossary: *Division and Classification*) What are they? Which one is the deadliest? Why?
3. What does Saukko say is the "trouble with rivers"? Why does she insist that we use the ocean as a dumping ground for as many toxins as possible?
4. In what way does rain act both as a cleanser and as a pollutant?
5. In her concluding paragraph, Saukko assures her readers that they can succeed in poisoning the earth if they upset what vital balance of nature?

Questions on Strategy

1. Saukko uses a process analysis in her argument. (Glossary: *Process Analysis*) What process is she describing? What steps does she list?

2. What kind of information does Saukko include in addition to the steps she discusses in her process analysis? What does this additional information add to her argument? Is it necessary information or could she have left it out?

3. The first sentence of the first paragraph of Saukko's essay is all she devotes to an introduction. What is the effect of this beginning and how well does it prepare the reader for the rest of the essay? (Glossary: *Beginnings*)

4. What is Saukko's purpose in writing this essay? (Glossary: *Purpose*)

Questions on Diction and Vocabulary

1. Satire is a literary form that uses wit, irony, or sarcasm to expose vice or folly. Which of those aspects of satire has Saukko employed in her essay? Why do you think she has chosen to treat so serious a subject in this manner?

2. Saukko uses the pronoun *we* throughout her essay. What effect does this create? Do you find it effective?

3. Refer to your desk dictionary to determine the meanings of the following words as they are used in this selection: *renew* (paragraph 1), *toxic* (1), *generates* (1), *persistent* (1), *injection* (2), *penetrate* (2), *contamination* (2), *lagoons* (3), *buffering* (6), *disperse* (7).

Writing Suggestions

1. Select a serious essay you have already written for one of your courses and write it again, this time using satire to get your point across. You will need to pay careful attention to your diction and your tone. How can you use satire in your writing without losing the serious intent of your original composition? Will your audience remain the same? Or will you find it easier to write satire if you imagine you are writing to your best friend, your parents, the editor of the local newspaper, or someone else?

2. Write an essay in which you compare and/or contrast the subject and style of Saukko's "How to Poison the Earth" with Judy Brady's "Why I Want a Wife" (pages 391–393).

Writing Suggestions for Argumentation

1. Think of a product that you like and want to use even though it has an annoying feature. Write a letter of complaint in which you attempt to persuade the manufacturer to improve the product. Your letter should include the following points:
   a. a statement concerning the nature of the problem
   b. evidence supporting or explaining your complaint
   c. suggestions for improving the product
2. Select one of the position statements that follow, and write an argumentative essay in which you defend that statement:
   a. Living in a dormitory is (*or* is not) as attractive as living off-campus.
   b. Grain sales should (*or* should not) be used as a political weapon.
   c. Student government shows (*or* does not show) that the democratic process is effective.
   d. America should (*or* should not) be a refuge for the oppressed.
   e. School spirit is (*or* is not) as important as it ever was.
   f. Interest in religion is (*or* is not) increasing in the United States.
   g. We have (*or* have not) brought air pollution under control in the United States.
   h. The need to develop alternative energy sources is (*or* is not) serious.
   i. America's great cities are (*or* are not) thriving.
   j. Fraternities and sororities do (*or* do not) build character.
   k. We have (*or* have not) found effective means to dispose of nuclear or chemical wastes.

l. Fair play is (*or* is not) a thing of the past.

m. Human life is (*or* is not) valued in a technological society.

n. The consumer does (*or* does not) need to be protected.

o. The family farm in America is (*or* is not) in danger of extinction.

p. Grades do (*or* do not) encourage learning.

q. America is (*or* is not) a violent society.

r. Television is (*or* is not) a positive cultural force in America.

s. America should (*or* should not) feel a commitment to the starving peoples of the world.

t. The federal government should (*or* should not) regulate all utilities.

u. Money is (*or* is not) the path to happiness.

v. Animals do (*or* do not) have rights.

w. Competition is (*or* is not) killing us.

x. America is (*or* is not) becoming a society with deteriorating values.

12
Language, Race, and Gender: A Casebook

The struggle for definition is veritably the struggle for life itself.

THOMAS SZASZ

When the language we use serves us well, it reveals itself to be at the very heart of what makes us civilized. We use speech and writing to communicate to each other what is dear to us—our differences and agreements, our fears and hopes, our demands and wishes, our seriousness and humor, our anger and our love. We use language, as well, to carry out our daily affairs, from the most mundane and trivial to the most politically demanding and spiritually important. Inasmuch as we use language to define ourselves, we also reveal no less than the common bond of our humanity through our speech and writing. We recognize each other as people, people who are sharing the same space and moment in time, hoping to learn from the past and looking toward the future.

When language fails to serve us well, it can become like the polluted air that hovers over many of our industrial centers. It impairs us, and we suddenly become all too aware of its presence. No longer is it invisible and healthful like fresh air. But just as there is some pollution that is invisible and goes undetected, there is some language whose bias is not immediately apparent. Language that consciously or inadvertently confines or diminishes others, that puts them down or abuses them in some way—whether because of race, ethnic origin, gender, sexual orientation, religion, age, or physical or mental impairment—also confines and diminishes the users of such language. To recognize the power of language both to liberate and to imprison is to come to some sense of the responsibility within each one of us to use language thoughtfully and carefully. Nowhere is there a greater need for sensitivity than in the area of race and gender.

None—no one—of us is able to use the English language, itself fraught with many built-in gender- and color-based biases, in a completely nonprejudicial way. We need constantly to hear from those who feel victimized by the language we use. They need to tell us where and how we might be putting them at a disadvantage, and we need to assess their claims and to act accordingly. For example, using *chairperson* or *chair* instead of *chairman* seems to correct the perception that all people holding the position named are male, whereas changing *history* to *herstory* to avoid *his* seems frivolous and perhaps explains why the term never gained acceptance. Similarly, athletic teams that carry the names *Braves, Redskins,* or *Indians* may be offensive to Native Americans, and the continued use of such terms may be insensitive and represent an act of defiance on the part of the owners of such teams. We need to be made aware of when our language becomes clouded with bias, where it is not as useful and productive as it might be. In short, we need to become sensitized to our language, to realize that language is not only transmitted but received, that it is used not only to realize our thoughts and feelings about who we are but to help others do the same.

It is the purpose of the essays in this casebook to begin the work of sensitizing us to the role language plays in racial and gender identity and understanding. In their theoretical explanations, and by the force of their examples, each author works toward an understanding of the complex network of human responses and conditions that creates an individual's racial and gender identity and the role that language plays in that process.

We open with a pair of essays that provide a theoretical understanding and definitions of basic concepts. The late Gordon Allport was for many years professor of psychology at Harvard University. In a selection from his classic book, *The Nature of Prejudice*, Allport discusses how the labeling process, verbal realism, and symbol phobia work to perpetuate prejudice and even create it. Alleen Pace Nilsen is a professor and administrator at Arizona State University. In the early 1970s she helped pioneer the study of sexist language. In "Sexism in English: A 1990s Update," Nilsen analyzes English words that express sexist assumptions about the differences between men and women.

In each of the next four selections, the writers explore what happens when people of one culture enter another. Edite Cunha, a 1991 graduate of Smith College, came to the United States from her native Portugal when she was seven. In her essay "Talking in the New Land," she recounts her difficulties in learning English and the emotional stress her bilingualism caused. In the next selection, Edward B. Fiske, former education editor for the *New York Times* and author of *Smart Schools, Smart Kids*, reports on the culture shock that many Hispanic students enrolled in American colleges and universities feel. Gloria Naylor, an essayist and novelist on the African-American experience, explores the many meanings of the word *nigger*. In her essay, "What's In a Name?" she examines the ways in which words can take on meaning depending on who uses them and to what purpose. Finally, Bette Bao Lord presents a positive and uplifting view of the immigrant experience. In her essay, "Walking in Lucky Shoes," she writes, "I do not believe that the loss of one's native culture is the price one must pay for becoming an American."

The last three essays focus on some aspects of language and gender. Maxine Hong Kingston, a novelist and first-generation Chinese American, narrates how she struggled as a youngster to find an "American-feminine speaking personality." "Finding a Voice" was taken from her best-selling autobiography *The Woman Warrior: Memoirs of a Girlhood Among Ghosts*. In a different vein, journalist and CBS news correspondent Bernard R. Goldberg strikes out against what he perceives as the new double standard. In "Television Insults Men, Too," an essay that first appeared in the *New York Times*, he argues against the current wave of man-bashing in television programming and advertising. Professor Deborah Tannen, a sociolinguist at Georgetown University and author of the best-selling books *That's Not What I Meant!* and *You Just Don't Understand: Women and Men in Conversation*, believes that it's no accident that men and women have difficulties talking to each other. Using examples from her extensive studies of the ways men and women talk, she argues that these misunderstandings may, in fact, be the result of distinctly different gender- and culture-based conversational styles.

Each author hopes to make us better able to see how language, rather than cloud, restrict, and diminish us, can liberate, invigorate, and advance our understanding of each other as individuals and social groups.

The articles included in this casebook have been selected to be used in conjunction with your own observations and experiences to assist you in writing a researched paper on the interrelationship of language, race, and gender. As you read each article, consider how the information and unique perspective of the author is supported and complemented, or even contradicted, by the other authors in the casebook. To start you thinking about possible paper topics, but by no means to exhaust the possibilities, we have provided a list of suggestions (pages 628–630). It may be a help to you to review our suggestions before proceeding with your reading so that you can acquaint yourself with the key issues raised in the articles. When you have finished your reading you can, of course, once again turn to that list of topics for ideas and inspiration for your own paper.

Writing the Documented Paper

A documented paper is not unlike the other writing that you have done in your college writing course. You will find yourself drawing heavily on what you learned about writing essays in our general introduction (pages 8–30). First you determine what you want to say, then you decide on a purpose, develop a thesis, consider your audience, collect your evidence, write a first draft, revise and edit, and prepare a final copy. What differentiates the documented paper from other kinds of papers is your research and how you acknowledge it. To assist you in writing your paper we have done the library work for you by collecting the nine articles in this casebook to use as a research base.

In writing a documented paper you will learn how to take useful notes, how to summarize, paraphrase, and quote your sources, how to integrate your notes into your paper, how to acknowledge your sources, and how to avoid plagiarism.

A good place to begin is to read each of the articles in this casebook. After you have completed your reading, you will be in a good position to decide upon a topic (either one of those suggested at the end of the unit or one of your own) and to develop a preliminary thesis—the main idea of what you want to say in your paper. At this point you'll be ready to begin carefully rereading those articles that directly relate to your topic.

Notetaking

As you read, take notes. You're looking for ideas, facts, opinions, statistics, examples, and evidence that you think will be useful in writing your paper. As you work through the articles in this casebook look for recurring themes and notice where the writers are in agreement and where they differ in their views. Try to remember that the effectiveness of your paper is largely determined by the quality—and not necessarily the quantity—of your notes. The purpose of a research paper is not to present a collection of quotes that show you've read all the material and can report what others have said about your topic. Your goal is to analyze, evaluate, and synthesize the information you collect—in other words, to enter into the discussion of the issues and thereby take ownership of your topic. You want to view the results of your research from your own perspective and arrive at an informed opinion of your topic.

Now for some practical advice on taking notes: First and foremost, be systematic in your notetaking. As a rule, write one note on a card, and use cards of uniform size, preferably 4 × 6-inch cards because they are large enough to accommodate even a long note on a single card and yet small enough to be easily handled and conveniently carried. More importantly, when you get to planning and writing your paper, you will be able to sequence your notes according to the plan you have envisioned for your paper. Furthermore, should you decide to alter your organizational plan, you can easily reorder your cards to reflect those revisions.

Second, try not to take too many notes. One good way to help you decide whether or not to take a note is to ask yourself "How exactly does this material help prove or disprove my thesis?" You might even try envisioning where you could use the information in your paper. If it does not seem relevant to your thesis, don't bother to take a note. Once you decide to take a note, you must decide whether to summarize, paraphrase, or quote directly. The approach that you take is largely determined by the content of the passage and the way you envision using it in your paper.

Summary

When you *summarize* material from one of your sources, you capture in condensed form the essential idea of a passage, article, or entire chapter. Summaries are particularly useful when you are working with lengthy, detailed arguments or long passages of narrative or descriptive background information where the details are not germane to the overall thrust of your paper. You simply want to capture the essence of the passage while dispensing with the details because you are confident that your readers will readily understand the point being made or do not need to be convinced about the validity of the point. Because you are distilling information, a summary is always shorter than the original; often a chapter or more can be reduced to a paragraph, or several paragraphs to a sentence or two. Remember, in writing a summary you should use your own words.

Consider the following long narrative paragraph in which Maxine Hong Kingston tells of her silence during her early years in American schools.

My silence was thickest—total—during the three years that I covered my school paintings with black paint. I painted layers of black over houses and flowers and suns, and when I drew on the blackboard, I put a layer of chalk on top. I was making a stage curtain, and it was the moment before the curtain parted or rose. The teachers called my parents to school, and I saw they had been saving my pictures, curling and cracking, all alike and black. The teachers pointed to the pictures and looked serious, talked seriously too, but my parents did not understand English. ("The parents and teachers of criminals were executed," said my father.) My parents took the pictures home. I spread them out (so black and full of possibilities) and pretended the curtains were swinging open, flying up, one after another, sunlight underneath, mighty operas.

—Maxine Hong Kingston, "Finding a Voice," page 604.

A student, wishing to capture Kingston's point without repeating her detailed account, wrote the following summary:

Summary Note Card

Childhood Silence

Kingston recalls that her teachers and parents did not understand her silence, thought that her pictures were a sign of depression, and didn't realize that she was using them as a way to fantasize.

Kingston, 604

Paraphrase

When you *paraphrase* a source you restate the information in your own words instead of quoting directly. Unlike a summary, which gives a brief overview of the essential information in the original, a paraphrase seeks to maintain the same level of detail as the original to aid readers in understanding or believing the information presented. A paraphrase presents the original information in approximately the same number of words, but in your own wording. In other words, your paraphrase should closely parallel the presentation of ideas in the original, but not use the same words or sentence structure as the original. Even though you are using your own words with a paraphrase, it's important to remember that you are borrowing ideas and therefore must acknowledge the source of these ideas with a citation.

How would you paraphrase the following passage from Deborah Tannen's book?

> Women who find themselves unwillingly cast as the listener should practice propelling themselves out of that position rather than waiting patiently for the lecture to end. Perhaps they need to give up the belief that they must wait for the floor to be handed to them. If they have something to say on a subject, they might push themselves to volunteer it. If they are bored with a subject, they can exercise some influence on the conversation and change the topic to something they would rather discuss.
>
> —Deborah Tannen, "'I'll Explain It to You': Lecturing and Listening," page 626.

The following note card illustrates how a student paraphrased the passage from Tannen:

Paraphrase Note Card

Solutions

When women believe that they have been put in a position of being a listener against their wills, they should try to take control of the situation instead of waiting for the other person to give them permission to speak. In extricating themselves from such conversations, women might consider asserting themselves by contributing their thoughts and opinions on the subject being discussed or by introducing a totally new subject, one that the women want to talk about.

Tannen, 626

In most cases it is better to summarize or paraphrase materials—which by definition means using your own words—instead of quoting verbatim (word-for-word). To capture an idea in your own words ensures that you have thought about and understand what your source is saying.

Direct Quotation

When you directly *quote* a source, you copy the words of your source exactly, putting all quoted material in quotation marks. When you take a quoted note, carefully check for accuracy, including punctuation and capitalization. Be selective about what you choose to quote; reserve direct quotation for important ideas stated memorably, for especially clear explanations by authorities, and for proponents of a particular position to argue in their own words. Consider, for example, the powerful testimony of Bette Bao Lord in speaking about her experiences with two distinct cultures:

> I do not believe that the loss of one's native culture is the price one must pay for becoming an American. On the contrary, I feel doubly blessed. I can choose from two rich cultures those parts that suit my mood or the occasion best.

—Bette Bao Lord, "Walking in Lucky Shoes," page 601.

Quotation Note Card

Culture

"I do not believe that the loss of one's native culture is the price one must pay for becoming an American. On the contrary, I feel doubly blessed. I can choose from two rich cultures those parts that suit my mood or the occasion best."

Lord, 601

On occasion you'll find a useful passage with some memorable wording in it. Avoid the temptation to quote the whole passage; instead you can combine summary or paraphrase with direct quotation. Consider the following passage from the concluding paragraph of Alleen Pace Nilsen's essay.

> Language is like an X ray in providing visible evidence of invisible thoughts. The best thing about people being interested in and discussing sexist language is that as they make conscious decisions about what pronouns they will use, what jokes they will tell or laugh at, how they will write their names, or how they will begin their letters, they are forced to think about the underlying issue of sexism. This is good because as a problem that begins in people's assumptions and expectations, it's a problem that will be solved only when a great many people have given it a great deal of thought.

—Alleen Pace Nilsen, "Sexism in English: A 1990s Update," page 576.

Note how the student in taking this note was careful to put quotation marks around all words that have been borrowed directly.

Quotation and Summary Note Card

Language / Thought

"Language is like an X ray in providing visible evidence of invisible thoughts." The more people think about the language they use the more they think about the underlying assumptions of those that use it. This is particularly true of sexist language.

Nilsen, 576

Integrating Quotes into Your Text

Whenever you want to use borrowed material, be it a summary, paraphrase, or quotation, it's best to introduce the material with a signal phrase—a phrase that alerts the reader that borrowed information is going to come. A signal phrase usually consists of the author's name and a verb. Well-chosen signal phrases help you to integrate quotations, paraphrases, and summaries into the flow of your paper. Besides, signal phrases let your reader know who is speaking and, in the case of summaries and paraphrases, exactly where your ideas end and someone else's begin. Never confuse your reader with a quotation that appears suddenly without introduction in your paper.

Unannounced Quote
Most Hispanic students are unprepared for what awaits them at many American colleges and universities. "The problems range from the anxiety of breaking close family ties to the loneliness and tensions inherent in finding their way in institutions built around an alien culture" (Fiske 588).

Integrated Quote
Most Hispanic students are unprepared for what awaits them at many American colleges and universities. According to Edward B. Fiske, former education editor at the *New York Times*, "the problems range from the anxiety of breaking close family ties to the loneliness and tensions inherent in finding their way in institutions built around an alien culture" (588).

How well you integrate a quote, paraphrase, or summary into your paper depends partly on varying your signal phrases and, in particular, choosing a verb for the signal phrase that accurately conveys the tone and intent of the writer. If a writer is arguing, use the verb *argues* (or *asserts*, *claims*, or *contends*); if the writer contests a particular position or fact, use the verb *contests* (or *denies*, *disputes*, *refutes*, or *rejects*). In using verbs that are specific to the situation in your paper, you bring your readers into the intellectual debate as well as avoid the monotony of repeating such all-purpose verbs as *says* or *writes*.

You should always try to use a signal phrase that fits the situation in your essay. The following are just a few examples of how you can vary signal phrases to add interest to your paper:

Alleen Pace Nilsen contends that ". . . ."
According to television news commentator Bernard Goldberg, ". . . ."
As Deborah Tannen has observed, ". . . ."
Edward B. Fiske, former education editor at the *New York Times*, emphasizes ". . . ."
Gloria Naylor rejects the widely held belief that ". . . ."

Other verbs that you should keep in mind when constructing signal phrases include the following:

acknowledges	compares	grants	reasons
adds	confirms	implies	reports
admits	declares	insists	responds
believes	endorses	points out	suggests

Documenting Your Sources

Whenever you summarize, paraphrase, or quote a person's thoughts and ideas, and when you use facts or statistics that are not commonly known or believed, you must properly acknowledge the source of your information. These acknowledgments are called *citations*. Your citations must consistently follow either Modern Language Association (MLA) or American Psychological Association (APA) style. The MLA documentation system is used in English and the humanities, while the APA system is used throughout the social sciences. (Your instructor will tell you which system to use.)

There are two components of documentation in a research paper: the *in-text citation*, placed in the body of your paper, and the *list of works cited*, which provides complete publication data on your sources and is placed at the end of your paper.

In-text Citations

Most in-text citations consist of only the author's last name and a page reference. Usually the author's name is given in an introductory or signal phrase at the beginning of the borrowed material and the page reference is given in parentheses at the end. If the author's name is not given at the beginning, put it in the parentheses along with the page reference. The parenthetical reference signals the end of the borrowed material and directs your reader to the list of works cited should he or she want to pursue a source. Consider the following examples of in-text citations from a student paper.

In-text Citation (MLA Style)

Citation with author's name in the signal phrase

> It is important to remember that words are not reality, but merely symbols of reality. **For as Naylor asserts,** "words themselves are innocuous; it is the consensus that gives them true power" **(596).** This is particularly true with labels that stereotype or categorize because, as a leading psychologist contends, "the living, breathing, complex individual—the ultimate unit of human nature—is lost to sight" (Allport 554). A single word can create a reality.

Citation with author's name in parentheses

In-text Citation (APA Style)

Citation with author's name and date in the signal phrase

> It is important to remember that words are not reality, but merely symbols of reality. For as **Naylor (1986)** asserts, "words themselves are innocuous; it is the consensus that gives them true power" (p. 596).

Citation with author's name and date in parentheses

> This is particularly true with labels that stereotype or categorize because, as a leading psychologist contends, "the living, breathing, complex individual—the ultimate unit of human nature—is lost to sight" **(Allport, 1979, p. 554)**. A single word can create a reality.

In both the above examples page references are to the articles as they appear here in *Subject and Strategy*. If you were using these sources from the newspaper and book in which they appeared, your page references would be to the originals.

List of Works Cited

LIST OF WORKS CITED ENTRY (MLA STYLE)

Allport, Gordon W. "The Language of Prejudice." *Subject and Strategy*. 6th ed. Eds. Paul Eschholz and Alfred Rosa. New York: St. Martin's, 1993. 553–563.

Naylor, Gloria. "What's In a Name?" *Subject and Strategy*. 6th ed. Eds. Paul Eschholz and Alfred Rosa. New York: St. Martin's, 1993. 596–599.

REFERENCES ENTRY (APA STYLE)

Allport, G. W. The language of prejudice. (1979). In P. Eschholz & A. Rosa (Eds.), *Subject and Strategy* (6th ed.) (pp. 553–563). New York: St. Martin's.

Naylor, G. What's In a Name? (1986). In P. Eschholz & A. Rosa (Eds.), *Subject and Strategy* (6th ed.) (pp. 596–599). New York: St. Martin's.

Because we have provided you with your sources in this casebook, all of your entries on your *List of Works Cited* will be for a

Works Cited

Allport, Gordon. "The Language of Prejudice" in
    The Nature of Prejudice. Cambridge, MA:
    Addison—Wesley, 1979, 178–187.
Cunha, Edite. "Talking in the New Land." *New
    England Monthly* Aug. 1990: 34+.
Fiske, Edward B. "The Undergraduate Hispanic
    Experience: A Case of Juggling Two Cultures."
    Change May/June 1988: 29+.
Goldberg, Bernard R. "Television Insults Men,
    Too." *The New York Times* 14 Mar. 1989: A29.
Kingston, Maxine Hong. "Finding a Voice" in *The
    Woman Warrior: Memoirs of a Girlhood Among
    Ghosts*. New York: Knopf, 1976, 163–169, 171–
    172.
Lord, Bette Bao. "Walking in Lucky Shoes."
    Newsweek 6 July 1992: 10.
Naylor, Gloria. "What's in a Name?" *The New York
    Times* 20 Feb. 1986: C2.
Nilsen, Alleen Pace. "Sexism in English: A 1990s
    Update." *Language Awareness*. 5th ed. Eds.
    Paul Eschholz, Alfred Rosa, and Virginia
    Clark. New York: St. Martin's, 1990, 277–287.
Tannen, Deborah. *You Just Don't Understand: Women
    and Men in Conversation*. New York:
    Ballantine, 1991. 123–148.

"work in an anthology" and follow one of the formats provided on page 550. If we had not collected these articles for you in this casebook and you had to locate them yourself in the library, your *List of Works Cited* at the end of your paper would be as shown above.

A Note on Plagiarism

The importance of honesty and accuracy in doing library research can't be stressed enough. Any material borrowed word-for-word must be placed within quotation marks and be properly cited; any idea, explanation, or argument you have paraphrased or summarized must be documented, and it must be clear where the paraphrased material begins and ends. In short, to use someone else's ideas whether in their original form or in an altered form without proper acknowledgment is to be guilty of *plagiarism*. And plagiarism is plagiarism even if it is accidental.

A little attention and effort at the notetaking stage can go a long way toward eliminating the possibility of inadvertent plagiarism. Check all direct quotations against the wording of the original, and double check your paraphrases to be sure that you have not used the writer's wording or sentence structure. It is easy to forget to put quotation marks around material taken verbatim or to use the same sentence structure and most of the same words—substituting a synonym here and there—and record it as a paraphrase. In working closely with the ideas and words of others, intellectual honesty demands that we distinguish between what we borrow—and therefore acknowledge in a citation—and what is our own.

While writing your paper, be careful whenever you incorporate one of your notes into your paper; make sure that you put quotation marks around material taken verbatim, and double check your text against your note card—or better yet, the original if you have it on hand—to make sure that your quotation is accurate. When paraphrasing or summarizing, make sure you haven't inadvertently borrowed key words or sentence structures from the original.

Finally, as you proofread your final draft, check all your citations one last time. If at any time while you are taking notes or writing your paper you have a question about plagiarism, consult your instructor for clarification and guidance before proceeding.

The Language of Prejudice

Gordon Allport

Without words we should scarcely be able to form categories at 1
all. A dog perhaps forms rudimentary generalizations, such as
small-boys-are-to-be avoided—but this concept runs its course on
the conditioned reflex level, and does not become the object of
thought as such. In order to hold a generalization in mind for
reflection and recall, for identification and for action, we need to
fix it in words. Without words our world would be, as William
James said, an "empirical sand-heap."

Nouns That Cut Slices

In the empirical world of human beings there are some two and 2
a half billion grains of sand corresponding to our category "the
human race." We cannot possibly deal with so many separate en-
tities in our thought, nor can we individualize even among the
hundreds whom we encounter in our daily round. We must group
them, form clusters. We welcome, therefore, the names that help
us to perform the clustering.

The most important property of a noun is that it brings many 3
grains of sand into a single pail, disregarding the fact that the same
grains might have fitted just as appropriately into another pail. To
state the matter technically, a noun *abstracts* from a concrete reality
some one feature and assembles different concrete realities only
with respect to this one feature. The very act of classifying forces
us to overlook all other features, many of which might offer a
sounder basis than the rubric we select. Irving Lee gives the following example:

> I knew a man who had lost the use of both eyes. He was called a "blind
> man." He could also be called an expert typist, a conscientious worker,
> a good student, a careful listener, a man who wanted a job. But he
> couldn't get a job in the department store order room where employees
> sat and typed orders which came over the telephone. The personnel

man was impatient to get the interview over. "But you're a blind man,"
he kept saying, and one could almost feel his silent assumption that
somehow the incapacity in one aspect made the man incapable in every
other. So blinded by the label was the interviewer that he could not be
persuaded to look beyond it.

Some labels, such as "blind man," are exceedingly salient and   4
powerful. They tend to prevent alternative classification, or even
cross-classification. Ethnic labels are often of this type, particularly
if they refer to some highly visible feature, e.g., Negro, Oriental.
They resemble the labels that point to some outstanding incapacity—*feeble-minded, cripple, blind man*. Let us call such symbols
"labels of primary potency." These symbols act like shrieking si-
rens, deafening us to all finer discriminations that we might otherwise perceive. Even though the blindness of one man and the
darkness of pigmentation of another may be defining attributes for
some purposes, they are irrelevant and "noisy" for others.

Most people are unaware of this basic law of language—that   5
every label applied to a given person refers properly only to one
aspect of his nature. You may correctly say that a certain man is
human, a philanthropist, a Chinese, a physician, an athlete. A given
person may be all of these; but the chances are that *Chinese* stands
out in your mind as the symbol of primary potency. Yet neither
this nor any other classificatory label can refer to the whole of a
man's nature. (Only his proper name can do so.)

Thus each label we use, especially those of primary potency,   6
distracts our attention from concrete reality. The living, breathing,
complex individual—the ultimate unit of human nature—is lost to
sight. As in the figure, the label magnifies one attribute out of all
proportion to its true significance, and masks other important attributes of the individual. . . .

A category, once formed with the aid of a symbol of primary   7
potency, tends to attract more attributes than it should. The category labeled *Chinese* comes to signify not only ethnic membership
but also reticence, impassivity, poverty, treachery. To be sure, . . .
there may be genuine ethnic-linked traits, making for a certain
probability that the member of an ethnic stock may have these attributes. But our cognitive process is not cautious. The labeled category, as we have seen, includes indiscriminately the defining at-

tribute, probable attributes, and wholly fanciful, nonexistent attributes.

Even proper names—which ought to invite us to look at the individual person—may act like symbols of primary potency, especially if they arouse ethnic associations. Mr. Greenberg is a person, but since his name is Jewish, it activates in the hearer his entire category of Jews-as-a-whole. An ingenious experiment performed by Razran shows this point clearly, and at the same time demonstrates how a proper name, acting like an ethnic symbol, may bring with it an avalanche of stereotypes.

> Thirty photographs of college girls were shown on a screen to 150 students. The subjects rated the girls on a scale from one to five for *beauty, intelligence, character, ambition, general likability.* Two months later the same subjects were asked to rate the same photographs (and fifteen additional ones introduced to complicate the memory factor). This time five of the original photographs were given Jewish surnames (Cohen, Kantor, etc.), five Italian (Valenti, etc.), and five Irish (O'Brien, etc.); and the remaining girls were given names chosen from the signers of the Declaration of Independence and from the Social Register (Davis, Adams, Clark, etc.).
>
> When Jewish names were attached to photographs there occurred the following changes in ratings:
>   decrease in liking
>   decrease in character
>   decrease in beauty
>   increase in intelligence
>   increase in ambition
> For those photographs given Italian names there occurred:
>   decrease in liking
>   decrease in character
>   decrease in beauty
>   decrease in intelligence
> Thus a mere proper name leads to prejudgments of personal attributes. The individual is fitted to the prejudice ethnic category, and not judged in his own right.
>
> While the Irish names also brought about depreciated judgment, the depreciation was not as great as in the case of the Jews and Italians. The falling of likability of the "Jewish girls" was twice as great as for

"Italians" and five times as great as for "Irish." We note, however, that the "Jewish" photographs caused higher ratings in *intelligence* and in *ambition*. Not all stereotypes of out-groups are unfavorable.

The anthropologist, Margaret Mead, has suggested that labels 9 of primary potency lose some of their force when they are changed from nouns into adjectives. To speak of a Negro soldier, a Catholic teacher, or a Jewish artist calls attention to the fact that some other group classifications are just as legitimate as the racial or religious. If George Johnson is spoken of not only as a Negro but also as a *soldier*, we have at least two attributes to know him by, and two are more accurate than one. To depict him truly as an individual, of course, we should have to name many more attributes. It is a useful suggestion that we designate ethnic and religious membership where possible with *adjectives* rather than *nouns*.

Emotionally Toned Labels

Many categories have two kinds of labels—one less emotional 10 and one more emotional. Ask yourself how you feel, and what thoughts you have, when you read the words *school teacher*, and then *school marm*. Certainly the second phrase calls up something more strict, more ridiculous, more disagreeable than the former. Here are four innocent letters: m-a-r-m. But they make us shudder a bit, laugh a bit, and scorn a bit. They call up an image of a spare, humorless, irritable old maid. They do not tell us that she is an individual human being with sorrows and troubles of her own. They force her instantly into a rejective category.

In the ethnic sphere even plain labels such as Negro, Italian, 11 Jew, Catholic, Irish-American, French-Canadian may have emotional tone for a reason that we shall soon explain. But they all have their higher key equivalents: nigger, wop, kike, papist, harp, canuck. When these labels are employed we can be almost certain that the speaker *intends* not only to characterize the person's membership, but also to disparage and reject him.

Quite apart from the insulting intent that lies behind the use of 12 certain labels, there is also an inherent ("physiognomic") handicap in many terms designating ethnic membership. For example, the proper names characteristic of certain ethnic memberships strike us as absurd. (We compare them, of course, with what is familiar and therefore "right.") Chinese names are short and silly; Polish names intrinsically difficult and outlandish. Unfamiliar dialects strike us as ludicrous. Foreign dress (which, of course, is a visual ethnic symbol) seems unnecessarily queer.

But of all these "physiognomic" handicaps the reference to color, 13 clearly implied in certain symbols, is the greatest. The word Negro comes from the Latin *niger* meaning black. In point of fact, no Negro has a black complexion, but by comparison with other blonder stocks, he has come to be known as a "black man." Unfortunately *black* in the English language is a word having a preponderance of sinister connotations: the outlook is black, blackball, blackguard, black-hearted, black death, blacklist, blackmail, Black Hand. In his novel *Moby Dick*, Herman Melville considers at length the remarkably morbid connotations of black and the remarkably virtuous connotations of white.

Nor is the ominous flavor of black confined to the English lan- 14 guage. A cross-cultural study reveals that the semantic significance of black is more or less universally the same. Among certain Siberian tribes, members of a privileged clan call themselves "white bones," and refer to all others as "black bones." Even among Uganda Negroes there is some evidence for a white god at the apex of the theocratic hierarchy; certain it is that a white cloth, signifying purity, is used to ward off evil spirits and disease.

There is thus an implied value-judgment in the very concept of 15 *white race* and *black race*. One might also study the numerous unpleasant connotations of *yellow*, and their possible bearing on our conception of the people of the Orient.

Such reasoning should not be carried too far, since there are 16 undoubtedly, in various contexts, pleasant associations with both black and yellow. Black velvet is agreeable, so too are chocolate and coffee. Yellow tulips are well liked; the sun and moon are radiantly yellow. Yet it is true that "color" words are used with chauvinistic overtones more than most people realize. There is certainly condescension indicated in many familiar phrases: dark as a nigger's pocket, darktown strutters, white hope (a term originated when a white contender was sought against the Negro heavyweight champion, Jack Johnson), the white man's burden, the yellow peril, black boy. Scores of everyday phrases are stamped with the flavor of prejudice, whether the user knows it or not.

We spoke of the fact that even the most proper and sedate labels 17 for minority groups sometimes seem to exude a negative flavor. In many contexts and situations the very terms *French-Canadian, Mexican,* or *Jew,* correct and nonmalicious though they are, sound a bit opprobrious. The reason is that they are labels of social deviants. Especially in a culture where uniformity is prized, the name of *any* deviant carries with it *ipso facto* a negative value-judgment. Words like *insane, alcoholic, pervert* are presumably neutral designations of a human condition, but they are more: they are finger-pointing at a deviance. Minority groups are deviants, and for this reason, from the very outset, the most innocent labels in many situations imply a shading of disrepute. When we wish to highlight the deviance and denigrate it still further we use words of a higher emotional key: crackpot, soak, pansy, greaser, Okie, nigger, harp, kike.

Members of minority groups are often understandably sensitive 18 to names given them. Not only do they object to deliberately insulting epithets, but sometimes see evil intent where none exists. Often the word Negro is spelled with a small *n,* occasionally as a studied insult, more often from ignorance. (The term is not cognate with white, which is not capitalized, but rather with Caucasian, which is.) Terms like "mulatto," or "octoroon" cause hard feeling because of the condescension with which they have often been used in the past. Sex differentiations are objectionable, since they seem doubly to emphasize ethnic difference: why speak of Jewess and not of Protestantess, or of Negress and not of whitess? Similar overemphasis is implied in the terms like Chinamen or Scotchman; why not American man? Grounds for misunderstanding lie in the fact that minority group members are sensitive to such shadings, while majority members may employ them unthinkingly.

The Communist Label

Until we label an out-group it does not clearly exist in our minds. 19 Take the curiously vague situation that we often meet when a person wishes to locate responsibility on the shoulders of some out-group whose nature he cannot specify. In such a case he usually employs the pronoun "they" without an antecedent. "Why don't they make these sidewalks wider?" "I hear they are going to build a factory in this town and hire a lot of foreigners." "I won't pay this tax bill; they can just whistle for their money." If asked "who?" the speaker is likely to grow confused and embarrassed. The common use of the orphaned pronoun *they* teaches us that people often want and need to designate out-groups (usually for the purpose of venting hostility) even when they have no clear conception of the out-group in question. And so long as the target of wrath remains vague and ill-defined specific prejudice cannot crystallize around it. To have enemies we need labels.

Until relatively recently—strange as it may seem—there was no 20 agreed-upon symbol for *communist*. The word, of course, existed but it had no special emotional connotation, and did not designate a public enemy. Even when, after World War I, there was a growing feeling of economic and social menace in this country, there was no agreement as to the actual source of the menace.

A content analysis of the Boston *Herald* for the year 1920 turned 21 up the following list of labels. Each was used in a content implying some threat. Hysteria had overspread the country, as it did after World War II. Someone must be responsible for the postwar malaise, rising prices, uncertainty. There must be a villain. But in 1920 the villain was impartially designated by reporters and editorial writers with the following symbols:

alien, agitator, anarchist, apostle of bomb and torch, Bolshevik, communist, communist laborite, conspirator, emissary of false promise, extremist, foreigner, hyphenated-American, incendiary, IWW, parlor anarchist, parlor pink, parlor socialist, plotter, radical, red, revolutionary, Russian agitator, socialist Soviet, syndicalist, traitor, undesirable.

From this excited array we note that the *need* for an enemy (some- 22 one to serve as a focus for discontent and jitters) was considerably more apparent than the precise *identity* of the enemy. At any rate, there was no clearly agreed upon label. Perhaps partly for this reason the hysteria abated. Since no clear category of "communism" existed there was no true focus for the hostility.

But following World War II this collection of vaguely inter- 23 changeable labels became fewer in number and more commonly agreed upon. The out-group menace came to be designated almost always as *communist* or *red*. In 1920 the threat, lacking a clear label, was vague; after 1945 both symbol and thing became more definite. Not that people knew precisely what they meant when they said "communist," but with the aid of the term they were at least able to point consistently to *something* that inspired fear. The term developed the power of signifying menace and led to various repressive measures against anyone to whom the label was rightly or wrongly attached.

Logically, the label should apply to specifiable defining attri- 24 butes, such as members of the Communist Party, or people whose allegiance is with the Russian system, or followers, historically, of Karl Marx. But the label came in for far more extensive use.

What seems to have happened is approximately as follows. Hav- 25 ing suffered through a period of war and being acutely aware of devastating revolutions abroad, it is natural that most people should be upset, dreading to lose their possessions, annoyed by high taxes, seeing customary moral and religious values threatened, and dreading worse disasters to come. Seeking an explanation for this unrest, a single identifiable enemy is wanted. It is not enough to designate "Russia" or some other distant land. Nor is it satisfactory to fix blame on "changing social conditions." What is needed is a human agent near at hand: someone in Washington, someone in our schools, in our factories, in our neighborhood. If we *feel* an immediate threat, we reason, there must be a near-lying danger. It is, we conclude, communism, not only in Russia but also in America, at our doorstep, in our government, in our churches, in our colleges, in our neighborhood.

Are we saying that hostility toward communism is prejudice? 26 Not necessarily. There are certainly phases of the dispute wherein realistic social conflict is involved. American values (e.g., respect for the person) and totalitarian values as represented in Soviet practice are intrinsically at odds. A realistic opposition in some form will occur. Prejudice enters only when the defining attributes of *communist* grow imprecise, when anyone who favors any form of social change is called a communist. People who fear social change are the ones most likely to affix the label to any persons or practices that seem to them threatening.

For them the category is undifferentiated. It includes books, movies, preachers, teachers who utter what for them are uncongenial thoughts. If evil befalls—perhaps forest fires or a factory explosion—it is due to communist saboteurs. The category becomes monopolistic, covering almost anything that is uncongenial. On the floor of the House of Representatives in 1946, Representative Rankin called James Roosevelt a communist. Congressman Outland replied with psychological acumen, "Apparently everyone who disagrees with Mr. Rankin is a communist." 27

When differentiated thinking is at a low ebb—as it is in times of social crises—there is a magnification of two-valued logic. Things are perceived as either inside or outside a moral order. What is outside is likely to be called communist. Correspondingly—and here is where damage is done—whatever is called communist (however erroneously) is immediately cast outside the moral order. 28

This associative mechanism places enormous power in the hands of a demagogue. For several years Senator McCarthy managed to discredit many citizens who thought differently from himself by the simple device of calling them communist. Few people were able to see through this trick and many reputations were ruined. But the famous senator has no monopoly on the device. As reported in the Boston *Herald* on November 1, 1946, Representative Joseph Martin, Republican leader in the House, ended his election campaign against his Democratic opponent by saying, "The people will vote tomorrow between chaos, confusion, bankruptcy, state socialism or communism, and the preservation of our American life, with all its freedom and its opportunities." Such an array of emotional labels placed his opponent outside the accepted moral order. Martin was reelected. . . . 29

Not everyone, of course, is taken in. Demagogy, when it goes too far, meets with ridicule. Elizabeth Dilling's book, *The Red Network*, was so exaggerated in its two-valued logic that it was shrugged off by many people with a smile. One reader remarked, "Apparently if you step off the sidewalk with your left foot you're a communist." But it is not easy in times of social strain and hysteria 30 to keep one's balance, and to resist the tendency of a verbal symbol to manufacture large and fanciful categories of prejudiced thinking.

Verbal Realism and Symbol Phobia

Most individuals rebel at being labeled, especially if the label is 31 uncomplimentary. Very few are willing to be called *fascistic, socialistic,* or *anti-Semitic.* Unsavory labels may apply to others; but not to us.

An illustration of the craving that people have to attach favorable 32 symbols to themselves is seen in the community where white people banded together to force out a Negro family that had moved in. They called themselves "Neighborly Endeavor" and chose as their motto the Golden Rule. One of the first acts of this symbol-sanctified band was to sue the man who sold property to Negroes. They then flooded the house which another Negro couple planned to occupy. Such were the acts performed under the banner of the Golden Rule.

Studies made by Stagner and Hartmann show that a person's 33 political attitudes may in fact entitle him to be called a fascist or a socialist, and yet he will emphatically repudiate the unsavory label, and fail to endorse any movement or candidate that overtly accepts them. In short, there is a *symbol phobia* that corresponds to *symbol realism.* We are more inclined to the former when we ourselves are concerned, though we are much less critical when epithets of "fascist," "communist," "blind man," "school marm" are applied to others.

When symbols provoke strong emotions they are sometimes re- 34 garded no longer as symbols, but as actual things. The expressions "son of a bitch" and "liar" are in our culture frequently regarded as "fighting words." Softer and more subtle expressions of contempt may be accepted. But in these particular cases, the epithet itself must be "taken back." We certainly do not change our opponent's attitude by making him take back a word, but it seems somehow important that the word itself be eradicated.

Such verbal realism may reach extreme length. 35

The City Council of Cambridge, Massachusetts, unanimously passed a resolution (December, 1939) making it illegal "to possess, harbor, sequester, introduce or transport, within the city limits, any book, map, magazine, newspaper, pamphlet, handbill or circular containing the words Lenin or Leningrad."

Such naiveté in confusing language with reality is hard to comprehend unless we recall that word-magic plays an appreciable part in human thinking. The following examples, like the one preceding, are taken from Hayakawa.

The Malagasy soldier must eschew kidneys, because in the Malagasy language the word for kidney is the same as that for "shot"; so shot he would certainly be if he ate a kidney.

In May, 1937, a state senator of New York bitterly opposed a bill for the control of syphilis because "the innocence of children might be corrupted by a widespread use of the term. . . . This particular word creates a shudder in every decent woman and decent man."

This tendency to reify words underscores the close cohesion that 36 exists between category and symbol. Just the mention of "communist," "Negro," "Jew," "England," "Democrats," will send some people into a panic of fear or a frenzy of anger. Who can say whether it is the word or the thing that annoys them? The label is an intrinsic part of any monopolistic category. Hence to liberate a person from ethnic or political prejudice it is necessary at the same time to liberate him from *word fetishism*. This fact is well known to students of general semantics who tell us that prejudice is due in large part to verbal realism and to symbol phobia. Therefore any program for the reduction of prejudice must include a large measure of semantic therapy.

Sexism in English: A 1990s Update

Alleen Pace Nilsen

Twenty years ago I embarked on a study of the sexism inherent   1
in American English. I had just returned to Ann Arbor, Michigan,
after living for two years (1967–69) in Kabul, Afghanistan, where
I had begun to look critically at the role society assigned to women.
The Afghan version of the *chaderi* prescribed for Moslem women
was particularly confining. Afghan jokes and folklore were blatantly sexist, such as this proverb: "If you see an old man, sit down
and take a lesson; if you see an old woman, throw a stone."

But it wasn't only the native culture that made me question wom-   2
en's roles, it was also the American community.

Most of the American women were like myself—wives and   3
mothers whose husbands were either career diplomats, employees
of USAID, or college professors who had been recruited to work
on various contract teams. We were suddenly bereft of our traditional roles: some of us became alcoholics, others got very good
at bridge, while still others searched desperately for ways to contribute either to our families or to the Afghans. The local economy
provided few jobs for women and certainly none for foreigners;
we were isolated from former friends and the social goals we had
grown up with.

When I returned in the fall of 1969 to the University of Michigan   4
in Ann Arbor, I was surprised to find that many other women
were also questioning the expectations they had grown up with.
In the spring of 1970, a women's conference was announced. I
hired a babysitter and attended, but I returned home more troubled
than ever. The militancy of these women frightened me. Since I
wasn't ready for a revolution, I decided I would have my own
feminist movement. I would study the English language and see
what it could tell me about sexism. I started reading a desk dictionary and making notecards on every entry that seemed to tell
something about male and female. I soon had a dog-eared dictionary, along with a collection of note cards filling two shoe boxes.

Ironically, I started reading the dictionary because I wanted to   5
avoid getting involved in social issues, but what happened was

564

that my notecards brought me right back to looking at society. Language and society are as intertwined as a chicken and an egg. The language a culture uses is telltale evidence of the values and beliefs of that culture. And because there is a lag in how fast a language changes—new words can easily be introduced, but it takes a long time for old words and usages to disappear—a careful look at English will reveal the attitudes that our ancestors held and that we as a culture are therefore predisposed to hold. My note cards revealed three main points. Friends have offered the opinion that I didn't need to read the dictionary to learn such obvious facts. Nevertheless, it was interesting to have linguistic evidence of sociological observations.

Women Are Sexy; Men Are Successful

First, in American culture a woman is valued for the attractiveness and sexiness of her body, while a man is valued for his physical strength and accomplishments. A woman is sexy. A man is successful. 6

A persuasive piece of evidence supporting this view are the eponyms—words that have come from someone's name—found in English. I had a two-and-a-half-inch stack of cards taken from men's names but less than a half-inch stack from women's names, and most of those came from Greek mythology. In the words that came into American English since we separated from Britain, there are many eponyms based on the names of famous American men: *Bartlett pear, boysenberry, diesel engine, Franklin stove, Ferris wheel, Gatling gun, mason jar, sideburns, sousaphone, Schick test,* and *Winchester rifle.* The only common eponyms taken from American women's names are *Alice blue* (after Alice Roosevelt Longworth), *bloomers* (after Amelia Jenks Bloomer), and *Mae West jacket* (after the buxom actress). Two out of the three feminine eponyms relate closely to a woman's physical anatomy, while the masculine eponyms (except for *sideburns* after General Burnsides) have nothing to do with the namesake's body but, instead, honor the man for an accomplishment of some kind. 7

Although in Greek mythology women played a bigger role than they did in the biblical stories of the Judeo-Christian cultures and 8 so the names of goddesses are accepted parts of the language in such place names as Pomona from the goddess of fruit and Athens from Athena and in such common words as *cereal* from Ceres, *psychology* from Psyche, and *arachnoid* from Arachne, the same tendency to think of women in relation to sexuality is seen in the eponyms *aphrodisiac* from Aphrodite, the Greek name for the goddess of love and beauty, and *venereal disease* from Venue, the Roman name for Aphrodite.

Another interesting word from Greek mythology is *Amazon*. According to Greek folk etymology, the *a* means "without" as in *atypical* or *amoral*, while *mazon* comes from *mazos* meaning "breast" as still seen in *mastectomy*. In the Greek legend, Amazon women cut off their right breasts so that they could better shoot their bows. Apparently, the storytellers had a feeling that for women to play the active, "masculine" role the Amazons adopted for themselves, they had to trade in part of their femininity.

This preoccupation with women's breasts is not limited to ancient stories. As a volunteer for the University of Wisconsin's *Dictionary of American Regional English (DARE)*, I read a western trapper's diary from the 1930s. I was to make notes of any unusual usages or language patterns. My most interesting finding was that the trapper referred to a range of mountains as *The Teats*, a metaphor based on the similarity between the shapes of the mountains and women's breasts. Because today we use the French wording, *The Grand Tetons*, the metaphor isn't as obvious, but I wrote to mapmakers and found the following listings: *Nippletop* and *Little Nipple Top* near Mount Marcy in the Adirondacks; *Nipple Mountain* in Archuleta County, Colorado; *Nipple Peak* in Coke County, Texas; *Nipple Butte* in Pennington, South Dakota; *Squaw Peak* in Placer County, California (and many other locations); *Maiden's Peak* and *Squaw Tit* (they're the same mountain) in the Cascade Range in Oregon; *Mary's Nipple* near Salt Lake City, Utah; and *Jane Russell Peaks* near Stark, New Hampshire.

Except for the movie star Jane Russell, the women being referred to are anonymous—it's only a sexual part of their body that is mentioned. When topographical features are named after men, it's probably not going to be to draw attention to a sexual part of their bodies but instead to honor individuals for an accomplishment.

For example, no one thinks of a part of the male body when hearing a reference to Pike's Peak, Colorado, or Jackson Hole, Wyoming.

Going back to what I learned from my dictionary cards, I was 12 surprised to realize how many pairs of words we have in which the feminine word has acquired sexual connotations while the masculine word retains a serious businesslike aura. For example, a *callboy* is the person who calls actors when it is time for them to go on stage, but a *callgirl* is a prostitute. Compare *sir* and *madam*. *Sir* is a term of respect, while *madam* has acquired the specialized meaning of a brothel manager. Something similar has happened to *master* and *mistress*. Would you rather have a painting by an *old master* or an *old mistress*?

It's because the word *woman* had sexual connotations, as in 13 "She's his woman," that people began avoiding its use, hence such terminology as *ladies' room, lady of the house,* and *girls' school* or *school for young ladies*. Feminists, who ask that people use the term *woman* rather than *girl* or *lady*, are rejecting the idea that *woman* is primarily a sexual term. They have been at least partially successful in that today *woman* is commonly used to communicate gender without intending implications about sexuality.

I found two hundred pairs of words with masculine and feminine 14 forms, e.g., *heir-heiress, hero-heroine, steward-stewardess, usher-ush-erette*. In nearly all such pairs, the masculine word is considered the base, with some kind of a feminine suffix being added. The masculine form is the one from which compounds are made, e.g., from *king-queen* comes *kingdom* but not *queendom*, from *sportsman-sportslady* comes *sportsmanship* but not *sportsladyship*. There is one—and only one—semantic area in which the masculine word is not the base or more powerful word. This is in the area dealing with sex and marriage. When someone refers to a *virgin*, a listener will probably think of a female, unless the speaker specifies *male* or uses a masculine pronoun. The same is true for *prostitute*.

In relation to marriage, there is much linguistic evidence show- 15 ing that weddings are more important to women than to men. A woman cherishes the wedding and is considered a bride for a whole year, but a man is referred to as a groom only on the day of the wedding. The word *bride* appears in *bridal attendant, bridal gown, bridesmaid, bridal shower,* and even *bridegroom*. *Groom* comes from the Middle English *grom*, meaning "man," and in the sense is seldom used outside of the wedding. With most pairs of male/female words, people habitually put the masculine word first, *Mr. and Mrs., his and hers, boys and girls, men and women, kings and queens, brothers and sisters, guys and dolls,* and *host and hostess,* but it is the *bride and groom* who are talked about, not the *groom and bride.*

The importance of marriage to a woman is also shown by the 16 fact that when a marriage ends in death, the woman gets the title of *widow.* A man gets the derived title of *widower.* This term is not used in other phrases or contexts, but *widow* is seen in *widowhood, widow's peak,* and *widow's walk.* A *widow* in a card game is an extra hand of cards, while in typesetting it is an extra line of type.

How changing cultural ideas bring changes to language is clearly 17 visible in this semantic area. The feminist movement has caused the differences between the sexes to be downplayed, and since I did my dictionary study two decades ago, the word *singles* has largely replaced such sex specific and value-laden terms as *bachelor, old maid, spinster, divorcee, widow,* and *widower.* And in 1970 I wrote that when a man is called *a professional* he is thought to be a doctor or a lawyer, but when people hear a woman referred to as *a professional* they are likely to think of a prostitute. That's not as true today because so many women have become doctors and lawyers that it's no longer incongruous to think of women in those professional roles.

Another change that has taken place is in wedding announce- 18 ments. They used to be sent out from the bride's parents and did not even give the name of the groom's parents. Today, most couples choose to list either all or none of the parents' names. Also it is now much more likely that both the bride and groom's picture will be in the newspaper, while a decade ago only the bride's picture was published on the "Women's" or the "Society" page. Even the traditional wording of the wedding ceremony is being changed. Many officials now pronounce the couple "husband and wife" instead of the old "man and wife," and they ask the bride if she promises "to love, honor, and cherish," instead of "to love, honor, and obey."

Women Are Passive; Men Are Active

The wording of the wedding ceremony also relates to the second 19 point that my cards showed, which is that women are expected to play a passive or weak role while men play an active or strong role. In the traditional ceremony, the official asks, "Who gives the bride away?" and the father answers, "I do." Some fathers answer, "Her mother and I do," but that doesn't solve the problem inherent in the question. The idea that a bride is something to be handed over from one man to another bothers people because it goes back to the days when a man's servants, his children, and his wife were all considered to be his property. They were known by his name because they belonged to him, and he was responsible for their actions and their debts.

The grammar used in talking or writing about weddings as well [20] as other sexual relationships shows the expectation of men playing the active role. Men *wed* women while women *become* brides of men. A man *possesses* a woman; he *deflowers* her; he *performs*; he *scores*; he *takes away* her virginity. Although a woman can *seduce* a man, she cannot offer him her virginity. When talking about virginity, the only way to make the woman the actor in the sentence is to say that "She lost her virginity," but people lose things by accident rather than by purposeful actions, and so she's only the grammatical, not the real-life, actor.

The reason that women tried to bring the term *Ms.* into the lan- [21] guage to replace *Miss* and *Mrs.* relates to this point. Married women resent being identified only under their husband's names. For example, when Susan Glascoe did something newsworthy, she would be identified in the newspaper only as Mrs. John Glascoe. The dictionary cards showed what appeared to be an attitude on the part of the editors that it was almost indecent to let a respectable woman's name march unaccompanied across the pages of a dictionary. Women were listed with male names whether or not the male contributed to the woman's reason for being in the dictionary or in his own right was as famous as the woman. For example, Charlotte Brontë was identified as Mrs. Arthur B. Nicholls, Amelia Earhart as Mrs. George Palmer Putnam, Helen Hayes as Mrs. Charles MacArthur, Jenny Lind as Mme. Otto Goldschmit, Cornelia Otis Skinner as the daughter of Otis, Harriet Beecher Stowe as the sister of Henry Ward Beecher, and Edith Sitwell as the sister of Osbert and Sacheverell. A very small number of women got into the dictionary without the benefit of a masculine escort. They were rebels and crusaders: temperance leaders Frances Elizabeth Caroline Willard and Carry Nation, women's rights leaders Carrie Chapman Catt and Elizabeth Cady Stanton, birth control educator Margaret Sanger, religious leader Mary Baker Eddy, and slaves Harriet Tubman and Phillis Wheatley.

Etiquette books used to teach that if a woman had *Mrs.* in front 22 of her name, then the husband's name should follow because *Mrs.* is an abbreviated form of *Mistress* and a woman couldn't be a mistress of herself. As with many arguments about "correct" language usage, this isn't very logical because *Miss* is also an abbreviation of *Mistress.* Feminists hoped to simplify matters by introducing *Ms.* as an alternative to both *Mrs.* and *Miss,* but what happened is that *Ms.* largely replaced *Miss,* to became a catch-all business title for women. Many married women still prefer the title *Mrs.,* and some resent being addressed with the term *Ms.* As one frustrated newspaper reporter complained, "Before I can write about a woman, I have to know not only her marital status but also her political philosophy." The result of such complications may contribute to the demise of titles, which are already being ignored by many computer programmers who find it more efficient to simply use names, for example in a business letter: "Dear Joan Garcia," instead of "Dear Mrs. Joan Garcia," "Dear Ms. Garcia," or "Dear Mrs. Louis Garcia."

The titles given to royalty provide an example of how males can 23 be disadvantaged by the assumption that they are always to play the more powerful role. In British royalty, when a male holds a title, his wife is automatically given the feminine equivalent. But the reverse is not true. For example, a *count* is a high political officer with a *countess* being his wife. The same is true for a *duke* and a *duchess* and a *king* and a *queen.* But when a female holds the royal title, the man she marries does not automatically acquire the matching title. For example, Queen Elizabeth's husband has the title of *prince* rather than *king,* but if Prince Charles should become king while he is still married to Lady or Princess Diana, she will be known as the queen. The reasoning appears to be that since masculine words are stronger, they are reserved for true heirs and withheld from males coming into the royal family by marriage. If Prince Phillip were called *King Phillip,* it would be much easier for British subjects to forget where the true power lies.

The names that people give their children show the hopes and 24 dreams they have for them, and when we look at the differences between male and female names in a culture, we can see the cumulative expectations of that culture. In our culture girls often have names taken from small, aesthetically pleasing items, e.g., *Ruby*, *Jewel*, and *Pearl*. *Esther* and *Stella* mean "star," *Ada* means "ornament," and *Vanessa* means "butterfly." Boys are more likely to be given names with meanings of power and strength, e.g., *Neil* means "champion," *Martin* is from Mars, the God of War, *Raymond* means "wise protection," *Harold* means "chief of the army," *Ira* means "vigilant," *Rex* means "king," and *Richard* means "strong king."

We see similar differences in food metaphors. Food is a passive substance just sitting there waiting to be eaten. Many people have recognized this and so no longer feel comfortable describing women as "delectable morsels." However, when I was a teenager, it was considered a compliment to refer to a girl (we didn't call anyone a *woman* until she was middle-aged) as a *cute tomato*, a *peach*, a *dish*, a *cookie, honey, sugar,* or *sweetie-pie*. When being affectionate, women will occasionally call a man *honey* or *sweetie*, but in general, food metaphors are used much less often with men than with women. If a man is called a *fruit*, his masculinity is being questioned. But it's perfectly acceptable to use a food metaphor if the food is heavier and more substantive than that used for women. For example pin-up pictures of women have long been known as *cheesecake*, but when Burt Reynolds posed for a nude centerfold the picture was immediately dubbed *beefcake*, c.f., *a hunk of meat*. That such sexual references to men have come into the language is another reflection of how society is beginning to lessen the differences between their attitudes toward men and women.

Something similar to the *fruit* metaphor happens with references to plants. We insult a man by calling him a *pansy*, but it wasn't considered particularly insulting to talk about a girl being a *wallflower*, a *clinging vine*, or a *shrinking violet*, or to give girls such names as *Ivy, Rose, Lily, Iris, Daisy, Camellia, Heather,* and *Flora*. A plant metaphor can be used with a man if the plant is big and strong, for example, Andrew Jackson's nickname of *Old Hickory*. Also, the phrases *blooming idiots* and *budding geniuses* can be used with either sex, but notice how they are based on the most active thing a plant can do which is to bloom or bud.

Animal metaphors also illustrate the different expectations for 27 males and females. Men are referred to as *studs*, *bucks*, and *wolves* while women are referred to with such metaphors as *kitten*, *bunny*, *beaver*, *bird*, *chick*, and *lamb*. In the 1950s we said that boys went *tomcatting*, but today it's just *catting around* and both boys and girls do it. When the term *foxy*, meaning that someone was sexy, first became popular it was used only for girls, but now someone of either sex can be described as a *fox*. Some animal metaphors that are used predominantly with men have negative connotations based on the size and/or strength of the animals, e.g., *beast*, *bull-headed*, *jackass*, *rat*, *loanshark*, and *vulture*. Negative metaphors used with women are based on smaller animals, e.g., *social butterfly*, *mousy*, *catty*, and *vixen*. The feminine terms connote action, but not the same kind of large scale action as with the masculine terms.

Women Are Connected with Negative Connotations; Men with Positive Connotations

The final point that my notecards illustrated was how many pos- 28 itive connotations are associated with the concept of masculine, while there are either trivial or negative connotations connected with the corresponding feminine concept. An example from the animal metaphors makes a good illustration. The word *shrew* taken from the name of a small but especially vicious animal was defined in my dictionary as "an ill-tempered scolding woman," but the word *shrewd* taken from the same root was defined as "marked by clever, discerning awareness" and was illustrated with the phrase "a shrewd businessman."

Early in life, children are conditioned to the superiority of the 29 masculine role. As child psychologists point out, little girls have much more freedom to experiment with sex roles than do little boys. If a little girl acts like a *tomboy*, most parents have mixed feelings, being at least partially proud. But if their little boy acts like a *sissy* (derived from *sister*), they call a psychologist. It's perfectly acceptable for a little girl to sleep in the crib that was purchased for her brother, to wear his hand-me-down jeans and shirts, and to ride the bicycle that he has outgrown. But few parents would put a boy baby in a white and gold crib decorated with frills and lace, and virtually no parents would have their little boy wear his sister's hand-me-down dresses, nor would they have their son ride a girl's pink bicycle with a flower-bedecked basket. The proper names given to girls and boys show this same attitude. Girls can have "boy" names—*Cris, Craig, Jo, Kelly, Shawn, Teri, Toni,* and *Sam*—but it doesn't work the other way around. A couple of generations ago, *Beverley, Frances, Hazel, Marion,* and *Shirley* were common boys' names. As parents gave these names to more and more girls, they fell into disuse for males, and some older men who have these names prefer to go by their initials or by such abbreviated forms as *Haze* or *Shirl.*

When a little girl is told to *be a lady*, she is being told to sit with 30 her knees together and to be quiet and dainty. But when a little boy is told to *be a man* he is being told to be noble, strong, and virtuous—to have all the qualities that the speaker looks on as desirable. The concept of manliness has such positive connotations that it used to be a compliment to call someone a *he-man*, to say that he was doubly a man. Today many people are more ambivalent about this term and respond to it much as they do to the word *macho*. But calling someone a *manly man* or a *virile man* is nearly always meant as a compliment. *Virile* comes from the Indo-European *vir* meaning "man," which is also the basis of *virtuous*. Contrast the positive connotations of both *virile* and *virtuous* with the negative connotations of *hysterical*. The Greeks took this latter word from their name for *uterus* (as still seen in *hysterectomy*). They thought that women were the only ones who experienced uncontrolled emotional outbursts, and so the condition must have something to do with a part of the body that only women have.

Differences in the connotations between positive male and neg- 31 ative female connotations can be seen in several pairs of words that differ denotatively only in the matter of sex. *Bachelor* as compared to *spinster* or *old maid* has such positive connotations that women try to adopt them by using the term *bachelor-girl* or *bachelorette*. *Old maid* is so negative that it's the basis for metaphors: pretentious and fussy old men are called *old maids*, as are the leftover kernels of unpopped popcorn, and the last card in a popular children's game.

Patron and *matron* (Middle English for *father* and *mother*) have 32 such different levels of prestige that women try to borrow the more positive masculine connotations with the word *patroness*, literally "female father." Such a peculiar term came about because of the high prestige attached to *patron* in such phrases as *a patron of the arts* or *a patron saint*. *Matron* is more apt to be used in talking about a woman in charge of a jail or a public restroom.

When men are doing jobs that women often do, we apparently 33 try to pay the men extra by giving them fancy titles, for example, a male cook is more likely to be called a *chef* while a male seamstress will get the title of *tailor*. The armed forces have a special problem in that they recruit under such slogans as "The Marine Corps builds men!" and "Join the Army! Become a Man." Once the recruits are enlisted, they find themselves doing much of the work that has been traditionally thought of as a "women's work." The solution to getting the work done and not insulting anyone's masculinity was to change the titles as shown below:

waitress	orderly
nurse	medic or corpsman
secretary	clerk-typist
assistant	adjutant
dishwasher or kitchen helper	KP (kitchen police)

Compare *brave* and *squaw*. Early settlers in America truly admired 34 Indian men and hence named them with a word that carried connotations of youth, vigor, and courage. But they used the Algonquin's name for "woman" and over the years it developed almost opposite connotations to those of *brave*. *Wizard* and *witch* contrast almost as much. The masculine *wizard* implies skill and wisdom combined with magic, while the feminine *witch* implies evil intentions combined with magic. Part of the unattractiveness of both *witch* and *squaw* is that they have been used so often to refer to old women, something with which our culture is particularly uncomfortable, just as the Afghans were. Imagine my surprise when I ran across the phrases *grandfatherly advice* and *old wives' tales* and realized that the underlying implication is the same as the Afghan proverb about old men being worth listening to while old women talk only foolishness.

Other terms that show how negative we view old women as 35

compared to young women are *old nag* as compared to *filly*, *old crow* or *old bat* as compared to *bird*, and of being *catty* as compared to being *kittenish*. There is no matching set of metaphors for men. The chicken metaphor tells the whole story of a woman's life. In her youth she is a *chick*. Then she marries and begins *feathering her nest*. Soon she begins feeling *cooped up*, so she goes to *hen parties* where she *cackles* with her friends. Then she has her *brood*, begins to *henpeck* her husband, and finally turns into an *old biddy*.

I embarked on my study of the dictionary not with the intention 36 of prescribing language change but simply to see what the language would tell me about sexism. Nevertheless I have been both surprised and pleased as I've watched the changes that have occurred over the past two decades. I'm one of those linguists who believes that new language customs will cause a new generation of speakers to grow up with different expectations. This is why I'm happy about people's efforts to use inclusive language, to say *he or she* or *they* when speaking about individuals whose names they do not know. I'm glad that leading publishers have developed guidelines to help writers use language that is fair to both sexes, and I'm glad that most newspapers and magazines list women by their own names instead of only by their husbands' names and that educated and thoughtful people no longer begin their business letters with "Dear Sir" or "Gentlemen," but instead use a memo form or begin with such salutations as "Dear Colleagues," "Dear Reader," or "Dear Committee Members." I'm also glad that such words as *poetess, authoress, conductress*, and *aviatrix* now sound quaint and old-fashioned and that *chairman* is giving way to *chair* or *head*, *mailman* to *mail carrier*, *clergyman* to *clergy*, and *stewardess* to *flight attendant*. I was also pleased when the National Oceanic and Atmospheric Administration bowed to feminist complaints and in the late 1970s began to alternate men's and women's names for hurricanes. However, I wasn't so pleased to discover that the change did not immediately erase sexist thoughts from everyone's mind, as shown by a headline about Hurricane David in a 1979 New York tabloid, "David Rapes Virgin Islands." More recently a similar metaphor appeared in a headline in the *Arizona Republic* about Hurricane Charlie, "Charlie Quits Carolinas, Flirts with Virginia."

What these incidents show is that sexism is not something ex- 37 isting independently in American English or in the particular dictionary that I happened to read. Rather, it exists in people's minds. Language is like an X ray in providing visible evidence of invisible thoughts. The best thing about people being interested in and discussing sexist language is that as they make conscious decisions about what pronouns they will use, what jokes they will tell or laugh at, how they will write their names, or how they will begin their letters, they are forced to think about the underlying issue of sexism. This is good because as a problem that begins in people's assumptions and expectations, it's a problem that will be solved only when a great many people have given it a great deal of thought.

Talking in the New Land
Edite Cunha

Before I started school in America I was Edite. Maria Edite dos   1
Anjos Cunha. Maria, in honor of the Virgin Mary. In Portugal it
was customary to use Maria as a religious and legal prefix to every
girl's name. Virtually every girl was so named. It had something
to do with the apparition of the Virgin to three shepherd children
at Fatima. In naming their daughters Maria, my people were expressing their love and reverence for their Lady of Fatima.

Edite came from my godmother, Dona Edite Baetas Ruivo. The   2
parish priest argued that I could not be named Edite because in
Portugal the name was not considered Christian. But Dona Edite
defended my right to bear her name. No one had argued with her
family when they had christened her Edite. Her family had power
and wealth. The priest considered privileges endangered by his
stand, and I became Maria Edite.

The dos Anjos was for my mother's side of the family. Like her   3
mother before her, she had been named Maria dos Anjos. And
Cunha was for my father's side. Carlos dos Santos Cunha, son of
Abilio dos Santos Cunha, the tailor from Saíl.

I loved my name. "Maria Edite dos Anjos Cunha," I'd recite at   4
the least provocation. It was melodious and beautiful. And through
it I knew exactly who I was.

At the age of seven I was taken from our little house in Sobreira,   5
São Martinho da Cortiça, Portugal, and brought to Peabody, Massachusetts. We moved into the house of Senhor João, who was our
sponsor in the big land. I was in America for about a week when
someone took me to school one morning and handed me over to
the teacher, Mrs. Donahue.

Mrs. Donahue spoke Portuguese, a wondrous thing for a woman   6
with a funny, unpronounceable name.

"*Como é que te chamas?*" she asked as she led me to a desk by   7
big windows.

"Maria Edite dos Anjos Cunha," I recited, all the while scanning   8
Mrs. Donahue for clues. How could a woman with such a name
speak my language?

In fact, Mrs. Donahue was Portuguese. She was a Silva. But she ⁹
had married an Irishman and changed her name. She changed my
name, too, on the first day of school.

"Your name will be Mary Edith Cunha," she declared. "In Amer- ¹⁰
ica you only need two or three names. Mary Edith is a lovely name.
And it will be easier to pronounce."

My name was Edite. Maria Edite. Maria Edite dos Anjos Cunha. ¹¹
I had no trouble pronouncing it.

"Mary Edith, Edithhh, Mary Edithhh," Mrs. Donahue exagger- ¹²
ated it. She wrinkled up her nose and raised her upper lip to show
me the proper positioning of the tongue for the *th* sound. She
looked hideous. There was a big pain in my head. I wanted to
scream out my name. But you could never argue with a teacher.

At home I cried and cried. *Mãe* and *Pai* wanted to know about ¹³
the day. I couldn't pronounce the new name for them. Senhor
João's red face wrinkled in laughter.

Day after day Mrs. Donahue made me practice pronouncing that ¹⁴
name that wasn't mine. Mary Edithhhhh. Mary Edithhh. Mary
Edithhh. But weeks later I still wouldn't respond when she called
it out in class. Mrs. Donahue became cross when I didn't answer.
Later my other teachers shortened it to Mary. And I never knew
quite who I was. . . .

Mrs. Donahue was a small woman, not much bigger than my ¹⁵
seven-year-old self. Her graying hair was cut into a neat, curly bob.
There was a smile that she wore almost every day. Not broad.
Barely perceptible. But it was there, in her eyes, and at the corners
of her mouth. She often wore gray suits with jackets neatly fitted
about the waist. On her feet she wore matching black leather shoes,
tightly laced. Matching, but not identical. One of them had an
extra-thick sole, because like all of her pupils, Mrs. Donahue had
an oddity. We, the children, were odd because we were of different
colors and sizes, and did not speak in the accepted tongue. Mrs.
Donahue was odd because she had legs of different lengths.

I grew to love Mrs. Donahue. She danced with us. She was the ¹⁶
only teacher in all of Carroll School who thought it important to
dance. Every day after recess she took us all to the big open space
at the back of the room. We stood in a circle and joined hands.
Mrs. Donahue would blow a quivering note from the little round

pitch pipe she kept in her pocket, and we became a twirling, singing wheel. Mrs. Donahue hobbled on her short leg and sang in a high trembly voice, "Here we go, loop-de-loop." We took three steps, then a pause. Her last "loop" was always very high. It seemed to squeak above our heads, bouncing on the ceiling. "Here we go, loop-de-lie." Three more steps, another pause, and on we whirled. "Here we go, loop-de-loop." Pause. "All on a Saturday night." To anyone looking in from the corridor we were surely an irregular sight, a circle of children of odd sizes and colors singing and twirling with our tiny hobbling teacher.

I'd been in Room Three with Mrs. Donahue for over a year when 17 she decided that I could join the children in the regular elementary classes at Thomas Carroll School. I embraced the news with some ambivalence. By then the oddity of Mrs. Donahue's classroom had draped itself over me like a warm safe cloak. Now I was to join the second-grade class of Miss Laitinen. In preparation, Mrs. Donahue began a phase of relentless drilling. She talked to me about what I could expect in second grade. Miss Laitinen's class was well on its way with cursive writing, so we practiced that every day. We intensified our efforts with multiplication. And we practiced pronouncing the new teacher's name.

"Lay-te-nun." Mrs. Donahue spewed the *t* out with excessive 18 force to demonstrate its importance. I had a tendency to forget it.

"Lay-nun." 19

"Mary Edith, don't be lazy. Use that tongue. It's Lay-te"—she 20 bared her teeth for the *t* part—"nun."

One morning, with no warning, Mrs. Donahue walked me to 21 the end of the hall and knocked on the door to Room Six. Miss Laitinen opened the door. She looked severe, carrying a long rubber-tipped pointer which she held horizontally before her with both hands. Miss Laitinen was a big, masculine woman. Her light, coarse hair was straight and cut short. She wore dark cardigans and very long, pleated plaid kilts that looked big enough to cover my bed.

"This is Mary Edith," Mrs. Donahue said. Meanwhile I looked 22 at their shoes. Miss Laitinen wore flat, brown leather shoes that laced up and squeaked on the wooden floor when she walked. They matched each other perfectly, but they were twice as big as Mrs. Donahue's.

"Mary Edith, say hello to Miss Laitinen." Mrs. Donahue stressed 23 the *t*—a last-minute reminder.

"Hello, Miss Lay-te-nun," I said, leaning my head back to see 24 her face. Miss Laitinen was tall. Mrs. Donahue's head came just to her chest. They both nodded approvingly before I was led to my seat.

Peabody, Massachusetts. "The Leather City." It is stamped on the 25 city seal, along with the image of a tanned animal hide. And Peabody, an industrial city of less than fifty thousand people, has the smokestacks to prove it. They rise up all over town from sprawling, dilapidated factories. Ugly, leaning, sixties, the tanneries were in full swing. The jobs were arduous and health-threatening, but it was the best-paying work around for unskilled laborers who spoke no English. The huge, firetrap factories were filled with men and women from Greece, Portugal, Ireland, and Poland.

In one of these factories, João Nunes, who lived on the floor 26 above us, fed animal skins into a ravenous metal monster all day, every day. The pace was fast. One day the monster got his right arm and wouldn't let go. When the machine was turned off João had a little bit of arm left below his elbow. His daughter Teresa and I were friends. She didn't come out of her house for many days. When she returned to school, she was very quiet and cried a lot.

"*Rosa Veludo's been hurt.*" News of such tragedies spread through 27 the community fast and often. People would tell what they had seen, or what they had heard from those who had seen. "*She was taken to the hospital by ambulance. Someone wrapped her fingers in a paper bag. The doctors may be able to sew them back on.*"

A few days after our arrival in the United States, my father went 28 to work at the Gnecco & Grilk leather tannery, on the corner of Howley and Walnut streets. Senhor João had worked there for many years. He helped *Pai* get the job. Gnecco & Grilk was a long, rambling, four-story factory that stretched from the corner halfway down the street to the railroad tracks. The roof was flat and slouched in the middle like the back of an old workhorse. There were hundreds of windows. The ones on the ground floor were covered with a thick wire mesh.

Pai worked there for many months. He was stationed on the 29 ground floor, where workers often had to stand ankle-deep in water laden with chemicals. One day he had a disagreement with his foreman. He left his machine and went home vowing never to return. . . .

Pai and I stood on a sidewalk in Salem facing a clear glass doorway. The words on the door were big. DIVISION OF EMPLOYMENT SECURITY. There was a growing coldness deep inside me. At Thomas Carroll School, Miss Laitinen was probably standing at the side blackboard, writing perfect alphabet letters on straight chalk lines. My seat was empty. I was on a sidewalk with *Pai* trying to understand a baffling string of words. DIVISION had something to do with math, which I didn't particularly like. EMPLOYMENT I had never seen or heard before. SECURITY I knew. But not at that moment.

Pai reached for the door. It swung open into a little square of tiled floor. We stepped in to be confronted by the highest, steepest staircase I had ever seen. At the top, we emerged into a huge, fluorescently lit room. It was too bright and open after the dim, narrow stairs. *Pai* took off his hat. We stood together in a vast empty space. The light, polished tiles reflected the fluorescent glow. There were no windows.

Far across the room, a row of metal desks lined the wall. Each had a green vinyl-covered chair beside it. Off to the left, facing the empty space before us, was a very high green metal desk. It was easily twice as high as a normal-size desk. Its odd size and placement in the middle of the room gave it the appearance of a kind of altar that divided the room in half. There were many people working at desks or walking about, but the room was so big that it still seemed empty.

The head and shoulders of a white-haired woman appeared to rest on the big desk like a sculptured bust. She sat very still. Above her head the word CLAIMS dangled from two pieces of chain attached to the ceiling. As I watched the woman she beckoned to us. *Pai* and I walked toward her.

The desk was so high that *Pai*'s shoulders barely cleared the top. Even when I stood on tiptoe I couldn't see over it. I had to stretch and lean my head way back to see the woman's round face. I thought that she must have very long legs to need a desk that high. The coldness in me grew. My neck hurt.

582 • Edite Cunha
582 • Edite Cunha

"My father can't speak English. He has no work and we need 35
money."

She reached for some papers from a wire basket. One of her 36
fingers was encased in a piece of orange rubber.

"Come around over here so I can see you." She motioned to the 37
side of the desk. I went reluctantly. Rounding the desk I saw with
relief that she was a small woman perched on a stool so high it
seemed she would need a ladder to get up there.

"How old are you?" She leaned down toward me. 38

"Eight." 39

"My, aren't you a brave girl. Only eight years old and helping 40
daddy like that. And what lovely earrings you have."

She liked my earrings. I went a little closer to let her touch them. 41
Maybe she would give us money.

"What language does your father speak?" She was straightening 42
up, reaching for a pencil.

"Portuguese." 43

"What is she saying?" Pai wanted to know. 44

"Wait," I told him. The lady hadn't yet said anything about 45
money.

"Why isn't your father working?" 46

"His factory burned down." 47

"What is she saying?" Pai repeated. 48

"She wants to know why you aren't working." 49

"Tell her the factory burned down." 50

"I know. I did." The lady was looking at me. I hoped she wouldn't 51
ask me what my father had just said.

"What is your father's name?" 52

"Carlos S. Cunha. C-u-n-h-a." No one could ever spell *Cunha.* 53
Pai nodded at the woman when he heard his name.

"Where do you live?" 54

"Thirty-three Tracey Street, Peabody, Massachusetts." *Pai* nod- 55
ded again when he heard the address.

"When was your father born?" 56

"Quando é que tu naçestes?" 57

"When was the last day your father worked?" 58

"Qual foi o último dia que trabalhastes?" 59

"What was the name of the factory?" 60

"Qual éra o nome da fábrica?" 61

"How long did he work there?" 62

"Quanto tempo trabalhastes lá?" 63

"What is his Social Security number?" 64

I looked at her blankly, not knowing what to say. What was a 65 Social Security number?

"What did she say?" Pai prompted me out of silence. 66

"I don't know. She wants a kind of number." I was feeling very tired 67 and worried. But *Pai* took a small card from his wallet and gave it to the lady. She copied something from it onto her papers and returned it to him. I felt a great sense of relief. She wrote silently for a while as we stood and waited. Then she handed some papers to *Pai* and looked at me.

"Tell your father that he must have these forms filled out by his 68 employer before he can receive unemployment benefits."

I stared at her. What was she saying? Employer? Unemployment 69 benefits? I was afraid she was saying we couldn't have any money. Maybe not, though. Maybe we could have money if I could understand her words.

"What did she say? Can we have some money?" 70

"I don't know. I can't understand the words." 71

"Ask her again if we can have money," Pai insisted. *"Tell her we have* 72 *to pay the rent."*

"We need money for the rent," I told the lady, trying to hold 73 back tears.

"You can't have money today. You must take the forms to your 74 father's employer and bring them back completed next week. Then your father must sign another form which we will keep here to process his claim. When he comes back in two weeks there may be a check for him." The cold in me was so big now. I was trying not to shiver.

"Do you understand?" The lady was looking at me. 75

I wanted to say, "No, I don't," but I was afraid we would never 76 get money and *Pai* would be angry.

"Tell your father to take the papers to his boss and come back 77 next week."

Boss. I could understand boss. 78

"She said you have to take these papers to your 'bossa' and come back 79 *next week."*

"We can't have money today?" 80

"No. She said maybe we can have money in two weeks." 81

"Did you tell her we have to pay the rent?" 82

"Yes, but she said we can't have money yet." 83

The lady was saying good-bye and beckoning the next person 84 from the line that had formed behind us.

I was relieved to move on, but I think *Pai* wanted to stay and 85 argue with her. I knew that if he could speak English, he would have. I knew that he thought it was my fault we couldn't have money. And I myself wasn't so sure that wasn't true.

That night I sat at the kitchen table with a fat pencil and a piece 86 of paper. In my second-grade scrawl I wrote: Dear Miss Laitinen, Mary Edith was sick.

I gave the paper to *Pai* and told him to sign his name. 87

"What does it say?" 88

"It says that I was sick today. I need to give it to my teacher." 89

"You weren't sick today." 90

"Ya, but it would take too many words to tell her the truth." 91

Pai signed the paper. The next morning in school, Miss Laitinen 92 read it and said that she hoped I was feeling better.

When I was nine, *Pai* went to an auction and bought a big house 93 on Tremont Street. We moved in the spring. The yard at the side of the house dipped downward in a gentle slope that was covered with a dense row of tall lilac bushes. I soon discovered that I could crawl in among the twisted trunks to hide from my brothers in the fragrant shade. It was paradise. . . .

I was mostly wild and joyful on Tremont Street. But there was a 94 shadow that fell across my days now and again.

"Ó Ediiiite." *Pai* would call me without the least bit of warning, 95 to be his voice. He expected me to drop whatever I was doing to attend him. Of late, I'd had to struggle on the telephone with the voice of a woman who wanted some old dishes. The dishes, along with lots of old furniture and junk, had been in the house when we moved in. They were in the cellar, stacked in cardboard boxes and covered with dust. The woman called many times wanting to speak with *Pai*.

"My father can't speak English," I would say. "He says to tell 96 you that the dishes are in our house and they belong to us." But she did not seem to understand. Every few days she would call. "Ó Ediiiite." *Pai*'s voice echoed through the empty rooms. Hear- 97 ing it brought on a chill. It had that tone. As always, my first impulse was to pretend I had not heard, but there was no escape. I couldn't disappear into thin air as I wished to do at such calls. We were up in the third-floor apartment of our new house. *Pai* was working in the kitchen. Carlos and I had made a cavern of old cushions and were sitting together deep in its bowels when he called. It was so dark and comfortable there I decided not to answer until the third call, though that risked *Pai*'s wrath.

"Ó Ediiite." Yes, that tone was certainly there. *Pai* was calling 98 me to do something only I could do. Something that always awakened a cold beast deep in my gut. He wanted me to be his bridge. What was it now? Did he have to talk to someone at City Hall again? Or was it the insurance company? They were always using words I couldn't understand: liability, and premium, and dividend. It made me frustrated and scared.

"You wait. My dotta come." *Pai* was talking to someone. Who 99 could it be? That was some relief. At least I didn't have to call someone on the phone. It was always harder to understand when I couldn't see people's mouths.

"Ó Ediiiite." I hated Carlos. *Pai* never called his name like that. 100 He never had to do anything but play.

"*Que ééé?*" 101

"*Come over here and talk to this lady.*" 102

Reluctantly I crawled out from the soft darkness and walked 103 through the empty rooms toward the kitchen. Through the kitchen door I could see a slim lady dressed in brown standing at the top of the stairs in the windowed porch. She had on very skinny high-heeled shoes and a brown purse to match. As soon as *Pai* saw me he said to the lady, "Dis my dotta." To me he said, "*See what she wants.*"

The lady had dark hair that was very smooth and puffed away 104 from her head. The ends of it flipped up in a way that I liked.

"Hello. I'm the lady who called about the dishes." 105

I stared at her without a word. My stomach lurched. 106

"*What did she say?*" *Pai* wanted to know. 107

"*She says she's the lady who wants the dishes.*" 108

Pai's face hardened some.   109

"*Tell her she's wasting her time. We're not giving them to her. Didn't* 110
you already tell her that on the telephone?"

I nodded, standing helplessly between them.   111

"*Well, tell her again.*" *Pai* was getting angry. I wanted to 112
disappear.

"My father says he can't give you the dishes," I said to the lady. 113
She clutched her purse and leaned a little forward.

"Yes, you told me that on the phone. But I wanted to come in 114
person and speak with your father because it's very important to
me that—"

"My father can't speak English," I interrupted her. Why didn't 115
she just go away? She was still standing in the doorway with her
back to the stairwell. I wanted to push her down.

"Yes, I understand that. But I wanted to see him." She looked 116
at *Pai*, who was standing in the doorway to the kitchen holding
his hammer. The kitchen was up one step from the porch. *Pai* was
a small man, but he looked kind of scary staring down at us like
that.

"*What is she saying?*"   117

"*She says she wanted to talk to you about getting her dishes.*"   118

"*Tell her the dishes are ours. They were in the house. We bought the* 119
house and everything in it. Tell her the lawyer said so."

The brown lady was looking at me expectantly.   120

"My father says the dishes are ours because we bought the house 121
and the lawyer said everything in the house is ours now."

"Yes, I know that, but I was away when the house was being 122
sold. I didn't know . . ."

"*Eeii.*" There were footsteps on the stairs behind her. It was *Mãe* 123
coming up from the second floor to find out what was going on.
The lady moved away from the door to let *Mãe* in.

"Dis my wife," *Pai* said to the lady. The lady said hello to *Mãe*, 124
who smiled and nodded her head. She looked at me, then at *Pai*
in a questioning way.

"*It's the lady who wants our dishes,*" *Pai* explained.   125

"*Ó.*" *Mãe* looked at her again and smiled, but I could tell she 126
was a little worried.

We stood there in kind of a funny circle; the lady looked at each 127
of us in turn and took a deep breath.

"I didn't know," she continued, "that the dishes were in the 128 house. I was away. They are very important to me. They belonged to my grandmother. I'd really like to get them back." She spoke this while looking back and forth between *Mãe* and *Pai*. Then she looked down at me, leaning forward again. "Will you tell your parents, please?"

The cold beast inside me had begun to rise up toward my throat 129 as the lady spoke. I knew that soon it would try to choke out my words. I spoke in a hurry to get them out.

"She said she didn't know the dishes were in the house she was away 130 *they were her grandmother's dishes she wants them back."* I felt a deep sadness at the thought of the lady returning home to find her grandmother's dishes sold.

"We don't need all those dishes. Let's give them to her," *Mãe* said in 131 her calm way. I felt relieved. We could give the lady the dishes and she would go away. But *Pai* got angry.

"I already said what I had to say. The dishes are ours. That is all." 132

"Pai, she said she didn't know. They were her grandmother's dishes. 133 *She needs to have them."* I was speaking wildly and loud now. The lady looked at me questioningly, but I didn't want to speak to her again.

"She's only saying that to trick us. If she wanted those dishes she should 134 *have taken them out before the house was sold. Tell her we are not fools. Tell her to forget it. She can go away. Tell her not to call or come here again."*

"What is he saying?" The lady was looking at me again. 135

I ignored her. I felt sorry for *Pai* for always feeling that people 136 were trying to trick him. I wanted him to trust people. I wanted the lady to have her grandmother's dishes. I closed my eyes and willed myself away.

"Tell her what I said!" *Pai* yelled. 137

"Pai, just give her the dishes! They were her grandmother's dishes!" 138 My voice cracked as I yelled back at him. Tears were rising.

I hated *Pai* for being so stubborn. I hated the lady for not taking 139 the dishes before the house was sold. I hated myself for having learned to speak English.

The Undergraduate Hispanic Experience: A Case of Juggling Two Cultures

Edward B. Fiske

Michael Sanchez grew up in Coolidge, Arizona, a community of 1
6,800 persons 52 miles southwest of Phoenix. A good student in
high school, he enrolled in Arizona State University in 1983 as a
business major with the dream of becoming the first member of
his family to earn a college degree.

Two years later Mr. Sanchez put his dream on hold. He found 2
the university, where the student population is more than six times
that of his hometown, to be "cold and impersonal." He couldn't
find an advisor to help him sort out his academic program, or a
group that would make him feel he belonged at Tempe; the lack
of Hispanic professors left him without reason to believe that Hispanics could advance to become academic leaders.

"I was really overwhelmed," he confesses. Mr. Sanchez returned 3
home and enrolled in a nearby community college, which he likes
because it is smaller and more personal. Soon, he hopes to transfer
to Arizona State to try again.

For many Hispanic students the most serious problems are not 4
those they confront getting into college but those they face once
they get there. The problems range from the anxiety of breaking
close family ties to the loneliness and tensions inherent in finding
their way in institutions built around an alien culture. Some Hispanic undergraduates complain of subtle or not-so-subtle discrimination. Even those from secure and privileged backgrounds are
often thrown off-balance by finding themselves identified as belonging to a "minority" group for the first time.

Culture shock is a reality for many, if not most, Hispanic college 5
students when they first set foot on an American college campus.
For some the shock comes simply from being thrown on their own
in a large institution. Ron Lopez grew up in Pacific Palisades, a
middle-class suburb of Los Angeles, where his father is a high
school teacher and his mother a counselor at a local community

college. He set his sights on the University of California at Los Angeles.

"UCLA was overwhelming," he says. "It was just big. I had to ₆ work and live on my own. It was a real shock. My first two years were outrageous. I was working so hard at the academics and at my job—I was spending at least twenty hours a week at the job— that was just hardship, serious hardship."

Add to that the cultural differences. Angelina Medina, a 21-year- ₇ old marketing major at the University of Texas at San Antonio, observes that Hispanics from the barrios on the south and west sides of the city are readily identifiable in a university where most students are middle-class whites. "They dress differently," she says. "They drive different cars, low to the flow."

Since curricula rarely reflect Hispanic interests, even the class- ₈ room can contribute to a sense of alienation. "We validate other cultures by studying them but we don't extend that same validation to Chicanos," observes Maria Meier, a senior international relations major at Stanford University who would like to see aspects of Latino culture worked into that university's controversial general education program.

Since Hispanics often come from weaker high schools, failure in ₉ the classroom is a frequent occurrence. Vladimir Garcia grew up in New York City and was recruited by Boston University because of high math scores on standardized admissions tests. But when he got there he found that he wasn't prepared for a fast-paced urban university. "A lot of people were shocked that I was Hispanic and was from New York, and here I was an engineering student," he says. "My first month was my loneliest month ever. I felt like I was alone. But once I failed, I found I wasn't alone." Mr. Garcia eventually switched from engineering to economics and, thanks to a stint at Lehman College in New York City, expects to get his BU diploma.

Academic disillusionment can come in other forms. Hispanics ₁₀ who reach colleges are used to being considered part of an elite— which they are. "The Mexican-American students that come to the University of Texas think that they have it made, because they were stars in high school," says Consuelo Trevino, a counselor in the dean's office at UT. "When they start competing, they realize that they're competing with stars. It's a big shock."

Hispanic college students say that discrimination is pervasive in 11
American colleges and universities, sometimes in subtle ways,
sometimes overtly. The stereotypes of Hispanics fed by television
and the movies persist—Latinos as dope peddlers and pimps, people who wear their pants low and just arrived by swimming across
some river.

"I've been stereotyped out the wazoo," says Jake Foley, a 22- 12
year-old Mexican-American accounting student at the University
of Texas who grew up in the Rio Grande Valley. "People will joke
around—at least, I hope they're joking—and say, 'Oh, he's Mexican, hide your wallet.' Or, 'Do you have a switchblade?' Or, 'Do
you go out and buy velvet posters of Elvis?' They're insulting you
in a public setting without knowing who you are, what you've
done, what you've accomplished. You grow up around 4,400 Mex-
ican-Americans, and you don't think you're different. You don't
know you're different until people point it out."

Efrain Ramos, a 21-year-old government major at Notre Dame, 13
recalls his freshman year when students on his dormitory floor
decided to adopt a Mexican theme for a dance. "They were talking
about putting a stream down the hall and distributing green cards,"
he said. "That got me really mad. I get very offended by that kind
of stuff." Now that his feelings are known on such matters, he
added, "people are cautious around me."

Cynthia Salinas, who graduated from Indiana University last 14
year, chalks such incidents up mainly to ignorance. "I never really
came across any prejudice or racial slurs—just some misunderstanding of who I was," she says. "Was I from another country?
They asked me if I was from Spain."

Other Hispanic undergraduates, however, have other tales to 15
tell. "I never really experienced racism until I got to this university," says Raul Mendez, a senior English major at UCLA who is
from New Orleans. "I was very ignorant." When he went to apply
for California residency, a move that would mean considerably
lower tuition bills, he encountered a "very antagonistic" clerk who
turned him down.

"I have a friend who arrived at the same time I did, lived in the 16
same dorm I did, and applied for residency when I did, but she
was white," Mr. Mendez reports. Even though he had a California
driver's license and a part-time job, he said, "She got residency,

and I didn't. All the clerk would say was, 'Your papers are not qualified.'" Eventually, by appealing the decision, he got his residency.

Many Hispanic students feel themselves under pressure to con- 17 tinually justify their presence on a college campus, in part because of the existence of affirmative action programs. "We carry a stigma in a sense," said Irma Rodriguez, a 21-year-old senior at the University of California at Berkeley. "When I first came here as a freshman, a white undergraduate said to me, 'You're here, and my friend, who is better qualified, is not.'"

Mr. Mendez of UCLA says that he has heard the arguments 18 against affirmative action over and over and takes the position that majority students just don't understand the situation. "What they don't realize is that we have to fight other barriers than they do," he observes. "We're from a different culture. We have pressures on us not to lose our culture, while maintaining a status quo in this culture. That's a big pressure. Some people don't think it is, but it is. You lose your culture. You get branded as a sellout. People who argue against affirmative action often aren't aware of our backgrounds or how we feel. They don't understand where we're coming from. If they did, they'd realize that affirmative action has helped a lot of people."

The problem of how to balance participation in two cultures is 19 a continuing one, and each Hispanic student must make his or her own decision. Some join Hispanic social or political groups and affirm their heritage as overtly as possible. Others become "coconuts"—brown on the outside, white on the inside—but this leads to charges of "selling out."

Juggling two cultures is never an easy task. "I think I'm always 20 swimming against the current," says Lupe Gallegos-Diaz, a 26-year-old graduate student at Berkeley. "I feel as a Chicana that I always have to perform. I have to know my material, then deliver it in a forceful, articulate manner. Otherwise, you're stereotyped as not being able to cope." Even the most successful students are not immune from subtle forms of racism, says Mr. Lopez. "Sometimes that will take the form of someone's saying, 'You say you're Chicano, but you're not really like them. You're not the way they are.'"

Scratch a Hispanic college student, and you'll probably find 21 someone in his or her background who showed a special interest in them, who took them aside and gave them the aspiration and encouragement to go on to higher education. For Jorge A. Ontiveros, a student at Our Lady of the Lake College in San Antonio, it was the Hispanic doctor down the street where he grew up in Dallas. "He told me that I had to go to college," he says, "It was his way of putting back what he himself got."

Eusebia Aquino, a 1983 graduate of Wayne State University who 22 is now a nurse, arrived in this country from Puerto Rico at the age of six. She grew up in Detroit in a single-parent family and had to drop out of school for four years to help raise her eight brothers and sisters, but she was encouraged by the local priest to fulfill her academic promise. "I used to steal books from Holy Trinity Church," she says. "I couldn't read English, but I had a hunger to learn, so I would take them. I found out many years later that Father Kern would leave books out for me to take that he thought I'd like." The priest turned out to be more supportive than her high school counselor, who refused to give her application forms for Wayne State or the University of Michigan. "Instead, she said I should take a housekeeping job at the K-Mart downtown because that's what Hispanic women are supposed to do," she recalls.

Hispanic students say that they feel the absence of "role models" 23 once they get to predominantly Anglo colleges and universities. Julie Martinez, a senior at Stanford who is from a predominantly Hispanic working-class high school in San Antonio, wants to become an anthropology professor and says that the biggest improvement Stanford could make would be to have more Latino faculty members. "Just having them here makes a big difference," she observes. "They serve as role models. Before I came here, I had never seen a Mexican-American in a position where I wanted to be in ten years."

Not surprisingly, Hispanic college students are conscious that 24 they, too, become role models for their siblings or other younger Hispanics. Miss Aquino encouraged four of her brothers and sisters to get their high school equivalency diplomas, and three of them are now in college. Miss Martinez knows that her progress at Stanford is being watched closely by people in her hometown.

"Coming here was a really big deal," she says. "Everyone from 25 my community is watching me. If I do well, people will encourage their children to do well in school and go to college." Her status as a role model is complex, though, because of her aspirations to become an anthropology professor. "If I drive back in a beat-up little car in 15 years—even if I'm a university professor—they'll say, 'What good did it do her? All that money, all that work and time? That guy down the street who got a job at the grocery store was more successful.'"

A universal theme among Hispanics in American colleges is the 26 need for adequate support systems. This starts, of course, well before college. "Many Hispanics are first-generation college students with very little knowledge of exactly what the heck they are getting into," says Jose Anaya, a Mexican-born student from East Chicago at Indiana University and president of Latinos Unidos, a campus Hispanic group.

Mr. Anaya came to Indiana through the Groups Special Services 27 Program that takes students who might not be considered college material and puts them through a summer program to help shore up their academic and nonacademic skills. "I was scared and a little timid," he recalls. "I decided to find out if I could survive a large campus. The Groups Program offered me an opportunity without throwing me in the waters and saying 'swim or drown.'"

Miss Aquino found help in the Chicano-Boricua Studies Program 28 (CBS). "When I came to Wayne State, I felt totally isolated," she recalled. "There was no one who cared outside of CBS. I wasn't white enough to join white groups or black enough to join black groups, so I hibernated at the CBS offices." Without this backing, she added, "I would be barefoot and pregnant somewhere in the city."

This tendency to stick close to other Hispanics and to Hispanic 29 campus organizations is not unusual. "It's taken this long to establish the ethnic organizations, and students see that as being their thing," says Miss Meier of Stanford.

This may be one reason why Hispanics typically end up majoring 30 in the humanities and social sciences. "It might have to do with the fact that there are already more Latinos in social science or that are interested in literature," suggests Mr. Lopez of UCLA. "One thing that has characterized the Chicano movement in general is a great deal of continuity." Being part of a minority group can also have a profound effect on academic choices. "Perhaps it has something to do with growing up in a marginalized cultural group," he comments. "Maybe we study cultural things as a consequence of that. When you grow up in a marginalized group, even if you're becoming an intellectual, you're interested in understanding that."

One of the great strengths of Hispanic culture is the close family 31 relationships that it fosters, and these have a profound influence on the experience of Hispanic college students. Many will tell you how hard it was to break away from their families to come in the first place. "I have a lot of friends back home who are smart enough to be here and who could afford it through scholarships and their parents," says Alicia Estes, a 19-year-old Mexican-American at the University of Texas. "But because of the close family ties they have, their parents didn't want them to come."

Given the strength of family bonds, the first weeks and months 32 of the freshman year can be difficult. Mr. Ramos at Notre Dame says that at first he "couldn't control" his homesickness. "I couldn't concentrate when I was studying," he recalls. "We hold family very important. We're very attached to our families. I've heard it causes a great deal of drop-outs because they can't deal with homesickness."

University administrators tell stories of students going home for 33 Christmas vacation and not coming back, and Hispanic students seem more willing than students in similar economic situations to put aside their academic plans to help earn money for their family. "We are brought up to do things for the good of the family," says Antoinette Garza, director of library services at Our Lady of the Lake. "It is difficult for us to put ourselves first, even as an adult."

Hispanic cultural values sometimes come into conflict with those 34 that make for academic success. For Hispanics, looking someone in the eye is seen as a sign of disrespect, even if that person is standing in front of you in a classroom. "You're taught to be more humble and not to question authority," says Sylvia Garza at the University of Texas at San Antonio. "It's real hard to ask questions."

This can translate into a tendency not to make use of the aca- 35 demic resources available. "Minority students, and Hispanics in particular, are not prepared by high schools to be assertive enough, to make use of all the services this university has," says Alberto Torchinsky, dean of Latino Affairs at Indiana University. "Indiana

University doesn't extend a welcome mat to the Hispanic students. I'm sure other universities don't either."

But Hispanic college students are, almost by definition, resilient. 36 Mr. Lopez of UCLA is managing editor of *La Gente*, the Hispanic student newspaper, and he sees such activities as providing a higher sense of loyalty to his people. "To be a politically conscious Chicano gives me a sense of profound responsibility," he says. "We're working for better lives for our raza, which to me means access to socioeconomic mobility and to social justice. To me, being a Chicano student and activist just means pursuing fairness. Today, in this society, that's asking a lot."

Hispanic students are also increasingly conscious that, for all the 37 obstacles they face—inferior schools, insensitive high school counselors, stereotyping, and the like—a college education is worth the effort. "To me, being a Latino student means trying to succeed, using all the resources within my grasp," says Mr. Mendez of UCLA. "It means meeting others' expectations—peers and family members—to achieve what other Latinos were unable to achieve."

Miss Medina of the University of Texas at San Antonio, the youn- 38 gest of four children, all of whom have gone to college, put it best. "Our family doesn't have money or a business to pass down to our children," she says. "All we have is education. And that's something that no one can ever take from you."

What's in a Name?

Gloria Naylor

Language is the subject. It is the written form with which I've 1
managed to keep the wolf away from the door and, in diaries, to
keep my sanity. In spite of this, I consider the written word inferior
to the spoken, and much of the frustration experienced by novelists
is the awareness that whatever we manage to capture in even the
most transcendent passages falls far short of the richness of life.
Dialogue achieves its power in the dynamics of a fleeting moment
of sight, sound, smell, and touch.

I'm not going to enter the debate here about whether it is lan- 2
guage that shapes reality or vice versa. That battle is doomed to
be waged whenever we seek intermittent reprieve from the chicken
and egg dispute. I will simply take the position that the spoken
word, like the written word, amounts to a nonsensical arrangement
of sounds or letters without a consensus that assigns "meaning."
And building from the meanings of what we hear, we order reality.
Words themselves are innocuous; it is the consensus that gives
them true power.

I remember the first time I heard the word *nigger*. In my third- 3
grade class, our math tests were being passed down the rows, and
as I handed the papers to a little boy in back of me, I remarked
that once again he had received a much lower mark than I did. He
snatched his test from me and spit out that word. Had he called
me a nymphomaniac or a necrophiliac, I couldn't have been more
puzzled. I didn't know what a nigger was, but I knew that whatever it meant, it was something he shouldn't have called me. This
was verified when I raised 'my hand, and in a loud voice repeated
what he had said and watched the teacher scold him for using a
"bad" word. I was later to go home and ask the inevitable question
that every black parent must face—"Mommy, what does *nigger*
mean?"

And what exactly did it mean? Thinking back, I realize that this 4
could not have been the first time the word was used in my presence. I was part of a large extended family that had migrated from

the rural South after World War II and formed a close-knit network that gravitated around my maternal grandparents. Their ground-floor apartment in one of the buildings they owned in Harlem was a weekend mecca for my immediate family, along with countless aunts, uncles, and cousins who brought along assorted friends. It was a bustling and open house with assorted neighbors and tenants popping in and out to exchange bits of gossip, pick up an old quarrel, or referee the ongoing checkers game in which my grandmother cheated shamelessly. They were all there to let down their hair and put up their feet after a week of labor in the factories, laundries, and shipyards of New York.

Amid the clamor, which could reach deafening proportions— 5 two or three conversations going on simultaneously, punctuated by the sound of a baby's crying somewhere in the back rooms or out on the street—there was still a rigid set of rules about what was said and how. Older children were sent out of the living room when it was time to get into the juicy details about "you-know-who" up on the third floor who had gone and gotten herself "p-r-e-g-n-a-n-t!" But my parents, knowing that I could spell well beyond my years, always demanded that I follow the others out to play. Beyond sexual misconduct and death, everything else was considered harmless for our young ears. And so among the anecdotes of the triumphs and disappointments in the various workings of their lives, the word *nigger* was used in my presence, but it was set within contexts and inflections that caused it to register in my mind as something else.

In the singular, the word was always applied to a man who had 6 distinguished himself in some situation that brought their approval for his strength, intelligence, or drive:

"Did Johnny *really* do that?" 7

"I'm telling you, that nigger pulled in $6,000 of overtime last 8 year. Said he got enough for a down payment on a house."

When used with a possessive adjective by a woman—"my nig- 9 ger"—it became a term of endearment for her husband or boyfriend. But it could be more than just a term applied to a man. In their mouths it became the pure essence of manhood—a disembodied force that channeled their past history of struggle and present survival against the odds into a victorious statement of being:

"Yeah, that old foreman found out quick enough—you don't mess with a nigger."

In the plural, it became a description of some group within the community that had overstepped the bounds of decency as my family defined it. Parents who neglected their children, a drunken couple who fought in public, people who simply refused to look for work, those with excessively dirty mouths or unkempt households were all "trifling niggers." This particular circle could forgive hard times, unemployment, the occasional bout of depression— they had gone through all of that themselves—but the unforgivable sin was a lack of self-respect. 10

A woman could never be a "nigger" in the singular, with its connotation of confirming worth. The noun *girl* was its closest equivalent in that sense, but only when used in direct address and regardless of the gender doing the addressing. *Girl* was a token of respect for a woman. The one-syllable word was drawn out to sound like three in recognition of the extra ounce of wit, nerve, or daring that the woman had shown in the situation under discussion. 11

"G-i-r-l, stop. You mean you said that to his face?" 12

But if the word was used in a third-person reference or shortened so that it almost snapped out of the mouth, it always involved some element of communal disapproval. And age became an important factor in these exchanges. It was only between individuals of the same generation, or from any older person to a younger (but never the other way around), that *girl* would be considered a compliment. 13

I don't agree with the argument that use of the word *nigger* at this social stratum of the black community was an internalization of racism. The dynamics were the exact opposite: the people in my grandmother's living room took a word that whites used to signify worthlessness or degradation and rendered it impotent. Gathering there together, they transformed *nigger* to signify the varied and complex human beings they knew themselves to be. If the word was to disappear totally from the mouths of even the most liberal of white society, no one in that room was naive enough to believe it would disappear from white minds. Meeting the word head-on, 14 they proved it had absolutely nothing to do with the way they were determined to live their lives.

So there must have been dozens of times that *nigger* was spoken 15 in front of me before I reached the third grade. But I didn't "hear" it until it was said by a small pair of lips that had already learned it could be a way to humiliate me. That was the word I went home and asked my mother about. And since she knew that I had to grow up in America, she took me in her lap and explained.

Walking in Lucky Shoes

Bette Bao Lord

I confess. Novelists have a fetish. We can't resist shoes. Indeed, 1
we spend our lives recalling the pairs we have shed and snatching
others off unsuspecting souls. We're not proud. We're not particular. Whether it's Air Jordans or the clodhoppers of Frankenstein,
Imelda's gross collection or one glass slipper, we covet them all.
There's no cure for this affliction. To create characters, we must
traipse around and around in our heads sporting lost or stolen
shoes.

At 8, I sailed for America from Shanghai without a passing ac- 2
quaintance of A, B or C, wearing scruffy brown oxfords. Little did
I know then that they were as magical as those glittering red pumps
that propelled Dorothy down the yellow brick road.

Only yesterday, it seems, resting my chin on the rails of the SS 3
Marylinx, I peered into the mist for *Mei Guo*, Beautiful Country. It
refused to appear. Then, in a blink, there was the Golden Gate,
more like the portals to Heaven than the arches of a man-made
bridge.

Only yesterday, standing at PS 8 in Brooklyn, I was bewitched— 4
others, alas, were bothered and bewildered—when I proclaimed:

I pledge a lesson to the frog of
    the United States of America.
And to the wee puppet for witch's hands.
    One Asian, in the vestibule,
with little tea and just rice for all.

Although I mangled the language, the message was not lost. Not 5
on someone wearing immigrant shoes.

Only yesterday, rounding third base in galoshes, I swallowed a 6
barrelful of tears wondering what wrong I had committed to anger
my teammates so. Why were they all madly screaming at me to
go home, go home?

Only yesterday, listening in pink cotton mules to Red Barber 7 broadcasting from Ebbetts Field, I vaulted over the Milky Way as my hero, Jackie Robinson, stole home.

Only yesterday, enduring the pinch of new Mary Janes at my 8 grammar-school graduation, I felt as tall as the Statue of Liberty, reciting Walt Whitman: "I hear America singing, the varied carols I hear . . . Each singing what belongs to him or her and to none else. . . ."

Today I cherish every unstylish pair of shoes that took me up a 9 road cleared by the footfalls of millions of immigrants before me— to a room of my own. For America has granted me many a dream, even one that I never dared to dream—returning to the land of my birth in 1989 as the wife of the American ambassador. Citizens of Beijing were astounded to see that I was not a *yang guei ze*, foreign devil, with a tall nose and ghostly skin and bumpy hair colored in outlandish hues. I looked Chinese, I spoke Chinese, and after being in my company they accused me of being a fake, of being just another member of the clan.

I do not believe that the loss of one's native culture is the price 10 one must pay for becoming an American. On the contrary, I feel doubly blessed. I can choose from two rich cultures those parts that suit my mood or the occasion best. And unbelievable as it may seem, shoes tinted red, white and blue go dandy with them all.

Recently I spoke at my alma mater. There were many more Asian 11 faces in that one audience than there were enrolled at Tufts University when I cavorted in white suede shoes to cheer the Jumbos to victory. One asked, "Will you tell us about your encounters with racial prejudice?" I had no ready answers. I thought hard. Sure, I had been roughed up at school. Sure, I had failed at work. Sure, I had at times felt powerless. But had prejudice against the shade of my skin and the shape of my eyes caused these woes? Unable to show off the wounds I had endured at the hands of racists, I could only cite a scene from my husband's 25th reunion at Yale eight years ago. Throughout that weekend, I sensed I was being watched. But even after the tall, burly man finally introduced himself, I did not recognize his face or name. He hemmed and hawed, then announced that he had flown from Colorado to apologize to me. I could not imagine why. Apparently at a party in the early '60s, he had hectored me to cease dating his WASP classmate.

Someone else at Tufts asked, "How do you think of yourself? 12

As a Chinese or as an American?" Without thinking, I blurted out the truth: "Bette Bao Lord." Did I imagine the collective sigh of relief that swept through the auditorium? I think not. Perhaps I am the exception that proves the rule. Perhaps I am blind to insult and injury. Perhaps I am not alone. No doubt I have been lucky. Others have not been as fortunate. They had little choice but to wear ill-fitting shoes warped by prejudice, to start down a less traveled road strewn with broken promises and littered with regrets, haunted by racism and awash with tears. Where could that road possibly lead? Nowhere but to a nation, divided, without liberty and no justice at all.

The Berlin wall is down, but between East Harlem and West ₁₃ Hempstead, between the huddled masses of yesterday and today, the walls go up and up. Has the cold war ended abroad only to usher in heated racial and tribal conflicts at home? No, I believe we shall overcome. But only when:

We engage our diversity to yield a nation greater than the sum ₁₄ of its parts.

We can be different as sisters and brothers are, and belong to ₁₅ the same family.

We bless, not shame, America, our home.   ₁₆

A home, no doubt, where skeletons nest in closets and the roof ₁₇ leaks, where foundations must be shored and rooms added. But a home where legacies conceived by the forefathers are tendered from generation to generation to have and to hold. Legacies not of gold but as intangible and inalienable and invaluable as laughter and hope.

We the people can do just that—if we clear the smoke of ethnic ₁₈ chauvinism and fears by braving our journey to that "City Upon a Hill" in each other's shoes.

Finding a Voice

Maxine Hong Kingston

Long ago in China, knot-makers tied string into buttons and   1
frogs, and rope into bell pulls. There was one knot so complicated
that it blinded the knot-maker. Finally an emperor outlawed this
cruel knot, and the nobles could not order it anymore. If I had
lived in China, I would have been an outlaw knot-maker.

Maybe that's why my mother cut my tongue. She pushed my   2
tongue up and sliced the frenum. Or maybe she snipped it with
a pair of nail scissors. I don't remember her doing it, only her telling
me about it, but all during childhood I felt sorry for the baby whose
mother waited with scissors or knife in her hand for it to cry—and
then, when its mouth was wide open like a baby bird's, cut. The
Chinese say "a ready tongue is an evil."

I used to curl up my tongue in front of the mirror and tauten   3
my frenum into a white line, itself as thin as a razor blade. I saw
no scars in my mouth. I thought perhaps I had had two frena, and
she had cut one. I made other children open their mouths so I
could compare theirs to mine. I saw perfect pink membranes
stretching into precise edges that looked easy enough to cut. Sometimes I felt very proud that my mother committed such a powerful
act upon me. At other times I was terrified—the first thing my
mother did when she saw me was to cut my tongue.

"Why did you do that to me, Mother?"   4

"I told you."   5

"Tell me again."   6

"I cut it so that you would not be tongue-tied. Your tongue would   7
be able to move in any language. You'll be able to speak languages
that are completely different from one another. You'll be able to
pronounce anything. Your frenum looked too tight to do those
things, so I cut it."

"But isn't 'a ready tongue an evil'?"   8

"Things are different in this ghost country."   9

"Did it hurt me? Did I cry and bleed?"   10

"I don't remember. Probably."   11

She didn't cut the other children's. When I asked cousins and   12 other Chinese children whether their mothers had cut their tongues loose, they said, "What?"

"Why didn't you cut my brothers' and sisters' tongues?" 13

"They didn't need it." 14

"Why not? Were theirs longer than mine?" 15

"Why don't you quit blabbering and get to work?" 16

If my mother was not lying she should have cut more, scraped 17 away the rest of the frenum skin, because I have a terrible time talking. Or she should not have cut at all, tampering with my speech. When I went to kindergarten and had to speak English for the first time, I became silent. A dumbness—a shame—still cracks my voice in two, even when I want to say "hello" casually, or ask an easy question in front of the check-out counter, or ask directions of a bus driver. I stand frozen, or I hold up the line with the complete, grammatical sentence that comes squeaking out at impossible length. "What did you say?" says the cab driver, or "Speak up," so I have to perform again, only weaker the second time. A telephone call makes my throat bleed and takes up that day's courage. It spoils my day with self-disgust when I hear my broken voice come skittering out into the open. It makes people wince to hear it. I'm getting better, though. Recently I asked the postman for special-issue stamps; I've waited since childhood for postmen to give me some of their own accord. I am making progress, a little every day.

My silence was thickest—total—during the three years that I 18 covered my school paintings with black paint. I painted layers of black over houses and flowers and suns, and when I drew on the blackboard, I put a layer of chalk on top. I was making a stage curtain, and it was the moment before the curtain parted or rose. The teachers called my parents to school, and I saw they had been saving my pictures, curling and cracking, all alike and black. The teachers pointed to the pictures and looked serious, talked seriously too, but my parents did not understand English. ("The parents and teachers of criminals were executed," said by father.) My parents took the pictures home. I spread them out (so black and full of possibilities) and pretended the curtains were swinging open, flying up, one after another, sunlight underneath, mighty operas.

During the first silent year I spoke to no one at school, did not ¹⁹ ask before going to the lavatory, and flunked kindergarten. My sister also said nothing for three years, silent in the playground and silent at lunch. There were other quiet Chinese girls not of our family, but most of them got over it sooner than we did. I enjoyed the silence. At first it did not occur to me I was supposed to talk or to pass kindergarten. I talked at home and to one or two of the Chinese kids in class. I made motions and even made some jokes. I drank out of a toy saucer when the water spilled out of the cup, and everybody laughed, pointing at me, so I did it some more. I didn't know that Americans don't drink out of saucers.

I liked the Negro students (Black Ghosts) best because they ²⁰ laughed the loudest and talked to me as if I were a daring talker too. One of the Negro girls had her mother coil braids over her ears Shanghai-style like mine; we were Shanghai twins except that she was covered with black like my paintings. Two Negro kids enrolled in Chinese school, and the teachers gave them Chinese names. Some Negro kids walked me to school and home, protecting me from the Japanese kids, who hit me and chased me and stuck gum in my ears. The Japanese kids were noisy and tough. They appeared one day in kindergarten, released from concentration camp, which was a tic-tac-toe mark, like barbed wire, on the map.

It was when I found out I had to talk that school became a misery, ²¹ that the silence become a misery. I did not speak and felt bad each time that I did not speak. I read aloud in first grade, though, and heard the barest whisper with little squeaks come out of my throat. "Louder," said the teacher, who scared the voice away again. The other Chinese girls did not talk either, so I knew the silence had to do with being a Chinese girl.

Reading out loud was easier than speaking because we did not ²² have to make up what to say, but I stopped often, and the teacher would think I'd gone quiet again. I could not understand "I." The Chinese "I" has seven strokes, intricacies. How could the American "I," assuredly wearing a hat like the Chinese, have only three strokes, the middle so straight? Was it out of politeness that this writer left off strokes the way a Chinese has to write her own name small and crooked? No, it was not politeness; "I" is a capital and "you" is a lower-case. I stared at that middle line and waited so long for its black center to resolve into tight strokes and dots that I forgot to pronounce it. The other troublesome word was "here," no strong consonant to hang on to, and so flat, when "here" is two mountainous ideographs. The teacher, who had already told me every day how to read "I" and "here," put me in the low corner under the stairs again, where the noisy boys usually sat.

When my second grade class did a play, the whole class went 23 to the auditorium except the Chinese girls. The teacher, lovely and Hawaiian, should have understood about us, but instead left us behind in the classroom. Our voices were too soft or nonexistent, and our parents never signed the permission slips anyway. They never signed anything unnecessary. We opened the door a crack and peeked out, but closed it again quickly. One of us (not me) won every spelling bee, though.

I remember telling the Hawaiian teacher, "We Chinese can't sing 24 'land where our fathers died.' " She argued with me about politics, while I meant because of curses. But how can I have that memory when I couldn't talk? My mother says that we, like the ghosts, have no memories.

After American school, we picked up our cigar boxes, in which 25 we had arranged books, brushes, and an inkbox neatly, and went to Chinese school, from 5:00 to 7:30 P.M. There we chanted together, voices rising and falling, loud and soft, some boys shouting, everybody reading together, reciting together and not alone with one voice. When we had a memorization test, the teacher let each of us come to his desk and say the lesson to him privately, while the rest of the class practiced copying or tracing. Most of the teachers were men. The boys who were so well behaved in the American school played tricks on them and talked back to them. The girls were not mute. They screamed and yelled during recess, when there were no rules; they had fistfights. Nobody was afraid of children hurting themselves or of children hurting school property. The glass doors to the red and green balconies with the gold joy symbols were left wide open so that we could run out and climb the fire escapes. We played capture-the-flag in the auditorium, where Sun Yat-sen and Chiang Kai-shek's pictures hung at the back of the stage, the Chinese flag on their left and the American flag on their right. We climbed the teak ceremonial chairs and made flying leaps off the stage. One flag headquarters was behind the glass door and the other on stage right. Our feet drummed on the hollow stage. During recess the teachers locked themselves up in their office with the shelves of books, copybooks, inks from China. They drank tea and warmed their hands at a stove. There was no play supervision. At recess we had the school to ourselves, and also we could roam as far as we could go—downtown, Chinatown stores, home—as long as we returned before the bell rang.

At exactly 7:30 the teacher again picked up the brass bell that 26 sat on his desk and swung it over our heads, while we charged down the stairs, our cheering magnified in the stairwell. Nobody had to line up.

Not all of the children who were silent at American school found 27 voice at Chinese school. One new teacher said each of us had to get up and recite in front of the class, who was to listen. My sister and I had memorized the lesson perfectly. We said it to each other at home, one chanting, one listening. The teacher called on my sister to recite first. It was the first time a teacher had called on the second-born to go first. My sister was scared. She glanced at me and looked away; I looked down at my desk. I hoped that she could do it because if she could, then I would have to. She opened her mouth and a voice came out that wasn't a whisper, but it wasn't a proper voice either. I hoped that she would not cry, fear breaking up her voice like twigs underfoot. She sounded as if she were trying to sing through weeping and strangling. She did not pause or stop to end the embarrassment. She kept going until she said the last word, and then she sat down. When it was my turn, the same voice came out, a crippled animal running on broken legs. You could hear splinters in my voice, bones rubbing jagged against one another. I was loud, though. I was glad I didn't whisper. There was one little girl who whispered. . . .

How strange that the emigrant villagers are shouters, hollering 28 face to face. My father asks, "Why is it I can hear Chinese from blocks away? Is it that I understand the language? Or is it they talk loud?" They turn the radio up full blast to hear the operas, which do not seem to hurt their ears. And they yell over the singers that wail over the drums, everybody talking at once, big arm gestures, spit flying. You can see the disgust on American faces looking at women like that. It isn't just the loudness. It is the way Chinese sounds, ching-chong ugly, to American ears, not beautiful like Japanese sayonara words with the consonants and vowels as regular as Italian. We make guttural peasant noise and have Ton Duc Thang names you can't remember. And the Chinese can't hear Americans at all; the language is too soft and western music unhearable. I've watched a Chinese audience laugh, visit, talk-story, and holler during a piano recital, as if the musician could not hear them. A Chinese-American, somebody's son, was playing Chopin, which has no punctuation, no cymbals, no gongs. Chinese piano music is five black keys. Normal Chinese women's voices are strong and bossy. We American-Chinese girls had to whisper to make ourselves American-feminine. Apparently we whispered even more softly than the Americans. Once a year the teachers referred my sister and me to speech therapy, but our voices would straighten out, unpredictably normal, for the therapists. Some of us gave up, shook our heads, and said nothing, not one word. Some of us could not even shake our heads. At times shaking my head no is more self-assertion than I can manage. Most of us eventually found some voice, however faltering. We invented an American-feminine speaking personality. . . .

Television Insults Men, Too

Bernard R. Goldberg

It was front page news and it made the TV networks. A mother 1
from Michigan single-handedly convinces some of America's biggest advertisers to cancel their sponsorship of the Fox Broadcasting
Company's "Married . . . With Children" because, as she put it,
the show blatantly exploits women and the family.

The program is about a blue collar family in which the husband 2
is a chauvinist pig and his wife is—excuse the expression—a
bimbo.

These are the late 1980's, and making fun of people because of 3
their gender—on TV no less, in front of millions of people—is
déclassé. Unless, of course, the gender we're ridiculing is the male
gender. Then it's O.K.

Take "Roseanne." (Please!) It's the season's biggest new hit 4
show, which happens to be about another blue collar family. In
this one, the wife calls her husband and kids names.

"Roseanne" is Roseanne Barr who has made a career saying such 5
cute things as: "You may marry the man of your dreams, ladies,
but 15 years later you are married to a reclining chair that burps."
Or to her TV show son: "You're not stupid. You're just clumsy
like your daddy."

The producer of "Roseanne" does not mince words either: "Men 6
are slime. They say they're going to do 50 percent of the work
around the house, but they never do."

I will tell you that the producer is a man, which does not lessen 7
the ugliness of the remark. But because his target is men, it becomes
acceptable. No one, to my knowledge, is pulling commercials from
"Roseanne."

In matters of gender discrimination, it has become part of the 8
accepted orthodoxy—of many feminists and a lot of the media
anyway—that only women have the right to complain. Men have
no such right. Which helps explain why there have been so many
commercials ridiculing men—and getting away with it.

In the past year or so, I have seen a breakfast cereal commercial 9
showing a husband and wife playing tennis. She is perky and he
is jerky.

She is a regular Martina Navratilova of the suburbs and he is 10 virtually dead (because he wasn't smart enough to eat the right cereal).

She doesn't miss a shot. He lets the ball hit him in the head. If 11 he were black, his name would be Stepin Fetchitt.

I have seen a commercial for razor blades that shows a woman 12 in an evening gown smacking a man in a tuxedo across the face, suggesting, I suppose, that the male face takes enough punishment to deserve a nice, smooth shave. If he hit her (an absolutely inconceivable notion, if a sponsor is trying to sell a woman something) he would be a batterer.

I have seen an airline commercial showing two reporters from 13 competing newspapers. She's strong and smart. He's a nerd. He says to her: I read your story this morning; you scooped me again. She replies to him: I didn't know you could read.

I have seen a magazine ad for perfume showing a business- 14 woman patting a businessman's behind as they walk down the street. *Ms.* magazine, the Journal of American feminism, ran the ad. The publisher told me there was nothing sexist about it.

A colleague who writes about advertising and the media says 15 advertisers are afraid to fool around with women's roles. They know, as she puts it, they'll "set off the feminist emergency broadcast system" if they do. So, she concludes, men are fair game.

In 1987, Fred Hayward, who is one of the pioneers of the men's 16 rights movement (yes, there is a men's rights movement) studied thousands of TV and print ads and concluded: "If there's a sleazy character in an ad, 100 percent of the ones that we found were male. If there's an incompetent character, 100 percent of them in the ads are male."

I once interviewed Garrett Epps, a scholar who has written on 17 these matters, who told me: "The female executive who is driven, who is strong, who lives for her work, that's a very positive symbol in our culture now. The male who has the same traits—that guy is a disaster: He harms everybody around him; he's cold; he's unfeeling; he's hurtful."

The crusading mother from Michigan hit on a legitimate issue. 18 No more cheap shots, she seems to have said. And the advertisers listened. No more cheap shots is what a lot of men are saying also. Too bad nobody is listening to *them.*

"I'll Explain It to You": Lecturing and Listening

Deborah Tannen

At a reception following the publication of one of my books, I noticed a publicist listening attentively to the producer of a popular radio show. He was telling her how the studio had come to be built where it was, and why he would have preferred another site. What caught my attention was the length of time he was speaking while she was listening. He was delivering a monologue that could only be called a lecture, giving her detailed information about the radio reception at the two sites, the architecture of the station, and so on. I later asked the publicist if she had been interested in the information the producer had given her. "Oh, yes," she answered. But then she thought a moment and said, "Well, maybe he did go on a bit." The next day she told me, "I was thinking about what you asked. I couldn't have cared less about what he was saying. It's just that I'm so used to listening to men go on about things I don't care about, I didn't even realize how bored I was until you made me think about it." 1

I was chatting with a man I had just met at a party. In our conversation, it emerged that he had been posted in Greece with the RAF during 1944 and 1945. Since I had lived in Greece for several years, I asked him about his experiences: What had Greece been like then? How had the Greek villagers treated the British soldiers? What had it been *like* to be a British soldier in wartime Greece? I also offered information about how Greece had changed, what it is like now. He did not pick up on my remarks about contemporary Greece, and his replies to my questions quickly changed from accounts of his own experiences, which I found riveting, to facts about Greek history, which interested me in principle but in the actual telling left me profoundly bored. The more impersonal his talk became, the more I felt oppressed by it, pinned involuntarily in the listener position. 2

At a showing of Judy Chicago's jointly created art work *The Dinner Party*, I was struck by a couple standing in front of one of the displays: The man was earnestly explaining to the woman the 3 meaning of symbols in the tapestry before them, pointing as he spoke. I might not have noticed this unremarkable scene, except that *The Dinner Party* was radically feminist in conception, intended to reflect women's experiences and sensibilities.

While taking a walk in my neighborhood on an early summer 4 evening at twilight, I stopped to chat with a neighbor who was walking his dogs. As we stood, I noticed that the large expanse of yard in front of which we were standing was aglitter with the intermittent flickering of fireflies. I called attention to the sight, remarking on how magical it looked. "It's like the Fourth of July," I said. He agreed, and then told me he had read that the lights of fireflies are mating signals. He then explained to me details of how these signals work—for example, groups of fireflies fly at different elevations and could be seen to cluster in different parts of the yard.

In all these examples, the men had information to impart and 5 they were imparting it. On the surface, there is nothing surprising or strange about that. What is strange is that there are so many situations in which men have factual information requiring lengthy explanations to impart to women, and so few in which women have comparable information to impart to men.

The changing times have altered many aspects of relations be- 6 tween women and men. Now it is unlikely, at least in many circles, for a man to say, "I am better than you because I am a man and you are a woman." But women who do not find men making such statements are nonetheless often frustrated in their dealings with them. One situation that frustrates many women is a conversation that has mysteriously turned into a lecture, with the man delivering the lecture to the woman, who has become an appreciative audience.

Once again, the alignment in which women and men find them- 7 selves arrayed is asymmetrical. The lecturer is framed as superior in status and expertise, cast in the role of teacher, and the listener is cast in the role of student. If women and men took turns giving and receiving lectures, there would be nothing disturbing about it. What is disturbing is the imbalance. Women and men fall into this unequal pattern so often because of the differences in their interactional habits. Since women seek to build rapport, they are inclined to play down their expertise rather than display it. Since men value the position of center stage and the feeling of knowing more, they seek opportunities to gather and disseminate factual information.

If men often seem to hold forth because they have the expertise, 8 women are often frustrated and surprised to find that when they have the expertise, they don't necessarily get the floor.

First Me, Then Me

I was at a dinner with faculty members from other departments 9 in my university. To my right was a woman. As the dinner began, we introduced ourselves. After we told each other what departments we were in and what subjects we taught, she asked what my research was about. We talked about my research for a little while. Then I asked her about her research and she told me about it. Finally, we discussed the ways that our research overlapped. Later, as tends to happen at dinners, we branched out to others at the table. I asked a man across the table from me what department he was in and what he did. During the next half hour, I learned a lot about his job, his research, and his background. Shortly before the dinner ended there was a lull, and he asked me what I did. When I said I was a linguist, he became excited and told me about a research project he had conducted that was related to neurolinguistics. He was still telling me about his research when we all got up to leave the table.

This man and woman were my colleagues in academia. What 10 happens when I talk to people at parties and social events, not fellow researchers? My experience is that if I mention the kind of work I do to women, they usually ask me about it. When I tell them about conversational style or gender differences, they offer their own experiences to support the patterns I describe. This is very pleasant for me. It puts me at center stage without my having to grab the spotlight myself, and I frequently gather anecdotes I can use in the future. But when I announce my line of work to men, many give me a lecture on language—for example, about how people, especially teenagers, misuse language nowadays. Others challenge me, for example questioning me about my research methods. Many others change the subject to something they know more about.

Of course not all men respond in this way, but over the years I 11 have encountered many men, and very few women, who do. It is not that speaking in this way is *the* male way of doing things, but that it is *a* male way. There are women who adopt such styles, but they are perceived as speaking like men.

If You've Got It, Flaunt It—or Hide It

I have been observing this constellation in interaction for more 12 than a dozen years. I did not, however, have any understanding of *why* this happens until fairly recently, when I developed the framework of status and connection. An experimental study that was pivotal in my thinking shows that expertise does not ensure women a place at center stage in conversation with men.

Psychologist H. M. Leet-Pellegrini set out to discover whether 13 gender or expertise determined who would behave in what she terms a "dominant" way—for example, by talking more, interrupting, and controlling the topic. She set up pairs of women, pairs of men, and mixed pairs, and asked them to discuss the effects of television violence on children. In some cases, she made one of the partners an expert by providing relevant factual information and time to read and assimilate it before the videotaped discussion. One might expect that the conversationalist who was the expert would talk more, interrupt more, and spend less time supporting the conversational partner who knew less about the subject. But it wasn't so simple. On the average, those who had expertise did talk more, but men experts talked more than women experts.

Expertise also had a different effect on women and men with 14 regard to supportive behavior. Leet-Pellegrini expected that the one who did not have expertise would spend more time offering agreement and support to the one who did. This turned out to be true—*except* in cases where a woman was the expert and her non-expert partner was a man. In this situation, the women experts showed support—saying things like "Yeah" and "That's right"— far *more* than the nonexpert men they were talking to. Observers often rated the male nonexpert as more dominant than the female expert. In other words, the women in this experiment not only didn't wield their expertise as power, but tried to play it down and make up for it through extra assenting behavior. They acted as if their expertise were something to hide.

And perhaps it was. When the word *expert* was spoken in these 15 experimental conversations, in all cases but one it was the man in the conversation who used it, saying something like "So, you're the expert." Evidence of the woman's superior knowledge sparked resentment, not respect.

Furthermore, when an expert man talked to an uninformed 16 woman, he took a controlling role in structuring the conversation in the beginning *and* the end. But when an expert man talked to an uninformed man, he dominated in the beginning but not always in the end. In other words, having expertise was enough to keep a man in the controlling position if he was talking to a woman, but not if he was talking to a man. Apparently, when a woman surmised that the man she was talking to had more information on the subject than she did, she simply accepted the reactive role. But another man, despite a lack of information, might still give the expert a run for his money and possibly gain the upper hand by the end.

Reading these results, I suddenly understood what happens to 17 me when I talk to women and men about language. I am assuming that my acknowledged expertise will mean I am automatically accorded authority in the conversation, and with women that is generally the case. But when I talk to men, revealing that I have acknowledged expertise in this area often invites challenges. I *might* maintain my position if I defend myself successfully against the challenges, but if I don't, I may lose ground.

One interpretation of the Leet-Pellegrini study is that women 18 are getting a bum deal. They don't get credit when it's due. And in a way, this is true. But the reason is not—as it seems to many women—that men are bums who seek to deny women authority. The Leet-Pellegrini study shows that many men are inclined to jockey for status, and challenge the authority of others, when they are talking to men too. If this is so, then challenging a woman's authority as they would challenge a man's could be a sign of respect and equal treatment, rather than lack of respect and discrimination. In cases where this is so, the inequality of the treatment results not simply from the men's behavior alone but from the differences in men's and women's styles: Most women lack experience in defending themselves against challenges, which they misinterpret as personal attacks on their credibility.

Even when talking to men who are happy to see them in po- 19 sitions of status, women may have a hard time getting their due because of differences in men's and women's interactional goals. Just as boys in high school are not inclined to repeat information about popular girls because it doesn't get them what they want, women in conversation are not inclined to display their knowledge because it doesn't get them what they are after. Leet-Pellegrini suggests that the men in this study were playing a game of "Have I won?" while the women were playing a game of "Have I been sufficiently helpful?" I am inclined to put this another way: The game women play is "Do you like me?" whereas the men play "Do you respect me?" If men, in seeking respect, are less liked by women, this is an unsought side effect, as is the effect that women, in seeking to be liked, may lose respect. When a woman has a conversation with a man, her efforts to emphasize their similarities and avoid showing off can easily be interpreted, through the lens of status, as relegating her to a one-down position, making her appear either incompetent or insecure.

A Subtle Deference

Elizabeth Aries, a professor of psychology at Amherst College, 20 set out to show that highly intelligent, highly educated young women are no longer submissive in conversations with male peers. And indeed she found that the college women did talk more than the college men in small groups she set up. But what they said was different. The men tended to set the agenda by offering opinions, suggestions, and information. The women tended to react, offering agreement or disagreement. Furthermore, she found that body language was as different as ever: The men sat with their legs stretched out, while the women gathered themselves in. Noting that research has found that speakers using the open-bodied position are more likely to persuade their listeners, Aries points out that talking more may not ensure that women will be heard.

In another study, Aries found that men in all-male discussion 21
groups spent a lot of time at the beginning finding out "who was
best informed about movies, books, current events, politics, and
travel" as a means of "sizing up the competition" and negotiating
"where they stood in relation to each other." This glimpse of how
men talk when there are no women present gives an inkling of
why displaying knowledge and expertise is something that men
find more worth doing than women. What the women in Aries's
study spend time doing was "gaining a closeness through more
intimate self-revelation."

It is crucial to bear in mind that both the women and the men 22
in these studies were establishing camaraderie, and both were concerned with their relationships to each other. But different aspects
of their relationships were of primary concern: their place in a
hierarchical order for the men, and their place in a network of
intimate connections for the women. The consequence of these
disparate concerns was very different ways of speaking.

Thomas Fox is an English professor who was intrigued by the 23
differences between women and men in his freshman writing
classes. What he observed corresponds almost precisely to the experimental findings of Aries and Leet-Pellegrini. Fox's method of
teaching writing included having all the students read their essays
to each other in class and talk to each other in small groups. He
also had them write papers reflecting on the essays and the discussion groups. He alone, as the teacher, read these analytical
papers.

To exemplify the two styles he found typical of women and men, 24
Fox chose a woman, Ms. M, and a man, Mr. H. In her speaking
as well as her writing, Ms. M. held back what she knew, appearing
uninformed and uninterested, because she feared offending her
classmates. Mr. H spoke and wrote with authority and apparent
confidence because he was eager to persuade his peers. She did
not worry about persuading; he did not worry about offending.

In his analytical paper, the young man described his own be- 25
havior in the mixed-gender group discussions as if he were describing the young men in Leet-Pellegrini's and Aries's studies:

In my sub-group I am the leader. I begin every discussion by stating my opinions as facts. The other two members of the sub-group tend to sit back and agree with me. . . . I need people to agree with me.

Fox comments that Mr. H reveals "a sense of self, one that acts to change himself and other people, that seems entirely distinct from Ms. M's sense of self, dependent on and related to others."

Calling Ms. M's sense of self "dependent" suggests a negative view of her way of being in the world—and, I think, a view more typical of men. This view reflects the assumption that the alternative to independence is dependence. If this is indeed a male view, it may explain why so many men are cautious about becoming intimately involved with others: It makes sense to avoid humiliating dependence by insisting on independence. But there is another alternative: *inter*dependence. 26

The main difference between these alternatives is symmetry. Dependence is an asymmetrical involvement: One person needs the other, but not vice versa, so the needy person is one-down. Interdependence is symmetrical: Both parties rely on each other, so neither is one-up or one-down. Moreover, Mr. H's sense of self is also dependent on others. He requires others to listen, agree, and allow him to take the lead by stating his opinions first. 27

Looked at this way, the woman and man in this group are both dependent on each other. Their differing goals are complementary, although neither understands the reasons for the other's behavior. This would be a fine arrangement, except that their differing goals result in alignments that enhance his authority and undercut hers. 28

Different Interpretations—and Misinterpretations

Fox also describes differences in the way male and female students in his classes interpreted a story they read. These differences also reflect assumptions about the interdependence or independence of individuals. Fox's students wrote their responses to "The Birthmark" by Nathaniel Hawthorne. In the story, a woman's husband becomes obsessed with a birthmark on her face. Suffering from her husband's revulsion at the sight of her, the wife becomes obsessed with it too and, in a reversal of her initial impulse, agrees 29 to undergo a treatment he has devised to remove the birthmark—a treatment that succeeds in removing the mark, but kills her in the process.

Ms. M interpreted the wife's complicity as a natural response to the demand of a loved one: The woman went along with her husband's lethal schemes to remove the birthmark because she wanted to please and be appealing to him. Mr. H blamed the woman's insecurity and vanity for her fate, and he blamed her for voluntarily submitting to her husband's authority. Fox points out that he saw her as individually responsible for her actions, just as he saw himself as individually responsible for his own actions. To him, the issue was independence: The weak wife voluntarily took a submissive role. To Ms. M, the issue was interdependence: The woman was inextricably bound up with her husband, so her behavior could not be separated from his.

Fox observes that Mr. H saw the writing of the women in the class as spontaneous—they wrote whatever popped into their heads. Nothing could be farther from Ms. M's experience as she described it: When she knew her peers would see her writing, she censored everything that popped into her head. In contrast, when she was writing something that only her professor would read, she expressed firm and articulate opinions.

There is a striking but paradoxical complementarity to Ms. M's and Mr. H's styles, when they are taken together. He needs someone to listen and agree. She listens and agrees. But in another sense, their dovetailing purposes are at cross-purposes. He misinterprets her agreement, intended in a spirit of connection, as a reflection of status and power: He thinks she is "indecisive" and "insecure." Her reasons for refraining from behaving as he does—firmly stating opinions as facts—have nothing to do with her attitudes toward her knowledge, as he thinks they do, but rather result from her attitudes toward her relationships with her peers.

These experimental studies by Leet-Pellegrini and Aries, and the observations by Fox, all indicate that, typically, men are more comfortable than women in giving information and opinions and speaking in an authoritative way to a group, whereas women are more comfortable than men in supporting others. . . .

Listener as Underling

Clearly men are not always talking and women are not always 34
listening. I have asked men whether they ever find themselves in
the position of listening to another man giving them a lecture, and
how they feel about it. They tell me that this does happen. They
may find themselves talking to someone who presses information
on them so insistently that they give in and listen. They say they
don't mind too much, however, if the information is interesting.
They can store it away for future use, like remembering a joke to
tell others later. Factual information is of less interest to women
because it is of less use to them. They are unlikely to try to pass
on the gift of information, more likely to give the gift of being a
good audience.

Men as well as women sometimes find themselves on the re- 35
ceiving end of a lecture they would as soon not hear. But men tell
me that it is most likely to happen if the other man is in a position
of higher status. They know they have to listen to lectures from
fathers and bosses.

That men find themselves in the position of unwilling listener 36
is attested to by a short opinion piece in which A. R. Gurney be-
moans being frequently "cornered by some self-styled expert who
harangues me with his considered opinion on an interminable
agenda of topics." He claims that this tendency bespeaks a pe-
culiarly American inability to "converse"—that is, engage in a balanced give-and-take—and cites as support the French observer of
American customs Alexis de Tocqueville, who wrote, "An American . . . speaks to you as if he was addressing a meeting." Gurney
credits his own appreciation of conversing to his father, who "was
a master at eliciting and responding enthusiastically to the views
of others, though this resiliency didn't always extend to his children. Indeed, now I think about it, he spoke to us many times as
if he were addressing a meeting."

It is not surprising that Gurney's father lectured his children. 37
The act of giving information by definition frames one in a position
of higher status, while the act of listening frames one as lower.
Children instinctively sense this—as do most men. But when
women listen to men, they are not thinking in terms of status.
Unfortunately, their attempts to reinforce connections and estab-

lish rapport, when interpreted through the lens of status, can be misinterpreted as casting them in a subordinate position—and are likely to be taken that way by many men.

What's So Funny?

The economy of exchanging jokes for laughter is a parallel one. 38 In her study of college students' discussion groups, Aries found that the students in all-male groups spent a lot of time telling about times they had played jokes on others, and laughing about it. She refers to a study in which Barbara Miller Newman found that high school boys who were not "quick and clever" became the targets of jokes. Practical joking—playing a joke *on* someone—is clearly a matter of being one-up: in the know and in control. It is less obvious, but no less true, that *telling* jokes can also be a way of negotiating status.

Many women (certainly not all) laugh at jokes but do not later 39 remember them. Since they are not driven to seek and hold center stage in a group, they do not need a store of jokes to whip out for this purpose. A woman I will call Bernice prided herself on her sense of humor. At a cocktail party, she met a man to whom she was drawn because he seemed at first to share this trait. He made many funny remarks, which she spontaneously laughed at. But when she made funny remarks, he seemed not to hear. What had happened to his sense of humor? Though telling jokes and laughing at them are both reflections of a sense of humor, they are very different social activities. Making others laugh gives you a fleeting power over them: As linguist Wallace Chafe points out, at the moment of laughter, a person is temporarily disabled. The man Bernice met was comfortable only when he was making her laugh, not the other way around. When Bernice laughed at his jokes, she thought she was engaging in a symmetrical activity. But he was engaging in an asymmetrical one.

A man told me that sometime around tenth grade he realized 40 that he preferred the company of women to the company of men. He found that his female friends were more supportive and less competitive, whereas his male friends seemed to spend all their time joking. Considering joking an asymmetrical activity makes it clearer why it would fit in with a style he perceived as competitive. . . .

Mutual Accusations

Considering these dynamics, it is not surprising that many 41 women complain that their partners don't listen to them. But men make the same complaint about women, although less frequently. The accusation "You're not listening" often really means "You don't understand what I said in the way that I meant it," or "I'm not getting the response I wanted." Being listened to can become a metaphor for being understood and being valued.

In my earlier work I emphasized that women may get the impres- 42 sion men aren't listening to them even when the men really are. This happens because men have different habitual ways of showing they're listening. As anthropologists Maltz and Borker explain, women are more inclined to ask questions. They also give more listening responses—little words like *mhm, uh-uh*, and *yeah*—sprinkled throughout someone else's talk, providing a running feedback loop. And they respond more positively and enthusiastically, for example by agreeing and laughing.

All this behavior is doing the work of listening. It also creates 43 rapport-talk by emphasizing connection and encouraging more talk. The corresponding strategies of men—giving fewer listener responses, making statements rather than asking questions, and challenging rather than agreeing—can be understood as moves in a contest by incipient speakers rather than audience members.

Not only do women give more listening signals, according to 44 Maltz and Borker, but the signals they give have different meanings for men and women, consistent with the speaker/audience alignment. Women use "yeah" to mean "I'm with you, I follow," whereas men tend to say "yeah" only when they agree. The opportunity for misunderstanding is clear. When a man is confronted with a women who has been saying "yeah," "yeah," "yeah," and then turns out not to agree, he may conclude that she has been insincere, or that she was agreeing without really listening. When a woman is confronted with a man who does *not* say "yeah"—or much of anything else—she may conclude that *he* hasn't been listening. The men's style is more literally focused on the message level of talk, while the women's is focused on the relationship or metamessage level.

To a man who expects a listener to be quietly attentive, a woman 45 giving a stream of feedback and support will seem to be talking too much for a listener. To a woman who expects a listener to be active and enthusiastic in showing interest, attention, and support, a man who listens silently will seem not to be listening at all, but rather to have checked out of the conversation, taken his listening marbles, and gone mentally home.

Because of these patterns, women may get the impression that 46 men aren't listening when they really are. But I have come to understand, more recently, that it is also true that men listen to women less frequently than women listen to men, because the act of listening has different meanings for them. Some men really *don't* want to listen at length because they feel it frames them as subordinate. Many women do want to listen, but they expect it to be reciprocal—I listen to you now; you listen to me later. They become frustrated when they do the listening now and now and now, and later never comes.

Mutual Dissatisfaction

If women are dissatisfied with always being in the listening po- 47 sition, the dissatisfaction may be mutual. That a woman feels she has been assigned the role of silently listening audience does not mean that a man feels he has consigned her to that role—or that he necessarily likes the rigid alignment either.

During the time I was working on this book, I found myself at 48 a book party filled with people I hardly knew. I struck up a conversation with a charming young man who turned out to be a painter. I asked him about his work and, in response to his answer, asked whether there has been a return in contemporary art to figurative painting. In response to my question, he told me a lot about the history of art—so much that when he finished and said, "That was a long answer to your question," I had long since forgotten that I had asked a question, let alone what it was. I had not minded this monologue—I had been interested in it—but I realized, with something of a jolt, that I had just experienced the dynamic that I had been writing about.

I decided to risk offending my congenial new acquaintance in 49 order to learn something about his point of view. This was, after all, a book party, so I might rely on his indulgence if I broke the rules of decorum in the interest of writing a book. I asked whether he often found himself talking at length while someone else listened. He thought for a moment and said yes, he did, because he liked to explore ideas in detail. I asked if it happened equally with women and men. He thought again and said, "No, I have more trouble with men." I asked what he meant by trouble. He said, "Men interrupt. *They* want to explain to *me*."

Finally, having found this young man disarmingly willing to talk 50 about the conversation we had just had and his own style, I asked which he preferred: that a woman listen silently and supportively, or that she offer opinions and ideas of her own. He said he thought he liked it better if she volunteered information, making the interchange more interesting.

When men begin to lecture other men, the listeners are expe- 51 rienced at trying to sidetrack the lecture, or match it, or derail it. In this system, making authoritative pronouncements may be a way to begin an *exchange* of information. But women are not used to responding in that way. They see little choice but to listen attentively and wait for their turn to be allotted to them rather than seizing it for themselves. If this is the case, the man may be as bored and frustrated as the woman when his attempt to begin an exchange of information ends in his giving a lecture. From his point of view, she is passively soaking up information, so she must not have any to speak of. One of the reasons men's talk to women frequently turns into lecturing is *because* women listen attentively and do not interrupt with challenges, sidetracks, or matching information.

In the conversations with male and female colleagues that I re- 52 counted at the outset of this chapter, this difference may have been crucial. When I talked to the woman, we each told about our own research in response to the other's encouragement. When I talked to the man, I encouraged him to talk about his work, and he obliged, but he did not encourage me to talk about mine. This may mean that he did not want to hear about it—but it also may not.

In her study of college students' discussion groups, Aries found that women who did a lot of talking began to feel uncomfortable; they backed off and frequently drew out quieter members of the group. This is perfectly in keeping with women's desire to keep things balanced, so everyone is on an equal footing. Women expect their conversational partners to encourage them to hold forth. Men who do not typically encourage quieter members to speak up, assume that anyone who has something to say will volunteer it. The men may be equally disappointed in a conversational partner who turns out to have nothing to say.

Similarly, men can be as bored by women's topics as women can 53 be by men's. While I was wishing the former RAFer would tell me about his personal experiences in Greece, he was probably wondering why I was boring him with mine and marveling at my ignorance of the history of a country I had lived in. Perhaps he would have considered our conversation a success if I had challenged or topped his interpretation of Greek history rather than listening dumbly to it. When men, upon hearing the kind of work I do, challenge me about my research methods, they are inviting me to give them information and show them my expertise—something I don't like to do outside of the classroom or lecture hall, but something they themselves would likely be pleased to be provoked to do.

The publicist who listened attentively to information about a 54 radio station explained to me that she wanted to be nice to the manager, to smooth the way for placing her clients on his station. But men who want to ingratiate themselves with women are more likely to try to charm them by offering interesting information than by listening attentively to whatever information the women have to impart. I recall a luncheon preceding a talk I delivered to a college alumni association. My gracious host kept me entertained before my speech by regaling me with information about computers, which I politely showed interest in, while inwardly screaming from boredom and a sense of being weighed down by irrelevant information that I knew I would never remember. Yet I am sure he thought he was being interesting, and it is likely that at least some male guests would have thought that he was. I do not wish to imply that all women hosts have entertained me in the perfect way. I recall a speaking engagement before which I was taken to lunch by a group of women. They were so attentive to my expertise that they plied me with questions, prompting me to exhaust myself by giving my lecture over lunch before the formal lecture began. In comparison to this, perhaps the man who lectured to me about computers was trying to give me a rest.

The imbalance by which men often find themselves in the role 55 of lecturer, and women often find themselves in the role of audience, is not the creation of only one member of the interaction. It is not something that men do to women. Neither is it something that women culpably "allow" or "ask for." The imbalance is created by the difference between women's and men's habitual styles. . . .

Hope for the Future

What is the hope for the future? Must we play out our assigned 56 parts to the closing act? Although we tend to fall back on habitual ways of talking, repeating old refrains and familiar lines, habits can be broken. Women and men both can gain by understanding the other gender's style, and by learning to use it on occasion.

Women who find themselves unwillingly cast as the listener 57 should practice propelling themselves out of that position rather than waiting patiently for the lecture to end. Perhaps they need to give up the belief that they must wait for the floor to be handed to them. If they have something to say on a subject, they might push themselves to volunteer it. If they are bored with a subject, they can exercise some influence on the conversation and change the topic to something they would rather discuss.

If women are relieved to learn that they don't always have to 58 listen, there may be some relief for men in learning that they don't always have to have interesting information on the tips of their tongues if they want to impress a woman or entertain her. A journalist once interviewed me for an article about how to strike up conversations. She told me that another expert she had interviewed, a man, had suggested that one should come up with an interesting piece of information. I found this amusing, as it seemed to typify a man's idea of a good conversationalist, but not a woman's. How much easier men might find the task of conversation if they realized that all they have to do is listen. As a woman who wrote a letter to the editor of *Psychology Today* put it, "When I find a guy who asks, 'How was your day?' and really wants to know, I'm in heaven."

Suggested Research Paper Topics

1. Interview at least one person who speaks one language at home and another in school to learn what it was like to grow up bilingual. What problems did the person encounter? What benefits did the person see in being bilingual? Compare and contrast the responses you receive with the accounts given by Pedrosa, Fiske, Lord, and Kingston.
2. After a class discussion of terms that are used affectionately within a minority community, but are considered derogatory when used in the larger, outside community, write an essay in which you agree or disagree with Naylor's contention that "a word's meaning often depends on who says it."
3. What experiences have you had with Allport's "nouns that cut slices" and "labels of primary potency"? What are some of the nouns that cut slices and labels of primary potency that deal with gender? Write a paper in which you explain how you or a friend has been placed at a disadvantage by such biased language. Use the articles by Nilsen, Tannen, and Goldberg to support your observations.
4. Is understanding the dynamics of prejudice as revealed in our language helpful? Using at least three of the articles in this casebook, write a paper in which you discuss the power of language to shape society's attitudes toward women or a minority.
5. Charles Osgood, the popular CBS radio commentator, once wrote: "To hate somebody, to hate them enough to kill them, you must first dehumanize them in your mind. . . ." Write a paper in which

you explore the way that racial and gender epithets (derogatory terms) dehumanize people and place them in potential danger. Use the Allport and Nilsen articles, and at least one other, for both ideas and examples to use in your own paper.

6. Ethnocentrism can be defined as a tendency to view alien cultures with disfavor resulting in a sense of one's own superiority. Why has there been so much attention given to ethnocentrism lately? Using the articles by Cunha, Fiske, Lord, Kingston, and any others that you find useful, write a paper in which you explore the ramifications of ethnocentrism for minorities in the United States, making sure to touch upon language concerns wherever possible.

7. Using several articles in the casebook, write an essay in which you use the following statement by Gloria Naylor as your thesis: "Words themselves are innocuous; it is the consensus that gives them true power" (page 596).

8. Bernard Goldberg argues that it has now become fashionable to ridicule men, and he draws examples from television sitcoms and advertisements to support his contention. How is this anti-male bias similar to the sexism categorized by Nilsen? To what extent can some of the "male bashing" be explained by Tannen's discussion of conversational style differences?

9. Bette Bao Lord writes, "I do not believe that the loss of one's native culture is the price one must pay for becoming an American." What are your thoughts on this issue? Is it possible for one to become an American and still maintain one's native culture? If so, to what extent? What do the comments by Cunha, Kingston, and the students interviewed by Fiske suggest about the possibility of realizing this ideal?

10. Everyone can be placed in various categories according to sex, race, religion, cultural background, and even appearance. How would you categorize yourself? What is your own image of the categories to which you belong? How do outsiders view these categories? In what ways has language been used to stigmatize you or the categories to which you belong? How do you feel about the stigma? Using at least three articles in this casebook, discuss the concept of self image and the need to define oneself.

11. Listen to yourself and your friends in conversation for a week or two. Consider what, if any, gender-biased language or male/female differences in conversational style you've heard. Remember that sexist language can be anti-male as well as anti-female. What

conclusions can you draw from your investigation? How do your conclusions compare with those of Nilsen and Tannen?

12. What is "political correctness"? What does an understanding of language have to do with political correctness? Using at least three articles in this casebook, write an essay on race, gender, language, and political correctness.

Glossary of Rhetorical Terms

Abstract See *Concrete/Abstract.*

Allusion An allusion is a passing reference to a familiar person, place, or thing drawn from history, the Bible, mythology, or literature. An allusion is an economical way for a writer to capture the essence of an idea, atmosphere, emotion, or historical era, as in "The scandal was his Watergate," or "He saw himself as a modern Job," or "Everyone there held those truths to be self-evident." An allusion should be familiar to the reader, for if it is not, it will add nothing to the meaning.

Analogy Analogy is a special form of comparison in which the writer explains something unfamiliar by comparing it to something familiar: "A transmission line is simply a pipeline for electricity. In the case of a water pipeline, more water will flow through the pipe as water pressure increases. The same is true of a transmission line for electricity." See also the discussion of analogy in Section 7.

Analytical Reading Reading analytically means reading actively, paying close attention to both the content and structure of the text. Analytical reading often involves answering several basic questions about the piece of writing under consideration:

1. What does the author want to say? What is his or her main point?
2. Why does the author want to say it? What is his or her purpose?

631

3. What strategy or strategies does the author use?
4. Why and how does the author's writing strategy suit both the subject and purpose?
5. What is special about the way the author uses the strategy?
6. How effective is the essay? Why?

For a detailed example of analytical reading, see pages 6–8 in the Introduction.

Appropriateness See *Diction*.

Argument Argument is one of the four basic types of prose. (Narration, description, and exposition are the other three.) To argue is to attempt to convince a reader to agree with a point of view, to make a given decision, or to pursue a particular course of action. Logical argument is based on reasonable explanations and appeals to the reader's intelligence. See Section 11 for further discussion of argumentation. See also *Persuasion* and *Logical Fallacies*.

Attitude A writer's attitude reflects his or her opinion of a subject. For example, a writer can think very positively or very negatively about a subject. In most cases, the writer's attitude falls somewhere between these two extremes. See also *Tone*.

Audience An audience is the intended readership for a piece of writing. For example, the readers of a national weekly newsmagazine come from all walks of life and have diverse opinions, attitudes, and educational experiences. In contrast, the readership for an organic chemistry journal is made up of people whose interests and educations are quite similar. The essays in this book are intended for general readers, intelligent people who may lack specific information about the subject being discussed.

Beginnings See *Beginnings/Endings*.

Beginnings/Endings A *beginning* is that sentence, group of sentences, or section that introduces an essay. Good beginnings usually identify the thesis or controlling idea, attempt to interest the reader, and establish a tone. Some effective ways in which writers begin essays include (1) telling an anecdote that illustrates the thesis, (2) providing a controversial statement or opinion that engages the reader's interest, (3) presenting startling statistics or facts, (4) defining a term that is central to the discussion that follows, (5) asking thought-provoking questions, (6) providing a quotation that illustrates the thesis, (7) referring to a current event that helps to establish the thesis, or (8) show the significance of the subject or stressing its importance to reader.

An *ending* is the sentence or group of sentences that brings a. essay to closure. Good endings are purposeful and well planned. Endings satisfy readers when they are the natural outgrowths of the essays themselves and convey a sense of finality or completion. Good essays do not simply stop; they conclude.

Cause and Effect Analysis Cause and effect analysis is one of the types of exposition. (Process analysis, definition, division and classification, and comparison and contrast are the others.) Cause and effect analysis answers the question *why?* It explains the reasons for an occurrence or the consequences of an action. See Section 10 for a detailed discussion of cause and effect analysis. See also *Exposition*.

Classification Classification is one of the types of exposition. (Process analysis, definition, comparison and contrast, and cause and effect analysis are the others.) When classifying, the writer arranges and sorts people, places, or things into categories according to their differing characteristics, thus making them more manageable for the writer and more understandable for the reader. See Section 8 for a detailed discussion of classification. See also *Exposition* and *Division*.

Cliché A cliché is an expression that has become ineffective through overuse. Expressions such as *quick as a flash, dry as dust, jump for joy*, and *slow as molasses* are all clichés. Writers normally avoid such trite expressions and seek instead to express themselves in fresh and forceful language.

Coherence Coherence is a quality of good writing that results when all sentences, paragraphs, and longer divisions of an essay are naturally connected. Coherent writing is achieved through (1) a logical sequence of ideas (arranged in chronological order, spatial order, order of importance, or some other appropriate order), (2) the thoughtful repetition of key words and ideas, (3) a pace suitable for your topic and your reader, and (4) the use of transitional words and expressions. Coherence should not be confused with unity. (See *Unity*.) Also see *Transitions*.

Colloquial Expressions A colloquial expression is characteristic of or appropriate to spoken language or to writing that seeks its effect. Colloquial expressions are informal, as *chem, gym, come up with, be at loose ends, won't,* and *photo* illustrate. Thus, colloquial expressions are acceptable in formal writing only if they are used purposefully.

Comparison and Contrast   Comparison and contrast is one of the types of exposition. (Process analysis, definition, division and classification, and cause and effect analysis are the others.) In comparison and contrast, the writer points out the similarities and differences between two or more subjects in the same class or category. The function of any comparison and contrast is to clarify—to reach some conclusion about the items being compared and contrasted. See Section 6 for a detailed discussion of comparison and contrast. See also *Exposition.*

Conclusions   See *Beginnings/Endings.*

Concrete   See *Concrete/Abstract.*

Concrete/Abstract   A *concrete word* names a specific object, person, place, or action that can be directly perceived by the senses: *car, bread, building, book, John F. Kennedy, Chicago,* or *hiking.* An *abstract word,* in contrast, refers to general qualities, conditions, ideas, actions, or relationships that cannot be directly perceived by the senses: *bravery, dedication, excellence, anxiety, stress, thinking,* or *hatred.*

Although writers must use both concrete and abstract language, good writers avoid too many abstract words. Instead, they rely on concrete words to define and illustrate abstractions. Because concrete words affect the senses, they are easily comprehended by the reader.

Connotation   See *Connotation/Denotation.*

Connotation/Denotation   Both connotation and denotation refer to the meanings of words. *Denotation* is the dictionary meaning of a word, the literal meaning. *Connotation,* on the other hand, is the implied or suggested meaning of a word. For example, the denotation of *lamb* is "a young sheep." The connotations of lamb are numerous: *gentle, docile, weak, peaceful, blessed, sacrificial, blood, spring, frisky, pure, innocent,* and so on. Good writers are sensitive to both the denotations and the connotations of words and use these meanings to advantage in their writing.

Controlling Idea   See *Thesis.*

Deduction   Deduction is the process of reasoning from a stated premise to a conclusion that follows necessarily. This form of reasoning moves from the general to the specific. See Section 11 for a discussion of deductive reasoning and its relation to argumentative writing. See also *Syllogism* and *Induction*.

Definition Definition is one of the types of exposition. (Process analysis, division and classification, comparison and contrast, and cause and effect analysis are the others.) Definition is a statement of the meaning of a word. A definition may be either brief or extended, part of an essay or an entire essay itself. See Section 9 for a detailed discussion of definition. See also *Exposition*.

Denotation See *Connotation/Denotation*.

Description Description is one of the four basic types of prose. (Narration, exposition, and argument are the other three.) Description tells how a person, place, or thing is perceived by the five senses. Objective description reports these sensory qualities factually, whereas subjective description gives the writer's interpretation of them. See Section 3 for a detailed discussion of description.

Dialogue Dialogue is the conversation that is recorded in a piece of writing. Through dialogue writers reveal important aspects of characters' personalities as well as events in the plot.

Diction Diction refers to a writer's choice and use of words. Good diction is precise and appropriate—the words mean exactly what the writer intends, and the words are well suited to the writer's subject, intended audience, and purpose in writing. The word-conscious writer knows that there are differences among *aged, old,* and *elderly; blue, navy,* and *azure;* and *disturbed, angry,* and *irritated.* Furthermore, this writer knows in which situation to use each word. See also *Connotation/Denotation*.

Division Like comparison and contrast, division and classification are separate yet closely related mental operations. Division involves breaking down a single large unit into smaller subunits or breaking down a large group of items into discrete categories. For example, the student body at your college or university can be divided into categories according to different criteria (by class, by home state or country, by sex, and so on).

Dominant Impression A dominant impression is the single mood, atmosphere, or quality a writer emphasizes in a piece of descriptive writing. The dominant impression is created through the careful selection of details and is, of course, influenced by the writer's subject, audience, and purpose. See also the discussion in Section 3.

Draft   A draft is a version of a piece of writing at a particular stage in the writing process. The first version produced is usually called the rough draft or first draft and is a writer's beginning attempt to give overall shape to his or her ideas. Subsequent versions are called revised drafts. The copy presented for publication is the final draft.

Editing   During the editing stage of the writing process, the writer makes his or her prose conform to the conventions of the language. This includes making final improvements in sentence structure and diction and proofreading for wordiness and errors in grammar, usage, spelling, and punctuation. After editing, the writer is ready to type a final copy.

Emphasis   Emphasis is the placement of important ideas and words within sentences and longer units of writing so that they have the greatest impact. In general, the end has the most impact, and the beginning nearly as much; the middle has the least. See also *Organization*.

Endings   See *Beginnings/Endings*.

Essay   An essay is a relatively short piece of nonfiction in which the writer attempts to make one or more closely related points. A good essay is purposeful, informative, and well organized.

Evaluation   An evaluation of a piece of writing is an assessment of its effectiveness or merit. In evaluating a piece of writing, you should ask the following questions: What is the writer's purpose? Is it a worthwhile purpose? Does the writer achieve the purpose? Is the writer's information sufficient and accurate? What are the strengths of the essay? What are its weaknesses? Depending on the type of writing and the purpose, more specific questions can also be asked. For example, with an argument you could ask: Does the writer follow the principles of logical thinking? Is the writer's evidence convincing?

Evidence   Evidence is the data on which a judgment or argument is based or by which proof or probability is established. Evidence usually takes the form of statistics, facts, names, examples or illustrations, and opinions of authorities.

Examples   Examples illustrate a larger idea or represent something of which they are a part. An example is a basic means of developing or clarifying an idea. Furthermore, examples enable writers to show and not simply tell readers what they mean. The terms *example* and *illustration* are sometimes used interchangeably. See also the discussion of examples in Section 4.

Exposition   Exposition is one of the four basic types of prose. (Narration, description, and argument are the other three.) The purpose of exposition is to clarify, explain, and inform. The methods of exposition presented in this text are process analysis, definition, division and classification, comparison and contrast, and cause and effect analysis. For a detailed discussion of each of these methods of exposition, see the appropriate section.

Fallacy   See *Logical Fallacies.*

Figures of Speech   Figures of speech are brief, imaginative comparisons that highlight the similarities between things that are basically dissimilar. They make writing vivid and interesting and therefore more memorable. The most common figures of speech are:

   Simile—An implicit comparison introduced by *like* or *as:* "The fighter's hands were *like* stone."

   Metaphor—An implied comparison that uses one thing as the equivalent of another: "All the world's a stage."

   Personification—A special kind of simile or metaphor in which human traits are assigned to an inanimate object: "The engine coughed and then stopped."

Focus   Focus is the limitation that a writer gives his or her subject. The writer's task is to select a manageable topic given the constraints of time, space, and purpose. For example, within the general subject of sports, a writer could focus on government support of amateur athletes or narrow the focus further to government support of Olympic athletes.

General   See *Specific/General.*

Idiom   An idiom is a word or phrase that is used habitually with a particular meaning in a language. The meaning of an idiom is not always readily apparent to non-native speakers of that language. For example, *catch cold, hold a job, make up your mind,* and *give them a hand* are all idioms in English.

Illustration   See *Examples.* Also see Section 4.

Induction   Induction is the process of reasoning to a conclusion about all members of a class through an examination of only a few members of the class. This form of reasoning moves from the particular to the general. See Section 11 for a discussion of inductive reasoning and its relation to argumentative writing. Also see *Deduction*.

Introductions   See *Beginnings/Endings*.

Irony   The use of words to suggest something different from their literal meaning. For example, when Jonathan Swift proposes in "A Modest Proposal" that Ireland's problems could be solved if the people of Ireland fattened their babies and sold them to the English landlords for food, he meant that almost any other solution would be preferable. A writer can use irony to establish a special relationship with the reader and to add an extra dimension or twist to the meaning.

Jargon   See *Technical Language*.

Logical Fallacies   A logical fallacy is an error in reasoning that renders an argument invalid. Some of the more common logical fallacies are:

> *Oversimplification*—The tendency to provide simple solutions to complex problems: "The reason we have inflation today is that OPEC has unreasonably raised the price of oil."
>
> *Non sequitur* ("It does not follow")—An inference or conclusion that does not follow from established premises or evidence: "It was the best movie I saw this year, and it should get an Academy Award."
>
> *Post hoc, ergo propter hoc* ("After this, therefore because of this")—Confusing chance or coincidence with causation. Because one event comes after another one, it does not necessarily mean that the first event caused the second: "I won't say I caught cold at the hockey game, but I certainly didn't have it before I went there."
>
> *Begging the question*—Assuming in a premise that which needs to be proven: "If American autoworkers built a better product, foreign auto sales would not be so high."
>
> *False analogy*—Making a misleading analogy between logically unconnected ideas: "He was a brilliant basketball player; therefore, there's no question in my mind that he will be a fine coach."
>
> *Either/or thinking*—The tendency to see an issue as having only

two sides: "Used car salespersons are either honest or crooked."

See also Section 11.

Logical Reasoning See *Deduction* and *Induction*.

Metaphor See *Figures of Speech*.

Narration One of the four basic types of prose. (Description, exposition, and argument are the other three.) To narrate is to tell a story, to tell what happened. Although narration is most often used in fiction, it is also important in nonfiction, either by itself or in conjunction with other types of prose. See Section 2 for a detailed discussion of narration.

Objective/Subjective *Objective* writing is factual and impersonal, whereas *subjective* writing, sometimes called impressionistic, relies heavily on personal interpretation. For a discussion of objective description and subjective description, see Section 3.

Opinion An opinion is a belief or conclusion not substantiated by positive knowledge or proof. An opinion reveals personal feelings or attitudes or states a position. Opinion should not be confused with argument.

Organization In writing, organization is the thoughtful arrangement and presentation of one's points or ideas. Narration is often organized chronologically. Exposition may be organized from simplest to most complex or from most familiar to least familiar. Argument may be organized from least important to most important. There is no single correct pattern of organization for a given piece of writing, but good writers are careful to discover an order of presentation suitable for their audience and their purpose.

Paradox A paradox is a seemingly contradictory statement that may nonetheless be true. For example, *we little know what we have until we lose it* is a paradoxical statement. For a detailed discussion of paradox that includes additional examples, see Laurence Perrine's "Paradox," pages 6–7.

Paragraph The paragraph, the single most important unit of thought in an essay, is a series of closely related sentences. These sentences adequately develop the central or controlling idea of the paragraph. This central or controlling idea, usually stated in a topic sentence, is necessarily related to the purpose of the whole composition. A well-written paragraph has several distinguishing characteristics: a clearly stated or implied topic sentence, adequate development, unity, coherence, and an appropriate organizational strategy.

Parallelism Parallel structure is the repetition of word order or form either within a single sentence or in several sentences that develop the same central idea. As a rhetorical device, parallelism can aid coherence and add emphasis. Roosevelt's statement, "I see one third of the nation ill-housed, ill-clad, and ill-nourished," illustrates effective parallelism.

Personification See *Figures of Speech.*

Persuasion Persuasion, or persuasive argument, is an attempt to convince readers to agree with a point of view, to make a given decision, or to pursue a particular course of action. Persuasion heavily appeals to the emotions whereas logical argument does not. For the distinction between logical argument and persuasive argument, see Section 11.

Point of View Point of view refers to the grammatical person of the speaker in an essay. For example, a first-person point of view uses the pronoun *I* and is commonly found in autobiography and the personal essay; a third-person point of view uses the pronouns *he, she,* or *it* and is commonly found in objective writing. See Section 2 for a discussion of point of view in narration.

Prewriting Prewriting encompasses all the activities that take place before a writer actually starts a rough draft. During the prewriting stage of the writing process, the writer selects a subject area, focuses on a particular topic, collects information and makes notes, brainstorms for ideas, discovers connections between pieces of information, determines a thesis and purpose, rehearses portions of the writing in the mind and/or on paper, and makes a scratch outline. For some suggestions about prewriting, see pages 9–14 in the Introduction.

Process Analysis Process analysis is a type of exposition. (Definition, division and classification, comparison and contrast, and cause and effect analysis are the others.) Process analysis answers the question *how?* and explains how something works or gives step-by-step directions for doing something. See Section 5 for a detailed discussion of process analysis. See also *Exposition.*

Publication The publication stage of the writing process is when the writer shares his or her writing with the intended audience.

Publication can take the form of a typed or a
a dittoed or xeroxed copy, or a commercially
What's important is that the writer's words
amounts to their final form.

Purpose   Purpose is what the writer wants to accon
ticular piece of writing. Purposeful writing seeks
ration), to *describe* (description), to *explain* (process a
nition, division and classification, comparison and c
cause and effect analysis), or to *convince* (argument).

Revision   During the revision stage of the writing proc
writer determines what in the draft needs to be develop
clarified so that the essay says what the writer intends it to
Often the writer needs to revise several times before the essa
is "right." Comments from peer evaluators can be invaluable in
helping writers determine what sorts of changes need to be
made. Such changes can include adding material, deleting material, changing the order of presentation, and substituting new
material for old.

Rhetorical Question   A rhetorical question is asked but requires
no answer from the reader. "When will nuclear proliferation
end?" is such a question. Writers use rhetorical questions to introduce topics they plan to discuss or to emphasize important
points.

Rough Draft   See *Draft.*

Sequence   Sequence refers to the order in which a writer presents
information. Writers commonly select chronological order, spatial order, order of importance, or order of complexity to arrange
their points. See also *Organization.*

Simile   See *Figures of Speech.*

Slang   Slang is the unconventional, very informal language of particular subgroups in our culture. Slang, such as *zonk, split, rap,
cop,* and *stoned,* is acceptable in formal writing only if it is used
purposefully.

Specific/General   *General words* name groups or classes of objects,
qualities, or actions. *Specific words,* in contrast, name individual
objects, qualities, or actions within a class or group. To some
extent the terms *general* and *specific* are relative. For example,
dessert is a class of things. *Pie,* however, is more specific than
dessert but more general than *pecan pie* or *chocolate cream pie.*

od writing judiciously balances the general with the spe-
. Writing with too many general words is likely to be dull
d lifeless. General words do not create vivid responses in the
ader's mind as concrete specific words can. However, writing
hat relies exclusively on specific words may lack focus and direction, the control that more general statements provide.

Strategy   A strategy is a means by which a writer achieves his or
her purpose. Strategy includes the many rhetorical decisions that
the writer makes about organization, paragraph structure, syntax, and diction. In terms of the whole essay, strategy refers to
the principal rhetorical mode that a writer uses. If, for example,
a writer wishes to show how to make chocolate chip cookies,
the most effective strategy would be process analysis. If it is the
writer's purpose to show why sales of American cars have declined in recent years, the most effective strategy would be cause
and effect analysis.

Style   Style is the individual manner in which a writer expresses
his or her ideas. Style is created by the author's particular selection of words, construction of sentences, and arrangement of
ideas.

Subject   The subject of an essay is its content, what the essay is
about. Depending on the author's purpose and the constraints
of space, a subject may range from one that is broadly conceived
to one that is narrowly defined.

Subjective   See *Objective/Subjective.*

Supporting Evidence   See *Evidence.*

Syllogism   A syllogism is an argument that utilizes deductive reasoning and consists of a major premise, a minor premise, and a
conclusion. For example:

All trees that lose leaves are deciduous. (*major premise*)
Maple trees lose their leaves. (*minor premise*)
Therefore, maple trees are deciduous. (*conclusion*)
See also *Deduction.*

Symbol   A symbol is a person, place, or thing that represents
something beyond itself. For example, the eagle is a symbol of
America, and the bear, a symbol of Russia.

Syntax   Syntax refers to the way in which words are arranged to
form phrases, clauses, and sentences as well as to the grammatical relationship among the words themselves.

Technical Language Technical language, or jargon, is the special vocabulary of a trade or profession. Writers who use technical language do so with an awareness of their audience. If the audience is a group of peers, technical language may be used freely. If the audience is a more general one, technical language should be used sparingly and carefully so as not to sacrifice clarity. See also *Diction*.

Thesis A thesis is a statement of the main idea of an essay. Also known as the controlling idea, a thesis may sometimes be implied rather than stated directly.

Title A title is a word or phrase set off at the beginning of an essay to identify the subject, to capture the main idea of the essay, or to attract the reader's attention. A title may be explicit or suggestive. A subtitle, when used, extends or restricts the meaning of the main title.

Tone Tone is the manner in which a writer relates to an audience, the "tone of voice" used to address readers. Tone may be described as friendly, serious, distant, angry, cheerful, bitter, cynical, enthusiastic, morbid, resentful, warm, playful, and so forth. A particular tone results from a writer's diction, sentence structure, purpose, and attitude toward the subject. See also *Attitude*.

Topic Sentence The topic sentence states the central idea of a paragraph and thus limits and controls the subject of the paragraph. Although the topic sentence most often appears at the beginning of the paragraph, it may appear at any other point, particularly if the writer is trying to create a special effect. Also see *Paragraph*.

Transitions Transitions are words or phrases that link sentences, paragraphs, and larger units of a composition in order to achieve coherence. These devices include parallelism, pronoun references, conjunctions, and the repetition of key ideas, as well as the many conventional transitional expressions such as *moreover, on the other hand, in addition, in contrast,* and *therefore*. Also see *Coherence*.

Unity Unity is achieved in an essay when all the words, sentences, and paragraphs contribute to its thesis. The elements of a unified essay do not distract the reader. Instead, they all harmoniously support a single idea or purpose.

Writing Process The writing process consists of five major stages:

prewriting, writing drafts, revision, editing, and publication. The process is not inflexible, but there is no mistaking the fact that most writers follow some version of it most of the time. Although orderly in its basic components and sequence of activities, the writing process is nonetheless continuous, creative, and unique to each individual writer. See pages 8–30 in the Introduction. See also *Prewriting, Draft, Revision, Editing,* and *Publication*.

Index